Career Planning Today

Hire Me!

Fourth Edition

C. Randall Powell
Indiana University — Bloomington

KENDALL/HUNT PUBLISHING COMPANY
4050 Westmark Drive   Dubuque, Iowa 52002

Cover illustration by Ron Wheeler

Table of Contents

- -

Guide to Selected Topics

● ●

Preface

● ●

This book has one overriding purpose: It is to help you find career happiness. Happiness (or job satisfaction if you prefer) comes from doing things you enjoy. What you choose to do to earn a living contributes to your happiness or lack of it.

Career Planning Today is a book from which you can learn a lot the first time through, and more importantly, it is a reference book which you may find yourself coming back to over and over. It is designed as a guide that sets you on a course which occasionally may need redirection.

The focus of the book is on planning. Planning involves developing a systematic approach to the direction you want your working life to take. The approach described in this book not only sets the plan but shows you how to implement it as well.

The approach of this book goes beyond the one-shot job hunt. It shows you how to be continually in charge of your career; not how to temporarily deal with a current problem.

Many people complain about our free enterprise employment system in the U.S. They regard it as backward. Yet, millions of people use the system each year and are very successful.

The system may not be the problem; the problem may be in how people use the system. The strategies and techniques suggested here assume the system is going to be around a long time and thus you must learn how to make it work for you.

Subtle humorous illustrations and cartoons dot the manuscript. The purposes of the illustrations are to drive home key points and lighten your day. The response to the earlier editions was overwhelmingly positive from both placement professionals and career planners. The illustrations and cartoons may help you identify personally with the message.

It is important for you to know something about the author of a non-fiction book. You should know where I am coming from when I make the recommendations and suggestions given in the text.

Who am I? I humbly call myself a career professional. I have devoted part of my life to helping career planners and job seekers set and achieve personal career objectives. I have devoted another part of my life to helping organizations locate employees who can help them satisfy their organizational goals.

I am a university faculty member and college placement officer who is not paid by either the employer or the potential employee. I have no personal monetary stake in bringing these parties together. I earn a faculty member's salary from Indiana University. It is fun, interesting, and quite educational to sit on the sidelines and coach and observe both sides simultaneously.

My position has opened doors for me that I do not believe could have been opened in any other way. I have worked with inexperienced entry-level college graduates, and I have worked with executives who were seeking chief executive officer positions. I have worked with organizations seeking executives to whom they are willing to pay hugh salaries. On a daily basis I work with organizations desiring to hire experienced and inexperienced candidates in the $30,000 to $90,000 salary range.

I manage one of the largest college placement programs in the nation. It is a hectic work environment that attempts to relate to hundreds of employers, recent college graduates, and experienced alumni. It can be described as a massive brokering operation which works quite effectively and efficiently.

I also have the opportunity to observe and study the employment system. In the final analysis, employment is a very personal business for both the employer and the employee. Both of them need a little help in finding each other.

During the Eighties, a colleague, Dr. Don Kirts at Lafayette College, and I finished a text titled *Career Services Today*, which was published by the College Placement Council, Inc. *Career Services Today* was written as a handbook for people practicing in our profession of career planning, placement, and recruitment. That book sparked my interest in writing a career book for the average job hunter.

Several years later I was elected and served as president of the Midwest College Placement Association, the largest regional association of employers and college personnel people in the nation. I continue to serve as a leader in the profession. These experiences have been helpful to me in meeting and understanding career professionals.

My career has taken me into literally hundreds of corporations, banks, retail firms, educational institutions, and government agencies. I have talked to thousands of people in all types of career fields about their jobs and how they got there. I have talked to people at the very top of the largest organizations in the U.S., and I have talked to the lowest level of employee.

It is nearly impossible to describe the extent of the research that has gone into this book. The research was not the esoteric, empirical type that uses the computer to crunch a batch of numbers. It was thousands of open-ended, probing questions to people who have "been there." It was a thorough, practical investigation of work settings, career fields, and job search methods.

I constantly met with search firm executives, employment agency owners, college placement experts, career counselors, and others who would let me pick their brains. I badgered hundreds of human resource managers who are responsible for hiring thousands of managerial, technical, and professional people.

This book will help you to achieve career satisfaction through a realistic approach to career planning.

The basic ideas in this book were first published in 1974 in *Career Planning and Placement Today*. I am indeed proud that this book has had such a long, successful history over the years, but there have been very significant improvements over these years also. This edition contains many new illustrations, updated facts, new techniques and ideas, as well as a new graphically illustrated text.

HIRE ME! is about gaining a competitive edge in the job market, but more importantly, it focuses on developing a strategical plan for your life. You will learn more techniques than you have time to use. The goal is to create a plan that you can realistically use over and over in your life.

HIRE ME! will work for you just as it has for thousands of others. Clearly you must pull together your strengths and credentials into a **strategic plan**, and then master the **tactics** gained from reading this book.

The work is not difficult, but it is time-consuming. This resource book is mostly about action, not some philosophical theory. The roots are implanted in a solid theory framework, but the theory is left for the professional counselors to worry about. By spending your time applying the principles and techniques taught here, you will maximize your effort to find a successful career beginning.

A sound strategic career plan turns dreams into reality. The early topics on self-assessment and career exploration expand your horizons for entry into the real world. The thrust is to get you to set goals, take charge of your life, implement some job search techniques and strategies, locate your current niche, and start progressing.

I urge you to discuss your concerns with career professionals at the college which you attended. You will get more in-depth insights than can be offered here. I see this book as merely the starting point for information. Others more knowledgeable than I can fill in some of the gaps.

The first edition was publised over 25 years ago. The new technologies have totally altered our profession. I am anxious to see the next century bring some time saving changes to the entire career planning process. Thanks to everyone for their input to this text.

**Partner:
Your Professional
Career Consultant**

Acknowledgments

● ●

There is no way I could personally acknowledge by name all of the individual contributors to this book, but in no way am I ungrateful for the hundreds of contributions. There are, however, a limited number of people who made my life fuller and this book richer.

No words can express my gratitude and respect for the late Professor J. D. Snider, my colleague and mentor for many years. Without Doug's prodding, cajoling, suggesting, inspiring, and encouraging me, none of my publications would have come to fruition.

Many of the concepts, strategies, and techniques owe their birth to Professor Snider, who is recognized as one of the earliest deans of our profession. His philosophical thinking and gentle management style influenced my approach more than any other factor. It was a sad day when we lost such a great leader.

My greatest ally in this writing business has been Mrs. Frieda Robertson. Her official title before retirement was Office Manager at our Indiana University Placement Office, but that role is dwarfed in significance when compared to her other role as contributor-editor-organizer-critic and friend. I especially want to thank her for bringing all of my publications, especially this one, together in an organized, meaningful, and timely fashion.

The "Ralph Crabtree" cartoons depict the woes and joys of career planning and job searching. The concerns and apprehensions of "Ralph" and his friends reflect many of our attitudes. I am most grateful to Ralph's creator, Ron Wheeler, for capturing the feelings that so many of us experience as we go through the career planning process.

I want to thank the thousands of students at several hundred universities who used, abused, cussed, and discussed much of the original material. The feedback from old and young students in my various career planning classes improved the quality of the final product.

Writing is a time-consuming process. At times it meant being away from the office. Over the years, I have had a super staff who have ably taken over some of my duties when I had to meet pressing deadlines. I have always been very fortunate in working for university deans who strongly support my efforts.

Besides Frieda, I must recognize Mr. Scott Zanger, who did some of the typing and entered the entire manuscript into desktop publishing software. We prepared many new graphics, cartoons, and illustrations in this edition. He spent hours designing, scanning, and laying out each page. In spite of the many rewrites that I continually provide, his graciousness made the effort of striving for better perform-ance worthwhile. The excellent rapport with Scott and his expertise took away much of the boredom often present in writing a manuscript of this magnitude.

I happen to be a collector. I save everything that comes across my desk in this field. As a result, I have incorporated hundreds of great ideas which I have received over the years from my colleagues, mentors, and detractors. I have thanked them all individually and now wish to acknowledge them in print.

With thousands of copies of my books in circulation, almost every colleague in my profession has had a crack at critiquing and making a contribution. The mail continues to bring in praise and criticism from them, which I very much appreciate. I wish I could acknowledge them all individually.

In the final analysis, the responsibility to organize and interpret materials rests with the author. I deserve a kick where errors exist and where I may have taken too much liberty at interpreting others. I accept the responsibility for these shortcomings. I hope to correct them in subsequent editions.

In closing, this book must be dedicated to my family. Only a family knows the strains and hard work that go into producing a publication of this magnitude. My three sons, "C.R.," James, and Ryan, and daughter, Katie, all had to give up some of dad's time so he could stay working on this project.

My wife Kathy has been wonderful. Our real estate properties that she manages plus the family commitments keep us really hopping. This family really works hard together and Kathy is super in putting all of our diverse demands in an organized perspective. Very few writers have enjoyed any stronger support than I have received.

I hope that this book proves very useful for the thousands of young people who read it and use its ideas to achieve their goals.

C. Randall Powell, Ph.D.
Indiana University
Bloomington, Indiana

PLANNING YOUR CAREER

Career planning or job hunting? Perhaps you need to make some career changes. Too many individuals plunge right into the job search.

Job hunting is part of a broader career planning process. You may need to step back, take time, and review your personal situation before just assuming that the solution is a new job.

Part 1 is essential reading. Your goal is to maximize your chances for a successful career decision. Sound career decisions demand advance planning. If you jump from job to job without regard for long-term strategic planning, you may be paying some significant costs for your long-term career success.

Part 1, "Planning Your Career," lays the foundation for this book and is what makes this book different from the hundreds of job hunting books on the market. It asks you to take charge of your working life by stepping back from the tree so you can get a glimpse of the forest.

With the big picture in mind, you can begin to make more intelligent decisions that may affect your working life for many years. The focus of Part 1 is career goal setting.

Part 2, "Exploring Your Career Options," helps you implement the decisions you made in Part 1. This section permits you to monitor the plans and decisions you made by establishing feedback monitoring information so earlier decisions can be fine tuned. The end results are some realistic job targets, albeit preliminary.

Part 3, "Developing Your Job Search Tools," is designed to help you prepare the tools for your job search and implement a planned strategy for achieving your goals. Part 3 covers resume preparation, cover letter design, networking, search strategies, prospecting, interview preparation, presentations, and employment communications.

When integrated together, all parts of this book put you in control of your working life. Planning, organizing, and controlling your career provides the basic input for the guiding principle in this book. The goal-directed behavior that emerges from this career plan approach is the basic lesson.

Planning, organizing, and controlling your career works extremely well if you follow the strategies and techniques offered. Once the overall plan is well grounded, this book can then become a quick reference handbook which you may return to many times in your career reviewing and job search phases of career planning.

Throughout the text, hundreds of websites and pages are identified with a URL address as of the beginning of 1999. The addresses often change. You may have to locate the site, if it still exists, by using a search engine like Yahoo.com or excite.com.

Career Planning:

Assessment – Exploration – Placement

Is "Career Planning" just another name for "Job Hunting"? The past has taught us a lot about careers. The following words are part of our vocabulary and need no definitions: Overeducated . . . Underemployed . . . Pink Slip . . . RIF . . . Displaced Worker . . . Affirmative Action . . . Protected Class . . . Out-placement . . . Baby Boom . . . Enrollment Decline . . . Job Competition . . . Foreign Competition . . . Glut of Job Seekers . . . Outplaced . . . Downsized.

The wealth of a nation is not just its natural resources; it is also its people. The world is not only changing; it is moving in "future shock" proportions.

You simply cannot shuffle into and out of jobs indiscriminately. The situation calls for much forethought. *Hire Me!* offers an action plan.

Career Planning

Career planning is an individual activity. In a free society, no giant bureaucratic organization dares chart courses for you to follow. You cannot survive happily for very long unless you take responsibility for the course of your life.

The declining lifespan of many jobs (and even entire career fields) demands a personal planning posture. The short job lifecycles may force you to make "rolling decisions" annually in order to regenerate new career options.

Career planning is not just a new name for job hunting. Career planning is conceptually and practically different. Job searching is only one component of career planning.

The future is not limited to your "formal" education. The future is lifelong education which continually renews the capabilities and energies that you use in earning a secure livelihood.

The job search is only one part of your career plan.

AND ANOTHER THING LITTLE ONE . . . IT'S NEVER TOO EARLY TO CONSIDER A CAREER IN MEDICINE.

3

//WEB.TIP//

www.petersons.com
Peterson's Education and Career Center
Locates colleges/advice on applying/campus news/ many links

Planning Ahead

Exciting productivity advancements imply that more work will be done with the human mind than with physical skills. Automation is common in manufacturing, marketing services, and finance. Technology is spreading to all industries and career fields.

The starting point for tomorrow's careers are the specific jobs of today. Tomorrow's skills will likely build upon those required in today's jobs. Career planning is a process that changes over time.

Career planning is a bold, exciting, new approach. It will enrich the lives of young and old alike. Planning implies more work now, but the returns throughout life will pay excellent dividends.

The jobs of today may not be the jobs of tomorrow.

The Work Setting

The future . . . what will it hold? The world of work holds open a massive array of work possibilities. Work is a significant part of your life.

Success is often defined in terms of significant work achievements. Even newspaper obituaries cite these past achievements daily.

From about age 20 until age 60, the American value system places great importance upon work activities. Work is frequently defined as the process through which you earn the resources that allow you to live in a manner to which you desire.

Career planning is an ever-changing, individually controlled activity.

The great philosopher Voltaire once said that work "spares us from three great evils: boredom, vice, and need."

The proper work *activity* and work *environment* can be sources of much satisfaction in life.

Life Decisions

Three of the most important decisions people make in life relate to buying an automobile, investing in a home, and choosing a marriage partner. Hours, days, weeks, and months are spent making these decisions. Every aspect is usually analyzed very thoroughly. Those decisions usually have long-term impacts on happiness.

Deciding what to do tonight and the decision about where to go next Saturday night are important to most people. Many hours go into making "Saturday night" types of decisions.

Work is too important to leave to chance. Nonetheless, thousands of people let their lives haphazardly fall into work activities and allow important decisions to be made for them by others and by happenstance.

Why not spend some time planning for a lifetime of work activity? Is that not just as important as the decision about which car, stereo, or house to purchase?

Why do most people spend so much time on the minor decisions in life and so little time on decisions that can mean so much? Your quality of life is greatly enhanced by a job which makes sense to you.

Your career is a series of work activities that you enjoy.

Significance of Planning

Career planning is directed toward those individuals who are seeking careers in managerial, technical, or professional fields. Although applicable to a very wide age range, the most directly affected age category is the 20 to 40 age range.

Most positions in the fields we will deal with in this book currently pay salaries in the $30,000 to $90,000 range, depending upon the required education level and experience, the type of position, and supply/demand. Assuming a starting salary of $40,000 annually at age 22 and a 5% increase per year until retirement at age 65, a person could earn *several million* dollars in a lifetime.

Career decisions are *significant* decisions! Perhaps no other decision that an individual makes has such a major impact on economic well-being.

Satisfaction comes from knowing that you recognized the challenge and then took a deliberate course of action to achieve your career, life, and personal goals.

How much time should you spend in analyzing your life's work endeavors?

Life Planning

You are not restricted to one career for your whole life! A person may carry out several unrelated work roles over time. Why can't you be a business executive, a doctor, and an architect in your lifetime?

Planning involves setting goals that can be realistically achieved. Goals motivate us.

The basis of life planning is setting achievable personal objectives. Career planning is a major element of life planning. For some work-oriented people, life planning is career planning. The two are always interrelated.

//WEB.TIP//

usnews.com
U.S. News and World Report
Objective college rankings/ links to colleges/objective advice/many statistics.

Career Jargon

Career planning professionals throw a fair share of jargon at people they counsel. There are several words which when taken out of context have multiple meanings.

Job. A job is a work situation taken for the purpose of earning wages for completing a task, a series of tasks, or a definitive piece of work. A job frequently is temporary in nature and the word seldom implies a long-term commitment to a given type of work. A job rarely requires a long training period for mastery of the work assigned. However, a job can be the starting point or intermediate step in your career.

Career. A career is a work experience that you elect to pursue during a significant period of time in life. A career involves a relatively long-term commitment to a given work activity. A career requires a significant level of formal education, training, and background for satisfactorily performing in the work area. It may involve a series of related job experiences.

Planning. Planning means devising a scheme for doing, making, or arranging a project, program, or schedule. Planning is a process that occurs over time and one that adjusts itself when new information becomes available.

Planning involves charting a course of action and then adjusting the course as the situation changes from the originally hypothesized projection.

What Is Career Planning?

Career planning is an activity that occurs throughout your working lifetime. It is futuristic. Career planning is distinct from life planning in that it does not initially attempt to integrate a broader array of planning variables such as early childhood, family, religion, values, leisure, retirement, and other personal goals.

Career planning is a sub-component of life planning that draws upon many of the same background variables, but it focuses attention on the *work activity* and *work environment.* There are many instances in which career and life planning cannot be completely separated.

Career planning reverts to solely job hunting unless three activities are addressed individually and in concert.

Assessment, exploration, and search form the framework of sound career planning. The concept builds a method of appraising career potential, exploring various alternatives, and implementing an action plan designed to achieve a predetermined set of career goals.

Career decisions influence your life for many years.

You need a plan to achieve your goals.

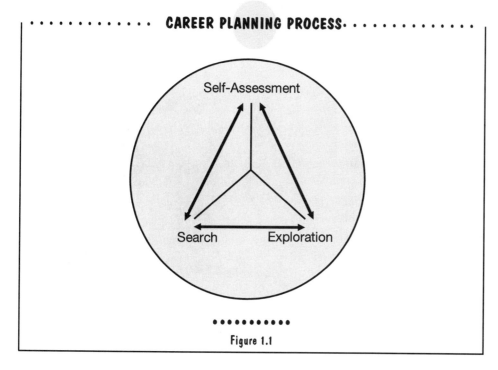

CAREER PLANNING PROCESS

Self-Assessment

Search   Exploration

Figure 1.1

Career planning is a process that draws upon three major planning activities: self-assessment, career exploration, and job placement.

Self-Assessment

The purpose of career decision making is to aid you in obtaining a career position consistent with your academic training, past work experiences, personality, abilities, aptitudes, values, and interests.

Your self-assessment is a sound understanding of all your personal characteristics.

Socrates referred to this understanding with the term "know thyself." This is a process through which you come to know yourself better.

The self-assessment is an activity that all of us should do on a regular basis, perhaps yearly. It is a structured event that forces you to amass a wealth of information about yourself from a variety of sources.

Only after assembling all of the pieces of information together can you begin to step back and develop a big picture. These elements can then be used to identify broader trends useful in plotting future directions.

The collecting, analyzing, and evaluating of information about **you** creates a much higher level of awareness about *all* your personal qualities, especially about your life goals.

A framework organizes thoughts in a

Know thyself!

YOU DON'T MIND IF I PICK UP A FEW TIPS DO YOU? I'M CONSIDERING A MEDICAL CAREER MYSELF.

meaningful way and permits a much more detailed specification of background characteristics.

Although this process is essentially a personal decision, you may wish to enlist the aid of advisors, friends, and numerous publications. Exercises, projects, tests, and other instruments aid in the drawing out of your attributes in a way that they can be organized and meaningfully related to your career options.

Career Exploration

Career exploration is a process of elimination.

What types of career options are available to someone with your background and interests? The number of options is often staggering. Although the self-assessment helps narrow the list by discarding conflicting options, the list is usually still long.

Exploration starts with a massive list of potential alternatives. You then develop an array of information on each alternative, and based upon the results of your self-assessment, you begin to sort out those of only marginal interest.

Even after the sorting process, many of us discover that there are many things we could enjoy doing. That is where the real in-depth investigation begins.

Career exploration means . . .
. . . Investigating your career options in a systematic manner.

For every option, you will discover a wealth of information. Information will flow to you from a variety of sources. Unfortunately, there is no single information source available to reference. The internet and library will be your best sources.

Career exploration involves digging into a mass of information with the objective of narrowing the scope of career alternatives. Thousands of alternatives may be discarded on the basis of job title alone.

Job Search

The search process begins with a preliminary decision to seek employment in a given career option. Your *"tentative"* decision may be revised several times as you test your decisions.

The search and placement process also adds information to your self-assessment and career exploration as you progress farther and deeper into this third phase of career planning.

The self-assessment and career exploration steps are never complete.

The terms job placement, employment, hunting, and search are fairly interchangeable, with "search" being the most professionally acceptable term today.

In this exciting age of technological change, human growth, and personal enrichment opportunities, career planning can never be a static process.

Job searching is convincing another person to hire you. The individuals in the work setting with whom you will relate must be convinced that your goals are compatible with their goals. Work gets accomplished best when there are common objectives.

Even if you decide to become self-employed (such as in a profession or business owner), the goals that you establish for your life endeavor must still be consistent with your own personal goals.

Many people view the search or placement phase as simply "job hunting." They consider it to be resume preparation, cover letter creation, contact sourcing, interviewing, and offer negotiating. Yes, it does include these basic activities, however, those are short-run techniques. They are not the necessary sound "strategic planning" which contributes to real job satisfaction.

Search is a sales activity. Successful selling begins with finding a need (or desire) and closes with satisfying the customers' desires.

Search success depends upon matching your goals with an employer's job requirements. Perfect matches rarely occur. Your odds for personal success increase substantially if you can bring your goals as close as possible with those of a potential employer, your customer.

Finally, the employment process is decision oriented. Success depends upon career goals matching job requirements. Without compromise, the match may never occur. Employment calls for a firm decision at a given point in time.

Time pressures force career choices. Time places pressure on the need for compromise. A preplanned time and decision framework permits a rational decision process based upon a realistic evaluation of the current work environment.

Search must be viewed in the total framework of the career planning process. A search strategy without a self-assessment and career exploration connotes getting a job at any cost and taking whatever is available.

Integrated Concepts

Each of the three major career planning process components may be completed initially as an independent project. But the career planning process cannot be optimally successful without viewing each activity as part of an integrated system.

Important feedback loops in each component tend to reinforce or modify earlier preliminary decisions. There is a continuous recycling of information and thus adjustment and modification of earlier decisions.

Career planning is a dynamic process that will occur throughout your working life.

The Job Search employs tools, techniques, and strategies designed to locate a career position that best matches your self-assessment with the career options you have chosen to explore.

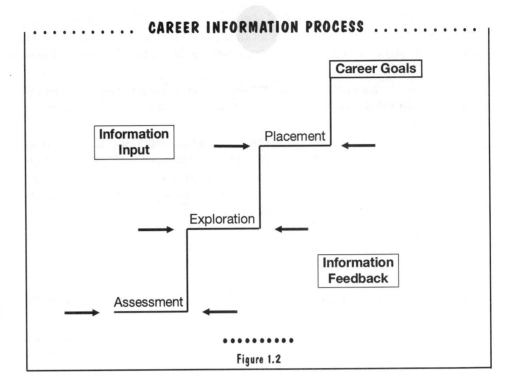

Figure 1.2

The variances between your "I want to" and "I am qualified to" force compromises.

Compromise

As the career planning process continues, compromises occur. Your self-assessment leads to a much more accurate view of yourself, and the picture becomes more and more clearly defined as new information is added from your career exploration activity.

The job search activity feeds real world career information into the model. As a result, specification and clarification, adjusted by necessary compromises, begin to firm up an overall career plan.

Feedback Loops

Career planning is completed upon acceptance of a career-related assignment with a specific employer. Another phase sets in as work-related experiences add new information to the process.

Re-evaluation phases continue throughout life. The new information continually is fed back into the career planning model and you make appropriate adjustments.

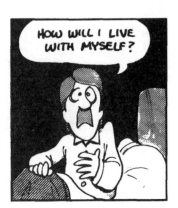

Process

Career planning can be viewed as a logical, patterned sequential approach to the task of assessing, analyzing, and deciding how you want to perform in a work setting.

Career planning is a series of events that recur over and over through a planned pattern controlled by you. Sound career planning is designed to renew itself continually over time.

Individual Activity

Career planning is an individual exercise. You are the center. You possess a unique set of values, philosophy, personality, interests, intelligence level, education, and work experience background.

A major role of a career counselor is to assist an individual in drawing out all basic characteristics and understanding the nature of these characteristics in relationship to career alternatives.

WOULD YOU RATE YOUR CAREER AS... (A) EXTREMELY REWARDING ... (B) MILDLY REWARDING ... (C) MODERATELY REWARDING ... OR (D) A TOTAL BUMMER.

You move forward, process data, and feed results back.

Work-Centered

Career planning is more than an understanding of self. It is also an understanding of the *world of work.* Only by understanding occupational options are you in a position to objectively correlate your personal characteristics with employment realities.

Career planning is a way of thinking about the future. It is not simply a sterile academic exercise of matching personal characteristics and job possibilities in order to ascertain your ideal niche.

The implementation of a career plan involves actual employment in a work setting. There are continual evaluation and feedback loops that clarify the adequacy of the employment decision or suggest a reassessment of the entire career planning process. This dynamic process continues throughout life.

Decision-Oriented

What am I going to do with my life? This is a heavy but relevant question. Some people tend to postpone the most critical decisions they must face. Procrastination is a way of life for many people.

Career planning is decision-oriented. Decision making is a skill that can be mastered. Like all decisions, career decisions require information. Information is available, but it must be requested and then processed in proper fashions.

People procrastinate because they do not see a way to get a handle on a problem. You want to make career decisions, but the magnitude of the decision is often overwhelming. What if you make the wrong decision? Is no decision better than a bad decision? Why do you even have to make any decision?

There are no perfectly bad or perfectly good decisions in choosing a career. The situation is never black or white. There are thousands of shades of grey. Most people convince themselves that the decisions they made were good ones; and they usually are.

After making a decision you tend to mobilize your resources and make subsequent decisions which assure that the first decision was right.

Decision making takes career planning to an action-oriented level. Decision-makers take career planning out of an academic exercise and into a practical, necessary activity. In its most elementary form, decision making is a six-step process:

1. Define the problem
2. Develop alternative solutions
3. Establish evaluative criteria
4. Evaluate alternatives
5. Make a decision
6. Evaluate decision

Decisions are modified as new information is collected and evaluated.

A closed loop connects the evaluation, the decision, and the review of the original problem. This "rolling" process can be used on the smallest sub-component of the problem area as well as on the largest element of the total decision.

Compromises

A decision must be made at designated points in time. Even procrastination becomes a decision after a certain amount of time.

Career decision making involves compromises. The compromise solution impacts upon other people, personal preferences, and hypothetical concepts.

There rarely is a perfect solution. This systematic, analytical process of decision making molds a realistic and acceptable match between the world of work and personal goals.

Career Planning Defined

Career planning seeks answers to four questions:

1. What do I want to do?
2. What can I do?
3. What needs to be done?
4. How can I get the job I want?

If you could always provide definitive answers to these basic questions, career planning would always be optimally achieved.

Marketing Fundamentals

If a marketing expert were dealing with a specific product, some basic marketing fundamentals would be quickly applied by answering these questions:

1. What do you have to offer?
2. Who needs it?
3. How do you make them want it?

Career decisions require a much more complex approach. Yet every approach must begin with a first step. The first step is often the hardest. Career planning must be approached one step at a time.

Career planning offers a logical, structured, and sequential method in career decision making. This method builds upon a theory-based framework proposed by leading career theorists.

The largest laboratory in the world is the job market. This is not some "pie in the sky" academic theory, but an approach which has stood the test of time in a real world setting. It works!

This career planning model offers a fresh look at career decisions. There is much interrelatedness within a complex set of variables. Conceptually, the model focuses attention on the three concepts of self-assessment, career exploration, and placement. Information is fed into one or all of these components.

Based upon a process of integration, compromise, work settings, and goal specification, career decisions are reached, assessed, and reassessed over a lifetime of work.

Your laboratory is the job market.

Career Planning Theory Sets the Foundation

Career planning is built upon a strong theory base. Considerable research in career guidance and vocational theory supports the dynamics of the relationships among the many interacting variables of career decision making.

Theory is more of a subject for guidance counselors, but you will eventually come into contact with a career counseling professional. Consequently, it is important to recognize and appreciate the foundation upon which their advice is built.

The professional counselor can be extremely valuable in helping assess and evaluate your capabilities and in providing guidance and referral to related career resources. The counselor's work is tied to research that relates to several decades of analysis.

Many people start to think about what they want as a vocation early in life, often before their teens. A great many personal factors, in addition to external forces, appear to influence the various career choices that are made. Theories range from astrological happenings to paternal handling of young children. The widest accepted theories are known as developmental theories of vocational choices.

Framework

A vocational theory is important because it helps us to understand the how and why of certain life sequences that assist in the selection of appropriate occupational endeavors. A theory shows a systematic relationship between certain variables and helps to define relevancy.

A theory helps you understand why you make certain career decisions.

A theory develops a system of classification and structuring of concepts that can be used to predict outcomes. A good theory is most often based on extensive empirical referents which means that the propositions in a theory are logically supported by prior research and/or experience.

Several theorists have attempted to systematize the results of their investigations into the career development process. Certain theorists have significantly influenced the direction of research and have stimulated innovative practices.

Among them are Eli Ginzberg (who reported the results of his investigations in *Occupational Choice: An Approach to a General Theory* in 1951) and John L. Holland, who in 1966 set the stage for new empirical studies with his book, *The Psychology of Vocational Choice*. The major aspects of these positions are presented as examples of the thought-guiding career development activities. They are not meant to be exhaustive and certainly do not cover the entire range of theories.

Ginzberg's Theory

Dr. Eli Ginzberg and his colleagues at Columbia University first proposed their theory of occupational choice in 1951. Their theory attempted to explain how the multiplicity of factors within the environment and forces within the individual act and react on each other so that individuals finally resolve the problem of their vocational choice. Three major concepts in Ginzberg's theory form the vocational choice framework: process, irreversibility, and compromise.

Vocational development is a process because it changes over time, and these time periods may be delineated into various life stages. The first stage is a "fantasy stage" (before age 11) in which children believe they can become whatever they desire. The next stage is a "tentative stage" (age 11-17) in which the young adult begins to develop values, interests, qualifications, and a more stable personality. Choices often evolve and change during this second stage.

The final stage is described as a "realistic stage" in which the individual begins to integrate interests, capabilities, and values. These factors are used to evaluate the real environment, a process that can be broken into these three periods—exploration, crystallization, and specification.

In the exploration period, individuals acquaint themselves for the last time with career alternatives in a highly realistic context. During crystallization, clear vocational patterns begin to form based upon the successes and failures experienced in the exploration period. Choice follows.

During specification the individual delimits the choice and elaborates by selecting a specific career, college major, or graduate school specialty. During the college years, many students roam through these three periods before deciding on a specific career direction.

Ginzberg sees the choice as being largely irreversible because reality pressures introduce major obstacles.

After a major commitment, such as the decision to pursue a career in teaching or in law, there are often serious emotional barriers to a shift in plans because the change can take on the quality of failure or at least present a threat to self-esteem.

With significant technological change in our society, Ginzberg's "irreversibility" has been challenged. Evidence suggests that people do change career directions multiple times, often being forced to by technological changes in their profession.

The third major concept in Ginzberg's theory is that the vocational choice represents a compromise. The individual tries to choose a career that can make as

GINZBERG THEORY BASICS

1. Vocational development is a process.
2. The choice is largely irreversible.
3. The choice represents a compromise.

• • • • • • • • • •

Figure 1.3

Specification clarifies your career decisions.

much use as possible of personal interests and abilities in a manner that will satisfy the most values and goals.

The person must weigh the opportunities and environmental limitations and then assess the extent to which a maximum degree of satisfaction in work and life can be secured. The individual attempts to balance abilities, interests, and values against real environment career alternatives and thus make appropriate compromises.

Throughout the entire process, it is evident that many compromises and trade-offs from earlier positions must be made as new information is obtained. Many choice points cannot be reentered due to limitations of time, technology, opportunities, abilities, and other reality factors which contribute to the irreversible nature of the vocational choice process.

The theory allows for persons to make career-related changes. In so doing, however, they often must build on earlier decisions and developmental accomplishments.

In general, Ginzberg's theory has stood the test of extensive empirical research.

Holland's Theory

According to Holland's Theory, vocational preferences and interests are expressions of personality. The choice of an occupation expresses an individual's motivation, knowledge of a particular occupation, and personal abilities. Stereotypes are used throughout this theory.

Persons within a given vocation have developmental histories and personalities that are similar. Due to the many personal similarities among those who enter and persist in a given occupation, it follows that the characteristic patterns of communication and interaction established will form a unique work environment.

To the extent the work environment and worker's personality are congruent, the prediction is for increased satisfaction, stability, and achievement in relation to the vocational choice.

The theory makes three assumptions: that people can be characterized by particular types of personalities, that environments in which people live and work

Compromise is an integral part of career development.

//WEB.TIP//
www.icis.indiana.edu/icis/
merkler.html
Merkler Style Preference Inventory
Helps you to understand your style of learning and working/pinpoints values and interests/suggests careers based on Holland's "RIASEC."

· · · · · · · · **HOLLAND'S VOCATIONAL PREFERENCE THEORY** · · · · · · · ·

Personality Types   Work Environment Characteristics

Pairings Over Time

Pairings Based Upon Individuals Searching for Compatible Work Environment

· · · · · · · · · · ·
Figure 1.4

resemble model environments, and that the pairing of people with compatible environments allows for the prediction of vocational choice, stability, and achievement.

A personality type is described as a cluster of personal characteristics defining how an individual typically copes with life's tasks.

For purposes of the theory, *persons* are categorized into six types:

- Realistic
- Intellectual
- Social
- Conventional
- Enterprising
- Artistic

The six types form models by which an individual's pattern of behavior may be compared for relative similarity. Although the scheme identifies the individual's major personality type, it also allows for more complex configurations where patterns of behavior reflect similarities to different types in varying magnitudes.

There are six corresponding *work environments*:

- Realistic
- Intellectual
- Social
- Conventional
- Enterprising
- Artistic

Generally, persons of the same type are found in each of the environments. The characteristics of a particular environment reflect the personal attributes of individuals in that group.

The main thrust of the theory is that persons move toward work environments that permit them to develop abilities, project personal values, and become involved in activities of interest. This movement toward a compatible work environment usually occurs over a period of time.

Interactions of persons with environments belonging to the same type or model tend to promote better personal stability and satisfaction.

People tend to project views of themselves and views of the world of work onto occupational titles. Holland analyzed hundreds of occupational titles and classified them into the six occupational "environments."

Holland also proposed that self-knowledge operates to increase or decrease the accuracy with which a person makes a vocational choice. This leads to two major hypotheses which he has empirically supported.

1. Persons with inaccurate self-knowledge make inadequate choices more frequently than do persons with more accurate self-appraisals.
2. Persons with more information about occupational environments make more adequate choices than do persons with less information.

Thus Holland concludes that a person's vocational behavior can be explained by the interaction of the personal orientation and the occupational environment. The **adequacy** of this choice relates to the level of self-knowledge and the level of occupational knowledge.

Theory Summary

Although there are a number of other important theories of vocational choice, these two theories provide the concepts needed for understanding the importance of regular career planning.

Ginzberg's theory helps to understand where you presently are in the vocational development process and what compromises will likely be necessary.

Holland's theories stress the importance of having an accurate self-concept and emphasize that a high level of occupational knowledge is needed for making a sound career decision.

Conclusion
• •

Career planning is more than a buzz word. It is a way of thinking about the choices that you must make in career decision making.

Career planning impacts on all ages. There is no single age group to which the concepts best apply. Career planning is a circular process that recycles itself over and over again as people face recurring life changes.

Ours is a dynamic world that changes career choices regularly. The planning cycle forces us into a lifetime of adjusting.

Career planning is a process that occurs many different times in everyone's life. No one is immune. It is a systematic way of looking at career decisions, which are no longer singular events that occur only when one graduates from high school or college.

The basic concept revolves around a self-assessment, a career exploration, and a placement plan. Compromise, time constraints, and economic pressures force decisions throughout the process.

Self-assessment is knowing yourself. It is a process that can be learned. The goal is to create the highest possible level of self-awareness.

Career exploration is a searching and investigative activity. Only if you understand the alternatives is there a reasonable chance of a fair analysis for career choice. The process involves a systematic collection of information about career options.

Search is the process of transferring the exploration process to the real market place. It involves implementing a plan designated to meet a specific career goal which has been transformed into an entry-level, middle-level, or top-level assignment in the managerial, technical, or professional career arenas.

Search activities consist of resumes, letters, contacts, interviews, and job offers.

Through the techniques of introspection, self-evaluation, and psychological testing, individuals can be classified into the six personal orientations and, thus, be matched with a compatible occupational environment. Individuals making vocational choices search for work environments that satisfy their personal orientations.

Career planning integrates the results of the self-assessment, career exploration, and placement processes. This integration lays the foundation for a continuous flow of information designed to keep career planning up-to-date.

If properly conceived and executed, career decision making will be a series of minor adjustments on a rolling basis. Such an adjustment process allows for a maximum level of career satisfaction. Should there be a need for a major career thrust change, the components will be in place at all times to meet the situation.

Self-Assessment:

Methods – Personal Qualities – Projects

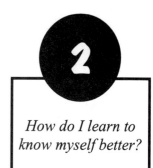

How do I learn to know myself better?

Any major library has hundreds of books on the job hunting process. Nearly all of them recommend starting the job search with an analysis of goals. It is virtually impossible to start a journey without some idea of the destination.

Telling you to set some realistic career goals seems logical enough, but that is a long way from where you must start. How do you go about setting career goals? "To be successful in life" is just not specific enough for potential employers who want to know, "What can you do for me now?"

Self-Assessment

Purpose

A self-assessment is the starting point. A self-assessment is a detailed, thorough analysis of your background, interests, and aspirations. Literally hundreds of factors go into the analysis.

The reason you prepare a self-assessment is to determine the most important criteria to use in analyzing your potential career options. The goal is to arrive at an optimal (not a perfect) match between personal desires and your career alternatives.

There could reasonably be many career fields that would satisfy your needs and desires. Career planning is a decision-oriented process that proposes to rank order your list of career options. The results of your self-assessment will be used extensively in your interviews.

Definition

The self-assessment is a mental exercise. It involves putting thoughts on paper and then prioritizing them in an order that is useful in appraising career directions.

Conducting a self-assessment is actually taking a personal inventory. First, make a list of the items in your "inventory." Then assign a value in terms of quantity, quality, and relative importance to each item. There are many methods that aid in this stock-taking process.

Your self-assessment is your personal balance sheet of assets and liabilities.

I'LL JUST LAY RIGHT HERE AND DIE AND GET IT OVER WITH NOW

Few, if any employers hire managerial or professional applicants solely on the basis of information on resumes or application blanks. Most employers want collaborative evidence to prove that you have the ability to perform the assignment in a superior manner. Employers obtain that collaborative evidence via reference checks, personal interviews, and tests.

Employers have devised elaborate methods to determine your abilities, motivation, and potential to achieve.

Your resume helps to indicate whether or not you are qualified to do a given job.

The crucial factor they must determine is your motivation level. **Will** you work hard and get along well with others?

There are small clues in the education and work experience sections of your resume that reveal motivation. Usually the motivational factors are determined via personal interviews, tests, and conversations with people who know you well.

Reality Check

A properly performed self-assessment boosts your confidence level significantly. You feel more certain about your skills and capabilities.

Self-assessment exercises polish your awareness of the skill set that you own and develop materials which you will use later in an interview presentation.

A regularly conducted self-assessment often signals to you that the time is appropriate to consider a major career or job change. It forces the employment change by alerting you to the fact that your career satisfaction should be much higher. The results assist in formulating a new direction in your life that may maximize your longer-term career satisfaction.

Goal Setting

The result of your self-assessment culminates into a statement of your goals. Before you jump into the work of conducting the self-assessment, you need to convince yourself of its value.

It is impossible to hit a target that you have not set up. Whether your goals are personal, career, financial, social, or spiritual, they cannot be achieved until you convince yourself that goal setting is important.

Goals must be written. Broad concepts in your mind cannot be translated into meaningful specifics. Goals cannot be wandering generalities if they are to be met.

Goals must be quantifiable into some specific time frame. It is best to break goals into both long-term goals and short-term goals so that incremental progress can be measured for motivational purposes.

Goal attainment needs a regular review process which can serve as a feedback vehicle to force you to stay on your tasks or allow you to reassess your goals in light of new developments.

The self-assessment concept works. Millions of people are involved in personal goal setting. Even your employer will demand adherence to organizational goals that were realistically established—perhaps with your input—over a pre-defined period of time. Most work goals carry annual time parameters. Yours should, too!

You may find that your various goals conflict. A resolution results after you write them down in each category, quantify them, and add the time dimension. Convincing yourself of the value of goal setting is the first step in employing the self-assessment techniques recommended in the following pages.

Your self-assessment is a precursor to establishing personal goals. Your efforts make sense only to the extent that they satisfy some pre-defined objectives. Your mission in life should be to establish **SMART** goals.

- Smart goals are **Specific.**
  General and vague goals are unacceptable.
- Smart goals are **Measurable.**
  Can you tell when you have met your goals?
- Smart goals are **Attainable.**
  Unrealistic goals cause a feeling of failure.
- Smart goals are **Relevant.**
  Your goals must relate to what you want out of life.
  What is relevant for others may not be appropriate for you.
- Smart goals are **Trackable.**
  Can you observe your goals being achieved?
  Is there a feeling of accomplishment as you progress?

Smart goals demonstrate your commitment to excellence. Your success relates to your ability to set and measure meaningful goals.

· · · · · · · · · · ·
Figure 2.2

Goals come after your self-assessment.

Self-Assessment Techniques

· ·

There is no one best way to conduct a self-assessment. Several different methods can be employed independently or in concert to reach the same conclusions.

Counselors

High school and college career counselors frequently offer personal guidance in the self-assessment. Professional career consultants offer the same service for a fee.

These professionals supplement their first impressions by skillful probing and analyzing psychological tests. Psychological tests provide data which cannot easily be obtained in personal interviews.

Websites

The www.jobweb.org/catapult/assess.htm website of this professional association offers a variety of assessment tools, some of which require a fee. The career development manual provides a template and exercises to assist in choosing a career, beginning with self-assessment and continuing through tips for acquiring practical work experience and, finally, undertaking a job search. A career interest assessment service is available for a fee; the assessment entails completion of an interest inventory, which then is matched with the interest patterns of various occupational groups to determine which career path an individual would be likely to enjoy. Additional services include a career success map, which is an online career focus testing profile that gives individuals and company managers a guide for career

METHODS OF SELF-ASSESSMENT

- Autobiography
- Personal Inventories
- Psychological Tests

· · · · · · · · · · ·
Figure 2.3

decisions, and career web assessment, which offers the job seeker career planning assistance, including a variety of self-assessment tools.

U.S. News

By searching the www.usnews.com site for information on careers, colleges, graduate schools, financial aid and scholarships, and campus life you will discover more career planning ideas and a great interest and skills test. This site allows you to conduct line-by-line comparisons of schools for admissions, demographics, financial aid, and more. For those conducting job searches, the site provides over 1,000 career profiles, a listing of "*hot* job tracks," advice on using want ads, search engines, and headhunters. The Campbell Interest and Skill Survey is one of the best assessment instruments. There is also advice on resumes, cover letters, interviews and salary negotiation.

You can use these websites and others to help you interpret the results of several tests you may find available on the web.

Publications

A wide variety of publications, mostly in workbook format, are used in organizing and synthesizing data about you. With all of this help available from both professional counselors and publications, the key word to remember is "self." A self-assessment must be conducted by you.

Self-assessment is a do-it-yourself project. The result is a very private matter. Information is drawn from a variety of reputable sources. Ideas and opinions from friends, teachers, employers, parents, neighbors, clergy, relatives, and others aid in the fact-gathering process. Inquiring offers great insights which improve the *accuracy* of the self-assessment.

Your self-assessment must be written.

The self-assessment is a writing project. It is not an exercise that can be stored in your memory in an unorganized fashion.

The self-assessment probes deeply into your inner feelings and is not a document to be shared indiscriminately with employers. It reveals your personal strengths and weaknesses.

An understanding of your liabilities is critical in sound career decision making, but it is not necessarily appropriate for the job search process. The end product of the self-assessment is a realistic self-appraisal that can be used with career information.

Self-assessment techniques fall into three categories: Autobiographies, Personal Inventories, and Psychological Tests.

Autobiography

An autobiography is written in narrative form, in contrast with the outline format of a resume. It is a personal story. The usual starting point is around the age of 16 and the story continues chronologically up to the present.

Some approaches do not use a chronological pattern. Some people prefer to document their life history under such headings as family experiences, professional work activities, education, work experiences, etc. Others prefer to orient the analysis to values, interests, personal qualities, and skills.

The approach matters very little. What is important is the writing down of thoughts that relate to the past. The past is a good predictor of the future. The analysis delves into the reasons past decisions were made. Future decisions are likely to draw upon the same set of decision criteria.

```
...............  PSYCHOLOGICAL TESTS  ...............

    Type of Test                    Measures

    • Intelligence      • Abstract reasoning and capacity for mastering problems
    • Achievement       • Extent of knowledge in a given field
    • Aptitude          • Potential for acquiring specific types of knowledge
    • Interest          • Stock taking of likes, dislikes, skills
    • Personality       • Emotional makeup, stability, and adjustment

                        • • • • • • • • • • •
                             Figure 2.4
```

Inventories

Inventories are checklists. Their value lies in the fact that they help you identify the words that best describe your values, interests, personality, skills, etc. The checklist of words or phrases help you understand the meaning of the concept. The words help jog your memory.

Career workbooks often use inventories as an aid in helping you identify factors which you feel relate to you. In addition to clarifying the meaning of the characteristic, inventories often provide a system of classifying variables.

Inventories help draw out specific strengths and weaknesses. These characteristics assist you in assessing why you behave as you do and assist in predicting your future actions.

Psychological Tests

Another important tool used in the self-assessment is psychological testing. Psychological tests are tools used by a career counselor trained in the use of tests. Tests are measuring devices that add new bits of information which career counselors use in developing a clearer picture of you.

Test effectiveness depends largely on the counselor's knowledge of the scope and limits of the tests used.

Fees are usually associated with administration of psychological tests, and they vary widely depending upon the number and type of tests administered. It can get expensive when a counselor's time is factored into the cost.

Shop around for these services. Visit websites yourself and take the more common, self-interpreted tests first.

Tests are predictors of future performance.

The pre-test instruction, the test administration, and an extensive personal analysis of the results can take several hours of a career counselor's time. Some professional career counselors charge $50 to $200 per hour for their time.

Tests are most frequently used by high school and college career counselors as an aid in career decision making. The counselor can more accurately recommend specific career fields.

The use of tests by employers for *selection* purposes appears to be growing again after a period of waning. It is expensive to prove that a given test is a valid predictor of career performance but worth the cost. Many employers use tests.

Counselors provide a professional interpretation of the results but leave the career choice decisions in your hands. Testing does not provide decisions. It provides fruitful information.

Types of Tests

Career counselors typically administer one or more of five major types of tests. These are summarized in Figure 2.4. These five types of tests are grouped according to the functions they perform.

THAT'S RIGHT, MOOCHER, I'M UNEQUIVOCALLY, INCONTESTABLY, INDISPUTABLY, UNMITIGATEDLY INDUBITABLY READY FOR THAT VOCABULARY TEST.

Achievement tests measure mastery of a given subject such as mathematics, English, chemistry, and so forth. Achievement tests attempt to measure actual learning in a specific subject matter after a period of instruction. They provide an objective measure of progress and thus are helpful to career counselors in assessing skill levels and abilities which might later be related to specific career endeavors.

Aptitude tests purport to measure certain personal characteristics which might indicate the capacity to acquire some specific knowledge or skill. Aptitude tests try to predict future success in a given field of study. These tests measure the capacity to acquire certain skills or proficiencies based on innate ability and past experience.

Aptitude tests are most likely to be the type an employer would use in personnel selection. Aptitude tests cover a wide range of abilities related to most work areas.

Interest inventories indicate the extent of similarity between a person's interests/preferences and those of persons already successfully employed in a specified occupation.

The underlying principle is that the more similar the interests, the greater your chances of work satisfaction and job success.

Intelligence tests are primarily concerned with complexity, level of difficulty, quality, and rate of mental activity. The score represents measures of intellectual functioning in an abstract reasoning manner. Intelligence tests are rarely used in career counseling.

Personality tests measure emotional makeup, stability, and the degree of life adjustment. They are helpful in eliciting feelings, values, and motives. They measure social poise, intrapersonal characteristics, and maturity. A career counselor using personality measures must be highly trained and experienced in competently administering and interpreting these tests.

Norms test is a standardized set of measurements of a person's responses to a group of tasks or questions. More general inferences can be drawn later from the measurements. Interpretation of test scores give a base which provides statistical comparisons later.

A norm is the typical score for a specified population group. For example, a mechanical aptitude score might be compared to the mechanical aptitude of a group of successful mechanical engineers. Every test has a test manual and other literature which support the tests and provides information to the career counselor.

I'M GIVING UP BEFORE I REALLY EVEN GET STARTED.

The test score is meaningful only when it is used properly by an expert. It must be compared to an appropriate population group. When the norm concept is not properly understood, there is great risk in drawing incorrect conclusions.

In general, the population sample on which the test has been standardized should relate as closely as possible to the age, socio-economic status, educational level, etc. of the individual being tested.

Reliability. Reliability refers to how consistently a test measures the same characteristic in successive measurements. A given individual should get approximately the same results each time the test is taken. The publishers of most commercial tests have gone to great lengths to insure reliability within all norm groups.

Validity. Validity determines the extent to which the test measures what it purports to measure. Validity measures how well the results of the test correlate with the given criterion.

For example, an MBA aptitude test score should correlate highly with actual academic achievement. If the test predicts a high level of academic success, the later academic grades will be high if the test is valid.

Summary of Assessment Methods

There are many methods which produce accurate pictures of the characteristics making up the self-assessment. Measures of values, interests, personality, and skills are rarely precise. Experts can aid in the assessing of the measurements and can even offer suggestions on how the pieces might fit together. However, only you can legitimately pull all of the factors together and form an accurate self-assessment.

There is no method of measurement that brings all of the factors together in a nice, neat package. Your career decision will be an educated guess. The degree of risk in your career decision can be minimized by you being as objective as possible in your self-assessment interpretation. It is your life at stake.

Identify Your V.I.P.S.

You may possess the same educational background and similar work experiences as others. What makes you unique are your *motivational* factors.

An evaluation of motivational factors is subjective, but these factors can make a unique fit for particular occupational fields. Thus, an assessment of them is important. They cannot be accurately identified and evaluated without your total cooperation.

Four frequently referenced personal qualities which aid in the analysis of a realistic fit into various occupational fields are your **V**alues, **I**nterests, **P**ersonal Qualities, and **S**kills.

PERSONAL QUALITIES: THE VIPS

Values
Interests
Personality
Skills

Figure 2.5

Your VIPS reveal your motivations.

INTERVIEW VALIDITY

Directly or indirectly, employers evaluate each of the personal VIPS. Their classification schemes may be slightly different, but they are getting at the heart of the matter nonetheless. The employers' objective is to develop an accurate image of you.

College career counselors and executive search experts are in unique positions to listen in on recruiters' conversations about candidates whom they have evaluated. Their eavesdropping includes some interesting discussions about candidates' backgrounds. In many cases, candidates never think about themselves in such descriptive terms. Those descriptive terms recruiters use most frequently relate directly to the VIPS.

Employers' analyses are occasionally wrong. How valid is a job interview? Valid or not, the interview supporting tests, and recommendations are the basis of most employment decisions. The employer can not afford to make many mistakes. A misinterpretation of the VIPS by you or the employer can have long-term, undesirable consequences.

Starting Points

Education, work experience, family, and environment are the major factors influencing values, interests, personality, and skills (your VIPS). Education, work, family, and environment go back to very early years in your life. Early experiences shape your views of yourself. These are projected in career choices.

Once your VIPS become set, they are difficult to change. Skills can be manipulated easier, but even skills are difficult to rearrange and expand once values, interests, and personality are entrenched.

Career goal setting is the ultimate purpose of career planning. Goal setting emanates from VIPS. VIPS are then integrated with real world career options.

Importance of VIPS

Most people find it difficult to write or speak about themselves in terms of their values, interests, personal qualities, and skills. You may stammer when asked:

- What are your values?
- What are your interests?
- Describe your personality.
- Identify your best skills.

Why are these questions so difficult? They seem quite important. They are much more important than the mundane items that appear on most resumes. They obviously have a great bearing on career planning.

Education and work experiences play important roles in career selection. However, nothing plays a greater role in career selection (from either the employer's or the employee's perspective) than your personal VIPS.

No matter what the career field, there is always an oversupply of applicants seeking positions in it. Nearly every job has more than one applicant for it.

THAT'S NO WAY TO TACKLE THE JOB SEARCH PROCESS.

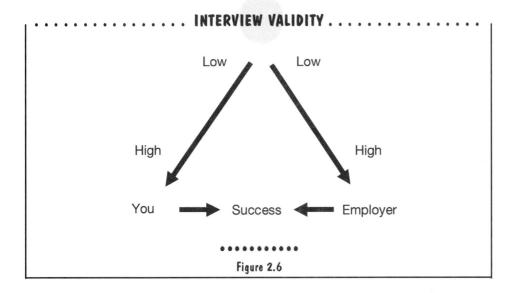

Low   Low

High   High

You → Success ← Employer

Figure 2.6

For a given opening in a technical, professional, or managerial position, chances are high that there will be several applicants with adequate education and work experience backgrounds.

How does an employer decide who gets the job? The decision is nearly always based on an appraisal of your personal VIPS. The VIPS have the most direct bearing on your ability and desire to accomplish work at the managerial, technical, and professional level.

Does every individual with great credentials get a job offer after every interview? Of course not! Some applicants get nice letters that say, "I am sorry but your qualifications and interests do not match the. . . ." Why? The reason can most often be traced to an evaluation of the VIPS.

Many people barge right into the search stage of career planning. What's wrong with that? They have failed to assess the very points that potential employers will be evaluating.

Decision Responsibility

The employer's *job* decision can become a *career* decision for you. You can easily get locked into a career or job which is not right for you.

Responsibilities and salaries tend to increase as you mature and progress. It becomes more difficult to leave a "well-paying job." Unhappiness results. Sound decisions by both you and the employer are essential.

Whether accurate or not, the employer processes information from you as truth. Through your interview comments you relay information to employers.

The employer makes decisions on the basis of the information received in the interview, on the resume, tests, and from others who know you.

Many applicants receive turndowns from employers for jobs for which they are eminently qualified. They may have the right combination of education, experience, and the personal VIPS but yet fail to communicate an accurate picture.

Conversely, many applicants receive job offers and accept employment in jobs for which they are only marginally qualified. This happens when applicants transmit inaccurate pictures. Employers and employees both come out losers when these employees later fail to produce on the job.

Every job has several applicants.

CAREER SUCCESS FACTORS

- Know Yourself
- Know Your Options
- Set Goals
- Create a Plan
- Execute Your Plan

Figure 2.7

Increasing the validity of the job interview is more important to you than to the employer. Although the employer may suffer some economic loss, you have far more to lose.

The validity of an interview for both parties is greatly increased if both parties know specifically what they are seeking.

How can the validity be high if you do not really know what you want? It can't.

The self-assessment phase of career planning controls the goal direction decision. Your analysis of your VIPS starts the self-assessment.

Communicating Your VIPS

Communicate the truth about your VIPs.

Employers are addressing the interview validity issue. Most recruiters go through rigorous interview training programs. Trained recruiters are better at the selection process.

You must also get better at packaging the truth. That is not done by interview coaching, polishing the truth, or deceptive packaging. Those things increase the ratio of offers to interviews, but they fail to increase the quality of the career decision. Superficial window dressing hurts more than it helps.

One fundamental marketing principle is that you cannot sell a product if you don't know the product and believe in it. Selling a product without a thorough knowledge of the product comes back to haunt the seller. The self-assessment is a process designed to get to know the product better.

Skills
• • • • • • • • • • • • • • •

Skills are individual talents which enable a person to perform a given activity. Skills can be both taught and learned.

How proficient are you in each skill that you possess?

Within a skill, there are degrees of proficiency. The situation is not usually one of skill or no skill, but is one of the degree to which one can perform a given activity. Most skills can be greatly improved by practice. Practice builds mastery.

The range of skill ability extends from "some awareness and ability" to "excellence or mastery." Skills gained through education vary widely depending upon an extensive set of circumstances including level of education, major field of study, reputation of institution, etc.

Nearly every managerial, technical, or professional job description lists a variety of skills that the employer considers important in accomplishing an assignment.

Within a job description, employers tend to list every conceivable skill that would be helpful in completing assignments. Rarely are "all" of these skills really necessary and rarely do employers attempt to specify the degree of excellence required in every skill. Often these skill listings scare away applicants needlessly.

Lack of acceptable skills is one of the most common reasons employers give for rejecting job applicants. The truth, however, is that values, interests, and personality are the real factors that cause most employers to reject candidates.

Skill Acquisition

The required skills for any career field can be clearly determined. Any job applicant who has completed a reasonable degree of homework will know before going into a job interview whether there is or is not a "skill" match.

```
. . . . . . . . . . . . . . . . . . . SKILL TYPES . . . . . . . . . . . . . . . . . . .
```

People Skills.
Mentoring	Negotiating	Instructing
Supervising	Persuading	Speaking

Data Skills.
Synthesizing	Coordinating	Analyzing
Compiling	Copying	Comparing

Things Skills.
Setting-Up	Controlling	Operating
Tending	Feeding	Handling

```
. . . . . . . . . . .
```
Figure 2.8

A carpenter does not apply for a job as a surgeon, of course, but there are "shades of grey." Employers seldom find perfect skill matches. You will seldom find a perfect skill match. Compromise by both parties is necessary.

Most skills are derived from education, but the level of educational attainment frequently fails to spell out the specific skills attained. For example, a four-year liberal arts education equips an individual with hundreds of skills that are directly career relatable, yet nowhere in the description of educational background is the skill or the level of the skill articulated.

Education is not the only source of skills. Skills also come from work experience, from personal life experiences, and from play activities.

The "Perfect 10" for a job seldom occurs.

Types of Skills

Skills break down into three groups:

- Data
- People
- Things

The *Dictionary of Occupational Titles* (U.S. Government Printing Office) is the first and last word on relating skills to specific occupations and jobs. Many of the skills specified in this book are found in thousands of job descriptions in all types of organizations that hire people. Each individual skill is defined in the *D.O.T.*

Many employers use a point system for specifying the skill difficulty level of the job. It is not uncommon for this point system to be used in the more sophisticated organizations for establishing salary grades.

A career position beyond your capacities is just as lacking in satisfaction as a position below your capacities. Being over-employed is not more beneficial to happiness than being under-employed. Both cause problems.

Skills Inventory

A skills inventory is an essential element in the self-assessment. Questions like "What do I have to offer?" and "What new skills do I need?" are pertinent.

A personal skill inventory requires thought and guidance. Figure 2.9 aids by identifying the skills most commonly referenced in descriptions of career fields. The overall goal is to find the career field that optimally coincides with your current and future capabilities.

NO ONE CAN SAY I DON'T HAVE MY VALUES STRAIGHT, MOM. I'VE GOT FAMILY RANKED NEAR THE TOP OF THE LIST, RIGHT AFTER MONEY.

An important dimension in both resume preparation and interview presentation is explaining to a potential employer your level of proficiency in certain basic skills. Figure 2.9 outlines many of the skills that employers try to evaluate when evaluating candidates for professional level positions.

What is your level of expertise for each skill noted? An enlightening exercise is to carefully evaluate your abilities by assigning a letter grade for yourself on each skill.

Values

Values are feelings. Feelings relate to facts, things, people, and even broad concepts. What is important in life? Some people might say family, friends, love, security, comfort, community, and leisure. Others might say career, money, time, education, marriage, etc.

Values help people make choices. They tend to prioritize the factors in our lives. They determine the relative importance of things which impact upon daily life. We are all a little different in our value perceptions.

Values Clarification

Value specification and clarification will help you understand yourself and guide future planning. Values help you understand colleagues and friends by building meaningful relationships.

There are no right and wrong values in a free society. Values derive from the way an individual has been taught. Values create the ability to accept certain norms and accepted standards of personal and group behavior.

Defining your values helps you get a handle on your self-assessment. If decisions, especially career decisions, are based upon a value system, it is clearly important to elaborate to yourself a definitive statement of the principles which guide important decisions in your life.

...AND ATTACK THE JOB HUNT WITH ALL VIGOR...

SKILLS INVENTORY FOR PROFESSIONAL POSITIONS

___ Accomplishing	___ Expediting	___ Promoting
___ Accounting	___ Fashioning	___ Pushing
___ Acquiring	___ Following Directions	___ Questioning
___ Acting	___ Following Orders	___ Rapport
___ (Analyzing)	___ Foresight	___ Reading
___ Assembling	___ Implementing	___ Relating
___ Building Things	___ Informing	___ Researching
___ Calculating	___ Initiating	___ Resolving Conflicts
___ Classifying	___ Innovating	___ Responding
___ Competing	___ Investing	___ Representing Others
___ Compiling	___ Inspiring	___ Reviewing
___ Computing	___ Instructing	___ Selling
___ Composing	___ Leading	___ Serving Others
___ Constructing	___ Lecturing	___ Setting-Up
___ Coordinating	___ Making Things	___ Speaking
___ Counseling	___ Managing	___ Structuring
___ Creating	___ Manipulating	___ Synthesizing
___ Dealing	___ Merchandising	___ Systematizing
___ Decision-Making	___ Motivating	___ Supervising
___ Demonstrating	___ Muscular	___ Talking
___ Designing	___ Number Manipulation	___ Teaching
___ Dexterity	___ Negotiating	___ Testing
___ Developing Ideas	___ Operating	___ Training
___ Directing	___ Organizing	___ Working - Mental
___ Discovering	___ Participating	___ Working - Physical
___ Editing	___ Persuading	___ Working with Ideas
___ Empathy	___ Planning	___ Working with Others
___ Evaluating People	___ Physical Handling	___ Working with Things
___ Evaluating Projects	___ Predicting	___ Writing
___ Examining	___ Problem Solving	___ Visualizing
___ (Excelling)	___ Programming	___ Verbalizing

Figure 2.9

Each employing organization has its own value system which is described as a "corporate culture." What is it? Would you fit in it?

The holding of certain beliefs influences your behavioral pattern. Actions may be explained by recognizing your value system. You make choices about how you want to live based upon your system of values.

To make a better career decision, start by clarifying the basis upon which your decisions are made.

Everyday life situations call for thought, decision making, and reasoned action. Different individuals find different solutions to identical problems. Your actions are based on your beliefs, attitudes, and values.

Attitudes, beliefs, and values impact upon people's decisions and actions. Some types of careers are incompatible with some people's values. Values help to determine the relative level of satisfaction a person derives from a career.

Rank order your top ten values.

Classifying Values

Figure 2.10 identifies an array of values. Values take on added meaning when one begins to classify them. Each item in the list could be placed on a personal like/dislike continuum. They could also be ranked in order of importance to you. The list is certainly not all-inclusive, but it is representative of values that many people regard as important.

· · · · · · · · · · **"WORK VALUES — HAPPINESS IS . . ."** · · · · · · · · · ·

Achievement	Location
Advancement	Love
Adventure	Marriage
Aesthetics	Money
Affluence	Morality
Art	Music
Authority	Objectivity
Autonomy	Pace
Avocation	Personality
Association	Physical Appearance
Beauty	Politics
Career	Possessions
Change	Prestige
Comfort	Pressure
Commitment	Race Discrimination
Community	Recognition
Computers	Religion
Creative	Rules
Culture	Security
Dependence	Sex
Drugs	Social Good
Education	Solitude
Esteem	Sports
Ethics	Stability
Family	Status
Flexibility	Study
Food	Subjectivity
Friends	Time
Health	Tradition
Home	Travel
Hobby	Truth
Honesty	Understanding
Importance	Variety
Independence	War/Peace
Intelligence	Wealth
Involvement	Welfare
Leadership	Work Ethics
Leisure	

· · · · · · · · · · · ·

Figure 2.10

...AND BLUFF MY WAY INTO A JOB.

One way to get a handle on the self-assessment is to first ask the question "How important is (this value) to me?" A one-line written statement is an adequate response. By the end of that brief exercise, you will begin to see how you make decisions.

Values Appreciation

It is not necessarily imperative that people who share common working hours and similar types of jobs maintain the same value structure. It is important, however, that work partners be tolerant of each other's values. Otherwise, the ensuing discord could have major disruptive effects on work performance.

Success is a main concern in career planning. Becoming involved in an unpleasant work situation is not a sound idea, especially if the situation can be avoided. Although you might be very tolerant of another person's viewpoints, they might not be tolerant of yours.

An example of this conflict can be found in the case where a "black/white mentality" locks horns with a "laissez-faire mentality." Each party believes his or her point of view is the proper one. Why should you get boxed into that corner when proper career planning can help avoid such unpleasant work situations?

Interests
• • • • • • • • • • • • • • • • • • • •

Interests are the things you like or dislike doing. Interests usually spring from a person's underlying value set. People attach more value to things they like to do and less value to things they do not like to do.

Values tend to be very stable over a lifetime, but interests change frequently. The range of interests a person may have is nearly unlimited. What is enjoyable in one period of life is not necessarily enjoyable in later periods of life.

Interests Influence Decisions

Current interests should not be quickly turned off in a self-assessment because they are less permanent. What you like to do in the short-run has a major bearing on what you are willing to do in the long-run. Careers change as interests change.

Interests profoundly influence career choice. You want to enjoy the work you are doing. Meaningful employment is a major contributor to career satisfaction. Interests may be less profound and esoteric than values, but they nonetheless influence which position you are willing to accept.

How well do your values coincide with others in your work group?

Your interests may change over the years.

Prioritizing Interests

For each of the activities listed in Figure 2.11, you could assign a high/low numeral to denote your personal interest. Some people have a very wide variety of different interests, whereas others have a great depth of interest in only a few activities.

The variable that narrows interests for most people is time. Time forces you to pick and choose among a variety of interests. You might enjoy boating, tennis, and football equally well, but due to only 2 to 3 hours of available playing time each day, you must choose only one of the activities per day.

Career interests and personal interests jell frequently. As Mark Twain suggested, "Why can't a person do for a living what he would otherwise do for a summer vacation?" Although play and work occasionally conflict, they frequently complement each other as well.

Career planning means coming to grips with your interests. One can improve his or her chances for career satisfaction if there is a logical, reasoned relationship between interests and career. Self-assessment involves determining the degree of your interests in various activities.

. . . . **INTERESTS** . . . .

Acting	Moving
Athletics	Outdoor Activities
Avocations	Planning
Being Alone	Playing
Being with Others	Reading
Challenging Limits	Relating
Competing	Relaxing
Controlling	Singing
Coordinating	Solving Problems
Creating Concepts	Solving Puzzles
Creating Things	Speaking
Deciding	Sports
Helping Others	Traveling
Hobbies	Working
Listening	Working with Hands
Managing	Working with Mind
Meeting People	Writing

. . . .

Figure 2.11

Personal Qualities

Judgments about people influence employment decisions. These judgments impact career decision making. You must assume that judgments about your personal qualities are reasonable, justified, honest, and motivated by a desire to see you succeed in a given career field.

Subjective Factors

In spite of the many laws designed to protect certain classes of employees, subjective factors still play a major role in hiring decisions. You must assume that there are valid supportable facts for using subjective factors in employment decisions.

Subjective factors influence employment decisions. It would be foolhardy to ignore the fact that personality is a key variable in the decision of whether to enter a career in the performing arts or a career in marketing. Certain personality types have a better chance of success in a given career field than other personality types.

Measuring personality is a very complicated process. Very expensive and elaborate tests have been developed to define, describe, and evaluate personality patterns. It often takes an expert to provide an accurate appraisal of personality variables.

For most career decisions, an in-depth personality analysis is not necessary. But a realistic understanding of your personal qualities helps in the evaluation process.

Personal Descriptors

You should try to evaluate your personal qualities. Figure 2.12, "Personal Descriptors," offers an excellent aid in assisting you in identifying the most important variables to review.

Regardless of the career field, every interviewer completes some sort of evaluation form after an interview. Rarely is an employment decision made without an interview. The resume and application blank usually adequately describe your work history and educational level. The interviewer's role is to describe your skills and personal qualities.

Time limits the extent of an interview write-up and evaluation. The majority of interviewers quickly jot down key words that appear descriptive of the person.

Hopefully, what is written is accurate and valid. Fortunately, you are in charge, not the interviewer. The impression left in the interviewer's mind comes directly from you. The interviewer's write-up can be greatly influenced by you.

Communicating Personal Qualities

As a serious career planner, you want the truth written down. Before a true description can be relayed, you must have a plan as to what information you want to transmit. If garbage is transmitted, garbage will be written down and decisions will be made (by both parties) on invalid information.

The personal quality component of the self-assessment plays a major role in the hiring decision. Even assuming a perfect combination of education, experience, and skills, a job offer in a career field is not assured.

An employer's assessment of personal qualities is a key factor in the employment decision. Some experts suggest that this assessment is 90 percent of the decision.

How do you measure your personal qualities?

//WEB.TIP//

www.keirsey.com
Keirsey Temperament Sorter
Web based instrument of 36 questions/presents 16 personality types and information on how to interpret results/many counseling sites use this well-known test.

Every interviewer fills out an evaluation form on you that describes your personal qualities.

You must influence the employer's evaluation of your personal qualities.

············ PERSONAL DESCRIPTORS ············

___ Able	___ Enthusiastic	___ Practical
___ Achiever	___ Expressive	___ Pragmatic
___ Active	___ Extrovert	___ Precise
___ Adaptable	___ Fair	___ Progressive
___ Aggressive	___ Flexible	___ Punctual
___ Alert	___ Follows Through	___ Questioning
___ Aloof	___ Follower	___ Quiet
___ Ambitious	___ Forceful	___ Rambler
___ Analytical	___ Free	___ Rational
___ Animated	___ Friendly	___ Realistic
___ Articulate	___ Gentle	___ Reasonable
___ Attractive	___ Giving	___ Relaxed
___ Beautiful	___ Glib	___ Reliable
___ Bold	___ Gregarious	___ Respectful
___ Bright	___ Hard worker	___ Responsible
___ Calm	___ Honest	___ Secure
___ Carefree	___ Honorable	___ Selfish
___ Caring	___ Humorous	___ Self-confident
___ Certain	___ Imaginative	___ Self-reliant
___ Challenger	___ Independent	___ Self-starter
___ Cheerful	___ Ingenious	___ Sensitive
___ Cleaver	___ Innovative	___ Serious
___ Cocky	___ Inspiring	___ Sharp Dresser
___ Competent	___ Intellectual	___ Shy
___ Competitive	___ Intuitive	___ Sincere
___ Confident	___ Introvert	___ Singable
___ Conforming	___ Judgmental	___ Skillful
___ Conscientious	___ Kind	___ Speaker
___ Controlled	___ Knowledgeable	___ Sociable
___ Challenging	___ Leader	___ Soft talker
___ Cooperative	___ Lively	___ Sophisticated
___ Courteous	___ Logical	___ Stable
___ Creative	___ Loyal	___ Striver
___ Decisive	___ Mature	___ Superficial
___ Dependable	___ Methodical	___ Supervisor
___ Determined	___ Meticulous	___ Supportive
___ Dignified	___ Non-committal	___ Systematic
___ Disciplined	___ Observant	___ Tactful
___ Direct	___ Optimist	___ Tenacious
___ Diplomatic	___ Organized	___ Tolerant
___ Discreet	___ Organizer	___ Traveler
___ Do Gooder	___ Original	___ Trustful
___ Doer	___ Overweight	___ Trusting
___ Domineering	___ Patient	___ Tough
___ Driver	___ Perceptive	___ Wise
___ Effervescent	___ Perfectionist	___ Workaholic
___ Efficient	___ Personable	___ Writer
___ Emotional	___ Persuasive	___ Youthful
___ Energetic	___ Pessimist	___ Zestful
___ Enterprising	___ Pleasant	

· · · · · · · · ·

Figure 2.12

WAIT A MINUTE, RALPH. YOU'RE WORTH PLENTY.

You must have a firm grasp on your personal qualities. Are your personal qualities consistent with those of the majority of people currently in the profession? How would you know if you had not assessed your own personal qualities and knew what information to share with an interviewer in order to obtain a fair and accurate employment decision?

What personal qualities appear to be desirable in specific career fields? There is little information available due to the subjective nature of the topic. It is difficult to find this data written in books, the web, or pamphlets.

Several psychological test publishers and university researchers have done extensive study in this area. Analysis of the norm groups of the tests forms the best single source of information.

One other good source is people who are currently working in the career field. For the average person, informational interviewing is probably the best way to obtain personality profiles.

Observation and probing questions can provide fairly accurate pictures. But do not base your assumed profile on only one or two informational interviews. You need a variety of collaborative data on each occupational area that you are considering.

Self-Assessment Career Action Projects

Career planning starts with the self-assessment. The only way for you to begin a self-assessment is to physically put words on paper. Everyone needs some aid in conducting the analysis.

Career projects are designed to provide a logical framework for thought and action to aid you in achieving a fair self-assessment.

Career projects offer a means of dealing with a complex situation. The career projects build a progressive story about you. As the story unfolds, a wealth of information falls out as if a novel were developing.

This is not solely a project in self-analysis. You will find real applicability for the results when you later move into the search phase of career planning. The self-assessment career projects contain answers to hundreds of interview questions which you will later face.

The benefit of the career project in self-assessment is directly proportional to the amount of time, thought, and effort put into it. The impact that the efforts have on career planning is significant. The result is truly worth the effort expended.

Are your personal qualities consistent with others working in the field?

KEY DECISION POINTS BY TYPE OF EXPERIENCES

- Education
- Work History
- Personal Events
- Social/Professional Activities

Figure 2.13

Autobiography Project

When written in sufficient depth, an autobiography is one of the most effective methods of self-assessment. Unlike the resume, the autobiography is not simply a brief summary which lists events and achievements; rather it is written in a prose style as a story. The purpose is to logically draw out variables that relate to an understanding of the self.

Chronological Narrative. The narrative describes all significant events in your life. It documents all important episodes where turning-point decisions occurred. To make certain all key points receive appropriate attention and nothing is left out, you should start by writing the narrative in a historical, chronological sequence of events placing special emphasis on *key decision points*.

Along with the time sequence of events, the key decision points form the outline of the biography. These decision points may be education, family, personal events, or job related episodes. This phase of the autobiography can vary from a minimum of three typed pages to as much as twenty pages depending upon your background and the depth of analysis you wish to pursue.

It is important to give an explanation and rationale for the various life transitional points. This analysis brings out important value considerations. These values produce the interest levels which have great influence on career satisfaction.

A straight narration of a life sequence rarely achieves the overall objective of self-understanding. Values, interests, and personal qualities surface only after a thorough analysis of life decisions. Write down the *rationale* for key decisions in the sequence of events.

Regrouping. This analysis starts with a regrouping of the chronological events. Rework the analysis under the following headings:

- education
- work experiences
- family background
- professional/social/civic activities

The regrouping should be written in a highly organized but narrative style. Again, discuss the "why" of each decision made.

The major reason for the regrouping is to put the results into an organized framework which later becomes the basis of the search phase of career planning. Your skills and interests begin to form a pattern which makes the later interview presentation and resume preparation flow into a harmonized communication package.

The *education* section must not be simply a listing of events. There must be an explanation of the *rationales* for your educational decisions and then an evaluation of those decisions after the training was completed.

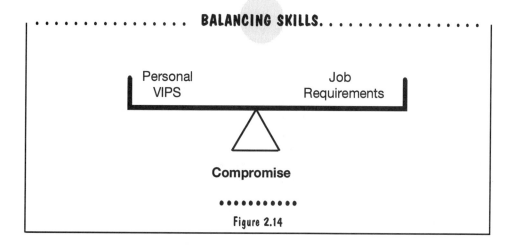

Personal   Job
VIPS   Requirements

Compromise

Figure 2.14

Try to cover such points as grades, choice of educational institution, majors, courses, faculty, etc. Cover the decisions that you had the option of making.

Your previous *work* experience includes full-time, part-time, and summer experiences. Your attitude toward work says much about your work ethic and career value structure. Discuss both good and bad experiences.

Try to show how each work activity benefitted you. Describe your duties and responsibilities in great depth by analyzing typical days, weeks, and months. Discuss the relationships you had with supervisors, peers, and subordinates. Highlight key points of advancement and responsibilities given and/or taken. No job was too insignificant to cover in this analysis.

Why did you make the decisions that most impacted your life?

The reason for covering *personal events* and *social/professional/civic activities* is to draw a value and interest profile.

Your flexibility of choice was probably greater in these activities than in any work or educational endeavor. How did these choices differ? Why did you elect these activities? How did family background influence these independent choices?

Your family and social background activities have equipped you with certain skills that education and work could never have provided. What have you learned from these situations? Would you consider what you have learned to be valuable skills? Are the skills applicable to work environments?

The regrouping of the chronological autobiographical narrative provides new insights for your decision making. Why did you make certain decisions? Would you make the same decisions again? These insights begin to bring out your basic value system, your interests, and your personal qualities.

You will draw upon these insights in your employment interviews and resume preparation.

IT REMINDS ME OF A LONG TIME AGO ...BEFORE BALL POINT PENS.

Deliverable. Provide at least one typewritten page each for work experience, education, family background, and civic/professional/social activities. Try to have at least one single-spaced, typewritten page for each of these four categories.

The autobiography, written in the two different formats, will serve as the basis for future career planning decisions.

SURE! I'VE GOT PLENTY OF TIME TO HELP YOU ASSESS ALL OF YOUR STRENGTHS, KIP... MY BUS DOESN'T COME FOR ANOTHER TWO MINUTES.

Fewer than half of all college graduates earn degrees in fields directly related to a specific managerial, technical, or professional position.

Skill Identification Project

This project is designated to assist you in identifying your skills, the degree of competence you possess in those skills, and ways to illustrate that you have the skills.

Job descriptions describe a basic set of qualifications required to do a job. There is occasionally another set of qualifications which are "preferred" but are not required. Qualifications may be specified in terms of education or prior work experience.

What an employer is really seeking is a *set of skills*. Education and experience frequently serve to develop those skills. However, skills can be developed in a variety of ways. The means by which skills have been acquired are not always evident in a formal listing of a person's background experiences and schooling.

You need to know what skills you have and what levels of competence you possess. Don't assume that employers know which education class and work experience fostered basic skills.

Identification. Skills can be identified. Figure 2.9 gives an inventory of the skills which are most widely requested of individuals seeking managerial, technical, and professional positions. Many of these skills are developed by means other than formal education and/or formal work experience.

Read each skill noted in Figure 2.9. Make a list of those that you feel you possess. Leave room beside each skill on your list to make a note of your level of competence and how you obtained the skill.

Competence. Using your list of skills, give yourself a letter grade of "A" through "C." Try to force your ratings into a normal distribution of grades (A = Excellent; B = Above Average; C = Good/acceptable). Try to create an equal number of A, B, and C skill levels. You probably will not give yourself any "D"s or "F"s since you will have eliminated those when you identified your skills.

Source. As you grade yourself, make some brief comments about each skill. Write three or four sentences about how you obtained the skill. Identify the method you employed to acquire and improve the skill. Be specific. Make references to specific sources and circumstances, such as courses, jobs, and formal and informal activities.

SO WITH ALL THAT TRAINING, WHY DO I FEEL LIKE I DON'T KNOW ANYTHING?

Examples. You now have a good idea of your various skills and the levels of your competence in them. Your thoughts now need to be organized in a manner that can be readily utilized in career planning.

You need to be able to recite your most desirable skills quickly and in a confident, supporting manner, especially in an interview.

Figure 2.9 lists skills in alphabetical order. However, you need to deal primarily with your "A" and "B" competence levels of skills.

Rank your twelve best skills. Forget about whether or not your skills are job-related. The job-related aspect becomes relevant only after the self-assessment. Rank order your skills in the way you feel they are best. Put your best skills at the top.

Deliverable. Select any four of your twelve best skills. Write each skill name at the top of a separate sheet of paper along with your competency rating in that skill. Write one single-spaced, typewritten page of analysis for each skill. Assume that you are explaining to an interviewer how you acquired the skill.

Explain how you acquired the skill and how you assess your level of competence. It is best to provide support for your level of competence rating by giving an example.

Your skills might have been developed through participation in a class project, a term paper, a laboratory assignment, a tutorial activity, cultural experiences, social organizations, family activities, civic responsibilities, work experience, etc. Pull out some mini-experiences. Explain the circumstances. Show how the skill was used.

Ideally, your highest-rated skills and those required for an occupation should relate exactly. In our imperfect world this rarely happens, however. Employers never find the "ideal candidate," and you rarely find the "ideal career." Compromises are made by both parties. There are usually some reasonably close matches.

The "resume" and "job description" do a fair job of initial selection. The interview process does the fine tuning that fits the pieces together.

It is not unusual for a job candidate to have every skill needed and yet not get the job. Why? It could be that the skill has not been communicated to the employer by the candidate.

The employer assumes the skills are missing unless shown otherwise. This project has you list these skills so that you can make effective use of them in subsequent job interviews. You must show each skill and how it relates to the job.

· · · · · · · · · · · · · · **CORPORATE CULTURES VARY.** · · · · · · · · · · · · · ·

Aloof	Laissez-faire
Aristocratic	Militaristic
Bureaucratic	Old-fashioned
Click-your-heels	Parental
Creative	Pompous
Cut-throat	Pressure
Developmental	Prestigious
Free-wheeling	Sink or Swim
Hierarchical	Supportive
Intense	Team-oriented
Ivory Towerist	Technocratic

· · · · · · · · · · ·

Figure 2.15

Values Clarification Project

Over a period of many years, you develop a unique way of thinking. A personal philosophy appears to develop and mature during the teen and college years. It evolves from family, religious, social, and cultural relationships and environments. These philosophical views will influence your future work settings.

It is not necessarily imperative that the people with whom you share your working hours maintain the same value structure. It is important, however, that you and your work partners be tolerant of each other's values because intolerance can lead to discord which has major disruptive effects on work performance. Conflicts are not healthy for success.

Since success is one of your main concerns, it makes sense to analyze exactly where you stand. You may be quite tolerant of others' viewpoints, but employees presently working with a potential employer may not be as tolerant. A "nuts and bolts" type of person can run at odds with a "thinker" or "dreamer."

This means that you must first develop a high level of awareness of your own value structure. Others are not likely to be in as good a position to assess your capacity to fit in with the environment. By knowing your values, you are much better prepared to chart the lay-of-the-land when you test the potential work setting.

The most difficult aspect of value analysis is assessing the potential work environment. What is needed is an assessment of the "personal feeling" you get when you approach the work setting. Do you feel comfortable with the people for whom you work? Are your attitudes in a no-conflict situation with your peers?

In the abstract, there is no way to analyze the values and philosophies of one work setting. It must be done with a personal visit and/or a temporary work situation. This testing of the work setting is most frequently possible in cooperative education, internship, summer, and part-time employment circumstances. Consulting exposures also helps.

Figure 2.10 gives you a series of work values. What is your basic philosophy toward work? What attitude will others perceive that you are bringing to the work situation? You must know where you stand if you desire to achieve any high level of career success and happiness.

Identifying Values.   How do the work values in Figure 2.10 affect you? First, read through the entire list of values in Figure 2.10. Try to discern how each word affects you. Go back to the top of the list and begin to quantify your feelings through use of a "like-dislike" scale. Using the scale below, place a numeral beside each value label.

1 = Extremely important to me
2 = Important to me
3 = Of some concern to me
4 = Not important

Regrouping.   Now list all of your 1-rated work values on one sheet of paper, all of your 2-rated values on another, and so on until you have four separate lists. Search for common denominators in each category. Discuss the similarities in each like-rated group of work values.

Limiting yourself to one page for each of the four groups, analyze what you have uncovered. Are your values consistent within and between groups?

Conclusion.   Discuss your ideal work setting. Go into specific values which you feel your colleagues must have in common with you. Does your analysis suggest any special probing that you should do when you approach a new work setting? How comfortable do you feel knowing that you have a certain value set?

Deliverable. Prepare a one-page, single-spaced, typewritten statement for each of your four work value groups. Identify each group and give a brief statement showing the origin of each group of values. Explain why they are important to you and how they will impact upon your career decisions.

Interest Inventory Project

Many colleges and high schools have a department that administers a variety of career-related tests and inventories. These inventories and tests are very useful in helping you gain a better understanding of yourself.

Psychological tests are not the panacea that will show you exactly which career field is right for you. They are simply very valid and reliable guides which greatly aid in helping people make more prudent decisions.

Interest inventories are very popular among career counselors. They offer some specific content relevant to career questions. These inventories are not tests of aptitude. They indicate only the extent of similarities between a person's interests and those of people who are successfully employed in specific occupational groups.

One popular inventory used by professional career counselors is the Campbell Interest Inventory. The output reports are largely self-interpretable, so the feedback of results is well facilitated. They usually require only a small amount of time of the counselor, except for the integration of the results into the overall self-assessment.

The Self-Directed Search (S.D.S.) is another interest-related career counseling tool based on Dr. John L. Holland's theory of personality types and environment models. It is self-scored and self-interpretable with a reasonable level of professional instruction.

The use of these interest inventories leads to a systematic exploration of various career fields. The results tell you which career group has interests similar to yours. It then leaves the follow-up career exploration to you.

There really is no good substitute for taking an interest inventory. Make arrangements to take one or all of these inventories. Most university counseling services can provide an interest inventory for you. There is often a small charge for this service.

Analysis. After the results are available, meet with a professional career counselor and examine the results. Take notes. You may not get to keep the test. Write down all suggestions given. Record recommendations. Request whatever written material is available to you.

The career counselor offers one opinion only. It is usually very accurate in terms of the reporting of the test results. The *action* to be taken as the result of the output is subjective.

When you have all the facts, *you* are the decision maker. Good counselors will suggest avenues for you to explore further. They will not give you many concrete answers to your career questions.

Deliverable. You have the data. Now you must analyze it. Write an analysis of the results using the basic outline in Figure 2.16 in three to five single-spaced, typewritten pages.

The interest inventory provides additional pieces of information for the self-assessment. The interest information must be integrated with skills, values, interests, and personal qualities before conclusions are drawn.

INTEREST INVENTORY ANALYSIS OUTLINE

1. Factual Results
2. Analysis of Results
3. Analysis of Counselor's Recommendations
4. Disagreements Discussion
5. Planned Follow-up

• • • • • • • • • • •

Figure 2.16

The interest inventory is an aid for follow-up and investigation, but it must not be the only piece of information you use for career decision making.

Personal Descriptors Project

Judgments about a person are made quickly, often in only part of a thirty-minute interview. After an interview, what descriptors would a recruiter use to communicate your potential to his or her boss?

Descriptors are personal qualities. Whether for a new job, advancement, or performance appraisal, people are reviewed by others. A written description is usually made.

Successful job performance is more than education, experience, and skills. Motivational characteristics are just as important. Personal quality assessment is a beginning step in an evaluation of motivation. Will you, given your skills, actually perform up to your highest potential?

What will be written about you? How can you be sure that it is accurate? You must project a true image if you expect an accurate assessment.

It is impossible to cue your evaluator if you do not have a plan yourself. An evaluator gets information from you. Do you have an accurate image of yourself? How can you relay this information?

Be honest with yourself. An accurate description is essential.

Identify Descriptors.   The list of descriptive words given in Figure 2.12 is often used by counselors, teachers, employers, and others in describing people they must evaluate. The descriptors are used by people who have not seen you but who must make decisions about you. These decisions might relate to hiring, promoting, developing, or firing you.

Use the list in Figure 2.12 to identify the descriptive words that most nearly could communicate your personal qualities to other people. Place a number from 1 to 4 beside each descriptor, depending upon how well it describes you (1 = strongly describes; 2 = moderately describes; 3 = weak descriptor; 4 = false descriptor). Carefully evaluate every word as you process through the list.

There are about 150 descriptors and four classifications. Try to force your numbering into equal groupings. Use about 40 ones, 40 twos, etc., but it is not necessary for the groups to be exactly equal.

Listing.   You should have 30 to 40 ones. Personal qualities are not factors that can easily be ranked from high to low. You either perceive of yourself as having the quality or as not having that quality. This is not to say that other people's perceptions of your qualities are identical to your own perceptions.

List the descriptors which you have identified as strongly descriptive. List those that you have identified as moderately descriptive. Before you finally type the two lists, jocky the lists back and forth if necessary.

This project is designed to help you prepare an accurate picture based upon your own perceptions of yourself. To add strength and validity to your personal analysis, you are asked to support your conclusions with concrete examples. An interesting variation of this project is to ask a close friend or relative to make the same evaluation about you.

Communicating.   It is relatively easy to identify the factors that you feel best describe you to others. Communicating an impression that you want others to draw from your conversations and their observation of you is more difficult, however.

How do you get another person (who often may not know you at all) to identify the same personal qualities that you selected in your listings? You would look foolish parroting out "Boy Scout" attributes about yourself. Who would believe you? Why should they believe you?

Communicate your qualities via examples. What instances in your life reveal specific attributes? One or two situations or stories about episodes in your life might communicate a number of different personal qualities.

Pick the two personal qualities which you value most highly. Think about situations in your life which have portrayed those qualities in you. For example, look at "honest." Tell about the time you returned ten dollars to a supermarket after discovering you were given too much change when you got home from shopping. Describe that entire sequence of events.

In other words, tell true stories about your life. Describe those stories in such a way that another person quickly sees the quality you have identified without your coming right out and saying that you consider that to be your most important quality. Write each story in about 4 to 5 typewritten paragraphs on one page for each quality.

Expanding.   After describing two different situations, go back and see if they describe other personal qualities you possess. Using each of the stories, write down any other descriptors that you feel the stories illustrate.

It is possible to develop four or five brief episodes from your life experiences that reveal the qualities which you want an evaluator to conclude.

Deliverable.   On the top half of a single sheet of paper, type the forty descriptors which you feel best illustrate your traits in rank order. Draw a line midway through the page and type the next forty best descriptors (in rank order) on the lower half of the page. Look over this list of eighty qualities and begin thinking how, in an interview, you might use personal events that happened in your life to describe these personal traits to a recruiter.

Your next step in this action project is to type three more single-spaced pages that use "stories" or anecdotes that happened in your life which reveal qualities that you possess.

Each page should have a different story of four to six single-spaced paragraphs. You should draw the stories from your classroom experiences, extracurricular activities, home life, work background, or other episodes in your life.

As you type these stories, leave a two-inch margin on the left side of the page. After you finish typing each story, re-read them to see which qualities (chosen from the first page) that you feel the stories illustrate. In the two-inch left margin of the three stories, go back and type in the personal descriptors which you feel each paragraph illustrates.

You will find this project to be an excellent item to review just prior to each interview which you take.

Summary
The self-assessment is clearly a multifaced project. It takes time. It takes perseverance. It is hard work, and there are no shortcuts. Doing the self-analysis is critical to making a sound career decision with positive long-term benefits.

The summation of this involved effort is a clear statement of self-understanding. A sound, well thought-out self-analysis is the best prescription for a happy working life.

A self-assessment plan integrates education, experiences, skills, values, interests, and personal qualities.

One-third of your career planning model is now complete. The next phase is an exploration of potential career alternatives based upon the results of the self-assessment.

Career Exploration:

Process – Realities – Markets

What is available?

The job hunter asks: What's available? The employer asks: What job do you want? It is like the classic chicken and egg confrontation which always results in an impasse.

Either you or the employer must compromise.

The issue goes much deeper. You do not want just *any* job. In reality, you are not willing to let an employer pick a career for you. Most job hunters have some idea of what they want. The purpose of playing coy is to get the employer to "show his hand" so that a broader selection is available.

Few employers will display an array of jobs and say "take your pick." They have too much at stake. A poor placement is expensive to the employer.

A successful placement implies that the applicant really wants the job and is willing to work hard to be successful. The employer seeks some indication of motivation.

The best evidence of motivation is a candidate's understanding of his/her capabilities and the knowledge of how to apply that understanding to a specific job.

You must set a goal and then prepare a convincing story that forces the employer to believe that you are motivated to succeed on the initial job as well as in broader goals later in your career.

An employer's open invitation to interview invites too many unqualified and improperly motivated candidates to apply for a job. The selection process can then become extremely tedious for the employer.

Employers improve the selection process by directing some of the responsibility back onto the job seeker. Forcing the job seeker to sort out things *first* enhances the quality of the selection process.

A job seeker without goals is lost. Employers will not set goals for you. To get around this, some job seekers tell white lies. They express goals of anything and everything. A trained recruiter sees through that facade quickly with only five minutes of questions.

You must set your goals *first*.

Goals range from broad life expectations to specific job titles. Specific job titles are necessary at the time of the job interview. There may be several slightly different job titles of interest to you, but they must have a common thread tying them together.

In most cases, people who seek careers in managerial, technical, or professional types of jobs require some level of college education. Most managerial, technical, or professional assignments imply a commitment to a career.

There are "levels of responsibility" within a given career field which means that you may specify a job title on a *continuum* from entry level to top levels.

The career planning concept demands that you set specific goals. The responsibility for setting entry, intermediate, and long-term goals cannot be left to the employer. Employers will not accept that responsibility and you should never give it up.

Your career goal is to obtain the perfect job that satisfies your broader goals in life.

You must set your goals first. Without goals you are lost.

Exploring the World of Work

I'VE WORKED OUT A JOB HUNTING SYSTEM, ALL RIGHT, BUT I'M STILL NARROWING THE SCOPE.

Career exploration is a process of accumulating information about the world of work.

Specific job decisions must eventually be made. Decisions require choices. Career options must be developed. Developing these options is the essence of career exploration.

Career exploration is collecting data about types of opportunities in managerial, technical, and professional career fields.

Your goal is to create the highest possible level of career awareness. The only constraints on this activity are your time, money, and interest. A wealth of career information is available.

Systematic Process

Develop a systematic process for collecting the information you need to make the best possible job for you. Use this process forever.

It often takes some digging to collect career information even when you know exactly what type of information you seek. Because of this, a consistent methodology needs to be developed.

A system is needed for collecting, processing, and evaluating the information. Not all bits of the research effort will be of significant value. In fact, some of the data will be largely worthless.

Some career information sources have greater credibility than others. Just because it is published does not mean it is accurate.

Collecting. The first phase of collecting may well begin before college and continue throughout your lifetime. A specific time, however, needs to be set aside to do some stock-taking.

WHAT AM I SAYING? OF COURSE I KNOW PLENTY!

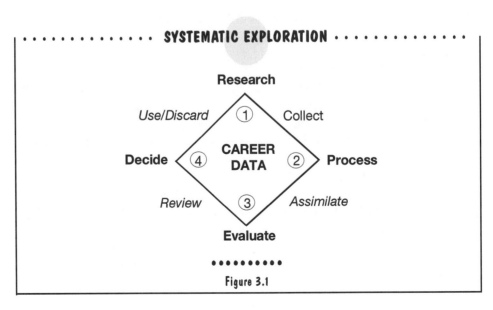

· · · · · · · · · · · **SYSTEMATIC EXPLORATION** · · · · · · · · · · · · ·

Research

Use/Discard ① Collect

Decide ④ **CAREER DATA** ② Process

Review ③ Assimilate

Evaluate

· · · · · · · · · ·

Figure 3.1

Your motivation and career interest levels usually peak when you find yourself seeking employment. The *systematic collecting* should begin each time you approach this decision point.

The key to systematic exploration is writing the information in a form that can be processed. Information flows from a variety of sources and in varying quantity, quality, and format. The data should be cleaned, filtered, and arranged to achieve a logical organization.

Evaluating. The purpose of the evaluation is to make some decision using the collected data. The evaluation represents an integration of hundreds of variables from both the self-assessment and the exploration.

Integrating. Most individuals face important compromises during this integrating process. Some refuse to compromise between reality and fantasy. Others restart the career information collection process as they reject the career field. Still others go through the self-assessment process again.

Deciding. In the end, some type of decision filters out. The decision becomes the career objective statement on a resume. After the career objective statement, focus centers on several appropriate assignments. The search action is close to being utilized, but there still may be further specification and clarification of career interest. The *clarifications* continue throughout the search process.

The career planning process (assessment—exploration—search) occurs over time. The process can be condensed into four weeks or expanded into four years. Logic suggests that the longer the time, the better the refinement and integration with reality.

You may collect data as specific as a job in a given organization or as general as a broad definition. The goal of systematic exploration is to create a high level of awareness about many different career alternatives.

Involve yourself in an in-depth investigation into a given career option. This systematic process can be repeated with other career options.

People collect career information all the time. Even through simple observation of a

The resume career objective statement emerges from a systematic exploration of career information facts.

WOULD YOU MIND IF I OBSERVED? I'M INTERESTED IN A CAREER AS A BUTCHER.

medical center television program, for example, information is collected. Every day people are observed in action in various occupations, and that information is mentally processed.

Unfortunately, not all information which is processed is accurate. Bad information can be worse than no information.

Career information exists in many places in several forms. Career information presents problems when it is not displayed in a logical format. Bits and pieces here and there seldom add up to sound data unless they are recorded in a usable form.

The data must be summed up in a manner that can aid in the clarification of career objectives.

Relevant Data

Collecting information by a systematic approach expedites the process. The scheme depicted in Figure 3.2 can be helpful in sorting out relevant from irrelevant information. Searching for specific data on a given career field permits you to scan a much greater volume of information about the career field in which you have an interest. In contrast, taking a look at all of the career possibilities often confuses people because of the massive amount of information available.

Titles. The *Dictionary of Occupational Titles* (*DOT*), published by the U.S. Government Printing Office, lists over 20,000 job titles. Different titles can relate to similar duties, because titles and descriptions are not universally accepted.

There are many government sites on the Internet that provide information on jobs. One such site is www.usajobs.opm.gov and other Department of Labor sites: www.dol.gov.

For example, the job titles of financial analyst, budget specialist, cost accountant, and credit analyst could all have the same descriptions of duties. Job titles are often not very descriptive so you should not rely on titles alone.

Descriptions. Job descriptions give a summary of the job and list various duties and responsibilities. A job description indicates what the job is and how the employer does it. It also gives various reporting relationships which can be helpful in observing upward mobility.

The Internet contains many job listings with job descriptions. The site www.jobdescriptions.com might also be helpful.

Career Paths. When assessing career information, you want to investigate the chances and routes for upward mobility. Some jobs lend themselves to mobility more than others.

The need for advancement is more important to some people than others. For some professionals, such as lawyers, veterinarians, and doctors, advancement is almost defined out of the job. In contrast, people in business management continue to strive for promotions.

CAREER PROFILE

- Title(s):
- Description:
- Duties:
- Responsibilities:
- Qualifications:
- Outlook:
- Training:
- Advancement Path:

• • • • • • • • • • •

Figure 3.2

Training Possibilities.   Jobs vary in their provisions for training. Some offer formal, sophisticated training programs; others are mostly on the job. For individuals desiring training opportunities, this type of career information is often important.

Outlook.   The number of people needed in various occupations and specific jobs is an important factor to evaluate.

For example, there are very few astronomers and many teachers, so landing a teaching job may be somewhat easier than finding work as an astronomer. The supply/demand ratio is another factor related to career outlook that needs evaluation.

Sources of Information

People and publications (hardcopy or webcopy) provide the basic sources of career information. People in occupations and career positions serve as role models to which potential aspirants might relate.

Most career knowledge comes from observing people in their day-to-day lifestyles. But appearances can be deceiving, so observation should not be the only source of career information.

Publications can also be poor because many times people write books without the best of resources. Your best plan is to use both people and publications and then personally integrate the information.

People.   Interviewing people in selected career fields provides a "real world" appreciation of the duties and responsibilities within the fields. One or two opinions in a field, however, can be misleading, because practitioners are often biased. It takes care to see through the enthusiasm and pride to glean out the negatives as well as the positives.

Perhaps the one best way to learn about an occupation is to work with people in the field as a sub-professional through a cooperative education or professional practice program. A ten- to fifteen-week work experience usually permits one to see most aspects of the field. The trend toward using these experiential types of programs in educational programs appears to be growing.

Publications.   You may not be fortunate enough to have the opportunity to observe, act, and react with people in careers in which you have an interest. If that is the case, you will have to turn to written documents.

Publications are often superior to personal interaction because the information is more broad-based. Most publications are written after taking observations from large numbers of people in the occupation.

Public and university libraries contain hundreds of books on many different career fields. The card catalog is the place to start.

Most professional associations publish books, booklets, and pamphlets about careers. Although libraries contain some of these, it is appropriate to write to associations directly. Many college placement offices maintain supplies of such materials to give away.

SOURCES OF CAREER INFORMATION

People
- observation
- interviews
- experiential

Publications
- associations
- employers
- computer files

•••••••••••

Figure 3.3

The U.S. Government also prints similar types of information which are available in libraries, college placement offices, or from the Government Printing Office.

Many large employers of college graduates, whether business, government, or education, publish brochures that describe career opportunities for college graduates with their organizations. Although you sometimes must read through the sales pitch, these brochures often give the most up-to-date descriptions of career fields.

The brochures are available from college placement offices and by writing to organizations directly.

The Handbook. The most useful of the government publications which you should review is the *Occupational Outlook Handbook for College Graduates,* which is published periodically. It gives a brief description and the current outlook for nearly every position sought by college graduates.

The *OCC* is excellent for labor market re-entrants and career-changers as well. It provides the following information on every occupation listed.

The *OCC* is printed in many different locations on the Internet. Use any search engine to locate a copy.

The "*Nature of the Work*" section introduces you to the career field. It provides a brief description of the duties, assignments, and day-to-day work activities of people in the career field. The description helps to provide a view of the scope of the field. It frequently correlates the work to related occupations and gives an expanded list of job titles.

Many occupations are performed only in selected parts of the nation. In many occupations, different areas of the country impact upon the nature of the work. Where applicable, the "*Places of Employment*" section gives the size of the work force by regions of the country.

The "*Qualifications*" section (including training, other qualifications, and advancement) is similar to the requirements section of an employer's job description. It lists the skills necessary to do the job. Such items as physical requirements, educational degrees, advanced training, specific courses, licensing requirements, and so forth, are given. Personal qualities of people in the field occasionally are specified.

The "*Employment Outlook*" section gives information on the supply and demand variables with a rationale for determining your employment chances. This section discusses growth as well as replacements needed in the foreseeable future. It covers the areas of the career field where special skills may be advantageous in improving the likelihood of employment.

The "*Earnings and Working Conditions*" section gives an indication of beginning rates usually paid to new entrants into the occupation. There are often benchmark averages given at midpoints and high ends of the salary ranges. Where applicable, it often gives the average salary of the comparable position of experienced people working for the federal government.

In many career fields there are professional associations that offer additional career literature. The "*Sources of Additional Information*" section refers you to additional booklets and pamphlets available from these associations as well as from the government. It provides addresses of specific organizations to contact.

The *Occupational Outlook Handbook* is the best and most resourceful publication available for initial exploration of a career field. There are many other excellent sources of information, but few sources rival the *Handbook* for preliminary data. Most of the other sources will expand and help build depth of understanding about a given career field.

One caution must be advised. Do not base your career decision solely on this source of information. The one- to three-page description for each occupation is inadequate to use alone.

The primary value of the *Handbook* is that it helps to identify specific career fields which might be of interest to you. As a follow-up investigative approach, use people and other publications to provide the in-depth detail required for decision-making purposes.

Find the *OCC* on www and review it.

Job Market Realities

No career counselor would suggest that you should canvass the job market, discover the field with the greatest number of current job openings, and then create a background to insure that you can get a job in that field. On the other hand, few counselors would recommend that you close your eyes to job market realities.

A rational career decision recognizes the labor market. Projecting the supply of labor market entrants is nearly an impossible job. Forecasting the number of jobs available in any field during a specific period of time is a very imprecise science.

The job market forecast often influences career decisions.

There is no known way at this time to produce a reasonable supply-demand balance in a free society. Free market principles apply to labor as well as products. Rapid technology changes and society needs make job market planning nearly impossible. For example, you might truly enjoy working with the old DOS computer operating system, but it has phased out. You should move to a newer operating system.

The job outlook by occupation is *one* of the variables that you must factor into a career decision. The job outlook, however, must not be the overriding variable. There are jobs available in almost every field. However, the time that you take to identify openings and then convince an employer to hire you may not be proportionate to the level of your interest in the job.

Supply/Demand Relationships

The relationship between "supply" of job candidates and "demand" for them necessarily influences career decisions. No prudent individual permits supply-demand relationships to dictate a career choice; yet, the prudent person cannot afford to stand naive to the complex and uncertain characteristics of supply and demand factors generated by changing market conditions.

The analysis of the marketplace becomes part of the career planning process. The market will not control your job choice but it should influence it.

I'M WORRIED, LORY. WHAT IF I WIND UP AS A "SUPPLY" AND NOT A "DEMAND"?

Demand.   The demand side of the equation is largely influenced by economic factors. This is true whether jobs are in the private or public sector of the economy. The public sector must rely on revenues which come from taxing individuals and corporations. Tax revenues decline in periods of slow or no growth in the economy.

Although the nation has had a full-employment law for several decades, unemployment still rises rapidly during recessions. The numbers of professional, technical, and managerial jobs do not increase during recessions, and that has a negative influence on job availability during those periods.

Given the imprecise ability to predict the state of the economy in the short run, it is nearly impossible to forecast the number of new jobs being created during any immediate (within 18 months) period of time. Over a longer time period (3 to 5 years), economic planners hold a better forecasting record.

In essence, the economists level-out the cyclical nature of the economy over longer periods of time. Therefore, it is possible to better forecast long-range demand variables and estimate the number of new jobs to be created within a three or more year timeframe.

The *number of people* in an occupational group depends to a large extent on the demand by others for their services. Some occupations will thus be in growth periods, in terms of new entrants to the field, while others may be declining.

The general economic level could be booming while employment is declining in occupations for which the need for the employee's services is declining.

Changes in industrial *growth rates* also affect the availability of jobs in certain occupations. Many occupations are directly related to certain industries. For example, a major decline in automobile manufacturing is sure to negatively influence the demand for mechanical engineers because a high percentage of them work in that industry.

The selection of an occupational field is closely related to the selection of an industry in which one plans to work.

Using information on the demand for goods and services, advances in technology, changes in business practices, and other factors, government economists can estimate the number of workers who will be employed in an occupation if present trends continue. Such estimates are based upon some realistic assumptions about

Growth rates in various occupations are influenced by related industries' economic outlook.

...BUT I'VE ALSO GOTTEN SOME TOP LEVEL TRAINING...

world stability, economic conditions, technology, social value stability, government policies, etc.

In the aggregate, the U.S. Department of Labor can fairly accurately estimate the increase in the number of positions available in the managerial, technical, and professional fields. These projections are based on the number of people currently in occupations, expected retirements and deaths, and the upgrading of lower-level positions. Replacements and upgrading are fairly predictable.

The difficulty arises in forecasting the economy, the stability of which is the underlying assumption for manpower projections. The estimate for growth in a particular occupation can thus vary considerably in any given year.

On the demand side, growth in jobs created is one of the variables economists consider. Retirements, deaths, and other labor-market-exit reasons such as illness, return to school, child rearing, etc., all enter into the analysis of the availability of job openings. Based upon time-tested statistical methods, census data, and labor market surveys of major employers, the availability of openings can reasonably be estimated.

A sophisticated set of techniques aid economists in determining the "demand for people" side of the equation. To the extent that the underlying assumptions do not change, projections can be reasonably estimated and they normally fall within a predicted range of error.

Supply. The supply of candidates entering a given occupation is more accurately predictable. Most professional, technical, and managerial assignments require a college degree, advanced training, or special skill development. The U.S. Department of Education regularly collects information on enrollments in various types of educational institutions and they have done this for many years.

Over time the Department has a reasonable idea of the number of trained people who never enter the occupation for which they trained, those who leave the occupation, and those who are otherwise not available. Because most occupations require several years of training and individuals often specify their intentions upon entering the program, there is a reasonable estimate of the newly trained entrants.

Colleges produce the largest number of new entrants into an occupation each year. By factoring in a reasonable estimate for returning entrants who have temporarily left the occupation to raise families, to obtain additional schooling, due to illness, etc., a reasonable estimate of supply is possible.

Consensus. During the next decade, most experts are forecasting a reasonable balance in the supply of candidates and demand for their services.

Even though the experts forecast a near balance in total during the next decade, great dislocations may occur in certain occupational fields and in certain college major areas. Many occupations require specific fields of study, but many other fields of academic study do not directly correlate to specific occupations. The mix of candidate qualifications may not match the occupational requirements.

In practice, the mix problem produces extreme shortages of qualified people in some occupations and creates a pool of highly trained people vying for a limited number of openings in certain other occupations.

In a free society, the only factors dictating a college major are the interest of the individual student and the resources of the educational institution. The job market might temporarily influence the selection, but given a minimum of four years' leadtime and the uncertainties of the economy, few students base their choice of a college major entirely on job possibilities.

Recent evidence, though, suggests that the labor market is becoming one of the many factors that students consider in selecting college majors. Because certain

Job applicant supply forecasts are reasonably accurately estimatable.

The supply of applicants for professional jobs will be in near balance with the demand for them in the next few years.

The supply/demand in specific occupations may produce extreme shortages of certain professionals.

MORE EDUCATION = LESS UNEMPLOYMENT

More education has always reduced the probability of unemployment according to figures released by the U.S. Government in publications like the *Occupational Outlook Quarterly* and the *Monthly Labor Review* magazines.

Education has become an increasingly important criterion for success in the job market. Although the supply of both high school and college graduates has grown significantly in the past years, there has almost always been a relatively greater increase in demand for college graduates. The trend of lower unemployment rates for college graduates suggests that employers highly value education attainment.

In addition, the growth in occupations that require a college degree has traditionally been greater than those requiring only a high school degree. Business cycle fluctuations impact college graduates less because the high school graduates tend to work in blue collar manufacturing jobs which are more susceptible to swings in employment changes. College graduates tend to work in service sector jobs which are less susceptible to downturns.

It is likely that the competitive advantage held by college graduates will continue in the future.

major subjects relate more to given occupations, a decided shift toward vocationally related majors appears to be a trend at many colleges.

A few years ago, less than 12 percent of college students elected to major in business, in contrast to over 20 percent today. Very few seats go begging today in a number of other vocationally attractive fields like engineering, journalism, and the sciences.

Many college students elect to major in subject areas where the potential for employment is less than favorable. Many people believe that the purpose of higher education is primarily to develop the whole individual and that less concern should be placed on the particular academic major.

The concept of a liberal education implies that any individual properly prepared can adapt to the work environment with a minimum of difficulty.

Whatever a person's point of view, few people argue with the importance of collecting career information before making long-term investments in time, money, and other resources.

Employment Projections

If you agree that supply and demand variables are two pieces of information that you must factor into your career planning model, you are probably wondering how to obtain such information.

Short Term. For short-run impressions, newspapers and news magazines do a fair job of printing stories based on opinions of people who are close to the employment scene.

Good journalists use reliable sources that they have come to know over a period of years in such employment reporting. To some extent, the reporters' research for a story saves you valuable time. On the other hand, some of their sources may not be totally reliable.

I'VE HEARD THIS IS A VERY COMPETITIVE FIELD.

There are great short-term employment fluctuations in given geographical areas, and many fields change rapidly. You should, therefore, do some investigation on your own before accepting feature articles in current periodicals as the total picture.

The type of people closest to the employment scene are college placement professionals, major employers of people in given occupations, employment agency counselors, and search firm consultants. Few people want to be bearers of anything but good news.

College faculty members want to perpetuate their employment, so their perception of the market is always that it is good. Placement professionals believe their graduates are superior because of the reputations of their schools, so things are usually rosy-appearing to them. Keep a critical mind as you read about employment projections.

If you have access to any of these sources, use them, but do not rely on everything they say as truth. Put the ideas and comments from the various sources together and see what the consensus suggests. By consulting four to six different people close to your occupational area, and merging their opinions with news stories, you can begin to put a true short-term picture together.

Long Term. For career decision-making purposes, you want more than a short-term view of the situation in your occupational area of interest. What does the three- to five-year outlook hold? What about ten years out?

For such longer-term projections you will need to turn to government economists who make careers of studying such concerns. Again, like the short-term supply-demand picture, the figures are suspect, but given all options, the best guess is the opinion of experts who continue to study the situation occupation by occupation.

The government experts tend to be much more objective than the people who write books and articles extolling the virtues of their professions, but you also need the ideas and opinions of people in the occupation. In spite of all their faults, long-term projections by unbiased experts add a needed element of credibility.

On a regular basis the U.S. Bureau of Labor Statistics prepares a report titled "The Job Outlook in Brief." The report forecasts openings by several hundred occupations through the next decade. This report when supplemented with the Bureau's *Occupational Outlook Handbook for College Graduates* is the most authoritative report on the long-term manpower outlook.

A thorough understanding of the job market realities is an integral part of sound career planning and job search.

The "Occupational Outlook Quarterly" is one of the most authoritative periodicals available on supply and demand. See the www for a copy.

OCCUPATION TABLE

Accountants
Actuaries
Air traffic controllers
Airline pilots
Anthropologists
Architects
Architects: Landscape
Astronomers
Bank Officers
Buyers (retail)
Chemists
Chiropractors
City managers
Claim representatives
Clergy
Computer programmers
Computer systems analysts
Computer specialists
Construction inspectors
Correctional officers
Counselors College
Counselors Employment
Counselors Rehabilitation
Counselors School
Credit managers
Dental hygienists
Dentists
Designers Industrial
Designers Interior
Dietitians
Drafters
Economists
Engineers
  General
  Aerospace
  Agriculture
  Biomedical
  Ceramic
  Chemical
  Civil
  Electrical
  Industrial
  Mechanical
  Metallurgical
  Mining
  Petroleum
Engineering technicians
FBI agents
Foresters
Food technologists
Forest technicians
Geographers
Geologists
Geophysicists
Health administrators
Health inspectors
Historians
Hotel managers
Inspectors (Manufacturing)
Insurance representatives

Lawyers
Librarians
Market research worker
Mathematicians
Medical lab. technicians
Medical record admin.
Merchant marines
Meteorologists
Newspaper reporters
OSHA workers
Oceanographers
Optometrists
Personnel
Pharmacists
Physicians
Physicists
Podiatrists
Police officers
Programmers
Psychologists
Public relations assistants
Purchasing agents
Radio and TV announcers
Range managers
Registered nurses
Sales representatives
  Automobile
  Manufacturing
  Real estate
  Retail trade
  Securities
  Travel agent
  Wholesale trade
Scientists
  Agricultural
  Atmospheric
  Biochemical
  Life
  Life and physical
  Marine
  Political
  Social
  Soil
Social workers
Sociologists
Soil conservationists
Speech pathologists
Statisticians
Supervisors
Surveyors
Teachers:
  College
  Secondary
  Elementary
Therapists:
  Occupational
  Physical
Urban planners
Veterinarians
Writers: technical

Figure 3.4

I AM VALUABLE TO AN EMPLOYER.

The Bureau has developed a listing of technical, professional, and managerial jobs for which a college degree or some college education is necessary. These jobs are listed and described in the Bureau's publications.

Using these government publications, the "Occupation Table" listed in Figure 3.4 was prepared. This represents one of the most

PERKINS, YOU'RE BEING REPLACED BY A COMPUTER...
MURPHY, YOU'RE BEING REPLACED BY A ROBOT...
AND, THORNTON, YOU'RE SIMPLY BEING REPLACED.

complete lists of occupations typically classified in technical, professional, and managerial position descriptions.

There are literally thousands of other jobs which people hold in the technical, professional, and managerial fields, so this is not an all-inclusive and exclusive list of career fields. However, it does represent a high percentage of the normally available opportunities. Many positions with slightly different titles can be related to the positions.

Projections of supply and demand by occupation are made by the U.S. Department of Labor's Bureau of Labor Statistics. The projections of long-term trends largely ignore short-term fluctuations caused by economic circumstances. As underlying assumptions change, the projections become less accurate.

Job outlook statistics by occupational field look so factual that the unenlightened may want to believe them as the unalterable truth. Always remember that "rough estimates" vary widely. Do not accept government projections at face value.

Even government planners readily admit the tenuous nature of forecasting the supply of jobs and the availability of job candidates in a short-run period of time. It is worthwhile to examine the figures in detail during the career exploration process, but refrain from making judgments until you have more facts.

Specific Jobs. In what occupations do the majority of professional, technical, and managerial people work? When you consider that the *Dictionary of Occupational Titles* lists thousands of specific job titles, you begin to realize that narrowing in on a specific occupation and then a specific job title is no simple exercise.

Nonetheless, the many thousands of job titles can be grouped into *clusters* of related jobs. These clusters can be further massaged into broad occupational categories that are more closely related to the one-quarter of the working population into which you want to fit your career namely the professional, technical, and managerial group.

The "Occupation Table" lists the specific occupational fields. The list is not inclusive of every imaginable appropriate career field, and it does not focus on narrower sub-specialties which are included in the broader classification. However, the list presents a fair listing of the majority, probably over eighty percent, of the available occupations in the professional, technical, and managerial fields.

Make a point of reviewing the list in its entirety. If you do not find the career field in which you have an interest listed, you should begin to make some more

Job forecasts are rarely accurate. The margin of error may be very high.

in-depth and specific supply-demand analyses of your own before investing a great amount of time in a field that may be so narrow that the demand is next to non-existent.

A significant amount of grouping has been done to narrow the list to a manageable number of occupations and career fields. There are many levels of responsibility and different job titles in each of these groupings.

The job titles listed can be misleading. The one word, "Occupation," is designed to start a chain reaction for further investigation and explode the single word title into its hundreds of meanings.

Magnitude.   It is human nature to look at projections and say you want to go where the greatest growth possibilities are likely to be. Most people have been conditioned to equate "growth" with "good," and in most instances there is a positive relationship.

But the "growth trend" is only one indicator of future job prospects. More jobs become available due to people leaving the labor force than to economic growth. Large occupations that are growing very slowly may offer more jobs than small, fast-growing occupations.

Growth Trends.   Some occupations will experience dramatic growth in terms of the number of jobs available while others will show declines in the next decade.

Based upon demand variables by occupation, the Bureau economists forecast the average yearly job openings anticipated for each occupation. For each occupation, they calculate the percent increase in number of jobs.

In career planning terms this means that if you elect to go into a "non-growth" field, the number of new entrants into your field is not going to increase any faster than the national average. It could mean that you may have to search harder to find employment initially in the field or when you change jobs within that field. The concept also may have some implications to *geographical* considerations as well.

The point is that you should be aware of the growth trends in employment in the career field that you select. How you elect to utilize that piece of information is a personal choice. It may have no impact whatever on your choice, and yet it may be a factor that forces you to look at other options.

Competitive Prospects.   Employment success depends on more than growth and the size of the work force. It also depends on the number of people competing for that same kind of position.

Many occupations correlate directly with academic subjects and formal training. A fairly accurate estimate of supply is available in this case.

For example, the supply of graduate electrical engineers is fairly easy to predict given that they are in college and have selected that major. The number of available seats is not growing rapidly, and most of them will be full. Both the number of labor market re-entrants and occupational drop-outs is low and predictable. There is a good estimate of supply of electrical engineers to compare to the number needed annually; thus a fairly accurate estimate of the supply-demand ratio is possible.

Other occupations have no correlatable college major on which to base an estimate of supply. For example, many liberal arts graduates will accept employment in sales, supervision, counseling, etc. Estimates in many occupations must simply be made on an aggregate basis given what is generally known about supply and demand relationships in these occupations.

Many people feel that the competitive prospects projections for employment in their chosen occupations mean very little because they have confidence that they will be among the chosen few even if the competition is extremely keen. Other

A positive growth trend in a career field does not always translate into better job prospects for you in that field.

Understand the competition for the job you seek!

I AM WORTH SOMETHING.

people prefer not to analyze the employment prospects until they complete a basic education. These are choices that you personally must make.

As a good career planner, you may conclude that competitive prospects mean nothing. You may also be at the other end of the continuum that believes that employment prospects are the whole ballgame.

Regardless of where you fall on this continuum, having the information available is sound career planning. How you use the information, if at all, is clearly dependent upon your values, interests, personal qualities, and skills.

//WEB.TIP//

www.careerxroads
CareerXRoads
Evaluate thousands of career sites/publishes an annual edition/updates via website/e-mail newsletter

Salary Concerns

One important element of career information is salary data. No one makes a career decision on the basis of one variable alone, but in every ranking of variables which are important to career choice, salary consistently ranks somewhere within the top ten factors.

The relative ranking of the factors important to career choice varies considerably based upon your personal value system.

Sources of Information

Finding hard, accurate salary information often requires perseverance and digging. Salary averages change rapidly.

Some people tend to resist releasing personal salary information even though the aggregation of personal data guarantees anonymity. People also tend to lie a little because they want others to feel that they (or those in their profession) are better off than others.

Authors of books seldom print salary averages because such information rapidly becomes obsolete. As a result, the best sources of salary information for you are survey data available from college placement offices, associations, want ads, and newspaper and magazine articles. There are several websites that contain salary information. Several sites are listed below. Your college Career Services Office website can probably provide you with additional links.

Salary Surveys. For the job seeker, valid salary information is difficult to obtain, but it is available readily to professional compensation experts who make it a practice to obtain comparative information. Corporate compensation experts are members of professional associations, which exchange information on a confidential basis.

Many different sources of comparative salary data are available if you investigate thoroughly.

Most employers are very well versed on the salary subject by given position classifications. There are very few career fields in which a compensation expert could not give you very accurate statistics based on educational background, years of experience, and level of responsibility.

A number of professional associations conduct salary surveys on an annual basis among their membership. Usually, you must be a member in order to receive the data. Given an area of interest, it is a good idea to get acquainted with several people currently working in the field. These people are in a position to answer questions on an individual basis or to help others obtain copies of salary surveys for you.

A few organizations publish salary surveys. For data processing workers, a trade magazine annually surveys its readers. Several other groups publish results in their publications. Each year, *Business Week* publishes salaries of top executives. A review of the periodicals in your area of interest may provide salary data.

Under the provisions of the Federal Pay Comparability Act of 1970, the government must set pay rates for federal white-collar workers that are comparable to those found in private industry. A survey is conducted to obtain information for comparative purposes. A bulletin giving the results of the survey is available from the Bureau of Labor Statistics.

For people who have worked five or more years, salary information is slightly more difficult and expensive to obtain. A readily accessible information is in classified want ads in newspapers and trade journals. Unfortunately, it is not always accurate because many employers advertise high salary ranges simply to encourage more applicants.

Entry Rates. The most accurate salary information available is that reported for college graduates who have recently entered the work force. It is extensive, accurate, and available for a very broad marketplace.

Although it is not directly applicable to most people with three or more years of work experience, the information does serve as a realistic base from which to make educated guesses.

Graduating students tend to be honest and cooperative in sharing salary information with each other. Their starting salaries usually fall within a narrow range. Most graduates report all offers they receive to their college placement offices with the position title and monthly base dollar amount.

Several hundred college career service offices participate in a national salary survey with the National Association of Colleges and Employers (NACE), a non-profit professional association. Periodically, each college placement office sends NACE survey data that gives the degree level, major subject, industry, and base salary for every offer reported for tabulating. Names are not sent.

Many employers—through the applicants' college career service office—also provide salary data to include in the survey.

In January, March, and July NACE prepares a multi-page report which is sent to participating colleges. Information is then released to the news media in the local area and posted on NACE's website. If you miss seeing the report, call or visit your college placement office for the current information.

Salary information released by the local placement office and NACE is a most valid source of salary statistics. Data are released by degree level, major field, functional field, and industry classifications. The NACE website is: www.jobweb.org.

Averages, medians, ranges, and the number of offers give you a wealth of new information to include in the career decision-making process.

LET ME PUT IT ANOTHER WAY... JUST HOW MUCH EVIL ARE YOU PLANNING TO PROTECT ME FROM IF I WORK HERE?

Salary Determinants

Salary levels are based on three major factors: employer policy, supply and demand, and the candidate's credentials.

Policy. Some employers view themselves as salary leaders and pay top dollar to attract supposedly the top graduates each year. Many employers hire many of the top candidates, place them in very competitive situations, watch the "cream" come to the top, and then keep the best and lay off the rest.

Other employers prefer to come in at the salary midpoint and hire candidates from a broad spectrum of backgrounds.

Many hire exactly the number of new employees they need and provide a development program to build the qualifications of those who are less productive.

Still other employers focus on hiring the "diamonds in the rough" who through perseverance and hard work will outperform the "barn-burners" at the top of the class. There are as many different employment and salary policies as employers.

Demand. The second major factor influencing salary levels is the local supply and demand situation. Salaries vary by parts of the country, economic conditions in certain sectors, environmental settings (urban/rural/suburban), and cost of living considerations. Salary schedules often center on the local factors, and new employees must be merged into the schedules with a minimum of disruption of existing staff relationships.

Credentials. Finally, your qualifications and competitiveness enter into the determination. Your worth may be dictated by considerations outside the immediate control of the employer.

The most influential factors are years of related work experience, education (degree, major, grades) and leadership potential.

Salary Basis

The majority of employers start with a base dollar amount depending upon degree level, academic major and experience. The base amount results from the employment policies and the supply-demand situation. The amount may be above or below national averages.

The local marketplace establishes the base salary for most positions.

CANDIDATE-RELATED SALARY FACTORS

- Degree Level
- Academic Major
- Work Experience
- Academic Record
- Leadership Activities

• • • • • • • • • • •

Figure 3.5

Calculations.

Amounts often referred to as "adders" make up the final figure. The "adder" amounts supposedly correlate with a judgmental opinion of what it might take to hire you, but yet they must be consistent with salaries being paid to current employees of the business. Few employers offer salaries that exceed the salaries of current employees who are doing similar work.

Generalizations about salary differences are usually wrong. Get the facts, not hearsay.

The most directly related "adder" is previous full- or part-time work experience, preferably former job-related experience. Some employers reward superior academic experience, while others use it only as a selection factor.

Most employers recognize other factors such as leadership activities, related interests, maturity, personality, and communication skills as part of the salary determination or selection factor. In essence, all of these add up to competitive variables that distinguish your offer amount from that of other job candidates.

Differences. National standards for starting pay in the private sector, state and local government, and education do not exist. Even the published federal government salary schedule contains elements of flexibility. Because of changing economic variables and individual competitiveness, free market forces determine rates of pay.

The number of years of highly productive work experience is the major determinant of salary growth.

Commonly held attitudes pertaining to certain sectors suggest that rates of pay contain some consistency. Many attitudes (such as "retailing is long hours and low pay," "teaching pays poorly but is secure," "oil companies pay exorbitant salaries," "public employment means low pay," etc.) represent no truth.

A low-paying sector of industry often contains several employers that represent salary leaders. The reason some industries pay more than others is often because they recruit more technical personnel where the demand exceeds the supply. Other industries may have most of their facilities in areas where there are high unemployment rates and hence pay less than the average.

Salary rates are employer and individual specific. You must estimate a reasonable range of your worth.

Trends. Salary rates change over time. In the past ten years, starting salary percentage increases kept slightly ahead of the rate of inflation.

There are so many uncontrollable influences on salary rates that you cannot realistically and accurately make forecasts.

Past trends suggest that starting salaries will increase by an annually compounded rate near the current rate of inflation. To avoid paying experienced people the same or less than starting college graduates, employers will probably increase salaries of the *"top"* performers in the range of two to four percent above the cost-of-living.

Given certain assumptions about inflation, job performance, job mobility, etc., to double one's starting salary in ten years is not an unreasonable prospect. It can be done by getting a seven percent salary increase every year, but that is far above normal expectation.

Salary Caveats. Salary information must be interpreted with care. In the final analysis, salary relates directly to job performance. Employers hire people to produce results.

College graduates get paid higher salaries for their "potential" performance rather than for their actual performance the first year on the job.

Starting salaries often exceed those of long-term blue-collar workers whose immediate contributions add more to the bottom line in the short run. Salaries paid to experienced employees are usually more indicative of the true market than those paid to inexperienced new employees.

In addition to the investment in salary and benefits, employers often lay out an additional investment of $30,000 to $40,000 in facilities, equipment, trainers, and supporting staff for every new "hire." The moment the potential for adding more than cost to the bottom line disappears, the prudent employer is faced with a termination decision.

Many new hires live on "potential" for six to eighteen months. At some point, your contribution must exceed your cost. The feedback comes in the form of the performance review.

In general, the higher the initial salary, the sooner the employer expects a reasonable contribution to the organization. In some assignments, particularly those above entry level, employers may expect an immediate contribution.

All of the concern about salary washes out quickly. Salary advancement depends upon performance. Within one year, no one remembers or cares about starting rates. Starting rates are determined by a rather inexact method. Any inequities usually disappear as rates are determined by more objective criteria related to job performance.

Some employers make paying lower than average salaries part of their employment philosophy. Their philosophy is to leave a wider latitude for rewarding top producers.

Usually the upward limit on salary progression is based on salaries of employees hired in the past one or two years in the same job classification. Many employers prefer to leave as wide a gap between the two groups as possible in order to provide motivation for the new hires to excel.

Jobs requiring significant experience are usually *not negotiable.* Salary desires may be asked before an offer is extended, but once the offer is extended, it is the rare employer who negotiates very much.

Some employers will withdraw an offer if there is a hint of salary negotiation for entry-level jobs.

Salary relates directly to job performance and the worth of the job to the organization.

Salary should not be a major concern. In the final analysis, the decision to join a given organization is usually based on factors more related to advancement potential, people, location, honesty, lifestyle, etc. In the short run, differences of $50 to $100 per month between employers impact little upon later career success which is the most important variable.

Salary can be a negotiable item for experienced hires. The starting point is normally your current salary. To entice an experienced employee, most firms expect to pay at least a 10 to 20 percent premium over his or her current salary. The percentage increase over current salary is rarely greater than 30 percent. The 10 to 30 percent increase range is the usual negotiating range.

Job Markets and Work Settings

You do not have enough time to explore all possible avenues of career choice, but you can bring together many of the variables that need to be explored.

Exploring can be accomplished by clustering a variety of related career fields based upon common elements in the work settings. Avoid relying on stereotypes.

Stereotypes influence images of work settings, organizational structures, and various career positions. Stereotypes may be false. The only way for you to determine the truth is to actively investigate each career option before deciding on a given course of action.

By looking at the broad context in which career choices must be made, you can better reveal and understand the various job choices. The goal is to explore career options as they relate to specific work settings and to destroy inaccurate stereotype images.

The employment climate is not identical for every work setting. That fact must be incorporated into your career decision-making process.

"Who can I work for with a major in my field?" is one of the most frequently asked questions by students of college career counselors. "What can I do with my background?"

You cannot explore *all* of the possibilities. You clearly must make some tentative decisions.

A starting point is to look at the possible *settings* for the work you choose to do and determine if and how specific settings mesh with your perception. A further step is to look at specific employment organizations.

An overlay of the "world of work" reveals five major work settings: government, education, not-for-profit organizations, private enterprise, and the professions. Within these work settings, there are major categories of occupations commonly referred to as white-collar, blue-collar, and service workers.

MAJOR WORK ENVIRONMENTS

- Education
- Government
- Not-For-Profit Organizations
- Private Enterprises
- The Professions/Self-Employment

• • • • • • • • • • •

Figure 3.6

Employment in government, education, and private business includes workers from each category. Most professionals (doctors, lawyers, etc.) are in private practice as independent entrepreneurs, but some of them work for employers in salaried capacities also in both the public and private employment sectors.

College-educated people are employed in all five of the major work settings. Within these occu-

I WOULDN'T MIND GOVERNMENT EMPLOYMENT. I WONDER IF THEY NEED AN AMBASSADOR TO TAHITI.

pational categories, college graduates most frequently work in white-collar jobs as managers, administrators, technical staff, professional sales, and in the professions. Analyze each work setting from a practical employment perspective.

Jobs in Education

The primary sources of employment in education are elementary, secondary, and higher education institutions, although related components include pre-school, vocational education, special education, proprietary schools, etc.

Most of the available jobs involve teaching, counseling, and administration, but educational institutions also hire a few people each year with special technical skills such as engineering, accounting, computer programming, and so forth.

Very few employment sectors in education forecast any significant growth in hiring. Because of high turnover and some retirements, several thousand job openings will develop, but the competition for each job is keen as qualified teachers, women returning to careers, and current graduates vie for these jobs.

Most school systems, including higher education, receive hundreds of applications for available jobs. Young, inexperienced candidates often obtain jobs sooner because of lower salary demands.

A tough job challenge should never deter you from entering a chosen profession. You should, however, recognize the competitive situation in order to best prepare a set of superior credentials and aggressively hit the job market.

Not all areas in education deserve the competitive rating given the field in general. Many experts regularly research the outlook for elementary and secondary

Private business, government, education, non-profit, and the professions provide jobs for nearly all employed professionals.

A tough job market should never deter you from your chosen endeavor. Jobs come to those who work smart at searching.

I'VE ONLY GOT A FEW MONTHS UNTIL GRADUATION, RALPH.

THEN ALL THOSE CORPORATIONS WILL BE FIGHTING EACH OTHER OVER ME.

BUT I CAN ONLY WORK FOR ONE, RALPH.

DON'T LET THEM DESTROY THEMSELVES OVER ME! I'M NOT WORTH IT!

· · · · · · REPRESENTATIVE FEDERAL EMPLOYMENT POSITIONS · · · · · ·

Accountant
Administrative Trainee
Aerospace Technologist
Air Traffic Controller
Alcohol Tax Inspector
Animal Husbandman
Architect
Archivist
Astronomer
Attorney
Bacteriologist
Biologist
Budget Analyst
Cartographer
Chemist
Claims Examiner
Community Planner
Contract Negotiator
Customs Inspector
Customs Specialist
Customs Technical Aide
Computer Programmer
Dietitian
Economist
Education Officer
Engineer
Entomologist
Equipment Specialist
Estate Tax Examiner
Financial Examiner
Food and Drug Inspector
Forester
Geodesist
Geographer
Geophysicist
Historian
Hospital Administrator
Housing Intern
Hydrologist
Illustrator
Intelligence Analyst
Internal Revenue Agent
Investigator
Landscape Architect

Librarian
Loan Examiner
Management Analyst
Management Intern
Manpower Specialist
Manual Arts Therapist
Marketing Specialist
Mathematician
Medical Record Librarian
Metallurgist
Meteorologist
Microbiologist
Museum Curator
Nurse
Oceanographer
Occupational Therapist
Park Ranger
Patent Examiner
Personnel Specialist
Pest Controller
Pharmacist
Physicist
Plant Scientist
Prison Administrator
Psychologist
Public Information
Range Conservationist
Realty Assistant
Refuge Manager
Revenue Officer
Social Insurance
Social Worker
Sociologist
Soil Conservationist
Special Agent
Speech Pathologist
Statistical Assistant
Supply Specialist
Tax Technician
Teacher
Therapist
Urban Planner
Veterinarian
Writer and Editor

· · · · · · · · · ·

Figure 3.7

teachers by teaching field. Your employment prospects can be enhanced greatly if you put two or more teaching specialties together.

You should consult your alma mater's educational placement office for the most current outlook, because the national picture is not applicable to all geographical regions.

Positions in elementary and secondary teaching almost always require a *teaching certificate*. More opportunities are available in inner-city locations than in suburban schools.

A doctorate is rapidly becoming a requirement in higher education. With the glut of doctorates in many fields, even community colleges and small colleges can often demand a doctorate. Although a doctorate is not currently required in many administrative assignments, the trend leans toward that direction.

Jobs in Government

Government employs over 20 million people in federal agencies, state governments, counties, cities, and municipalities. Governments hire people from nearly every occupational group. The federal government gets the most press coverage yet it employs only 20 percent of all government employees. State governments employ 25 percent and local governments over half.

As a greater percentage of federal money returns to local governments, employment at state and local levels is increasing while it is stabilizing or downsizing at the federal level.

Federal Jobs.   Federal employment practices may be characterized as: high competition for jobs; low attrition of current employees; internal attention to upward mobility programs; and budget reductions.

This means that it is necessary to start job campaigns early and to be well informed about available positions and procedures for application if you are interested in federal government employment.

Most new hires enter under the "General Schedule (GS) Classification" as professional, scientific, administrative, or support personnel. About 15 percent of all federal white-collar workers work in Washington, DC. Only two percent work overseas.

Your chances of employment depend upon how well you compare with others in experience and education, the geographical location in which you will consider employment, and the minimum grade (salary level) you will accept. You may effectively eliminate yourself from consideration by restricting location and/or grade on the application form.

Some agencies require a standardized test for inexperienced applicants with nontechnical degrees. These tests measure several ability areas (verbal, mathematical, judgmental, aptitude, etc.). You are referred on the basis of your scores to agencies listing vacancies which utilize the various ability categories.

Obtaining a job with the federal government requires a thorough knowledge of the process and an early start in the search process.

·····INDEPENDENT GOVERNMENT HIRING ORGANIZATIONS·····

Energy Research
Federal Reserve System
Central Intelligence Agency
Federal Bureau of Investigation
Foreign Service of the U.S.
International Monetary Fund
Judicial Branch of Government
Legislative Branch of Government
National Science Foundation
National Security Agency
Organization of American States
Tennessee Valley Authority
United National Secretariat
U.S. Mission to the U.N.
U.S. Nuclear Regulatory Commission
U.S. Postal Service
World Bank and IFC

··········

Figure 3.8

**TYPICAL
STATE EMPLOYMENT
FUNCTIONS**

Conservation
Criminal Justice
Education Programs
Elections
Employment Services
Financial Operations
Health Services
Highway Operations
Law Enforcement
Legislative Liaison
Mental Health Services
Parks and Recreation
Prison Operations
Social Welfare
Transportation
   Systems
Unemployment
   Services

··········

Figure 3.9

Appointments are usually made at the GS-5 and GS-7 levels, mostly at the lower level. Competition is intense.

Exams are given only a few times each year. You must take statements about deadlines very seriously.

Referral of candidates is done according to specific rules.

Occupations requiring technical degrees or specialized backgrounds are filled by individual agencies, and many do not require an exam. Some positions require written tests more related to the jobs. You often are evaluated on the basis of education, experience, and ability to reflect your credentials clearly and accurately on the application form.

You often must complete several application forms. Complete these legibly and with great care and detail, because answers are weighted in terms of the requirements for particular positions. Give much detail about extra-curricular activities, volunteer work, part-time experiences, and all full-time work. Successful candidates normally are geographically flexible. Patience is an important virtue. Start early.

Federal salary scales change annually. The rates are set to be competitive with comparable jobs in private industry. Rates are available on websites.

The federal government operates a system of federal job information centers located in most major cities. These centers provide current information about employment opportunities, open announcements, testing, and application centers.

Certain federal agencies manage separate hiring systems. These agencies and quasi-agencies must be contacted directly. Figure 3.8 gives a partial listing of some of the more active hiring groups.

State Government Jobs.   The size and scope of government operations vary considerably from state to state. States also differ in the processes by which they hire new employees.

Most states have personnel offices, but the functions are not always the same. Some certify and recommend candidates to agencies, some directly hire for agencies, and some provide a central application and candidate repository service.

There is no consistency among the states in the utilization of testing, position classification systems, publicizing of open positions, use of patronage, and recruitment. Each state personnel office must be contacted directly.

States obviously hire people for roles similar to those in the federal government, but the applicant has a maze of fifty states to contact in order to learn the rules of the games. Some states have residency requirements.

Local Government Jobs. Local governments (counties, cities, towns) offer employment opportunities in a variety of fields. Total employment in local governments dwarfs federal and state employment numbers combined. Although many governments have excellent merit or civil service systems, many have nothing equivalent and yet hire hundreds of people. It is common for individual agencies to do their own hiring, even at the managerial and professional levels. Patronage and residency requirements often constitute barriers for some applicants.

Locating vacancies can be an expensive and complex process. The best approach is to visit each local jurisdiction and talk with the person responsible for hiring in each agency.

Figure 3.10 identifies the services normally provided by local governments. A review of the services provided might give you an idea of how you could fit into the local government employment picture.

Not-For-Profit Organizations

A few organizations which employ college graduates do not lend themselves to the government or private organization classification. Most of these are not-for-profit corporations.

Not-for-profit hiring organizations include hospitals, museums, symphony orchestras, art galleries, professional associations, labor organizations, consumer unions, industry trade groups, lobby and special interest groups, foundations, trusts, convention centers, auxiliary enterprises of educational institutions, etc.

The number of job possibilities with these organizations is not large, but these organizations do need qualified people. They need accountants, public relations specialists, marketers, engineers, negotiators, coordinators, etc. Unfortunately, there is no organized employment market for them, so each unit must be contacted independently. Professional associations play an important role in the employment process. Review a number of relevant websites for specific information.

Private Enterprise

About 85 percent of all employment in the United States is outside the realm of government.

TYPICAL LOCAL GOVERNMENT SERVICES

Tax Assessment
Tax Collection
Elections
Courts
Law Enforcement
Urban Planning
Sanitation
Health
Social Work
Welfare
Roads and Streets
Parks and Recreation
Fire Protection
Public Records
Financial Services

• • • • • • • • • • •

Figure 3.10

//WEB.TIP//

americanexpress.com/ smallbusiness/
American Express
Online classifieds/business network directory/advice/ business tools/ business plans/customer identification assistance.

The private employment sector, largely business, offers the greatest number of jobs.

Most employment growth in our society during the next decade is likely to come in the private sector.

Even if you think employment in the private sector is not for you, you must at least investigate its opportunities. You may be forced by circumstances to seek employment in the private sector.

Work activities are similar in many various employment settings, but the methods you use to seek employment in different settings are very different. That does not imply that it is easier or more difficult to obtain a job in a given sector; rather, it means that the approach you utilize must be designed for the option you select.

Some jobs in the private sector have no counterparts in the public and quasi-public sectors and vice versa. In the vast majority of situations, however, the duties have common counterparts. You must understand the setting (and what it implies) before you can completely understand the jobs.

The work structures, organizations, and work concepts have similarities but are also very different in government, education, and private enterprise work settings. Concepts such as security, job performance, earnings, productivity, values, and interpersonal relationships have different meanings in the different work environments.

Private enterprise employment is such a strong probability for most people that it needs to be understood by everyone, regardless of whether they are seeking employment in that sector or not. Your life, regardless of the work setting you choose, is affected by people working in the private sector.

Organizational concepts such as industry groupings, organizational structure, functional careers, and responsibility levels should be thoroughly understood. The likelihood of your working in the private sector is great.

Work Environments:

Systems – Functions – Responsibility Levels

The private enterprise system provides more jobs for more people than all other employment sectors. The number of career opportunities in private business *far* exceeds those in government, education, social services, non-profit organizations, the professions, and all other employment possibilities.

The magnitude of private enterprise career possibilities is so overwhelming that it is extremely ill-advised for you to fail to seriously investigate them.

Private Enterprise System

Many people view private enterprise as consisting of only the giant American corporations, but private enterprise also includes thousands of small, privately owned businesses ranging from the corner grocery store to the local bank. Most private enterprises are small to medium-size organizations, and they are usually owned by the person or persons operating them. These businesses may have only two or possibly two thousand employees.

The free enterprise system permits doctors, lawyers, investors, writers, store managers, distributors, manufacturers, farmers—anyone—to establish an organization for the purpose of earning a living plus a reasonable profit by investing, and thus risking, their time and financial resources.

Most of America's giant corporations started as small, independently owned and operated organizations and grew over the years by the exercise of sound management practices.

Profit Corporations

A corporation is nothing more than a group of people working together toward the common goals of earning a good living for themselves and their colleagues in the enterprise, and of returning a reasonable rate of return to the individuals who have invested financial resources in the corporation.

Through mutual funds, the stock market, and insurance firms, private individuals own corporate America. This includes members of labor unions, employees, housewives, and millions of other private citizens. Most people in America own shares of major corporations either directly or indirectly.

Many people are indirectly stockholders in corporations and do not even realize it. If you have an asset base of any size, you probably have some funds invested in insurance policies and financial institutions.

In all probability, your financial success and retirement are greatly dependent upon the success of corporate enterprises because the businesses with which you deposit your capital invest in these organizations.

Corporations are people, not monolithic entities.

Not all countries of the world share in this concept nor in the principle of individual choice of employment. Our country's free enterprise system generates more career opportunities for people than all other forms of employment combined.

A major goal of many people is to eventually own and operate an entity they can claim as their own. The business might be a one-person private consulting firm, a ten-employee retail operation, or a multi-employee manufacturing firm.

Few people just starting out have the experience or financial resources to go into business for themselves, so most people must look to the larger organizations for the foothold they need in order to get started in their careers. The larger firms offer training and the chance to build a financial base.

Every business has a cadre (some large and some small) of professional, technical, and managerial personnel who guide the organization. Many of these people—not all—have college educations. With the passage of time, that cadre is being replaced and supplemented by a new generation of college-trained managerial professionals.

As new industries and firms create new products and/or services, greater opportunities for employment are generated. Today's entrants into private enterprise represent the leadership of tomorrow for these organizations.

Employer Websites

Nearly every employer has their own website, and most of them have a "CAREERS" section. Many even collect applications on line. Before interviews, and whenever you are just exploring, you should visit these sites.

Most sites have job descriptions of jobs an employer has open. This is a great opportunity for you to explore various career fields available within various firms.

Individual Proprietorships

What is the difference between an individual and a corporation? Legally, there is a body of laws that separate individuals and corporate entities, but from a working standpoint, there is no difference. The reasons individual owners of businesses form corporations are to facilitate the raising of capital to expand the organization and to limit personal and financial liability.

The reason investors are willing to provide financing is to obtain a rate of return greater than what is possible through investing in other things. Because the risk of loss is greater than that with a savings account, insurance, and other forms of insured savings, the anticipated rate of return is better.

Entrepreneurship is part of the American dream.

One major goal of many individuals is to someday own a business of their own. In surveys of recent college graduates, large percentages indicate that their goal is to start working for a large private enterprise, gain work experience, earn and save capital, develop knowledge in a specific field, and to eventually leave the corporation to start a new business.

An understanding of this basic work environment is a key element in career planning.

Non-profit Corporations

Not-for-profit institutions like labor unions, associations, cooperatives, museums, hospitals, etc., incorporate to provide a management vehicle for perpetual existence and to limit the liability of the board of directors and individual members and users. The non-profit organization also incorporates to avoid paying taxes.

There is a thin line between what non-profit corporations call "surpluses" and profit, but the difference is that profit corporations pay dividends to stockholders. Non-profit corporations plow earnings, if any, back into the organization for the benefit of their members and/or the publics they serve.

Free enterprise impacts your career planning. For practical purposes, the free enterprise system defines work settings and provides an overview of the entire world of work. Recognizing this concept permits you to see how the activities you want to do in order to earn a livelihood fit into the broad context of work.

The free enterprise system is a fundamental concept in employment.

Industry Groups

To help understand the composition of the U.S. work force and how you might fit into the overall design, private enterprise institutions may be viewed as either goods-producing or service-producing organizations. The U.S. Department of Labor further classifies these two groups into several major divisions according to the product or service.

Most of the nation's workers are in industries that produce services, which include education, health care, trade, repair, government, transportation, banking, and insurance. The production of goods, such as food, buildings, and minerals, requires less than one-quarter of the country's work force.

Salary Surveys often divide salary statistics by *"types of employer." A representative breakdown of types of employers or industry groupings is shown in Figure 4.1.*

Many investment services, such as Value Line, Moody's, Standard and Poor, and the like, classify employers into different groupings. There is no universally accepted classification due to mergers, new industries, and the potential use of a given classification.

Employment growth trends continue to be faster in service-producing industries.

In order to collect more career information, a helpful activity is to carefully review various industry groups and observe the relative size of employment in that group. Keep in mind that some industries are more "labor intensive" than others. Clearly, some industries employ more people in professional, technical, and managerial capacities than others.

Figure 4.1 is also useful for reviewing the number of different industries available for you to investigate for potential employment. With the growth of technology, some of these industries may even be subdivided into new industries, while others may have disappeared, and yet others may have consolidated with related fields due to technological advances.

Thousands of employing organizations dot the landscape of the nation. The potential for employment in private enterprise is enormous. Within each industry there are hundreds of large and small employers, and within each employing organization many different types of job opportunities exist.

Certain occupations are characterized by employment in a particular industry. For example, individuals who desire teaching jobs usually must seek employment in education. Urban planners work for governments. Advertising workers work in a small industry group. Nurses most often work for hospitals.

Your choice of an occupation and career field may dictate the industry in which you will work. Some people are comfortable with that specification, but others prefer to keep their options broader.

Your occupational decision must factor in your feelings about the type(s) of industry in which you wish to work.

Business and Services

Public Accounting	Hospitality
Advertising	Insurance
Banking	Retailing
Computer	Publishing
Consulting	Transportation
Financial	Utilities

Manufacturing and Industrial

Aerospace	Food
Agricultural	Purchasing
Automotive	Metals
Building	Petroleum
Scientific Instruments	Textiles
Pharmaceuticals	Tires
Business Machines	Chemicals
Electrical Equipment	

Government and Quasi-Government

Education	Federal
Health	State
Non-Profit	Local

· · · · · · · · · ·

Figure 4.1

Occupational Classifications

As industries grow in the next decade, changes will take place in the occupational structure. Many jobs will become more complex and specialized, and thereby an even greater number of occupational choices will be available. Studying broad occupational groups first helps you get a handle on how to approach a complex job market.

The government classifies workers into four large groups: white-collar workers, blue-collar workers, service workers, and farm workers.

Professional, technical, and managerial workers make up over half of the white-collar group. A very high percentage of workers in these groups hold college degrees.

Another component of the white-collar group is sales workers, and we are seeing an increasing number of workers in this category also who hold college degrees.

Most jobs in which you are interested, no doubt, are in the professional, technical, and managerial classifications. Fewer than ten percent of all employees in the blue-collar, service, and farm worker classifications hold college degrees.

For many years employers have classified employees as either salaried or hourly paid employees. Salaried employees are the smaller group and constitute mostly the white-collar workers.

Federal wage laws reinforce this distinction by defining which employees are to be covered under labor agreements, minimum wage laws, and other compensation and employment laws. Employees not covered by these laws are widely referred to as "exempt" employees and include most professional, technical, managerial, and sales personnel.

NOW **THAT** IS THE PROBLEM WITH TOP HEAVY MANAGEMENT.

Management Concepts

To survive, organizations must be managed in a manner that will insure their continued existence. As a result, private enterprise organizations set corporate goals just as individuals establish career goals. The goals can be motivated by profit, social, service, or survival interests, or combinations of these interests.

Many types of people from many occupations must work together in a harmonious work setting if the goals of the enterprise are to be met. Management is the vehicle for this cooperation and articulation. Management brings together people, financial resources, technology, and other resources in such a way as to insure attainment of the goals of the organization.

Management Structure

The management process demands that work be organized in a manner that efficiently allows the organization to meet its specified objectives. This organizational structure is important to you because it specifies how and where your particular skills and interests can be utilized. Organizational goals and individual goals are not necessarily in conflict. What is best for you may turn out to be best for the organization as well.

Every organization (including government agencies, hospitals, law firms, associations, small firms, and large businesses) operates within some type of management structure. A management structure avoids chaos and defines relationships between functions and people carrying out these functions.

When two or more people come together, *formal* and *informal* relationships develop, and after a time, the relationships usually evolve into a *hierarchy* or other organizational structure. Leadership roles emerge.

Functions.   Organizations are organized around the tasks to be accomplished. Work tasks can be classified by their function. Any particular task is directed at carrying out one of the three major functions:

1. **Creating** a product or service
2. **Distributing** a product or service
3. **Financing** a product or service

//WEB.TIP//

stats.bls.gov/ocohome.htm
Occupational Outlook Handbook
Employment projects/job descriptions/job requirements/sources for more info/compensation.

Your goals may be synonymous with the organization's goals.

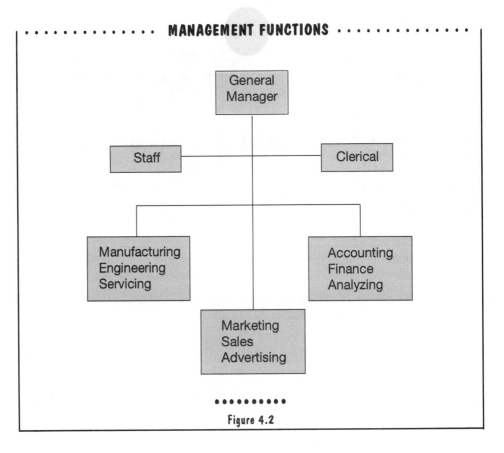

Figure 4.2

In most private enterprises that manufacture a product, these three functions represent *manufacturing*, *marketing*, and *accounting*. In a service organization, the manufacturing function is replaced by the service being provided. It may be called the *distribution* or *purchasing* function in retail and wholesale trade firms. Hundreds of people, or one single person, may be employed in these various functions, depending upon the size of the organization.

Where in the organization could your qualifications make the most significant contribution to both the organization and you?

What you decide to do is important, but equally important is how that activity fits into the *structure* of the organization which will eventually be the source of employment for you. If you know what contribution you can make and how it meshes with the goals of the organization, you are well on your way toward satisfaction in your career.

Career exploration is determining where in an organization your particular interests and skills best fit.

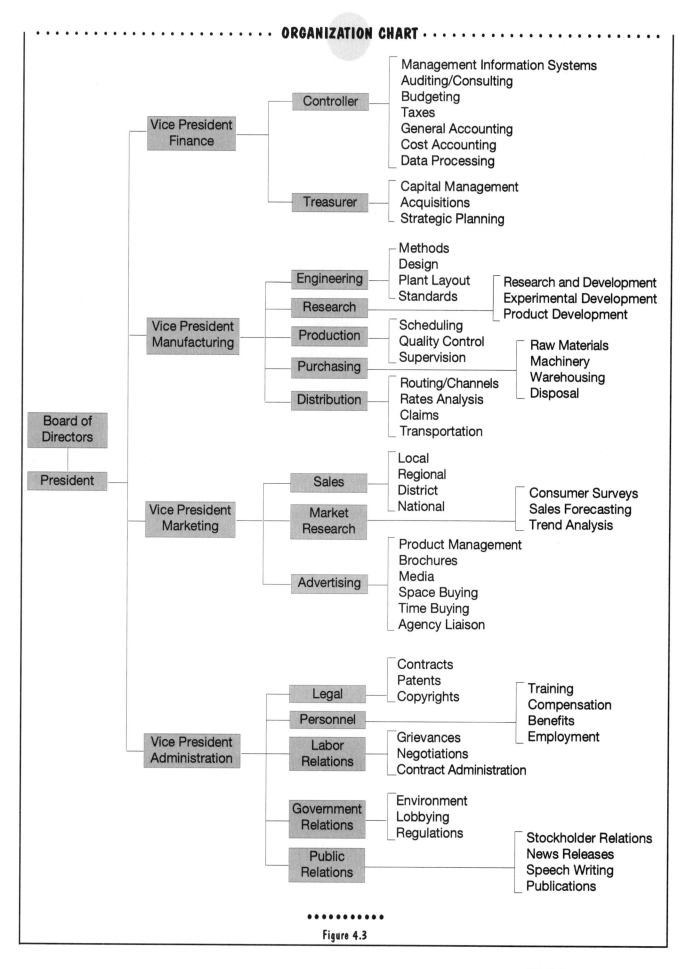

ORGANIZATION CHART

Vice President Finance
- Controller
  - Management Information Systems
  - Auditing/Consulting
  - Budgeting
  - Taxes
  - General Accounting
  - Cost Accounting
  - Data Processing
- Treasurer
  - Capital Management
  - Acquisitions
  - Strategic Planning

Vice President Manufacturing
- Engineering
  - Methods
  - Design
  - Plant Layout
  - Standards
- Research
  - Research and Development
  - Experimental Development
  - Product Development
- Production
  - Scheduling
  - Quality Control
  - Supervision
- Purchasing
  - Raw Materials
  - Machinery
  - Warehousing
  - Disposal
- Distribution
  - Routing/Channels
  - Rates Analysis
  - Claims
  - Transportation

Vice President Marketing
- Sales
  - Local
  - Regional
  - District
  - National
- Market Research
  - Consumer Surveys
  - Sales Forecasting
  - Trend Analysis
- Advertising
  - Product Management
  - Brochures
  - Media
  - Space Buying
  - Time Buying
  - Agency Liaison

Vice President Administration
- Legal
  - Contracts
  - Patents
  - Copyrights
- Personnel
  - Training
  - Compensation
  - Benefits
  - Employment
- Labor Relations
  - Grievances
  - Negotiations
  - Contract Administration
- Government Relations
  - Environment
  - Lobbying
  - Regulations
- Public Relations
  - Stockholder Relations
  - News Releases
  - Speech Writing
  - Publications

Board of Directors
President

Figure 4.3

A management structure organized around work functions is essential in any enterprise.

The complexity of management increases as the size of the enterprise grows. In a very small manufacturing concern, one person, such as the owner, might function as the chief manufacturing supervisor, the sales manager, and the chief accountant.

If the enterprise were to grow, however, other people would need to be hired to handle these functions. The owner could hire a certified public accountant to do the bookkeeping and use an independent sales representative to sell the product while personally supervising the manufacturing.

The owner usually discovers that it is more profitable to hire other people to handle these functions. The owner's role is then to supervise, or manage, all of the functions of the growing business.

As thousands of units come to be manufactured and sold, the need may arise for a national distribution network and new plants to handle the activity. The owner may elect to duplicate units in a distant city. New financing may be necessary. An engineer may be needed.

A research person might be useful to improve the product. Advertising experts could help to increase sales as well, as could a network of sales representatives to call on potential customers.

Credit may become necessary to help distributors carry inventories of the product. The organization may thus become a complex organizational structure of several hundred people, and bankers may begin to offer help with the new equipment, plant, and distribution financing.

This description of the growth potential of a small business illustrates the American free enterprise concept and explains the genesis of our economic foundations. The enterprise described could be a hospital serving a small town, a labor union, a public accounting firm, a school corporation, a retail store, or any of a thousand business entities.

The U.S. economy is a mature economy, but the growth of private enterprise still happens every day. Most people, particularly young professionals, usually first work for a mature or maturing organization as they progress in their careers. As experience is gained, many elect to go out on their own. Perhaps that is your long-term ambition. Others prefer to always work for an organization and not to assume the risk and time commitment inherent in working for themselves.

Organizational Charts.   Many private enterprises in the U.S. have attained gigantic proportions and extremely complex organizational structures. Nonetheless, the three basic functions are the same.

Few organizations could survive without effective organizational structures because a single individual's span of control reaches a point of diminishing returns.

To handle this problem, *authority* is delegated to others even though the *responsibility* continues to rest with the delegator of the authority. This is accomplished by breaking the unit into smaller sub-units with established reporting relationships.

This reorganization may be implemented by assigning managers to various sub-units that may be classified by a given line of products, groups of products, a geographical part of the world, or any other logical grouping. Within each sub-unit, you will find the three basic functions.

You can quickly see a pyramid structure developing which is integral to most organizations and their sub-units in government, education, and business. Most of these structures follow a hierarchical arrangement with managers and other professional people being in charge at the top levels.

Why is this managerial organizational structure important to you? What do you want your role to be? Are you manager potential? Are you a technical expert with no intention of climbing an organizational structure? Have you ever thought about this concept? These questions form the essence of career exploration.

This pyramiding concept is brought to reality when you look at an organization chart. Have you seen the organization chart of an employer for whom you worked? If you have, you have seen a diagram of a logical pattern of working relationships.

Figure 4.3 illustrates a typical organizational chart. See if you can identify where you might fit, and trace the path both up and down the chart.

Informal Relationships. Organization charts show only the formal structure. There are "dotted-line" relationships between many departments; these are the social relationships which are never shown. People from all parts of the organization meet and talk to one another. In most organizations, it is impossible to function only in one little niche.

Relationships rapidly expand in geometric proportions in all directions. A sound career decision demands that you understand informal organizational structures.

The entry-level electrical engineer meets with the vice president of marketing to discuss customer product concerns. The junior accountant meets with the sales representative to explain paper processing. A secretary screens telephone calls to protect the boss's valuable time.

A computer programmer discusses a production schedule problem with the manufacturing head. The public relations copywriter writes a speech for top management to deliver to a congressional subcommittee. The interrelationships are varied.

Can you afford to put on occupational blinders? Career exploration involves coming to understand both formal and informal relationships within organizations. It does not imply the use of "company politics" to get ahead; it means career survival in any work setting.

Your goal is to understand how management influences your career choices. To do this, you need a basic awareness of how the management process integrates all functions and facets of the employment process. This requires you to learn how industries and occupations interrelate.

It behooves you to mentally create a picture of how the concepts of functional organization and level of responsibility within functions and occupations impact upon various career alternatives that you might wish to consider.

The career field that you eventually select in all probability will require you to manage your career within the framework of a private enterprise. In order

SEVEN LEVEL PYRAMID

The corporate organization defines the relationship between the functions that employees perform.

THAT'S IT? AN "UNQUENCHABLE LUST FOR POWER"
...IS WHY YOU'RE INTERESTED IN MANAGEMENT?

to maintain control over your career destiny, you need to know how to direct an organization and how to plot a realistic career plan within the work environment you select.

Management Process

Regardless of whether you work in government, education, or private enterprise, your sphere of influence is limited by your ability to touch only a few people. Your actions can influence people above your level, your peers, and your subordinates.

You must manage your career within the confines of an *identifiable unit.* If you own a business, you have a target customer population that you can potentially influence. If you are an engineer working for a government agency, you have a population that describes your sphere of influence.

Only world leaders can impact upon large populations and resources, and even then only for a certain segment of the earth. Even decisions by the President of the United States rarely impact all people of the world.

What is your *sphere of influence?* What do you want it to be? What organizational units can you identify in which you could develop a "niche" to do the things that are of value to you? You need to identify the environment in which you want to work now, a few months hence, and in years ahead.

Once your world is identified, you must manage your career within the constraints offered by your world. Some worlds demand more self-discipline than others.

The word "manage" means to conduct, control, plan, and organize. **Management is an action-oriented process of planning, organizing, and controlling an operation, system, or group of people.** Management is a process, because it is an activity that occurs and recurs over and over, time after time.

Your Career Management

Career management is an on-going activity based upon the career planning concept. Career management is taking charge of your life by employing career planning techniques and processes in order to attain your personal objectives.

Management by Objectives. An objective is a goal, an aim, or a purpose. Missions are inherent in all types of organizations. Regardless of the statement of purpose, organizations must establish goals simply for survival purposes. Undirected organizations usually die after painfully paying a price in resource destruction.

Your personal career management should be no less goal-oriented. Otherwise, you may flounder aimlessly in your life as well as your career, and may not enjoy life to the fullest extent possible.

Career management is a process of career decision making that changes or modifies goals as new information becomes available. The information is "real-world" input, and it includes understandings about the concepts of management and organizations.

The management process begins with the setting of career objectives which are realistic, attainable, and consistent with self-understanding and career field realities.

Planning. A plan is a schedule of future activities designed in a systematic order so as to facilitate achievement of some stated objective. A career plan maps out an approach to be implemented in the future that will insure successful achievement of a prestated career goal.

Planning solves the "chicken and egg dilemma." Career planning sets up a dynamic process that continually searches for information. As information is

The informal relationships can be as important in career advancement as the formal relationships.

Take charge of managing your own career.

Career management is setting realistic, achievable goals within the context you want to operate.

YOUR WORK HAS IMPACT

Organizations invest billions of dollars in financial assets. These assets are tracked, analyzed, nurtured, and prepared to insure that they produce the highest possible financial return back to the organization. Yet, if you look at most organizations, you will not see one dime on their financial statement regarding an investment in human capital.

People run organizations. People employ other people. People manage financial assets to achieve a stated objective of the organization.

Aren't you dumbfounded at the lack of attention that most organizations pay to their most significant asset—their employees? Most organizations place a value on people called annual compensation and account for it in the category of operating expenses like pencils, computers, and other depletable expenses.

History records that organizations fail largely because of the ineptness of the people managing it. People, their employees, are organizations most important asset.

The record shows that employee compensation runs from low to high, but in recent years the spread between the top groups and the entry groups has narrowed significantly. The concept of a team working together to get a top quality job completed in a profitable way is emerging in our society.

Unless you elect to become a one-person organization (a dying phenomena) you will become part of the team of some type of organization. Hopefully, someday you will be among the select few at the top, but most people start somewhere along the way and make incremental contributions along the way.

In your chosen organization, you are not likely to change the accounting concepts and introduce long term human capital as an asset on the financial statement. The evidence is overwhelming that even supposedly stable organizations merge, reorganize, disband, or respond to new and different markets. Change is inevitable.

Along your career (or careers), expect to change employers several times. In fact, your skills will probably be completely outdated within three to five years if you do not renew them continuously. Some of the skill renewing will surely be on the job while other facets will result from employer sponsored training or formal programs in educational institutions.

Although human capital is an organization's most important asset, the merger mania of the past decade proves that organizations cannot exist to perpetuate themselves or their employees. The choice of where to spend your working life relates as much to personal life goals as it does to organizational objectives.

Organizations experience success (or lack of it) just as individuals experience success. The definition of organization success differs from your definition of success, especially when time parameters are introduced into the equation. In the ideal situation, the goals are completely compatible, but a common level of equilibrium is not likely to endure forever.

You may prefer to ride out periods of incompatibility for the sake of external reasons, such as security, stability, health, family, etc. The organization may cooperate during the difficult periods, but a wise approach is to be ready to sever ties if the mutual goals wander afar.

You have more invested in human capital than the organization. Your goal should be to maximize your own investment. If and when that demands a reassessment, you should be prepared to conduct the proper analysis. One purpose of this book is to teach you how to have a *strategic* and *tactical* career planning model handy in order to plug in the appropriate variables.

This is not to suggest that the concept of employee loyalty is now thrown out the window. It does imply that loyalty is a scale, not a blind dogma. Many factors go into career assessment, and loyalty will continue to be an important dimension.

Loyalty is a two-way street. Employing organizations in both public and private sectors have been stretching the concept of loyalty.

The future will continue to bring wide swings depending on both organizational and individual needs. Your goal should be to have a back-up position ready in the event it is needed. A sound career planning model with its attendant tools provides the necessary peace of mind.

received and evaluated, it is fed back into the cycle, and this permits a readjustment of the career goal which is based on reality.

Organizing. Organizing is creating a structure within which a planning and control system can operate. The organizational structure allows you to operate without concern for losing control of a given situation.

The organization sets limits of acceptable behavior and actions. Organizational settings are widely diverse. Although no two organizations may be identical, generalities and *standard operating procedures* (SOP) define the framework and style in which actions are taken.

Career management involves knowing and understanding the organizational structure in which you must complete duties specified by your occupation. The same career field in two different organizations may have completely different operating structures.

Motivating. The central factor controlling the management process is motivation. Above all else, *people* manage organizations. Some people work very hard, and others goof off. What makes you work hard? Different forces move different people.

Understanding your motivations gives you the ability to select the most compatible organization in which to work. Some management styles are very *disciplinary* in approach, and you may be the type of person who responds to that type of stimulation. Other management styles are *participative* and indeed, others are *laissez faire.*

You may perform best under the do-your-own-thing approach, or somewhere in between the two extremes. In any event, sound career management means selecting the right motivational climate.

Controlling. Control keeps the activity moving according to the plan and within the defined organizational setting. Controlling is taking charge of the situation in order to make it conform to predefined routines.

Effective controlling builds in a monitoring device that feeds information back into the planning, organizing, and motivating process to improve and fine tune the total system.

Career management uses career planning approaches to regulate and modify the feedback of career information. Just like the management process, the career control system provides for regulation of the process.

Select the right motivational climate for yourself.

The Management System

The management process is a complex set of interrelated activities which moves the organization toward its stated goals. Many organizations have the management process so ingrained in their basic characters that, regardless of top leadership, the systems run themselves.

A system is a coordinated set of events which serve in concert to achieve a mission. This concept is found in education, big corporations, labor unions, and nearly every organization in private enterprise regardless of the size.

The management process is an action-oriented process of planning, organizing, motivating, and controlling the operation system, or group of people. It is found in every phase of an organization including accounting, marketing, manufacturing, engineering, research, and even among professionals such as doctors, dentists, and nurses.

Management occurs at "low" levels as well as "high" levels in the organizational structure. It involves policy determination, decision making, responsibility assumption, and supervision of people and systems.

Career management and planning build upon the management concept. Do organizations run careers or do people run careers? Decide which way it is going to be for you.

Whatever you decide, you must decide with a full understanding of the implications. That means knowing more about how work is organized in our society.

> A system is a structured set of events designed to optimally achieve a predetermined goal.

Levels of Responsibility

The majority of us list *advancement* as one of the most important reasons why we select a given job over another job.

Greater financial rewards come as we progress higher in the organization structure of our employer. If one of your goals is to advance, then you must understand the concept of "levels of responsibility."

Your level of responsibility grows to the extent that you make increasingly greater and greater productivity gains to the organization. Your worth improves as the organization's financial goals (or other goals) improve.

Productivity

In all organizations, people are paid for what they contribute to organizational objectives. Assuming no inflationary price increases or productivity increases, in theory individual earnings would never increase or decrease.

If there is no productivity improvement, the only reason for an increase in earnings is to maintain a constant standard of living. In a world of inflation, for real earnings to rise, productivity must be increased.

Productivity does improve. As you perform a given task, you get better at it and your contribution to organizational goals increases. In fairness, the wise employer recognizes your contribution and increases your earnings consistently with your increased contribution.

Conversely, if your productivity declines, so should your earnings. In practice, salaries seldom decline absolutely, but they do decline relatively as inflation advances at a pace faster than their increase.

> Your earnings are directly tied to your performance and value. The greater your contribution, the higher you rise in the organization.

Promotion

Employers recognize your increasing productivity through earnings increases and promotion. A promotion implies greater responsibility and authority in addition to greater productivity. Assuming more responsibility and improving your productivity are the two basic ways for you to progress in an organization. If advancement is your ambition, then you must be prepared to do one or both of them.

To some degree, your position in the organizational hierarchy denotes your level of responsibility. Power and authority are tied to your ability to decide action independently or to supervise other people or projects.

In most organizations, you can readily identify four distinct levels of responsibility: labor, professional staff, management, and executive personnel. Where do you fit? Where do you want to fit?

Labor

The laws of our nation have fairly accurately defined who is labor and who is management. Labor includes workers who directly produce a product or service at the basic interface level. They are mostly blue-collar, service, and clerical workers. Although there are shades of grey, in most situations, you can usually define where a given group of workers fit.

Some blue-collar workers do succeed in working themselves out of blue-collar status into the management ranks. Other individuals in the labor classification would not accept management jobs if they were offered to them. Nationally, about half of these workers are unionized and take great pride in the skilled work that they do.

Professionals

Many large organizations, mostly manufacturing, banking, retailing, and professional service employers, create entry-level assignments for the specific purpose of providing entry routes for inexperienced professional, technical, and managerial aspirants into the organizations.

Many government agencies also identify a certain level of responsibility which they use to accomplish the same purpose.

Entry-level assignments are designed for individuals with no or limited work experience in the assignment field. Most of the people entering these assignments are just getting out of college or are starting over in new careers.

The entry position's function is to attract high-caliber people and to provide them with training for future development. The training relates as much to learning the organization's structure, system, and philosophy as it does to learning specific tasks.

Following the functional organization chart given in Figure 4.3 permits you to obtain a relative view of organizational life and just where you might fit in if you see yourself in this type of entry assignment.

In terms of level of responsibility, these positions fit into a groove just above labor status. This type of job frequently pays less than skilled blue-collar jobs, but it offers the chance to move high up the organizational ladder.

This small niche is not a long-term commitment; it is designed with a very short-term job life span, usually less than two years. In essence, these assign-

//WEB.TIP//

sbaonline.sba.gov
***Small Business
Administration***
Provides business counseling/facts on federal aid/ financing/resource locator.

WELL... DO YOU WANT TO BE LABOR OR MANAGEMENT?

ments are *junior* professional and managerial positions. The assignments are used for both bachelor- and master-degreed individuals.

These inexperienced professionals include engineers, accountants, computer programmers, systems analysts, financial analysts, personal assistants, sales representatives, buyers, production supervisors, junior scientists, and management trainees. They include assignments in hundreds of different fields but fit into the functional concept within the management structure.

Purpose. The employer's purpose in identifying certain positions as entry-level assignments is to provide technical and managerial talent for leading the organization in the future.

Few people start at the top. The age-old tradition is to start at the bottom and work up. Even a college degree does not alter that fundamental concept.

The entry-level assignment is not "rock bottom," but an intermediate step between blue-collar and white-collar; neither labor nor truly management, but destined to become management if everything progresses satisfactorily.

Upward Mobility. Employers hire new people for their *potential,* not necessarily for immediate productive results. Most want productive results quickly, but the basic thrust is to develop *long-term* managers, professionals, or technical experts to run the organization. Some of these employers stay with the organizations and go on to high positions, but others leave the organizations and go on to other jobs for various reasons.

No guarantee for advancement is given. Upward mobility is based on merit. Thus, upward mobility serves as the "motivational carrot."

Some employers hire more employees than they need because a certain level of failure is expected. Non-performers do not get promoted and either get terminated, leave, or remain on low-level assignments.

The professional entry-level concept works well for most organizations. Exact job titles vary depending upon the size and type of organization. In fact, some employees never realize they have been routed through entry-level assignments.

Depending upon the type of job, the industry, and the size of organization, some employers design specific management trainee positions which feed into more responsible positions.

Because most new hires lack interest in nonproductive "trainee" roles, some employers have abandoned the management trainee approach in recent years. They prefer instead to place the new professionals immediately in functional fields consistent with their prior training.

The entry-level assignment is used to introduce, smooth, and hasten the transition from an academic or other work environment to the specific employment environment.

TYPICAL ENTRY LEVEL JOB TITLES

- Trainee
- Analyst
- Coordinator
- Associate
- Assistant to ...
- Representative
- Intern
- Consultant
- Researcher
- Specialist
- Junior

• • • • • • • • • • •

Figure 4.4

CAREER PLATEAUS LIMIT PROMOTION

CAREER PLATEAUS

- Only one percent reach the top.
- Ninety-nine percent plateau.

LIMITS TO UPWARD MOBILITY

- Lean and mean programs.
- Competitive promotions.
- Baby boomers.
- Employment contraction.
- Sales plateaus.

Make peace with yourself or push forward.

Only 1 percent of career strivers ever reach the top in any organization. By definition, 99 percent of careers must plateau. Realistic career goal setting is wonderful, but the key component is the word realistic.

Do you have the ability, interest, stamina, and other qualities to reach the top? What is your definition of the "top"? Many people who supposedly reach the top admit the fun was in the rise, not the final achievement. Disappointment often follows people who attain their lifelong dreams.

Our society is facing significant limits on the age-old concept of upward mobility. The top is becoming even more elusive. Organizational cultures that espouse the "lean and mean" philosophy basically clear out the ranks of middle management from which top achievers must be drawn.

Promotions in organizations are becoming increasingly more competitive as baby boomers and their follow-up generation vie for recognition. Coupled with slower growth of traditional high flying organizations, the middle assignments get squeezed even further by economic cycles. Salary compression, caused by unions, and labor shortages at entry levels, is making upward mobility tough.

Most corporate cultures define all "non-promotional" rewards as immensely secondary. We have an "advancement mentality" which we keep perpetuating via encouraging people to respond to challenge, change, and new experiences.

This is an unrealistic strategy because by definition, even in the best of times, promotions are going to slow or cease. The law of average states that only one percent can reach the top in terms of promotion.

What is a career plateau? It is a flat place, but it could be at high levels as easily as at low levels. It means career stability which is not all bad. Reaching the end of the promotional ladder means that you are not going to gain significantly more power, responsibility, status or money.

A career plateau means that you are being recognized as a middle management, competent, career professional. The organization leaves you in the same job where you are highly productive, contribute significantly to the bottom line but does not promote you. Your contentment at that plateau may signal that you feel good about having expertly mastered a needed body of knowledge. You may love your job.

Career plateauing faces nearly everyone. The main difficulty is that the career plateau may deteriorate first into a feeling of endless cycles of repetition. Boredom can result. The next cycle is the attitude of "hating" to go to work. In our era of planned out-placement, rebalancing, and redeployment, the middle management professionals (usually in the 45 to 60 age range) feel the brunt of major changes.

Plateauing in organizations is inevitable. The way out is to leave the organization on your own before being gently forced out. The issue is whether to seek change or wait for it to impact upon you. Either way, sooner or later, everyone must develop a strategy to deal with these issues.

If you realistically accept this assessment—that you are not the top one percent—then your task is to make new commitments in other areas of your life. Your rewards must come from other than career related sources. The only way you lose is by permitting yourself to become psychologically paralyzed.

Most careers stabilize a number of times. You have the opportunity to accept the stability, make peace with yourself, or push yourself forward. It is your choice.

It is highly common for people to plateau, enjoy the stability, relish the feeling of expert productivity, and later re-start a new (or even different) career thrust. It is unrealistic to assume that you can plan for all of the eventualities.

The assignments are not lifelong commitments which pigeonhole people in the organization. They provide career direction in an initial job and can open multiple career paths which might be unavailable to other inexperienced and experienced employees.

Whether it is a training program or one of the more common direct placement assignments, an entry-level assignment can achieve several very important purposes for you. It will rapidly introduce you to the many people with whom you must work, both inside and outside the organization. It will also expose you to typical problems encountered by the employer in your area of expertise and to typical problems more germane to the total organization.

An entry-level assignment can provide a unique environment initially so you can become immediately productive and make a positive contribution to the organization's goals. You will be able to immediately begin applying your skills.

The employer is also going to be testing and challenging you in order to evaluate your potential for additional training and advancement. The entry assignment also

The entry-level position is designed to hasten your entry into a management assignment.

· · · · · · · · · · **TYPICAL MANAGEMENT-LEVEL JOB TITLES·** · · · · · · · · ·

Accountant	Inspector
Actuarial	Intern
Adjuster	Internal Auditor
Administrative Assistant	Investment Analyst
Advertising Assistant	Labor Relations Assistant
Agent	Laboratory Assistant
Analyst	Lawyer
Appraiser	Management Trainee
Assistant Buyer	Manufacturing Trainee
Assistant Director	Market Researcher
Assistant Manager	Marketing Assistant
Assistant to	Marketing Trainee
Auditor	Management Consultant
Bank Examiner	Officer
Budget Analyst	Personnel Assistant
Business Manager Assistant	Programmer
Claims Representative	Purchasing Assistant
Consultant	Sales Engineer
Copy Writer	Sales Representative
Cost Accountant	Scientist
Counselor	Social Worker
Credit Analyst	Specialist
Distribution Analyst	Statistician
Economist	Supervisor
Editor	Systems Analyst
Engineer	Tax Accountant
Executive Secretary	Teacher
Expediter	Therapist
Financial Analyst	Writer
Foreman	

· · · · · · · · · · ·

Figure 4.5

helps the employer to determine, with your input, just where in the organizational structure your abilities can optimally be utilized.

Actual Titles.   The most frequently referenced titles of management-level jobs appear in Figure 4.5. The list is not all-inclusive but represents about 80 percent of entry-level job titles used by business, government, and education employers. The titles may vary slightly depending upon type of job, industry, or size of the organization, but the assignments differ little in actual job content and purpose.

An entry-level assignment may have no relationship to later assignments, but there is usually a tie between initial duties and upward movement. Most organizations tend to move people through a variety of assignments, even in unrelated fields, yet common threads are often apparent and relevant to the individual's career paths.

In most successful careers there are detours which may last many months. Detours provide a broadening of experience that is helpful to the employee and to the employer.

Some organizations hire career development specialists whose role is to assist in the internal placement and career planning of employees. These individuals are in-house career consultants who assist employees in realistic career pathing within the organization.

The career consultant who is usually a high-level executive with several years of personnel and development experience in the organization, assists in these types of career decisions:

- to move you laterally for additional experience, or upward for promotion
- to move you to development programs for training
- to job counsel you for out-placement and employment with another organization

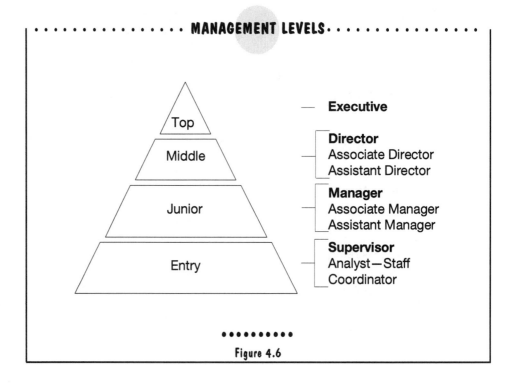

Figure 4.6

OBSOLETE CAREER PATH PLANNING

Understanding career paths, advancement, challenge, and so forth are all important aspects of career planning. Recent evidence, however, shows that very few people will start with an organization and spend the rest of their life working there. Further, with the social and technological changes within society, few people even stay in a chosen occupation for more than a decade or two.

We are a mobile society. Things continue to change. Your career pattern is likely to be much more diverse than that of your parents. No longer should you think about an organization or even career field where you will spend the rest of your life.

Many career experts suggest that life will become a series of different work experiences. The experiences are more likely to be bunched in terms of 5 to 15 year increments.

The terms, "career" and "profession" imply a longer period of energy directed to a given endeavor, but it may not imply a lifelong commitment. You may well want an instant job now and a different career change in a few years. There is clearly a less than definitive answer as to when you move from one work experience to another.

You may find yourself seeking re-education several times in your working life. These educational experiences may be in highly diverse arenas.

Nothing about careers is locked into concrete. The doctor of today may be the real estate mogul of tomorrow, and the accountant may turn out to be the architect in his second or third career. Nonetheless, these changes do not throw the need for career planning out the window.

The pace of societal change demands that you greatly compress the time horizons in traditional career planning. It is unrealistic for you to plan for a specific career change after ten years and outline that career. The forecasted career could have been eliminated by the rapid change in society, technology, and organizational needs.

In all likelihood you are going to have to be an instant responder. External events will likely force you into seeking a different job, a different employer, and maybe even a different career because your chosen field becomes obsolete.

Career planning means having a vehicle ready to address these changes when and if they occur. Career planning is a tool in your background that is designed to enable you to pick up and start anew whenever circumstances demand change.

Some areas of an organization serve as better entry-level points than others, in spite of the fact that entry-level placement normally does not dictate long-term commitment to that area.

On the other hand, employers like to hire people who map out career plans because that planning process demands the same type of objective analysis which is useful in making most decisions. *The analogy follows that people who can plan ahead for their own careers have the basic abilities necessary in planning for the organization's success.*

Cross-functional Training. History teaches that movement within organizations for highly successful managers often crosses functional lines but that successful career paths are usually functionally centered.

For example, the vice president of finance usually started in finance but may have worked several years in both the marketing/sales and production/engineering functions during his or her rise to top management. Engineers frequently spend some time in marketing and manufacturing assignments before assuming engineering management positions.

Employers like to hear a candidate express strong interest in a particular functional field. Without that strong initial interest, success in the functional field may not develop. A statement like, "I want to start in engineering but move into finance later," does not show sufficient interest in engineering to permit success in that field, so the person who says that will probably never get beyond low-level assignments.

Employers cannot guarantee upward mobility. Promotions for the first five years almost always occur in the starting functional field. Superior performance, measured by several promotions, permits cross-functional exposure later. Until the functional field is mastered, a cross-functional experience is probably not possible.

It is good advice to lay out a career path for five to ten years in a given functional field. Then after about five years you can begin to request reassignment to other functional fields. This strengthens your qualifications and indicates sincere interest. Consider enrolling in some evening courses in the other field which you feel would be a logical cross-functional experience.

International Exposure. Top management-level aspirants in a multinational organization need exposure to international operations at some point in their career paths. International experience is not a requirement for top management, but in some firms it is very helpful.

The corporation is not the place to look for an immediate overseas assignment. Most corporations look internally for management talent that has five to fifteen years of domestic expertise in a functional field, such as accounting, finance, sales, marketing, manufacturing, engineering, etc. These high-potential American employees are sent overseas to help solve specific problems.

Most employers fill overseas positions with nationals. Preference is given to nationals educated in the United States who wish to live in their home countries because employers have experienced fewer political, social, and economic problems with this policy. Overseas affiliates do their own hiring, normally without direction from the American headquarters.

The large multinational firms do send Americans overseas for short durations of six to twenty-four months to assist with particular problems and to develop management and technical expertise.

Americans wishing to gain international business experience should first accept functional employment with a corporation that has large international operations.

Upward mobility is earned, not guaranteed.

After exceptional career progress in a domestic functional assignment, a request to be transferred to the international division is more likely to be honored.

It is not always easy to obtain international or cross-functional training in today's organizations. However, long-term career success may depend on this exposure.

People who later become top-level executives will usually, at some point in their careers, have acquired cross-functional and international experience. Knowing the basics about several functional fields helps people in moving up in organizations.

If you have none or very little work experience, the entry-level professional assignment may be exactly what you need. The terms of your assignment will probably differ from those mentioned here, but they will follow these concepts.

Management

The next level of responsibility in most organizations is management. This includes engineers, scientists, accountants, marketing managers, plant managers, and a host of other professional, technical, and managerial people. This large class of people form the backbone of American corporations, financial institutions, hospitals, government agencies, etc.

Levels. Within management there are also various levels of responsibility. Titles in a technical area might be junior, assistant, associate, professional, senior, and executive, in that order. Titles in nontechnical areas frequently include: assistant, associate, assistant to, department head, group head, manager, and director, in that order.

If you have several years of work experience, you will probably bypass the entry-level job.

You must decide where within the levels of responsibility of the new firm you fit. For example, the position of controller in a small firm may not be equivalent to the position of assistant department head in a multinational firm. To best determine a rough fit, try to obtain relative salary information.

Technical and nontechnical managers constitute the backbone of every organization. Managers design, conduct, teach, coordinate, and implement the managing process. The term "management" (called "administration" in nonbusiness organizations) gets thrown around with little understanding of its true meaning.

What is a manager? When does one become a manager? Obviously, few (if any) people start their careers as managers because it takes time to gain the experience which is essential to managing and supervising.

There are various levels of management (junior, middle, top) in each specific function at each location. The entry-level assignment, usually related to a functional field, is the first rung of the management ladder.

Progression. Progression into various levels of management takes time which varies sharply among organizations and individuals. Some employers offer fast-track, sink-or-swim approaches, while others prefer slow methodically planned development programs.

Some employers prefer to rotate personnel frequently among various job functions, geographical locations, product lines, etc., to help them gain a wide exposure to people, organizational philosophy, and cross-functional training. Others prefer a strict upward progression in a given functional field.

Your ability to learn also impacts upon the speed of your upward mobility. Some people learn faster than others. Some fail and their employment is terminated.

Automatic tenure and salary increases are not common. Promotions come only after superior performance. Promotions can come in three months or take three years, depending upon merit considerations.

//WEB.TIP//

www.tbird.ed
Thunderbird International Management Program
Offers master's degree in international management/ some of best and most comprehensive links to international job related sites.

Because of some demographic changes in the United States population, upward mobility is not likely to be as rapid as it was the past two decades. The low birth rate of the depression and war years (1930–45) permitted that generation to practically fly into leadership roles and move into top management rapidly.

The middle management position voids were subsequently filled by the postwar baby generation. Due to the relative ages of young, middle, and top management today and the lack of major economic growth, one could predict much cross-functional movement within the lower and middle management ranks within the next decade in all types of organizations.

Not all individuals aspire to management responsibilities. Even though a high percentage of new hires want to move into the ranks of management later, it is not for everyone.

Management tends to be the highest paid individuals in business, government, and education, but many organizations build in a comparable reward structure for high technology, engineering, research, and professional personnel. With some employers you can remain a "professional" without the management pressure and earn comparable salaries.

Executive

The executive level of responsibility is for only a very small number of people, usually less than 1 to 3 percent of total employment. There is only one chief executive officer per organization. It is possible for both technical and nontechnical people to move into the executive ranks, and every profession points to their members who have made it.

Not everyone desires this type of position, even though it offers enormous prestige, status, and financial rewards. The pressures, stress, social demands, and total commitment to the organization is not for most people.

Executives often earn incomes of well over $200,000. In most organizations the route to the top is still up through the organization. Very few choose the "job hop" route to the top.

This is not a book about executive employment. The group of people most likely to find this publication of use are the entry-level and management-level participants, people earning $30 to $100,000. Ironically, however, individuals in executive ranks use the basic approach in preparing for a job change.

Conclusions

Your exploring process must encompass all types of employment settings including private enterprise. Where you want to work is a fundamental employment consideration. You should understand basic organizational structures in order to see how you can fit into the total scheme of activities.

Understanding the organizational management process permits you to develop your own career plan within a compatible environment. Career management is reality-based.

You must also incorporate into your plan some idea of the level of responsibility you desire initially and in the long term. You do not need to be so specific as to attach concrete time parameters to each level, but you should know the general direction and the steps which must be taken to reach the level of responsibility.

EXECUTIVE TITLES

- Owner
- Partner
- Chairman
- President
- Vice President

Figure 4.7

//WEB.TIP//

www.dbm.com/jobguide
The Riley Guide
Master list of links of hundreds of career resources/ cross-classified in hundreds of ways/brief reviews of websites.

MANAGEMENT CAREER EXPLORATION

This section on management careers is not for everyone. If your career decision is fairly well made, you may not need to read about the different aspects of management. If you have worked in a management capacity, this discussion is simply a review of what you already know.

The material is most applicable for young, inexperienced management aspirants and experienced people who have had no management training or experience. There are discussions of each of the basic functional fields and the position alternatives normally found in them.

This material is an integral part of the exploring process. The information is invariably discussed in job interviews.

Functional Focus

Six major work functions are found in the typical private enterprise organization: marketing, finance, manufacturing/service, engineering, research and development, and administration. The three central functions are marketing, finance, and operations (manufacturing). Within manufacturing, many firms include the engineering and research functions since they relate so closely to production operations.

These three functions dominate: creating the product or service (operations/production), financing the product or service (accounting and finance), and distributing the production or service (marketing).

Regardless of the type of sector (government, education, or business), there are counterparts for these three functions in each.

People with direct authority for one of these functions have *line* management authority. People employed in activities which assist these principle functions hold *staff* management functions.

Do you fit into marketing, finance, operations, engineering, or administration?

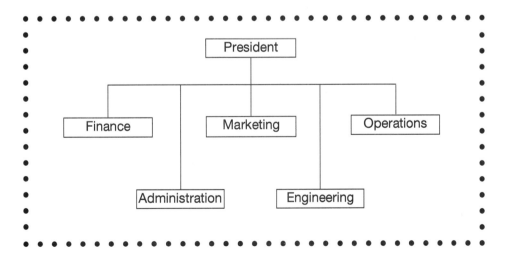

In general, line managers hold more power and authority and are paid more for comparable-level jobs than staff people. Experience in one or all of the line functions is normally required for advancement to executive status.

Most organizations' websites will provide additional detailed organizational structure. Surf to the sites of firms that interest you to see the specific style.

In some non-manufacturing organizations (banking, insurance, retailing, hospitals, associations, government, etc.) the operations (production) function may be replaced by a purchasing (buying) function or service activity.

Industry Focus

In most cases, your employment relates to one of the three basic functions regardless of the type of organization for which you work. Many times the function and the industry closely parallel each other. Your background may lend itself more to a given industry than to a given function.

Nonetheless, your *functional* interest is as much or more important than the *industry* in which you plan to work. For example, biology, chemistry, and zoology academic credentials relate very well to careers within the chemical, pharmaceutical, and health industries. Majors in English, journalism, and communications relate closely to publishing, printing, and advertising. Within the industries, however, people with those majors specialize in specific functional activities when they start to translate interests to real work assignments.

With the exception of a few specialized fields, such as accounting, engineering and marketing, few academic backgrounds correlate perfectly with job-related assignments.

Individuals who insist on relating academic credentials directly to jobs miss the whole point of a broad-based education. Engineers do not always start and stay in the engineering function; many start in marketing and may even switch to other non-engineering fields later.

Regardless of your academic credentials, you should take a close look at all of the basic functions and try to place yourself in the most appropriate function. Relate your self-assessment to real world assignments. You do not have to live forever in the narrow niche your academic credentials might at first glance dictate.

International Careers

The globalization of the economic world has clearly impacted every career field and occupation. As you review and explore various options for yourself, you need to factor in, as appropriate, how this economic change is influencing that career area.

Some employers expect top management to have completed an international assignment at some point in their career. Although it is not always a requirement for top level positions, this exposure is career enhancing.

As you follow-up and review career websites for your interest areas, notice if you see this global impact. It rarely impacts all career fields and even specific employers in the same way, but you will notice the changes over time. Plan for these influences in your own decision making.

Career Profiles

Your starting point is the preparation of career profiles—an analysis of careers in various functional areas within employing organizations.

Learn what is available. Relate various profiles to your background. Investigate industry settings as secondary, and more specific work environments. The more you

Investigate all of the career options for which you are qualified.

can relate your background to specific jobs in specific industries, the greater are your chances for employment and an enjoyable career.

Various career profiles are described within each basic management function to give you some real world information. It would be impossible to discuss *every* occupational profile or to give *complete* profiles in any single publication. To obtain depth of information, you must follow up your interest in a functional field, a specific position, and/or a specific industry with a vigorous research effort using many outside references.

Marketing Management

Marketing is the distribution of products or services from the source to the customer. No government, public enterprise, or private business can survive without effective distribution of goods or services to users and potential users.

Marketing invites consumers to sample a wide variety of products or services before they elect to devote resources to the purchase of them.

The customer exercises complete control. Competitive marketing provides a broad selection of goods and services at various levels of quality at the lowest possible prices. Everyone is a customer.

Millions of people in some way or another are involved in marketing every day. Although the concept is simple, its effect is immense and almost incomprehensible to people using other systems in other countries of the world.

Marketing System

The American marketing and distribution system is unique in its ability to serve the public. Anyone who travels outside the U.S.A. quickly recognizes that other countries can manufacture equivalent products, but that these products seldom reach the masses and thus bring them the necessities and conveniences of life as well as in the U.S.A.

The main difference is our distribution system which permits enormous savings through the economics of scale production.

The American marketing system is built upon the ideas, "Find a need and fill it," and "Do it better, faster, and cheaper than the other guy." And it must always be at a "better quality level." That competitive entrepreneurial spirit makes an enormous impact on our standard of living.

Significant Needs. The marketing function in private enterprise needs millions of talented people with both technical knowledge and superior ability to communicate. An individual who can combine technical competence with quality communicative skills will find

YOU KNOW... I USED TO BE COMPLETELY SOLD ON MARKETING, BUT NOW I JUST DON'T BUY IT.

financial opportunities in marketing which are difficult to match in any other form of employment.

Marketing is often the shortest route to management responsibility and authority.

Regardless of whether you possess a technical or non-technical background, marketing may be the right career for you. The distinct advantage for the person willing to work hard is that productivity is readily measurable and rewards directly follow performance.

In many other positions, keeping your salary up with inflation is a major goal. A successful person in marketing, however, beats the inflation syndrome by substantially outperforming the rate of inflation by regularly increasing sales. An employer has no option but to increase the marketing person's earnings substantially to retain him or her.

Marketing offers thousands of jobs to individuals with diverse backgrounds.

Channels of Distribution. Although there are hundreds of different channels of distribution for goods and services, for employment purposes you can look at two main avenues: wholesale and retail.

In the wholesale avenue the product or service is exchanged through a middle person, the wholesaler, who serves a broker role between the manufacturer and the end user. The retail market is where the product is sold directly to the end user.

Before the establishment of thousands of retail stores, products and services were often literally sold "door to door" or by "word of mouth." Most of that personal selling has now been replaced by many types of retail stores where the customer finds the seller rather than vice versa.

There are still a few large pockets of personal selling in stock brokerage, insurance, personal services, etc. but for the most part store retailing has replaced personal selling.

A product or parts of a product may have changed hands many times before it is ultimately sold to the consumer. For example, an automobile radio is a combination of parts and sub-assemblies which are manufactured by different firms and sold to the final assembler by various persons. In practice, the automobile firm may have purchased

ARE YOU A BUY OR A SELL?

only three items (speaker, antenna, and tuner) and put them together into the package that the end user purchased; while the speaker manufacturer had to buy paper, magnets, steel, and wire to construct the speaker assembly.

Most products have a lengthy chain of purchases of sub-parts before they reach the consumer. Someone sold the manufacturer the raw materials. The manufacturer shopped around for the lowest price for a given quality level just like a conscientious shopper would do at the supermarket. Sales people called on the manufacturer.

Raw materials are bought and sold. Partially finished components are bought and sold. Long before a product reaches the consumer, many transactions occur, and these transactions involve marketing people. This is part of a wholesale market.

Another part of the wholesale market is the *middle* person for a finished good. Developing a marketing network is an expensive process. Many times a manufacturer prefers not to develop a network of salespeople because further investment in production is more profitable than an investment in the sales network. Most manufacturers prefer not to create retail outlets for a single product line.

There obviously is a need for someone to coordinate the purchases of thousands of small stores with thousands of manufacturers. This is the function of the middle person, often called a *manufacturer's* representative. The representative is not employed by the manufacturer but is an independent person buying at one price and selling at another or obtaining a commission for completing each transaction.

Brokers are everywhere. Farmers do not sell lettuce directly to retail supermarkets. Clothing manufacturers use middle people rather than sell directly to every small retail store. Manufacturers of copper wire sell to firms who make electric motors who sell to washing machine manufacturers who use a distributor network to sell to small and large retail appliance stores.

You may fit into this whole marketing and distribution network. There are products that only technically trained people can sell, such as jet engines; but there are also products such as fiberglass insulation which may only require limited technical training which is easily supplied by the manufacturer.

An overwhelming number of products require no technical expertise to sell.

Thousands of people sell products/services in a business-to-business network without ever directly talking to the end consumer.

Wherever there are sellers, there are also buyers; and you may also fit into that part of the channel as well. Retail stores, large and small, need sophisticated buyers who forecast what the consumer market wants and needs. Manufacturers need purchasing agents for raw materials and sub-assemblies. Governments need buyers for products and contract negotiators for services.

Millions of people work in this buying and selling arena at various levels. Even professional people like doctors, lawyers, and psychologists must sell their services. Mechanics, plumbers, and masons must develop a reputation to convince consumers that their personal services are needed.

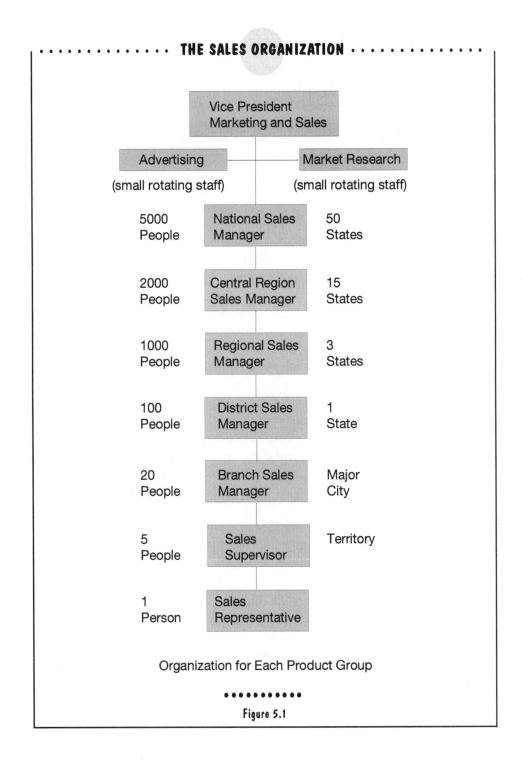

. . . . THE SALES ORGANIZATION . . . .

	Vice President Marketing and Sales	
	Advertising — Market Research	
(small rotating staff)		(small rotating staff)
5000 People	National Sales Manager	50 States
2000 People	Central Region Sales Manager	15 States
1000 People	Regional Sales Manager	3 States
100 People	District Sales Manager	1 State
20 People	Branch Sales Manager	Major City
5 People	Sales Supervisor	Territory
1 Person	Sales Representative	

Organization for Each Product Group

. . . .

Figure 5.1

As a consumer you have a choice of which products and services you want. Someone must sell you on going to a given store or calling a certain sales person.

Marketing is a wide-open career field which has great potential for its entrants. If this is of interest to you, take a look at some specific opportunities available in the career profiles that follow.

Sales Management

In nearly all business organizations, regardless of size, the major marketing assignment is that of sales representative. Before you can become a successful marketing executive you must spend some time in sales work learning about the products or services, customer attitudes, and how to handle front-line, direct relationships with customers.

Few employers hire and promote people into higher-level marketing management positions without some experience in sales. Figure 5.1 gives the typical marketing organizational structure.

Individual company websites often display the sales organization structure.

Organization. The old hard-sell approach is dead. Buyers are sophisticated today and are searching for *value* in terms of price, quality, and service.

The fast-talking, back-slapping, flashy-dressing salesperson does not meet today's needs, and few such people will find employment in today's environment. Customers want solid information based upon facts, guarantees, and service commitments, not public relation gimmicks.

Marketing is not confined to business organizations. The consumer demands no less service and information from public employees (federal, state, and local) political leaders, churches, hospitals, and cultural institutions. All organizations must express their wishes in a direct, logical, and well prepared way in both speaking and writing to their constituency.

Selling. The art of selling calls for person-to-person contact and problem-solving ability. This service-oriented activity requires skill, discipline, and analytic ability if it is to be competitive in our highly developed technologically based society.

Presidents, vice presidents, executives, professional people, partners, owners, directors, and all types of managers spend a great deal of their time in selling activities.

As you move into higher levels of responsibility in whatever career you choose, chances are that more and more of your time will be spent in some facet of the selling activity. Very few organizations can survive without the personal involvement of its leadership in the selling of products, services, or reputation of the organization.

Whether you are a teacher, engineer, dentist, scientist, or accountant, if your goal is to move into the highest levels of responsibility, you need to learn how to sell ideas, products, services, or abstract concepts. When you recognize that fact, the rest of the organizational structure begins to make sense.

In many respects, life consists of selling. People enjoy giving advice. They do it all the time.

Titles.   Because the salesperson's job is so broad, many different job titles have emerged. Many of the titles relate to *specific industries* and others relate to certain *occupations* in a particular industry group. As you move up the promotion ladder, the assistant manager and manager titles get added.

The most commonly used titles are sales representative, marketing representative, marketing consultant, service representative, technical specialist, sales consultant, special agent, account executive, field engineer, and manufacturer's representative.

Many of these titles are also appended with the names of specific products, geographical regions, and divisions of the organization.

Abstract of Duties.   Sales personnel, regardless of their levels of responsibility, are responsible for a wide range of specific duties. It is common for a salesperson to have the most *unstructured* job in the organization and most control over his or her use of time to complete an assignment.

Although it is neither all-inclusive nor descriptive of every salesperson's work, the following list of typical activities should give you a good idea of what a salesperson does.

> Makes contact with customers . . . consultant . . . takes orders . . . serves as liaison between two parties . . . plans requirements . . . forecasts sales . . . problem solver . . . projects supply and demand . . . researches markets . . . introduces new products . . . assists with inventory and production control . . . arranges delivery dates and methods . . . services clients' needs . . . settles complaints . . . trains new employees . . . develops new customers . . . checks on competitors' activities . . . prepares sales reports . . . serves as representative at trade meetings . . . arranges, coordinates, and sets up trade shows . . . influences produce or service design and price . . . assists in preparation of promotional materials . . . coordinates advertising . . . arranges public relations activities . . . trains new employees . . . develops solutions . . . solves customer problems.

To the customer, the marketing representative *is* the organization. At all levels, the marketing representative is part of the management team. Many marketing management decisions must be made in the field.

Requirements.   The requirements for entering the sales career field differ greatly by industry, product line, and specific employing organization, but some generalizations can be made.

Sales usually requires a college degree, but most organizations do not require a specific major. For some commercial and technical sales assignments, a masters degree may be required.

Very few specify exact academic training, but there are assignments where certain majors and degrees are helpful. For example, a semi-conductor firm might prefer an electrical engineer for marketing the newest and latest technical products to a sophisticated manufacturer of products using electronic components.

Liberal arts majors also make excellent marketing representatives. Their analytical thought pattern and communicative skills are highly beneficial.

PERSONALITY/PRODUCT MATCH

- Choose a product you believe in
- The product does not have to be in a "growth" field
- Know the product and possess the ability to learn it better
- Relate to the personality of your clients
- Be comfortable with your client's social status

• • • • • • • • • •

Figure 5.2

Most firms have elaborate training programs designed to teach the technical characteristics of the product or service to salespeople. Many firms require continuous training via seminars, correspondence study, and on-the-job training.

Conversely, some firms immediately place new hires out in the field to call on customers if they are sufficiently versed in sales techniques and product information. On-the-job training is common.

Sales positions require strong self-discipline because people often must set their own hours and work routines. The individual need not be the stereotyped extrovert, but an outgoing, mature, pleasant personality is extremely helpful.

The job requires some evidence of a helping nature because that is the essence of selling. Most firms desire excellent speaking ability. Strong skills are required in writing reports and promotional styles of writing.

At the entry level, prior work experience is rarely required, but most firms do seek prior selling and supervisory experience if the position is at a manager or higher level of responsibility. Employers frequently consider extracurricular activities, civic responsibilities or prior part- or full-time work experience which shows leadership potential. Most firms look for the ability to solve problems, supervise others, and make decisions.

Career Paths. The top-level position is vice president of marketing or sales. Many of the larger firms have several vice presidents for product lines, geographical areas, and functional departments. The regional and national sales manager positions are usually classified as executive status. All employers have many middle- and upper middle-level managers in the sales area which are paid extremely handsomely.

Managers are responsible for product planning, promotional design, advertising strategy, and staff administration. Managers supervise other managers, clerical personnel, market researchers, marketing staff assistants, and sales representatives, and often control large geographical areas and/or multiple product lines.

> **The most sought-after quality is the ability to think quickly and communicate solutions effectively. Hard working, self-motivated people with assertive personalities do extremely well.**

· · · · · · · · · **ACCOUNT EXECUTIVE PERSONAL QUALITIES** · · · · · · · ·

Strong ego
Persuasiveness
Independent drive
Self-starter
Patient listener
Belief in the products
Empathy with clients
Desire to find solutions
Accept rejection of product, not self
Helping others
Resilient attitude on peaks and valleys
Perseverance and challenge
Independent, minimal supervision
Positioning product power
Coping with uncertainty
Creative solutions

· · · · · · · · · ·
Figure 5.3

Managers are responsible for budget preparation, financial control, and sales production of significant dollar amounts. They often sell to large accounts as well.

Representatives begin to assume management responsibilities after one to three years of experience. About 30 percent of top executives come from marketing backgrounds. Individuals on management tracks often spend one to three years in *staff* assignments in marketing research, product management, and advertising.

Training. Almost all firms offer extensive management development, sales management, and sales technique and strategy training programs. These programs vary in length from a few days to two years of now-and-then programming. The product line, industry, and level and type of training dictate the length of the various programs.

Most training involves classroom work, seminars, evening home study programs, and on-the-job training with highly experienced managers. As one progresses in the field of sales, he or she is called upon many times to develop and train subordinates, drawing upon materials provided by the firm, academic texts, and personal experiences.

The training programs orient the new salesperson to the organization's product and/or service characteristics and specifications. The programs deal with organization policy, personnel practices, and provide exposure to internal resources in terms of people and materials. The training introduces the new people to customers, important industry contacts, and key people in the sales management organization.

Earnings. Earnings are usually expressed as a yearly salary which is paid in monthly installments. A sales representative often receives some attractive supplemental benefits such as an automobile and an expense account. Some firms pay a bonus at the end of the year based upon productivity during the preceding twelve months.

Earnings in sales can become very substantial in a very short period of time if you are especially productive.

It is not uncommon for a sales consultant to be earning significantly more than many of their managers due to incentive compensation.

After a few years, many firms will offer a commission or some other incentive plan that often increases earnings beyond that of much higher-level executives.

Although initial hiring earnings levels may not be as attractive as those in some technical fields within the same firm, a sales career can prove to be a faster track to substantial earnings later.

> **The incentive compensation and travel benefits make sales one of the most lucrative career options available.**

Outlook. No exact figures are available on number of people currently in the function, but it is well over a million people. Employment growth potential is one of the strongest characteristics.

Many openings are listed daily in almost every newspaper in every region of the nation. All manufacturers and service industries need qualified sales talent.

YES, THE SKY'S THE LIMIT IN SALES, AMY... HOWEVER EXPECT PARTLY CLOUDY THROUGHOUT THIS QUARTER WITH A SLIGHT CHANCE OF SHOWERS.

Nearly every industry and occupation group has a counterpart to the sales representative. The outlook is especially strong as many smaller employers upgrade positions. A degree is becoming essential for higher level talent.

The best sources of additional information are the *Occupational Outlook Handbook*, local libraries, employment brochures of major firms, job descriptions in classified ads, the world wide web, etc.

Sales is one of the best bets for liberal arts graduates hoping to make use of their communicative abilities. It is one of the highest-paying fields. The experience is directly applicable for individuals wishing to someday own businesses of their own.

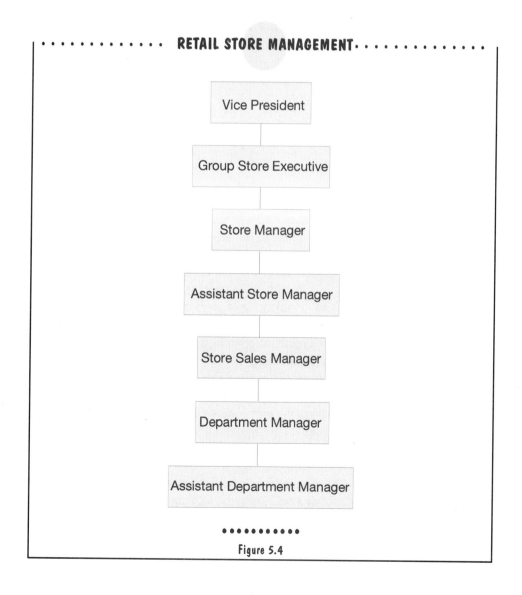

· · · · · · · · · · · · **RETAIL STORE MANAGEMENT** · · · · · · · · · · · · · ·

Figure 5.4

The drawback of some sales positions is that they often require extensive travel. Many sales representatives literally live on their expense accounts. The amount of travel required depends on the industry, type of product, and geographical territory to which the person is assigned. People located in major metropolitan areas may rarely need to travel overnight, while representatives in Nebraska may rarely be at home during the week.

Sales management is one of the largest and most attractive career fields for you to consider. Upward mobility is "wide open," and earnings relate closely to your productivity. A good salesperson's *job security* is enhanced by his or her ability to go just about anywhere in the U.S. and find employment readily, particularly with prior successful sales experience. Many dual-career couples consider this a most attractive field for one of the parties due to this career flexibility.

Retail Management

As lucrative and attractive as the sales area is to many people, there remains a strong aversion among others for the traveling, setting appointments, and talking with customers about product specifications.

Given the non-technical outlook of many of these people, they realize that the marketing function best suits their background, but they prefer that customers come to them.

The prospecting and calling on people they don't know do not seem to fit their basic dispositions. The field of retailing might be the ideal match for this group of people.

Career Paths. Most large department stores and the large national chain stores provide both entry-level programs for new entrants and hire experienced personnel for *management* positions. Many of the smaller retailers bring people into the business as assistant managers.

Retailing is a business that offers direct management responsibilities very rapidly. The scope of the early responsibility is probably unmatched in any other career field.

Retailing offers two distinct career paths: retail store management and merchandise buying. In day-to-day activities much of the distinction blurs, but in theory, these are two different functional areas of the business.

A third area is operations which includes the more technically oriented careers of accounting, presentation engineering, distribution, data systems, personnel, display, advertising, labor relations, facility management, etc.

Store Management. The organization of store management depends largely upon the size of the retail organization. Large operations, like Sears, J.C. Penney, K-Mart, Walmart, Target, etc. have structured training programs whose career paths typically follow the management hierarchy.

You should visit the website of each of these retailers. Surf to careers or employment, and see the specific options open to you.

After a training program which orients new managers to basic policies and procedures, a person may be assigned as an assistant department manager and follow the promotional path shown in Figure 5.4.

After becoming store managers, individuals can move between various sizes of stores or can be promoted to zone, regional, and corporate management positions and supervise several stores. Anywhere along the way, an individual can be selected for buying responsibilities.

Buying. Some people prefer to take the alternative career path of becoming a buyer who is more responsible for the selection, purchase, and promotion of the

There will always be many jobs in sales. Your best security is your own ability.

Many people prefer a job where the customer comes to them. They like to deal directly with the end user rather than middlemen.

Retailing offers one of the fastest entries into the management function. You are supervising people almost immediately.

merchandise that the store carries. If a particular line does not sell, the buyer is the person held directly responsible.

Store management people supervise people and manage the physical facilities, whereas buyers manage the product mix, image, and product promotions.

Both buying and store management hold comparable positions, so earnings potentials are not usually a consideration in selecting which route to consider.

Buyers often travel a great deal and can be away from home for two to four weeks on major buying trips. Store managers travel much less frequently.

Store managers may do some buying in terms of reorder to catalog selection, but buyers usually select the merchandise to be carried after consultation with store and sales managers to identify what customers in particular geographical or demographic settings want.

The key decision is the type of work you want to do.

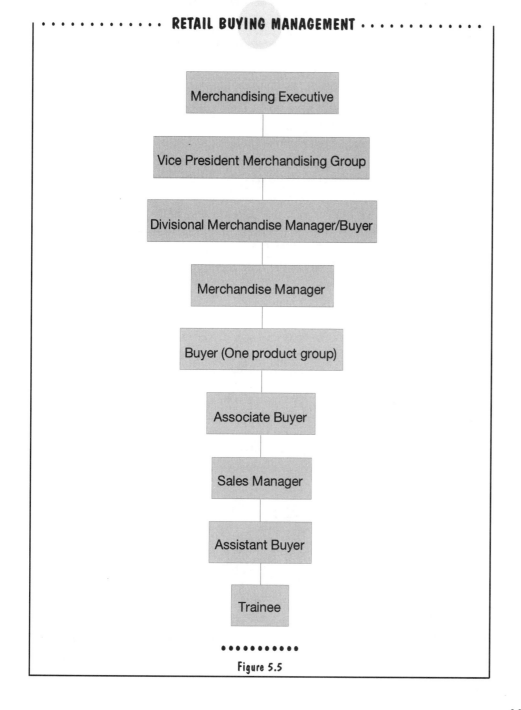

· · · · · · · · · · · · · RETAIL BUYING MANAGEMENT · · · · · · · · · · · · ·

Merchandising Executive

Vice President Merchandising Group

Divisional Merchandise Manager/Buyer

Merchandise Manager

Buyer (One product group)

Associate Buyer

Sales Manager

Assistant Buyer

Trainee

Figure 5.5

In the large chains buying is centralized, so the store manager often orders from a central distribution center merchandise most appropriate for his or her store. If goods can be purchased better elsewhere, the manager often has the authority to use outside sources. The magnitude of buying responsibility for a large chain is immense. The pressure on the buyer can be intense.

ACTUALLY I'M A BUYER FROM YOUR COMPETITION. I JUST WANTED TO SEE IF YOU WERE STILL CARRYING THE SAME LINE OF JUNK.

Many regional department stores do their own buying, as do small specialty shops. Buyers purchase merchandise to fit their unique markets and images. Although the dollar amounts may seem staggering, the sums invested do not often approach those of the chain store buyers.

Some department stores associate together and form buying cooperatives in some basic lines to insure lower cost and retail price competitiveness with the large chains.

It is not uncommon for you to become a buyer of several million dollars worth of goods in less than three to five years.

The time it takes to move from entry to buyer and other management posts is not predictable. It varies by store policy, size of store, product classification, and individual track records.

Beware of promises made about the time required for upward mobility. Many external and uncontrollable factors such as the weather, the economy, and availability of merchandise influence performance.

Abstract of Duties. Depending upon the store's policies, size, merchandise selection, and other variables, the distinctions between manager and buyer functions are often hard to recognize in actual practice. Listed below are some of the daily and periodic duties a retailer performs regardless of function.

Supervises sales workers . . . sells merchandise on floor . . . handles complaints . . . provides customer service . . . orders merchandise . . . meets with manufacturer's representatives . . . travels to buying markets . . . determines prices of merchandise . . . assists in advertising and promotional plans . . . analyzes market.

Prepares marketing and sales reports . . . manages and controls daily cash receipts . . . supervises inventory audits . . . trains sales workers . . . hires sales and clerical personnel . . . assists in advertising copy preparation . . . designs and supervises building of displays . . . shops competitors . . . operates as an independent profit center.

The smaller the organization is, the more likely are the functions to be intertwined. A family department store owner does everything from buying goods overseas to selling merchandise on the selling floor. The variety of duties is so diverse that people in the profession often find it impossible to describe a typical day. Each day may be a whole new experience.

Requirements.   People of all academic disciplines and degree levels and with a variety of prior work experiences work in retailing. In terms of academic background requirements, retailing is one of the most open fields.

The people-oriented nature of the business demands outgoing personality styles, high energy levels, drive, initiative, and independence. High levels of responsibility must be accepted quickly, so employers look for these background qualities in prior academic, work, social, and civic endeavors.

For some types of buying jobs, candidates need to have a flair for fashion, color coordination, fabric selection, and presentation methods (ala fashion stores), while for other types, persons may need more of a mechanical bent (ala an automobile center).

Training.   The time spent as a management trainee varies from six to eighteen months depending upon policy and candidate performance. It normally takes three to six years to reach the buyer/store management level.

Training begins with seminars but quickly goes on-the-job supplemented with regular seminars. Usually the first performance review is after six months and then there are annual reviews and annual salary increases thereafter.

Earnings.   Retailers have a reputation for starting with low pay and then substantially rewarding high performers with superior salaries. The reputation is not universally true. Large department stores and chains pay extremely competitive salaries in order to attract top students, while smaller retailers are usually slightly below average.

Buyers and store managers earn in the $75,000 to $150,000 range, depending upon performance, merchandise line, and gross sales. In several recent salary surveys, successful retail executives rank near the top of industry-wide pay scales which indicates substantial returns for high performers.

Outlook.   There are thousands of retail stores ranging from small specialty shops to the national chains. The need for people varies greatly with the economy. Demand for people drops substantially in slow economies and is extremely strong in normal and superior climates.

> **The most important criteria sought are leadership qualities, desire to interact with the general public, and strong ability to communicate verbally with people from all walks of life.**

. . . ESPECIALLY WHEN THEY'RE WRONG.

ADVERTISING AGENCY ORGANIZATION

— Executive Staff

— Market Research (Statisticians, field interviews, research design)

— Media Selection (Space and time buyers for newsprint, radio, television, and other media)

— Creative (Copy and production)

— Account Management (Sales to clients)

— Services (Merchandising and public relations)

— Operations (Personnel, training, accounting)

Figure 5.6

Opportunities are usually available in most geographical locations. Retailing is a strong field for the non-technically trained college graduate, especially liberal arts majors.

Because the skill transfer is so easy from one store to another, many dual-career couples plan for one of the parties to go into retailing if the other's career may be enhanced by frequent job moves.

For graduates who enjoy meeting people but dislike calling on customers, retailing may be a good choice; responsibility and earnings come rapidly.

Retailing may be especially enticing to individuals with an entrepreneurial flair who want to start their own businesses after gaining experience and acquiring a savings base.

Most retailers require employees to work 40 hours per week normally, but during certain periods like Christmas the workweek is often longer. There is often pressure, some travel for buyers, and night and weekend hours, but the challenge and attractive pay tend to negate some of the drawbacks.

The business is fast-paced and action-oriented which is why so many people right out of college enjoy starting their careers in retailing. Retailing can also be an attractive alternative for housewives returning to the labor market.

The number of jobs in retailing will always continue to be strong. The potential for high earnings after training is extremely high.

Advertising Agency

Many organizations, both public and private, use advertising agencies to assist in the selling and promoting of products and services to potential customers. All but the very largest of the consumer goods companies use advertising agencies rather than in-house advertising organizations.

There are many reasons for this lack of in-house activity, but one of the foremost is the continual need for new sets of creative ideas which can be inhibited by an in-house staff. The expense of maintaining a whole cadre of technical experts every few years is also a negative factor for most businesses.

Most organizations allocate percentages of their budgets for sending messages to given constituencies via various methods of communication. Ad agencies design these messages for delivery via media such as newspapers, magazines, brochures, radio, and television.

Most opportunities in advertising are with agencies rather than with the large industrial firms and government units.

Organization. Advertising agencies deal with the media of newspapers, magazines, business publications, outdoor billboards and signs, television, and radio by providing orders for space or time. The media run the copy or video tape provided by the agency at the frequency requested.

Media also work with clients in developing copy and programs, but the majority of employment opportunities on the creative side are with agencies. A few jobs are available with media in sales and production.

Figure 5.6 illustrates the organizational structure of the typical advertising agency. The chart gives some idea about the types of jobs normally available. An agency may produce displays, folders, booklets, catalogs, trade show exhibits, and premium programs for clients in addition to developing copy and programs for various media.

An agency is composed of various technical specialists who are involved in the planning, design, and production of marketing programs. Agencies are usually hired by high-level business executives whose roles are more those of coordinating than of executing.

The agencies make recommendations which the clients approve or disapprove. Few organizations attempt on a regular basis to challenge or greatly modify programs recommended by their agencies, for doing so negates the very reason the experts were hired.

After an advertiser appoints an agency, the goal of the agency is to make the firm's advertising budget allocation produce the desired results. If the agency does

not achieve the goal, it is not rehired. This creates a highly charged, volatile, competitive situation characterized by extreme pressure and excitement. Agency personnel need to be persons who can cope with and thrive on this pressure.

Employment opportunities exist in several major areas, or departments, of an ad agency. Within large agencies the seven areas are readily distinguishable, but in smaller agencies many of the functions are consolidated or even farmed out to free-lance consultants.

Once you understand the areas or departments and their functions, you will better see how your particular skills may fit into the agency organization.

Marketing Research. The market research function conducts surveys designed to provide information for decision-making purposes. Sophisticated research design techniques are employed to obtain accurate up-to-date data from the constituency being surveyed.

The research method may involve mail questionnaires, telephone queries, web based data, or door-to-door canvassing. Researchers analyze the responses and deliver elaborate reports to management.

Copywriting. The copywriter composes stories which hopefully will sell products, services, or ideas. Creativity, style, and content in writing are thus concerns of a copywriter, and people in this department spend much of their time reading, typing, editing, and reviewing copy.

Art and Layout. Agencies use graphic artists in the design of advertising whose jobs are to enhance the copy and improve the comprehension and recall of the material being presented.

Photographs serve a similar purpose. Agencies usually employ a staff of professional photographers and may call on a cadre of freelance photographers as well.

Television and Radio. The television and radio department produces the sound effects, video, audio, sketches, scenes, etc. for commercial messages. Creative designers come up with themes which production experts develop into radio jingles and messages or television spots.

This department hires engineers, writers, announcers, actors, and technically trained telecommunication specialists. Small agencies often contract much of this work to specialty firms or large radio and television stations.

Print Production. The planning and ordering of the plates used to produce magazines and newspapers happens in this department. These employees are experts in all phases of hard copy reproduction processes such as typography, printing, photoengraving, electroplating, and allied crafts.

Traffic. The traffic department plans the flow and timing of the various processes of the agency. Work for printing, radio and television, copywriting, art, layout, graphics, etc., must be coordinated in order to meet various production deadlines.

In some large firms this function is similar to a production line in an assembly plant and requires supervisors, technical planners, and expediters. All of the various components of a job are put together at this point.

Account Management. The account executive is the agency person in charge of direct contact with clients and serves as the liaison between the agency and its clients.

The account manager must have knowledge about both the agency's expertise and the client's problems, products, services, and other concerns. Although he or she is not the creative designer, the manager must act in a role involving all aspects of the finished product.

A strong analytic computer background and organized writing style are key criteria for personnel selection in marketing research.

The account executive is basically the salesperson who calls on regular and potential customers for the agency.

Outlook. Few agencies actively recruit people for their staffs because so many applicants continually contact them.

Agencies are in the attractive position of being able to select the very best qualified and talented people to join them.

If you are interested in pursuing employment in one of the departments in an agency, you must begin early on an aggressive approach to the job search process, because there is enormous competition for each opening.

Your starting point is the *Standard Directory of Advertising Agencies,* your telephone directory's yellow pages, and various websites.

Job requirements depend on the function you see yourself performing. Most employees are specialist-trained in their technical fields via courses and full- and part-time work experience.

It is necessary that you have a portfolio of your work and other credentials with you when you contact agencies. The majority of agencies are located in New York, Los Angeles, and Chicago, but larger metropolitan cities usually have a number of branches and smaller firms.

Levels of responsibility relate to time spent in the advertising business and the level of skill development. Very creative people can earn substantial sums early in their careers and then drop substantially later. Earnings are sometimes cyclical since they are related to performance and productivity.

Agencies tend to have very "flat" organizational structures.

Entry-level earnings tend to be below average due to supply and demand aspects of the employment picture in the industry. As expertise is developed, earnings increase rapidly though. Earnings are directly related at middle levels to contribution to the account being serviced. Substantial earnings are possible, but relatively few people earn great sums of money.

Upward mobility within an ad agency is not always a prime motivating force for employees, but the type of assignments given, recognition, and financial rewards are regarded as important and thus serve as motivation for them. Most personnel remain loyal to their technical expertise be it writing, research, photography, printing, sales, etc. Of course, people can and do elect to advance to management positions within their areas of expertise.

The advertising field is characterized by large numbers of people wanting to get in and an extremely limited number of openings. There is keen competition for jobs, so agencies simply wait for the most talented people to contact them.

Marketing Research

Some of the very large corporate firms maintain marketing research staffs, usually at the corporate headquarters. Generally, these staffs are quite small and consist of technical experts such as economists, statisticians, computer programmers, psychologists, and sociologists.

> **The number of job openings in advertising is typically very low.**

//WEB.TIP//

www.adguide.com
Adguide's Employment Site
Focuses upon entry level jobs for high school and college students/very fun and easy to use/advice.

IN THE OLD DAYS ... A THREE MARTINI LUNCH MEANT SOMETHING ELSE.

The role of the department is to prepare analyses of sales and other marketing data available within the firm or collected from external sources.

Duties. Market researchers collect, analyze, and interpret many kinds of data that may have been generated from questionnaires, general economic data, and/or internal sales records. The reports that market researchers prepare

ACTUALLY WE PREFER "RANDOM SAMPLE OF POTENTIAL CUSTOMERS TO "GUINEA PIGS."

may make recommendations to management on sales forecasts by product line, receptivity to brand names, plant locations, acquisitions, and advertising strategies.

Most employment is with large manufacturing and consumer goods companies, but advertising agencies and independent market research firms also maintain small staffs in marketing research. New York City has the largest number of market research analysts.

Requirements. A bachelor's degree in a semi-technical field is the normal basic requirement for employment, but many jobs require advanced degrees.

Market researchers must have exceptionally strong writing skills because much of their work requires preparing lengthy reports to management in decision-requiring situations. Courses in research methodology, statistics, english composition, speech, psychology, and advanced economics are essential.

Many firms require extensive sales experience of employees being moved into this area because sales experience is the best way to truly understand the product and the customers purchasing the product.

Advancement. Trainees usually start as market analysts if they have not come up via the sales route. Initial market analysis work involves collecting data from published sources; designing, administering, and coding questionnaires; and summarizing the results.

Later responsibilities include designing projects, writing reports, making presentations to management, and directing the efforts of several subordinates.

Top positions include marketing research director and vice president for marketing. It is usually not possible

LORY, IT'LL BE YOUR BABY... NURTURE IT, FEED IT, CARESS IT, LOVE IT, CODDLE IT, CARE FOR IT, RESPECT IT, AND ABOVE ALL ... **SELL** IT.

to advance to top executive status without some sales and marketing management experience with the firm.

The number of people needed in this field is not likely to be large in the next few years, but the number of such highly technically trained personnel is not likely to be great either. The few jobs available will most likely go to the most technically trained people. There will also be some temporary assignments in marketing research made to sales management personnel as firms attempt to broaden the horizons of sales personnel.

Product Manager

The product manager is the person responsible for coordinating every facet of the product's business including advertising, promotion, sales, pricing, packaging, manufacturing, distribution, budgeting, legal problems, and other concerns. This method of marketing is common primarily in consumer product companies. Some firms use the term "brand management" instead of product management.

Duties. The product management concept was pioneered at Procter and Gamble over fifty years ago as a means of focusing marketing attention on one

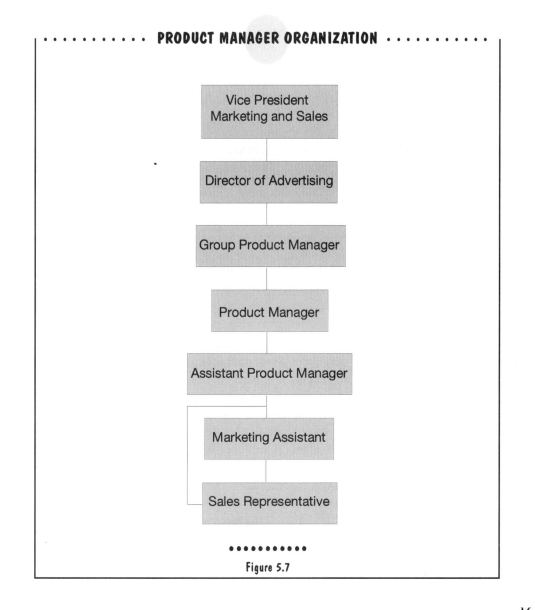

· · · · · · · · · · · **PRODUCT MANAGER ORGANIZATION** · · · · · · · · · · ·

Vice President Marketing and Sales

Director of Advertising

Group Product Manager

Product Manager

Assistant Product Manager

Marketing Assistant

Sales Representative

· · · · · · · · · ·

Figure 5.7

central group of people. This group (usually only three or four people) plans, develops, and directs the marketing efforts for a particular product.

The product group consists of the manager, an assistant, and one or two market analysts. This small group knows more about the product and how to increase consumer acceptance of it than anyone else in the company.

GOOD MORNING! I'M THE NEW HIGH TECH XLP 3000 COMPUTER, THE IDIOT STANDING NEXT TO ME IS JUST A SALES REP.

The product manager has the responsibility for developing an annual marketing plan, executing the advertising and copy strategy, planning and selecting media, planning sales promotions, coordinating package design, recommending product improvements, sizing packages, and analyzing sales and forecasting sales and profits.

Organization.   Most products of a given firm are consolidated into groups of three to six similar products. A product management team is assigned to each specific product or brand.

The new assistant product manager might coordinate the budget, track progress of a special test market, and/or write copy for submission to the manager. Assistants work with advertising specialists in copywriting, media, art, and package design, and participate in meetings with agency representatives.

Most assistants spend several hours at their desks each day analyzing reports, processing numerical data, and writing memos consolidating their efforts.

Advancement.   Before being promoted to assistant product manager, most people in this field have spent some time in sales usually selling a consumer product. The purpose of the sales assignment is to provide a broad understanding of products and how they are merchandised to consumers. After the sales experience comes a promotion to assistant product manager, an assignment usually held for three to five years.

Because the product management organization is a very flat structure, promotions are not frequent, but individuals do rotate from product to product. Promotions to group product manager and advertising manager are possible also. Many product managers later become account executives for advertising agencies.

Many firms do not start people directly in product management. These firms often require their people to have three to five years of sales experience before considering them for product management assignments. Some first use product management as a temporary assignment for three to five years before moving managers back into the line sales force as executives.

Figure 5.7 typifies an organizational structure. Very few companies use this approach, and most of those that do are consumer product firms such as Procter and Gamble, General Mills, General Foods, and Quaker Oats. Firms in the beer, wine, cigarette, and soft drink industries also use product managers.

Requirements. The annual need for people entering this field is very low, probably less than 200 people. There are thousands of fresh college graduates, particularly MBA-degreed people, plus hundreds of people with three to five years of sales experience vying for the limited number of openings. All openings are at entry level, and they usually require a good working knowledge about marketing and some sales experience in the consumer goods business.

Most firms require an MBA degree in marketing, although that is not yet a universal requirement. There is a strong need for sophisticated writing skills. With the current supply and demand situation, most firms can demand that candidates be in the top ten percent of their classes.

The competition for these few openings is likely to remain highly competitive for several years.

Financial Management

What can I do in finance?

Financing the product or service is an essential activity of all types of organizations. It encompasses a wide range of finance-related occupations, some of which have very little direct relationship to the basic accounting function.

Finance includes accounting for expenditures, budgeting for the future, analyzing past and planned expenditures, investing resources, banking, risk-sharing, and managing a complex combination of procedures, paper work, and the people running the operation.

The accounting and finance function employs people from all academic and work disciplines. Finance requires people who understand the big picture of the total organization.

Financial managers get a broad view of the organization because budget expenditures and prudent monitoring and planning for them extend across all functional lines. The function exists in both public service and private business.

The finance function includes most of the administrative activities involved in running the organization. The positions available include many assignments at various levels of responsibility and include accountants, auditors, budget analysis, financial analysts, credit analysts, banking specialists, insurance specialists, real estate specialists, investment analysts, computer programmers, systems analysts, tax experts, and an extensive array of managers.

Most assignments require some exposure to basic accounting and finance courses, but the depth of study varies greatly with the actual assignment. A real estate or insurance specialist might need only two courses of basic accounting and one course in finance, while a controller aspirant needs a full academic major of accounting and finance courses.

By surfing to specific employer websites and going to their employment section, you will gain more insight into specific jobs. After visiting a few of these, you will better see how your general (non-company specific) interests fit on your resume. This analysis gives you the big, broad picture.

Because the positions vary so greatly in duties, requirements, and career paths, they must be explored separately. The function cuts across all functional lines, which

Finance is the controlling mechanism of an organization.

Financial staff work in all sectors (government, private enterprise, and non-profit) as well as in all industry groups.

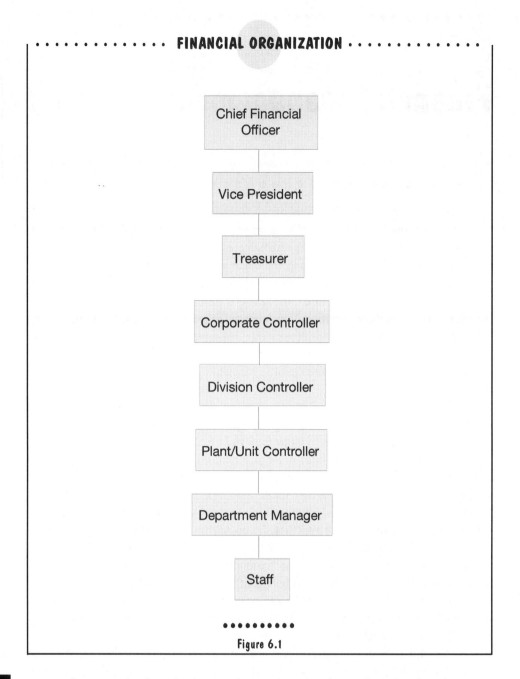

Figure 6.1

means, for example, that a budget analyst assigned to the engineering function must know the basics about engineering in addition to basic accounting.

The career profiles which follow provide adequate depth or information to help you determine if a particular position might be appropriate for your background and interests, but the information is not of sufficient depth to determine a firm career choice. It will be necessary to refer to additional sources for the depth you need for that decision.

General Accountant

More than sixty percent of all accountants do management accounting work, and twenty percent work as public accountants in independent accounting firms. The remainder work in government or teach at colleges and universities.

Because of growing interest in accounting and readily available jobs, the field has grown rapidly over the past decade. In fact, it has grown to the extent that over one million people are now working in the profession and it is one of the fastest growing occupations.

An accountant carries one of many different job titles depending upon the industry, level of responsibility, and type of accounting work he or she performs. All accounting is characterized by compiling, analyzing, and reporting on the financial condition of the many functions of an organization. Frequently used titles include industrial accountant, tax accountant, financial analyst, budget analyst, administrative assistant, cost accountant, auditor, and for high-level assignments, controller.

Career Paths. Figure 6.1 illustrates a typical financial organization and thus shows the upward career progress normally seen by most successful accountants. The usual entry-level positions are within the various operating departments shown in Figure 6.2.

Within each level of responsibility, staffs perform the basic work activities in the various operating departments. These staffs are managed by accounting *managers*, not bookkeepers.

Departments. Operating department managers usually report to a local controller and to a functional operating manager at the head office. This *dual* reporting relationship maintains functional integrity while providing for local operating control.

Financial accounting involves assignments in journal entry preparation, general ledger preparation, financial statement preparation, and analysis of these accounts.

A typical *cost accounting* assignment might involve estimating costs for a new product, preparing a cost analysis on an operating facility, setting cost standards for given products or services, analysis of operating variances, and projecting cost-trend data. These projects call for a thorough understanding of production processes, engineering methods, and new equipment plans.

Internal auditing provides independent, objective reviews of the financial and operational control functions of all levels of operation. In many organizations the department acts as an internal management consulting unit that makes recommendations to management for profit planning purposes. Auditing is the corporate watchdog and problem solver.

Tax departments prepare the employer's federal, state, and local tax returns for all legal entities and provides professional tax counsel on tax planning, tax laws, legislative interpretation, and court decisions. For many private enterprises, a good tax department saves substantial sums of capital resources annually.

Budgeting requires initial and continuing contact with division and department heads to

ACCOUNTING OPERATING DEPARTMENTS

- General Accounting
- Computer Systems
- Internal Auditing/ Consulting
- Credit Analysts
- Operating Budgeting
- Capital Budgeting
- Taxes
- Cost Control
- Pricing
- Insurance
- Investments
- Treasury

• • • • • • • • • • •
Figure 6.2

REALLY, THOUGH, OUR ACCOUNTANTS DO VERY LITTLE ACTUAL JUGGLING OF THE BOOKS, KIP.

develop a plan for a realistic expenditure of funds. Projections are based upon manpower requirements, operating efficiency, customer needs, and new plans.

Budget people consolidate reports from various units, analyze total impact, and make recommendations for sources and uses of funds consistent with the organization's mission and available resources.

The *chief financial officer* is responsible for safeguarding the organization's assets. This is accomplished through cash management, financing expansion plans, establishment of long-term debt requirements, supervision of investment portfolios, protection of foreign exchange exposure, credit analysis, credit collection, risk management, insurance, bank relations, and establishment of financial policies for all departments within the organization. The chief financial officer heads the organization's treasury department.

Positions. *The normal entry-level assignment is as an accountant. The assignment might be to any one of the operating departments. People frequently move between operating departments during the early stages of their careers to increase their breadth of organizational exposure and experience.*

One common assignment is to the position of *financial analyst.* This assignment is similar to that of an accountant but carries with it the potential for movement into a line accounting management function. A financial analyst reviews balance sheets and statements of financial condition and writes reports and/or makes presentations to management recommending and supporting certain financial courses of action.

The financial analyst works in the accounting and finance function, and his or her basic role is to analyze, recommend, and support a financial decision based upon concrete financial and market facts.

Financial analysts are found in both controller and treasury functions. The position is usually an interim assignment leading to a top-level financial management responsibility. Management uses the assignment to provide both breadth exposure to many areas and in-depth experience in a particular area. The position is often a training ground for grooming high-potential talent.

Financial analyst is the title most frequently given to MBA degree recipients as they enter the enterprise for their first assignment. The salary level is often above that of the typical entry-level accountant job, and employers usually assign the financial analysts to higher-level managers. In many instances they report to vice presidents and controllers.

After spending a short time as a financial analyst, most organizations assign the person to a line accounting function; often this is a supervisory, rather than an analytical assignment. Most financial analysts have strong accounting, finance, or banking backgrounds and the potential to move quickly into management assignments.

Abstract of Duties. The following list of typical duties of accountants and financial analysts gives you a good feel for a typical routine.

> Compile financial records . . . prepare financial reports . . . develop profit and loss statements . . . develop statements of financial operations . . . analyze financial reports . . . prepare budgets . . . conduct internal audits to insure adherence to acceptable accounting standards . . . manage cash resources.

> Prepare balance sheets . . . make financial decisions . . . prepare control procedures . . . create financial systems . . . design procedures and formal data for machine processing . . . write financial and credit reports . . . prepare capital investment plans . . . develop financial

The accountant and financial analyst basically perform very similar duties.

plans . . . work with bankers . . . supervise clerical, managerial, and technical personnel.

Requirements. For the highest-level positions in accounting, most employers want to see a full complement of accounting courses which is usually reflected by an undergraduate degree in accounting. Although an MBA degree in finance or accounting is extremely advantageous, the degree is not often listed as a requirement.

For upper-management accounting positions, very few firms accept anything less than five strong courses in accounting plus two courses in financial analysis.

For top jobs, many firms require certification as a "Certified Management Accountant" or a "Certified Public Accountant." The CMA and CPA certificates represent accomplishment in accounting beyond the basic academic training in college.

At the entry level, the bachelor's degree in accounting is normally required along with evidence of a strong ability to write concise, clear, and grammatically sound reports.

Many employers look for additional courses in financial analysis coupled with an internship, cooperative education experience, or similar practical experience, but they do not require these credentials. MBA degree-holders who have a large number of accounting courses often start as a financial analyst or "assistant to" an accounting manager.

Perhaps more than the accounting skills, employers look for evidence of strong communicative skills, written and verbal, as they promote and move people up into accounting manager positions. Partly for this reason, employers look for evidence of leadership via extracurricular activities, civic responsibilities, and other work experience.

Advancement. New accountants rotate through several operating departments and at various levels of reporting to obtain breadth of knowledge about the overall financial function. It takes three to five years, depending upon performance, openings, and size of organization, to attain the manager level.

In very small organizations the functions performed by the operating departments may be consolidated into the controllership function which makes movement from top to bottom of the organization relatively "flat."

During the early years, accountants may be given titles like financial analyst, budget analyst, assistant to, assistant department manager, or assistant controller. The levels of responsibility in some organizations are junior, staff, senior, and chief accountant for each operating department and within various plants, divisions, or headquarters.

Promotions every two to four years are quite common, and they almost always involve substantial earnings increases in addition to the normal merit and cost of living increases. As one

"Corporate financial analyst" is the most frequently used job title for the MBA candidates.

Advancement is frequently very rapid due to shortages of qualified talent.

advances, the pyramid becomes narrower and narrower, so the time span between promotions tends to become longer. Because of the pent-up need for qualified financial managers and executives, the earnings increases tend to be rather substantial even though title changes may not occur.

Training. Most employers provide some formal training at the entry level, the purpose of which is to show how the fundamental accounting principles taught in school relate to the employer's specific manner of building upon the basic skills.

Most employers attempt to maximize exposure to all accounting departments with an overview training program which relieves one from spending time in every department. A few employers rotate people through each department with two- to six-month assignments to accomplish the same purposes as the overview training.

Regardless of the method employed, most employers provide some type of in-house training (OJT, rotational, courses) supplemented with outside seminars and home office programs. The purposes are to expose one to all facets of the organization (both within accounting and within other functional areas), to provide an introduction to the people with whom one must work, and to provide experiences through which one will learn how to do and manage other functions.

As advancement comes, many organizations move people up in the function or laterally to a new function to broaden the learning process. In addition to building specific accounting skills, more attention is given to supervisory, management, and decision making skills as people are moved.

Outlook. There are over one million accountants employed in the U.S. at many levels of responsibility. The growth continues at a pace faster than that of most other occupations. The competition for each job opening is tempered by the fact that fewer new employees are entering the field than the field needs at this time.

The competition is reflected in entry-level and management-level salaries which are among the highest paid to any occupational group except engineers. The annual performance reviews normally result in further salary increases which appear to stay two to four percentage points above the current rate of inflation.

Promotions usually bring substantial pay boosts. Top financial managers are among the highest paid occupational groups.

Most initial jobs demand attention to detail because the work is of a project-related nature. This requires a special type of mental attitude. As one progresses, the daily routine slowly changes from the detail-orientation to one of managing people and resources.

Most jobs do not entail extensive travel, but when one reaches managerial assignments more travel is demanded. The major exception is the internal auditing function which often requires regular travel between various units, but this inconvenience is usually compensated for by financial considerations.

The accounting function offers enormous exposure to top management in all areas of all organizations (public and private), because every function has a need for accounting expertise. Preparing and making formal presentations to high-level management is a common activity of rising accounting managers.

Every major organization needs a strong management team in finance and accounting and this enhances employment possibilities and the chance for upward progress in the field.

The accounting and finance function often serves as a training ground for general management responsibilities later.

Public Accountant

Public accountants are independent practitioners who work on a fee basis for organizations needing financial records verified. Government regulations require many organizations to hire an independent third party to review financial records.

The three major functions of public accountants are to:

- Report the financial facts
- Attest to their authenticity
- Advise clients of alternate plans of action

Public accountants review an organization's financial records and given an *opinion as to the reliability* of the methods of accounting used by the organization and the *accuracy of the records kept.* Public accountants are *advice clients* on tax matters and other financial concerns, but basically they make after-the-fact analyses.

The organization's accountants then make recommendations and implement decisions for the future. Public accountants deal largely with historical data.

Organizations.   Most large public accounting firms are organized into three main units:

- auditing
- tax
- management consulting service

By overwhelming numbers, most people enter the firm via the audit staff, but a few who are highly trained in tax work do enter the tax department directly.

The management service unit serves in a capacity identical to that of a management consulting organization. It provides advice to clients for decision-making purposes. Most people in this function are highly experienced and/or educated in a specific technical area.

Many firms use a team approach to providing consulting services. The client receives technical advice from a variety of experts who individually would be impractical to hire for a short-term project. The accounting firm finds it profitable, however, because the team works on similar projects for many different clients.

Career Path.   Entry into public accounting is almost always at the entry-level assignment. Very few experienced people desire to start over with new firms, so most firms recruit a very high percentage of employees from college campuses. The promote-from-within concept is stronger in public accounting than in about any other industry. The typical career path is illustrated in Figure 6.3.

"Staff accountants"   usually begin in the audit branch of the firm. Although most firms have a tax and management service component which hire a few entry-level people, many often move people into one of these specialties internally. Only about 10–15 percent of the individuals beginning as staff accountants reach the top partner level but this varies by firm.

The initial training period is aimed at orientation and preparation for passing the CPA examination with supervisors meeting regularly with new employees to review work assignments and offer professional assistance.

Typically the staff accountant is given one area of the audit (verification of cash balances, inventories, receivables, etc.) and asked to evaluate the client's control procedures and to verify the accuracy of the figures.

The second level is the **"senior"** accountant, who assumes responsibility for field assignments and for supervising several staff assistants. The promotion comes in two to four years. The senior is rotated to a variety of jobs and assumes responsibility for small jobs. There are various levels of seniors, and most seniors stay at this level for two to four years.

The third level is the **"manager"** who maintains direct contact with the client's problems, personnel, organization, and accounting methods. Managers assign seniors and assistants to jobs. The manager, with the partner, writes the "management letter" to the client suggesting ways to improve operations.

Some firms have an intermediate level known as a **"supervisor"** before the manager stage. Most managers have five to eight years of experience before reaching this level and remain in the assignment four to eight years. Some plateaus exist at this level.

A few firms promote the manager to an intermediate step, often called **"principal"** or **"senior manager,"** a few years before they are given partnership status. In other firms, the word "principal" implies a position largely equivalent to a partner.

Consulting firms and divisions of the public accounting firms called "Management Advisory Services" often employ the job title "principal" in lieu of partner or just one step before partnership status.

The word "partner" implies ownership and hence a capital investment in the firm. Many times the principal does not have a financial investment in the firm.

A **"partner"** bears the responsibility of management and takes part in decision making and policy formulation. Final responsibility for servicing clients rests with partners. Partners maintain and foster relationships with accounts and deal with questions regarding fees, services, and recent developments in the industry.

There are also various levels of partners. It normally takes twelve to fourteen years to reach the partner stage.

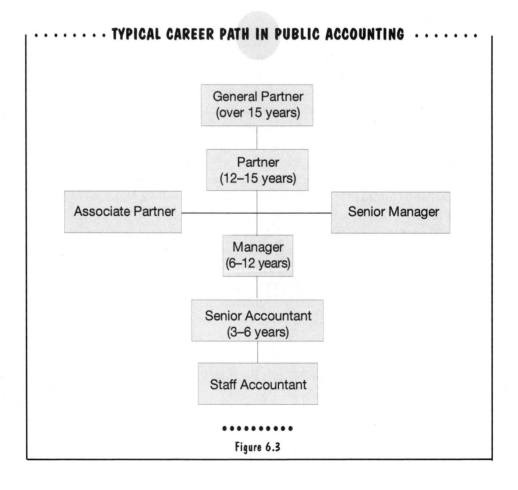

· · · · · · · · · **TYPICAL CAREER PATH IN PUBLIC ACCOUNTING** · · · · · · ·

Figure 6.3

Requirements.   Most public accounting firms require 24 to 30 semester hours of accounting courses and a four-year college degree. Many states require a five year accounting program to sit for the CPA exam.

Most seek graduates in the top 25 percent of the graduating class and rarely drop standards below 3.2 on a 4.0 scale. CPA firms need the assurance that employees can later pass the rigorous national CPA examination.

Public firms also turn down a high percentage of students in the top 25 percent of their class because it takes more than grades. Employees constantly meet with clients, so an outgoing personality and highly developed speaking skills are essential for future success. There are many reports to write and much public relations work to do with clients, so written communication abilities are extremely important in the selection process.

Compensation.   Public accounting offers superior earnings at every level. In addition to a higher than average starting salary, many firms offer employees several hundred dollars when they pass all parts of the CPA examination. Significant increases annually above the annual rate of inflation are not uncommon for partnership-track people.

With some firms, staff accountants can earn overtime, which increases the base salary on an annual basis by about 10 percent. At entry level, a master's degree increases the starting rate to about 10 to 20 percent above that offered to bachelor's degree candidates. Small regional firms often pay 15 to 25 percent less than the large national firms located in major metropolitan areas, but these salaries are usually very competitive and attractive given the location of the firm.

Senior accountants usually earn 50 to 70 percent more than beginning accountants, while managers can earn two to three times more money than accountants. Although senior partners in most large firms earn six-figure salaries, many of them make substantial regular contributions to the firm's capital base.

Outlook.   Entry into public accounting is almost always at the staff accountant level, and few people enter the field above the senior accountant level. If you do not start when you first complete your degree, later entry is very difficult unless you start your own firm.

Competition for entry into public accounting is competitive. There are many more qualified people trying to enter the profession than it can absorb. Location and school reputation play important roles in the selection process.

Less than 20 percent of those who start with a public firm remain for ten years. Attrition due to the attractiveness of other opportunities is high. More than half of the accountants who leave do so by the end of the third year, but nearly all of those who leave stay within the field of accounting.

THE INTERNAL CONSULTANT

The traditional concern of the internal auditor has been financial auditing which translates into the inside staff that checks up on managers and staff to insure the funds are not stolen or misallocated. Since the chief auditor often reports directly to an outside Board of Directors member who chairs the Audit Committee, the top management may also have reason to be wary of internal auditors.

Auditors may be viewed as a "necessary evil." They often have to tell top management that their baby is ugly. In recent years, the auditor's activities have broadened to include reviews of non-financial programs due to the independence of these well-respected staff members. An internal unbiased opinion is often difficult to obtain in large organizations.

The data in a computer has become an important tool used by auditors. Through examination of financial and non-financial data stored in computers, it is often easy to ascertain many improprieties. Once an area is identified, a more thorough investigation can be given.

The work of the internal auditor, (now the internal "consultant" in leading-edge firms), takes staff into nearly every department within the firm. From this vantage point, people get showcased throughout the organization. Top management often identifies new talent from this pool and hires from this important cadre of talented individuals as special opportunities arise. Often this results in a super monitoring relationship that continues for several years.

Consulting gives you a very broad perspective on the organization by permitting you to see many operations and feel the true underlying culture of the organization from several perspectives. After several years, you might find yourself heading such diverse areas as corporate finance, accounting control, acquisitions planning, corporate accounting, data processing, purchasing, or personnel.

The field welcomes majors from a variety of academic disciplines, but most organizations like to see four or five accounting courses supplemented with one to three courses in finance.

For some people, the major drawback is the amount of travel that is often required. It is common for assignments to last from one week to three months in locations outside the base station of the internal consultant. For some individuals with family commitments and responsibilities, this may not be desirable. For other individuals whose desire is to travel and experience many parts of the world, this is truly a special opportunity. A side benefit is that auditors often can live on an expense account and basically save much of their base salary.

More information about this opportunity can be obtained from The Institute of Internal Auditors, Altamonte Springs, FL 32715-1119.

Many individuals leave because of an extensive amount of traveling and the long hours, particularly during tax season. Many leave because they see that they do not have a chance for making partner with the firm, and others because the firm has encouraged them to look around for opportunities elsewhere. The tedious nature of auditing is another reason given for leaving an accounting firm.

Public accounting firms try to keep the more talented individuals and offer them as much opportunity as other organizations. Individuals on a partner track seldom leave.

Those that do leave do not always settle for a second-best firm. Some of the client firms with which they have worked are happy to have them join their staffs. This often works out to be an attractive arrangement for both the public accounting firm and the hiring employer.

As more and more employers adopt promote-from-within practices, the opportunity for the "recycled" CPA to join major firms in other than entry-level positions might be declining. Getting two to three years of work experience in public accounting before joining an industrial firm may not be the wave of the future; yet, a better opportunity to learn and a better chance for advancement is hard to find.

For further information, you should write the American Institute of Certified Public Accountants, 1211 Avenue of the Americas, New York, NY 10036.

Internal Auditor

The internal auditor is the industrial and government employer's counterpart of the public accountant. Auditors are internal *consultants*. It is their job to advise the appropriate parties regarding financial plans. Internal auditors go into every operation of a company or a government agency.

Duties. In addition to checking to see that all money is accounted for, auditors investigate the ways in which the money is being used. Auditors check the inventory valuation and investigate how well it is being secured and whether it is too small or too large in light of the organization's objectives. They conduct project analyses to determine whether there are appropriate numbers of workers on various jobs.

The consultant gets into tax matters, sales, purchasing, production, advertising, and any other area where particular projects need to be investigated. The auditor's role is not to direct, but to describe conditions and performance to management.

Nearly all organizations have an internal auditing function. The internal auditor is a full-fledged member of the management team. The rapid expansion of the field has come about through the growth in the number and size of public and private enterprises. Chief auditors sometimes report to the Board of Director's Audit Committee to guarantee independence.

As organizations grow, management is more and more removed from the physical running of things; therefore, there is a need for the checking and balancing provided by an internal auditing department.

Internal auditors take broad views of the company's policies and activities. Their work takes them into many departments. Internal consultants examine and appraise policies, plans, procedures, and records of various departments. They do not exercise direct authority over persons nor install procedures, prepare records, or engage in any other activities; what they do is audit inventory, payroll, and accounts receivable.

Internal auditors often travel from factory to factory, agency to agency, and branch to branch. The job requires the ability to concentrate on many details without losing sight of the broader perspective. It requires tact and maturity to probe for potential problems in a department while gaining the respect and confidence of people in the function being audited.

Requirements. The auditor is a generalist who usually reports to top management directly.

Many organizations require a degree in accounting and course work which develops strong abilities in human relations, public speaking, and report writing.

The consultant assists management in learning how well controls, policies, and procedures are working and to suggest solutions where there are deficiencies.

Auditors must have a "detective" type of awareness while probing for suggestions and ideas to improve the system being studied.

Many organizations consider the auditing function a training ground for managers in the finance, accounting, and administration areas. Employees frequently rotate people in and out of the function in order to give them an overview of the entire organization.

Management Information System (MIS)

Although the management information system (MIS) reports into the finance function in most organizations, this field cuts across nearly all organizational and functional lines. The larger the organization, the greater is its need for diverse and complex information systems. Effective cross-functionally integrated systems can control the operations of hundred of departments and make the work of thousands of people more meaningful.

Enterprise-wide systems are growing rapidly. They are fostered by technology driven firms like SAP, Oracle, Peoplesoft, IBM, etc. This rapid growth is likely to continue for years as enterprise-wide controls, in a global economy, become more essential.

Systems professionals develop, design, program, and implement computer and manual system networks that control many different operations in finance, production, engineering, marketing, and research. Systems may be installed in materials control, production planning, assembly operations, personnel planning, labor analysis, sales reporting, sales forecasting, cost accounting, financial analysis, payroll, and general accounting.

Management information systems personnel, whether at the analyst level or the manager level, work on the leading edge of change and improvements in management.

Duties.   MIS analysts plan, schedule, and coordinate the activities which are necessary for developing the systems, procedures, and processes which manipulate the data used to solve organizational problems.

Analysts collect and analyze data in order to formulate efficient patterns of information flow from sources to computer, to analyst, to manager, and to other end product areas. Although computers are not always used, most applications lend themselves to computer processing.

The MIS analyst defines the computer process which is necessary for changing raw data into useful information and then plans the distribution and use of the resulting information. The analyst develops process flowcharts and diagrams in detail format for the computer programmer.

The MIS analyst may work as part of a team or alone. In smaller installations, the positions of the system analyst and computer programmer are frequently combined, while other employers prefer to keep the job functions as separate activities. In any case, there must be a close working relationship between the systems analyst and the computer programmer.

Requirements.   A college degree with courses in business, accounting, programming, statistics, computer science mathematics, and/or other hard sciences is usually required unless the person has prior experience in data processing. Some employers do not require any specific academic major, but computer science majors receive high preference.

An advanced degree is rarely needed after one becomes employed because most firms offer in-depth training in consulting, programming, systems design, data base organization, communications, training process control, and management.

MIS POSITIONS

- Chief MIS Officer
- Data Processing Manager
- Assistant Manager
- Database Manager
- Project Team Leader
- System Analyst Manager
- Lead Systems Analyst
- Applications Manager
- Lead Programmer
- Systems Analyst
- Programmer
- Consultant

• • • • • • • • • • •

Figure 6.4

Because of the need to interact frequently with persons outside of the data processing function, good communication skills are necessary. Some firms give tests designed to evaluate numerical ability and the logical thought patterns which are necessary in the daily work setting. The most common test is a programmer aptitude test.

Advancement. The growth of the information systems area has been phenomenal in the past decade, and the future also looks promising. Many new jobs should open up, which will provide upward mobility for current systems analysts. The levels of responsibility in the field range from trainee to analyst to senior to chief and then into supervision, management, and executive responsibilities.

Because of the cross-functional exposure, some people move into other areas of the organization and then advance in very different career paths. Others prefer to remain in the programming and systems function indefinitely as experts on a given system and work with new generations of equipment and supporting systems.

The compensation for the systems experts is normally most attractive.

//WEB.TIP//

www.computerworld.com
Computer World Magazine
For the IT professional and CS, MIS, CIS student/news/ industry and company reports/career articles/ salary reports/classifieds.

Programmer

The programmer takes the work of the systems analyst and prepares specific instructions for the computer. The programmer prepares a detailed plan for solution of a data problem. This plan is a series of logical steps of computer instructions called a program which makes the computer perform the desired operations.

Duties. Computer instructions received by the programmer are in English, whereas the computer can only accept its machine language. Machine language is a set of procedures expressed in the number system basic to the computer. Programming languages are more definitive languages than the English language and thus bridge the gap between English and machine language.

Programming may require only a few hours for a simple data manipulation program or weeks and months for complex systems programs. A program may consist of as few as 20 instructions or encompass hundreds of pages of instructions.

Large programs are usually broken down into sections of basic procedural steps. Flow diagrams give an overview of complex programs which enable different programmers at different times to access and understand the original programmer's logic and subsequent construction pattern.

Advancement.
There are several levels of responsibility to which a programmer may aspire. The chief programmer plans, schedules, and directs all operations of a given section of programming. For example, one small section may be assigned to work only on sales reports, or a large section (which may have several units within it) may be assigned to the

...THIS IS McGRAFF WHO PROGRAMS OUR COMPUTERS AND THAT'S HINOWITZ, WHO PROGRAMS McGRAFF.

entire marketing organization. Because of the various sizes of units, even chief programmers may have different levels of responsibilities.

A lead programmer is usually an assistant to the chief programmer and as such supervises several other programmers in an assigned section. There are business, scientific, and system programmers whose responsibilities vary by the size and complexity of the projects assigned to them.

Many programmers move into systems work later in their careers and advance up into management responsibilities. Many move into management consulting roles.

Many employers make the programming section the first assignment for anyone coming into information systems management because programming is the basic building block upon which all systems are constructed. Having spent some time in programming greatly increases the credibility and acceptance of MIS managers by their subordinates, especially after they progress into management responsibilities.

Financial Institution

Financial institutions offer individuals the opportunity to move into the finance function without getting as heavily involved in accounting as would be necessary if he or she were to seek employment in the accounting function of a manufacturing firm.

Most larger financial institutions prefer to "grow their own" management talent and, as a result, it is very difficult to move into a position of authority there without rising through internal management steps.

Many smaller financial institutions do not have elaborate management training programs, so they look to the larger organizations to provide candidates for management positions if talent is not available internally.

Financial institutions include banks, credit unions, loan companies, savings and loan associations, insurance firms, stock brokerage firms, investment banking firms, investment advisory firms, and commercial and residential real estate businesses.

Titles.   Titles vary depending upon the type of financial institution, but the actual duties are often quite similar. Some of the titles include branch manager, lending officer, credit analyst, mortgage loan officer, appraiser, operations manager, trust administrator, and vice president of any number of various departments.

All financial organizations employ supervisors, data processing personnel, managers, accountants, auditors, and collection managers, and most offer management training programs.

Abstract of Duties.   If you decide to join a financial institution, you will most likely be involved in the following types of activities.

Evaluate credit . . . invest funds . . . provide financial advice . . . make decisions on installment, commercial, or real estate loans . . . appraise property . . . conduct marketing studies . . . evaluate risks . . .

FUNCTIONS IN FINANCIAL INSTITUTIONS

Major project finance
Energy lending
Installment lending
Cash management
Domestic private banking
Corporate lending
Correspondent banking
Trade financing
Asset based lending
Credit analysis
Factoring
International private banking
Construction lending
Residential real estate
Commercial real estate lending
Trust
Branch banking
Money market trading
Information systems

• • • • • • • • • • •

Figure 6.5

//WEB.TIP//

www.acm.org/cacm/careeropps
Association for Computing Machinery
Professional association publications/job leads in computer science.

plan investment programs . . . coordinate work flow . . . evaluate and design paper processing systems.

Manage people at all levels . . . sell services . . . carry out public relations activities . . . devise advertising strategy . . . conduct economic research . . . forecast economy . . . draw up contracts . . . service contracts . . . design forms . . . evaluate claims . . . process paperwork.

Buy and sell stocks and bonds for clients . . . analyze securities . . . provide customer contact and service . . . prepare periodic reports . . . maintain records . . . handle customer inquiries and complaints . . . develop budgets . . . implement cost control procedures . . . recruit and train personnel.

Requirements. A bachelor's degree in some phase of business administration is preferred, but institutions often hire candidates without business backgrounds especially if they have taken some accounting and/or finance courses.

Some money center banks primarily recruit MBA degree-holders for commercial lending, investment banking, and technical functions.

The paper flow is tremendous, so outstanding report writing skills are required. For jobs involving public contact, a pleasing appearance and good speaking characteristics are essential.

Many organizations require strong computer skills.

Career Path. Many financial institutions set aside several positions as professional entry-level positions. Training programs tend to rotate new salaried employees into a variety of different areas. A structured and planned on-the-job training program with key personnel identified as top trainers is common.

Some employers offer regular seminars with take-home assignments, but most simply encourage matriculation at local colleges and pay their employees' tuition for job-related courses.

The typical career path is:

1. Trainee
2. Assistant/Analyst
3. Department/Branch Manager
4. Junior Officer
5. Officer
6. Officer of a Major Division

Experienced personnel usually can move into the institution at appropriate levels of responsibilities. Officer ranks often carry vice president titles.

Earnings. Money center banks tend to be salary leaders. Most of them are located in large metropolitan areas. The large insurance firms and regional banks start employees at competitive salaries. Other smaller financial institutions tend to offer starting salaries slightly below the average but often provide excellent benefits and working conditions, less pressure, and greater job security.

Financial institutions have some of the best benefit packages. Salaries of officers with large banks are on the level of those paid by manufacturing firms. Salaries in smaller organizations often top out in the $70,000 to $100,000 range.

As the U.S. moves toward more credit card use and a "checkless" society evolves, more and more opportunities will emerge in this field. Financial institutions may add to their professional staffs while overall white-collar employment may drop.

Financial institutions are service-oriented and are highly competitive. This brings about pressure to develop new services for the public, and thus it is necessary to hire people to manage the functions.

Credit Manager

A credit manager has final authority in decisions to accept or reject credit requests after analysis of pertinent facts. The analyses may

MR. GRAVES, WITHOUT YOUR HELP, I COULD NEVER HAVE ADDED TO THE NATIONAL DEBT.

be conducted by the manager, assistants, or analysts, and they are based upon a prescribed set of analytical procedures.

Consumer credit is granted to the end product (or service) user, usually a private individual. Commercial credit is extended from one organization to another organization, often through an intermediary such as a bank or commercial lending company.

There are credit departments, (independent units which are usually organized as part of the accounting function), in every large private organization and in many government departments.

Duties.   The credit department personnel analyze detailed financial reports submitted by the applicant, conduct personal interviews with applicants, and review credit agency reports about past payment history.

Analysts check with banks and other lending firms where the firm or individual has deposits or previously was granted credit. Where detailed financial statements are not available, the credit analyst relies upon personal interviews, credit bureaus, and banks who can provide information.

High-ranking credit managers in large corporations are responsible for formulating broad credit policies and implementing procedures to insure compliance with sound principles of business. They establish uniform financial standards and determine the degree of risk the firm is willing to accept.

Credit managers establish office procedures, supervise analysts and office workers, and assign broad limits of credit responsibility to subordinates.

Requirements.   Most firms request a college degree, but a major in accounting is not normally specified if the person has taken two to four courses in the accounting and finance fields. Hires above the entry level usually have prior experience in a related field such as accounting, finance, lending, supervision, or data processing.

Credit department applicants must be able to analyze detailed financial information and draw inferences from it because it is necessary to maintain good customer relations, a pleasant personality is essential for credit department employees. The ability to write accurately and concisely is also important.

Career Path.   About half of credit managers work in wholesale and retail trade with the other half working for banks, loan firms, and large manufacturing organi-

The credit function is an essential activity in most organizations that sell products, services, or ideas.

zations. Inexperienced entrants into the profession usually start as analysts whose work is directed by a manager for three to nine months.

Some of the larger firms offer elaborate classroom instruction, seminars, and rotational training programs.

There are various levels of responsibility within the credit organizations in terms of dollar responsibility and number of people supervised. The option to move into other financial and marketing responsibilities opens avenues of upward progression for people in the credit function.

Security Analyst

The security analyst is a researcher involved with portfolio management and the analysis of bonds, stocks, and other forms of investments. The largest employers of security analysts are the large brokerage houses, often located in New York.

A few security analysts, however, do work for investment bankers, insurance companies, and the trust departments of some banks, especially banks in San Francisco, Chicago, and New York.

A security analyst is often assigned one type of industry to research through reading reports and interviewing corporate leaders. They prepare reports which are similar to those found in the *Value Line Investment Survey* and *Standard and Poor's Investment Service.*

Most of the financial reports are for internal use or for clients' needs and are not for the general public's knowledge. These positions normally require a high degree of technical expertise and an ability to write well.

The average analyst has been in the profession for many years and earns a substantial salary. During recent years there was a significant number of mergers and failures in the brokerage and investment business which sharply reduced the number of people in the profession as well as the number of openings for new employees.

Although the situation has improved, there is still much competition for each new investment analyst position from both experienced and inexperienced applicants.

Most security and investment analysts do not aspire to upward advancement in the typical manner of many other professionals. They prefer to remain in their profession doing analytical work, but some do leave to move into bank lending and security sales positions or to manage departments of analysts.

In addition to the security and investment analyst titles other titles used for these positions include portfolio manager, director of research, trust administrator, account manager, and broker. Typical promotions are from junior analyst to senior to consultant.

FINANCIAL PLANNER

Financial planners advise other individuals on financial matters. They earn income by charging a flat fee to their clients or they earn a commission on the sale of financial products and services that they recommend as part of a comprehensive financial plan. The largest contingent earn income by charging both a fee to clients and earning a commission from products.

Planners prepare a detailed financial plan for their clients to execute in short- and long-term time horizons. The advice involves personal budgeting, saving, and investment strategies. The plan often gives recommendations on tax planning, estate design, wills, stock portfolios, partnership arrangements, life insurance, and real estate holdings.

Because the clients who purchase these services demand experience and seasoned maturity, this is not a common job for young individuals coming right out of college.

The International Association for Financial Planning estimates that a very high percentage of their members are independent practitioners or partners in small firms. Individuals are certified (CFP) by the Institute for Certified Financial Planners in Denver. This is an excellent way to eventually hang up a shingle and start your own business.

A common career path is for you to start by finding employment in public accounting, banking, life insurance, customer financial firms, or securities brokerage firms. These industries frequently hire entry-level talent and offer extensive training in both sales and financial products.

Many financial planners originally began their careers as staff auditors, tax accountants, bank lenders, branch managers, insurance salespeople, mutual fund consultants, real estate agents, financial account executives, etc. The large firms in these industries provided the training needed, and their name lends credibility if you later become an independent practitioner in your community.

The majority of financial planners are in the 30 to 50 age range and earn above-average incomes. A major ingredient though is that you are a recognized professional whose future income is directly tied to ability. It is like running a small business of your own.

Sources of employment include investment counseling firms, mutual funds organizations, foundations, insurance companies, banks, brokerage houses, and special research firms. More than half of all analysts live and work in New York City, but other large metropolitan areas and money centers have employment opportunities in this field as well.

All employers require a significant commitment to the profession in terms of education and work experience. Work experience is usually gained first in tangential fields or through significant personal investment and research before entering this field. Most new entrants are over 25 years old and hold MBA degrees from prestigious business schools.

Security Sales and Trading

A security salesperson is one who buys or sells stocks, bonds, or shares of mutual funds for an investor. Security salespeople are often called customer brokers, registered representatives, or account executives.

Every salesperson must be registered as a representative of a brokerage firm according to the regulations of the security exchange where the firm transacts business. Before beginning salespeople can qualify for a registered representative position, they must pass the Security and Exchange Commission's general security examination.

Most employers do not require specialized training in a given academic major; however, courses in finance and investment subjects are usually helpful in securing employment. The same traits found in other types of sales personnel are required for this career field as well, but these traits must be coupled with a sound financial background to add credibility to the sales presentation.

Security sales personnel can advance into management positions, such as branch manager, mutual fund manager, etc., but most of them prefer to remain in sales. The reason for this lack of interest in advancing into management relates to the higher earnings potential in sales and the sheer excitement of the business. Most work with high net worth individuals.

Most successful security salespeople enjoy their work and earn substantial commissions. Their earnings are restricted only by their ability to increase the number and size of the accounts they serve.

A beginner usually starts by servicing accounts of individual investors and eventually may handle very large accounts such as those of institutional investors. Some experienced salespeople advance to positions as branch office managers who supervise the work of other salespeople while executing buy and sell orders for their own clients. A few salespeople eventually become partners in their firms.

Trainees are usually paid salaries until they meet licensing registration requirements and for a short time thereafter. Starting salaries in the field are competitive with those being offered to other recent college graduates.

Once a salesperson has completed the training, earnings are usually in the form of commissions from sales of securities. The size of commissions depends on the policies of the firm and the type of security bought and sold. Consequently, earnings fluctuate. Full-time security salespeople usually earn over $30,000 annually, and many earn much more.

The employment market for security salespeople has been very cyclical. When not weak it can be on a roller coaster hiring boom. A large number of brokerage houses regularly close or merge. Consequently, experienced security salespeople find themselves changing employers occasionally but there is little negative impact on their earnings.

Insurance

Insurance companies assume millions of dollars in risk each year by transferring liability for loss from their policyholders to themselves. Like individual policyholders, all types of organizations purchase insurance to cover the potential chance that a disaster may strike and bankrupt the organization.

Whether for personal or organizational protection, the insurance business is a major part of the financial planning program and, therefore, the industry needs many types of experts in this area. Conversely, organizations must employ experts in the finance and administration functions to evaluate their needs for protection. Organizations refer to this as risk management.

Careers abound in the insurance industry in many types of jobs, but learning some things about three types of employment (underwriters, sales, and claims) permits one to gain an understanding of the industry and how risk management careers may be found in all types of organizations.

Underwriters. Underwriters appraise and select risks their company will insure. This career is distinctly different from that of insurance agents. Underwriters analyze information in insurance applications, reports from loss control consultants, medical reports, and actuarial studies which describe the probability of insured loss. Routine applications may be handled by computers, but underwriters must also use considerable personal judgment in making decisions on risk.

Underwriters outline the terms of contracts, including the premium amounts.

Underwriters assume great responsibility, because their company may lose business to competition if they appraise risks too conservatively, and their company will have to pay too many future claims if their decisions are too liberal.

They correspond with policyholders and agents regarding information requests and cancellations and occasionally accompany salespeople on appointments with prospective customers.

Most underwriters specialize in one of four major categories of insurance:

- Life
- Property Damage
- Personal Liability
- Health

Life underwriters may specialize in group or individual policies. The property and liability underwriter may specialize in a type of insurance such as fire, automobile, marine, etc.

Claims Representatives. Fast and fair settlement of claims is essential to an insurance company if it is to meet its commitments to policyholders and protect its own financial well being. *Claims representatives investigate claims, negotiate settlements with policyholders, and authorize payments.*

When a casualty company (in contrast to a life insurance company) receives a claim request, the claim adjuster determines the amount of the loss and whether the policy covers it. Adjusters use reports, physical evidence, and testimony of witnesses in investigating a claim. When their company is liable, they negotiate and settle the claim.

In life insurance companies, it is the claim examiner who checks claim applications for completeness and accuracy, interviews medical specialists, verifies information, and calculates benefit payments.

Insurance Agents. *Agents sell policies that protect individuals and businesses against future losses and financial pressures. They help clients plan financial protection, advise them on investment strategies, and help them obtain settlements.*

Agents may sell and service life, casualty, or health policies, or a combination of those policies.

An agent may be either an insurance company employee or an independent agent who represents several companies. The latter is called a broker, but agents and brokers do the same things. Agents spend most of their time discussing policies with prospective and existing clients who may be organization executives or individuals buying personal protection.

Beginning agents are usually paid a competitive base salary for a reasonable period of time. After that time, earnings are based strictly on commissions, and productive agents can earn substantial commissions in a very short period of time. Few fields offer such a high level of earnings potential in such a short period of time.

Administration. Insurance firms manage thousands of policies and millions of dollars in assets, so they need many home office employees. The employees may specialize in customer relations, service, computer processing, accounting, investments, or actuarial science. The insurance industry has many of the same types of positions found in any large firm.

Insurance plays a large and important role in any organization. Experts are needed in the insurance industry and also in the organizations that must interface with the industry.

Because of the nature of most positions in this field, most employers require college degrees, but few specify particular major fields of study. Most insurance firms have training programs to teach new employees the duties and responsibilities of various assignments.

Operations, Engineering, and Research

7

What jobs are available in technical fields?

Most organizations which offer a product or service to customers employ people to perform the function that *creates* the product or service. The operation may be an assembly line, a mining operation, a product processing operation, a paper flow process, or any other activity which requires the services of many people doing repetitive and/or skilled tasks.

Engineers help create the systems that make an operation function smoothly.

Operations

The operations end of an organization is a management structure organized around the goal of producing a finished product or a service or accomplishing a series of tasks.

Banks manage an enormous flow of paperwork and deal with millions of individual personal transactions. Automobile plants assemble vehicles. Transportation firms manage motor vehicle fleets. Oil companies convert raw materials to products used by consumers and commercial organizations. Steel firms produce a basic commodity. Hospitals manage a patient flow process. Governments deliver services. All of these operations require people at all levels of responsibility.

Few organizations operate without a chain of command structure for managing people, materials, and other resources. This management function is called production, manufacturing, or operations, depending upon the industry and the type of activity which is involved.

The most common characteristic of the management of all operations is that people are supervised. The operation to which it is simplest to relate the function is the typical manufacturing organization. Although manufacturing is used as an example, you should realize that the same activities are performed in non-manufacturing organizations as well.

> **The operations (or production and manufacturing) function is the activity that manages people and other resources.**

NO KIP, THIS DOES NOT REQUIRE ANY EXTENSIVE MEDICAL TRAINING.

Functions

A production function is responsible for supervision and coordinating activities of people involved in the manufacturing process. This may involve thousands of employees in many different locations for large corporations or only a few employees in a department within a service organization. Figure 7.1 lists the eight functions most often found in operations.

Some of these functions are found in some organizations but not in others. Where these functions are found, various levels of responsibility exist within each function. There are analysts, specialists, and managers within each function.

Many organizations carry out cross-functional training so that individuals in the operations function are exposed to all eight functions. Other firms tend to develop professionals in the respective fields for the purpose of making each of them an expert or manager in one of the eight functions.

Production Management.   Production management is the function of directing the work of those who are responsible for producing and making products, and it is performed at various levels from first-line supervision to vice president.

Positions in production management afford high visibility and exposure to all levels of management including distribution, product planning, employee relations, finance, research, and marketing.

Most manufacturing firms have a 6- to 18-month training program in production management, with the length depending upon assignments covered and the individual's background and progress.

The first assignment might be as a first line supervisor directing 25 to 100 production employees. One may be assigned to special projects dealing in quality control, process control, product development, pollution control, or safety. Over time, most individuals gain exposure to various levels of management from supervisor to department manager to plant manager.

Production Planning.   Production planning involves the ordering of materials and supplies, the development and control of operating schedules, and the management of inventory in the firm's production facilities and distribution centers. The function uses sales estimates from marketing personnel, production capacity figures, labor agreements, and inventory levels to arrive at appropriate production levels.

The goal is to minimize total costs by smoothing manufacturing processes over time and by keeping inventories low while still maintaining required customer demands and service.

Purchasing. Purchasing is responsible for the placement and administration of orders, contracts, and other agreements for the procurement of goods and services.

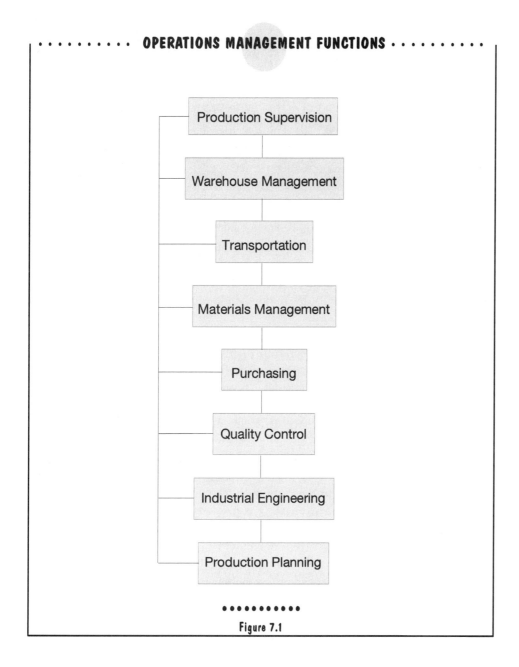

Figure 7.1

This includes negotiating with suppliers on matters of quality, service, and price features. Purchasing follows up and expedites in order to insure that the terms of various agreements are met.

Purchasing secures the materials, supplies, and equipment required for operation of the business or government agency. In addition to the actual buying of merchandise, it includes planning and policy activities.

It is the responsibility of the purchasing agent to buy materials of the right quality and in the right quantity, at the right time, and at the right price, from the right source, and with delivery at the right place.

Within any one firm the purchasing department includes the manager of purchasing, purchasing agent, assistant purchasing agent, buyers, assistant buyers, expediters, and traffic managers.

A purchasing agent must be willing and able to accept the responsibility for spending large amounts of money. He or she must be tactful in dealings with salespeople and have a good memory for detailed specifications.

Most employers, whether in business or government, who hire assistant purchasing agents at the entry-level position seek people with college degrees. Many employers fill needs internally by moving individuals from other areas into the purchasing function.

Warehouse Management.   Warehousing is the function that manages the warehousing and distribution operation to insure customer service levels. This includes developing and maintaining a close liaison with sales personnel to help assure a cooperative response to customer needs.

It also coordinates operations with planning, order processing, and transportation activities to allow for the timely, efficient, and orderly flow of finished product to customers.

Materials Management.   Materials management involves controlling the flow of materials from vendors to and through the production facility, to the warehouse and eventually to the customer. The objective is to insure that raw materials, partially processed materials, and finished products are at the right place, at the right time, in the right quantities.

Materials management involves contact with almost every phase of a manufacturing firm's operations and offers a unique insider's view of the various aspects of the firm. Materials management activities include purchasing, transportation, packaging, production planning, distribution, and order processing.

Transportation.   The physical distribution (as it is sometimes called), coordinates the movement of materials, supplies, and finished product to the production facilities, the warehouse, and the customer. This includes all phases of negotiations with carriers, their associations, and government regulatory bodies. The function also administers claims control, travel modes, and product movement.

Employment Characteristics

All of the individuals working in these functions usually report to a functional manager who reports to the equivalent of a plant manager, who is usually a high-level executive.

If there are multiple locations, a person in one function might move from one location to another within that function or move to another function at the same location. The move might depend upon the size of the organization, organization policy, and the individual's career interest.

Job Titles.   Many different job titles are used in the operations management function, so it is impossible to describe each specific job. Titles at the entry level might include foreman, analyst, inspector, planner, industrial engineer, systems analyst, expediter, assistant, scheduler, agent, dispatcher, etc.

Higher-level management job titles might include plant manager, superintendent, general foreman, department manager, engineer, chief, senior, etc.

Job titles are most frequently assigned with functional department names attached to them. For example, an assistant manager would carry the designation of the department to which he or she is assigned.

Duties. There are so many possible duties of people involved in the operations process that every aspect could never be completely described. Some of the specific duties are noted in the abstract below which is designed to provide some idea of the variety of assignments possible.

> Supervise production personnel . . . schedule work . . . review output quality . . . process raw materials . . . arrange transportation . . . order materials . . . analyze production processes . . . design production process . . . select transportation carriers . . . route raw materials and finished goods . . . manage warehouse . . . design control systems . . . analyze work methods of workers . . . develop quality standards.

> Improve efficiency of operations . . . conserve energy . . . design equipment . . . develop new products . . . establish safety standards . . . test products . . . design environmental control systems . . . create, design and implement engineering projects . . . create managerial control systems for cost reduction . . . buy production equipment . . . order raw materials.

Requirements. Essential skills for positions in operations management include the ability to work well with others; mechanical aptitude; ability to analyze products, equipment, and people problems; and ability to manage time well.

The person must be self-motivating, have a positive attitude, be imaginative, be assertive, and be a decision maker. The person must be able to take calculated risks based on sound analysis of technical and non-technical data.

Although many employers require technical or engineering academic backgrounds, many other firms look for leadership factors, coupled with educational backgrounds that involve the study of people. Even with applicants for non-technical positions, most employers still look for some mechanical aptitude and quantitative courses in the academic background.

A bachelor's degree in some phase of engineering is preferred, but employers often hire candidates with backgrounds in related fields such as industrial management, production, mathematics, physics, chemistry, and other fields that require the use of quantitative and analytic experiences.

ACTUALLY, BEING A PURCHASING **AGENT** ISN'T LIKE THAT AT ALL, CHUG.

A few non-technical candidates are hired in supervision, scheduling, warehousing, purchasing, and other fields where the technical, analytical thought process is not necessary. Some jobs require a strong people-orientation while others are analytical and project-centered. Some jobs require specific backgrounds in given disciplines of science or engi-neering, and many times people are promoted from blue-collar jobs into these management assignments.

Career Path. An entry-level assignment may be as part of a team project concerned with some aspect or problem area in production or operations design. Upward movement may be within a given professional field rather than into management if individuals in that field do not desire management responsibility.

It is common for individuals to remain plant professionals throughout their careers and to assume more complex projects as their experience warrants. The management option is to move into people supervision, systems or unit management, plant manager, superintendent, etc.

In the long run these people can become divisional manufacturing heads, research and development managers, and corporate vice presidents.

Training. Much of the initial training is on-the-job since candidates usually come in with high levels of technical competence. To maintain this high level of skill in a fast-changing technology, many organizations operate in-house technical centers through which employees are rotated on a regular basis.

These team-oriented projects help people keep current as they learn from each other. There are frequent plant and corporate level seminars. Most firms pay tuition for employees who want to continue their education on a part-time basis.

Salary. Individuals going into the field command earnings that are among the highest of all occupations. As long as the supply-demand trend continues to raise starting rates so rapidly, employees within the firms will continue to enjoy large pay increases.

Annual raises of 10 percent above inflation rates are not uncommon for the top 25 percent. Chief plant technical people and managers in middle management earn substantial salaries.

Entry level people entering this function will find top salaries, challenges, and long-term opportunity. All is not glory, though, because dirt, noise, long hours, shift work, daily change, people problems, production foul-ups, etc. are integral parts of the everyday picture.

Non-technical entrants need to begin early in their careers to prepare themselves technically in order to compete for the higher-level assignments. Top management in certain highly technical industries traditionally come from the engineering and manufacturing ranks.

Engineering

The engineering function built the American enterprise system to the apex of all industrialized nations of the world. Engineers created and developed technology to the fine-tune science that now provides us with one of the highest standards of living in the world.

The initial thrust related technology to the manufacturing process which brought about a highly productive system.

More recently, the same technological innovations applied in the manufacturing process have been extended to increasing the productivity of white-collar workers. There is a growing trend for engineers to be employed in service-providing industries as well as in the product producing industries.

Engineer

Engineering is one of the largest professional occupations. More than one million people practice the profession, and over 50,000 new people enter the field each year. Engineers are employed in all sectors of the economy, so if you desire to work in education, government, private industry, a non-profit group, or your own business, you should be able to find the appropriate work environment.

Most engineers specialize in one of the more than 25 areas recognized by professional societies. Each of the major areas is further subdivided, so specialization is exceedingly common. The largest engineering specialties are discussed briefly in the career profiles that follow, and they are the aerospace, chemical, civil, electrical, industrial, and mechanical engineering fields.

These areas were selected solely on the basis of the number of employment possibilities within them. Employment possibilities which are equally as attractive exist in most of the other engineering disciplines and their subspecialties.

Although by definition, a narrow specialty field limits the number of jobs available, it has the countering effect of balancing the opportunity by permitting one to become a "scarce" expert. Personality style and academic interests help to determine the engineering specialty a person chooses.

The duties and responsibilities of the various types of engineers differ substantially, but there are certain commonalities in other facets of the field. The requirements for entering the profession, career paths, and the general outlook are very similar in the various engineering specialties.

Requirements. A B.S. degree in the special field is required. In many technical fields, employers request a master's degree. For those individuals wishing to work in a research setting or at a university, a doctorate is a common requirement.

Career Path. Most engineers progress through the ranks of assistant, associate, senior, and executive engineer. Common paths involve heavy exposure to production, design, and research applications of technical knowledge.

Many engineers move into management positions at plant, division, and corporate levels later in their careers. For those electing the management route, the typical progression is from supervisor to manager to director. Many continue to advance into the executive ranks of vice president, chief operating officer, and chief executive officer.

Another common career path is for the engineer to move out of the manufacturing or analysis function of the operation and into the marketing function.

Many employers desperately need technically trained personnel to deal with customers and potential customers. This requires individuals who are intimately involved in all technical aspects of a product, service, or process. The work may entail direct selling, a service working relationship, or consulting work.

The upward mobility is nearly identical in the two different career paths. Which route to accept is largely a personal choice. Both routes can be extremely rewarding financially.

Outlook. In nearly all fields, the outlook is very good and superior to that found in most other occupations. Demand occasionally is influenced by short-term fluctuations in the overall economy, but the underlying strength indicates good opportunities for nearly all new entrants into the field of engineering as well as great mobility for experienced engineers.

The growth of complex manufacturing processes and automated work devices and services will keep the demand strong. The supply is expected to remain constant as nearly all seats in the colleges are currently occupied, and no new expansion in the colleges seems evident.

The recent phenomena of college students leaning toward more vocationally oriented courses of study suggests that the seats will remain filled. This relationship should have a stabilizing influence on employment in the engineering profession.

Earnings. The favorable supply and the demand situation should keep earnings growing faster than inflation. Engineers' salaries tend to start at much higher levels than those of most other disciplines. This initial advantage keeps others from catching up rapidly, but over time engineers' earnings as a group do tend to plateau. This plateau is at a rather high level compared to other occupational groups, however.

As a profession, engineers tend to be a highly mobile group; that is, they move to wherever the best opportunities are available. This mobility is among the highest for all occupational groups, and it has served as an explanation for the high earnings and rapid ascent to corporate leadership within the engineering profession.

Specialties. The many specialties in engineering enrich the scope of the opportunities available. The six basic fields whose profiles are presented next form the bulk of the job possibilities normally available, but there are hundreds of spin-offs associated with these six fields and other engineering specialties. The profiles are designed to present only a quick overview of the field and to spark enthusiasm for a more in-depth exploration.

Aerospace Engineers

Aerospace engineers work with all types of commercial and government aircraft and spacecraft including missiles, rockets, satellites, and airplanes. They develop products from the initial planning and design to the final assembly, testing, and maintenance. The actual duties relate to the following:

> Structural design . . . navigational guidance and control . . . instrumentation . . . communication gear . . . power distribution . . . theoretical flight simulation . . . stress analysis . . . design formations . . . field testing . . . manufacturing technology . . . aerodynamics . . . vibration analysis . . . cycle analysis . . . acoustics.

> Product life evaluation . . . performance testing . . . aeromechanics . . . thrust control . . . structural engineering . . . instrumentation testing . . . teardown analysis . . . maintenance and repair-ability . . . manufacturing assembly . . . quality control . . . cost-to-design analysis . . . manufacturing planning and processes . . . production supervision . . . production scheduling . . . space utilization . . . technical marketing . . . service engineering.

Chemical Engineer

Chemical engineers design, develop, and install processes that change the chemical or physical properties of materials to the forms needed in production processes. The chemical engineer turns a chemical process into an economical reality which will advance progress and still retain a reasonable profit for an industrial organization. They work in research, laboratories, and in manufacturing facilities.

Although most chemical engineers work for chemical and petroleum firms, nearly all industrial firms employ them in a variety of capacities. The employment outlook is extremely bright, and advancement continues at a rapid pace. Some of the typical duties are listed here.

HELLO, OPERATOR . . . GET ME THE CHEMICAL ENGINEER OVER AT THE PLANT.

Produce chemicals and chemical products . . . design equipment . . . design plants . . . devise methods of chemical manufacturing . . . operate pilot plants . . . develop new processes . . . improve current processes . . . reconstitute materials . . . participate in environmental control activities . . . analyze compounds . . . estimate costs . . . prepare budget requests . . . lay out facilities . . . install and "debug" production processes.

Design equipment for handling complex specialty or bulk chemical products . . . conduct testing programs . . . evaluate methods . . . supervise production personnel . . . manufacture and transport polymers, liquids, and gases . . . perform laboratory analysis . . . participate in technical marketing . . . carry out basic research.

Civil Engineer

Civil engineers design and supervise the construction of roads, harbors, airports, tunnels, bridges, water supply systems, sewage and waste systems, and buildings. Specific concerns in civil engineering include the following:

Surveying . . . facility layout . . . construction development . . . economical use of materials . . . functional structures . . . load bearing capacities . . . materials strengths and properties . . . water demand analysis . . . sewage capacities . . . distribution and collection systems . . . population trends . . . suburban growth trends . . . urban planning . . . municipal engineering.

Community social needs analysis . . . environmental impact . . . pollution control . . . impact statements and recommendations . . . materials testing . . . bridge design . . . highway construction supervision . . . street location and construction . . . contractor/government liaison . . . design requirements.

Nearly all types of manufacturing and construction firms employ civil engineers in every part of the nation.

Civil engineers work with architects, other engineers, government leaders, and industrial organizations in analyzing, planning, and constructing major projects. They often work outdoors as well as designing and writing elaborate plans and project proposals at their desks.

The employment outlook and earnings potential in civil engineering place it among the best-rated growth occupations for the next decade. The short-term demand for civil engineers can be highly cyclical depending upon construction expenditures, the supply of funds, and the general economy.

Electrical Engineer

Electrical engineers design, develop, and supervise the manufacture of electrical and electronic equipment. These include such things as

UH... TELL THEM TO SEND THE *TOP* FIELD ENGINEER

electric motors, generators, and communication equipment. Electrical engineers also design and operate facilities for generating and distributing electric power.

Electrical engineers generally specialize in electronics, computers, electrical equipment, communications, or power. There are several other subspecialties in which many elect to concentrate their study. Listed below are some of the activity areas in which electrical engineers spend time.

Power engineering . . . generation . . . transmission . . . distribution . . . application . . . manufacturing . . . machine design . . . hydro-electric power . . . design combustion systems . . . pollution analysis . . . nuclear generation . . . radiation . . . radioactive waste disposal . . . solar electrical production . . . collectors . . . power distribution networks . . . cost estimates . . . peak power loads . . . conductors . . . insulation . . . tower design . . . stress . . . power applications . . . illumination . . . light reflection, absorption, and distribution.

Communications engineering . . . information transmittal and delivery . . . audio and visual forms . . . signal channels design . . . amplification . . . transmission apparatus: relays, switches, keys . . . circuit design . . . switching systems.

Electronics engineering . . . computer technology . . . navigational controls . . . calculators . . . radar . . . radio signals . . . miniaturization . . . chips control application.

The common element in the work of all electrical engineers is the movement of the electron—electrical engineers harness its immense power by designing, developing, supervising, and controlling equipment, processes, and materials.

There are numerous opportunities available each year for entry-level and experienced engineers in all parts of the nation.

Industrial Engineer

Industrial engineers determine the most effective ways to use the basic factors of production, personnel, machines, and materials. They are more concerned with people and work organization than most other types of engineers. Industrial engineers may be employed in any type of industry from manufacturing to service industries such as banks, retail organizations, and hospitals.

Industrial engineers are employed in all geographical sectors of the nation, but they are most heavily concentrated in the heavily industrialized areas of the Midwest and the Northeast.

The increasing complexity of industrial operations, the expansion of autodated processes, and the continued growth of the economy will contribute to an increasing

These diverse activities make electrical engineering one of the fastest growing fields of engineering.

//WEB.TIP//

www.ieee.org
Institute of Electrical Engineers
Professional association has over 300,000 members/ database of professionals/ job descriptions with requirements/current news in the profession.

The major goal of industrial engineering is to improve operating efficiency, and this cuts across all industry and occupational lines.

demand for industrial engineers. The needs for scientific management, safety engineering, cost reduction programs, environmental pollution control, and increased productivity foster the continuing demand for industrial engineers.

The actual duties of industrial engineers vary greatly depending upon the industry and size of the work force, but the duties always relate to the goal of saving time, money, and other resources. Most industrial engineers have great latitude on how they approach this goal, but certain techniques are common across industries and work settings. The basic duties may be similar to those listed below.

OH ... AND TELL THEM I THINK I FOUND THE PROBLEM IN THE CENTRAL COMPUTER TERMINAL.

Design data processing systems . . . apply operations research techniques . . . analyze organizational reporting relationships . . . develop management control systems . . . install cost reduction programs . . . design production planning processes . . . coordinate quality control processes.

Organize physical distribution routes . . . conduct surveys . . . analyze plant location potentials . . . plan raw material acquisition arrangements . . . develop wage plans . . . install job evaluation programs . . . evaluate new operations . . . select equipment . . . examine make, buy, or lease alternatives . . . study work flow patterns.

Mechanical Engineer

Mechanical engineers are concerned with the production, transmission, and use of power.

The field of mechanical engineering incorporates:

- The conversion of energy from one form to another
- The design of all types of machines
- The instrumentation and control of all types of physical processes
- The control of human and machine environments

Activities of mechanical engineers include research, consulting, engineering instruction, applied research, design, testing, production, distribution, handling, and sales. Mechanical engineers are usually involved in many facets of these activities over their careers.

Mechanical engineers design and develop machines that produce and use power.

Mechanical engineers apply their scientific-technical backgrounds to problems that need solutions. They draw from such areas as statistics, dynamics, thermodynamics, heat transfer, gas dynamics, gas systems, electrical principles, instrumentation, materials processing, and computer technology. They creatively integrate ideas from each relevant area to solve specific problems.

Research and Developent

Most manufacturing firms maintain research and development functions in order to stay at the forefront of new product technology and invention. A hallmark of American progress has been the strong commitment to regular and sustained research activity. This is especially true of firms in high technology fields such as the chemical, petroleum, electronic, pharmaceutical, and computer industries.

Research activity includes the systematic and intensive exploration designed to expand the horizons of current knowledge in the field. Many times this research is initiated without reference to a specific application, but, of course, the purpose of the overall research activity is to provide for product improvement and the development of new products.

The research may be directed toward creation or modification of equipment, materials, systems, or techniques. Once a possible application is found via the research, development people design, produce, and test the new product or other application. There must be a close tie between marketing, manufacturing, engineering, and finance if the production process is to be utilized to its fullest.

Although the research and development function is best characterized by discussing its experimental activities, it nonetheless must eventually serve as a profit-producing center. The work must, therefore, be somewhat more application-oriented than that done by scientists in government and university research settings.

Once major development plans are set, the project is usually turned over to the engineering and manufacturing staffs if the marketing and finance functions see a profitable market.

Most individuals going into the research and development function hold advanced degrees in very specialized fields. Doctorate and post-doctorate degreed individuals find employment in research, but some master degreed people may be employed in the development phase.

Most research and development activity in industry is centralized and reports to top executive levels. Top management often closely supervises expenditures and encourages applied product, process, and new technology development in addition to new concept research.

Most firms maintain pilot test facilities, laboratories, professional service units, technical libraries, and appropriate offices. The corporate legal staff works closely with this unit in patent work.

The scientific occupations most frequently found in research and development include geologists, geophysicists, meteorologists, oceanographers, biochemists, astronomers, chemists, food scientists, and petroleum scientists. Most of these scientists specialize at great depth within their fields of study and their work is largely dependent on their specialty, the type of work, and any geographical considerations related to their occupation.

OKAY, OKAY, I'LL CHECK IT OUT... BUT WHO KEEPS THROWING A WRENCH INTO THINGS?

The number of job possibilities in these specialized fields is very low because of the very narrow specialization. Growth is expected to keep up or move faster than that of most other occupations. Most job seekers must be extremely flexible as to geographical location. The likelihood of multiple offers is uncommon except for established, highly recognized scientists.

NO, HE'S NOT A MAD SCIENTIST... JUST AN ANGRY ONE.

The protege concept is widely recognized as a channel for employment.

Most firms have several levels of professional scientific personnel grades. Typical job titles are:

- Scientist
- Research scientist
- Senior research scientist
- Research associate
- Principal research associate

Most titles carry the designation of the research *discipline* such as biochemist, chemist, physicist, geologist, etc.

Job responsibilities range from functioning as a project team member to the complete handling of projects that require more in-depth knowledge and are by nature more complex and challenging. Some scientists work as individualists and others function as group leaders.

Manager positions almost always exist in the research environment for people who have been on the staff for some time as technical persons. A common practice is to move into a managerial position after some years rather than opting to stay in a scientific role indefinitely.

The reward structure is extremely good for those taking either the scientist or managerial route. A few people also elect to leave the research and development environment for positions in manufacturing and marketing. A few even move into top executive ranks after many years of experience with a given organization.

I'VE DECIDED TO FORGET ABOUT A BETTER MOUSETRAP. I'M WORKING ON AN INFERIOR MOUSE.

Administration

8

What jobs using management skills are available?

Many technical and non-technical employees in all types of organizations aspire to management assignments as they progress in their careers. For very valid reasons few people start in management assignments, but through hard work and dedication those who desire positions in management can attain them.

In some industries and organizations, a few administrative-type jobs exist that do not have a close relationship with any functional management field. These positions are most often at the firms' headquarters and involve paper-processing rather than people-management. Employees' upward mobility is greatly advanced by moving to branches, plants, or other units that have a more direct line type of responsibility.

TYPICAL HUMAN RESOURCE POSITIONS

Vice President of Human Resources
Chief Human Relations Officer
Labor Relations Executive
Compensation/Benefits Executive
Labor Relations Director
Director of Personnel Services
Staffing Director

Organizational Development Manager
Compensation Manager
Benefit Manager
Safety Manager
Personnel Manager
College Relations Manager

Affirmative Action Manager
Recruitment/Employment Manager
Employment Interviewer
Training Coordinator
Compensation Analyst
Job Analyst
Safety Inspector

Figure 8.1

In most organizations, there are three functions that do not have counterparts in the marketing, finance, operations, engineering, and research areas. These three functions are:

- Personnel
- Public relations
- Legal staff

A few organizations also have very general management training programs that cross functional lines, and these are also explored in this section.

Human Resource Management

Personnel professionals are responsible for labor relations, employment, training, compensation, benefits, and personnel services. Personnel departments are rapidly becoming highly specialized, and a variety of experts are now being employed in each department.

Many organizations have changed the name of their department from personnel to human resources.

Legislation regarding labor relations, wage and hours, equal employment, safety regulation compliance, environmental health concerns, etc. has forced personnel management to become a much more technical area than it once was.

Many personnel offices have become a major paper-processing part of every organization, in contrast to its former emphasis on working with people. There is still a considerable amount of human interaction in these personnel offices, but much of the work carried out there is more related to meeting legal and technical requirements than it is with managing people.

The people managing process is now more the responsibility of managers in the finance, marketing, operations, engineering, and research functions.

More employers are seeing the need to bring highly trained personnel into their organizations. The idea of transferring a promising manager working in another function into human resource management for a two- or three-year broadening experience is also a viable option. There is a trend toward developing human resource specialists who want to remain in the human resource function throughout their careers.

The technical nature of modern human resources management requires organizations to hire people who are trained in labor relations or personnel management.

Even though the image of the HRD has improved greatly during the past decade, the number of people needed in the function is still quite small relative to the total number of employees an organization hires. There may be only one HR expert for several hundred other employees.

The Human Resources Department (HRD) has replaced the old Personnel Department in many organizations.

SAY, CLIFF, WHY DID YOU EVER GO INTO PERSONNEL, ANYWAY?
BECAUSE I LOVE TO WORK WITH PEOPLE.

HI! AM I (BELCH) TOO LATE FOR MY INTERVIEW?

HOWEVER THERE ARE SOME I LOVE WORKING WITH MORE THAN OTHERS.

Because HR related courses are some of the most popular courses on college campuses, there are many more qualified people with in-depth training in the field than there are jobs available. Many employers prefer to move people into personnel who have some supervisory experience in other functions.

The personnel function goes by many different names in various firms. It is known as human resource management, employee relations, industrial relations, and the most widely used term: personnel management. Once the size of a firm grows to over 100 employees, an independent personnel function is usually necessary.

Very large organizations may have several hundred people employed in the function with many sub-function specialists. Smaller organizations may have just one or two managers who wear many different hats. The major specialty areas are described below.

Employment.   The employment department is responsible for the recruitment of personnel for factory, office, sales, technical, and professional positions. They analyze jobs, prepare job descriptions and job specifications, administer tests, interview applicants, and refer selected applicants to specific openings.

They seldom do the actual hiring, because this is usually the responsibility of department managers. They often do the initial screen.

They also assist department managers in appraisal procedures for employees and executives. They are involved in transfers, promotions, terminations, layoffs, and exit interviews.

The employment function is the typical entry-level position for college graduates in human resources. Entering candidates should be familiar with each of these operations and should have some course work in industrial relations, labor relations, industrial psychology, and labor economics.

The duties of an employment manager or assistant might include the following:

> Hiring of hourly workers . . . screening of salaried personnel . . .
> coordinating college recruiting . . . writing classified ads . . . analyzing
> employment tests . . . conducting performance reviews . . . assisting
> in recommendations for reviews, promotions, and terminations.

Training.   Training departments orient new employees into the organization and provide training for present employees that will improve their skills. They are usually involved in supervisory training, executive development, presentation of visual aids, maintaining the company library, developing suggestion systems, preparing training manuals, and providing appropriate education for employees.

Training specialists may develop curriculum materials and teach courses in general areas, but in most cases they simply set the stage by bringing in experts (from within or external to the firm) to instruct employees in technical areas related to their jobs.

Few organizations maintain a resident faculty as a college would. *A training department serves as a catalyst; it brings individuals needing training and those capable of providing training together.* Training is a coordinating and liaison function in most organizations.

Compensation.   The function of the wage and salary administration department is to plan and administer an equitable wage and salary scale. *Consultation with managers determines the compensation policies which are then administered in compliance with various laws and regulations.*

This department makes periodic reports and conducts wage surveys. It is responsible for developing wage systems and supplemental compensation plans for new employees as well as current employees.

TRAINING PROFESSIONALS

The Training and Development Department of most large organizations that have 100 or more employees at a given site usually employs a staff member to assist with training activities. The American Society for Training and Development (ASTD) estimates that their members teach about 20 million courses each year. Staff professionals most frequently report to the Human Resources Department but can report to other line managers as well.

Nearly all professionals hold at least a bachelor degree, and the most favored majors include business, psychology, and education. A high percentage hold master's and some even doctor's degrees.

A trainer is not always the teacher. They are responsible for helping organize materials, recruit instructors, assist top management in instruction (both content and techniques), set up facilities, prepare audio and visual teaching aids, invite participants, arrange travel, and even assist in providing accommodations.

Sometimes the trainer is the instructor who must deliver a pre-defined body of knowledge to a group of people who are required by job descriptions to thoroughly know every detail of the material delivered. A logical extension of duties is the follow-up evaluation to insure that the material was in fact learned.

Some of the specific duties of the training profession might include the following:

- conduct workshops and seminars
- teach employees to use, repair, or sell equipment
- teach employees to operate complex equipment
- teach employees how to manage and lead
- design and write course modules
- readapt commercial programs to unique situations
- instruct on decision-making techniques and planning
- facilitate communications in learning groups
- prepare sophisticated teaching aids via computers
- prepare teaching aids, such as videotapes and slides
- supervise and train other professionals
- consult with senior technical and managerial staff on materials
- teach others how to deliver complex materials
- organize and manage large conventions and conferences
- create and design exhibits and learning models
- librarian for existing training programs
- maintain and set up teaching equipment, such as computers

There are many facets of this interesting career. Although the assignment only occasionally leads into "top management" positions, it offers an enjoyable career for the right person. The salaries are comparable to teachers and professors. You will not likely get rich in this occupation, but the pay is adequate and the job rewards intrinsically satisfying.

The competition to seek an entry-level position in this field is keen so many professionals start at other jobs in the organization and request a transfer to this area later.

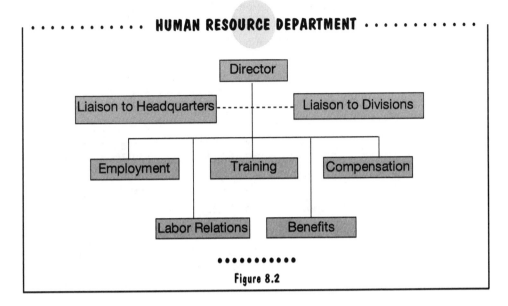

HUMAN RESOURCE DEPARTMENT

Director

Liaison to Headquarters ---------------- Liaison to Divisions

Employment   Training   Compensation

Labor Relations   Benefits

Figure 8.2

Compensation experts conduct wage surveys, maintain employment compensation records, devise complex pay plans for executives, and basically keep the organization competitive.

They manage elaborate wage and salary schedules and classification systems to insure fair and equitable treatment for all classes of employees. This activity usually requires some sophisticated advanced courses in compensation alternatives and knowledge of how laws are administered.

Benefits.   The benefits and services department administers the company insurance, disability, pension, and retirement programs, as well as a variety of other services for employees. It reviews requests for leaves, vacations, unemployment insurance, and severance pay.

Specialists in this field must understand social security regulations, administer fair vacation plans, and design legal, medical, and insurance policies. They administer pension plans in accordance with the most recent legislation.

Specialists may be involved in designing and purchasing group medical and life insurance plans for thousands of employees. They must be aware of the tax implications of the various benefit plans proposed and adopted and be able to explain in written form the tax ramifications to employees.

Labor Relations.   A complex set of laws, court decisions, and formal National Labor Relations Board rulings govern the relationship between management and labor. Labor relations people are experts on labor history and laws and on the interpretation of labor laws.

An elaborate system of management and labor relations has developed in our society over several decades, and over 20 million workers are now members of labor organizations.

Labor relations experts negotiate contracts periodically and then must live with the contracted rules and regulations until the next bargaining session.

Contract administration and interpretation constitute a form of private judicial arrangements in our labor force which requires a sound understanding of what can and cannot be done in the work environment.

Labor experts are involved in all phases of settling labor disputes which can arise daily. Most contracts spell out detailed grievance procedures to which both sides must adhere. The final step is arbitration and it often requires people with legal training.

Duties of Human Resources Manager. The various duties in the human resources function require far more than the ability to deal with people. Satisfactory performance requires a working knowledge of sophisticated techniques, methods, laws, and compliance regulations.

A large organization may have over a hundred different job descriptions for people employed in the personnel function. Some of these duties are summarized in the abstract below.

> Direct personnel programs . . . administer policies . . . set personnel objectives . . . interview salaried and hourly candidates . . . refer qualified candidates to department managers . . . write classified ads . . . travel to recruit people . . . develop recruiting itinerary . . . prepare manpower plan . . . conduct wage and salary surveys.

> Maintain employment records . . . compile statistics . . . devise complex pay structures . . . administer benefit programs . . . prepare payroll reports . . . know government wage regulations . . . know social security laws . . . handle employer grievances . . . participate in labor negotiations.

> Design and give orientation programs to new employees . . . administer job classification system . . . write job descriptions . . . design job performance evaluation systems . . . design forms . . . manage government compliance reviews.

Requirements. Most organizations require a bachelor's degree for entry into human resources, but some experienced people may move into HR from other departments of the organization. Many employers require master degrees in human resources.

Because complex government laws and regulations are creating a deep structure of specialists, most people will need some special training even after becoming employed with the organization. Hiring preferences are usually for those who are best trained and those with related human resource work experience.

Specific course work in industrial relations, labor relations, labor law, industrial psychology, HR management, employment, compensation, organizational development, and related areas greatly enhances your chances of finding employment in the field.

Some firms still hire generalists, but the trend is toward hiring specialists. You often must start as a specialist and work toward a career as a generalist later in your career.

Career Path. The entry-level job is usually as a personnel assistant or trainee. The first move may be to a position as an assistant department manager in one of the basic functions from which functional managers are selected. Many firms rotate personnel between functional fields, but the increasing complexity of OSHA, ERISA, EEO, FLSA, etc. is forcing some specialization.

Some firms use the human resource department as a 12- to 30-month temporary, rotational assignment for line managers.

Most training is on-the-job, supplemented by training seminars sponsored by professional associations. The upward mobility route is usually that of staying within the HR function and moving into executive status there.

Outlook. The number of candidates needed annually is very low. The supply of candidates greatly exceeds the demand; however, many of those applying do not have the necessary credentials.

Because of the heavy walk-in and write-in applicant traffic, very few employers actively advertise and recruit candidates even when an opening exists. The openings are often filled internally or through professional associations.

Because of this supply and demand situation, starting salaries in HR are below average, and the salary progression is often slower than in more direct line management functions. The earnings are modest but more than adequate to maintain an excellent standard of living. Most experts enjoy the type of work they do and are willing to accept lower levels of compensation as a result.

Candidates trained in human resources or labor relations have the best shots at available jobs.

Public Relations

Public relations employees build and maintain positive images for employers. Most public relations workers are employed by manufacturing firms, public utilities, trade and professional associations, labor unions, and governmental agencies. Others are employed by consulting firms and provide public relations services to clients for fees.

Duties.   Public relations personnel provide information to newspapers, magazines, radio, television, and other channels of communication. They also arrange speaking engagements and often write speeches for high-level officials. Much of their writing relates to news releases about promotions, retirements, and financial reports.

Many public relations people who are hired to work in the organization are writers or copywriters who have had experience with newspapers, magazines, or other communications media prior to joining the organization.

Beginners often maintain files of materials about company activities, scan newspapers and magazines for pertinent articles, and assemble information for speeches and pamphlets. As they progress, they get more difficult assignments such as writing press releases, speeches, and articles for publications. Some organizations publish internal publications.

Usually the promotion path is within the public relations function, although employees occasionally accept opportunities in marketing after gaining experience in public relations.

In addition to public relations departments within business and public service organizations, a number of other employers hire people with writing skills. Daily and weekly newspapers hire many of the people graduating from college with experience in reporting.

Newspaper reporters gather information on current events and use this to write stories for publication. Their reporting assignments can lead to jobs as editors.

Many newspapers require bachelor's degrees in journalism, although many of them will consider English majors or majors involving an extensive amount of writing experience.

//WEB.TIP//

www.shrm.org
Society for Human Resource Management
Job descriptions in HR/job listings, classifieds/profession materials to explore.

MY DAD NEVER FORGETS HE'S IN PUBLIC RELATIONS.

Professional courses in reporting, copywriting, editing, feature writing, and technical writing would be very worthwhile for persons aspiring to careers in newspaper work.

Some organizations hire technical writers. The technical writer organizes, writes, and edits material about science and technology in a form which is useful to those who need to use it.

Government agencies and business firms often must take some of their research and put it into terms that the average layman or business executive can read and understand. For those graduates who have degrees in scientific areas and the ability to write well, this is an avenue to consider.

Other sources of job leads for writers are weekly and monthly magazines and publishing companies. Although magazines often obtain their material from freelance writers, much of it has to be edited before it gets into print. Publishing firms hire writers to edit books and solicit new manuscripts for publication.

Requirements.   Many people joining public relations departments or public relations firms hold college degrees with majors in English, journalism, mass communications, telecommunications, or public relations. Sophisticated typing, word processing, and graphic arts skills are also required by many employers. Web experience is also helpful.

Individuals should have a measure of creative ability as well as the ability to express thoughts clearly and simply in speaking and writing. Employers always like to see some previous work experience in journalism or a related field, so it is advantageous for a candidate to have acquired some writing experience by working part-time.

Public relations jobs invariably require outstanding writing skills. Candidates who have majored in journalism, English, or radio and television will need a basic understanding of business and technical terms, but this should be easy for them to pick up. Whether they are writing copy, designing layouts, preparing news releases, or editing house organs or other internal publications, literary expertise is a major necessity.

Outlook.   There are many more applications for jobs than there are opportunities, but graduates having experience and top grades should apply. Public relations firms and public relations departments within businesses and government agencies do not usually advertise or recruit personnel openly, so special effort is required for finding an appropriate position.

Good writing skills are very valuable in many different occupations. If you have them, it is well for you to combine them with another functional field in management or an occupation that has more favorable employment prospects.

Legal Staff

The legal staff is almost always a very small department. Attorneys in the legal department deal with the organization's patent protections, law suits, real estate, tax considerations, labor contracts, and other legal concerns. Many firms do not have this function in house because they prefer to hire an external (often prestigious) law firm to handle problems on a retaining or as-needed basis.

Employment in this function is quite limited and required a law degree and admission to the bar. Most organizations hire experienced lawyers when they decide to add a person to their legal staff. Legal staff members are often recruited from the firm the organization uses for legal matters.

Given the keen job market, you must contact firms directly.

164   *Chapter 8*

Management Training

Many firms offer well-structured management training programs. The programs teach you about the basic management functions.

A common practice is to rotate new employees through several different management-track assignments to give them an overview of the organization. Management trainees wander around through various assignments learning and growing. This concept is used by smaller employers.

The turnover in management training programs tends to be excessive. As colleges provide more technical and vocationally trained people, the need for the program is declining.

The dissatisfaction of people in the programs and the increasing availability of candidates trained in functional areas forced most employers to abandon the concept.

Several industries have found the rotational approach to be very satisfactory. Management training programs are common in the industries of transportation, insurance, retailing, and some government organizations.

Most of these programs are short-term, lasting six to twelve months. Trainees tend to be moved into functional assignments as soon as possible.

For individuals who are undecided about their careers, these programs may be ideal. The number of them is limited, so it takes a great deal of searching to locate one. Many firms also call training programs in the marketing and sales function management training programs.

International Careers

The world has truly become a global inter-related economic powerhouse which significantly impacts careers. The Internet technology facilitates worldwide employment. For example, foreign students studying in the USA can find employment in their home region via an Internet-assisted job search.

The marketplace is indeed global. Yet, employment still tends to remain local. ABB's slogan: "Think globally, act locally," operates in the career arena also. There is an important management segment, even if currently small, that moves their career around the world as duty calls, especially if you work for a global enterprise.

Assignments. It is not unusual for these global enterprises to internally source experts for global assignment in non-home countries. Governments often place "red tape" in the way of this trend to protect local employment. A growing employment segment tends to build a global executive workforce. They often do this with short-term, 6–18 months, non-home country assignments.

You may be interested in these development rotations. You usually start in your home country which maintains the training and payroll commitment. After you gain 3–5 years' experience, language capabilities, and have a functional expertise like marketing, engineering, computer science, finance, etc., ask for the developmental transfer. These often put you in the "fast-track" career path within your organization.

Whether you are a USA citizen or Foreign National, the web can facilitate your goals. The information on specific jobs in specific countries is printed on the web. An employment/international/your specialty/search via a search engine like YAHOO can generate ideas.

Due to legalities, the job search most often starts in your home country and, once employed in a global concern, the international HR specialists can assist in facilitating your visa requirements. You often need the leverage of an employer to get the necessary work permits. You can't do it alone.

//WEB.TIP//

www.amanet.org
American Management Association
World's largest membership based management training organization/conferences, seminars, and events to attend/management resources/classifieds.

//WEB.TIP//

ciber.bus.msu.edu
MSU-CIBER
Michigan State U. international business resources/economic outlook/contacts/research.

//WEB.TIP//

www.ins.usdoj.gov
U.S. Immigration and Naturalization Service
Responsible for visas and work permits/forms/regulations/links.

Managing your own business encompasses marketing, finance, operations, and administration.

Work Permits. Most governments will not allow a foreign national to replace a locally qualified applicant so your employer must run the political gamut to prove your unique talents cannot be found locally. It is tough to play these politics in some countries but it is often done. That is why you need the clout (power) of a well-known employer, an expertise, applicable experience, and a burning desire from yourself and your employer to make the "global manager" idea work. Some industries carry more influence than others.

Regardless of your nationality, the wisest and most successful approach is initial employment in your home country in a functional specialty. You also need to know the visa laws. Many international websites can give you the knowledge you need to be successful. College recruiting and other employment methods are not nearly as productive as a web-based employment search which can focus your unique background to the direct international employment decision makers.

FRANCHISING FOR YOU

Every week in the Classified Ad Section of *USA Today* and *The Wall Street Journal* scores of franchising ads appear: "Be Your Own Boss," "Chance of a Lifetime." For an increasing number of entrepreneurial-minded individuals, franchising can be the ticket to a job and to prosperity.

The evidence clearly supports that franchising vastly increases the likelihood of success for the small business person. A franchise offers both security and flexibility not possible with other business ventures. The franchiser system has usually been tested in several markets, and the need for the product or service thoroughly researched and proven by the real marketplace.

The franchise formula is quite simple. A business (the franchisor) with an innovative product, service, or business concept offers exclusive territories to individuals (the franchisee). The franchisee invests an up-front fee ($15,000 to $500,000) and agrees to pay a monthly royalty (5 to 10 percent of gross sales). In return, the franchisor agrees to provide product, systems, training, support services, financial counseling, etc., but most important, a regional or national advertising and marketing effort.

About one third of all retail sales dollars in the U.S. are made through a franchised operation. The success of McDonald's, Holiday Inn, Dunkin Donuts, Roto-Rooter, Midas Muffler, and many, many others are legend. The oil, automobile, soft drink, and hospitality industries made this concept work well in its infancy.

Where is the next McDonald's? The American dream is real, and the potential for owning a successful franchise is a possibility for individuals with a penchant for hard work, commitment, management skills, and some start-up capital. Most major franchisors also want to see some experience but not necessarily in the same industry. The areas below offer great potential for franchising success.

- Cleaning services
- Copy services
- Fast food
- Hospitality
- Travel

- Petroleum products
- Accounting services
- Tax services
- Private communications
- Computer support

Like other businesses, the older, well-established franchises tend to be highly successful and more expensive to purchase. The newer ones tend to be smaller, less stable, but with a great idea and potential to grow. The franchise fee tends to be much less. The magical mix of product, service, distribution channel, marketing, and price creates a winning franchise system. Success also requires time to test the "format" and "quality people" to make the concept work well. Since this format cannot be trademarked, franchises are not without competition. The best franchises continually look over their shoulder to see who is coming up fast.

The success of franchising is clear. The trade association of franchisors, The International Franchise Association (IFA), claims that the annual failure rate is under 4 percent compared to a 13 percent rate for all new business. The usual statistic cited is that two thirds of all new businesses fail within five years. Most franchisors have a heavy stake in wanting to avoid failures since this determines their ability to gain more franchisees and thus grow in terms of sales and profits.

The IFA sponsors several trade shows each year where franchisors and potential franchisees can get together. You can get information on the location by writing to IFA, 1350 New York Avenue, NW, Washington D.C. 20005.

If you feel that franchising is a topic that you want to investigate further, one of the best sources of further information is *Franchise Opportunities Handbook.* You can obtain this in most libraries and by writing the Superintendent of Documents, U.S. Government Printing Office, Washington, D.C. 20402.

Few franchisors are interested in fresh, inexperienced persons, as well as older individuals. They prefer that you work two to five years (retailing and sales are great training), save some capital, and then contact them for information. Yet for the right person, they may place you with a current franchisee operation with the understanding that later you can go out on your own.

Franchising is not for everyone. It means months and years of very hard work including long hours. Not everyone becomes a millionaire, but the financial rewards usually are greater than that you receive by working for someone else. Aside from the money, the most consistent response from the franchisee you hear is that, "I enjoy being my own boss."

Career Decision Making:

Assessment – Exploration – Goals

Career management consists of decisions made over time that influence the direction of your work life. Each decision must be made independently of one another. You build each new decision on the base of earlier decisions.

What most people do not do is lay out a plan for future decisions that ties all decisions together.

Frequent, albeit small decisions get you involved in the mechanics of career planning.

Career Planning

Your goal is to learn how to manage your career as opposed to letting fate and fortune determine your destiny. The career management process begins with career planning. How do you tie together each career decision you make over time?

Self-Assessment

Career planning is a process that integrates an analysis of self with an analysis of the world of work. An in-depth investigation of the self develops a very high level of personal awareness about values, interests, personal qualities, and your skill attainment.

You have a broad overview of the world of work. It is composed of specific assignments and tasks which operate together to achieve stated organizational objectives.

Knowing yourself is important in your career decision making.

Decision Making

How do you develop objectives through a decision-making process? Before you begin the job search process you must establish specific personal career objectives. Not to do so leaves you wandering aimlessly searching for something without knowing what you are seeking.

I'VE HAD A LOT OF LUCK WITH MY CAREER... I'VE ALWAYS JUST FALLEN INTO SOMETHING.

169

Career decision making requires development of your career options.

Decision making is developing a set of alternatives and then evaluating the alternatives against a predetermined set of criteria. Your criteria are found in your self-assessment.

Career exploration is collecting information about careers of interest to you. An overview of management and how organizations function is critical to the investigation process. An awareness of organizations gives you the framework in which you must conduct your exploring.

A "management level" position, but not necessarily a supervisory career, is most likely your goal whether you are technically trained or liberally educated. This requires you to understand the management process, industry groups, occupational classifications, functional organization structure, and the level of responsibility concepts.

You must overlay your self-assessment on that framework and, through a pattern of logical investigation, discover which fields of career interest best suit you.

Career Profiles

Can you prepare a career profile for your special area of interest? A career profile is a fairly extensive summary of all information you collect about the career field of special interest to you.

In actual practice, depending upon your current level of job specification and responsibility level, you may prepare *several* different career profiles.

A career profile is the first step in exploring your career options.

A later analysis of these profiles will give you a wealth of information consolidated in one place for you to review in specifying which career field you feel is best suited to your self-assessment.

Figure 9.1 gives a brief description of the content that belongs in a career profile. The career profile gives various job titles, duties, requirements, career paths, training normally received on the job, earnings, the employment outlook, and any points that are peculiar to the career field.

Career profiles need to be developed within an organizational framework and functional field designations.

Where do you see your career profile resting within the organizational framework?

Career profiles fit somewhere within the organizational structure. Career profiles are not complete analyses, but they do offer ideas and suggestions that will cause you to investigate your profile in much greater depth as you get closer to the job interview.

Entry-Level Job Title(s): One-word or two-word descriptors.

Nature of the Work: Duties . . . activities . . . physical requirements . . . tools used . . . psychological demands . . . typical work period (hour/day/week/month) . . . structure and pattern of tasks . . . scope of responsibility and authority.

Working Conditions: Physical layout of environment . . . length of work periods . . . pressure level indoors/outdoors . . . nature of supervision . . . number of colleagues . . . team/individual work . . . geographic location . . . climate.

Qualifications: Education . . . experience . . . skills . . . values/interests/personality.

- **Education:** Level of general education . . . degrees . . . major subject areas . . . special education and seminars . . . technical training . . . honors . . . grade standards . . . on-the-job training . . . dates of education . . . special licensing requirements.

- **Experience:** Months of full-time work . . . nature of full-time work . . . internship training . . . related part-time work . . . apprentice experience . . . degree of relatedness of work.

- **Skills:** Equipment operation . . . selling abilities . . . interpersonal skills . . . physical skills . . . speaking . . . writing . . . numbers . . . accounting programming . . . research . . . dexterity . . . mechanics . . . scientific . . . organizing . . . planning . . . motivating . . . supervision . . . goal setting . . . decision making.

Values/Interests/Personality: Personality traits most frequently required . . . attitudes . . . variables found in people in the career . . . likes and dislikes.

Advancement: Initial assignment . . . mid-career job titles . . . high-level assignments . . . time between promotions . . . promotion criteria . . . examinations or licensing requirements for advancement . . . common indirect promotion ladders . . . horizontal mobility . . . related career fields . . . probable additional education required for mobility . . . geographical limitations on advancement mobility.

Career Demographics: Age of career incumbents . . . number in the field . . . geographic distribution . . . number in work units . . . net annual additions/deletions to the field.

Earnings: Starting rates . . . average annual increases . . . local compensation market . . . average promotion salary increases . . . overtime . . . bonuses . . . allowances . . . expenses . . . monetary benefits . . . life insurance . . . medical insurance . . . vacation . . . sick leave . . . retirement plan.

Non-Economic Benefits: Psychological income . . . job satisfaction . . . lifestyle . . . social mobility . . . advanced training . . . ease of mobility.

Disadvantages: Seasonal . . . irregular hours . . . frequent overtime . . . night work . . . hazards . . . location . . . environmental factors . . . pay . . . growth . . . limited advancement . . . overcrowded field.

Outlook: Present and future demand . . . need for career . . . stability during recessions . . . automation impact . . . geographic mobility . . . career mobility.

• • • • • • • • • • •

Figure 9.1

Exploration

You can systematically explore several career alternatives by accumulating specific career information on each alternative.

Through various "career exploration projects" you should conduct an in-depth study of a particular career field including specific employers. You should gather information through library research, web surfing, reading, and interviewing others.

ACCORDING TO THE COMPUTER, WE'RE BOTH PERFECTLY QUALIFIED TO MARRY RICH TYCOONS.

Career Objectives

You may initially investigate one field in great depth or conduct a superficial overview at first to ascertain which field you wish to explore in greater depth.

After you have completed the in-depth analysis you must correlate, compare, and relate your self-assessment with your findings. This integration of the self-assessment and the career field is critical to career goal setting.

Which career options should you be exploring?

The end product of this analysis is a career profile which can be translated into a specific career objective statement suitable for a resume, cover letter, or interview discussion. As the job search focuses in on industries, employers, and specific jobs, the career objective statement becomes more clarified and job-specific.

As this required crystallization occurs in your job search, your long-term goals must be kept intact so they can bloom again from the specific seed you are planting.

Integration

The integration of self and career demands specification of a related job at a level appropriate for your background. As you progress in the job, you should be able to progress on a path that leads to your long-term career goal and, thus, life satisfaction.

This does not imply that whatever job you accept must be the "perfect" match. You make certain compromises along the decision path. The job will get you started on a track that leads to where you eventually want to be.

Exploration Purposes

The purpose of completing an exploration project is to develop a very high level of career awareness about a given position, career field, industry, or even a specific employer. This career awareness is the only valid way to relate your self-awareness to your potential happiness in a chosen job and career field.

A second major purpose of this exploration is that you will learn how to approach the exploration process. The projects provide a practical working definition of career exploration.

You will learn a "*methodology*" of investigation about a single career field that will speed up projects in the future as you investigate additional career alternatives for yourself.

Before you select a single project to investigate, read through several of the projects in order to get an idea of what type of information you need to collect. Although it is not necessary to complete more than one project, it is important that you gain an understanding of how to "approach" the career exploration process.

It is recommended that you completely write out at least one project in order to obtain a feel for the commitment that a good investigation requires. This is serious business, and expending superficial efforts may be more damaging than not starting the project at all.

After reading the proposed project descriptions, you may discover that none of the projects fit your specific needs. Your area of career interest may not even be listed, so you may have to create your own project.

These particular projects will give you a feel for the depth of analysis and content which is needed in the career exploration.

The topic choices are almost limitless. Each suggested project is intended to take several hours of library and/or web researching and interviewing for information. To be effective, you must generate new information and then organize it in a manner that will be useful later as you approach the job search process.

The rest of this section describes several extensive career action projects. Read through each of them before you decide which one, if any, you wish to complete.

The purpose of your career exploration is to help you write a definitive career objective statement for your resume.

Exploration Projects

Career Profile

The purpose of this project is to prepare an in-depth analysis of the occupation for which you feel you are best qualified. It assures that you have identified one career field that initially appears to best match your values, interest, personal qualities, and skills.

Review at least two occupation related websites and two thorough articles

HONEST, OFFICER, I WAS JUST MAKING A THOROUGH EXPLORATION OF THE CAREER OPPORTUNITIES IN THE CAR RACING BUSINESS.

which describe the occupation. Identify the level of responsibility at which you would be most likely to seek employment.

Interview at least two people in the occupation at the level of responsibility you feel your background matches best. Based upon the information you gained through your review and your general knowledge, formulate a series of at least twenty questions to ask your interviewees. Record their responses later.

Contrast and compare the information obtained via the web and publications with that obtained from your interviews. Why do they differ?

Career Action Project. *Based upon the information obtained from all activities, prepare a career profile.* Follow the format and content suggested in Figure 9.1. Your career profile should be three to five single-spaced, typewritten pages when complete.

Compare your career profile to your resume.

Using your career profile, relate the information to your credentials, qualifications, and background, category by category.

Develop a convincing presentation on how your credentials and interests relate to the career profile. If and where different, describe what future education or work experience will bring the two into closer harmony. This presentation needs to be about two single-spaced, typewritten pages to complement the "Career Profile."

Management Training

Many career-undecided people who have done only minimal amounts of career exploration often say they are seeking management training programs. Indeed, most jobs, regardless of their functional field, do eventually lead into management.

This project is designed for the undecided person who is ready to explore the various assignments that lead into management.

Define management. Is it a noun or verb? Is management an art or a science? Scan an introduction to a management principles textbook to get a handle on these points. Show how the formal definition differs from your working definition of management. What is the functional difference between the following job titles: "general manager," "department manager," and "executive vice president"?

Pick an organization in business, a unit of government, or a quasi-public institution such as a hospital or university. Using the organization chart of the institution, describe all of the basic management functions that must be accomplished on a regular basis. List some of the position titles normally associated with the department or basic management function.

//WEB.TIP//

www.inc.com
Inc.Online
Inc. magazine articles/interactive worksheets/resource database/forum links to resources/city maps.

Which of these positions are normally regarded as entry positions and which require experience? Organization charts are usually available in annual reports and sometimes in recruiting brochures. If you are unable to locate them in these sources, you will need to approach a specific employer for the chart.

Review an employment brochure, website, or interview executives of two organizations in which you have an interest. Describe in as much detail as possible the format of their management career path programs.

Identify the qualifications needed to start in their programs. How long does it take to move into a management position? When you leave the initial assignment, do you immediately become a manager? When do you know you are in management and not just in one of the assignments leading to a management position?

The Occupational Outlook for College Graduates lists many occupations requiring college degrees. The OOC is on several websites. Select any three occupations for which you are qualified and give a brief summary of the qualifications required for entering the field.

Assume that you are going to interview for one of these jobs. Using the phone book's *yellow pages*, various websites, and other sources, make a list of ten potential employers. First, assume that you are the recruiter for the position and that you must interview twenty applicants for it. As recruiter, make a list of the ten most important things you will be looking for during each interview.

Second, evaluate yourself using the ten most important items. Give both positives and negatives. This should be similar to your actual interview presentation. Last, return to the role of recruiter and write up an "Interview Report." Play the recruiter's role and write a formal memo recommending yourself for further interviews to your hypothetical boss, and support it with documentation from the "Interview Report." Chapter 18 includes several examples of reports which many employers use.

Management Action Project. *Write a two or three page management-level job description for the position that you will be seeking in one of the organizations that you identified. Use the "Career Profile" as your guide.*

Using two of the evaluation forms used by recruiters (copied from this book), evaluate yourself for the position. Be as verbose in your evaluation as possible, drawing upon the results of your hypothetical interview and your resume. *Use two different evaluation forms to give yourself two different evaluation perspectives.*

When you finish, write one page summarizing your qualifications for the management position which is exactly the job of a recruiter.

Sales Management

Each year, over 100,000 openings are available in professional sales. The high salaries, travel, expense accounts, automobiles, and job autonomy offered by many of these positions are attractive benefits. The purpose of this project is to provide an understanding of the field of professional sales.

There are at least four sales occupations described in the *Occupational Outlook for College Graduates*. Read and summarize these descriptions. Select two firms that employ sales representatives and read and summarize their recruiting brochures and employment websites, and formally interview two different sales managers. Contrast what the government publication says about the jobs with what the employers say.

In some people's minds, the professional sales occupation has low job status and prestige but high pay and good lifestyle. Is this characterization correct? Why do you think it is so widespread?

There is the attitude that a professional sales career is a waste of a college degree, yet employers insist that all their new front-line representatives have degrees. Why are employers so "gung-ho" on the degree when many of their good, older sales-people have only high school diplomas? If you were a company executive, how would you respond to these issues? Would you require the college degree? Why?

Sales Action Project. Assume that you are the employment manager for a large organization that anticipates sales doubling in three years. Management asks you to recruit fifty new people. You need to know what to look for when interviewing the applicants. *As the employment manager, you must write a brief job description and a set of specifications for the job.* You will send out recruiters who must know what to look for and what to ask. Develop a packet of information and instructions to give to your recruiters. It should contain job descriptions, job specifications, and an evaluation form on which to evaluate each candidate interviewed.

Now assume that you are one of the interviewees. Evaluate yourself based upon the job specifications. Be fair and give ratings for both your strengths and your weaknesses. Write the recommendation that you think the recruiter would give using any two of the evaluation forms given in Chapter 18.

Upon completion of this project, you should have written several single-spaced typewritten pages. These include a two- or three-page "Career Profile," a one-page interview presentation that matches your credentials with the career profile, and two different "Recruiter Evaluation" forms, filled out recommending you with concrete reasons for the sales assignment.

Marketing Management

Many people without technical skills narrow their job interests to either a job that deals with people or a job that is analytical in nature. This project is designed for those individuals with an interest in dealing with people.

The purpose is to introduce you, in some detail, to one of the basic functions of management—marketing.

Select any basic marketing textbook and summarize the major functions in marketing. What is marketing management? Does the textbook give an idea of how long it takes the beginning sales representative to work up into a management assignment? How does one know when he or she has "arrived" in management?

Using the marketing textbook as a reference, show the inter-relationships among advertising, marketing research, and sales. How much experience in each of these functions must a person have before he or she can be considered for a management position?

Sales appears to be the most common and essential function in marketing. Many firms have only the sales function listed on their organization charts. Explain how this can occur when college textbooks place so much emphasis on the other functions. Why do college professors write so much about non-sales functions in marketing and so little on preparing people to sell a product or service?

Review several sales manager job advertisements on 2–3 corporate employment websites.

Scan through a sales management textbook and notice the responsibilities of the sales executive. Based upon this quick review, list the characteristics a sales executive should possess, from analytical skills to people skills.

Can the characteristics needed for the job be learned, or must people naturally have that happy, backslapping, jovial personality in order to be a success?

Select a relatively large organization for which you would consider working. Read its annual report, employment website, a web-based stock report evaluation, and an employment brochure or job description and then interview one of its sales managers.

Briefly identify all of the principal products or services and explain the marketing training program. Which marketing activities seem to be stressed in the brochure?

Contrast the marketing program of this organization with that of a smaller manufacturer. Explain how small firms continue to be so profitable with only a few people employed in the whole marketing organization. For which firm would you prefer to work? Why?

Analyze what organizations seek in hiring people for assignments in marketing. Discuss the program of rotation among the various marketing departments in the organization you just reviewed.

Show where your background characteristics are weak and strong in relationship to what employers are seeking in people they feel have marketing management potential. This should be a presentation similar to what you might give in an interview situation.

Marketing Action Project. Many questions were posed in this project. You need to develop a minimum of three to five typewritten pages in a report that addresses these concerns. As you write responses to several of these questions, insert information about yourself that illustrates how your background fits into the field of marketing.

Another approach is to be very organizational-specific by writing a "Career Profile" that fits the specific organization's job description. Under each section of the "Career Profile," discuss your qualifications and interests by describing how the two fit together.

At the end of each section of the "Career Profile," insert a new section titled "Presentations." That series of paragraphs will illustrate the match. This should also be a minimum of three to five typewritten pages. Use the "Career Profile" description in Figure 9-1.

Retailing

Thousands of people begin their careers every year with the long-term goal of someday owning their own businesses. Many will achieve their goals eventually by starting retail businesses.

The training offered in a retail management development training program can be an ideal beginning toward meeting that long-term ambition. The purpose of this project is to introduce and expose you to one of the largest industries in the world: retailing.

Your library contains books, career literature and course textbooks on retailing and merchandising. Give a definition of retailing and discuss the types of retail business based upon website and library research.

Summarize and briefly discuss the various functions in running a retail business. Try to develop a strong understanding of the basic functions including service, buying, selling, supervision, etc. Prepare an interview presentation that demonstrates a high level of retail awareness. Describe what you know about retailing.

Relate each of the basic retail activities to your personal background, training, and experience. Explain why you might be suited for a career in retailing. Show your entrepreneurial spirit by citing examples of it in your own life.

Select two national chain stores and two urban department stores. Obtain literature on their training programs from websites and interview two managers. Analyze the financial position of each organization and describe the operations.

Describe the training programs offered for new hires at the management level. Prepare a well-documented presentation of the training programs and where they lead.

What are the personal requirements for a retailing career? Discuss college degree and major, work experience, activities, grades, personality, etc. Try to determine the starting salaries in retailing and attempt to show salary progress.

Using a web search engine and/or the *Business Periodical Index* you can find a list of trade journals in various fields of retailing. These journals and websites often contain classified ads for high-level job openings that give job titles and information about required experience and salary levels.

Read articles in retail trade journals about a company in which you have a special interest. Use the world wide web. Summarize the articles. Contrast what the articles say about the company with what the employment brochure or website says.

Describe the store management function and the buying function in retailing. Which is more important? Why? Which function best suits your background? Why?

Retailing Action Project. *Prepare a presentation that integrates your background with the field of retailing. Make a convincing case for why the employers you select should hire you.*

Pose several specific questions that an employer may ask and provide convincing responses. Write down your limitations which the employer might focus upon and describe how you propose to counter each of them with your strong points.

Your project should be at least three to five single-spaced, typewritten pages to be effective. *You might wish to incorporate the "Career Profile" (in Figure 9.1) into the analysis as a part of the project.*

The information you collected for your research on the project should be used as supporting data which you might want to save in a file folder.

Banking

Banking (and the broader financial services industry) is an industry that has attracted a large number of people from diverse academic backgrounds. It is a field that you may wish to explore.

Refer to textbooks on "Money and Banking" and "Commercial Banking." Identify and briefly explain the activities and functions performed in commercial banking. Contrast commercial banks with other types of financial institutions, such as savings and loans, credit unions, investment banks, and Federal Reserve Banks.

Using employment brochures, websites, or annual reports from three large banks, identify the internal organizational structures. What are the various departments? Are their training programs designed for training in all departments, or are they more oriented to single departments? Describe the management training programs of three major banks based on interviews with employees and web surfing.

The big banks are often viewed as salary leaders for college graduates. What was the average offer to college graduates last year, and where does banking rank among the industries in terms of salary? How do banks compare in fringe benefits? Why do smaller banks have such a different image?

Select a major city in the United States and identify the three largest banks in that city. How can the sizes of banks be measured? What are some of the advantages and disadvantages of working for a large money-center bank as opposed to a medium-sized or small bank? Describe the operations and organizations of the three large banks.

Banking Action Project. Identify at least one position in a bank for which you want to be considered. *Describe the duties and activities in this position (after a training program if you are inexperienced). What are the job qualifications (grades, degree level, major, personality, experience, etc.)?*

Your banking job description should be at least two single-spaced, typewritten pages long. The "Career Profile" in Figure 9.1 might be used as a guide in preparing this job description. You should try to answer many of the questions posed above for banking.

Your interview presentation must respond to answers that you feel an interviewer is likely to ask. Anticipate these questions. Use the research that you collected to provide answers to these questions.

Simultaneously, you must integrate elements of your background into these hypothetical questions. This will let the interviewer know that you have prepared for your interview by researching the firm.

Prepare a presentation that intelligently relates your background to organizational needs.

Develop a single-spaced, two or three page typed report that explains and supports your interests in banking. These will be the same answers that you will give to questions in the interview. It reveals your knowledge about banking and gives your strong points for being the person that the interviewer should hire.

General Accounting

Several books on accounting careers are available in most public libraries. Professional Accounting associations have great websites. Select two books or websites and thoroughly read them. Given your background, at what level of responsibility would you fit? Based on your research, develop an in-depth job description for a position in accounting.

The U.S. Department of Labor puts out two publications that provide information on accounting: *The Occupational Outlook Handbook* and the *Occupational Outlook in Brief*. Read and summarize these reports. How does the government information relate to the two books you read? Are the statistics on the profession consistent? These publications are on several websites.

Discuss the differences in the jobs of the bank examiner, the internal auditor, and the public accountant. They all conduct audits using acceptable accounting methods, but there are variances in the assignments. What are they, and are the requirements and qualifications for the three jobs the same? Does an Internal Revenue Agent do the same job?

The corporate controller is a key executive on the management team.

Review the job of the controller, its requirements, and the types of accounting background experiences which are necessary for this position. Outline the typical controller's career path.

Select the employment brochures or websites of five industrial and/or government organizations and read the openings available for accounting and finance people. List these organizations and, beside the name of each, write the various job titles and a brief description for each.

Based on web research and information from your placement office, discuss the salary outlook for accounting majors in various industries. Using the *Wall Street Journal* and the classified ad section of a major metropolitan newspaper, describe the most common job for the highest-paid financial executives.

Based on your advertisements review, what is the average amount of experience required and the salary range for the controller position? Identify benchmark salaries by years of experience and identify a position in which you would be interested.

Accounting Action Project. Using the research that you have just completed, prepare a "Career Profile" that is at least two or three single-spaced typewritten pages in length. You may use any of the organizations that you researched as a guide and integrate what your research showed into the firm's job description. Use Figure 9.1.

Using the job description or "Career Profile" as a guide, the next step is to prove how well your background matches the job description. In essence, you are matching your resume with the job description.

Prepare at least a two page, single-spaced, typed report that identifies your strongest qualities and how they match the needs of the accounting job description. Be specific. Take your top ten qualities and relate them to elements on the job description. If there are major limitations in your background that the job description prefers, show how you intend to address these limitations.

Public Accounting

What is public accounting? Describe the industry. Outline the various departments within the public accounting firm. Describe the duties, responsibilities, and relationships among the various levels of management.

What is the method of supervision? How specialized do auditors become? How is responsibility assumed and shared among the various levels of management and among peers? What responsibilities do auditors have to clients?

Describe the duties, responsibilities, and daily activities of the entry-level job in public accounting. Describe in detail all of the typical functions a new person would perform during the first two years on the job. How much diversity and specialization exist?

Does the new person have decision-making authority, or does the new person play primarily an advisory role and perform nitty-gritty "dog work"? Do the same for the next level of responsibility.

Outline the various job requirements for a position in public accounting including education, grades, certification, ability to travel (length and frequency), personality, time commitments, location, age, and so forth. Discuss the role of teamwork.

What is the typical career path to partnership in public accounting? For each level of management, describe the duties and responsibilities. Identify characteristics of partners. Discuss the role of turnover in the industry.

How do these questions relate to your goals? Does your personality fit with this type of work? How interested are you in both the initial and the long-term assignments? Do you consider yourself a decision maker or basically an advisor? How do your interests relate to public accounting? Summarize why or why not public accounting is the career field for you. Contrast public and private accounting and show why you feel that your background is best-suited to one or the other.

Public Accounting Action Project. Using the "Career Profile" (in Figure 9.1) as a guide, prepare a two or three page single-spaced, typed report for a position in the public accounting field. You may use an entry-level or an advanced job in any of the basic functional areas. Be as specific as possible as to the job, the location, and even the firm if you have identified a preferred choice.

Your summary "Career Profile" should address many of the questions posed above. Your research into the industry and a specific firm should provide you with some detail upon which to make a decision about the compatibility of the industry and your background.

On one page make a list of all of the areas of compatibility. Indicate beside each factor how your characteristics best match. On another page make a similar list of the areas of incompatibility and indicate how you plan to address these limitations.

On the last page write a summary evaluation about yourself and the firm. Assume that you are the initial interviewer and that you must write a convincing case to your supervisors about why this person (you) should be hired.

Engineering

Engineers tend to have more definitive career profiles than most other occupational fields. Why is this? Are there factors in the education and work experiences of engineers that cause a close tie between the profile and the self-assessment? What are they?

Engineering majors usually have a fairly concrete understanding of what their profession is all about by their senior year in college. Yet many begin to agonize over whether to go into design, process, applied, field sales, management, etc. There are many ways to apply an engineering background in the work setting.

There are decisions on whether to specialize or remain broad. Is it better to remain a generalist or to become an expert? There are fields within the engineering specialty and industry specifications that make these decisions more complicated than one would initially suspect.

Select a sub-specialty within one of the major engineering fields, and describe its duties and responsibilities in great depth based upon reading in textbooks and interviews of practitioners in the field. Compare the information from the books and the practitioners.

Study the design, process, application, and sales aspects of your technical field. What characteristics in your background relate to those in each of these areas? Which factors would help you resolve the decision on which approach to take? Where do you fit best? Why?

A great concern of many engineers is the potential for obsolescence of their knowledge within five years after graduation. Is this a possibility in your field? What will you do to face this issue? Be specific on exactly how you will keep current. Lay out a specific plan.

Engineering employment tends to be highly cyclical. There are many openings during boom times and engineers are laid off during recessions. What plans are you taking to address this situation?

Engineering Action Project. *Based upon all of these concerns, prepare a "Career Profile" following the format given in Figure 9.1.* Incorporate your decisions reached above into the "ideal" career profile.

Describe how your technical background best fits with this profile as if you were doing so in an interview situation.

Prepare a hard-hitting presentation of about two to three single-spaced, typed pages in length that integrates your background with the career profile.

Human Resource Management

A number of jobs in human resource management (HRM) are available each year to job candidates with proper training in the field. The purpose of this project is to explore the opportunities which are available and the requirements for those openings.

The HRM department of an organization consists of a relatively small number of people. These people are employed in the following HRM departments:

- Labor relations
- Wage administration
- Employment
- Benefits and insurance
- Training and Development
- Publications
- Management development
- Performance appraisal
- Equal employment
- Compliance regulations
- Security and safety
- Affirmative action

Define each of these areas and describe the daily activities of people working in them. Identify the qualifications, education, interest profile, personality, etc.,

required of individuals working in each area. Base your comments on a college textbook in "Human Resource Management" and professional association websites.

Based on information in the *Occupational Outlook Handbook* and the *Occupational Outlook in Brief* from the U.S. Department of Labor, what are the estimated numbers of annual openings? Using additional sources, determine the long-term outlook for employment in human resources.

Using web, newspaper, trade journal advertisements, and personal information interviews, determine the typical starting salary and the average salary of HR managers. What is the typical advancement path in the field? How do salaries in HRM compare with those in accounting, marketing, and other professional fields?

Select two major employers and review their job descriptions, employment brochures, and websites. Based upon your research in the HRM field, critique the descriptions, brochures, and websites. What type of employers are more likely to offer job opportunities in HRM?

Based upon your review of the field, explain why your background is ideally suited for a career in HRM. Develop a strong presentation that you can use in your interviewing for a HRM job. Draw upon your technical skills, values, interests, and personal qualities that are best related.

HRM Action Project. On two single-spaced, typed pages write a brief description of the specific duties and responsibilities of a person working in each of the HR departments listed above. *Define each department and describe the specific activities that managers do in each.*

Develop a two or three page "Career Profile" for one of the positions in HRM for which you feel that you would be qualified. If you can identify a specific job opening in a firm, use that as a guide.

Lastly, explain in a one or two page evaluation why you are the best qualified person for such a position. This would be similar to the presentation that you would use in any interview. One approach that you could use is to try to anticipate the series of open-ended questions that an interviewer is likely to ask and provide a reasoned response to each of about eight to ten questions.

Public Relations

Public relations employees build and maintain positive images for their employing organizations. Public relations staffers work closely with newspapers, magazines, radio, and television, so they often have extensive training in media. Many create websites.

Many people who are unaware of what the function really involves say they want to go into public relations when they are really more interested in the marketing function. The purpose of this project is to help you decide if you are interested in and qualified for a career in public relations.

Describe the principal duties and responsibilities of the chief public relations person in a major organization. In the past few years there have been several articles in the *Wall Street Journal* and other business periodicals about the profession. Summarize and critique two articles in the field.

The *Business Periodical Index* in your library and professional association websites would be good sources of articles. Read a college level textbook on public relations and summarize the main functional areas.

Scan through two books or articles in the library about careers in public relations. What are the typical job titles of beginners? What are the qualifications, education, skills, personality, appearance, and special interests of people entering the field? Where are most of the jobs located?

Give some information on salaries and describe the most typical career path. From newspaper and professional journal advertisements, what are the experience requirements and salary levels of top public relations personnel? What is the employment outlook? Use association websites.

Public relations people are often accused of creating false, but glowing images. This media image building often runs counter to people's demands for truth and openness. If you were employed in the field, how would your value system face this issue?

Public Relations Action Project.   Given that you want to advance in this field, describe how your background is suited for a public relations career. *Design a concise summary of your background and experience to appeal to a public relations executive who currently has a job opening at your level of expertise.*

Use web search engines to identify specific job openings in public relations. Use these job descriptions in your analysis.

Make it a creative and innovative presentation that is sure to attract interest and get you the interview you desire. From your current level of education and experience, discuss how and when you might realistically expect to break into (or advance upward to) the field of public relations.

By design, this project is very open-ended. There would need to be a great deal of creativeness and cleverness used to help you open the door into this arena.

The goal is to encourage you to write five creatively designed, single-spaced, typewritten pages about the profession and show how your credentials best relate.

You may wish to use the "Career Profile" (Figure 9.1) as a guide and your resume as your qualification record. The important aspect of this project is to explain in a graphical and creative writing style why you are the best qualified candidate for a specific type of job opening in the field.

Career Book Review

All libraries include recent books on various career fields. Select any book about a career field in which you have an interest and read it. You may substitute a professional association website instead of using a book.

Book Review Action Project.   Write a review that provides a summary plus a critical analysis. Discuss what you wanted to know that the book did not cover. Note whether you are more or less interested in the career field after reading the book or website and explain why.

Develop a presentation that integrates your self-assessment with the information you derived from the in-depth analysis of the career field. *Using the career profile in Figure 9.1 show relationships between your background and the career field at every level of concern.*

Based upon this analysis, identify several likely employers within your geographical area of concern. *Describe how you would methodically show that your background relates to the career field.*

Assume that you were having a job interview in this field and as you tell about your background characteristics relate them to the career profile headings.

Your report should be at least five single-spaced, typed pages in length to be most helpful.

Graduate Study

Many people decide to attend graduate school to obtain an advanced degree (MBA, JD, MS, etc.) either immediately following undergraduate training or after several years of work experience.

The reasons for doing this should be thoroughly investigated before the decision is made. The purpose of this project is to conduct the analysis. Read the chapter on "Continuing Education," before completing this project.

Graduate Study Action Project. Describe the type of position you wish to hold after graduate school and give supporting evidence that the degree is essential for obtaining the position.

//WEB.TIP//

www.collegeboard.org
The College Board
The SAT folks have a super search engine that zooms you to college sites/application process and pertinent college info.

Which schools will you consider for this type of program and how do you rate their degree programs? What is the placement record of graduates from the various programs? Analyze the placement outlook with hard evidence, not generalizations.

What are some of the criteria used in selecting a school (e.g., hours required, cost, location, aid, reputation (define), difficulty, etc.)? Which criteria are most important to you and why?

Visit the website of several schools and compare three schools on criteria that are important to you. Calculate the cost of the programs and estimate your return on the investment.

What are some of the admission requirements and how does your background stack up in relation to them? Would it be better to have some more relevant work experience before entering this program?

Outline the academic program of study for you at each school. Appraise your chances of getting accepted.

Prepare an admissions strategy with fallback positions at each step in the process. Plan your academic program course by course.

Analyze your present education, work experience, job interests, background, and personality in relation to the *daily* duties, *general* responsibilities, and *specific* job activities of the job for which the further education would train you.

Download and print the application of one school from its website. Complete that application including "To whom it may concern" reference statements.

Develop a career profile (as shown in Figure 9.1) for the position to which you aspire, that integrates your new background (with the advanced degree). This project should be at least five single-spaced, typed pages in length to be most useful to you.

Industry and Employer Analysis

Assume that there is a specific employer for whom you wish to work. The purpose of this project is to better prepare you for an interview by enhancing your knowledge of the available opportunities and your understanding of how your background meets the requirements of the potential employer.

Select an employer and then thoroughly research that employer from their career employment website. Also research the industry in which it operates.

Identify other major employers in the same industry. Investigate some of the current problems which are common to the industry and specific to that particular organization. Are there pressing concerns that may impede progress in the industry? Is there current legislation which is important to the industry?

Project trends in the industry that could stimulate or restrict growth. Show how population growth, economic trends, legal concerns, and technological developments may influence the industry. Relate these to your employment prospects.

Industry Action Project. *Identify and describe the position in which you wish to be employed by the organization.* Present the organizational structure of the organization and its size (assets, sales, employees, etc.) and rank in the industry. Show where your specific job goal fits into the organizational framework.

Use the firm's website and at least one web-base independent source for specific information.

Identify the organization's range of products and/or services, and support an outlook for its sales growth. Who is the competition and how strong is it? Where are its various locations? How strong is its financial foundation?

Discuss any development program for the position you are seeking. How long is it and to what position does it lead? Describe the duties and responsibilities of the job you want and evaluate your chances for advancement.

Summarize your findings and relate them in a positive fashion to your education, background, interests, and personality. Use the "Career Profile" in Figure 9.1 as a guide in structuring the relationships.

Go to the *Business Periodical Index* in your library and record all of the articles that have been written about the organization in the past two years. Use the WWW to do the same type of research.

Select articles that have appeared in the most widely circulated publications such as *Fortune, Forbes, Barron's, Wall Street Journal, Business Week, Nation's Business,* etc. Read and summarize these articles.

Read a recent analysis of the company's stock and internal growth potential in one of the leading investment research services, such as *Value Line, Moody's,* or *Standard and Poor.* These, too, are available in most libraries and the WWW. For smaller firms you may have to call a brokerage house and ask them to send you a research report. Summarize the reports.

Obtain a copy of the employer's latest annual report and contrast it with the investment reports. Report on the various product lines and internal operating divisions. Identify the additional information you were able to obtain about the firm from the annual report. Does the annual report fairly portray the company's prospects? Offer a critical analysis.

Evaluate the employer's *employment brochure* (if available). Summarize it and critically respond to the following questions. Does the brochure define and describe the available openings? Are qualification requirements fully explained? Is the training program explained? What additional information should the brochure contain?

The *employment brochure* can often be obtained from your college placement office or by writing the organization's central HR department. It is often on the firm's website also.

If possible, try to obtain a copy of the organization's employee publication (house organ, company newspaper, etc.) and comment on how much new knowledge this adds. *After all of your research is complete, write a list of ten questions pertinent to your employment with the firm that have not been answered.*

If possible, obtain an interview with a company employee to get answers to your questions. Record the results of that interview.

The purpose of this project is to help you carry out important research before your first interview with the organization. With the experience you gain using the methodology outlined here, your later research on other firms is likely to be much less time-consuming but just as essential.

This project will also strengthen the validity of the career exploration and self-assessment that you employed to arrive at your current career decision.

Summarize your research on the organization based upon the research and analysis suggested above. Focus on the single employer and its industry. Illustrate how your credentials fit both the industry and this employer.

This report should be at least five single-spaced, typed pages in length if you are to remember all of the appropriate details. Your comments should be supported with the research that you collected.

This is the type of analysis summary that you should prepare prior to each of your interviews.

Summary

Formal career planning projects are important learning devices. Forcing yourself to write out a detailed, several-page analysis involves a commitment. You are about to make some extremely important decisions that may have a lasting impact upon your career.

The time you invest in a serious written analysis will be well worth the effort.

After reading through the projects you may not have discovered an "appropriate" topic. However, you will have gotten a flavor of the approach to career field exploration. As a result, it should be fairly simple for you to write a career project specific to your situation.

Write it. Complete it. By doing so you will learn what you need to know before approaching the next step in career planning.

DEVELOPING YOUR JOB SEARCH TOOLS

The focus of Parts 1 and 2 was goal-setting. You have now spent considerable time assessing your basic values, interests, personal qualities, and skills. You should also be extremely aware of your actual career alternatives now.

Hopefully you have integrated your assessment and your exploration and have established some specific direction(s) for your career. The purpose of Part 3 is to show you how to achieve your career plans and goals.

Part 3 helps you develop a plan to meet your objectives. The recommended strategies build upon those of "Planning Your Career" and "Exploring Your Options." Each strategy or technique sets into motion an approach that has worked for thousands of others, and the approach will also work for you.

Resume Preparation Techniques

Purpose – Strategy – Design

The resume is the most important tool in your effort to find a job. In the final analysis, it is a sales brochure designed to present your capabilities in the most favorable light to potential employers. You need to learn the secrets of developing a piece of paper that is designed to sell your potential to employers.

With millions of resumes in circulation, you would think that there would be no secrets. Yet, hundreds of HR professionals say that the lack of an effective resume is the number one reason why they turn people away before the interview.

The basic idea is to structure the resume in such a way that the potential employer is convinced that you are the ideal candidate for an available opening. "Broad brush" resumes that simply chronologize the facts about you are seldom effective.

Sending out bland resumes indiscriminately is like shooting in the dark: You may get lucky, but luck is not an effective approach to use after a major investment in your education.

The basic idea in resume design is to structure it in such a way that it convinces the potential employer that you are the perfect match for a position that is open or anticipated.

A resume is an individually designed document that summarizes your background. It is intended to demonstrate your fitness for a particular position or array of related positions. It is your passport to job interviews.

The resume is your most important communication tool and it is close to impossible to land an assignment of a technical, professional, or managerial type without one.

Targeted resumes are most effective in getting interviews.

THE ONE-MINUTE RESUME

The competitive reality of the job market dictates that there are many qualified applicants for every job opening. An employer obviously prefers to interview several candidates for each opening, not just a single applicant. There rarely is enough time to interview every technically qualified applicant. Who gets through the sixty-second resume scan?

A targeted resume increases your odds of getting the interview appointment. Over 95 percent of job hires are first introduced via a resume. This marketing brochure is the single most important tool in your job search.

The resume focuses attention on the most attractive and applicable aspects of your background. It forces the reader to conclude that you are an ideal applicant for a given assignment.

The purpose of the resume is to obtain a job interview; it is not designed to get you a job offer. All you want is a chance to tell your story in person and to elaborate on your qualifications.

The resume opens the door, but it does not close the sale. Targeted resumes focus on your goals, interests, and motivations. They explain *why* you have confidence in your abilities.

Resumes are used in many ways. Distribution strategies boil down to the following uses:

Networking.   Making contact with all friends and friends of friends who are in a position to assist in arranging an interview.

Informational Interviewing.   Making contact with individuals employed in the field you desire with the expressed purpose of data collection, but realizing that these contacts may eventually produce job interviews. Networking and informational interviewing provide you access to the "hidden job market."

Advertisements.   Responding to "help wanted" ads which offer access to about 15 percent of the available job openings.

Mail Campaigns.   Targeting cover letters with resumes to employers most likely to have openings in your area of interest.

Cold Calling.   Contacting personnel and operating managers directly to inquire about employment possibilities.

Third Party Assistance.   Arranging with agencies to set up interview appointments for you.

Ample advice on timing the approach, meeting the right person, and interview positioning dominate popular thought on the use of these approaches. The one thing all strategies have in common is the need for a quality resume.

Preparation Techniques

Many employers receive hundreds of resumes each day from many sources and the time they have available for reviewing them is quite short; rarely more than a cursory one or two minutes each.

Consequently, an employer absorbs a great deal of information about you in those few seconds and you must direct attention to the few items that are most likely to positively influence their decision.

Goals.   The goal is to get your resume read in great detail and, unless you have done your homework, the odds are against your getting it read completely. It is only by knowing what the employer is seeking and then directing your resume to fit those criteria that you have a reasonable chance of getting your resume read more thoroughly.

Matching.   The concept of matching key criteria means that you must deliver your resume to the right decision-maker. The decision-maker who makes the first cut is most likely screening for skills, career interest, major subject, degree level, and job titles. These are the items that must stand out first and foremost on your resume.

Door Opener.   The employer will not hire you on the basis of your resume alone; it merely serves to whet the employer's appetite. The employer will want to set up an interview with you. Although the resume is a critical step in the job search process, it can only be relied upon to open a door.

Use of Resumes

There are many good reasons for writing your credentials on a piece of paper. The resume will follow you and serve you well in many ways for years. Whether in the job market or not, you should always maintain an up-to-date resume.

There are many times when you can make good non-employment uses of your resume—from the time when you want to secure bank credit to when you need to provide information for speech introductions.

A good resume packages your credentials in a manner that will convince a potential employer that you must be interviewed. The sales-oriented resume focuses attention on the most attractive and applicable aspects of your background. It forces the reader to conclude that you are an ideal applicant for a given assignment.

Because the resume is a sales presentation, it must truly reflect all of your credentials in an honest, truthful, and professional manner. How you intend to use the resume is important in design considerations.

Cold Calling Card. Cold calling is a course of action that involves making personal visits to a number of firms. You are hoping that even though you had no formal appointment, you will be able to speak with an employment decision-maker.

This is a frustrating way to look for a job because there is a very high probability that you will get turned down without ever having seen anyone, but, nonetheless, it does work.

A good resume can greatly improve your odds of obtaining the interview. If there is an opening and if your background fits, you normally will get an interview then or an appointment time for one later.

Unlike the ad response where you know an opening exists, you are gambling on an available opening. Secondly, even if there is an opening, you are gambling that your carefully-constructed resume will match. The odds are clearly against you when compared with the circumstances where you know an opening exists and can somewhat structure your background to fit the opening.

A well-constructed resume improves your odds, and if you have the time, this direct approach can produce interviews. If you do get the interview, the resume will facilitate and aid the interview process. If you fail to land an interview, many employers will keep your resume on file in the event an opening develops later.

Answering Employment Ads. Job leads can come to your attention in many ways, and some of the most common are want ads in newspapers, websites, trade journals, association newsletters, and job bulletins from college and alumni career service offices.

An employer wants and expects to receive resumes with cover letters in reply to the ad. Most ads draw many resumes, particularly when they are for attractive job openings. An employer does not want to screen through irrelevant data.

Will your resume match a brief set of job specifications? Keeping your resume concise aids this matching process and increases your odds of being screened in, not out.

Although a separate resume does not have to be prepared for answering each job ad, the better you can show that your credentials match the specifications for a particular job, the better your chances are of obtaining an interview.

A broadly-designed resume does reduce your work because it can be used in applying for many types of jobs. But it also has the distinct disadvantage of putting your resume into a class with all of the other also-rans because of its lack of a clear-cut match with any one job.

RESUME USES

- Calling card for multiple circumstances
- Servicing academic and work references
- Conversing with counselors
- Disseminating to network contacts
- Responding to job leads
- Introducing to employment agencies
- Answering employment advertisements
- Broadcasting to potential employers

• • • • • • • • • • •

Figure 10.1

The purpose of your resume is to introduce you. It is not your total sales presentation.

Broadly-focused resumes, in contrast to job-focused resumes, are less likely to get through the initial 60-second glance.

Your goal is to make the employer's selection decision easy. If your credentials are recorded in an organized way, it permits the employer to quickly ascertain your fitness for the position. Thus, you are much more likely to be called for an interview.

Agency Calling Card. If your job search process involves using an employment agency, executive search firm, or college placement office, you will be asked to submit a resume.

Unless you are an engineer, sales manager, computer specialist, or other highly-sought-after individual, you will have to decide which type of resume to submit. It must be a broad-based resume since you have no idea of the eventual circulation; however, broad-based resumes are not generally effective. You have to make a judgment call.

The agency needs guidance on what type of job you want. They will not refer your resume to the world. It will be selectively circulated. Do not let an agency make career decisions for you. You should tell them where you want your resume sent.

The more specific you are about the type of job you want, the fewer times your resume will be referred. However, when it is referred you will stand a better chance of securing an interview than do those applicants whose resumes are vague and general.

Most people develop multiple resumes. One of your resumes should include a broadly-focused job objective (or no objective). Other resumes should be more focused on specific jobs. The agency may need the *generic* version for referral purposes, but when you interview, remember to give the potential employers your job-focused version.

Direct Mail Piece. Canvassing a potential job market by sending a cover letter and resume is an approach used by many in a job search. For this approach to be effective, a special mailing list and specifically-targeted career thrusts are required.

The resume serves as your advertising brochure. It explains what you have to offer and how your services can meet the needs of the employer.

References. Whether or not you elect to place recommenders (references) on your resume, you will want to maintain a repertoire of former employers, colleagues, teachers, etc. who are willing to say positive things about you. These recommenders are frequently called by potential employers.

What will your recommenders say about you? You can influence what they say by providing them with a very thorough and complete resume. Most will flip to your resume when contacted and use it to provide the potential employer data.

Some recommenders will read your complete resume. This is one situation where a multiple page resume might be useful.

Although you may feel confident that these people will say good things about you, you do not know exactly what they will say or how they will say it. It

I CAN TELL BY YOUR RESUME, EVE, WE HAVE SOMETHING IN COMMON... MY KIDS LIKE PEANUT BUTTER, TOO.

is easy for others to get facts about you slightly and unintentionally incorrect. Their information may be inconsistent with what you told the employer.

In order to avoid such difficulties, always keep your closest recommenders supplied with up-to-date versions of your resume. They will feel more comfortable and you will know that the facts are correct.

Contacts. A good job search strategy demands that you have many people working on your behalf. You need certain people to recommend you for specific jobs. These contacts are your personal sales representatives. These relationships are extremely important to you in the job search process.

A contact may send out your resume to an employer they think might like to interview you, or simply may make a few remarks about you in a letter, telephone call, or personal conversation. However, no matter what method the contact uses, they need an up-to-date resume in order to be aware of your current qualifications and goals.

Your resume is a central part of your specific job search strategy. It must be strategically planned in order to be most effective.

> **Carefully plan how you intend to use your resumes. You need different resumes to use with agencies, references, direct mail, and personal network contacts.**

BREAKING THE SCAN TRAP

Targeted resumes assist in breaking through the scan test by convincing employers that your employment will make a difference.

Will your employment make a difference? Average talent abounds and you are not average. Effective resume presentations package your credentials in an honest approach designed to convince the employer to invite you for an interview.

The resume is not your whole sales pitch. Its purpose is to get you the interview. The purpose of the *interview* is to get you the offer. Recruiters look for items to screen you out, not in. Too much bait may provide tidbits that can be used to eliminate you, and too little bait may offer a weak lure. You need balance.

The hiring manager has several screening factors in mind in reviewing resumes. When you hit one of those screening factors, you inch the door open a bit further. As your story unfolds, you add to the factors that you suspect the screener is seeking. The first scan is in looking for what you want to do.

Format

There is no one accepted way or format for preparing a resume. Unlike company application forms and standardized college interview forms, the resume is given in a free format and can highlight your assets while minimizing your limitations. Standard forms force you to give all data requested, regardless of how it bears on qualifications.

The resume *differs in principle* from standard forms. Application forms screen you *out*. Effective, free-form resumes screen you *in*.

Application forms present basic facts about background in an organized scheme so that employers can rapidly screen on key factors and readily compare the qualifications of the various candidates competing for a given job opening.

Structure. The resume is not a letter or a bibliography written in a narrative format. It is closer to an outline for a major speech about you.

The purpose of the structure is to highlight the positive points that will screen you in. The idea is to draw the reader's attention to a few basic and extremely important elements in your background.

The structuring of these critical elements directs the attention of the reader on them. They positively influence the employer to consider you further.

Traits. The purpose of the structure is to highlight the positive points for rapid screening. The idea is to draw the reader's attention to a few basic and extremely important elements in your background.

The structuring of these critical elements forces the reader's attention on them so that they positively influence the employer to consider you further.

Appearance. A five-second glance at a resume leaves an impression. The content may be ideal, but if the initial impression is poor, the resume may never be read. Organization of several key elements aids the initial impression, but neatness also generates a pleasing appearance.

The resume must be typed with a word processor or an electric typewriter. Misspelled words are totally unacceptable.

Graphically, the resume should be easy to follow and pleasing to the eye. Excessive narrative, smudges, extraneous marks, etc., are unacceptable. A well-constructed resume uses ample white space in a neatly blocked pattern to facilitate reading by the employer.

Construction Methods. In an initial 60-second scan, an employer's eye will pick up four to six key points on a resume. With what five points do you want to hit the employer?

After you determine your five most important points, you can lay out your resume in such a way as to force the reader's eye to focus on those five points with the initial glance.

You can move the reader's eye to certain points by use of well-chosen design techniques. White spaces move the eyes and capitalization focuses attention on a given area. Capitalization of a whole word is more vivid than capitalizing only the first letter. Lower-case letters indicate that the fine print should be read for more details.

In addition, underlining and boldfacing are effective ways to consistently emphasize the foremost points in the various elements. Be consistent with underlining and bolding but do not overdo it. A three-inch long underline is followed by a shorter length. A long underline in the education element might be followed by a long underline in the experience element. Within each element, if you use underlining more than once, make the lines progressively shorter.

The purpose of the resume is to introduce you to the employer and help you obtain an interview. It is more of a *sales* brochure.

The outline structure allows you to attract attention to elements of your background that you believe will entice the employer.

TRAITS TO EXPRESS

- Attitude
- Career direction
- Character
- Confidence
- Enthusiasm
- Involvement
- Leadership
- Maturity
- Motivations
- Organization
- Personality
- Self-expression
- Social skills
- Work desire
- Work habits

• • • • • • • • • • •

Figure 10.2

An indention tends to tell readers that detail may follow. The reverse indicates that the material above is more important, so look at it first. You want to keep readers from overlooking indentions, so use bullets, dashes, asterisks, etc., to keep their eyes moving. These techniques tend to indicate that the detail is also important.

Resumes do need some detail to support the main points, but long

AFTER CAREFUL EXAMINATION, KIP, I'D HAVE TO SAY YOUR RESUME IS WOEFULLY INADEQUATE.

narrative-style paragraphs tend to clutter resumes. In order to avoid this, never make a paragraph longer than four sentences. If you must go longer, use multiple paragraphs.

This approach is particularly effective under education if you want to expand on subjects, projects, or extracurricular activities when there is a lack of work experience. If you have been out of school for several years, you might want to downplay education and expand on work experience instead.

Incomplete sentences can be used to expand upon detail. If you want to say more but still keep the resume short, you can write out complete sentences and then go back and eliminate all extraneous words such as "and" and "the," some phrases, pronouns, and prepositions, and still retain the key verbs and nouns. In addition, to separate key points, you can run them together with the use of triple dots (ellipses).

Section Size.   Resumes are composed of a series of sections, such as education, activities, work experience, etc. It is desirable to allot a balanced amount of space to each element, but for many people that is not practical or wise.

For example, if your strength is your educational background, you should devote more space to that element than to any other. That will serve to draw the reader's eye to that part of your resume and force them to read more of the detail there.

However, if you have extensive work experience and your schooling is several years behind you, you might devote little attention to education. Emphasizing your **skills** is most important. You should devote the most space in describing your skills.

Section Order.   There are some accepted practices in the ordering of the resume elements. The identification and career objective are always at the top, and references, if used, are always at the bottom. The body of the resume tells about your education, activities, and work experience.

Education and experience are frequently reversed. The area to which you devote the largest amount of space should be the most important element. Place the more important section first.

Length.   The length of your resume should be dictated by three things:

- Extensiveness of background
- Potential use of the resume
- Key points to be emphasized

Ideally, your resume should be just one page if its major use is to serve as a screen to obtain an interview.

Graphic Considerations

- White or off-white paper
- Concise
- One/two pages
- Quality paper
- 8-1/2 x 11 size
- Balanced sections
- Error free
- Print or type
- Quality copy
- Ample white space
- Centered text
- Outline format
- Underlined section heads
- Capitalized body points
- Bullet point features
- Neatly blocked

• • • • • • • • • • •

Figure 10.3

No matter how extensive your background, the employer is looking initially for only a few key variables. After securing an interview, however, it might then be advantageous to give the interviewer a multi-page resume at the time of the interview.

Recommender Exception. If you have been working full-time in your career field, it is appropriate to put together a two- to three-page resume. This should be in *addition* to the one-page synopsis. Your two- to three-page resume is best given to your references and people who know you well who might be instrumental in referring you to potential employers.

College students with extensive leadership and activities as well at meaningful work experiences often prepare two page resumes. Again, this is in *addition* to the one-page resume. This is best shared with personal contacts who you know will take the time to read it and with employers after you have had success with the initial interview. Three page resumes are worthless.

A resume is not a life or work history. It is a short, informative summary. (It is a French word which means "short"; a long expansion of the resume is called a vita.) Nevertheless, there are many reasons for preparing a two page resume (never longer than 2 pages).

When a multi-page resume is used, the cover letter tends to become the brief summary. As a rule of thumb, you rarely require more than a one page resume.

There are some professional field exceptions to these generalities. Performers, academicians, scientists, high-level executives, writers, etc., often must submit multi-page resumes or portfolios. To a great extent, much of this is dictated by the employment processes within those professions.

Paper. Resumes should always be copied onto 8 1/2" x 11" paper. Legal size paper is acceptable, but it is not recommended and is seldom used. Smaller paper tends to get lost in piles, and large-size resumes get pitched because they will not fit conveniently in in-boxes or files. Also, fancy folds, odd shapes, and other gimmicks designed to get attention should be avoided.

Copying. The most flexible resumes are those produced using word processing equipment. Never use fan-fold paper or print with a dot matrix printer. Whenever possible, use a very high quality printer.

You should reproduce your resume using a high quality copy machine. Typeset resumes look attractive, but you lose a great deal of flexibility in adjusting to the employer's needs. The expense, plus the inflexibility, argues against typeset resumes.

Most experts recommend using a word processor with a laser printer. You can also use desktop publishing software to get the typeset "look" if desired.

When copying your resume, avoid using colored paper. If you want to be a little different, consider only off-white tones, light earth tones, and light gray. The majority of all resumes are reproduced on twenty-pound white bond stock paper with an average rag content.

Photographs. Few resumes have photographs attached. However, if you prefer to use a photograph, place a 2 1/2" x 3" passport size photograph in the upper right-hand corner.

Pictures present problems for a number of reasons. It is against the law to discriminate against job applicants on the basis of race, sex, religion, age (over 40), or national origin. A picture can identify those variables.

By law, an employer cannot require a photograph until after the hiring process is completed. In addition, some states have laws against employers having candidate's photographs in employment files before they are hired.

Incidently, in Europe and other parts of the world, the normal convention *is* to include a photograph on your resume. When in Rome . . .

The only legitimate reason for a photograph being placed on a resume is to enhance recall. This can be quite important if you are applying and interviewing for a job that has many qualified applicants.

Your qualifications will be quite similar to other applicants. Personality will play an important part in the decision process. With so many applicants, the employer could have a problem remembering you. Thus, the picture would help to recall you and your conversation.

Inclusion of a photograph on a free-form resume is unusual. Whether to include it or not depends on interviewing circumstances and personal values.

Writing Services.   There are a number of firms that, for a fee, will write your resume for you. As with tax returns, you must supply all of the information, including your goals and your intended use of the resume.

Given this information, they will design a polished, professionally packaged resume. It will look great and emphasize your most important assets if it is prepared by a reputable organization.

However, a really good resume must be written by you. Experienced recruiters can easily spot professionally prepared resumes, and often these are the first to be discarded because they are often not a sincere reflection.

Remember that your resume is a sales device. You will likely spend several hours working on it. It must present a positive image but not an insincere, glittery impression.

If you have above average writing ability, you should try to prepare the resume yourself. If you question your abilities, consult an expert. If you go to an expert, make sure to provide an extensive amount of data on every element of your resume.

Printing Services.   Copy and printing services regularly provide copies of resumes for job applicants. Most of these services simply set up the resume, let you correct a rough draft copy, and then run the number of copies you order.

Some services also employ expert typists who will type resumes on quality word processors or desktop publishers. The process can range in cost from $30 to more than $80. In units of 50 copies or more, reproduction costs run from $.05 to $.25 per copy.

Advice.   Even if you use resume writing and printing services, you basically must do all of the work of putting the resume together. Most people wind up doing three to five drafts before they get a resume with which they are pleased. During this trial and error stage, it is a mistake to rely solely upon your own judgment. Advice is usually free. Seek it. Use the suggestions in your next draft.

Teachers, counselors, and placement officers see hundreds of

> **A photograph can help you after an interview by aiding the interviewer's recall abilities.**

UH... I DID MENTION IN MY RESUME THAT I SOMETIMES GET A LITTLE NERVOUS.

· · · · · · · · · · · · · BASIC RESUME FORMATS · · · · · · · · · · · ·

Chronological — Presents work experiences and educational background in reverse time sequence with a statement about each relevant episode.

Functional — Catalogs under major skill-set headings major areas of involvement that draw upon work experiences, education, and personal background. Dates and details may not be presented sometimes, but the skill is usually documented by reference to the individual's background.

Targeted — Presents abilities and accomplishments in a highly focused method that targets directly into a specific job, functional field, or industry group. The targeting occurs in the construction of the career objective statement. A targeted resume can be used in conjunction with either the chronological or functional resume formats.

• • • • • • • • • •

Figure 10.5

resumes. These are the people to go to for advice. If you know someone in the Human Resource department of a medium or large organization, solicit his or her advice.

Do not overlook your friends and colleagues. Although they may not be experts, they can offer suggestions which may prove helpful, particularly in design, presentation, and how you say things.

In the final analysis, the document you finally assemble must be a true reflection of you. Work on your resume until you reach the point where you feel extremely proud of it. You will probably then find yourself improving it year after year.

Types of Resumes

The two most common forms for resume design are "chronological" and "functional." The chronological resume is blocked into sections categorized by source of skills (education, work, activities, etc.). The functional resume is categorized by the skills possessed (managing, writing, research, etc.). The work experience, education, activities, etc. are all discussed under each functional heading rather than vice versa.

The attention-grabbing, targeted resume may be used with either the chronologically-designed resume or the functional resume. The job objective focuses attention on the initial match. The details used to strengthen the match between your credentials and job qualifications are presented later in the body of the resume.

Chronological Design. This skill-based approach catalogs education, activities, and work experiences in a manner that describes your skills and personal qualities in about the same order as they occurred. These events in your education, activities, and work sections are listed in order of most recent first within the three major headings.

Functional Design. This skill-based approach lists and categorizes your skills first and then illustrates the events that shaped the particular skill being described. You draw upon your education, activities, and work experiences to support your abilities. Your particular skills are used as section headings within the resume body.

Technical Skills	Functional Skills	Administrative Skills
Accounting	Distributing	Analyzing
Computer	Engineering	Controlling
programming	Financing	Coordinating
Designing	Managing	Delegating
Engineering	Manufacturing	Directing
Foreign languages	Marketing	Leading
Legal	Operations	Managing
Mathematics	Purchasing	Motivating
Public relations	Researching	Organizing
Reporting	Selling	Planning
Speaking	Supervising	Presenting
Teaching	Training	Programming
Writing/editing		

· · · · · · · · · · ·

Figure 10.7

Most college graduates tend to use the chronological approach. Some career field changers or re-entrants into the labor market prefer the functional approach.

Basically, the same information is placed on each resume, but it is organized differently. In actual practice, most resumes are hybrids of the two varieties. Over 95 percent of resumes are initially categorized by chronological sections rather than skills possessed.

The advantage to the functional approach is that it quickly spotlights marketable skills for the employer to review. This format emphasizes growth and development of the skills being marketed. Jobs not extremely relevant to career goals can be played down. Some people use this technique for hiding spotty employment records.

· · · · · · · · · · · · FUNCTIONAL RESUME EXAMPLE· · · · · · · · · · · ·

Writing Skills
- Compiled and published reports on the topics of . . .
- Earned awards on the clever design and depth of contrast presented on the following publications . . .
- Wrote over 20 articles for the college newspaper, largely on the topics of . . .
- Edited 50 articles over a period of years and recently compiled them into a new book titled . . .

Managing Skills
- Hired and trained 12 research assistants
- Managed a staff of 30 people
- Responsible for a budget of $58,000

· · · · · · · · · · ·

Figure 10.8

COMPUTER-GENERATED RESUMES

There are several computer-generated resume software packages available. Most of them offer a self-contained tutorial on how best to develop your resumes. Since there is no standard resume format or accepted norms in the fields, the computer program developers must basically select what they consider to be a more than adequate resume consistent with the constraint that it must fit a multitude of different types of backgrounds.

Essentially, the tutorial lock-step pattern is equivalent to reading a good book on resume preparation. There are several advantages that the computer approaches offer:

- Easy to make changes and more flexible than typeset
- Handle the formatting issues and design for you
- Cover all essential elements
- Graphically layout in an appealing manner
- Provide a rigorous pattern for inputting data

Some of the disadvantages include:

- Not as flexible as word processor/typewriter
- Expensive to purchase
- Requires access to specific computer configurations
- Resume print quality dependent upon printer quality
- Offer fear to the computer illiterate crowd

If you are comfortable with a simple computer word processor, these programs make the resume preparation a more pleasant task. If you want to be more creative a word processor can be just as effective. However, many students need the tutorial advice. Most college placement offices and software retail stores can help you locate resume software packages.

The chronological approach is familiar to all employers, so it is favorably regarded by them. The simple, direct structure even guides employers in the interview process. Strong emphasis is placed on previous employers and the descriptions of the jobs done for them.

The chronological approach is better accepted and serves the needs of more people than the functional approach. Examples of both approaches are illustrated. Use whichever form fits your personal preference.

Web HTML Resumes

Many websites allow you to load your resume onto their sites. They often charge an employer a reasonable fee to search for resumes on their website. It is usually free for you to upload your resume onto such a site.

Many college career service offices also allow you to upload your resume onto their website. They have developed their own "web resume book" or purchased such a service from a vendor. Thousands of employers are moving away from the "resume view" process using hard copy resume books. It is so much easier, and more effective, just to scan a resume database for the "keyword strings" or "selected criteria" to "pre-identify" potential applicants to interview.

The www has changed the way that thousands of employers now select job candidates. Most of the traditional ideas still work but if you don't avail yourself of the latest technology, you could lose opportunities for interviews.

Selection Criteria. Most job descriptions give specific job-related requirements and the HR staff typically does their first screen on these required variables. Listed below are some of the variables that employers often use in this initial screen.

- Degree Level
- Major
- Minor
- GPA
- University Name
- Technical Skills
- Location Desired
- Minimum Salary Desired
- Years of Experience
- Language Proficiency
- Date Available
- Full-/Part-Time
- Internships
- Professional Organizations
- Areas of Job Interest

It is very easy to scan through resumes with software looking for key variable or word strings. The full resume is reviewed only after it matches all of the job-related criteria.

Data Fields. Rather than scan through actual resumes, some websites request that you complete a database. You are given several tables with drop-down choices to select with your mouse. This constructs a database which allows web-based software to much more rapidly scan thousands of resumes in a shorter time period. Within seconds, employers could select "qualified" candidates and download or print resumes.

You want to place your data and resumes on many of these sites. All sites intuitively lead you through the process of entering data into their servers. On most sites the data can be entered in less than 15 munutes.

HTML Resumes. Many sites allow you to upload your actual resume to their server so employers can print a copy once your skills and abilities in the database match their needs. This upload/download facilitates the employer's access to you for further resume screens and internal distribution by HR staff to live hiring managers. You can then be contacted via telephone, fax, or email (preferred) for subsequent interviews.

The World Wide Web requires information to be in HTML format so your word processed resume must be converted to this format. In most cases, you can maintain the same "look" on your resume.

All major word processors allow you to "save" your resume in HTML format. Once you do that, you often must view your resume and do some minor html coding to ensure that centering, columns, tables, tabs, line spaces, etc. are as you intended. You then can upload your HTML resume to the site.

Many people don't have a good knowledge of HTML so there are other ways to get a properly designed resume uploaded. Some sites present you with templates that are small boxes and tables in which you replace the "sample info" with your own data. They are very easy to use and then automatically submit. The boxes may be the standard resume elements:

- Career Objective
- Education
- Activities
- Honors
- Skills
- Internships
- Work Experience
- References

Once you "fill in the blanks," you click a submit button which sends your resume forward. You can then, with your password, print out your own resume. Some sites allow multiple resumes for different career objective resumes.

Writing HTML Resumes.   There are several excellent HTML editors that you can use to prepare your resume without the use of the preformated templates. These give you great functionality so you can use any style or format that fits your needs.

Microsoft FrontPage, Netscape Composer, and Corel all provide excellent HTML editors. They function exactly like the word processor with which you are already familiar. The resume is already saved in HTML and, thus, you maintain your exact "rich text look" after you upload your resume.

Summary.   Each website operates a little differently but the concepts are all the same. You should load your resume onto as many sites as you have time to review. It's easy. It's free. The employer pays a fee on a subscription, advertising, search, or other novel way. Take advantage of this opportunity to broadly circulate your resume.

Image Creation

A resume is words, and many words have multiple meanings. Some words have more positive connotations than others. You must make *every* word on your resume count because wasted words can spoil your chance for success. A resume is not a hastily thrown together document.

Word selection is critical.

Your resume must be a reflection of your personality and interests as well as a description of the specific skills you have earned via education and work experience. Words that connote achievement and expertise give meaning and life to your resume. Your resume should not be just a collection of bland nouns and verbs. The resume reflects you.

Words to Avoid.   Your goal is to avoid as many unnecessary words as possible while including important words that are likely to influence the employer's decision. Words such as "I," "he," and "we" are superfluous and should be eliminated. One way to avoid this pitfall is by starting sentences with verbs.

Words can reflect the positive image you have of yourself and express the confidence you have in your abilities. Resume writing is one activity where it doesn't pay to be humble; patting yourself on the back is part of resume-building. Certain words connote success. Use them generously.

Any words that denote failure or unsatisfactory performance must be avoided. Words such as "fail," "no," "less," "low," "none," etc. should never be part of your resume vocabulary.

HI-TECH RESUMES

Nothing is likely to completely replace the traditional one-page paper resume soon, but innovative and creative approaches to the concept are now possible with recent technological advances. Some of these are noted below. These include personal ads, video resumes, computer generated resumes, data base resumes, and web entered resumes.

Video/Audio Ad. If a 30- to 60-second ad can sell hamburgers, why not you? Some news stations have successfully experimented with this concept for years. The basic idea is for you to appear in front of a camera and offer a brief resume and a statement of your job interests. The typical commercial goes like this:

> Hello, my name is **[Name].** Are you seeking an experienced **[job title]** with a thorough knowledge of **[major category of skills]**? I am seeking a new career opportunity in **[specific job interest areas].** I have **[statement of top three achievements at work or school].** I have a **[degree level]** degree in **[major fields]** from **[college]** with a strong academic performance record of **[grades].** Please call me at **[telephone number]** if you have an opportunity that fits a person with my talents.

These ads have been used on commercial television, cable stations, and as resume introducers. They must be done professionally to be effective, but producing a home version can add some important learning experiences. Some universities and private firms have spliced versions together from individuals in similar job interest areas and marketed them to employers as video resume books.

They do add the visual appearance, communication aspects, and some personality attributes when used in conjunction with the proper resume. Because of the time and equipment needed to view these and the boring nature of the visual presentation, the jury is still out on the effectiveness of this approach.

Video Resumes. Many individuals have experimented with the concept of a 15- to 30-minute videotape that essentially covers all points in the resume. The starting point in the production process is a high-quality resume.

These need to be produced professionally with multiple cameras to be effective. A head and shoulders shot for even 5 to 10 minutes does not make a quality product. The most effective video resumes show various clips of you in work, education, and social activities roles with your voice superimposed over the action shots.

A quality product is very expensive due to script development, equipment needed, studio time, and professional advice. Few employers have the time to preview hundreds of these as they do in the 60-second resume scan. Their use is usually limited to certain situations where you have already been screened in as a viable candidate.

The purpose of the video resume is to permit your personal qualities to come through by bringing the paper skill base to life. A quality production shows your ability to communicate, personality attributes, and personal leadership potentials. Videos are rarely effective for screening purposes. With all the coaching, some employers question the usefulness of the over-rehearsed presentations.

Data Base Resumes. Many services provide an opportunity for you to place your complete resume into a massive data base. Employers pay a fee to access these files in a search on key screening variables. The most frequently screened variables are job interest, degree, major, grades, prior related experience, location interests, and so on.

The converse of this is your using your personal computer to scan a data base to search for potential employers that match your desires.

These services charge a fee for you to store your data and possibly a fee to update or review it. Employers pay for hook-up time. These fees are fairly modest.

If you have the credentials which are in great demand, you are more likely to be contacted via such a program. If your background is of a more general nature or your salary demands are high, your chances of being selected decline considerably. Since there are so many private services available, you should thoroughly evaluate each one in relationship to the probability of their employer users accessing your particular resumes.

Summary. High technology is entering the job match business, so the future will undoubtedly improve the results of these efforts. Satellite video interviewing and electronic referral of both data base and video resumes will be a massively-used reality someday. The choice to employ and pay for these innovative approaches to an old problem remains a personal decision based on a cost/benefit analysis.

RESUME GAMES

Numerous books and articles have been written advocating different approaches to the traditional chronological resume. There are advocates of market letters, extensive cover letters, sales brochures, brief personal portfolios, targeted resumes, functional resumes, and hundreds of other non-traditional forms of employment qualification record displays.

Yet, through decades, the overwhelming favorite of employers remains the basic chronological resume.

Over 90 percent of all jobs filled at the professional, technical, and managerial levels are required to provide a basic background resume. Although no single format or form has emerged, the basic structure has remained unchanged.

A primary reason why employers keep resumes on file has nothing to do with the applicant's qualifications. The Equal Employment Opportunity Commission simply suggests that employers retain all unsolicited resumes for several months to help document potential discrimination claims. This recommendation has prompted the majority of large employers to computerize their resume retrieval systems.

When a job opening exists, the first source of qualified candidates is an internal search followed by referrals from current employees. The next screen is a search of the resume data base, usually on selected skill-based fields.

Unless you have a carefully thought-through strategy and rationale for using a non-traditional resume, the best advice is to stay with the chronological resume. The test of time is on your side, whereas resume games rarely make it through the prying screen of the professional human resource officer or experienced manager.

If possible, avoid passive verbs and substitute verbs with growth, movement, and driving images. In addition, remember that cliches and flowery phrases never add strength to a resume.

Action Words. Employers want producers. They like movers because the driving person tends to be the most productive. The essence of a good employee is getting a job done efficiently and accurately while being aware of other's feelings and concerns.

Words that show action on your part convey the image of a successful doer. You should use as many of the Action Words as possible in order to bring life to your resume and cover letter.

```
···············ACTION WORDS················

accelerate        evaluate         originate        significant
adapt             expand           participate      set up
administer        expedite         perform          solve

analyze           found            plan             strategy
approve           generate         pinpoint         structure
coordinate        increase         program          streamline

conceive          influence        propose          successful
conduct           implement        prove            supervise
complete          initiate         provide          support

control           interpret        recommend        train
create            improve          reduce           touch
delegate          launch           reinforce        work

develop           lead             reorganize
demonstrate       lecture          revamp
direct            maintain         responsible

effect            manage           revise
eliminate         motivate         review
establish         organize         schedule

··········
```

Figure 10.9

Action words can be coupled with nouns or used as descriptors of what you have done or are capable of doing. When tied to your educational achievements, work experience, activities, interests, and plans, the action words provide amazing evidence of your capabilities.

Self-descriptive Words.   How would you describe yourself? Try to think of 20 words that would give someone else a good idea of your personality and attitude. You should work as many of these words as possible into your resume if you want the reader to get a good idea of what you offer.

Very few jobs have only one applicant applying. You will be among *several* technically well-qualified applicants. An employer must make a choice. That choice is usually determined by what the employer thinks the applicant *can do* and *will do*.

The impression left by your resume will determine if you are invited for an interview. People who can confidently state their level of skills, interests, and attitudes stand better chances of being selected from a group of other qualified applicants.

It is better to risk sounding cocky than ignoring the strong interest of the potential employer. Avoid the humble approach.

Several self-descriptive words are illustrated. Although it is perfectly acceptable to use some of these words in describing yourself, it is preferable to first identify the words that you feel are most descriptive. Then think of educational episodes, work experience, and/or activities that illustrate the descriptors and illustrate these qualities via resume examples.

SELF-DESCRIPTIVE WORDS

active	economical	personable
adaptable	efficient	pleasant
aggressive	energetic	positive
alert	enterprising	practical
ambitious	enthusiastic	productive
analytical	extroverted	realistic
attentive	fair	reliable
broad-minded	forceful	resourceful
conscientious	imaginative	respective
consistent	independent	self-reliant
constructive	logical	sense of humor
creative	loyal	sincere
dependable	mature	sophisticated
determined	methodical	systematic
diplomatic	objective	tactful
disciplined	optimistic	talented
discrete	perceptive	traveler

Figure 10.10

GOAL-DIRECTED BEHAVIOR

A positive decision about you will occur only if there is ample evidence that you have more than the minimum talents to handle the assignment. Resumes tend to focus too much on "can-do" factors instead of "will-do" factors.

Can-Do Factors. Your skills that result from academic curriculums, extracurricular activities, and work experiences illustrate that you may be well qualified to handle the position. Most employers want to know more about you than *technical* capabilities. Most job-related failures do not relate to weak skills.

Will-Do Factors. Real job success comes from inner motivations, common personal values, related interests, and appropriate personality attributes. An effective presentation of these will-do factors creates a desire by the potential employer to want to talk to you further.

Therefore, the resume must package together more than a finite set of technical skills. You must also go beyond *saying* that you are a highly-motivated person. You must *illustrate* in a non-boastful manner that you also possess the personal qualities that are necessary for job success.

Employers review resumes looking for balance in a person's life. Employers want to see individuals who can juggle several balls in the air, make efficient use of time outside the classroom, and progress in summer and part-time work experiences.

DESIGN TO HIGHLIGHT TRAITS

Since the *visual* impact of a resume is often what captures the scanner's attention, design to appeal to scanners, not readers. Rarely are more than two pages scanned.

The resume should be graphically centered and balanced with equal amounts of type and white space. Underlining, capitalization, and bullet points move the reader's eye to the points you wish to emphasize. Some of the resume preparation services that typeset your resume are excellent at graphical presentation, but typeset is expensive and difficult to quickly alter.

As you fill in the detail, focus on relevant, concisely stated points that emphasize skills and *accomplishments*. Your superior performance capabilities, personality attributes, and leadership traits need to be interwoven into the description of your background statements. The fine print supports your emphasized claims.

A professionally prepared resume with bullet points initially captures attention. After the first impression, it is resume content that convinces the employer to interview the applicant.

The one-minute scan permits only four to seven key points to hit the reviewer's eye. Focusing on more than seven points risks a high probability of a "no interest" response. Once the attention has been captured, you can begin to fill in details.

Once the recruiter stops scanning and starts reading, your emphasis needs to focus on personal traits rather than just a recitation of your skills. Traits such as work habits, maturity, confidence, social awareness, and motivation must be presented.

Lengthy and verbose resumes turn off employers. Keep your resume short and crisp. Assist the employer in developing a match in terms of interest, degree, major and other accomplishments that accentuate positive experiences and leadership characteristics.

Proven Power Words. After your interview, the employer always writes a constructive evaluation that cites the results of the interview. Many interviewers prefer to sum up the interview with a few words that describe you. These words tend to be high impact words that connote multiple meanings when read by other reviewers.

These "proven power words" are listed below. These words may be used to sell your abilities to others in the organization. The powerful thrust of each word emphatically implies that the interviewer is sold on you. You are a winner.

- Successful
- Seasoned producer
- Proven record
- Results oriented
- Go-getter
- Problem solver
- Self-starter
- Goal driven

WORDS CREATE IMAGES

Resume scanners look for words which describe you as a *go-getter, producer, hard worker, responsible,* and *decisive* individual. These action words imply that you are achievement-oriented, assertive, and yet respectful of other's opinions and actions. Certain action words, when incorporated into the description of your education, activities, and work experiences, influence the impression you leave.

Verbs. Verbs such as *analyze, approve, direct, influence, manage, plan, establish, create, supervise,* etc., connote leadership traits. Most career fields need those characteristics.

Descriptors. We rarely desire to describe ourselves as assertive, ambitious, creative, or systematic. But you can use descriptive words to discuss your educational background, personal leadership activities, or work experiences in which you had a major role. By implication, the reader assigns these attributes to you, not just to the experience.

Adjectives. Qualifying adjectives may be used to add impact to your accomplishments. In the body of your resume you will use real situations with names, titles, dates, etc. to describe an experience that illustrates your skill levels.

Numbers. You should use numbers whenever possible to describe the *magnitude* of your achievements. Some examples might include:

- Increased output by 30 percent in three months
- Managed a staff of 20 professionals
- Expanded sales by 10 percent in six months
- Made significant improvements in . . .
- Developed dynamic program on . . .
- Created major contributions including . . .
- Supervised development of . . .

Adverbs. High-impact adverbs can enhance accomplishments. These adverbs might include words such as *effectively, aggressively, tactfully, successfully, fairly, equitably, quickly, energetically,* and *objectively.*

Impact. These high-impact words add *credibility* to your accomplishments. They respond to questions that a reviewer might have in mind and provide meaningful specifics. These influential words and phrases, if carefully, honestly, and objectively selected, should be used within each resume paragraph.

- Street fighter
- Aggressive
- Team player
- People person
- No-nonsense person

How can you incorporate these proven impactful words into your resume? They can be helpful if they accurately describe you. The inclusion must be done subtly and with finesse or the wrong impression may be reached and your resume discarded.

Like the self-descriptive words, you must use them in *descriptions* of educational experiences, outside activities, job duty descriptions, and events noted on your

- Design for skimmers, not readers.
- Graphically center, balance, and outline text.
- Construct on 8-1/2 x 11 white bond paper.
- Eliminate all errors — perfect.
- Use underlining, capitalization, and bullet points.
- Create "white space" on each page.
- Be positive, avoid negatives.
- Keep the points concise, yet complete.
- Focus on relevant data only.
- Emphasize skills and capabilities.
- Incorporate buzz words about your field.
- Use action words, not passive verbs.
- Use the pronoun "I" sparingly.
- Stress accomplishments.
- Use examples to illustrate personality traits.
- Let actions denote leadership traits.
- Illustrate skills by course specifications.
- Highlight abilities by performance episodes.
- Personalize by showing uniqueness.
- Critique as an advertisement.

···········

Figure 10.11

resume. As you describe the situation and story about your background, you use these words. The second level use of these words will often drive the reader to subconsciously ascribe the descriptor to you indirectly.

Package the Truth Subtly. A creative targeted resume makes effective use of carefully selected words. These key words add perspective to the mundane detail. They present an honest, sincere, humble view of your background. This image that you project should target upon your values, interests, personal qualities, and skills.

Values. What distinguishes you from others with similar skills? *Values* are those principles that we hold dear which do not significantly change over time. Employers tend to generalize about your philosophical leaning on work ethics, motivational traits, social awareness, and professional perspectives.

Interests. Career success comes easier if you truly enjoy the activities required to handle assignments expected of you on the job. Hopefully, your interests are similar to successful people in your chosen career field. Targeting these common *interests* encourages the resume scanner to slow down and take note of your likes and dislikes.

Personal qualities. Certain career fields require unique attributes that transcend the basic ability to do a given task. Recruiters scan for the best, not just adequate, *personal qualities*. You must focus on descriptions of your education, activities, and work experiences that reveal characteristics such as personality, teamwork, social poise, maturity, responsibility, loyalty, work ethics, and major commitments.

Skills. Resume writers often spend an inordinate amount of space describing job-related skills. Most applicants who get to the interview stage possess the basic set of skills needed to handle the position. Be careful in overstating the obvious in the limited space available. It is your *unique* set of values, interests, and personal qualities that truly make you a very special applicant. You must acknowledge your job-related skills but not dwell on the obvious.

Door-Openers. The best qualified people are not the only people who get the interview. Skills open doors but the person who is eventually hired may not have the highest degree, possess the most directly-related college major, or enjoy the highest grades. The resume packages the total individual, not just the skill-based components. Effective resume presentations subtly display a wide range of character attributes.

Resume Contents

Selling – Selling – Selling

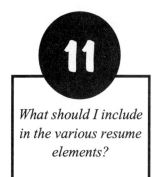

Nearly all initial contacts with a potential employer are first introduced via a resume. The resume is your number one tool in your job search toolbox.

A resume uses an outline format in contrast to a narrative writing style. Most resumes have six to nine major sections with the length depending on your individual background.

SALES BROCHURE

The number and type of headings used depend upon your background, career interests, and personal preference. It is not necessary to use all the headings. Some headings can be consolidated or even omitted. The two major headings are always *education* and *work experience* because these offer the most job-related criteria.

Each of the various sections has several subcomponents. Although each section is constructed independently, there is a close relationship among the various sections. The item that ties them all together is the *career objective*.

Each section is written with the goal of enhancing the career objective. In addition, each element should show the potential employer how that part of your background further supports your suitability for the position being sought.

Identification

The goal of your resume is to convince the potential employer to initially contact you and to continue contacting you until you receive a job offer and accept it. You want to make the contact process as simple as possible.

This section includes your name, various addresses, and telephone numbers.

Telephone Numbers. There is a trend for employers to use the telephone extensively—and often exclusively—in the employment process. It is crucial that you leave a number where you can always be reached.

Telephone calls are quick and convenient. A brief telephone interview often provides a review of your interests, communication ability, and career goals. If you are a difficult person to reach because of your busy schedule, you should invest in a telephone answering machine or service.

Your career objective statement summarizes how you desire to use your talents described under "Work" and "Education."

Objective

Telephone calls, along with emails, are almost always used to negotiate appointment times. They are an essential part of the search process.

Most calls come during the normal business hours of 8:00 a.m. to 5:00 p.m. If you are not available during those hours, you should indicate when you are available in parentheses. Many employers will call you in the evening if you recommend they do so. If you prefer not to be contacted at work you should so indicate.

If you are unable to be reached by telephone, leave the number of a friend or relative who will be able to reach you. Indicate to the employer that the message will be relayed to you as soon as possible.

Work Address. If you can be contacted at work, list your work address and telephone number. This greatly expedites communications with potential employers. If you do not wish any employment communications going to your work address, do not include it on your resume.

Current Address. This is the address to which you want all employment inquiries mailed. You should always include the zip code.

Permanent Address. This is the address of someone who will always know how to reach you. Many employers may not follow up with your resume immediately but will contact you later. Thus, it is in your best interests to leave an audit trail. It is frequently a parent's address.

email. Most resumes include the email address, typically after the current address, since many resumes are served to HTML and loaded onto websites. It is common to see a hyperlink on the mail.

Career Objective

Your career objective is one of the most important element of your resume. Ideally, every other section is related to the goals you have set or stated.

Few employers will take the time to interview you if there is not a job currently available or no prospects for one. When there is an opening, employers invariably have several candidates who are well qualified to do the job. A statement of strong interest in the position is the one thing employers use when deciding which candidates to interview.

Nearly every resume screened for consideration by the employer has the basic set of qualifications. The second screen is on interests and motivation. The best source of that information is the career objective statement.

Desirability. Placing a career statement on both your resume and your cover letter gives a potential employer a firm idea of what you want to do. Additionally, if your cover letter and resume are separated (as is often the case), there will be no confusion as to your career goals.

A few experts advise people not to place their career objectives directly on their resumes. The reasoning is that it restricts the scope and usefulness of the resume. They reason that with the options left open, the employer might recommend a position for which you would be qualified.

Another group of experts strongly disagree with that line of reasoning. At the resume stage in the career planning process you are no longer "shopping around." You know what you want. Many studies suggest that goal-directed behavior is much more likely to produce positive results.

The shopping-around stage is preliminary to the resume and interview stage. A broad-scope resume is not as effective as one that focuses on a specific goal. The usefulness of a specific resume is indeed limited, but that does not need to handicap you.

You can and should develop several specific resumes to use in specific instances.

Placing the career statement on the cover letter does give a potential employer a firm idea of what you want to do. On the other hand, the design of the resume may be too general to support the statements made in the cover letter.

Employers often remove the cover letters and send the resumes out to different managers. These managers may not follow up positively if there is not a strong goal statement with the resume. Most managers look for strong desire and interest on a resume to indicate that the individual is motivated to do a given assignment.

Placement.   The career objective statement is always placed at the top of the resume. If there is no match between open jobs and your goals, many employers will read no further.

Your goal is to interest the employer in reading your whole resume. There are techniques of writing career statements so that they are both specific and yet broad enough to cover a wide array of assignments.

One way is to make the short-term goal very close to the title of the job that you know is open and to then write intermediate and long-term goals in much more general tones. You are more likely to at least get an interview if you do this. You can use the interview to feel out the employer on other possibilities close to your immediate interests.

Multiple Resumes.   One common misconception is that you should prepare only one resume and use it in applying for all types of jobs. Although that is an inexpensive plan, it is seldom the most effective approach.

Most people have multiple career interests even after doing a very thorough job of career planning. It is ludicrous to assume that there is one and only one job that is right and perfect for you.

Everyone has varied interests and can be successful in many different types of jobs. In fact, many people fall into jobs by luck which turn out to be perfect matches.

A thorough self-assessment and career exploration does help to narrow the field. A specific goal statement greatly aids in narrowing the scope of job possibilities. Specification helps you manage a previously mind-boggling array of options.

The job search is what forces the specification. A statement of what you want helps you develop a plan for achieving goals.

Most people can easily handle a job search that includes three or four different resumes. Which resume to use or send depends on the nature of the contact and what you know about the job to which your contact has access.

Job Targeting.   Interviews are difficult to obtain. The time and money spent obtaining an interview are often quite significant. If you can write a resume to perfectly fit a position you know is open, you will greatly increase the likelihood of an interview.

TARGETED OBJECTIVES

Write your job objective for your future supervisor and add skills and abilities that reveal your *potential* for assisting that person in doing a better job. Your future boss needs to know what you want to do. The boss matches candidates against criteria that are necessary to effectively handle challenging assignments.

Employers cannot take time to read every word in every resume, so they tend to focus their attention on the career objective. They are not impressed by flowery phrases and cliches and most recommend simply highlighting the key elements.

The targeted resume produces an instant match for your future supervisor. You must explain *what* you *want* to do and *why* you are the *ideal* candidate for the position. Depict yourself as the solution to problems.

The major disadvantage to the targeted resume is that you may have to prepare several different versions to match your multiple career field interests. However, with modern word processing programs and personal computers, that is a very minor detail. You direct different resumes to different employers.

A typical career objective statement in a targeted resume might look similar to the following:

> <u>Brief Job Title.</u>   Seeking a position as a _____ in the industry which would make use of my proven abilities in _____, _____, and _____.

The resume scanner assumes that you have the abilities to do the job which you know from your research probably exists. The reader further assumes that you will later illustrate your credentials in the body of your resume. You have created some initial interest and have encouraged the reviewer to read further.

Some recruiters feel that a major turn-off is having *too much* information. Employers want you to boil down the resume to the essentials because their hiring decision rests largely on the interview, not the resume.

Your confident statement implies interest in the firm, knowledge of the field, and skills necessary to perform the required tasks. Next, be convincing in a statement of your skills and interests. The career objective statement should be placed near the top of your resume (after name and address) where it can be among the first screening factors reviewed.

Some opponents of targeted resumes suggest that the career objective statement may quickly screen you out of consideration if the firm has no current opening in your area of interest. This logic assumes that the reader will screen you in for some other assignment for which your credentials might be applicable. That logic also assumes that an employer is a counselor trying to find a good match for you. Unfortunately, those hopeful gestures are often just wishful thinking. Most employers will not be reviewing resumes without trying to fill specific job openings.

The education, activities, and work experience sections of your resume form the heart of your story. The information provided proves that you have the proper credentials, including basic skills gained through specific courses and on-the-job experiences. The resume headings focus attention on the details that explain your can-do and will-do credentials. The body of your resume will prove that you have the capabilities to do the job stated in your objective statement.

• • • COMMON JOB TITLES USED ON CAREER OBJECTIVE STATEMENTS • • •

Financial Titles

Accountant	Economic Analyst	Mortgage Lender
Appraiser	Economist	Operations Manager
Bank Trainee	Financial Accounting	Programmer
Branch Manager	Financial Analyst	Public Accounting
Budget Analyst	Financial Institutions	Real Estate
Claims Representative	Financial Intern	Securities Trader
Commercial Lending	Industrial Accounting	Systems Analyst
Cost Accounting	Information Systems	Tax Manager
Credit Analyst	Insurance	Tax Specialist
Data Processing	Internal Auditor	Treasury Analyst
Database Manager	Internal Consultant	Trust Administrator
Department Manager	Investment Analyst	Underwriter

Marketing Titles

Account Executive	Field Engineer	Sales Analyst
Ad Copywriter	Leasing Agent	Sales Assistant
Advertising Sales	Manufacturers Representative	Sales Consultant
Agent	Market Analyst	Sales Manager
Assistant Buyer	Market Researcher	Sales Representative
Brand Assistant	Marketing Assistant	Securities Trader
Brochure Developer	Marketing Representative	Service Manager
Broker	Marketing Show Coordinator	Store Management
Commercial Advisor	Merchandiser	Technical Sales
Commercial Sales Assistant	Product Assistant	Technical Sales Engineer
District Manager	Retailing	Technical Specialist

Operations Titles

Aerospace Engineering	Laboratory Assistant	Quality Control
Chemical Engineering	Lodging Industry Trainee	Research Scientist
Civil Engineering	Logistics Coordinator	Restaurant Management
Computer Scientist	Mechanical Engineering	Setup Assistant
Electrical Engineering	Operations Manager	Supervisor
Electronic Engineering	Production Scheduling	Technical Manager
Facility Manager	Purchasing	Transportation Manager
Industrial Engineering	Purchasing Agent	Warehouse Manager
Industrial Management		

Administrative Titles

Attorney	Lobbyist	Public Relations Writer
Benefits Manager	Management Trainee	Report Writer
Brochure Developer	Media Coordinator	Technical Writer
Compensation Analyst	News Manager	Training Facilitator
Corporate Attorney	Personnel Assistant	

• • • • • • • • • • •

Figure 11.1

Why risk sending a vague and general resume when you could send a specially designed resume for each known job opening? It only takes a few additional minutes of your time to develop multiple resumes, and it may mean the difference in securing an interview.

Although other parts of your resume may change when you use job targeting, the major impact will be on your career objective. You should try

to make your career statement sound somewhat like the job description of the job you are targeting.

Using exact job titles and specific words from the job description is too obvious so take care in making it somewhat generic. You should make your statement sound like you are sending it to several similar organizations.

Geographical Restrictions. Geographical restrictions may be placed under personal background or in the career statement section. If you do decide to place a geographical restriction on your resume, you should carefully evaluate the reasons for doing so.

One of the most common reasons for geographical restrictions is the dual-career couple issue. Other reasons often stated relate to health, family roots, and lifestyle concerns. However, reasons such as "prefer sunshine" or "like to be near the ocean" are not valid reasons. These statements show immature attitudes.

If you do have a valid reason for a restriction, you have several options. One option is that you never mention it and simply confine your search process to a certain area. Another option is to simply note the restriction as a "preference" and keep your options open. A third option is to state a restriction and not explain it.

From a career and job standpoint, it is preferable not to list geographical restrictions or even preferences on your resume. Where you have legitimate concerns, however, the best advice is to explain your reasons for the restriction.

Length. The maximum length of a career statement is one paragraph of not more than four sentences, or approximately 60 words. In order to attract attention, the first words are key words—a job title or a group of titles.

This title is often underlined or capitalized for emphasis. Remember, this is a major resume-screening factor for employers, and it can make a significant impact on whether or not the rest of your resume is read.

Technical Jargon. Many people apply for jobs for which they are unqualified, and this is irritating to employers. For example, many people apply for jobs in personnel without any background or courses in labor relations, employment, interviewing, etc. By stating your knowledge of the field, the employer will know you are qualified.

Every field has an array of words that refers to what is done in the field. Using as many of these "buzz words" as possible in the restricted space available on your resume enhances the employer's awareness and interest. The employer quickly realizes that you have a high degree of knowledge as well as an interest in the field. You are not just another shopper.

Using jargon establishes your credibility. It shows knowledge of the field which encourages the employer to read further. Since the career objective is one of the first things the eye sees on the resume, it is important that you utilize jargon. Your goal is to get your resume read. Examples of "buzz words" are given in the "Sample Career Statements" in Figures 11.3 and 11.4.

GEOGRAPHICAL PREFERENCES MAY HELP

Many experts make a geographical restriction sound like a major negative handicap in the job search process. In reality, many employers prefer to see the stability. If you have a sound, mature reason for seeking employment in a given community, many employers might well screen your resume for consideration over the person who might be considered a "job hopper."

When you must use a geographical limitation, it should be no more than two sentences. It may be placed at the end of the "career objective statement" or in the "Personal" section of your resume.

Some possible ways to incorporate a geographical preference into the objective statement are listed below.

- Prefer to locate in the Minneapolis area for family reasons. My fiance and I have several relatives in the vicinity, and we prefer the climate and other advantages of the twin city area.
- For lifestyle and personal reasons the New York City area is a major preference.
- Planning to stay in the tri-cities community to assist ailing family member.
- Preference is to remain in the general vicinity of my hometown of Dallas but would consider a transfer if requested.

Although statements like this can be limiting, the restriction is often necessary for personal reasons. Many employers in the area would welcome a person who has a strong commitment to the area. A personal obligation does not always have to create a negative reply when there are extenuating circumstances.

Most experts recommend leaving a geographical restriction (or preference) out of your career objective statement. By limiting your job search to a given community, you are in essence committing to the area without telling the employer that you would be willing to relocate if necessary. You might feel differently about the relocation issue if and when you really have to face that decision.

Interest. The job title (or titles) that you use establishes your area of interest. The employer knows the meaning of the job title, and assumes that you do too.

By using a particular job title on the resume, you effectively expand the employer's interest in you. Job titles save space and at the same time describe your interests.

Individuals with prior work experience in the field do not need to use as many "buzz words." In the work experience description, jargon and concepts are obvious. Conversely, individuals with only educational credentials must use several "buzz words."

The level of job you specify automatically expands the employer's understanding of your interests. Stating the *level* sought implies that you have had a wealth of prior experience in the field.

GOALS INTEGRATE YOUR BACKGROUND

The major portion of your resume simply catalogs information by explaining how and when you developed your set of skills. You need to provide a potential employer the rationale for *why* you made the decisions that your resume describes.

Goal statements add meaning to the choices that you made earlier. They explain that there was rational thought that went into your maturing process. Your life did not just stumble along in a haphazard fashion. You influenced the direction by the jobs you took, the courses you selected, the people with whom you associated, and so on.

You made the decisions because it built an important part of your background that can now be used in the job that you are seeking. No employer is likely to hire you simply because you need a job. Lots of people need jobs. Can you explain why you want the specific job that is open and why you are the best qualified person for it?

Many people have a problem writing career objective statements. The cop-out to the goal definition challenge is to walk away and put nothing on the resume. Unfortunately, wandering generalities seldom find lifetime career success.

The challenge is finding the proper balance in a career statement. Some people write a statement that is so vague and ill-defined that employers sense a great deal of immaturity. Who wants to hire a person who has not given much sincere thought to what they want to do in life to earn a living?

Conversely, some people write a statement that is so specific that the likelihood of such a job being open is extremely remote. It marks a lack of adequate career exploration for an MBA degree holder with a major in marketing to say he or she wants to find a product management job in a remote community where no consumer goods firms are located.

You can be well qualified for a specific job but define yourself out of consideration by narrowing your focus to extreme limits. Advanced education can limit prospects also. PhD candidates occasionally drive taxis because their specialty area became obsolete.

The secret to writing a successful career objective statement is **balance**. You must balance your credentials and interests against the reality of the job market in your geographical area of interest.

JOB LEVELS

- Executive
- Partner
- Vice President
- Director
- Assistant Director
- Manager
- Assistant Manager
- Analyst
- Coordinator
- Trainee

Figure 11.2

Although you will later elaborate on this in the "Work Experience" section, a brief statement of level automatically moves your resume to a different level of credibility and consideration.

An example of this is the job title of controller. The employer automatically assumes that you have experience as an accountant, auditor, budgeter, cost analyst, assistant controller, etc. All of these previous job titles enhance the employer's understanding of your credentials.

The job title is all you need to establish the employer's interest. Other parts of the resume build upon this later. Your cover letter, if applicable, also expands upon this interest.

Management Trainee. Prefer a medium-size firm that rotates new employees through the sales, finance, and operations functions and makes final assignments to one area within several months based upon a joint assessment of personal talents and firm needs. Strongest area may be in marketing since best course work is in the humanities and social sciences which develop extensive writing, presentation, and interpersonal communication skills. Very flexible in relocations, especially international tours, which might draw upon my multilingual talents. Aspire to become a senior manager or partner in a service industry organization.

Sales Representative. Wish to begin my career in an assignment that offers contact with the public, structured on-the-job training, exposure to management, and a quality product or service. After training and some experience, plan to move into management assignments involving training, hiring, customer service, advertising strategy, analyzing research studies, and supervising others.

Industrial Sales Representative. Desire a position that utilizes technical background in physics, chemistry, and mathematics. Although not limited, industries most applicable include electronics, chemical, drugs, and oil. Special talents in aiding the technical interface between firm and customer. Aspire to become an operating marketing manager with responsibility for budgets, marketing plans, and decision-making responsibilities.

Commercial Sales Representative. Desire extensive contact with customers and regular exposure to management to help build upon talents of facilitating relationships. Prefer on-the-job training that quickly introduces products and services. After training and experience, seek a promotion into first line management that involves recruiting, hiring, training, and motivating subordinates. Prefer experience doing a line management career in some staff assignments, such as advertising, market research, and merchandising.

Brand Assistant. Want responsibility of coordinating advertising, pricing, packaging, forecasts, distribution channels, profits, etc. of a consumer goods product line. Previous sales experience should aid in coordinating programs with the sales force. Strong analytical skills and good writing skills coupled with experience hopefully will permit advancement to product manager.

Product Management. After experience in sales force management, desire staff level responsibilities in advertising coordination, pricing, packaging, and market research. Prefer involvement in a consumer or commercial product line with multiple distribution channels for specific well-known brands. Wish to use strong analytical skills, copywriting abilities, and assertive personal characteristics in initial assignments.

Sales Engineer. Interested in industries such as electronics, electrical machinery, office products which can use my engineering training. Desire to serve as a technical service liaison with customer contact. Intermediate goal is to move into higher levels of responsibility from both a technical and managerial viewpoint.

Retailing. Interested in joining a department, chain, discount, or specialty store in a structured management training program. Prefer exposure to a wide variety of product or service lines. Desire experience in sales, supervision, buying, and other facets of retailing. Eventually hope to advance into either store management or the merchandising function.

Retail Buyer. Plan to start in a management development program with an upscale fashion retailer that rotates associates through the buying, store management, and operational aspects of a hectic and exciting environment. Desire assignments in merchandising, advertising, sales, customer service, and supervision. As a senior executive, desire to buy merchandise on a global basis and manage large multi-employee operations

Public Relations Assistant. Interested in copy writing, editing, writing speeches and news releases, photography, graphics, etc. Desire experience on organization's internal and external publications. Good writing and speaking skills with communications background should assist in advancement to a management position within the public relations department.

Personnel Assistant. Expect to begin job in the human resources department of a unionized manufacturing concern to gain experience in the functions of labor contract administration, employment, recruitment, compensation, benefit programs, training programs, and performance management. Long-term goal is to become a general HR officer.

Management Consultant. Drawing upon previous work experience in accounting systems, plan to start in the management service function of a large public accounting or national consulting firm. Desire to use academic courses in accounting, finance, and systems in analyzing data, writing proposals, writing analytical reports, and making specific recommendations to client organizations. Eventually wish to be involved in strategic projects involving product positioning, acquisitions, divestitures, and organizational design.

• • • • • • • • • •

Figure 11.3

Accountants. Considering opportunities in both public and industrial firms. Enjoy the client contact in public and the management potential in industry. Desire variety of experiences in auditing, cost, tax and finance. Based upon experience, long-term goal is to move into a chief financial office position or partner with a public firm.

Industrial Accountant. Plan to start with a manufacturing or service concern. Prefer on-the-job training in a variety of rotated assignments. Desire some experience in internal auditing, cost accounting, credit analysis, investment analysis, tax preparations, and the treasury functions.

Public Accountant. Desire to join a large to medium size firm where there is training in auditing, taxes, and management service. Prefer a professional training oriented firm that keeps staff current through regular seminars and publications. Aspire to partnership within a reasonable period of time. Eventually plan to work in financial and technology consulting engagements at a senior level.

Corporate Accountant. Desire a position with a large prestigious industrial firm that leads controllership candidates through the technical departments like internal auditing, management accounting, financial systems, tax preparation, financial reporting, and information management. With over 30 hours in finance, systems, and accounting course work, expect to employ talent in a progression of positions leading to senior financial management responsibilities. Willing to relocate frequently including international rotational assignments that draw upon multiple language fluencies developed in various academic programs and academic studies.

Systems Specialist. Plan to accept an initial job as a programmer or systems analyst which can make best use of my quantitative background. Interested in computer hardware/software firms and software service firms. Special interest in marketing and finance applications. Prefer the role of systems consultant to several departments or customers.

Technology Consultant. Wish to begin in computer systems and programming to expand on academic training but later hope to merge technical skills with management ambitions. Plan to draw upon a strong background in web design, computer programming, data structures, and information systems management. Seeking initial work in systems support, MIS consulting, web applications, and internal and external client relations which require unique interpersonal skills, presentation abilities, and technical competencies.

Financial Analyst. Desire to join an organization that assigns complex financial projects to new employees immediately. Interested in analyzing projects involving capital cost, cash flow, capital investments, tax verifications, financing methods, pension fund security analysis, pricing, cost comparisons, profit and loss and balance sheet analysis, international consolidations, interest rates, monetary policy, etc. Eventually wish to move into the controllership function.

Corporate Financial Analyst. Seeking an assignment in an international manufacturing firm which demands a strong course background in accounting, finance, and computer systems supported with nearly two years of related work experience. Coursework in advanced accounting, financial structures, financial analysis, budgeting, taxes, and risk assessment serve to prepare for managing a controllership or treasury function.

Consumer Banking. Goal is to become a senior bank operating officer. Initially desire to gain experience in branch management, operations, trust, and installment lending. Strongest asset is in the commercial lending function where can conduct complex credit analysis and meet commercial customers. At some point, an experience in international banking would be important.

Commercial Banking. Long-term goal is to progress to a senior operating officer of a large financial institution. Desire to gain experience in branch banking, installment lending, investment banking analysis, commercial lending, credit analysis, trust administration, cash services, mortgage lending, customer relations, and internal operations supervision. The competitive commercial lending function draws upon considerable technical skills acquired in course work in finance, accounting, economics, and communications.

Production Assistant. Goal is to start in any one of several areas in manufacturing including scheduling, industrial engineering, first line supervision, inventory control, physical distribution, purchasing, quality control, etc. Prefer an employer who permits one to rotate through various functions because eventually wish to move into operations management.

• • • • • • • • • • •

Figure 11.4

Industry. Many individuals have very strong ties to particular industries. By staying within a given industry, an individual can build expertise. Developing an image as an expert in an industry in your career field is one method of assuring job security and advancement.

For example, there are many aspects of the semi-conductor industry which are common to other engineering fields. An electrical engineer can transfer his or her skills to several different industries. It might be wise, however, for a person working in the semi-conductor industry to remain in that industry.

Some people build their careers around an industry. For example, a merchandise buyer is limited to jobs in the retail store industry if he or she wants to remain a fashionwear buyer. Discussing the industry in the career statement shows an awareness of the field.

Other examples of industries in which there are strong loyalties include banking, insurance, transportation, higher education, health care, and real estate. Specifying your interest in an industry will enhance your acceptability to employers in that industry.

Advancement. Many employers want some evidence of how realistic your ambitions are. Do you understand the typical promotion path? How realistic are your timetables? Are you thinking about a job just for today or are you planning for the future as well?

Goals are tied to timeframes. Your career statement should have an immediate job objective but it should also show some evident awareness of typical promotion avenues.

No one is going to hold you to your statement. It changes over time. All you are saying is that you have seriously thought about the future and have analyzed it in relation to the position for which you are now applying. In addition, your statement shows much about your interest, attitude, and ability to plan. These are important factors evaluated by the employer.

Education

Employers seek people who know how to do specific tasks. The tasks may be very broad or extremely narrow; they may be highly technical or extremely subjective or creative. Such skills come from training and work experience.

The more relevant education is to the career statement, the more space you should devote to it. Thus, more recent education must be described in greater depth than education received several years ago.

Institution. The full name of the institution should be given. If the institution is not a well-known school, you should give a brief description of its mission and size. Conversely, if the institution is a nationally-known leader in its field, you might

EDUCATION DEVELOPS SKILLS

What can you do? Your series of planned academic courses prove that you have the necessary skills to handle your career objective. Based upon a mastery of specific courses, you have learned how to accomplish certain tasks. Resume scanners tend to look for the following things:

Academic Performance. Grades are used as a predictor of intelligence, teamwork abilities, personality characteristics, perseverance, and other attributes of challenging situations.

If you have strong grades, emphasize them. If your grades are weak, draw upon trends, certain subjects, and other grade-related items to bolster the same predictors that grades supposedly address.

Breadth. Part of a sound academic experience is to learn a little about many things. A broad-based liberal arts education shows a recruiter that your communication skills and intellectual awareness meet acceptable standards.

Depth. No employer seeks a narrow-minded "nerd," but a mastery of some discipline can be indicative of the ability to comprehend a complex subject area in sufficient depth to approach a state-of-the-art mentality. The study of a field in depth, such as thirty or more semester credit hours, is a positive indication of strong cognitive skills.

A major concern in society today is that high executive officers want managers to hire the well-rounded liberal arts individual while the front-line manager needs an individual with sufficient skills to accomplish specific duties with a minimum of training time. The resume screener must attempt to balance both needs. Structure your layout to address both concerns.

Most recent college graduates fail to write enough about their educational experiences. The years of hard work deserve significant resume space. Comment on the following:

Institution. Describe the type of college, its history, and what creates its current reputation as a superior learning center. List your most recent education first.

Dates. Record the dates attended as your actual or anticipated graduation date.

Academic Subject Areas. Your major field of study denotes your *technical* capabilities. Credits in all your fields of study should also be noted. Discuss specific courses, term projects, team exercises, honors curriculum topics, and so on.

Academic Achievement. Most employers view this as the grade point average but there are many ways to present evidence of your ability to comprehend complex material. Employers search for evidence that you are bright, articulate, and willing to work hard to accomplish difficult tasks.

If your grades are not at the top of your class, you can illustrate noteworthy academic achievements, point to grade trends, or offer evidence of specific accomplishments in your major or certain courses.

Not all employers seek top grades. They prefer to have you note that you worked long hours while attending school or developed your leadership abilities. Build a strong case for your ability to excel later using educational examples of past achievements.

Achievements Attest Skills. Incorporating action words into an explanation paragraph under "Education" improves your image as an achiever. There is nothing negative about not being a scholar (most resume readers were not scholars themselves), but a few academic pursuits that describe your intellectual credentials offer evidence that you can succeed on the job. Provide convincing evidence that you can handle the job demands.

ACCOMPLISHMENT STATEMENTS EXCITE

Accomplishment statements provide the action and excitement that you want your resume to show. They are most frequently used in the body of your "Education," "Activities," and "Work Experience" sections of your resume if you are using the chronological resume style.

Focus

If you are using the functional resume style, you will order your achievement statements under one of your three to five functional headings. It is common to have three or four accomplishment statements under each functional heading.

Magnitude

Accomplishment statements almost always relate to work, school, activities, or personal achievements. They go beyond just describing *what* you did. They describe the *magnitude* of your achievements.

How

In describing what you did (the event) and magnitude (the extent), you might wish to also describe *how* you accomplished the achievement. It is common to incorporate adverbs to add emphasis to your illustration.

Time

Most accomplishments are completed within a specified period of *time*. Normally, this is stated in annual terms but it is acceptable to use semesters, months, weeks, days, or even minutes to define your time parameter.

Style

Your goal is to emphasize your special achievements by capturing the employer's eye almost instantly. Accomplishments are more important than most of the other details on your resume. You capture attention by the style of your presentation.

Action

You must first be very selective on which of your achievements that you intend to highlight and then use action verbs to describe the event. Write in bullet point style for emphasis and stay in the present tense if possible.

Verbs

You can specify how you achieved your mission by using the "ing" on your verbs. For example, you could use words such as consolidating, coordinating, organizing, creating, installing, raising, promoting, etc. to impact on action orientation as to how you met your goals. Your accomplishment statements should always draw upon the action verbs.

Key Words

The key words, shown in Figure 11.5, add a powerful visual impact to your achievements.

Results

Your goal is to highlight the **results** of your achievements. If the results can be quantified, you will add a sense of validity to your statements. Express the accomplishment results in terms of percentages, dollars, units, and numbers of people involved. This adds a validity dimension. Try to use standard, acceptable business terminology and avoid any technical jargon.

Direction

To identify the direction of the change you should use words such as increased, raised, enhanced, saved, maintained, or lowered, saved, and stabilized if the downward direction is a positive.

Summary

Most people find it advantageous to first develop the chronological resume sections before tackling the accomplishment statements. These statements flow much easier once you identify where and how they fit into your resume. You will find the samples quite useful after you have your base written.

Acted as liaison to . . .
Administered plan created to . . .
Attained a referral rate of xx percent . . .
Automated billing requirements for . . .
Chaired a task force to develop . . .
Compiled statistics proving . . .
Completed project $x,xxx under budget in x months
Conducted management activities of . . .
Conducted studies on . . .
Consolidated regular reports of . . .
Counseled large group of . . .
Created financial model that . . .
Created financial plan used to . . .
Created a new product image with . . .
Cut production time by xx percent by . . .
Designed equipment for . . .
Designed project promotional plan which . . .
Developed new procedures to . . .
Developed a unique program that . . .
Directed activities which . . .
Directed a consumer research study which . . .
Directed the department staff of xx that . . .
Discovered problems which . . .
Established reporting procedures for . . .
Facilitated training on WWW which . . .
Generated increased morale of team by . . .
Held the best closing rate of xx percent . . .
Implemented computerized system to . . .
Improved productivity by . . .
Increased earnings xx percent in six months by . . .
Initiated a clever campaign designed to . . .

Installed a process that . . .
Interviewed candidates seeking . . .
Managed, organized, staffed, and trained . . .
Managed xx engineers in project which . . .
Marketed new concept in . . .
Performed financial analysis designed to . . .
Personal actions achieved . . .
Planned and directed a team of xx staff who . . .
Planned marketing strategy used to . . .
Promoted new technique which . . .
Provided services which . . .
Purchased $xx,xxx of . . . for . . .
Rated in top ten performers for xx years
Received x promotions in x years
Recruited talent for . . .
Redefined a process that . . .
Reduced expenditures by . . .
Reorganized the function which . . .
Reorganized work patterns which . . .
Served on major . . .
Serviced a team of physicians who . . .
Sold new concept to top management by . . .
Sold xx,xxx units in two months by . . .
Strengthened organization by . . .
Supervised a staff of . . .
Taught training programs for . . .
Traveled extensively to . . .
Voted as "Best Leader" by co-workers . . .
Wrote market plan designed to . . .
Wrote proposal that achieved . . .
Wrote xx publications in the field of . . .

• • • • • • • • • • •
Figure 11.5

want to emphasize it by capitalization and/or underlining. You might want to describe its preeminence in your field

You do not need to give a complete address of the institution on your resume. The employer will request the address when an offer is imminent in order to confirm your attendance. However, the exact dates that you attended the institution should be indicated on your resume.

Degree Earned. Upon completion of a formal course of education, a degree, diploma, or certificate is normally earned. You should begin with the highest degree earned. For each degree, you should devote space on your resume to indicate the degree level earned.

If the degree greatly enhances your employability, be sure to underline it for emphasis. Always indicate the exact date the degree was earned.

Major Subject. Indicate the subject area in which you concentrated your education. If the subject area is related to your career objective, you might wish to identify a number of the specific courses with credit hours and grades listed beside them.

EDUCATIONAL CLARIFICATIONS INFLUENCE RECRUITERS

GRADES

- Grades the past three terms have been 3.0, 3.25, and 3.6 which show deep interest and special abilities in the major field where most courses now are being taken.
- Grades reflect the fact that financial needs require a work commitment of 30+ hours per week to earn expenses to complete the degree.
- Academic performance has excelled in courses that draw heavily upon communication and teamwork abilities. Grades in the humanities have been very strong; recent grades in analytical courses have improved significantly.
- Grade performance has improved steadily after a poor first year GPA caused by illness and immaturity. Have maintained at least a "B" average the last three terms.
- Overall grades rank in the top quarter; grades in my major have been 3.65, which is near the top in a highly competitive program.

COURSE WORK

- Double major in finance and marketing to enhance my technical and analytical skills which should aid in the goal of moving into a management assignment later.
- Many human resource courses involve term projects which draw upon several courses in information systems.
- Presentation skills have been enhanced by taking several courses in such areas as speech, theater, television, mass communication, and broadcast journalism.
- Course work has included two internships, one of which earned academic credit in addition to teaching about day-to-day commitments.
- Studied Spanish extensively and supplemented this fluency and cultural awareness with courses in business.
- Plan to use business and analytical skills to function in international environments after the skills are improved by actual work in the domestic environment.
- Completing 24 hours of accounting and 12 hours of finance.
- Job related topics studied include cost accounting, capital budgeting, electronic auditing, advanced taxation, and investment analysis.
- Need two courses to complete a second major in economics.
- Liberal arts education has been supplemented with courses in marketing, sales management, retailing, basic accounting, and computer programming.
- Communication and business teamwork abilities developed in several honors seminars should improve skills in decision making. The honors courses are small classes with senior faculty who competitively selected course participants.
- Strong scientific, engineering, and technical course background supported by college activities that indicate leadership capabilities in a compassionate social setting.

GLOBAL

- Studied abroad for one year in Latin America and visited several multinational corporations in "real world" educational projects supervised by local faculty and professors in the United States.
- Lived with a local family for six months in France while participating in a student exchange program. This exposure provided a significant learning opportunity which created a strong appreciation for other cultures, different environmental conditions, and improved language fluency considerably.
- Participated in several courses designed to provide an awareness of different cultures, economic conditions, and business methods in other societies.
- Worked closely with a faculty advisor who is an internationally recognized expert on East-West trade relations. Fluent in Japanese, which resulted from a military assignment.

ACTIVITIES SPOTLIGHT YOU

If you have been out of college for more than three years, extracurricular activities may not be important to include as a special resume heading. Most recent college graduates, however, need to include this section in order to show what they have done with their non-class time besides study. It is designed to reveal your values, interests, and personal qualities.

What ethical, moral, and philosophical points of view do you value most highly? Did you do things that focuses attention on money, self-improvement, personal fun, social distraction, commitment, sharing with others, etc.?

What you do with your disposable time often reveals your motivations, maturity, responsibility levels, and mental well-being. Make certain that what you highlight relates to your job objective.

Traits. What activities excited you and induced you to work hard? Did you excel in these extracurricular activities? Describing an event or series of events tends to reveal important motivational traits. You are likely to carry these same interests with you to the workplace.

Work consumes a major portion of your waking hours. If you are not doing something that you enjoy, you are inviting some unpleasant experiences and playing with potential failure. If you are a leader and socially dominant person, you may find yourself in a difficult situation if the position does not offer an outlet for your energies and for your personal qualities.

Diversity. The types of activities that you draw upon include a wide range of participatory experiences. These may include musical groups, campus politics, Greek organizations, professional associations, special interest organizations, campus journalism, and student management boards.

You may have been involved in a variety of committees such as commencement, curriculum, homecomings, alumni events, and campus programs. Athletic group activities qualify for consideration, even if not done at varsity levels. Put performing arts in that category also.

Leadership. In describing your involvement in these activities, you want to focus on leadership roles and experiences where you were singled out as an achiever. Use titles such as secretary, treasurer, vice president, president, chairperson, scholar, assistant, coordinator, and the like to describe your involvement.

Describe how many people work for and with you in completing a mission. Illustrate teamwork and note in a numerical way the magnitude of your successful activities.

Recruiters screen for leadership characteristics such as participatory athletic activities which aid in developing a well-rounded person.

Employers seek individuals who possess a high level of social awareness that reveals you as a well-rounded individual that others respect, follow, and enjoy having around. In describing your activities, try to provide evidence of being an assertive, outgoing, pleasant, team-oriented person.

Assertiveness. Err on the side of describing yourself as a bold, forceful, brazen, domineering, aggressive person. On paper, that description is more likely to translate into an assertive, confident, team player who gets action by working with and through other people.

The modest, humble attitude receives more points in the interview, whereas the heavy approach works better on paper. Few employers seek introverted, wimpy, shy, introspective people. The gentle, deferring, polite, mild mannered approach rarely generates interviews.

Regardless of the type of job, you are far ahead to emphasize strong, assertive, personal social qualities. Don't try to be modest!

Group Participation

Academic Assistant	Dorm Organization	Singing Groups
Academic Clubs/Groups	Ethnic Organizations	Sororities
Bands and Orchestras	Fraternities	Technical Societies
Campus Newspapers	Interfraternal Groups	Union Boards
Campus Political Party	Professional Association	Women's Organizations
Debate Team	Scholastic Fraternities	Yearbook Programs

Noncampus Groups

Big Brothers/Sisters	Hospital Aide	Service Clubs
Commerce	Junior Achievement	Social WorK
Flying Clubs	Music Societies	Teacher's Aide
Foundations	Nonprofit Groups	United Funds
4-H Clubs	Religious Groups	Youth Groups
Health Care	Scouting	Youth Sports

Sports: Varsity/Intramural

Archery	Handball	Soccer
Baseball	Lacrosse	Swimming
Basketball	Polo	Tennis
Football	Racquetball	Track
Golf	Rowing	Volleyball
Gymnastics	Rugby	Wrestling

Leadership Roles

Board Member	Representative	Team Leader
Committee Chair	Secretary	Treasurer
President	Staff Assistant	Vice-president

Committees

Alumni	Commencement	Homecoming
Athletic	Faculty	Major Event
Curriculum	Foundation	Steering

Political

Campus Politics	Precinct Worker	Young Republicans
League of Voters	Young Democrats	Voter Registration
Lobbying		

Performing Arts

Bands	Symphonies	Toastmasters
Plays	Orchestras	Lecturing

· · · · · · · · ·

Figure 11.6

ACCOMPLISHMENTS HIGHLIGHT YOUR SKILLS!

The functional resume emphasizes the skills that you believe to be the most important in your background and the most important in the job you seek. It also focuses on the personal qualities which you consider to be your strongest assets.

The primary headings include your key skill areas. Sometimes this resume is called a "*skill-based resume*." Your skills may be grouped under one or more of the following skills areas.

Technical Skills.   These include writings, mathematics, foreign languages, speaking, mechanical, computer programming, accounting, engineering, design, teaching, and so on.

Functional Skills.   The functional skills center around the basic functions of organizations. These include marketing, finance, manufacturing, management, operations, purchasing, distribution, engineering, research, data processing, etc.

Administrative Skills.   These include planning, organizing, motivating, directing, delegating, managing, controlling, maintaining, leading, analyzing, coordinating, presenting, programming, etc.

The skill-based resume often integrates these skill areas within the major section of the chronological resume. For example, within education, you may want to use some of the headings above and use your courses to illustrate the skills you have attained. The same approach could be used under the "Activities" section.

The more common approach is to state your career goals and then immediately under them write three to five skill headings. Under each skill heading you will give three to five accomplishments, events, and other activities that support your position.

In addition, if you studied under a major, well-known instructor or a person who is a prominent national figure in their field, it is frequently desirable to mention that information on your resume.

What constitutes a major or minor varies considerably from college to college. Using number of credit hours and specific course titles, spell out your background. Many colleges allow a great latitude on electives and what

WELL, KIP, YOU CERTAINLY DO HAVE SOME UNUSUAL HOBBIES ... TAPE RECORDING SNOWFALLS, PHOTOCOPYING LITTER, CONNECTING THE DOTS ON DALMATIONS ...

courses are counted in your major. You should describe your specific course selection to aid the employer's evaluation of your specific skills.

Minor Subject. Many institutions require graduates to elect both a major and a minor field of study. If the minor field adds to your credentials for the job you are seeking, you should include it on your resume. Describe the number of hours that constitute a minor. List these courses.

Relevant Courses. You may have taken courses that were not part of your major or minor field but are relevant to the type of position you are seeking. You should indicate the course titles, number of credit hours, and possibly the grades if they are strong.

Academic Performance. Employers put significant importance on academic performance, especially for individuals without relevant work experience. Grades are an indication of competence and achievement level.

Although many studies show that future success has little relationship to grades, many employers still rely on grades as indicators of potential.

If you have been out of school five or more years, including grades on your resume may not be crucial. An exception to this is if you were a superior student or earned academic recognition in your field.

If you recently graduated, you will probably want to include grades on your resume. If there was a positive upward trend in your grades over time, mention it. In addition, if you worked many hours while attending school, mention the effect it had on your grades.

If your grades are better in your major, indicate those grades separately. If there was a positive upward trend in your grades, you should acknowledge that also. If an illness, family tragedy, or personal problems negatively impacted on your grades during a given period, you might wish to describe the situation.

Other Achievements. If you have any other achievements that are noteworthy and applicable to the position you are seeking, you should mention them. These include such things as academic honors received, writings published, and participation in athletics, theater, and music, as part of your academic course credit hours.

Activities
• •

Extracurricular activities are likely to be more important for people with less than five years of work experience since leaving school. If you do not have a significant amount of work experience, activities outside the classroom mean a great deal. Employers want to know what you have done with your non-class time.

Certain values, interests, personality, and other variables important in performing on a job are developed outside of the classroom. Employers want to see how your outside interests have developed you because they do not want people with

☽ WORK REVEALS MATURITY

Your ultimate goal is to show how your past work experiences coincide with your targeted job objective. Even if you do not have the directly-relatable professional prior work experience, you must nonetheless examine the qualities that the employer needs to handle the initial job opening and then draw upon your experiences that demanded similar qualities.

Your education provided the required *skill base*. Your summer work and part-time jobs taught you discipline, positive work habits, responsibility, reliability, and organizational activities. You need to assist the resume reader in translating these mundane duties into positive learning episodes in your total development.

Your goal is to subtly describe yourself as a hard worker, responsible person, and highly motivated individual who is willing to perform to the peak of your abilities. Your goal is not to prove yourself as a perfectly skill-qualified applicant. More than likely you will be entering a training assignment where they want the opportunity to develop your talents to fit their unique needs.

The job description is where you need to shine. The two to four sentences, usually one paragraph per job, describe the qualities you gained by the work experience. Use descriptive words that by implication place descriptive adjectives onto your credentials. Discuss the magnitude of the responsibilities, advancement, recognition by supervisors, opportunity for teamwork, and relating to many people with diverse backgrounds.

Do not hesitate to describe menial tasks such as counter work, maintenance, life guard, waitressing, cleaning, factory labor, flunky duties, hard physical labor, bookkeeping, typing, sales clerk, order taker, etc. Your willingness to do these tasks in order to assist in the goal of paying for your education reveals otherwise hidden information about your values, goal direction, motivations, and personal qualities.

narrow frames of reference. Additionally, activities help develop your total social awareness.

Participating in activities shows that you are willing to accept responsibility. This responsibility is often manifested in the assuming of leadership roles.

If you plan on using extracurricular activities to support your nonacademic credentials, you should outline the information similar to the work and education sections.

You should name the organization and tell something about its membership. Indicate what responsibilities you had beyond being a member and list the years you participated in the group.

Indicate the overall purpose of your group and what occurred in your meetings and events. Be specific about the achievements of your group and why you are proud to mention it.

Figure 11.6 identifies both college and other activities that you should draw upon in describing what you have accomplished.

ACTIVITIES: THE SOCIAL SIDE

Activities and honors indicate your leadership, professional interests, commitments, beliefs, and social orientation. Properly positioned and stated, the real social side of your background can come alive. Here are some examples:

- **SAE Social Fraternity,** *President,* xxxx–xx; worked about 20 hours per week to manage many responsibilities of a 100 member facility.
- **College Radio Station,** *Announcer,* xxxx–xx; introduced and interviewed personalities and edited and delivered news broadcasts on a regular basis for about 10–15 hours per week to a local student audience of about 2,000 listeners.
- **Beta Gamma Sigma,** *Treasurer,* xxxx–xx; this accounting honorary has 380 members and runs over 20 professional programs each year. Manage a budget of $3,000 per year. Last year, we managed a large job fair on campus.
- **Student Union Board,** *Vice Chair,* xxxx–xx; this policy-setting 12-student board reviews a $32 million budget that includes a 200-room hotel, food service, and recreation facilities. Chair the Audit and Food Service Committees.
- **SAE Social Fraternity,** *President,* xxxx–xx; worked about 20 hours per week to manage many responsibilities of a 100-member facility.
- **MBA Association,** *Chair,* Professional Activities Committee, xxxx–xx. This committee of the 500-member association is responsible for hosting over 50 senior executives who make presentations to our group each year. The committee is responsible for invitations, marketing, hosting, and other logistics. Chair supervises over 20 different members.
- **Finance Guild,** *Vice President,* xxxx–xx. This student group coordinates several programs between 300 finance students, 25 faculty, and scores of senior financial managers. The professional programs of the group cover current issues and topics which are discussed in lively group settings of 25–75 participants each.
- **Phi Gamma Delta Social Fraternity,** *Treasurer,* xxxx–xx. Our fraternity earned superior academic recognition during the four-year period and the 150 members were very involved in the Greek life on campus. Elected to the Policy Board of the Interfraternity Council during senior year.
- **Indiana Daily Student,** *News Reporter,* xxxx–xx. Wrote several news articles based upon wire news, TV feeds, and interviews. Won an award for reporting on an issue involving investment policy of the I.U. Foundation.

Include the organization name, your role, dates involved, and a brief description. For credibility, cite numbers like members, participants, budget amounts, jobs, etc. For clarity draw relationship to other resume elements.

Successful
Behaviors
Sell Well
- Relate to Curriculumn
- Show Accomplishments of Group
- Highlight Performances and Presentations
- Describe Team, Not Just Individual Success
- Reveal Any Global Aspects

The goal in resume design is to impress. Forget modesty. Recruiters need to evaluate your social side, leadership credentials, and organizational skills. Provide the evidence to tell the honest story. Truth comes from past behaviors.

Work Experience

The "Work Experience" section of your resume tells more about you than you might realize. The actual information listed is minor in comparison to the underlying story told about your values, personality, interests, maturity, and abilities to relate to others. Work experience implies social awareness, responsibility, and leadership.

Work experience is just as important to the recent college graduate as it is to the individual who has fifteen years of work experience. Experience is important in describing skills acquired by work that are applicable to the job being sought.

Type of Work. Work type falls into six basic categories: full-time, part-time, cooperative education, internship, summer, and military. Volunteer work is usually listed under "Professional Endeavors," but it may also be listed under "Work Experience."

Listing. All full-time experience should be listed. However, it is not crucial to list all part-time jobs; only list those that are relevant. Many people simply state "numerous part-time jobs," and then describe what they did to earn money for their college degree.

The employer is trained to look for employment gaps. Your resume should give employment starting and ending dates, and you will undoubtedly be questioned as to what you did in between your jobs.

Content. This section should include employer's name, location, employment dates, job title, brief job description, and level of responsibility. The most widely accepted method of listing experience is in reverse chronological order (most recent first).

The employer is not looking solely for the quality or quantity of jobs you have held, but rather information that supports the idea that you are a hard worker.

Employer. The first item will be the employer, location, and dates of employment. Often the employing organization will be capitalized or underlined for emphasis. If you are circulating your resume beyond the area where the name of the employer is recognized, you might want to give a brief description of the organization. This usually includes the type of business, the product or service, and figures relating to size: employees and sales.

RESPONSIBILITY LEVELS

Geography	Magnitude/Numbers
Unit	Budget dollars controlled
District	Employees supervised
Regional	Facilities managed
National	Assets managed
International	Major divisions managed

Figure 11.7

Sometimes people do not want their current employer to know they are actively seeking a different job. Giving the name of your employer invites a potential employer to call. You can describe your current employer but indicate that you do not want your current employer contacted by stating "Please do not contact without permission."

Anytime you put yourself into the job market there is some risk that your current employer will find out. When you first start circulating your resume you should make plans about what to do if the word gets to your employer. With so many trade associations, including human resource management association meetings, word can spread quickly that a certain person is looking around. There are no guarantees of autonomy. Don't expect privacy.

Descriptive Title. A job title says a lot about what you do, but the duties under the same job title may vary greatly from employer to employer. The job title is a significant word on your resume. It is almost always underlined or boldfaced to highlight its importance.

If your part-time job did not have a title, make up a title (one to three words in length) that is descriptive of what you did. If your full-time job title is not very descriptive or is misleading, consider changing it to a more descriptive title. You might indicate in the description that you made a clarifying change so you will not have "honesty problems" with subsequent reference checks.

Duties. Descriptions of what you do in your present job and what you did in previous jobs are imperative no matter how menial it might sound. Even include descriptions for part-time jobs you choose to use if you are a recent college graduate.

The descriptions are typed in lower case letters in either sentence or sentence fragment form. Avoid the use of the word "I" if possible. You are trying to get the employer to read the fine print. You want it to say something important so that positive action will follow.

There should always be at least a one-sentence description for each listing. If it exceeds four sentences, a new paragraph should be started. It is important to use the "action-oriented" and "self-descriptive" words.

If your work experience is related to that being sought, emphasize the skills you have acquired that relate to the career objective.

If the work is not directly related to the career objective, describe some of the "value" that you have received from the work. When the skills do not apply, turn to a description that ties into the subjective qualities that you know the employer is seeking.

Young people with limited work experience must show qualities such as willingness to work hard, earning for a goal (education), maturity, leadership, etc. To do this, list all of the verbs that describe your primary and secondary duties. Write up a description of a typical day. Write about

ANY OTHER SPECIAL SKILLS THAT WEREN'T ON YOUR RESUME, CHUG... BESIDES FROG IMITATIONS.

some of the experiences you had on some unusual days. Step back and think about what you learned.

Why was the job important to you? Start assembling some key phrases. Only then should you go back and write a description. As you write, keep in mind what you want the employer to learn about you from that description. Many people can turn the job titles of "general laborer," "production assembler," and "counter clerk" into some impressive learning experiences.

Responsibility Level.   The responsibilities you had are part of the detailed job description, but they often need to be listed in a separate paragraph. The responsibility level adds credibility to what you say about yourself.

Include some facts like number of people supervised, sales dollars, budget level, decision latitude, and the title of the person to whom you reported.

Responsibility implies that you possess certain skills. These may be technical or people-oriented. Describe any process you control. Indicate the management abilities you possess.

In short, build up your level of responsibility to the highest possible level. Make it honest and give yourself the maximum amount of credit.

Training Received.   Many jobs are literally training programs for future responsibilities. What are you learning in your current job? What did you learn from previous jobs? It is important to list these skills in the description. Listing the skills subtly imply that you possess them.

Many jobs require that you take refresher courses and other advanced training to improve your skills. Many employers pay for you to attend programs outside of the work setting. State these if appropriate.

If your job allowed you to be part of a professional or trade association, discuss your participation and role in conferences, seminars, etc.

If applicable to the job being sought, describe the various skills that you have acquired through formal learning experiences. You could discuss this either in the work experience or education sections.

Salary Issue.   Many resume experts used to recommend that people list starting and ending salaries of previous jobs on the resume. The purpose of this was to indicate a progressive upward mobility. In some cases job titles and levels of responsibility are not always true reflections of the worth of the individual to the firm. Nonetheless, salary is a universally comparable variable between jobs.

Depending on an applicant's record of salary advancement, the current salary is to be regarded as a bargaining base. An employer knows that you would not normally take less than you are currently earning. This is not necessarily true any longer as lifestyle and dual-career considerations have changed many value structures.

A rule of thumb is that it takes at least a 20 percent increase to entice a person to change jobs if a geographical move is involved. If an employer knows your current earnings from the resume and could not match a 20-percent increase, a job interview invitation would not be forthcoming.

The practice of including salary on resumes is not used very often today. If this is a major concern in a special instance, it is best discussed in the cover letter.

It is not very difficult for an employer to ascertain your current earnings. Employers are well aware of the market value for someone with your credentials and can locate your current earnings by a retail credit check.

Leaving Reasons.   Why you left your last job is not a good selection variable for any employer to use in deciding whether or not to invite you for an interview.

Do not include any reference to your current salary on your resume.

COLLEGE JOBS DO IMPRESS!

None of the jobs listed below are "professional" in nature but as you read them, you draw value judgements about each person. Recruiters also did these same jobs themselves in getting their degree. Mundane work situations can be turned to positive images. You learn in all work situations. Notice how the work is positioned to show a learning, responsibility, relationship, goal, was achieved in these.

Trendsetters Indianapolis, IN xx/xx to Present
Sales Clerk As school schedule permits, work 10–20 hours per week with local women's fashion shop. Duties include sales, cash control, gift wrapping, display, merchandising, customer service, and floor supervision. Worked full-time the past two summers; commission aspect of pay permits significant earnings potential. Top-paid part-time clerk recognition for past six months. Do limited fashion modeling for store in local ads.

Maxi Discounts Fort Wayne, IN Summers xx-xx
Bookkeeper Worked full-time the past two summers at this family owned electronic discount center which is the fastest growing store in the region. Frequently returned to work during holidays, school breaks, and peak weekend periods. Started as a sales clerk and moved through cashiering, personnel, credit, security, marking, stocking, loss prevention, merchandising, advertising coordination, and many other areas. Invited into the finance function when supervisors learned of coursework in accounting and systems. Helped develop several new control procedures and suggested some new software applications which I installed.

ABC Ceramics Cincinnati, OH 5/xx to 8/xx
Tile Setter Handled grout work, tile cutting, and layout for bathrooms, kitchen, and entry floors and halls. Usually worked without supervision within four weeks. Earned funds for senior year.

Mega Dealer Cincinnati, OH 5/xx to 8/xx
Lotman Worked in various assignments in this dealership that sells 5,000 vehicles per year. Checked in new and used vehicles, cleaned vehicles, repaired minor mechanical problems, moved vehicles, and handled some new car preparation for customers.

Fast Foods Cincinnati, OH 5/xx to 8/xx
Restaurant Associate Started in shift work. Served customers during very hectic periods. Worked with a team of 30 people under stress and many pressure points. Cleaned floors, tables, and other equipment. Occasionally prepared food. Awarded "Associate of the Week" plaque for six consecutive weeks.

Numerous Part-Time Jobs Hometown IN 5/xx to Present
Various Assignments Held many part-time jobs while enrolled full-time in college. As a financially independent person, worked at least 30 hours per week to provide support for college. Jobs included sales clerk, general labor, security person, waiter, bus boy, cashier, attendant, fast food, etc. In the past six years, worked for numerous employers, but the past year has been with a local security firm where night work permitted time off in the day for attending class.

Indiana University Bookstore Bloomington, IN 8/xx to Present
Sales Clerk Work about 10 hours per week selling and handling students' needs for books, supplies, equipment, and software. Responsible for special computer inventory control system which permits placing direct orders. Worked many hours during peak periods since freshman year and now supervise and train a group of about 10 other part-timers.

Jones Construction Jefferson, IN 5/xx to Present
General Laborer This local construction firm builds single- and multiple-family housing in a three state area and is owned by family members. Worked here every summer and at other breaks since 16 years old. Typically worked 50–60 hours per week which generated income to pay for the next school year.

Duties have included truck driver, carpenter, electrician, plumber, roofer, errand person, installer, carpet layer, and other tasks associated with residential construction. Given the opportunity last summer to supervise a crew of five people on a large apartment project. Worked 60 hours per week and learned about personal capacities, commitments, people management, and other lessons which proved to be extremely valuable.

Don't minimize your past work relationship. Reveal how you grew in all of your situations. Your past perseverance is indicative of future successes.

..... VOLUNTEER SERVICE LEARNING-WORKING ACTIVITIES .....

- Athletic Clubs
- Big Brothers
- Big Sisters
- Chamber of Commerce
- Commercial Groups
- Community Kitchens
- Flying Clubs
- Foundations
- Fund Raising
- 4-H Clubs
- Habitat for Humanity
- Health Boards
- Hospital Volunteer
- Junior Achievement

- Music Societies
- Non-Profit Groups
- Professional Associations
- Red Cross
- Religious Groups
- School Volunteer
- Scouting
- Service Clubs
- Social Clubs
- Social work/Organizations
- Trade Groups
- United Fund
- Youth Group
- Youth Sports

•••••••••••

Figure 11.8

Listing the reason you left your last job takes up valuable resume space that could best be used for other purposes more germane to the invitation decision. If it comes up, the best time to discuss your reasons for leaving past jobs and your current job is in the job interview. Don't volunteer the reasons on the resume or interview but be prepared to address the question.

.... RECOGNITIONS ....

- Civic awards
- College scholarships
- Achievement certificates
- Leadership certificates
- Elected offices
- Professional licenses
- College achievement awards
- Service clubs acknowledge-ments
- Grade excellence awards
- Corporate training seminars
- Leadership recognitions
- Athletic leadership
- Association officer
- Employer service

- Employer performance
- Academic excellence
- Rank in class
- Employer incentive award
- Peer review acknowledgement
- Special license
- Social club merits
- Job accomplishments
- Competitive performances
- Writing awards
- Public service
- Elected official
- Public speaking awards
- Campus politician
- Musical performances

•••••••••••

Figure 11.9

# STORIES SELL

Most people enjoy reading short stories about other people's experiences. Even in casual conversations, the topic often covers anecdotes about mutual acquaintances or ourselves. These are usually interesting and entertaining. Why not use this approach in the resume and interviewing to get your credentials described in a story manner?

You can draw upon stories that relate to the three most important sections of your resume. The "Education," "Work Experience," and "Activities" components lend very well to story telling.

Education. Your educational background builds the skill base that you must use on the job for which you are applying. You may wish to select a special subset of the college courses you took and describe why you selected this unique group in your program plans even though all of them were not "required" in the curriculum.

You may wish to describe a single course (or groups of courses, such as your major or minor) where you accomplished a superior performance. You may want to cover your role as a team leader (or member) or cover the major term paper, class project, or other significant events in which you personally excelled and produced a meaningful paper, performance, or product.

Instead of focusing on a special course, you may prefer to highlight an episode in which you earned a special academic recognition. This may have involved a formal presentation, plaque, certificate, accommodation letter, etc. A common approach is to tell a story behind the recognition, what made it special, or the ceremony itself.

Work Experience. Most jobs are rather routine most of the time, but occasionally a special day (or period) occurs. It may involve a snafu, surprise event, unique challenge, or unusual happening. Perhaps you learned an important lesson from the event which enhanced your awareness of your technical and/or interpersonal capabilities, revealed your social poise under pressure, or opened up the strength of your character traits.

These real life events (stories) offer a much more revealing aspect of your background to potential employers in an interesting way. Your routine work activities show your skills, maturity, work ethics, commitment to organizational goals, teamwork, and other factors that the employer needs to observe. These same factors can come out in an effective story.

Activities. The main reason for activities being shown on a resume is to highlight your social interaction, your leadership abilities, and your ability to communicate effectively with others. If you just list or describe the activities, the reader has to *infer* that you possess these traits.

Your activities do not have to be college or academic related. You can draw from everyday life activities that might evolve around family, accidents, living arrangements, hobbies, sports, professional endeavors, etc. What happened in your life that can better illustrate the traits above?

Motivations. Why did you work hard or excel in a given activity? What got inside you to force you to produce excellence? Saying that you are a highly motivated person adds nothing. Where is the proof? What is the answer to why?

Some things cannot be effectively stated directly without your coming across the wrong way, but stories can get your message across without awkwardness.

Sometimes one or two significant events can change your life. It always involves other people. These events or happenings may be more convincing to an employer than a mundane description.

A story often captures attention quicker and reveals more succinctly the points that you wish to illustrate. When used in either the resume or the interview, these *stories* may more effectively deliver the message you wish to communicate.

Interesting stories sell.

Professional Activities

Today's work environment has fostered the strong desire in people of like interests to affiliate. This has come about due to social and professional concerns. These affiliations bring people together for seminars and conferences and involve them in writing for professional colleagues and the general public in order to promote science and public awareness.

People involved in these endeavors deserve recognition for their efforts. Like many other items on the resume, a statement of involvement in professional associations adds an important element of information for a potential employer to evaluate.

Affiliations. Biologists, chemists, engineers, educators, personnel managers, purchasing agents, accountants, doctors, and thousands of other people in various other occupations have seen the need to organize in professional societies. The acronyms like AAA, AMA, NEA, CPA, etc. run the gamut. Some groups are nationally known and others are hardly recognizable. The memberships of these groups range from millions to less than a hundred members.

Most professional organizations sponsor publications and programs for their membership. Many of them are deeply involved in the employment process. In fact, you must be a member of some of these in order to gain entry into certain professions.

Most have excellent websites for their members. They provide outstanding information and facilitate networking.

If you are involved in one or more of these national organizations and are a leader in a regional or local group, you should acknowledge this on your resume. Involvement in many of these organizations greatly enhances your credibility and can be a major factor in the consideration of your being interviewed.

Civic Concerns. If you are involved in civic activities and organizations, these should be shown on the resume. These programs say important things about your values and concerns for others. If you have been a leader in some way in these civic programs, your extent of involvement should be stated. Figure 11.8 gives examples of civic activities.

Publications. In many technical and professional fields, individuals must publish in order to be recognized as contributors to the profession. This is especially true of writers, scientists, and faculty in the prestigious institutions of higher education.

When applying for positions in these professions, it is important to mention your publication record because this is one of the first factors an employer is likely to consider.

Resumes that list a long string of publications are relevant only in certain professions. Most resumes do not list publications. If you have had one or two significant publications, it might be appropriate to list them. If the publications were irrelevant to the position, the only value in listing them would be to illustrate achievement.

Recognitions. Based upon significant achievements, you often are granted some type of certification that recognizes your performance level. These awards may come from teachers, work superiors, peers, teams, civic groups, government, employers, and professional affiliations.

If your superior performance merited a formal recognition by your associates, it should be acknowledged somewhere on the resume. Figure 11.9 gives some examples of the recognitions often cited.

You may wish to incorporate a special section of your resume to note your accomplishments, particularly if there are three or more that you wish to cite. If you were given a plaque, framed certificate, letter, certificate, trophy, etc., you may wish to highlight the recognition to emphasize your commitment to excellence.

Many of these awards are made in public ceremonies. It might be appropriate to discuss the event and some of the notes that you used in your acknowledgements.

Instead of a special dedicated resume section, you may prefer to incorporate these recognitions into the body of your "Academic," "Activities," or "Work" sections of your resume. Some experts believe that the section location strengthens and verifies your overall credentials. Some experts suggest that you locate your recognitions in the "Personal" section.

Where to locate your recognitions is not as important as ensuring that they are clearly acknowledged. Just make sure that you include them somewhere in your resume. The recognitions prove your performance capabilities and verify your interest and personal traits.

Recognitions define you as a responsible, hard working, highly motivated person. These are qualities that are impossible to state directly. This subtle approach still leaves no doubt about your commitment to goals that you value.

Personal
● ●

Personal background is found in less than 10 percent of all resumes today. Personal information usually includes height, weight, health condition, date of birth, status, family background, and religion. Most of these items are rarely requested anymore because they can be discriminatory and irrelevant to an employment decision.

Some people now use the personal section to discuss hobbies, sporting activities, and avocations. Although these points can be interesting and an important part of a person's personal life, they may not be relevant for your resume.

Whether or not to include them depends upon the space available, the relationship to the career statement, and personal preference.

Many people are now discussing their family background under personal information. The occupation of the father and mother still greatly influences career choice. Parental contacts greatly aid in resume distribution.

If your father or mother was part of a professional, technical, or managerial profession, your employment could be enhanced by that fact. Employers might reason that if you grew up in a similar work setting you could make the necessary adjustments more readily than an individual who is a complete stranger to the work setting.

Many dual-career couples are using this

YOU SEEM QUITE CAPABLE TO ME, KIP...DESPITE WHAT YOUR REFERENCES SAID ABOUT YOU.

REFERENCES SPEAK FOR YOU

Putting "References furnished upon request" at the bottom of your resume is a cop-out. It says to the reader that right now in your life you do not know many important people who are willing to vouch for you. As a recent college graduate, if you ever needed help in getting started, now is one of the most important times in your life to draw upon other people willing to help you.

Provide Access. References listed on the resume are less important if you have over five years of work experience. Your access to the "hidden job market," where eighty percent of the jobs are, is through your contact network. You need some sales representatives working with you. Let potential employers know who is willing to speak on your behalf.

There are three types of references for you to use:

- **Academic.** Professors, teachers, counselors, and administrators who have gotten to know you well in college are usually eager to help you.
- **Work.** Direct supervisors, staff persons, and even higher-level officers who have seen you in action often want to be asked to support your case for employment.
- **Character.** Well-placed friends of friends, neighbors, family contacts, community leaders, etc. who have known you for a long time and have observed your growth are more than willing to speak on your behalf.

More people obtain employment by *word of mouth* than any other method. Your references are the most important people you know and they want to see you succeed. If they are willing to provide you permission to use their name or write a "to whom it may concern" reference letter for you, take advantage of the opportunity.

Open Doors. Names screen you in for consideration more often than they screen you out. If your references are willing to be contacted frequently on your behalf, it is not your responsibility to protect their time.

Few employers contact references until they are serious about your employment chances and, when they do, a positive reference statement is most important in getting you the interview. If the recruiter happens to know the reference, that will influence the decision, providing that there is a job match.

Show Credibility. References add credibility to the nice things you are saying about yourself. Even if references are never contacted, the implication is that "these individuals will back up what I am saying about myself."

You may vary the references in your targeted resume approach. The norm is three or four references per resume, and you undoubtedly have more than four. Select which references to use based upon who you are selectively contacting with your targeted resume. Always place references as the last element on your resume.

Always give your references a copy of your most current resume. Copy them on related employment correspondence. Keep them informed of your progress and eventual success. Remember to thank them irregardless of their influence in your final job placement.

Positive words about you generate most of your interviews.

part of the resume to state their plans. Rather than use the career statement, they prefer to state a geographical preference, common employer requests, and other problems unique to the working couple.

References

Many resumes list three or four references in one of the traditional formats. As job markets soften, references become more useful.

Rather than interviewing hordes of people, many employers simply call a reference or two before proceeding with arrangements for an interview. This is particularly common in professions where the members know each other well. In this case, a reference who advises an employer to interview you almost assures your chances of being called for an interview.

References are not always contacted. In most cases, references are not called until you have been interviewed and an offer is imminent.

Government agencies and educational institutions prefer to contact a central source, such as a college placement office, to request references. Business employers tend to simply call the references and talk directly with them on the telephone.

Permission.   Make certain that you have specifically asked people to serve as references for you and that you have sent them up-to-date resumes as soon as they are available. Always include telephone numbers and email addresses to facilitate contact. Most teachers, neighbors, friends of the family, and former supervisors are pleased to be asked to serve as references. Hopefully, you have cultivated several faculty members when you were in school.

Letters and Forms.   Many references prefer to send a letter to your college career services office or write a "to whom it may concern" type of letter. Most college offices are willing to maintain such a file. There is occasionally a small charge for this service.

The "to whom" type of letter is more convenient for you but, of course, it does not carry the credibility associated with a confidential evaluation.

Types.   References come in three types:

- Work
- Academic
- Personal

You should always have at least one reference in each category. Whatever the type of reference, the person must know you very well. It is extremely embarrassing to have a reference who admits to only knowing you superficially.

You should select references whose credibility is extremely high. The higher the professional standing, the better the reference. Professors, teachers, counselors, former employers, community leaders, bankers, business executives, business owners, lawyers, and people employed in the occupation you are seeking make excellent references.

A reference listed on a resume says, *"This person knows me well and is willing to say good things about me."* There is an implied positive feeling whether or not the reference is even contacted. If for no other reason than this implied approval, it can be important to list references on resumes.

Omission.   Some resume experts recommend not placing reference names on the resume. The logic is that references would be very unhappy about being contacted continually about you. Another reason is that a certain individual's name could be as negative to the reader as it is positive. Another consideration is that

> Reference names can often assure that you will get called for an interview.

references are seldom contacted before the initial interview so one should use the resume space more efficiently.

The proponents of this line of reasoning recommend placing a *"References furnished upon request"* statement at the bottom of the resume. Opponents argue that that begs the question. If you have good references willing to lend their name to you, you should seriously consider taking advantage of their potential influence.

Another compromise approach is to indicate that references are on file in your college placement office. You should indicate on the resume where to write for copies of the confidential references, if your college offers that service.

No perfect solution exists as to whether or not to list references on the resume. It is a personal decision. In many cases, inclusion or exclusion comes down to whether or not you have space for them without increasing the resume length by another page.

"References furnished upon request" is a redundant statement.

· · · · · · · · · · · · · · · · · **RESUME QUIZ** · · · · · · · · · · · · · · · ·

HOW DOES YOUR RESUME RATE?

Appearance: Is it enticing? Do you want to read it?
Layout: Professional style, graphically presented?
Length: Can you get same effect if it is shorter?
Relevance: Has extraneous material been deleted?
Writing Style: Is everything grammatically correct?
Action: Do sentences begin with action verbs?
Specificity: Is there focus instead of generalities?
Accomplishments: Are your most outstanding abilities presented?
Completeness: Have you left out important data?
Goal Directed: Does the employer know what you want immediately?
Audit Trail: Can an employer find you later?
Truth: Do you avoid inflating the truth?
Impact: Do you imply self-confidence?
Documentation: Can statements be verified?
Relationships: Have references been informed?

· · · · · · · · · ·
Figure 11.10

Resume Career Action Project

Recommender Resume

Prepare a complete three or four page resume that incorporates an in-depth presentation of all aspects of your background. The second part of this project requests a one-page version. This long resume will be suitable to give to your references and recommenders who are likely to read a very thorough resume about you.

The purpose of this recommender resume is to give your references a complete picture of you to use in preparing a "to whom it may concern letter" on your behalf. This gives you a clearer impression ahead of time of what they are likely to be saying about you. You are putting some of the words on paper for them to use in rephrasing for the recommendation letters and the telephone calls they receive.

This type of resume would be useful to enclose with graduate school applications. It would be suitable to share with potential employers where you know that you are over the one-minute scanning process. Some interviewees use this resume to include in thank you letters after the preliminary interview went well. Some interviewees leave it at the end of the preliminary interview as part of their interview presentation.

You may use either the chronological or functional resume style. Since this is not part of your targeted resume approach, it is not necessary to include a career objective statement when you actually use it, but for purposes of this project you must include one of your targeted career objective statements.

If you are having difficulty writing three pages, start repackaging your official transcript in a way that better states the skills that you possess. You can do this by grouping related courses or explain several of the more relevant courses in greater depth. Discuss the course content, teaching approaches used, projects required, and your performance in the courses.

CLOSE THE SALE

The targeted resume approach works for thousands of job seekers. Use it with the chronological or functional resume styles. When used discriminately with creative job search strategies, targeted resumes open doors to the personal interview appointment. A concise, one to two page, goal-directed resume cannot replace your interview, but it can get your foot in the door.

By clever use of graphical considerations, you can focus the reader's attention on the five to seven most important selling points in your background. Strong, assertive statements of your skills and personal qualities imply that you can and are willing to work hard to be a success in the position that you know the employer is seeking to fill. Create your own luck in your job search by using the targeted resume design approach.

The targeted resume is your advantage over the masses.

Another way to expand the resume is to tell what you learned from your activities and work experiences. Go into some depth by describing stories that illustrate your traits. You may also wish to expand on your personal background in order to illustrate your VIPs.

Do not use more than six references on the recommender resume. Your last page can have written information on it in addition to the references.

After you complete the three or four page resume, go back and prepare a single page resume that you may actually use in circulating to potential employers. Try to be very creative in content and design. This is designed for you to use in contacting employers.

Hopefully, you will have a tough time boiling your long resume down to the short version. Your goal is to make the short version just as action oriented but in a much compressed version that does not omit important elements of your background.

In both resumes you will want a graphically appealing outline that balances print with white space. Try to get about 75 percent of the paper printed with about half-inch margins all around the pages. Each page should be appropriately centered including the last page which should be at least two-thirds full.

There should be a remarkable contrast between your two resumes. Mentally make a list of your five to ten most important qualities and ask if they can be quickly perceived by the reader with a quick glance. Study the contrast to see how you might improve these in your next revision.

Submit this action oriented project to one of your closest references and ask for a critique.

Summary
• • • • • • • • • • • • • • • • • • • •

There are many ways by which your resume can be improved, and a number of ideas have been suggested. You should use some empathy to appreciate the point of view of the employer. This involves an interpretation of the characteristics felt to be important in the job and then stressing these points in your resume.

You should avoid including unnecessary data. You must emphasize essential information, but make certain your resume is complete and well spaced on one page. Unnecessary words should be eliminated. Whenever possible, incorporate the use of action words and self-descriptive episodes into your resume. The key is positive conciseness.

Emphasize eye appeal. Use some artistic talent in designing your resume that appeals as well as informs. Your resume should be uncluttered, neatly blocked, and organized so that key points can be quickly identified by the reader. Proper use of graphical considerations will improve the overall "look" of your resume.

Your resume should be a credit to your creativity and ability in self-expression. It is an advertisement designed to sell your ability and potential and not just your past experience and schooling.

Over 95 percent of all employment hires are introduced by resumes, so you must take special care in constructing yours. It should focus on what can and will be done for the employer, based upon the evidence of past accomplishments presented. You should focus on positive results from past behaviors.

In summary, be prepared to spend several hours in preparing your written sales presentation. The resume is your best advertisement. If it succeeds in getting you the interview, you will be ready to close the sale with an equally well-designed oral presentation.

By using these guidelines—and your common sense—you should be able to develop a very effective sales oriented resume.

- - - - - - - - - - - - - **DESCRIPTIVE CAREER PHRASES** - - - - - - - - - - - - -

. . . use skills such as _____, _____, and _____ in . . .

. . . work in functional areas of _____, _____, . . .

. . . interested in industries of _____, _____, . . .

. . . obtained related skills from courses in _____, _____, . . .

. . . hold _____ years experience in _____, _____, . . .

. . . exploring areas of interests like _____, _____, . . .

• • • • • • • • • •

Figure 11.11

Sample Resumes

How do various resumes look?

One of the best ways to learn about how to prepare an effective resume is to review some quality sample resumes. You should not try to emulate any of these resumes without first understanding basic resume preparation and design techniques. You need to understand why these resumes are effective.

These samples use the design approaches recommended earlier and integrate many preparation suggestions. Several different formats are shown, but this section is not intended to offer all possible format variations.

Use samples as guides.

These resumes are offered for you to use as potential illustrations of what can be done.

This extensive set of resumes is adapted from resumes of real individuals and have been modified extensively to protect confidentiality and illustrate certain techniques.

There are resumes of individuals with over 20 years of experience boiled down to one page. Rarely is a two-page resume needed to be successfully screened in for an interview appointment.

Just as you can talk yourself out of a job offer, you can provide too much data on a resume which recruiters use to screen you out of consideration.

You may prefer to eliminate the Career Objective Statement when you are not targeting your resume.

Nearly all of the samples are illustrated with the targeted job objective shown. Of course, the objectives may be frequently modified or changed if you are sending your resume to different types of employers. The career objective can readily be completely reworded or even eliminated if desired.

Most of the resumes are illustrations of individuals with zero to four years of experience after earning a degree, but there are also samples of individuals with many years of experience to give format variations.

There are resumes illustrating hundreds of different types of educational institutions and job experiences. Whether your interests are in the public, private, professional, or non-profit sector of the economy, the various sectional examples within the resumes should offer a wealth of ideas upon which to base your own resume.

It is very common to omit references.

Brenda S. Allen

123 Cypress Drive
Louisville, KY xxxxx
(xxx) xxx-xxxx
email@email.com

OBJECTIVE

Advertising Account Executive: Seeking an assignment that uses my extensive years of advertising and sales experience in working with clients in consumer products.

SKILLS AND EXPERIENCE

Marketing/Advertising

- Increased local agency volume by 173% over previous year.
- Handled sales volume of $10.5 million covering the state of Kentucky.
- Presented company programs to national accounts such as Sears & Roebuck, General Motors, etc.
- Assisted salespersons with promotional activities.
- Made field visits to answer customer inquiries for several clients.
- Addressed issues on warranty, promotions, procedures, and product data in promotional design.
- Created retail promotional displays which generated double digit sales increases.
- Designed store layouts based on review of electronic sales surveillance results.
- Advised dealers on product promotion.
- Designed yellow pages ad copy, layouts in trade magazines, and consumer catalogs.

Management/Organizational

- Organized a territory that was vacant for 2 years into a very profitable territory.
- Re-established customer trust on accounts that had been previously underserviced.
- Trained new employees in agency policy, procedure, and product knowledge.
- Developed schedule for servicing accounts which generated significant sales increases.
- Prepared weekly reports on sales volume, expenses, promotional and competitive activities.

EMPLOYMENT

Account Executive. Advertising Galore Associates, Louisville, KY.
Small advertising agency serving manufacturing firms located in the State of Kentucky (xx/xx–xx/xx).

Telemarketing Directory Representative. Transwestern Publishing Company, Louisville, KY.
Sold yellow page advertising (x/xx–x/xx).

Photographic Assistant. Kentucky State University.
Photographed, developed, and printed photographs for internal and external publications (xx/xx–xx/xx).

EDUCATION

B.S., Journalism - University of Louisville, Louisville, KY, xxxx.

JOHN ARTSEY

123 Artful Avenue
Indianapolis, IN xxxxx
xxx-xxx-xxxx
art@email.edu

CAREER OBJECTIVE

Graphic Design and Advertising: Desire an entry level position that will provide exposure to all aspects of the advertising industry in relation to graphic design. Eventually, hope to move into management assignments including creative research and design work in advertising

EDUCATION

John Herron School of Art, Indianapolis, IN (8/xx to 5/xx)
Indiana University, Bloomington, IN (8/xx to 5/xx)
Bachelor's Degree in Fine Arts and Education in May, xxxx

ACTIVITIES

Sigma Pi Fraternity executive officer, xx/xx
Winner of most outstanding pledge award, xx/xx
Winner of Daniel mental attitude award, xx/xx
Public Relations chairman during last school year
Pledge educator, xx/xx to xx/xx
Active in intramural sports such as basketball, football, and volleyball
Member of the National Art Education Association (NAEA)

EXPERIENCE

Freelance Graphic Designer.
Freelancer. Work with several advertising agencies in the Indianapolis area on a contact basis doing work for business ads and product brochures.

<u>Designed and painted</u> a winning entry in the International Scholastic Achievement in Art Awards in xxxx held in Copenhagen, Denmark.
<u>Designed logos</u> for athletic teams, T-shirts, local business student groups since high school.
<u>Sign painter</u> for various businesses in the community. Sold water color prints of special athletic scenes to students.
<u>Experienced</u> with computer graphic design, photo, and video software.

Brown County Playhouse, Nashville, IN (Summer seasons xxxx–xxxx).
Supervisor of stage scenery painting and construction crew. Organized about 30 different students for each event.

REFERENCES

Dr. Thomas Craft	Prof. James Rowe	Ms. Sally Bright
President	Fine Arts Department	Owner
NAEA Association	John Herron School of Art	Bright Themes Agency
125 Madison Ave.	125 Meridian St.	Keystone Square
New York, NY xxxxx	Indianapolis, IN xxxxx	Indianapolis, IN xxxxx
xxx-xxx-xxxx	xxx-xxx-xxxx	xxx-xxx-xxxx
craft@email.com	rowe@email.com	bright@email.com

Scott Behrman

Present Address
125 E. 19th Street
Bloomington, IN xxxxx
xxx-xxx-xxxx
behrman@email.edu

Home Address
Two Amherst Place
Columbus, IN xxxxx
xxx-xxx-xxxx
parents@email.com

Career Objective

Advertising, Assistant Account Executive. Interested in assisting with client planning strategies, client studies, media relations, coordination with agency internal departments, and direct creative client presentations with a local agency working with consumer products.

Education

INDIANA UNIVERSITY, SCHOOL OF TELECOMMUNICATIONS
Earned a B.A. in xxxx, Advertising. Have Minors in Fine Arts and Spanish, with 30 hours of Business integrated courses. Fluent in Spanish. Graduated in top quarter of class.

Campus Activities

Indiana University Student Association: Work in the Public Relations Department doing artwork and layout for brochures and pamphlets. Reorganized the webpage at www.indiana/student. Recently elected as an Off-Campus Senator, and sit on various committees, such as Anti-Apartheid and Health, Safety, and Leisure. **I.U. Advertising Club:** Working presently in the creative department, on a campaign for Nestle Crunch, as a member of National Student Advertising Competition. Designed web ads for club patrons.
I.U. Improvisation and Comedy Club: Developing skills of improvisational communication and comedy.

Work Experience

Entrepreneur: Started a franchise for a car polishing service and proceeded, with my partner, to run every aspect of the business. Doing paperwork, advertising, marketing, interviewing, and labor gave me the opportunity to learn the basics of how a business is run, as well as develop valuable skills in marketing and advertising. Also learned the meanings of the words organization and responsibility, which I now know to be the key to any successful venture. Designed company logo that hangs in our office and appears in all of our advertising. Colleagues consider me to be extremely creative and highly motivated.

References

Dr. Bernard Greenberg
Chief of Surgery
St. Martin Hospital
Indianapolis, IN xxxxx
(xxx)xxx-xxxx
green@email.com

Sharon Grainer
Academic Advisor
I.U. Student Services
Bloomington, IN xxxxx
(xxx)xxx-xxxx
grain@email.edu

Andrew Paine
Co-Owner
Fastwash
Bloomington, IN xxxxx
(xxx)xxx-xxxx
paine@email.com

SALES MANAGEMENT WITH SOME MINOR EXPERIENCE SAMPLE

DERRICK DAVIS

123 Linden Drive
Houston, Texas xxxxx
www.personal.com

(xxx) xxx-xxxx Home
(xxx) xxx-xxxx Office
davis@email.com

OBJECTIVE

Sales Management. Results-oriented professional seeks a sales position which will utilize and challenge proven sales skills. Prefer to utilize technical skills by staying in energy, chemical, pharmaceutical, and related industries.

ACCOMPLISHMENTS & ACHIEVEMENTS

- Increased sales by 15% over quota for 5 out of 7 years for a Fortune 500 company.
- Won salesman of the year award two times as well as salesperson of the month awards over 10 times in formerly underperforming territories.
- Received extensive training by United Chemicals and various suppliers in product knowledge and marketing techniques, including web catalog sales support.
- Participated in quality improvement program and Xerox Professional Selling Skills Seminar: certificated in both programs.
- Improved credibility, built customer rapport and helped customers save money by reformulating products which reduced raw material costs and enhanced product performance.

PROFESSIONAL EXPERIENCE

xx/xx
to
xx/xx

United Chemicals, Petrochemicals Division, Houston, Texas.
Senior Sales Representative for Petrochemicals

Responsibilities: maintain existing accounts, develop and expand on customer base, assist customers in meeting environmental requirements, improve profitability by increasing sales volume, develop customer rapport.

Territory: Houston area and approximately 150 mile radius of southeastern Texas. Volume approximately $14.5 million in annual revenue. Previous territory included Baltimore/Washington, D.C. metroplex with control of an annual sales revenue $2.5 million.

EDUCATION

xx/xx
to
xx/xx

Bachelor of Science degree . . . Southern Methodist University . . . December xxxx.
Major: Biological Science . . . Minor: Chemistry
Earned excellent grades in major study fields. Extremely knowledgeable with technical terminology. Very active in sports of all types. Excellent health. Open to travel and relocation. Interned in sales with local firm for academic credit.

REFERENCES

Available upon request.

INDUSTRIAL SALES WITHOUT EXPERIENCE SAMPLE

Resume of JOE E. DOE

Present Address
University Quadrangle
Apartment 3-K
Bloomington, IN xxxxx
xxx-xxx-xxxx
doe@indiana.edu

Home Address (Parents)
James J. Doe
123 Wells Avenue
Indianapolis, IN xxxxx
xxx-xxx-xxxx
doej@corp.com

Career Objective

Sales Representative. Wish to begin my career in an industrial firm where the products to be marketed are of a semi-technical nature. Eventually hope to become a high-level marketing executive in a high tech firm with strong marketing orientation.

Education

Indiana University School of Business (8/xx to 6/xx)
B.S. degree in Business Administration, June. On Dean's List two semesters out of the last three semesters . . . Overall grade average of 3.1 . . . Took elective courses in cost accounting, systems analysis, sales management, industrial sales, marketing strategy, retailing, and advertising . . . play with e-commerce websites frequently.

Purdue University College of Engineering (8/xx to 6/xx)
Started college with the idea of becoming a mechanical engineer . . . Took several hours in chemistry, physics, calculus, and engineering principles while at Purdue . . . Overall grade-point average was a B+ . . . Because interests were found to be more people oriented, transferred to Indiana University at end of sophomore year.

Campus Activities

Pledged and initiated into SAE social fraternity at Purdue . . . Actively participated in basketball and baseball intramural sports . . . Played these sports as a varsity letterman in high school . . . Reporter for the **Exponent** (campus newspaper) my sophomore year.

Active member of the I.U. Student Foundation both years at I.U. . . . Active in campus politics (second highest votes for senior class president) . . . Public relations chairman of Promise Party, junior year . . . Part-time disc jockey on Quad radio station . . . Captain of baseball and basketball intramural teams . . . Worked on SAE Fraternity website design 2–4 hrs. per week.

Work Experience

Part-time Janitor, Indiana University (8/xx to 6/xx)
Worked ten hours each week to provide spending money while at college . . . Superior was pleased with my industry . . . In spite of the low status and pay, learned much about people relations in this task . . . Supervised the "swing" people who came into my area of the building.

General Laborer, Indiana State Highway Department (last four summers)
Worked 50 to 70 hours per week . . . Cut grass, patched ruts, dug ditches, drove tractor, shoveled rock, put up signs, flagman, etc. . . . Earned and saved enough money to pay tuition for two semesters.

Background

Brought up in Indianapolis . . . have three brothers . . . father works for U.S. Post Office . . . lettered in two sports (basketball and baseball) in high school.

References

Dr. C. R. Powell
Prof. of Bus. Admin.
Indiana University
Bloomington, IN xxxxx
xxx-xxx-xxxx
powell@email.edu

Mr. D. Blair
Asst. Basketball Coach
Indiana University
Bloomington, IN xxxxx
xxx-xxx-xxxx
blair@email.edu

Mr. James Jackson, Director
Halls of Residence
Indiana University
Bloomington, IN xxxxx
xxx-xxx-xxxx
jack@email.edu

Date: xx/xx

HIGH LEVEL MARKETING EXECUTIVE SAMPLE

CHARLES DRINKWELL

Home:	304 Jones Street Nashville, IN xxxxx xxx-xxx-xxxx drinks@email	Business:	National Sales Manager John Beam, Inc. Gnaw Bone, Indiana xxxxx xxx-xxx-xxxx

OBJECTIVE

Sales Executive/Marketing Manager/Vice President, Marketing Position

SALES MANAGEMENT

Devised and supervised sales promotion projects for large business firms and manufacturers, mostly in the manufacturing field. Originated newspaper, radio, website, and television advertising and coordinated sales promotion with public relations and sales management. Analyzed different markets and costs. Developed sales training manuals. Taught Sales Training As Sales Executive and Promotion Consultant, handled a great variety of accounts. Sales potentials in these firms varied from $5 million to $30 million per year. Was successful in raising the volume of sales in many of these firms 30 percent within the first year.

SALES MANAGEMENT

Hired and supervised sales staff on a local, area, and national basis. Established branch offices throughout the United States and developed uniform systems of processing orders and salesrecords. Promoted new products as well as improved sales of old ones. Developed sales training program. Developed a web based catalog system involving internal inventory control to facilitate movement of different stock between branches.

MARKET RESEARCH

Devised and supervised market research projects to determine sales potentials, as well as need for advertising. Wrote detailed reports and recommendations describing each step in distribution, areas for development, and plans for sales improvement.

SALES

Retail and wholesale. Direct sales to consumers, jobbers, and manufacturers. Sold hard goods, including small motors and electrical appliances.

ORDER CLERK

Received, processed, and expedited orders. Set up order control system which was adopted for all branches.

FIRMS

xx/xx to Present	**John Beam, Inc.** Nashville, Indiana	National Sales Manager (7 years)
xx/xx to xx/xx	**Jack Allen Widgets Co.** Indianapolis, Indiana	Product Manager, Market Research Staff, Sales Promotion Manager (10 years)
xx/xx to xx/xx	**Pfeiffer Bros. Electronics** Uptown, Indiana	Sales Manager, Sales Representative (3 years)

EDUCATION

Indiana University, Kelley School of Business, B.S., xxxx; Major: Marketing Management

JOHN L. FULLER

1234 Aspen Trail, Fresno, California xxxxx

(xxx)xxx-xxxx   fuller@email.com

OBJECTIVE   Key executive position in marketing management or general management with an industrial products firm.

SUMMARY   Twenty plus years of diverse, multi-disciplinary management experience with broad-based exposure and expertise in the various facets of marketing, operations, sales, and general management in industrial and commercial products.

Demonstrated ability to profitably expand mature business and to manage corporate assets for superior productivity. Proven analytical, conceptual, technical, and people skills.

EXPERIENCE

HEAT RECOVERY PRODUCTS   VICE PRESIDENT
Fresno, California   DIRECTOR OF MARKETING
www.heat.com   xxxx to Present (9 years)

- Reversed the 14% decline in unit sales volume in the two year period preceding employment. Increased unit sales volume 41% and total sales revenue 78% in the subsequent two year period.

- Developed marketing strategies to exploit existing product opportunities in present and new markets, including commercial, industrial, and institutional. Strategies focused on an expanded product line with exclusive options and differentiable product features, multiple model selections, and complementary new products.

- Conceptualized and implemented an aggressive product diversification effort. Supplementary HVAC products were acquired on a representation basis and now comprise approximately 20% of total sales revenue.

- Established a national sales representation network to market industrial/commercial ceiling fans and air handling, air cleaning, heating, and ventilation equipment.

- Identified and developed private label accounts in three new markets, i.e., Agricultural, Church, and Direct Mail, resulting in a 50% increase in private label unit sales volume.

COMMERCIAL PRODUCTS INTERNATIONAL   BUSINESS DEVELOPMENT MANAGER
Denver, Colorado   Jan., xxxx – Sept., xxxx (2 yrs)

- Identified and exploited complementary business opportunities in new but related markets resulting in a 10% increase in special OEM sales.

- Devised a simplified marketing strategy to upgrade, restructure, and optimize the performance of mature strategic business units.

- Developed comprehensive business assessments relative to participation in high growth and high profit consumer and industrial product markets.

- Assumed a leading role in the identification, strategic assessment, and financial analysis of complementary business acquisitions.

INDUSTRIAL PRODUCTS INTERNATIONAL
Indianapolis, Indiana

MARKETING MANAGER
PRODUCT MANAGER
March, xxxx – Dec., xxxx (3 yrs)

- Created a $10MM new market by modifying an existing product to meet specific customer needs in the farm equipment market resulting in a 50% increase in unit sales volume.

- Managed the successful launch of two new "engineered" products for the farm and truck markets and managed the phase out and disposition of several mature and outdated product lines.

- Supervised an innovative and persuasive advertising/sales promotion program to create demand for engineered products at the OEM level and to exploit burgeoning Aftermarket sales opportunities.

FARM INDUSTRIES, INC.
Calgary, Alberta
Canada

OEM SALES MANAGER
MARKET RESEARCH MANAGER
June, xxxx – March, xxxx (2 yrs)

- Increased OEM private label farm equipment sales by 30% and expanded non-captive distributor sales by 35%. Improved product line gross margin by 50%.

- Conceived and developed a comprehensive marketing strategy/gameplan predicated on product diversification, market dispersion, and risk diffusion for the strategic business unit(s).

- Identified a new product opportunity which resulted in a $4.5MM gross sales contribution, produced a more balanced product line, and supported expansion into new geographic markets.

FARM EQUIPMENT GROUP, INC.
Bakersfield, California

SENIOR BUYER
ASSISTANT BUYER
June, xxxx – June, xxxx (4 yrs)

- Authored and negotiated comprehensive purchase agreements and manufacturing contracts for construction, farm, industrial, and material handling equipment resulting in a $1.0MM gross profit contribution.

- Initiated and implemented effective measures to monitor and control external manufacturing projects resulting in a $450,000 cost avoidance.

- Reduced material purchase costs 6% on assigned key commodities/component.

EDUCATION

MBA (Marketing)	xxxx	UCLA
Masters (Mechanical Engineering)	xxxx	California State College
B.S. (Mechanical Engineering)	xxxx	California State College

LESLIE GOLDBERG

123 Main Street Apt 3B	Silver Springs, VA xxxxx www.goldberg.com	(xxx) xxx-xxxx gold@email.com

OBJECTIVE

SALES. Seeking a position where strong personal drive, high productivity, computer abilities, and well developed communication skills are desired. Prefer structured on-the-job marketing training program that provides exposure to sales techniques. After training and experience, desire to move into management assignments involving hiring, training, supervising, and motivating others.

EDUCATION

University of Virginia (xx to xx)   **Communications**
Charlottesville, VA xxxxx   GPA 3.4/4.0

Blacksburgh Community College   **General Studies, xxxx to xxxx**

RELEVANT COURSES

Journalism   Television Production
Public Speaking   Theater
Composition   Technical Writing
Graphic Arts   Photography
Computer Introduction   Web Programming

ACTIVITIES

Business Investors Club; Marketing Club, fund raising chairperson; Judicial Board member; Honor Society (elected officer).

EXPERIENCE

Green Olive Bar, Charlottesville, VA, xx/xx to Present
Bar Manager. Worked evenings and weekends while enrolled full-time. Sales increased 25 percent per year while I worked as evening/weekend manager. The owner has 25 employees and in his absence, I manage the bar. Designed part of the recent renovation which resulted in a 50 percent customer increase.

Work about 30 hours per week, year-round, which has caused me to take 5 years to complete the 4 year degree.

ACCOMPLISHMENTS

- Superior academic record in communications and illustration
- Earned 100 percent of college expenses via part-time employment
- Maintained departmental website

PERSONAL

Plan to relocate to the Washington, D.C. area where family resides. Prefer to travel and willing to work long hours. Will consider relocating to any area.

REFERENCES

Mr. Larry Hannah   Professor Charles Brice
Owner   Communications Department
Green Olive Bar   University of Virginia
Charlottesville, VA xxxxx   Charlottesville, VA xxxxx
xxx-xxx-xxxx   xxx-xxx-xxxx

SALES CONSULTANT AT ENTRY LEVEL SAMPLE

MICHAEL J. GRIMM

Campus:
Lambda Chi Alpha
123 3rd Street
Bloomington, IN xxxxx
(xxx)xxx-xxxx
grim@email.edu

Home:
123 Blue Ridge
Allentown, PA xxxxx
(xxx)xxx-xxxx

CAREER OBJECTIVE: *Commercial Sales Consultant.* Wish to use financial and computer skills in the selling of financial products. Desire to consult with potential customers who need financial software. Eventually wish to manage the consultive selling role in a financially oriented firm.

EDUCATION: **Indiana University School of Business, Bloomington, IN. (8/xx to 5/xx)**
B.S. degree in Finance, May, xxxx.
Have accumulated 33 hours above amount required for graduation. These hours include courses in Biology, Chemistry, Physics, and Computer Science which, when integrated with 30 hours of finance and accounting courses, provide a unique background.

ACTIVITIES: **Lambda Chi Alpha Social Fraternity**
• **President** - responsible for 120 members, overlooking duties of officers, planning meetings, and discussing future direction of the fraternity with alumni. Have also planned and controlled a budget of $500,000. (xx/xx to xx/xx)
• **Secretary** - performed activities such as filing fraternity records, maintaining records, and recording minutes. (xx/xx to xx/xx)
• **Greek Week Chairman** - responsible for organizing and motivating fraternity member's involvement in Indiana University's Greek Week. (xx/xx to xx/xx)
• **Intramurals** - softball, volleyball, basketball, football, soccer (always involved).
Interfraternity Presidents Council
• **Representative.** Discussed and voted on policies affecting Indiana University's fraternities. (xx/xx to xx/xx)
• **Leader.** Attended Greek Leadership Seminar twice in Junior and Senior years.
Operation SMART
• **Trainer.** Counseled high school students about the effects of cigarette smoking in Freshman year.

WORK EXPERIENCE: **Nicks English Pub, Bloomington, IN**
(Summer xx)   **Bartender** - worked 15 hours per week serving mostly students and alumni customers.
(Summer xx)   **Delta Delta Delta Sorority, Bloomington, IN**
House Maintenance - performed daily duties averaging 14 hours per week during senior year. Responsible for general maintenance and inventory materials of the sorority.
(Summer xx)   **Asbestos Control, Inc., Allentown, PA**
Laborer - worked 55–65 hours per week. Prepared buildings for the removal of asbestos and also worked in the warehouse filling job orders.
(Summer xx)   **Allentown High School, Allentown, PA**
Crew Supervisor - worked 40 hours per week. Responsible for organizing duties for 6 high school students and reporting daily activities to high school supervisor. Daily duties included painting, grass-cutting, and furniture moving.

REFERENCES: Furnished upon request.

ALICIA HURST

Purdue Villas
125 Dunn Street
West Lafayette, IN xxxxx
(xxx)xxx-xxxx
hurst@email.edu

c/o Dr. John Hurst
19100 Warfield Avenue
Birmingham, MI xxxxx
(xxx)xxx-xxxx

CAREER OBJECTIVE

IT Consulting Sales. Desire to use my electrical engineering and computer science background in a consulting capacity. Interested in assisting with the specification of technical design parameters and communicating between my employer and customer. Long term, plan to manage an IT consultive staff of experts to work with clients on enterprise-wide IT initiatives.

EDUCATION

BS, Electrical Engineering, Purdue University, (xx/xx to xx/xx).

- o Graduated in top 10 percent of EE class.
- o EE class treasurer
- o Spent sophomore year studying abroad on EE program in Switzerland.
- o Specialized in computer software systems design, specializing in enterprise-wide projects.
- o Graduating with 20 extra hours of academic credit in EE.
- o Worked part-time on Professor Lau's chip technology research.
- o Worked about 15 hours per week as a student assistant in the EE computer research lab.
- o Completed an unusual one-year internship for both academic credit and salary.
- o Took 12 hours of accounting and finance courses.

COMPUTER COURSES

Computer Programming	Database Structures	Advanced Programming
Systems Analysis	Enterprise Programming	E-Commerce
Web Technologies	Networking	ORACLE

RELATED EXPERIENCE

Systems Engineer Intern, EDS Corporation, Anderson, IN, xx/xx to xx/xx (one year).

Worked as the Systems Analyst in the development of an on-line Financial Forecasting System. Communicated extensively with users. Defined their needs, current work flows, and data flows in order to define system requirements. Made recommendations for improvement. Assisted IT managers on database applications.

Assisted in the design of a new computer system. Set up file structure, system flow and structure. Generated programming specifications, screen layouts, and report formats. Responsible for the progress of the project, reporting status to management, and system documentation. Gained experience in oral presentations to top management.

REFERENCES

Prof. Chin Lau	Dr. James Price	Ms. Sharon Deal
Electrical Engineering	Electrical Engineering	Director
Purdue University	Purdue University	EDS Corporation
West Lafayette, IN xxxxx	West Lafayette, IN xxxxx	Anderson, IN xxxxx
(xxx)xxx-xxxx	(xxx)xxx-xxxx	(xxx)xxx-xxxx
lau@email.com	price@email.edu	deal@email.com

RETAIL STORE MANAGEMENT-EXPERIENCED SAMPLE

DAVID JAMES

1234 Oriental Court
Chicago, IL xxxxx
(xxx) xxx-xxxx
james@email.com

CAREER OBJECTIVE:

Store Manager. Plan to continue career in field of retailing. Enjoy supervising both people and programs in a fast-paced work setting with challenges and opportunities.

EDUCATION:

Oklahoma State Univ, School of Business (xx/xx to xx/xx)
- Earned a BS degree in marketing in May, xxxx
- Achieved a solid top quartile GPA in marketing courses
- Tutorial assistant in retail course during senior year
- Wrote 40 page business plan for proposed new retail shop in our community for a senior entrepreneurial course
- Minored in mass communication and advertising
- Elected two extra courses in public speaking.
- Member, Toastmasters Intl.

University of Northern Illinois, Dekalb (xx/xx to xx/xx)
- Started college with idea of becoming a Chemist but after taking several hours of chemistry, biology, physics, and calculus, transferred to Oklahoma because my interests were more people oriented.
- All courses taken transferred since I earned no grade less than a "C" in a very rigorous curriculum.

WORK EXPERIENCE:

Assistant Store Manager, National Drug Stores, Inc. (xx/xx to xx/xx)
Supervise, manage, and motivate 30 full and part-time employees. Work about 50 hours per week doing the following:
- Maintain and improve customer relations
- Hire, train, motivate employees
- Solve internal and external problems
- Prototype high technology store.
- Increased sales and earnings by at least 10 percent every year.

Management Trainee, National Drug Stores, Inc. (xx/xx to xx/xx)
Completed 26 week intensive development program that included both OJT and Seminar Training. During this period, the class of 15 trainees did the following:
- Opened and closed stores in real environments.
- Became proficient at how to run a large operation in profit centered stores.
- Learned policies and procedures on buying products, supervising others, and accounting for inventories.

Yellow Pages Representative, Telephone Inc. (xx/xx to xx/xx)
Worked about 20 hours per week while in school and 50 hours per week during summer selling advertising. Organized accounts, set-up appointments, presented facts, and closed sales. This provided an excellent source of income while attending college. Earned 100 percent of my own education expenses. Received numerous letters of recognition praising my ability to maintain good customer relations in a pleasant, personable, and diplomatic manner.

OUTSTANDING SKILLS:

Past employers and faculty members often described me as possessing especially strong credentials in the following areas:

- Leading	- Organizing	- Teaching
- Managing	- Scheduling	- Presenting
- Reliability	- Communicating	- Listening

REFERENCES:

Furnished upon request.

SALES REPRESENTATIVE ENTRY LEVEL SAMPLE
KATLIN JONES

Campus Address (until x/xx/xx)
Stadium Apartments, #2A
Collegeville, US xxxxx
xxx-xxx-xxxx
joness@email.com

Permanent Home Address
123 River Road
Hometown, US xxxxx
xxx-xxx-xxxx
dad@bus.com

Job Target
Sales Representative in Consumer Goods Industry which utilizes my proven abilities
in marketing, organizing, and managing people and projects.

Education
Big State University, College of Arts and Sciences, Collegeville, USA.
B.S. Degree, Economics major with Communications minor, June, xxxx.

Earned a 3.1 GPA overall with a 3.5 average in economics. Selected to participate in an honors class in economic history in my senior year. Team wrote a 30 page business plan which was submitted to a national association contest. Some of my most relevant courses included the following:

Communicating: Public Speaking, Mass Communications, Persuasion Techniques
Managing: Sales Management, Computer Programming, Marketing Principles, Technology
Writing: Prices and Markets, Income and Employment, Money and Banking

During my senior year, several of my academic accomplishments received recognition in the school newspaper. Actively participated in the 200-member journalism society when served as MC at awards banquet.

Spent my sophomore year on an international exchange program in Spain. I lived with a large family and assisted in managing the household activities and their small retail grocery business. Wrote a cultural experience report. Earned transfer credit from a local Spanish university.

Campus Activities
— Elected captain of the tennis team as a junior when the team won the regional championship
— Lead my sorority to campus athletic honors for two years
— Wrote an article that won top recognition for our 15,000 copy distribution campus newspaper
— Effectively contributed to the economics student advisory board two years, a faculty-elected position
— Aggressively campaigned for student senator and received 2,200 votes in senior year
— Worked for Governor's successful re-election committee within the campus community

Work Experience
Smith Associates, x/xx to Present, Secretary, 15 hours per week
- — Created word-processed documents and uploaded to website
- — Transcribed court proceedings and file briefs
- — Trained other part-time clerical assistants
- — Searched for related cases on legal computer networks on the world wide web
- — Received letter of appreciation from a senior partner

Mom's College Shop, Sales Associate every summer since high school, 40 hours per week
- — Served a variety of college-age customers on a daily basis
- — Developed strong personal customer base among teenaged customers
- — Earned significant commissions which paid college tuition
- — Managed store last two summers during owner's vacation period: opened and closed store
- — Purchased $1 million of holiday merchandise at summer Apparel Mart last year

SALES REPRESENTATIVE ENTRY LEVEL SAMPLE

Sara Smith

Campus Address (until 6/1/xx)
Pigskin Apartments
Apt. 2-B
Bloomington, Indiana 47401
xxx-xxx-xxxx
smith@email.edu

Home Address
Care of James K. Jones
123 Front Street
Chicago, Illinois 60601
xxx-xxx-xxxx
mom@email.com

CAREER OBJECTIVE

Sales Representative. Objective: To start career with a firm that markets computer products (or similar products/ services) . . . Work has exposed me to most computer equipment and software . . . Relate well to office management personnel because understand their problems . . . Enjoy the discipline and autonomy of sales . . . Desire a high technology firm with training designed to offer management advancement potentials.

EDUCATION

Indiana University, College of Arts and Sciences, Bloomington, Indiana (xx/xx to xx/xx)
Will earn the A.B. degree in Economics, June, xxxx . . . Hold a 3.8 overall grade average and have earned all A's in Economics . . . Minor field is in journalism . . . Anticipate election to Phi Beta Kappa.

University of Illinois, Circle Campus, Chicago, Illinois (xx/xx to xx/xx)
Began college as a part-time student while I worked as a full-time sales clerk in a local clothing store . . . Transferred to I.U. with 30 credits after one year . . . Earned a GPA of 3.0.

CAMPUS ACTIVITIES

Captain of the Women's varsity tennis team for two years. Member and officer in Kappa Delta Sorority (social) . . . Night editor in junior year of the *Indiana Daily Student* campus newspaper . . . Historian of Mortar Board, a senior women's honorary . . . Selected as advisor to President Ryan my senior year . . . Active in the I.U. Student Foundation program, particularly the "Little 500," a bicycle race whose proceeds provide scholarships.

WORK EXPERIENCE

Jane's College Shop, Junior Sports Wear, 8/xx to present (Every semester for last 3 years)
Sales Clerk, part-time . . . Worked approximately 10 to 15 hours per week servicing customers . . . Frequently assisted the manager-owner in designing advertisements and promotional displays . . . During my last three months, often supervised and scheduled other clerks when the owner was out of town.

Treasure Place Gift Shop, (Every summer since high school)
Various assignments . . . Mother owns this unique gift shop in a tourist area just north of Chicago . . . Specialize in items from the Scandinavian countries . . . Have done everything from sweeping out the storeroom daily to helping select merchandise at the semi-annual trade shows . . . Show customers around, handle some of the daily accounting, develop displays, manage part-time salespeople, do all correspondence, etc.

PERSONAL

Have traveled extensively in Europe and lived one year during high school in Japan . . . Can operate most office equipment including copiers, calculators, microfilm equipment, and computers . . . Type 70 wpm . . . Know desktop publishing, html, and some computer programming . . . Speak Spanish and Japanese.

JENNIFER HARDY

Campus Address (until x/x/xx)　　　　　　　　　　　**Home Address**
Pigskin Apartments, #2B　　　　　　　　　　　　　　　123 Front Street
College Town, USA xxxxx　　　　　　　　　　　　　　Hometown, USA xxxxx

xxx-xxx-xxxx　　　　　　　　　　　　　　　　　　　　xxx-xxx-xxxx
hardy@email.com　　　　　　　　　　　　　　　　　　mom@email.com

Career Objective

Sales Representative. Wish to start career with a firm that markets consulting services . . . My part-time clerical work has exposed me to computer equipment and software . . . Relate well to management personnel . . . Aspire to manage a large technical sales force.

Education

Big Time University, College of Arts and Sciences, College Town, USA, xxxxx
Will earn the A.B. degree in Economics, June, xxxx . . . Hold a 3.3 overall GPA . . . Earned 3.5 GPA in Economics . . . Minor field in Journalism (3.5 GPA) with focus on web design and use.
Key Courses:

- Prices and Markets
- Income and Employment
- Money and Banking
- Systems Design

- Labor Economics
- Mass Communications
- Telecommunications
- Computer Programming

- Electronic Marketing
- Accounting
- Marketing
- Web Design

Local University Circle Campus, Hometown, USA xxxxx
Began college as a part-time student while worked full-time . . . Transferred to Big Time Univ. with 30 credits after one year . . . Earned 3.1 GPA . . . Took summer courses in technology field during summers.

Campus Activities

Captain of the women's varsity tennis team for two years . . . Member and **officer** in Kappa Delta Sorority (social) . . . Night **editor** in junior year of the *Daily Student* campus newspaper . . . **Historian** on Mortar Board, a senior women's honorary . . . Selected as **advisor** to University President my senior year . . . **Campaign manager** for senior class president . . . Maintained webpage for sorority last year.

Work Experience

John H. Jones, Attorney at Law, x/xx to present (Junior and senior years)
Part-time secretary . . . Handle filing, take dictation, transcribe tape recordings of proceedings, type contracts and other legal documents . . . Train other part-timers . . . Learned to operate most common office equipment and computers . . . Met sales representatives, other vendors, and clients.

Jane's College Shop, Junior Sport Wear, x/xx to x/xx (Sophomore year)
Sales clerk, part-time . . . Worked 10 to 15 hours per week servicing customers . . . Frequently assisted manager in designing ads and displays . . . Supervised others.

Treasure Place Gift Shop, Every summer since high school
Various assignments . . . Mother owns unique gift shop in a tourist area north of Home Town . . . Specialize in Scandinavian items . . . Helped select merchandise at trade shows . . . Handle daily accounting . . . Develop displays . . . Supervise workers.

References Available

DEBORAH CLARK

Campus Address (until x/x/xx)
Pigskin Apartments, #2B
College Town, USA xxxxx
xxx-xxx-xxxx
clark@email.edu

Home Address (Mother)
123 Front Street
Hometown, USA xxxxx
xxx-xxx-xxxx
mom@email.com

OBJECTIVE: **Sales Representative.** Wish to start career with a firm that markets computer products or services . . . previous work has exposed me to computer equipment and software . . . relate well to office personnel . . . aspire to manage a large technical consulting staff.

FUNCTIONAL SKILLS AND ABILITIES

SELLING: Courses in Marketing, Data Processing, Accounting, Money and Banking, Prices and Markets, Income and Employment . . . Achieved an overall 3.3 GPA and 3.6 GPA in my major of Economics . . . Sales clerk in college town sportswear store while working 10–15 hours per week . . . Sold gift items in parents' gift store and purchased merchandise at trade shows from professional salespersons . . . Operated office equipment and computers in part-time job . . . understand office products and service field well . . . Frequently interacted with professional salespersons who called on our office.

SUPERVISING: Captain of women's varsity tennis team for two years . . . Officer in social sorority . . . Campaigned for senior class president . . . Managed retail store in absence of owner . . . Trained part-time workers in law office . . . Selected as an advisor to the university president . . . Assigned increasing levels of responsibility in full and part-time jobs held while in college.

ORGANIZING: As a part-time secretary in a law firm, handled filing, correspondence, contracts, and other important legal documents . . . Managed time effectively as worked part-time . . . Participated in campus activities . . . Achieved above average grades (3.3 GPA) . . . Assisted store manager in designing ads and displays . . . Worked in hectic seasonal rush periods during summers and vacation periods in family's gift shop . . . Maintained a website.

EDUCATION: Big Time University, AB in Economics, June, xxxx.
Local University, 30 credit hours, Freshman year.

WORK EXPERIENCE: John H. Jones Attorney, Part-time Secretary (xx/xx to xx/xx)
Jane's College Shop, Part-time Sales Clerk (Sophomore year)
Treasure Place Gift Shop, Sales Clerk (Summers since xx/xx)

PERSONAL: Speak Spanish . . . Computer literate . . . Willing to relocate . . . Earned 70 percent of college expenses . . . Enjoy public speaking.

STEPHEN H. KRIVICKAS, II

Present Address
1234 Graham Place
Madison, WI xxxxx
xxx-xxx-xxxx
kriv@email.edu

After August 10, xxxx
125 Ashton Drive
Christian, WI xxxxx
xxx-xxx-xxxx

CAREER OBJECTIVE:

Sales Development Program. Seeking Sales Representative position with a well-respected firm that offers a training program offering training in pricing, promotion, distribution channels, account management, sales techniques, and supervision. Prefer an industry that can best use my science background.

EDUCATION:

UNIVERSITY OF WISCONSIN, Madison, Wisconsin
Bachelor of Science, May xxxx   — Overall GPA: 2.80
Major: Biology (30 credits)   — GPA: 3.33
Minor: Business (15 credits)   — GPA: 3.48

WORK EXPERIENCE:

Camera Inc.
Clifton, WI
(Summer of xxxx)

ORDER PROCESSOR
— Took, processed and checked product orders for customers and sales reps
— Processed product returns which sometimes exceeded more than $200,000
— Helped compile a daily returns and orders report
— Studied the product line to handle customer questions and complaints
— Learned telemarketing software package quite well

Listening Line
Madison, WI
(Fall Semester, xxxx)

HOTLINE VOLUNTEER
— Trained to "actively" listen and identify a caller's special needs and/or problems
— Referred callers to the appropriate support agencies
— Developed good communication skills and ability to deal with a variety of people

Kelsey Manufacturing
Osh Kosh, WI
(Summer of xxxx)
(Summer of xxxx)

ASSEMBLY LINEMAN AND MAINTENANCE
— Worked as part of a team to produce a high quality product
— Cleared and cleaned machines to ensure proper operation
— Exposed to a variety of manufacturing operations including product production, shipping and quality control

Molded Plastics
Christian, WI
(Summer of xxxx)
(Summer of xxxx)

MACHINE OPERATOR
— Worked 50 hours a week
— Assisted in quality control by checking product for defects
— Learned how to work hard and follow instructions

HONORS AND ACTIVITIES:

— Traveled extensively and worked in Ireland
— Who's Who Among College Student Leaders
— Volunteer WQA Disc Jockey
— Advertising Club Secretary

— Elected Dorm Senator
— Intramural Soccer Referee
— United Way Volunteer
— Enjoy Chess, Risk and other strategy games
— Paid 75% of college expenses

REFERENCES: Please call   Prepared xx/xx

Andrew K. Martin

123 Beacon Woods Place	Fort Carson, Utah xxxxx	(xxx) xxx-xxxx martin@email.com

OBJECTIVE

Marketing Manager position in an organization where there is a need to expand markets and develop new marketing concepts through the use of market research, product planning, web commerce, and persuasive selling skills.

MARKET DEVELOPMENT

Establish new business opportunities by researching and targeting those markets that would most likely benefit from innovative transportation services. Develop and manage projects by gathering pertinent data, provide appropriate analytical support, and present programs in both written and verbal form to upper management and prospective clients. Research and design new methods of presenting programs. Organize and manage implementation of projects. Meet with new customers once a month.

RESULTS: *Assisted department in surpassing goals set by management in developing new business last year by 35%. Met personal objectives established by superior for new business development each of last 4 years.*

MANAGEMENT

Design procedures for support personnel to ensure optimum level of **customer service**. Review problematic areas. Execute effective solutions. Assist in researching, developing and implementing computerized reports for both project development and management of existing programs.

RESULTS: *Assured Programs met desired targets by monitoring and maintaining the most efficient use of resources. Often complimented for accurate and complete record keeping.*

WORK HISTORY

American Transport, Fort Carson, Utah
Manager, Commercial Marketing Department, xxxx–Present (4 years)
Area Sales Planner, xxxx–xxxx (2 years)
Fleet Coordinator, xxxx (2 years)

EDUCATION

Indiana University School of Business, xxxx.
Earned a Bachelor of Science degree in Marketing.
Appeared on Dean's List four semesters.
College expenses financed by employment throughout both academic year and summers.

PERSONAL DATA AND OTHER FACTS

- Highly active in nature sports.
- Avid home computer enthusiast
- Enjoy camping, fishing, photography and computers.
- Enjoy accepting and completing challenging projects.

SYSTEMS MARKETING CONSULTING ENTRY LEVEL SAMPLE

c/o John C. Myers (Father)
2015 N. Main Street
Santa Clara, CA xxxxx
xxx-xxx-xxxx
myersj@email.com

JACK E. MYERS
Campus View Condos
123 Park Avenue
Palo Alto, CA xxxxx
xxx-xxx-xxxx
myers@email.com

OBJECTIVE	**Systems Marketing.** Desire a position that integrates my technical computer skills with my external leadership abilities. Strong communication talents might best be utilized in the marketing function.
EDUCATION	**Walsh College, Palo Alto, CA (xx/xx to xx/xx)** BS, Mathematics with Computer Science minor. GPA: 3.2/4.0

RELEVANT COURSES

Analytical	**Communication**
Assembler (3 hrs)	Public Speaking
C++ (6 hrs)	Composition
Calculus (15 hrs)	Technical Writing
Statistics (6 hrs)	Psychology
Data Structures (6 hrs)	Mass Communication
Operating Systems (3 hrs)	

HONORS	Kappa Mu Epsilon (Math honorary) Dean's List (3.7 GPA, xxxx and 3.6 GPA, xxxx) Top Senior Project Award (Class presentation)
ACTIVITIES	**Campus Recruiter**; One of 3 seniors selected to assist in recruitment of high school scholars. **Special Olympics**; Volunteer coordinator for 4 years. **Boys Club**; Coach 9–12 year olds in basketball and soccer. **Concert Choir**; Tour throughout the West Coast.
EXPERIENCE	**REC/TEC Software, Silicon, CA (xx/xx to Present)** *Contract Programmer/Installer.* Work on a contact basis writing computer programs and help install hardware and software with small business networking clients. This has been an off/on job while in school. Owner has offered me a full-time job upon graduation which I declined.
	Campus View Condos, Palo Alto, CA (xx/xx to Present) *Maintenance.* Do odd jobs around the complex to help with housing expenses.
PERSONAL	Experienced with small server network and web installations. Spent last summer in Japan. Prefer to locate in Silicon Valley.

Melissa Roth

Danish Imports	123 Main Street
100 S. Main	Norman, Oklahoma xxxxx
Kansas City, MO xxxxx	(xxx)xxx-xxxx
(xxx)xxx-xxxx	roth@email.edu

OBJECTIVE

RETAILING. Seeking an assignment with a fashion department store offering a training program that rotates through operations, distribution, advertising, display, sales, customer service, and buying. Desire to advance through the general merchandise manager track or the large store manager track. My assertive style, outgoing personality, and supervisory skills should aid in my long-term success in retailing.

SKILLS

Resolved customer problems satisfactorily in retail environment.
Organized task forces of team members in sorority leadership events.
Solved analytical financial problems using software in part-time jobs.
Taught training program in use of Microsoft Office products.

EDUCATION

UNIVERSITY OF OKLAHOMA, Norman, OK, xx/xx to xx/xx
B.S., Psychology, May, xxxx, 2.7 GPA (4.0=A)
- o Motivational Psychology
- o Consumer Policy
- o Buyer Behavior
- o Advertising
- o Accounting
- o Computers in Psychology

Attended workshops and proficient in all Microsoft Suite products and many web related design browsers and development tools like HTML and Frontpage.

CITY OF LONDON POLYTECHNIC, London, England, xx/xx to xx/xx
Completed 16 credit hours of liberal arts courses that emphasized aspects of British culture and art. Traveled extensively through Europe independently the following summer.

ACTIVITIES

Alpha Epsilon Phi Social Sorority: Internal Spirit Committee Chairperson (Organized spirit and motivational activities for house meetings and events); **Senior Representative** (Organized social events and acted as liaison between live-in and live-out house members); **Philanthropic Chairperson** (Supervised sponsorship of several Refusnik families living in the Soviet Union); **Junior Class Treasurer**.

Danforth Center, Kansas City: When home on vacations and summers, volunteered to assist medical professionals in group and individual therapy; supervised patients in physical therapy; contributed to staff discussions about specific patients in order to collectively consider appropriate treatment.

EXPERIENCE

DANISH IMPORTS, Kansas City, KS (since high school)
Numerous Assignments. Mother owns this gift shop located in the largest specialty mall in tri-state area. Specialized in Danish and Norwegian gifts ranging from crafts to top quality woolen goods. Participated in four foreign-buying trips. Some of my roles have been personal selling clerk, inventory receiving and marking, bookkeeping, store analysis, managing advertising, hiring and buying. Gained a great deal of knowledge about retailing in this practical setting but also took some related academic courses in college. Hours worked varied from 5 to 50 depending on seasons and family needs.

CRAIG SIMMONS

Blair Hall-333
Emory University
Atlanta, GA xxxxx
(xxx)xxx-xxxx
simmons@email.com

Sarah Simmons (mother)
123 Gran Haven Lane
Rome, GA xxxxx
(xxx)xxx-xxxx

CAREER OBJECTIVE	**Sales Consultant.** Wish to use my background in biology, chemistry, and mathematics to market technical products that are designed and built to the customer's specifications. My excellent ability to communicate technical jargon in non-technical terminology should prove valuable in a customer liaison role. Eventually wish to consult on large multi-million dollar projects that are cooperative arrangements between designer, builder, and end user.
EDUCATION	**B.S. August, xxxx, Emory University, Atlanta, Georgia** Major: Biology Minor: Psychology and Chemistry Coursework: •Organic Chemistry •Endocrinology •Calculus IV •Inorganic Chemistry •Microbiology •Statistics •Social Psychology •Motivational Psych •Physiology
COLLEGE ACTIVITIES	**Active member of Sigma Alpha Epsilon Fraternity (9/xx – 5/xx)** •Rush Chairman - Recruited potential members. Organized and planned semester rush schedule. •Social Chairman-Planned and organized social functions and dances. Collected and budgeted social funds. •Intramural Sports-Captain of basketball and member of football, softball and volleyball teams. •Bike Coach-Organize, manage and coach bike team. **University Student Foundation** (10/xx–5/xx) •Special Projects Committee •Telephone Solicitor •Pre-Med Committee •Alumni Field Trip Host
WORK EXPERIENCE	**Lab Technician**, Emory University, Atlanta, GA Worked about 10–15 hours each week preparing lab for classes, cleaning equipment, reordering supplies, and monitoring use. Assisted Professor Walsh in his experiments on various amino acids and typed several of his research papers that were delivered at professional conferences. (From sophomore year through senior year) **Head Kitchen Steward**, Sigma Alpha Epsilon Fraternity, Atlanta, GA Responsible for kitchen facilities and supervision of 10 employees. Work closely with house manager in planning weekly menu, ordering and purchasing of food. (8/xx–present) **Customer Service**, Consumer Products, Rome, GA Delivered products to customers in Chicago area. Handled complaints. Inspected, repaired, or replaced merchandise. Made on-site sales. (3 summers of xxxx, xx and xx)

BILL WILLIAMS

1632 Holloway Avenue
Ft. Wayne, Indiana xxxxx
xxx-xxx-xxxx
will@email.com

Professional Objective	**Retail Store Sales Manager or Buyer.** Ultimate goal—Manager of major retail store for large national chain or Merchandise Manager for department store chain.
Education xx/xx to xx/xx	**BS, xx/xx, INDIANA UNIVERSITY, KELLEY SCHOOL OF BUSINESS** Major: Marketing . . . Minor: Mass Communication — Special emphasis on retail sales and merchandising. — Considerable work in accounting and data processing.
Experience xx/xx to xx/xx	**L.S. AYRES, Fort Wayne, Indiana** **Assistant Manager.** In charge of all advertising and copy layout for this large department store. Work closely with all buyers in planning sales campaigns. Materially assist manager in working out modernization plans for basement floor. Have taken two trips to Dallas, Texas, to assist in selection of men's suits and shoes. Sales volume is over $12 million in both departments that I manage.
xx/xx to xx/xx	**J. C. WHITE & COMPANY, South Bend, Indiana** **Retail Shoe Sales.** Started as clerk in Elkhart store. After six months, moved to South Bend outlet as Assistant Manager. Responsible for all display work, newspaper advertising, and sales promotion. Sales volume is over $8 million.
Summer Work	Earned 50 percent of total college expenses selling vacuum cleaners and cooking ware on commission for four summers.
Military Service	**UNITED STATES ARMY, xx/xx to xx/xx** **Communications Specialist.** After graduation from college, enlisted in the Army. Spent most of the time in Europe working as a communications and personnel relations officer.
Background	Brought up in northern Indiana area. Active in community affairs such as Junior Achievement, Boy Scouts, and active alumnus of Indiana University. Member of a social fraternity. Have traveled extensively throughout the Midwestern and Southern United States.
Interest	Primarily interested in hiking-outdoor activities and conservation societies, e.g., Sierra Club, Save the Redwood Foundation, Audubon Society, etc.
References	Captain J. Tough J. C. White, President Dr. John Smart U.S. Army J. C. White and Co. Professor, Retailing Ft. Leonard Wood 300 Main Street Indiana University Waynesville, MO xxxxx South Bend, IN xxxxx Bloomington, IN xxxxx xxx-xxx-xxxx xxx-xxx-xxxx xxx-xxx-xxxx tough@email.com white@email.com smart@email.com

BRANDY ANN TOUGHSKIN

Campus Address	**Permanent Address**
Mountain View Apartments	1400 Michigan Avenue
Winding Way Boulevard	Apartment 25C
Bloomington, IN xxxxx	Chicago, Illinois xxxxx
xxx-xxx-xxxx	xxx-xxx-xxxx
brandy@email.com	

CAREER OBJECTIVE

RETAIL BUYER DEVELOPMENT PROGRAM. Wish to begin career with a trend-setting department store or fashion women's specialty store. Prefer to start on a training program that will give me experience in store operations, advertising, point of purchase display presentations, sales training, supervision, and exposure to the buying function. Ambition is to advance into a buying position, general merchandise management, and retail store management.

EDUCATION

INDIANA UNIVERSITY, TEXTILE MERCHANDISING, A.B., MAY, xx/xx. Minored in Business. Maintained a B+ average in my major and a B average overall which included courses in the following fields:

¤ Home Economics	¤ Computers in Business	¤ Web technologies
¤ Retailing	¤ Advertising	¤ Merchandising
¤ Accounting	¤ Management Principles	¤ Sales Management

During my junior year, I did a 10-week fashion internship with Izod Manufacturing in which I earned six credit hours and learned about clothing manufacturing, quality methods, modeling, colors, merchandising, trade shows, etc.

EXTRACURRICULAR ACTIVITIES

Delta Gamma Social Sorority: *President; Treasurer; Rush Chairperson. Vice-President of Panhellenic: Responsible for changing rush system* for all sororities. Indiana Daily Student: *Editor* and reporter for two years. Union Board Trustee: Assisted in *managing* a very large Student Union operation. Hobbies: *Singing and acting* in college theatre; play on women's *intermural basketball team.*

EXPERIENCE

MARSHALL FIELD AND CO.
College Board
Chicago, Illinois

Selected by a group of fashion buyers to sit on a board with six other college seniors. We assisted buyers in selection of new holiday fashion merchandise in the junior area. Each of us had the opportunity to accompany a buyer on a trip to New York during the summer of xxxx.

SEARS, ROEBUCK AND CO.
Sales Clerk
Evanston, Illinois

Each summer from my high school senior year until my junior year in college, I worked as a full-time sales clerk at a store near my home. Since I was often vacation relief, I was exposed to most facets of retailing from hard goods to soft goods. (xx/xx to xx/xx)

PART-TIME

As my academic load and schedule permitted, worked part-time for Limited College Shop, a young women's specialty store. Worked from sophomore year until present when needed as a sales clerk. Had a variety of duties including sales, security, cash control, display, gift wrapping, minor supervision, etc.

REFERENCES FURNISHED UPON REQUEST

JOAN MARIE BROWN

123 Quad Court
Howard University
Washington, DC xxxxx
xxx-xxx-xxxx
brown@email.com

c/o James Brown
110 Pleasant Run
Valley Forge, PA xxxxx
xxx-xxx-xxxx
stables@email.com

CAREER OBJECTIVE:

Brand Assistant. Seeking an assignment with a consumer products firm in the product management function. After training and experience in sales, desire to gain training and experience in ad agency relations, packaging, pricing, costing, sales forecasting, data analysis, point of sale display design, couponing strategies, and advertising media planning depending upon channel of product distribution.

SUMMARY OF QUALIFICATIONS:

- Involved in the development of a corporate sales program to supplement membership sales.
- Demonstrated an excellent ability for organization, time management, and achievement of goals.
- Instrumental in initiating, closing, and following up sales in full and part-time jobs.
- Utilized marketing skills and successfully aided in the design and implementation of a fund-raising program.
- Considered a major contributor to the team effort by encouraging competition and goal setting.

EDUCATION:

MBA, xx/xx, University of Virginia, Charlottesville, VA

- Earned recognition as top 10 percent of marketing class.
- Graduate Assistant in Marketing Department. Taught in consumer behavior lab.
- Marketing term project: Introduction of a peach-flavored soft drink. Our team researched the market, produced a prototype product, launched it in a local test market, tested consumer reaction, determined market potential, set up advertising, filed application for a brand trademark, and took the project up to the actual production. Product died when analysis revealed the market was not ready for the peach taste.

BS, xx/xx, Howard University, Washington, DC

- Studied a broad course in the liberal arts with emphasis on communication skills.
- Maintained a 3.3 GPA/4.0 and scored in top quartile on GMAT test.
- Wrote articles for the newspaper and maintained a highly graphical website in admissions office.
- Worked part-time in admissions on recruitment materials.

WORK EXPERIENCE:

SCANDINAVIAN HEALTH AND RACQUET CLUB, Washington, DC

Program Director/Sales Representative, (xx/xx to xx/xx)

Responsible for marketing and selling memberships based on benefit and need. Continued client follow up is through design and implementation of individualized programs. Have consistently obtained over 115 percent of monthly sales quota, over 85 percent of service quota, and received Sales Employee of the Month, August and October, Top Servicer of the Month, August.

OLAN MILLS, Tyson's Corner, MD

Sales Representative, (xx/xx to xx/xx)

Sales Trainer

Accountable for managing a studio and meeting personal sales quotas, while teaching Trainees proper sales, marketing, and management techniques. Conducted periodic reviews and supplemental training. These methods resulted in 12 Top Sales Average of the Week and 10 Top Studio of the Week awards.

HUNTER HILL STABLE, Fort Valley, VA

Assistant Manager to Groomer, (xx/xx to Present)

This position required strong organizational abilities and willingness to accept responsibilities. Various duties included training horses, teaching riding lessons, managing the care of horses, supervising employees, initiating horse sales, and organizing horse shows. Owned by family. Worked there part-time all my life.

Cornell Quad Ithaca, NY xxxxx xxx-xxx-xxxx kers@email.edu	**MICHAEL L. KERSHAW**	One Langford Drive Lynnville, MA xxxxx xxx-xxx-xxxx

CAREER OBJECTIVE

Market Research Assistant. Desire an entry-level position with a consumer products manufacturer. Interested in consumer data collection, analyzing buyer behavior, statistically analyzing data, forecasting sales, computer modelling, and presenting of research results to management. Possess outstanding writing skills and presentation abilities which should prove invaluable in communicating research results to top management for decision-making purposes.

EDUCATION

Cornell University Ithaca, NY	8/xx – 5/xx	M.B.A. (Marketing)
Tufts University Medford, MA	9/xx – 5/xx	B.A. (Economics)
London School of Economics London, England	1/xx – 5/xx	(Economic/Political Studies)

ACTIVITIES

Graduate.....................................* Director of Marketing for the Cornell Entrepreneur Conference
* Co-founder and editor of MBA Orientation newsletter
* Chairman of the Marketing Club's Recruitment Development Committee
* Member of the MBA Executive Forum Program—Host speakers
* Participant in various intramural sports

Undergraduate............................* Vice President Economic Club. Hosted President's Economic Advisor
* Chaired committee to improve security within University's dormitories
* Active in various state and federal political campaigns
* Travel in every state and most countries of Europe
* Play varsity soccer on top rated Tufts team

EXPERIENCE

Transportation and Exchange Director
Citizens Energy Corporation
Boston, MA
5/xx – 1/xx (3 years)

Coordinated the transportation of 55 billion cubic feet of natural gas on 17 of the nation's largest intra- and interstate pipelines for the firm's subsidiary, Citizens Gas Supply Corporation. Responsible for the initial development and operation of this department. Assisted in development of the firm's promotional material.

National Coordinator
Home Oil Transfer Program
Boston, MA
10/xx – 5/xx (Intern)
5/xx – 8/xx (15 months full-time)

Arranged for the collection of residential and commercial waste oil and its distribution to low income and elderly people in six Northeast states. Supervised the activity of 12 independent oil dealers. Managed the daily operations as well as assisted in the program's long-term strategic planning. Frequently marketed the program to oil dealers, public utilities, and charitable organizations. Promoted the service to state governments and local municipalities.

Operations Manager
International Ice Cream Corporation
Boston, MA
(Summers; junior/senior years)

Supervised the daily operations of the Boston area office for New England's largest independent ice cream distributor. Directed the deliveries of 15 truck drivers. Developed methods for improving the effectiveness of the sales and accounts receivable departments. Assisted in the formation and management of a co-operative advertising venture.

125 S. Ocean View
Seattle, WA xxxxx
xxx-xxx-xxxx
white@email.com
(Campus)

LARRY V. WHITE

c/o Larry White, Sr.
125 S. Lake View
Salt Lake City, UT xxxxx
xxx-xxx-xxxx
white@emial.com

OBJECTIVE

Financial Sales Position. Seeking a marketing opportunity that will integrate my financial skills with my strong sales experiences. Prefer to sell financial products/services that utilize my computer abilities for decision analysis coupled with personal judgment. Long term goal is to manage a financial services organization.

EDUCATION

M.B.A. Finance, University of Washington, Seattle, WA, May, xxxx, 3.5/4.0.
B.S. Economics, Westminster College, Salt Lake City, UT, May, xxxx, 3.5/4.0.

SPECIAL TRAINING

- Xerox Sales Training Course
- Computerland Sales Training Course
- Securities Training Course
- Registered Securities Trader

AWARDS/ACTIVITIES

- Graduate Assistantship, 15 hrs. weekly
- Kodak Scholarship & Leadership Award (MBA)
- Graduated Cum Laude at Westminster
- Full-time student/full-time employee simultaneously
- Investment Club Officer (MBA)
- Church leadership responsibilities
- Provided 100% educational expenses

PROFESSIONAL EXPERIENCE

UNIBANCTRUST BOND DEPT., Chicago, IL   Summer, xxxx
Summer Intern

Responsibilities: Recommending ideas (derivatives, swaps, options, etc.) to existing institution accounts, and prospecting for additional accounts. Assisting at the trading desk. Assisting in creating a complete marketing program for safekeeping securities portfolio pricing, analysis, and accounting record keeping. Analyzing the Discount Brokerage business.

Achievements: Designed two brochures and slide presentations for marketing a portfolio safekeeping, accounting, and pricing marketing program. Motivated the Discount Brokerage department to radically alter their commission schedule based on an exhaustive analysis performed for the department. Gained substantial knowledge about the securities industry.

OPTIONS FINANCIAL, Salt Lake City, UT   xx/xx to xx/xx (18 months)
Stock Broker

Responsibilities: Analyzing stocks and mutual funds and determining which are the most appropriate investments for my clients. Clients were local upper middle income professionals. Left to earn the MBA degree.

Achievements: Passed Series 7 Exam after completing a 3-month training course. Attained over $40,000 in gross sales my second month and was the 2nd highest producer in an office of 15 representatives for the year.

COMPUTERCITY, Salt Lake City, UT   xx/xx to xx/xx (3 years)
Computer Sales

Responsibilities: Prospecting and developing large accounts. Selling microcomputers, networks, and software. Became very network proficient.

Achievements: $1,000,000 salesperson each year with the top sales award in last year there. Closed the 2nd largest contract in our firm's history with Utah Life Insurance Company. Awarded trip to Florida for highest sales volume in firm my first year.

MARY RENEE ANTOINE

Campus Address: Ash Center - B121
Tucson, AZ xxxxx
(xxx) xxx-xxxx
anton@email.com

Home Address: 12 Circle Drive
(after May 7) Indiana PA xxxxx
(xxx) xxx-xxxx

CAREER OBJECTIVE

International Finance. Seeking an entry level position in one or more of the following specialties: economic analysis, financial analysis, cost analysis, and international economic, research, and business relations. Desire a challenging position which will develop my skill in analysis and decision-making with the objective of a constructive career in a global work setting.

EDUCATION

University of Arizona, College of Arts and Sciences, Tucson, Arizona (xx/xx to xx/xx)
B.A. degree in Economics/French, May, xxxx
3.75 G.P.A./4.0 scale, Phi Beta Kappa
- Golden Key Honor Society, junior-senior class
- Alpha Lambda Delta, freshman honor society
- Phi Eta Sigma, freshman honor society
- Residence Scholar Program

Council on International Education Exchange Program, Rennes, France (xx/xx to xx/xx)
Semester overseas study program in international economics, University of Arizona and local university.
21 hours course work in economics and extensive written report upon returning to UA.
Housed with French family for 12 months and shared in all household duties.

COURSE HIGHLIGHTS

Money, Banking and Financial Markets
Theory of Prices and Markets
Theory of Income and Employment
Finite Mathematics
Statistics
Analytical Geometry and Calculus

Computer Science
International Economics
International Monetary Economics
  (including Balance of Payments Accounting)
Environment and Resource Economics
  (emphasis on cost/benefit analysis and policy formation)

CAMPUS ACTIVITIES

Intramural sports; softball (4 yrs), flag football (3 yrs/captain 1 yr), volleyball (1 yr), basketball (1 yr)
Governor, dormitory unit (1 semester), elected Resident Assistant for next 2 years
"Extravaganza" group song and dance competition (1 yr), group won top prize for production in xxxx

WORK EXPERIENCE

Residence Halls Cafeteria, University of Arizona
Dining room assistant, supplier, and general cafeteria worker (2 yrs), 10–15 hrs/wk

York Steak House, Indiana, Pennsylvania
Waitress, new employee trainer, and food preparer (3 yrs), summers and holidays, 10–15 hrs/wk

REFERENCES

Dr. Chu Chang
Economics Department
University of Arizona
Tucson, AZ xxxxx
(xxx) xxx-xxxx
chang@email.edu

Dr. Frances Viegnes
French Department
University of Arizona
Tucson, AZ xxxxx
(xxx) xxx-xxxx
vieg@email.edu

Dr. Donald K. Freeman, Chairperson
Economics Department
Indiana University of Pennsylvania
Indiana, Pennsylvania xxxxx
(xxx) xxx-xxxx
free@email.edu

John E. Jones

Present Address
123 Smith Road
Anytown, USA xxxxx
xxx-xxx-xxxx
jones@email.com

Home Address
R. R. 25, Box 25
Anytown, USA xxxxx
xxx-xxx-xxxx

Professional Objective

Accountant or Financial Analyst
An immediate goal is employment on an accounting or finance staff of a large industrial firm or public institution that will provide a wide exposure to different financial problems. Eventually wish to become controller of a major organization after obtaining some experience as both an analyst and manager in areas such as capital budgeting, treasury, auditing, systems, taxes, cost control, operating budgets, etc.

Education

xx/xx
to
xx/xx

INDIANA UNIVERSITY GRADUATE SCHOOL OF BUSINESS
Master of Business Administration degree in June, xxxx, Finance. Have taken a large number of courses in telecommunications, technology, and business analysis with the idea of developing a strong background in management information systems. Earned a 4.0 in my major subject and held a 3.65 average overall. During the second year of the program, taught the basic accounting courses as a teaching assistant. Treasurer of the MBA Association that year. College expenses were financed by the assistantship and the military.

xx/xx
to
xx/xx

THE OHIO STATE UNIVERSITY COLLEGE OF ADMINISTRATIVE SCIENCE
Earned the B.S. degree in June, xxxx, with a major in accounting. Grades in the accounting averaged 2.8. Overall GPA was 2.5 although earned a 3.5 my last two quarters. Took 35 semester hours of accounting courses, Vice-President of the Accounting Club during senior year. Pledged the Phi Psi social fraternity my freshman year and elected president my junior year. Played intramural basketball every year to stay in shape.

Work Experience

Part-time. Employed as a part-time sales clerk for about 10 hours per week every quarter while at OSU in the campus bookstore.

Summers. Worked summers while in undergraduate school as a welder in my uncle's tool and die shop. This position, plus my part-time work, paid for 75 percent of college expenses as an undergraduate.

Military
xx/xx
to
xx/xx

U.S. ARMY - Commissioned as a 2nd Lieutenant in September, xxxx, after completing ROTC at OSU. Began active duty by attending Signal Corps at Ft. Gordon and Ft. Monmouth, New Jersey. Served as communications officer in Japan. Also spent one year in Europe. Currently 1st Lieutenant in the active reserves which keeps me in touch with military advanced telecommunications technology.

References

Dr. Joe Smith
Professor of Finance
Indiana University
Bloomington, IN xxxxx
xxx-xxx-xxxx
smith@email.edu

Dr. Curt Jones
Professor of Accounting
Ohio State University
Columbus, OH xxxxx
xxx-xxx-xxxx
jones@email.edu

Dr. James Monroe
President
Gnaw Bone State Bank
Gnaw Bone, IN xxxxx
xxx-xxx-xxxx
monroe@email.com

Glenn Nigh

Campus Address
245 S. High Street
Master Quad-B125
Lexington, KY xxxxx
(xxx)xxx-xxxx
nigh@email.edu

Alternate Address
c/o Sally High (Mother)
128 Bard Street
Louisville, KY xxxxx
(xxx)xxx-xxxx
Fax: (xxx)xxx-xxxx

GOAL:

FINANCIAL INSTITUTION TRAINEE. Interested in rotating through several areas such as branch management, trust, installment lending, mortgage lending, data processing, marketing, customer services, card services, brokerage, and commercial lending. Would prefer some exposure to international banking later in my career and/or work in Spanish speaking locations.

EDUCATION:

UNIVERSITY OF KENTUCKY, Lexington, KY, xx/xx to xx/xx
Economics major with a minor in Spanish. Earned 3.4 gpa. Key Topics:

Money and Banking	International Economics
Federal Reserve	Computers in Business
Financial Institutions	Accounting
Advanced Spanish	Comparative Systems

Spent one year in Spain in the University of Kentucky Overseas Program. Very proficient in reading, writing, and speaking Spanish.

ACTIVITIES:

AISEC, Chairman. This international association of students in economics and business seeks internship in the U.S. for foreign students. Our counterparts overseas find employment for U.S. students in their home country. Our chapter placed 20 Americans in Europe and found 20 internships for European students in the U.S. I worked in Spain for a bank for 2 months while living with a local family.

Scuba Diving Club, Treasurer. Active in promoting and managing this 80-member club. Group meets monthly for diving lessons and tripplanning events. In xxxx, lead a team of 12 students from our club and another university club in an underwater exploratory investigation of the reefs surrounding the East End, Grand Cayman Islands.

EXPERIENCE:

RIO DE JANEIRO, SAN PAULO, SANTA CATARINA TRAVEL
In xxxx (summer), organized and lead an expedition of U.S. students through independent travel and economic research with Professor Antonio Perez, economics department. Teams developed business plans the next semester. Earned credit.

FLOWERS BY NIGH, Owner, xx/xx to Present
Established a small entrepreneurship to distribute flowers to sorority sisters on all sorts of special occasions with Spanish singers. Financed all of my own education from this venture. Have 20 part-time employees on a contract basis. Have a business website at www.spanishflowers.com.

REFERENCES:

Available

DERK OSENBERG

327 W. Ottawa
Sycamore, IL 60178
xxx-xxx-xxxx
osen@email.edu

CAREER OBJECTIVE

Financial Institutions. Seeking a management training program position which would provide training in operations, insurance, investments, supervision, financial analysis, and lending.

EDUCATION

Duke University, School of Public Administration, Durham, NC (x/xx to x/xx).
B.S. degree in Public Policy, May, xxxx. Course work included economics, finance, production, marketing, and strategic management. Maintained a B+ average in my major field of study.

American University, Washington, D.C. (x/xx to x/xx).
Earned a 4.0 in a work and study program which consisted of government and economic courses. Required a 50 page research paper. Worked briefly as an intern for an economist at the Federal Reserve Bank.

ACTIVITIES

Member of the Delta Chi Social Fraternity; Served as Activities Chairman. President of the College Republicans. Martin County of Indiana Republican Precinct Committeeman. Executive Director of the Federation of College Republicans (statewide office). Participated in intramural football, basketball, and cross country to stay in shape.

EXPERIENCE

Intern, Congressman J. Pierport Morgan's office (x/xx to x/xx).
Responsible for researching and answering questions from constituents. Conducted web related research on policy issues for legislative assistants.

Intern, Secretary of State of North Carolina (x/xx to x/xx).
Assigned duties included the review and revision of the duplicate Vehicle Title Research procedures, assisting in the development of a departmental budget presentation, and several short-term tasks dealing with different branches of state government. Worked on website designed to capture input on corporate registrations on-line.

Page, State of North Carolina (Summer, xxxx).
Worked up to 15 hours a day, seven days a week, assisting legislators in the House of Representatives.

Research Assistant, Research Genetics (Summer xxxx).
Involved working in a team of six researchers sourcing web data for a powerpoint presentation to a legislative committee on aging.

REFERENCES

J. Pierport Morgan
United States Congressman
500 Cannon Building
Washington, D.C. xxxxx
xxx-xxx-xxxx
morgan@email.gov

Martin L. Collins
Dir of State Gov't Affairs
Independent Ins Agents of America
Washington, D.C. xxxxx
xxx-xxx-xxxx
collins@email.gov

Dr. Richard King
Dean of Students
Duke University
Durhan, NC xxxxx
xxx-xxx-xxxx
king@email.edu

Paul Pruitt

Present Address	**Permanent Address** (Parents)
123 Main Street	432 S. Court Street
Lawrence, KS xxxxx	St. Charles, IL xxxxx
xxx-xxx-xxxx	xxx-xxx-xxxx
pruit@email.edu	Fax: xxx-xxx-xxxx

OBJECTIVE

COMMERCIAL BANKING DEVELOPMENT PROGRAM. Prefer to start with a large regional bank that offers a strong commercial lending development program that will make use of my talents in analysis, finance, writing, and presentations. Trying to balance my financial skills with my communication skills. Calling on commercial customers, selling services, and conducting credit analysis fits my interests and abilities.

EDUCATION

B.S. DEGREE IN FINANCE, MAY, xxxx
***University of Kansas**, School of Business, xx/xx to xx/xx*
- Earned a 2.9 GPA on 4.0 system
- Completed 24 credit hours in accounting and finance
- Elected extra hours in speaking, journalism, and psychology
- Selected team leader in senior project group
- Nominated by faculty advisor to President's Council
- Participated in semester abroad program in Zurich

ACTIVITIES

Flying Club; hold a private pilot's license
Investment Club; participated in real portfolio selections
Intramural Sports; basketball and soccer
Campus Marathon; fairly good runner, practice daily

EXPERIENCE

STATE BANK, St. Charles, IL, xx/xx to xx/xx
Summer Job. Worked in customer service. Handled minor bookkeeping, met new customers, opened checking/savings accounts, relieved tellers, and ran check sorters. Ended summer by working one week as the president's assistant.

ST. CHARLES COUNTRY CLUB, St. Charles, IL
Caddy. Worked full-time the summers between freshman and sophomore years. Extra tips earned provided funds for college.

GAMMA PHI BETA SORORITY, Lawrence, KS
Part-Time Jobs. Served as waiter, dishwasher, cook's assistant, clean-up, etc. for two hours every day to earn funds for college expenses.

REFERENCES

Mr. James Jones	Dr. Keith Smart	Ms. Kathryn Shank
President	Finance Department	President
State Bank	Univ. of Kansas	GPB Alumni
St. Charles, IL xxxxx	Lawrence, KS xxxxx	Lawrence, KS xxxxx
xxx-xxx-xxxx	xxx-xxx-xxxx	xxx-xxx-xxxx
jones@email.com	smart@email.edu	shank@email.edu

MICHELLE QUINN

Parent's Address
123 Main Street
St. Paul, MN xxxxx
xxx-xxx-xxxx

Campus Address
123 Campus View
Austin, MN xxxxx
xxx-xxx-xxxx
quinn@email.edu

CAREER OBJECTIVE

BANKING. Desire to join a bank development program which offers rotational training in departments such as operations, cash management, trust, commercial lending, mortgage lending, and branch banking.

EDUCATION

CRAIN UNIVERSITY, SCHOOL OF BUSINESS, Austin, MN, xxxx
BS Degree with a major in finance. Major included 12 hours of accounting and 12 hours of finance where my GPA was 3.5/4.0. Overall GPA of 3.0 reflects a very poor freshman year when I had a serious automobile accident that took me away from studies for several weeks.

Provided for 80 percent of my college expenses by working a variety of jobs and assuming responsibility for several student loans. Received the Ruth Stall Scholarship in senior year. Relevant courses included:

- Financial Accounting
- Cost Accounting
- Intermediate Accounting
- Income Tax
- Statistics
- Spreadsheet/database

- Financial Management
- Money and Banking
- Financial Institutions
- Financial Analysis
- Computer Programming (C++)
- Web Technologies

ACTIVITIES

FINANCE CLUB, President. Coordinate the responsibilities of six officers and 150 members, arrange industry leadership presentations, conduct meetings, organize social and professional activities, and supervise club trips to major financial centers during my junior and senior years.

DELTA GAMMA SOCIAL SORORITY. Pledged this 160 member during my sophomore year and participated in all activities while living in the house. Served as treasurer during my junior year.

EXPERIENCE

xx/xx to xx/xx
MIDWEST BANKCORP, Austin, MN
Summer Intern. This paid internship involved assisting the mortgage loan officer in sales, pricing, analysis, approving, and closing FHA loans for clients of local builders. Completed some of the spreadsheet analysis and much of the paper flow. Made one credit presentation to loan committee at end of program. Gained excellent experience in using several software loan analysis packages.

xx/xx to xx/xx
NUMEROUS PART-TIME JOBS, Austin, MN
Held a number of part-time jobs while carrying a full-time course of study. Worked in several university offices doing clerical tasks, word processing, computer processing, serving other students, and whatever was asked of me. Worked 10–15 hours per week on average but supervisors frequently requested longer hours during peak periods. Learned about interacting with others in the pressure work setting.

REFERENCES AVAILABLE

ALLISON BAKER

125 S. Third Street
New Haven, CT
xxx-xxx-xxxx
baker@email.com

OBJECTIVE

FINANCIAL ANALYST. Seeking to return to full-time employment after a five-year absence to raise two children. My two years of experience as an accountant after a B.S. degree and three years as a financial analyst after the MBA degree in finance qualifies me to resume my career full time as a financial analyst. Prefer to remain within an hour's drive of New Haven.

QUALIFICATIONS/SKILLS

o Accounting	o Web Mastering	o Forecasting
o Financial Analysis	o Programmer	o Budgets
o Taxes	o Spreadsheets	o Cash Flow
o Auditing	o Technical Reporting	o Mortgage Lending
o Credit Analysis	o Public Speaking	o Bilingual (Spanish)
o Supervision	o Training	o Teaching

ACCOMPLISHMENTS

o Organized a non-profit child care facility in our community.
o Maintained financial skills by working part-time for local Tax Service.
o Served as volunteer budget auditor on local hospital board.
o Managed a portfolio for local investment club of 35 members.
o Assist church members in home loan financing strategies on a volunteer basis.
o Administer a church budget of $500,000 annually (part-time).

EXPERIENCE

ICB Industries, New York City   xx/xx to xx/xx

Assistant Treasurer. Managed short-term cash flows of $100 million per year with 3 money center banks and investment banks. Made recommendations on placement of long-term funds of $5 billion supported by analysis of projected economic directions and plans of corporation.
Financial Analyst. Worked on consolidations of financial statements from various subsidiaries with the goal of minimizing tax consequences. Led a small team of accountants and attorneys working on a proposed acquisition of a competitor which materialized as a result of our analysis. Extensive spreadsheet analysis in budget preparation and analysis.

Worldwide Public Accountants, Washington, DC   xx/xx to xx/xx

Staff Accountant. Worked as an auditor on two major corporate accounts and several smaller firms for two years. Resigned to return to obtain the MBA degree.

EDUCATION

University of Connecticut, MBA, Finance, xxxx
University of Maryland, BS, Accounting, xxxx
University of Madrid, Year Abroad Program, xxxx

REFERENCES AVAILABLE

FRED S. SHAW

1234 Andrew Avenue
Apartment 509
Tallahassee, FL xxxxx

(xxx)xxx-xxxx (Home)
(xxx)xxx-xxxx (Work)
shaw@email.com

CAREER OBJECTIVE

Assistant Controller. After three years working in public accounting and earning both the CPA and MBA degree, career interests have shifted into corporate accounting. Prefer to become the line decision maker instead of the advisor, consultant, and reporter. Enjoy supervising other financial professionals and conducting financial analysis. Strong technical credentials and a positive people orientation. Aspire to be a chief financial officer.

EDUCATION

MBA, Finance, August, xxxx, University of Florida

Courses (18 credit hours) in finance including financial management, strategic corporate financial plan and policy, cash management, investment management, special markets and strategies, and public finance and budgeting. Proficient in web technology and enterprise wide systems like SAP. Earned MBA while working full time.

BS, Accounting, August xxxx, Florida State University

Courses (31 credit hours) in accounting including intermediate and advanced financial accounting, cost accounting, auditing, taxation and accounting systems. Total undergraduate credit hours include 24 credit hours of graduate and honors courses. Wrote undergraduate (honors) senior research papers on oil and gas accounting and bankruptcy prediction with financial ratios.

Honors

Graduated with Honors and Distinction in Accounting (GPA 3.6/4.0).
Member, Beta Gamma Sigma (National Scholastic Honorary Society)
Consultant, accounting department website.

WORK EXPERIENCE

Senior Management Accountant, Big Eight Accountants, Tallahassee, Florida (xx/xx to date)

Conduct audits and reviews of manufacturing, banking, retail and service organizations. Prepared audit reports and management letters. Prepare corporate and individual income tax returns. Assist clients in accounting and tax matters. Supervised installation of networked computers and software in accounting and tax analysis functions for clients. Completed over 80 credit hours of professional education in accounting, auditing and taxation.

Graduate Assistant, Accounting Department, University of Florida, Gainesville, Florida (xx/xx to xx/xx)

Assisted faculty in academic research, and gained experience in using the extensive library and web resources and information networks (Dow Jones News Retrieval System). Administered and graded examinations for the department. Used department websites and computer software in compiling data and reporting analysis.

Audit and Management Intern, Big Eight Accountants, Miami, Florida (Summer, xxxx)

Directed and carried out audits of manufacturing, banking, service and non-profit organizations. Supervised and monitored the work of junior audit interns. Prepared and reviewed audit workpapers. Prepared audit reports and management letters. Studied and evaluated accounting systems, and introduced new or revised systems and procedures based on findings. Assisted in consulting assignments relating to project analysis, capital budgeting, and website design.

REFERENCES

Furnished upon request.

SENIOR FINANCIAL MANAGER SAMPLE

John W. Smith

Business Address	**Home Address**
Controller's Staff	1000 West Oak Street
ABC Electronics	Indianapolis, IN xxx:
One Market Square	xxx-xxx-xxxx
Indianapolis, IN xxxxx	smith@email.com
xxx-xxx-xxxx voice	(Feel free to contact
xxx-xxx-xxxx fax	me at work)

OBJECTIVE:

SENIOR FINANCIAL OFFICER. To become Controller, Treasurer, or Vice President, Finance, of a medium-sized manufacturing organization located in the Midwest.

EXPERIENCE:

ASSISTANT CONTROLLER, ABC ELECTRONICS, INC., Indianapolis
Corporation manufactures electronic components and has a sales volume of $360 million in three Midwestern plants with a double digit sales growth annually.

xx/xx to
Present

Responsible for supervising the accounting functions including cost accounting, tax accounting, telecommunications, web technology, data processing, and budgeting. Duties involve supervision of cost analysis, inventory control, budget preparation, tax advising, etc. Principle projects involved:

(5 years)

— Established an effective system of activity based cost analysis that led to a major change in product pricing and an increased profit.
— Redesigned cash management system which greatly reduced need for short-term funds, thereby, increasing ROI.
— Recommended major acquisitions program that led to merger with a compatible manufacturing company.

Promoted from Financial Analyst to Manager of Cost Accounting to Director of IS in 3 year period. Promoted to assistant controller 2 years ago.

xx/xx to
xx/xx

SENIOR MANAGER, JONES AND COMPANY, CPA'S, Louisville
A medium-size regional firm with two national accounts, several local OTC firms, and many local organizations. Reputation as a strong information technology practice.

(3 years)

Started as a Junior Accountant on the audit staff and progressed to Senior Manager in only 3 years. Duties involved audits, tax preparation, SEC registrations and systems design. Spent several months in the Management Services Department working with the installation of a Peoplesoft application.

EDUCATION:
xx/xx to
xx/xx

MASTER OF BUSINESS ADMINISTRATION, INDIANA UNIVERSITY, Bloomington, IN
Completed degree in xx/xx. Concentrated in finance and information systems. Earned a G.P.A. of 3.75. Elected to Beta Gamma Sigma. Passed all parts of C.P.A. examination before Finance Guild.

xx/xx to
xx/xx

BACHELOR OF SCIENCE, ACCOUNTING, UNIVERSITY OF NOTRE DAME, South Bend, IN
Completed 33 credit hours in accounting and 12 hours in finance. Treasurer of Alpha Beta Delta Social Fraternity during my junior and senior year. Active in campus politics. Maintained a 3.1 G.P.A. overall.

PERSONAL:

Born in Jeffersonville, Indiana. Played varsity basketball at Notre Dame. Very mobile situation.

REFERENCES:

Furnished on request. Please do not contact current employer without my permission.

FINANCIAL OFFICER MIDLEVEL SAMPLE

1234 West Chargin Avenue
Cleveland, Ohio xxxx

CONFIDENTIAL

Home: xxx-xxx-xxxx
Work: xxx-xxx-xxxx
email: thor@email.com

─── **LAURA THORESEN** ───

OBJECTIVE

International Finance Officer. For personal reasons, must move to the New York City area. Seeking a position with a major international money center financial institution where an extensive international financial background in commercial banking can be optimally utilized. Please be discreet in contacting me at work.

EMPLOYMENT

xx/xx – Present   **The International/Ohio Trading Bank, Cleveland**

International Services: Assistant Vice President
Present Duties: (5 years), Domestic, international business development, cross sell other bank services. Responsible for all Exim/FCIA financing; approve L/C's, acceptances, FX with domestic officer. Forfeiting, countertrade via correspondents. Assist budget preparation, monitor profit plan, interact with operations to monitor and increase fee income. Results: new/increased lines, totalling $6–12 MM yearly.

Prior Duties: (5 years), responsible for Latin American reschedulings/watch list, Europe/M.E. correspondent relationships. Previously - export/import loans including FCIA/Exim; Washington, D.C. liaison; economic files, country risk studies supervision; marketing plan; profit, liability reports. Developed, edited export-import newsletter and doubled circulation in a year, established library, prepared export bibliography.

Training: Assigned to credit department for 2 years. Credit analysis, reports for loan committees. Prepared handbook on international spreading, financial instruments, evaluation of country risk. Developed proficiency in 5 languages.

EDUCATION

Finance Program   Enrolled in the distance learning MBA Program at the University of Toronto where I take one relevant course each term.

M.A.: Master of Arts   **Middle Eastern Studies, 8/xx, Indiana University.**
                             NDEA Summer Workshop, Intensive 2nd Year Arabic. Georgetown University. First Honors. Studied at American University in Egypt for 18 months.

A.B.: Bachelor of Arts   **French, 6/xx, Indiana University.** Scholarship, Dean's List. Lived in France for one year with family friends. Elementary Japanese, Chinese. University of Maryland Overseas/Extension. National Merit Letter of Commendation.

PUBLICATIONS

"Cultural 'Basics' on Doing Business in Latin America," *The International Banker*, 12/4/xx.
"Evaluating Currency Risk Factors to International Banking," *The Financial Times*, 8/12/xx.

SEMINARS

Presentations on analyzing country risk, creative financing/countertrade, financing international trade to local college, university classes, trade groups, domestic bank officers. Attended Eximbank, Xerox and Richardson Group selling, numerous specialized export seminars.

CIVIC

Member, Regional Development Board TIBTA Board; Member and past Publicity Subcommittee Chairman, Cleveland World Trade Association; Past Member, Export Advisory Council to Cuyahoga County Board of Commissioners; Foreign Credit Group, North Central Ohio Foreign Trade, Ohio Foreign Commerce Association, Women's City Club.

GREG WILSON

Campus Address	**Home Address**
25 Varsity Lane	125 South Union Street
Bloomington, IN xxxxx	Indianapolis, IN xxxxx
(xxx)xxx-xxxx	(xxx)xxx-xxxx
wilson@email.com	

CAREER OBJECTIVE

INVESTMENT BANKING. To obtain an analyst position at a major investment banking firm in New York City. Interested in participating in recommendations based upon financial analysis to be used in new debt considerations, security evaluation, underwriting, investment recommendations, credit analysis, acquisition analysis, risk assessments, merger analysis, net worth appraisals, and new security underwriting potentials.

EDUCATION

MBA, Finance, Indiana University, xx/xx to xx/xx.
- Earned a 3.85 GPA on 4.0 system with all "A" grades in finance.
- Organized investment club field trip of 30 MBA candidates that visited six different investment banking firms in New York City.
- Hosted partners from Goldman Sachs and Morgan Stanley during speaking presentations on campus.
- Relevant subjects — MBA program:

o Investment Analysis	o Portfolio Management	o Option Theory
o Financial Analysis	o Speculative Markets	o Long-Term Finance
o Capital Markets	o Portfolio Theory	o Short-Term Instruments
o Security Analysis	o Valuation Theory	o Financial Models

BA, Political Science and Economics, Northwestern University, xx/xx to xx/xx.
- Graduated with Honors (Magna Cum Laude) with a 3.8 GPA on a 4.0 system.
- Earned Phi Beta Kappa with a double major.
- Improved upon Spanish high school courses with 10 more hours.

ACTIVITIES

SIGMA CHI Social Fraternity at Northwestern University.
Vice President. Managed all major events, directed committee work, and maintained order and adherence to house policies.
Chairman, Renovations Committee. Designed and coordinated successful renovation of all non-bedroom areas of the house. Duties included purchasing, hiring contractors, supervising construction, and adherence to schedules and budgets. Other responsibilities:

o Rush Chairman	o Public Relations Committee
o Pledge Trainer	o Inter-Fraternal Council, Rush Chairman
o Student Judicial Board	o Admissions Orientation Host

President, IU MBA Investment Club, xx/xx to xx/xx.
Major activities of the club involved a trip to New York City, hosting investment banking speakers. Served on team managing a real line investment portfolio for the School of Business of over $3 million which had a 28% return during our supervision.

EXPERIENCE

MBA Summer Internship, Goldman Sachs, New York, xx/xx to xx/xx.
Selected to participate in a rotational analytical program along with 10 other MBAs from 5 top MBA schools. Worked on two major acquisitions for a Fortune 100 firm.
Staff Consultant, Arthur Andersen, Chicago, xx/xx to xx/xx.
Trained for four months to develop financial and computer skills at world renowned development center. First assignment was working with a team of consultants and a Fortune 500 firm management group on a system of converting to a checkless payroll system. Next assignment was on a cafeteria benefits program for another larger firm. When resigned to attend MBA Program, was working with a team that developed a computerized model for investing short-term cash flows for a firm's treasury department.

PUBLIC ACCOUNTING SAMPLE

KATHRYN K. DONOVAN

Current Address:
1234 Parkview Avenue
Springtown, MO 12345
(xxx) xxx-xxxx
don@email.com

Permanent Address (Parents)
1234 Forest Drive
Chesterfield, MO 12345
(xxx) xxx-xxxx

CAREER OBJECTIVE

Public Accountant. Desire a position in a medium or large office of a public accounting firm in the St. Louis, Minneapolis, or Kansas City areas. An extensive 30 semester credit hours in accounting and 5 courses in English coupled with 2 internships have provided a solid foundation for most areas in public accounting. After experience in auditing and taxation, prefer to gain consulting responsibilities.

EDUCATION

Indiana University, School of Business, 9/xx to 5/xx
B.S. Degree, Accounting major and English minor
- Earned a 2.8 GPA (4.0 = A) but have a 3.5 GPA in accounting courses.
- Relevant courses include advance auditing, advanced tax, technical writing, and 15 other courses in accounting and English.
- Completing the CPA coaching course now and planning to sit for the CPA exam in May.
- Assisted English department with website development.

ACTIVITIES

Women in Business. Chairperson, Membership Committee, xx/xx to xx/xx.
- Increased membership from 1000 to 1200 last year
- Hosted two CEOs at Professional Development Seminars
- Nominated for Vice President this year

Student Activities. Spend about 10 hours per week in activities.
- Assist in student fund raising for School of Business and other alumni programs
- Played flute in university pep band at all I.U. basketball games
- Handle accounting and budgeting for Housing Association

EXPERIENCE

Part-Time
9/xx to Present

Fine Cuisine, Bloomington, IN
Waitress
Worked about 10–20 hours during evenings and weekends to provide incidental expenses for college. Top service to customers guaranteed preferred weekend hours where tip income was greatest.

Summers of
Junior and
Senior years

A.M. Associates, Lincoln, MO
Office Assistant
Performed a variety of clerical duties including computer data entry and minor programming at this small investment banking firm. Worked closely with brokers on compiling proposals in public finance department last summer. Conducted a spreadsheet analysis on a new issue recently.

REFERENCES

Professor Thomas Davis, Accounting Department, Indiana University, Bloomington, IN xxxxx, (xxx) xxx-xxxx.
Professor Henry Bowers, English Department, Indiana University, Bloomington, IN xxxxx, (xxx) xxx-xxxx.
Ms. Sharon Neely, Owner, Fine Cuisine, Bloomington, IN xxxxx, (xxx) xxx-xxxx. (neely@email.com)
Mr. J. P. Banker, Managing Partner, A. M. Associates, Lincoln, MO xxxxx, (xxx) xxx-xxxx. (bank@email.com)

JOHN M. KOETTERING

Foster Quad-B205
Ohio State University
Columbus, OH xxxxx
(xxx) xxx-xxxx
koet@email.com

4055 Candlewood Drive
c/o Marie Jonas (Mother)
Newburgh, OH xxxxx
(xxx) xxx-xxxx

CAREER OBJECTIVE

Accountant. Seeking an entry level accounting or finance position that utilizes my accounting, computer, and writing skills. Prefer to work in high technology manufacturing or service industries in the vicinity of a major city in Ohio, Indiana, or Michigan.

EDUCATION

The Ohio State University, Columbus, OH, xx/xx to xx/xx
Plan to receive the B.S. degree in Accounting in May, xxxx. Earned a 3.25 GPA on an A = 4.0 system.
- Relevant courses include:

8 Accounting Courses	3.4 GPA
3 Finance Courses	3.6 GPA
3 Computer Courses	3.3 GPA
3 Communication Courses	3.0 GPA

- Grades improved steadily since my freshman year when earned only a 2.5 GPA.
- Earned 40 percent of college tuition via a resident assistantship and part-time work.

ACTIVITIES

Beta Alpha Psi, Accounting Honorary Fraternity, membership committee
Entrepreneurship Academy, Consulting club helping local businesses
Foster Quad, Education Advisory Committee, assistant chairperson
Student Association, Judicial Board jurist for three trials

WORK EXPERIENCE

Boise Cascades, Accounting Intern, Columbus, OH, xx/xx to xx/xx
- Served as a support accountant for the marketing department . . . prepared month end journal entries on a mainframe . . . participated in inventory audit and reconciliation . . . started work on corporate website.
- Earned six credit hours by writing a financial capital investment analysis which was an independent study project managed by Professor Tiller for which the grade of "A" was received.

The Ohio State University, Halls of Residence, Columbus, OH xx/xx to Present
- Manage a floor of 55 residents since sophomore year.
- Act as personal and academic counselor.
- Enforce university regulations set by Dean of Students.
- Coordinate educational, social, and career programming.
- Work about 10–15 hours per week.

Numerous summer and part-time jobs, Newburgh, OH
- Driving range attendant at local country club.
- Sales associate at automotive center.
- Counter clerk at Fast Food Central.
- Worked 40–50 hours per week every summer.

REFERENCES

Ms. Sharon Hayhurst
Residence Life Coord.
Foster Quad
The Ohio State Univ.
Columbus, OH xxxxx
xxx-xxx-xxxx
hay@email.edu

Dr. Mike Tiller
Professor
Accounting Department
The Ohio State Univ.
Columbus, OH xxxxx
xxx-xxx-xxxx
till@email.edu

Dean R. Bradley
Dean of Students
Bryan Hall
The Ohio State Univ.
Columbus, OH xxxxx
xxx-xxx-xxxx
brad@email.com

ACCOUNTANT ENTRY LEVEL SAMPLE

GREGORY G. MOTE
12 South Third Avenue
Sunnydale, California xxxxx
xxx-xxx-xxxx
mote@email.com

OBJECTIVE

HEALTHCARE ACCOUNTING. An immediate goal is employment on the accounting and finance staff of a large public hospital or related health care facility. Eventually wish to attain a high-level chief administrative or operating officer after obtaining additional experience in capital and operating budgets, taxes, government insurance, receivables, contacts, etc.

EDUCATION

UNIVERSITY OF OREGON
Eugene, OR xxxxx
xx/xx to xx/xx

Public Administration
B.S., xxxx, 2.85 gpa (A=4.0)
Concentration in Finance and
accounting with 21 hours of courses

ACTIVITIES

- Healthcare Finance Association
- Knox Country Humane Society
- Lions Club-Service Committee Chair

- Varsity Baseball (3 years)
- Student Congress Senator
- Delta Upsilon (Treasurer)

HONORS
- Recipient of Joseph C. Smith Foundation Scholarship
- Voted MVP by baseball teammates
- Managed $100,000 fund raising event for fraternity for senior award

EMPLOYMENT
GOOD SAMARITAN HOSPITAL
Sunnydale, California

INTERN ACCOUNTANT
April, xxxx to Present

Worked in the departments of General Accounting, Payroll, Accounts Payable, and Insurance. Involved in the scheduling, reporting, and managing of 6 clericals and 2 exempt employees with a budget of $30 million dollars. Given much latitude in independent decision-making and application of sound financial policies and procedures in working with staff. Reported to the Assistant Controller.

BLUE CROSS INSURANCE
Eugene, Oregon

INTERN ACCOUNTANT
xx/xx to xx/xx

Started as a junior auditor and progressed through 3 different assignments. Learned about the uniqueness of the health care financial system. Worked on a task force to realign the computerized claim processing procedures.

UNIVERSITY HOSPITAL
Eugene, Oregon

PART-TIME
October, xxxx through graduation

This part-time job paid for much of my education. Worked in the back office doing everything from filing, typing, copying, errands, etc. During my senior year, assisted the controller with a new receivables processing program which involved extensive PC spreadsheet analysis. Usually worked 15 to 20 hours per week while enrolled as a full-time student. Worked nearly full-time during 2 summers and carried part-time course load.

PERSONAL

Prefer to relocate to the Pacific Northwest. Willing to relocate. Past employers have agreed to serve as references.

ANNE MARIE SUMMERFELT

123 Garrison Hall
DeKalb, IL xxxxx
(xxx)xxx-xxxx (Campus)
sum@email.edu

Five Circle Drive
Carmel, IN xxxxx
(xxx)xxx-xxxx (Home)

CAREER OBJECTIVE

Accountant   Seeking position as a staff accountant with a corporate organization or public accounting firm. Desire exposure and training in auditing, tax, review and analysis of financial statements, and information systems. Eventual goal is to manage engagements and conduct consulting assignments. Sitting for C.P.A. exam in November.

EDUCATION

NORTHERN ILLINOIS UNIVERSITY, DEKALB, ILLINOIS, 8/xx–5/xx. Earned a B.S. in Accounting, completing thirty hours of accounting coursework. 2.8/4.0

BUTLER UNIVERSITY, INDIANAPOLIS, INDIANA, 8/xx–5/xx. Worked toward a B.S. in Accounting. Transferred to Northern Illinois University after first year with thirty-two credit hours.

Have been entirely responsible for college expenses through work/study and summer jobs, grants, scholarships, and loans. Worked 10–25 hours per week during academic terms and full time every summer since junior year in high school.

HONORS AND ACTIVITIES

Received Rotary, Tri-Kappa, and Amoco Scholarships.

Willkie Women's Co-operative.
Participated in a university program that offered reduced housing rates in exchange for janitorial and kitchen work in co-op building. Also served as Treasurer and was responsible for recording and maintaining accurate financial records for Women's Co-op.

Navigators Campus Ministry.
Participated in Bible Studies, fellowship hours, and other miscellaneous activities.
Alpha Phi Sorority. (Butler University). Actively participated in house and pledge class activities.

WORK EXPERIENCE

Secretary/Clerical Worker, Northern Illinois University (9/xx – 6/xx and 8/xx – 5/xx).
Typed questionnaires and reports, entered data into computer, and performed tasks related to research projects for Professor of Education. In xx/xx, also began working for the Department of Curriculum and Instruction. Maintained department's financial records, updated prospective and current students' files, and performed miscellaneous filing, typing, and various other duties. Have extensive word processing, spreadsheet, and database experience. Recognized as outstanding work/study student for last academic year.

Waitress, Indiana Beach, Inc., Monticello, Indiana (every summer).
Began work as bus person and kitchen pantry assistant. Promoted to waitress at end of first summer. Accepted added responsibilities of cashiering and hostessing during last summer. Have supervised up to 10 summer student helpers.

REFERENCES AVAILABLE

COLLEEN W. DIETRICK

Present Address
Graham Dorm
Brookings, SD xxxxx
(xxx)xxx-xxxx

Permanent Address
Three Deerfield Drive
Sioux Falls, SD xxxxx
(xxx)xxx-xxxx

CAREER OBJECTIVE

Human Resource Assistant
Seeking placement in manufacturing or service sector. Desire exposure to all areas of the organization establishing a solid foundation in the employee - management relationship. Desire human resource functional experience in recruitment, selection, training, compensation, and industrial relations.

EDUCATION

SOUTH DAKOTA STATE UNIVERSITY, School Of Public Administration, Brookings, SD
B.S., Industrial Relations (Psychology minor)   8/xx–8/xx
Courses include Recruitment Selection, Wage and Salary Administration, Managing Behavior in Organizations, Models of Job Motivation, Performance Appraisal, Labor Relations, and Collective Bargaining. VP of student chapter of the Society of Human Resource Management and help publicize meetings via groups website.

EXPERIENCE

METAL CRAFT, Brookings, SD
Payroll Clerk   Currently Working
Working independently 15–20 hours per week. In charge of all payroll duties and forms plus additional requested reports and bank reconciliation. Learning about HR in small firm.
STATE BAKERY, Sioux Falls, SD
Baker's Helper   5/xx–1/xx
Worked 35–40 hours per week during vacations as a production line employee. Mastered majority of positions with the responsibility of giving breaks and vacations to full-time employees. Exposed to the functions of a labor union and its relationship with management.
CITY DIVING CLUB, Sioux Falls, SD
Diving Coach   Currently Working
A nonprofit organization developing young people and promoting diving. Responsibilities include attaining goals through working with young people and parents to apply technical and motivational techniques. Worked on and off part-time for 4 years.

ACTIVITIES

o Varsity Swimming Team 4 years. MVP senior year.
o Vice President Dormitory floor for 3 years. Served as RA senior year.
o Intramural Sports - football, springboard diving, gymnastics, swimming.
o Human Resource Association, Chair, Professional Development Committee

REFERENCES

Dr. Tim Gray
Professor of Mgmt.
SD State University
Brookings, SD xxxxx
(xxx)xxx-xxxx
gray@email.edu

Mr. Mike Baldwin
Production Manager
State Bakery
Sioux Falls, SD xxxxx
(xxx)xxx-xxxx
bald@email.com

Ms. Susan O'Neal
Head Swim Coach
Brookings High
Brookings, SD xxxxx
(xxx)xxx-xxxx
oneil@email.edu

PAULA T. PRALL

123 West Avenue
Toledo, Ohio 43606
(xxx) xxx-xxxx
prall@email.com

OBJECTIVE	**Human Resource Manager.** Wish to utilize interpersonal, communication, and organizational abilities in Human Resource Management. Interests include: recruitment and selection, training and development, employee and labor relations, EEO and affirmative action, and wage and salary administration.
RELEVANT EXPERIENCE	**Recruitment and Selection** Participate in the screening, interviewing, and selection of managers and support staff. Assist in the recruitment of intercollegiate student athletes. Interview prospective students and their parents. Select scholarship recipients. **Training and Development** Create and teach the Internship Seminar. Taught a course in Organizational Behavior. Organize and conduct preregistration programs for more than 1000 new business students each year. Lead training programs and serve as resource person for faculty advisors. **Employee and Labor Relations** Provide career counseling and academic advising. Interact with individuals at all levels in the organization. Assisted with new employee orientation sessions. Conducted some exit interviews. Completed courses in Labor Law at The University of Toledo School of Law. **EEO and Affirmative Action** Member of committee responsible for recruitment of minority students. Participated in Hispanic Parent Workshops. MBA curriculum included course in EEO Law and Affirmative Action. Assisted in preparation of EEO/AA reports. **Wage and Salary Administration** Assist staff in job reclassification efforts. Conducted benefits surveys. Wrote a manual for the position of Personnel Assistant. **Administration/Supervision** Supervise program advisement staff. Oversee maintenance of confidential records. Complete research projects. Develop publications and produce multi-media presentation. Serve on a variety of implementation and advisory committees.
EMPLOYMENT HISTORY	**College of Business Administration** **UNIVERSITY OF AKRON, Akron, OH xx/xx to xx/xx** **Director of Program Advisement** Organize and coordinate advising programs for undergraduate students in AACSB-accredited program. Supervise advising staff. Participate in College and University committees. (xx/xx–present) **Internship Coordinator** Design and teach the Internship Seminar, a course which focuses on the improvement of oral and written communication skills. Coordinate departmental internship activities. (xx/xx–Present) **Instructor** Taught Human Resource Mangement, an upper-level Management course required of all College of Business Administration students. Instructed one section per semester in addition to administrative responsibilities. (xx/xx – xx/xx) **Personnel Assistant** The Associates Company, Cleveland, OH (xx/xx – xx/xx)
EDUCATION	**Master of Business Administration, May (xx/xx – xx/xx)** **UNIVERSITY OF MICHIGAN, Ann Arbor, MI** Major: Human Resource Management. Worked at Associates while in part-time MBA Program **Bachelor of Science in Business Administration, May xxxx** **JOHN CARROLL UNIVERSITY, Cleveland, OH** Major: Psychology Minor: Sociology

ELECTRICAL ENGINEER LIMITED EXPERIENCE SAMPLE

KAREN B. STILES

Home Address
233 Milkyway Drive
Apartment 5-D
Columbia, Maryland
xxx-xxx-xxxx
stiles@email.com

Business Address
N.A.S.A.
Goddard Space Center
Greenbelt, Maryland
xxx-xxx-xxxx
stiles@email.gov

Permanent Address
% John B. Stiles (Father)
10250 Ocean View
Winter Haven, Florida
xxx-xxx-xxxx

OBJECTIVE:

ELECTRICAL ENGINEER. Interested in the circuit design of complex digital computer systems that provide control mechanisms for automatic manipulation. Desire to further develop proficiency in software design, microprocessor based subsystems, and information teletransmission. Eventual goal is to manage a technical operation of an electronically controlled operation for commercial satellites.

EDUCATION:
xx/xx
to
xx/xx

B.S., ELECTRICAL ENGINEERING, GEORGIA TECH, JUNE, xxxx
Studied under Dr. Warner VanBauer, who fostered my interest in the microprocessor field. Earned a straight A average in all electrical engineering and computer science courses. Gained experience on several types of mainframe and server computers and assisted in the design of a forward generation of digital technology used in satellite data transmission.

ACTIVITIES:

Avid computer hobbiest . . . built several computer networks at home . . . enjoy motorcycling on weekends . . . financed college education via several scholarships . . . activities include:
— Women's Glee Club
— Delta Delta Delta Social Sorority (Treasurer)
— Society of Women Engineers (Vice President)
— Institute of Electrical and Electronics Engineers

EXPERIENCE:
xx/xx
to
Present

ELECTRICAL ENGINEER, NASA GODDARD SPACE CENTER
Started two years ago as junior engineer working on cryogenic test procedures for LSI devices. Conducted evaluations on solid state detectors and support electronics. Within six months promoted to the microprocessing division to design circuitry for advanced telecommunications applications.

During the past year I have been working as a project engineer with a team of scientists on a classified guidance system. I function as the applications person on the team. I enjoy this technical work, but I prefer an environment where I can eventually gain some management experience and work on projects with commercial application.

Summer
(3 years)

TECHNICAL SALES ENGINEER INTERN, IBM CORPORATION
Spent the summer between my junior and senior year in college working in field service with customer engineers. This was basically an electronic troubleshooting role working with large scale computers installed at customer facilities.

REFERENCES:

Dr. Warner VonBauer
Chairperson
Electrical Engineering
Georgia Institute of Technology
Atlanta, Georgia
xxx-xxx-xxxx

xx/xx · vonb@email.gov

Dr. Karen Glaver
Research Scientist
NASA
Goddard Space Center
Greenbelt, Maryland
xxx-xxx-xxxx
glaver@email.gov

CHEMICAL ENGINEER ENTRY LEVEL SAMPLE

WILLIAM R. BRENNEN

Campus Address	**Parent's Address**
2819 Long Lane	George R. Brennen (father)
Columbus, Ohio xxxxx	25 N. Main Street
xxx-xxx-xxxx	Topeka, Kansas xxxxx
brennen@email.com	xxx-xxx-xxxx

Objective

Chemical Engineer. Desire to obtain a position in plant technical service or chemical process engineering. As I advance, I prefer to gain experience in both production engineering and research design. Long-term is to manage a large chemical plant operation in a refinery or in the chemical industry.

Education

B.S., Chemical Engineering, Ohio State University, June, xxxx. Have earned a B average in all course work and a B+ average in all engineering courses. Excelled in courses requiring hands-on application experiences. Have taken a number of courses in Industrial Management. College related activities include the following:

— American Institute of Chemical Engineers (Campus Chapter, Vice Pres.)
— National Society of Black Engineers
— Tau Beta Pi

Actively participate in intramural football and basketball. Board member of the Black Student Union. Elected to Student Senate during my junior year.

Experience

Chemical Engineer Intern, Procter and Gamble Company, Summer, xxxx. Worked with a team of process engineers over the summer and was exposed to a variety of different types of assignments. Helped make some plant facility process modifications, worked in quality control, assisted in project cost analysis, observed process control trouble-shooting, helped write an environmental impact statement, and assisted some lab technologists on a heat recovery study.

Various Part-Time Jobs. During summers, school breaks, and part-time during the school year (up to 10 hours per week) held a number of part-time jobs. Worked as a bus boy, mail clerk, sales clerk, and restaurant cook to earn spending money for college. Tuition and board was paid for by a variety of scholarships and loans.

References

Dr. Robert Walton	Mr. Walter A. Hopkins	Dr. Stephen Kent
Professor of Chemical Engineering	Project Engineer	Superintendent of Schools
Ohio State University	Procter and Gamble	Topeka School Corporation
Columbus, Ohio xxxxx	Center Hill Road	Topeka, Kansas xxxxx
walt@email.com	Cincinnati, Ohio xxxxx	kent@email.edu
	hop@email.com	

LESLIE DIANE HELPING

4231 Pictureview Lane
Cincinnati, Ohio xxxxx
xxx-xxx-xxxx
help@email.com

Career Objective:
Mechanical Engineer. Seeking a position as a project engineer in either a design or analysis type of setting. Prefer some exposure to research and development as progress up to a project manager position. Eventually desire to progress into an engineering management function where can be responsible for supervising both technical and non-technical personnel. An applications oriented type of person.

Education:
University of Cincinnati, B.S., Mechanical Engineering, June, xxxx
U.C. is an alternating quarters co-op educational program which integrates course work and job experience. During last 4-1/2 years maintained a 3.5 G.P.A. on a 4.0 scale.

Activities:
» Vice President, Phi Kappa Social Fraternity
» Varsity Women's Basketball Team during freshman year
» Active member of following engineering societies:
    American Society of Mechanical Engineers (Secretary, junior year)
    Society of Automotive Engineers
    Tau Beta Pi - engineering honor society (inducted junior year)
    Engineering Tribunal

Paid for 90 percent of my education through co-op earnings. Very active in Junior Achievement in high school, college intramural sports, and Greek activities.

Experience:
Toledo Edison Company, Nuclear Power Station, Oak Harbor, Ohio.
Did all coop experience with this facility. Worked as a shift foreman, assistant operations engineer, and project engineer. Duties included testing procedures, system workdowns, drafting, project design, plant improvement studies, budget drafting, simulations, computer analysis, and computer programming. Installed several control robotic computers.

Over the various quarters was given increasing levels of responsibility. Last quarter, was responsible for training and supervising some new incoming co-op students and part-time technicians. One memorable quarter had an opportunity to assist a nationally recognized research design engineer from a consulting firm.

References:

Dr. Francis Tame
Professor of Mechanical Engineering
University of Cincinnati
Cincinnati, Ohio xxxxx
xxx-xxx-xxxx
tame@email.com

Mr. Wayne Evans
Engineering Operations
Manager
Toledo Edison Company
Nuclear Power Station
Oak Harbor, Ohio xxxxx
xxx-xxx-xxxx
evans@email.com

Mr. David Radwin
Vice President, Engineering
Toledo Edison Company
Toledo, Ohio xxxxx
xxx-xxx-xxxx
rad@email.com

SCOTT M. BARNETT

Campus Address
701 E. 19th Street, Apt. 125
Bloomington, IN xxxxx
(xxx)xxx-xxxx
barn@email.com

Permanent Address
125 Winding Way
Anderson, IN xxxxx
(xxx)xxx-xxxx (voice)
(xxx)xxx-xxxx (fax)

CAREER OBJECTIVE

Commercial Systems Consultant. Seeking an opportunity to serve as a systems advisor between a client and employer's hardware, software, and customer-designed financial systems. Enjoy the challenge of integrating standard systems with some enhancements to meet a client's unique needs to cut costs, increase productivity, increase profit margins, or expand sales potential. Long term, would enjoy managing a group of creative and innovative people designing custom financial products and services using existing components and systems.

EDUCATION

Indiana University, School of Business, Bloomington, IN (8/xx to 5/xx)
B.S. degree in Finance, May. Have an overall grade point average of 3.12 on a 4.0 scale. Coursework includes 15 hours of accounting and 12 hours in systems and computer programming. Have taken 6 elective courses that emphasize communication skills. Senior project was a web design for a campus department.

ACTIVITIES

- Senior Club Co-Chairman - Lambda Chi Alpha Social Fraternity. Planned and organized senior social events.
- Greek Week Chairman - Responsible for organizing my fraternity's involvement in Indiana University's Greek Week.
- Rush Committee - Responsible for recruitment of new fraternity members.
- Intramural Sports (softball, basketball).
- Student Athletic Board - Involved with promotion of Indiana University men's baseball team and women's volleyball.
- Finance Club - Regularly attend bi-weekly social and professional events.
- I.U. Sing - Participated in annual university musical for 2 years.

EXPERIENCE

(8/xx–1/xx)

(6 months)

Data Systems-Anderson, IN
Finance Intern. Responsibilities included analyzing the profit and loss statements, fiscal budget forecasting, reconciling expenses, and preparing spreadsheets and small databases. Worked 50–60 hours per week on a pressure deadline project.

(Summer–xxxx)

Supermarkets, Inc., Anderson, IN
Clerk. Performed general duties such as bagging groceries, cleaning the store, and stocking shelves. Worked 30 hrs./wk.

(Summer–xxxx, xxxx)

Anderson Park Department, Anderson, IN
Landscaper. Responsible for keeping city parks attractive by trimming grass and planting flowers. Worked 40 hrs./wk.

REFERENCES

Mr. Larry Blane	Mr. James Clever	Mr. Dan Mitchell
President	Account Manager	President
Supermarkets, Inc.	Data Systems	National Bank
Anderson, IN xxxxx	Anderson, IN xxxxx	Anderson, IN xxxxx
(xxx)xxx-xxxx	(xxx)xxx-xxxx	(xxx)xxx-xxxx
blane@email.com	clev@email.com	mitch@email.com

JOHN P. PETERSEN

502 S. Wood
New Haven, CT xxxxx
xxx-xxx-xxxx
pete@email.com

123 W. 123rd St. (Parents)
Overland, KS xxxxx
xxx-xxx-xxxx

CAREER OBJECTIVE

Information Systems Consultant. Desire to enter a training program in the information systems department of a medium to large organization. Plan to use my skills in finance, programming, and managing to eventually manage an IS facility on the east coast. Prefer some international exposure overseas somewhere in my career.

EDUCATION

Yale University, New Haven, CT, B.S. Computer Science, xxxx
- Completing a five year course of study that included a semester abroad in the London School of Economics in xxxx, with a certificate of international management.
- Earned a 3.2 gpa with class list status the past three semesters.
- Proficient in both Spanish and French.
- Computer languages: Assembly, C++, SQL.
- Skilled in several database web enabled software packages.

ACTIVITIES

International Student Association, Orientation Chairperson, xx/xx to xx/xx
Assist foreign nationals first matriculating in the basics orientation seminars. Taught 20 seminars in both Spanish and French to over 100 students from 15 different countries. Helped promote seminars on website.

Delta Upsilon Fraternity, Alumni Relations Chairperson, xx/xx to xx/xx
Responsible for alumni correspondence, alumni record management on web, donation solicitations, and planning homecoming events. Maintained records in MS-ACCESS.

Listening Line Volunteer, Telephone Counselor, xx/xx to xx/xx
Serve as a team member of a 25 person support group that offered a confidential serve designed to help others solve their own problems. Helped collect statistics on the service which received an average of 75 calls per week from on and off-campus. Worked about 5 hours per week during peak periods for the interdenominational campus ministry group that sponsored the program. Helped program the call management system.

EXPERIENCE

NCR Corporation, Summer Programmer Intern, Dayton, OH, (xxx to xxxx)
Performed system pricing analysis for the Logistics Division, modified, created, and analyzed programs using a 4th generation language. Met with two different user groups several times to discuss projects, to suggest ideas, and to discover problem resolutions. Earned 6 hours of course credit while working full-time.

Numerous Part-Time Projects, Programmer Consultant, Yale University, (xx/xx to xx/xx)
Worked about 10 hours most weeks in working independently for academic departments, individual faculty, and local businesses. Usually picked-up small programming jobs using EXCEL, ACCESS, HTML, and other application software. Set-up new computers for people and taught them how to run equipment and software.

PERSONAL

Prefer to locate near New York area and plan to work part-time on an MBA degree in MIS at Columbia where I have already been accepted into the evening program.

JANE D. BISHOP

123 Riverview Drive
Cincinnati, Ohio xxxxx
(xxx)xxx-xxxx
bishop@email.com

OBJECTIVE

Operations Management. Wish to join an established manufacturing firm where talents in first-line supervision, inventory management, quality control, personnel hiring and motivating, production scheduling, and warehouse management can be effectively utilized. Prefer to work in an operation where the total number of employers is in the 1,000–1,200 employee range. Eventual desire to manage a major manufacturing facility.

EDUCATION

BS, xxxx, Georgia Tech, Atlanta, GA, xx/xx to xx/xx
Industrial Management. Topics covered:

o Supervision		o Personnel Selection/Motivation
o Purchasing	o Work Measurement	o Productivity Enhancement
o Production Planning	o Inventory Control	o Technical Reporting
o MRP	o Just in Time (JIT)	o Cost Containment
o Operations Incentive	o Quality Maintenance	o Operations Scheduling
o Systems Design		o CAD/CAM

ACTIVITIES

Dean's Academic Advisory Board of five appointed students. **Departmental Newsletter Publisher,** managed production. **Campus Blood Drive,** organized donor schedules.

WORK EXPERIENCE

Industrial Internship, Check Printers, Inc., Cincinnati, OH (last semester). This Fortune 500 firm is the largest printer of bank checks in the world. The process is highly automated with sophisticated magnetic inks and precision printing on a very short demand schedule. Given a first-line supervisor's job after a 3-week orientation.

> o Supervised 24 employees producing 25,000 checks daily.
> o Selected, trained, and evaluated 20 part-time laborers each week.
> o Met a rigid deadline every day.
> o Audited standards and procedures hourly for compliance.
> o Scheduled maintenance and repair between jobs.
> o Communicated with marketing and plant managers daily.
> o Forecasted man-hours needed for next day's production.
> o Dealt with labor union representatives.

This extremely demanding and pressure-packed assignment proved to be one of my most exciting activities.
Assembly Line Laborer, Injection Molders, Inc., Cincinnati, OH (summer xxxx). Worked second and third shifts as vacation relief. Ran many different types of injection molding machines in a high volume, precision quality non-union job shop. Worked extensive overtime hours.
Carpenter and Laborer, Rose Contractors, Cincinnati, OH (summer xxxx). Used carpenter skills in framing structures, room additions, and interior finishings. Excellent at detail trim, so handled trim on most jobs. By end of summer, became foreman of a small crew on an interior finishing project. Worked 50–65 hours per week to earn funds for college.
Numerous unskilled construction jobs on a part-time basis in the Atlanta area. Worked on many different construction crews doing new construction and remodeling. Generally worked 20 hours per week while in college.

JERROLD P. SOUTER

MOQ 3333
Camp Lejeune, North Carolina xxxxx
xxx-xxx-xxxx

OBJECTIVE

Operations Management. To pursue a career in management utilizing skills in financial services, administrative procedures, training and personnel policies.

EDUCATION

Boston University, Boston, Massachusetts
MBA in Operations Management to be awarded in xxxx (distance learning)
Coursework includes: Production Management, Marketing Management, Logistics, Computer Programming, Systems Consulting, Human Resources
The Ohio State University, Columbus, Ohio
BS in Marketing, xxxx
Highlights: Market Research, Advertising Management, Accounting, Systems Design, Sales Management, Retailing, Operations Management

PROFESSIONAL EXPERIENCE

Management

Held complete responsibility for disbursing all monies, maintenance of pay records, travel records. Supervised handling of discrepancies in pay and supervised completion of necessary forms to correct pay discrepancies. Successful management techniques achieved 100% reenlistment among subordinates.

Personnel Policies

Supervised and directed activities of eight enlisted personnel and one officer. Supervised subordinate supervisory personnel, determined staffing requirements and routinely conducted performance evaluations.

Quality Control

Supervised departmental work practices and programs to insure compliance with established standards; initiated/recommended changes to preclude error.

Administrative Support

Entrusted with disbursing bi-monthly payroll for 3200 Marines in 10th Marine Regiment, a total of well over $2 million; overall supervision of pay section, including records maintenance, correspondence.

Training

Kept apprised of disbursing policies and procedures for special exercises and briefed high ranking officers as required; established and maintained line of communication between superiors and other personnel; prepared and presented several training seminars for enlisted personnel with uniformly outstanding results.

Research

Utilized comprehensive research skills to compile and analyze data on pay problems and consistently substantiated payments

WORK HISTORY

xx/xx to present
(4 years)

UNITED STATES MARINE CORPS
First Lieutenant. Experienced in leadership and decision making of increasing scope and responsibility. Possesses hands-on, in-depth experience in personnel management and financial planning. Have traveled extensively throughout the world. Studied MBA part-time in a distance learning environment on land and sea.

xx/xx to xx/xx
(1 year)

D'ARCY, MacMANUS AND MASIUS ADVERTISING AGENCY, St., Louis, Missouri
Media Assistant. Conducted nationwide competitive services surveys for such national accounts as Anheuser-Busch and Red Lobster. Conducted market research, compiled data, presented comprehensive reports on market research to clients. Left to complete military commitment after one year.

LEGAL OFFICE WITH EXPERIENCE SAMPLE

RONIKA HELGA
3535 South Dearborn Avenue
Chicago, Illinois xxxxx
(xxx)xxx-xxxx
helga@email.com

OBJECTIVE

Assistant Corporate Attorney. Plan to build upon my legal training and private firm work experience with medium to large corporate clients. Prefer the corporate staff role to the independent practitioner.

EXPERIENCE

Corporate Associate, Rooking and Pounding, Chicago, xx/xx to Present. Investigate, negotiate, and make recommendations for this large, highly prestigious and reputable law firm.
- Concentrate in securities, real estate, and secured lending.
- Advise clients, close transactions, and maintain files and relationships.
- Involved in negotiating and drafting the following instruments:

•Employment Agreements	•Tax Assessment Appeals
•Real Estate Contracts	•Loan Documentations
•Commercial Leases	•Securities Compliance
•SEC Registrations	•Dispute Resolution

- Occasionally involved in courtroom litigations.

Summer Intern, Mortgage Lending Federal Savings, Chicago, xx/xx–xx/xx.
Worked every summer while in law school. Responsibilities included updating loan files, assisting at mortgage closings, preparing board reports, documenting and verifying of client statements.

EDUCATION

Indiana University, School of Law and School of Business, Bloomington, Indiana, xxxx–xxxx
J. D./MBA Degree, completed in June, xxxx.
Concentrated in Corporate Law and Corporate Finance.
Completed both degrees simultaneously in four years instead of five years.
Graduated in top quartile of both J. D. and MBA classes.
- **Teaching Assistant.** Taught undergraduate business law, xxxx, to 500 sophomores. Graded papers and reviewed articles for Professor Michael Perkins.
- **Managing Editor,** *Indiana Law Journal*, xxxx. Revised, edited, and proofed manuscripts for publication. Advised associates on writing.
- **Researcher,** *Indiana Law Journal*, xxxx. Worked with editors to accelerate publication schedule; revised, proofed and edited manuscripts.
- **Author of Note,** "Tender Otter Legal Battle Continues," *Indiana Law Journal*, xx/xx, co-authors discussed regulation issues.

Northwestern University, Evanston, Illinois, xx/xx to Present
B.A., Political Science, xx/xx.
Minored in Economics and Spanish. Ranked in top 10 percent of graduating class. Involved in the following activities:

•The Daily Northwestern (Reporter)	•Blood Bank (Volunteer)
•Delta Zeta Sorority (Activities Chairman)	•Judicial Review Board
•Student Government (Senator)	•Poly Sci Club (Secretary)

MANAGEMENT TRAINEE ENTRY LEVEL SAMPLE

KIMBERLY JEANNE CUNNINGHAM

123 Arrowhead Drive
Apt 2B
Skokie, Illinois 60187

Home (xxx)xxx-xxxx
Work (xxx)xxx-xxxx
cunng@email.com

CAREER OBJECTIVE

Management Trainee. To obtain entry-level position in the Chicago area where training program will provide the applicable management and leadership skills used to effectively and efficiently manage people, products, and services. Desire to draw-upon technical credentials and human resource talents.

PROFESSIONAL EXPERIENCE

Pension Coordinator, Hewitt & Associates, Evanston, Illinois, September, xxxx to present. Small Employee Benefit Consulting Firm specializing in selling primarily Guardian Life and Disability Insurance. Responsible for annual administration of approximately 120 Defined Benefit and Defined Contribution Pension Plans. Includes assisting clients in preparation of year end asset and census forms; reviewing and distributing annual valuations, employee statements, contribution approval forms and form 5500-C; and preparation of plan documents and amendments to documents to comply with IRS regulations. Leaving after 6 months due to staff reductions from a merger.

Receptionist, Hewitt & Associates, Evanston, Illinois, Summer, xxxx. Responsible for the following: answering multi-line phone system, typing and word processing, implementing new filing system, purchasing all office supplies, billing clients and recording payments, payment of corporate expenses and reconciliation of corporate checkbook, and continually updating rolodex files on computer program.

EDUCATION

Northwestern University School of Journalism, Evanston, Illinois.
B.S., December xxxx, with a major in Journalism and a minor in Psychology. Maintain a 3.3 GPA in a very competitive environment. Helped maintain website for school newspaper.

UNDERGRADUATE EXPERIENCE

Loan Operations Clerk, Bank of Skokie, Skokie, Illinois, Christmas Break, xx/xx, February xxxx – May xxxx. Responsible for providing information on the status of loans. Organized and maintained efficient records of all loans by developing a more efficient filing system. Had complete control of the security of certificates of deposit, bonds and notes. Developed familiarity with all types of installment loans. (Full-Time Temp)
Tax Information Clerk, DuPage County Treasurer, Wheaton, Illinois, Summer of xxxx. Responsible for providing tax information to the public, title companies, lawyers, realtors, and mortgage companies. Recorded payments of taxes manually and through data entry. Most of all learned how to function in a professional environment through developing personal traits such as maturity and self-respect.

UNDERGRADUATE ACTIVITIES

Wildcat Songleader. Primarily responsible for organizing, motivating, and instructing a sorority/fraternity team in a musical production for the University Auditorium stage. Arranged, staged, and choreographed total production to try to obtain top placement in annual Sing contest. Our group effort resulted in winning 2nd in one division and 3rd overall.

Delta Zeta Social Sorority • Serenade and Pairing Coordinator • Parliamentarian • Ritual Guard • Intramurals • Ticket Representative • Greek Leadership Retreat • Songleader

NU Student Foundation • NU Match Sprints Committee Member • Annual Blood Drive

PAUL J. ROTH

Olson Hall
Notre Dame University
Notre Dame, IN xxxxx
(xxx)xxx-xxxx
roth@email.com

817 S. Ironwood Dr.
Niles, MI xxxxx
(xxx)xxx-xxxx
(Parents)

**PROFESSIONAL
OBJECTIVE**

Management Training Program. Desire an entry-level position, which would make use of my education and experience in organizing, leadership and direct customer contact. Would be interested in sales training with a food broker, packaged goods distributor, or suppliers of products to supermarkets.

EDUCATION

University of Notre Dame School of Business, (xx/xx to xx/xx)
B.S. Degree in Marketing, May xxxx
Earned a 3.4 GPA overall. Course work includes:

o Sales Management
o Accounting (2 semesters)
o Retailing Management
o Public Speaking
o Computer Programming (2 courses)

o Buyer Behavior
o Advertising and Promotion
o Retailing Buying
o Consumer Marketing Policy
o Professional Writing

ACTIVITIES

o Elected Vice-Governor of 50 member dorm floor
o Active Member on the Board of Governors for University Quad
o Active in intramural sports including basketball, softball, and football
o Member of intramural all-sport championship team
o Dedicated runner, run 4 days per week, actively participate and volunteer in road races

WORK EXPERIENCE

City Supermarket #4, Niles, MI (xx/xx to xx/xx)
Worked two years for supermarket while in high school; Have worked every summer and college break since then; Earned one-third of college expenses. Frequently work during college holiday breaks.

Frozen/Dairy Assistant, (Summer xxxx), 45 hrs./week
Responsible for stocking, ordering, and taking inventory of frozen/dairy foods
Maintained direct contact with grocery sales representatives
Supervised dairy department during manager's vacation period

Night Crew Stocker, (Summer of xxxx), 45 hrs./week
Responsible for ordering, setting, stocking and facing grocery aisles
Unloading and unpacking semi-trailers
Designed and built grocery displays

Courtesy Captain, (Summer xxxx), 36 hrs./week
Reported directly to management on front-end activities and personnel
Supervised and trained 10–15 part-time employees
Scheduled and coordinated work assignments, breaks and lunches

REFERENCES

Professor Robin Werner-Simon
Economics Department
University of Notre Dame
Notre Dame, IN xxxxx
(xxx)xxx-xxxx

Mr. Joseph Albricht
President
City Supermarket
Niles, MI xxxxx
(xxx)xxx-xxxx

Mr. Jim Green
Manager
City Supermarket
Niles, MI xxxxx
(xxx)xxx-xxxx

Cover Letter Design:

Purpose – Content – Techniques

How do I match my cover letter with my resume?

Cover letters serve as introductory sales letters to potential employers. They always accompany resumes. A good cover letter motivates the potential employer to read the attached resume and subsequently invite you to interview for the position you are seeking.

Many employers receive hundreds of cover letters and resumes each day. Most employers can interview only a small fraction of the people who write requesting interviews. Employers use cover letters as the first screen in deciding how to respond to job applicants.

Only a few carefully worded letters stand a chance of getting through an employer's one-minute screening maze. Yet, every day this method accounts for hundreds of actual hires. Certain well-planned strategies and meticulous letter writing techniques increase your odds of obtaining an interview.

COVER LETTER DESIGN

Attention
+
Job Objective
+
Qualifications
+
Achievements
+
Interests
+
Motivation
+
Personality
+
Aggressive Close

= equals =

Results

Figure 13.1

301

The ultimate purpose of a cover letter is to motivate an employer to invite you for a job interview. A good cover letter introduces you to the employer and shows why you are one of the best candidates applying for a job with the organization.

As with a resume, a cover letter is not designed with the goal of obtaining a job offer initially. All you want the cover letter to do is help you get your foot in the door.

To a degree, the cover letter expands upon the resume, but it also does one additional thing. It adds personal flavor to your approach.

The cover letter brings the resume to life by pointing out that there is a real live person contacting the employer on a personal basis. The cover letter is more than a bland piece of paper.

A good cover letter represents you as a warm, pleasant, talking human being who is seeking a more personal conversation. The cover letter says, "Let's be friends." It goes beyond saying, "I need a job from you." The tone should be one of modest confidence.

Unfortunately, most cover letter writers have difficulty in communicating personal warmth. Most cover letters simply repeat the information which is on the resume, so they fail to achieve a greater purpose than resumes without cover letters would.

Designing an effective cover letter requires finesse. Your poise, polish, and maturity stand out to the degree that you have those qualities and the ability to communicate in written form.

Later, you will use networking and the internet to determine your distribution list. A quality cover letter is the first priority. Technology will greatly help with broadcasting both your cover letter and resume.

Developing the right touch is an art, and it may take hours of planning time to achieve the ideal wording. As with most employment methods, certain well-thought-through techniques and strategies can improve the chances of the cover letter achieving its planned purpose.

The purpose of the cover letter is to request an interview, not to get an offer.

A good cover letter indicates a personal warmth not found in the resume.

HOW DO YOU LIKE THIS JUST FOR FUN, AMY, "DEAR MULTINATIONAL BENEVOLENT CONGLOMERATE, WHOSE PRODUCTS MAKE LIFE RICHER FOR ALL OF US,"

Is an email cover letter appropriate? Normally not because it is not personal enough nor formal enough. There are exceptions though. If the job lead resulted from a website, email inquiry, or ad that requested email, then it is appropriate. Otherwise, stick with the more acceptable snail mail.

Strategic Planning Ideas

A planned series of events starts the approach to effective cover letter writing. Who should receive the cover letter? How do you locate the right contact? Once you know which contact is the decision-maker, how do you move that person to do what you want?

A cover letter is a perfectly word processed document like a resume. Use your spell and grammar checkers before printing. Print on a very high quality laser or ink jet printer. Individually sign each letter after it's printed.

Personalize. Personalizing the cover letter helps it get read. Few employers respond positively to letters addressed to "Sir" or "Madam." There is no personal reason for sir or madam to respond. If "Mr. Jones" receives a letter, however, responsibility for some type of reply is established with him.

Personalizing cover letters means that they must be individually typed and personally signed by you. Mass-produced letters rarely get more than "form letter 13" replies.

A typed letter implies a time commitment on your part which most recipients appreciate. An accepted norm in our society is that one courtesy deserves another. It is psychologically more difficult for an employer to respond to a personal letter with a form reply. Although many employers will still not reply, personalization increases your odds of receiving a reply.

Uniqueness. Another strategy is to create a unique setting in your letter so that a form reply will not be sufficient. There are several techniques for doing this.

The idea is to force the employer to write or dictate a personal letter back to you. If you can accomplish this, the likelihood of an interview is enhanced.

A letter that causes an employer to become interested in seeing what type of person you are increases your chances of getting an interview. Make your letter stand out from the run-of-the-mill cover letters. Usually, a statement of qualifications alone will not accomplish this.

Mentioning unusual experiences or interests, or employing a different writing style may interest the employer. Remember that these interests must be job related in order to appeal to the employer.

Target. A cover letter written in a manner that shows a special reason for wanting to work for the particular employer stands a better chance of special consideration. A strategy that implies "I really want to work for you above all others" appeals to the employer's loyalty to his or her organization.

A letter that shows ties between your background and this particular employer enhances your chances of success.

Enthusiastic. Employers like outgoing, enthusiastic people. A positive, enthusiastic tone in a cover letter is contagious.

Enthusiastically written letters say, "I like you!" and imply to the employer that the feeling is mutual. This type of initial rapport can inspire the employer to contact you.

Establish a personal relationship with the reader that says that we have mutual interests.

Construction Techniques

These strategies are broad concepts, and translating the above ideas into real words on a piece of paper can be difficult. No single letter can fit everyone.

The cover letter must be written by you with a great deal of contemplation. There are certain techniques that can aid in the writing of effective cover letters.

WELL, IT IS EVIDENT FROM YOUR COVER LETTER THAT YOU CERTAINLY ARE VERY CREATIVE.

Long cover letters bore their readers.

The employer's goal is to sort through the day's mail searching for people whose backgrounds would most effectively help the organization.

Only a few seconds are available for rapidly screening the day's mail. The longer the letter, the less likely it becomes that it will get its few key points across to the busy employer.

Conciseness

A cover letter must be a personally prepared, one page letter. It should be printed on high-quality personalized stationery or high-quality 8.5 x 11 inch bond paper.

At the maximum, a good cover letter rarely goes beyond five paragraphs of three to five complete sentences each. The sentences, unlike those in the resume, must be grammatically perfect.

Many of the techniques you employed in designing the resume also should be used with the cover letter.

The key idea in both cases is to show "accomplishment." A hard-hitting statement of accomplishments can illustrate very important subjective factors which are normally evaluated only in an interview.

The subjective factors are best discussed in an interview, but incorporating them into the cover letter encourages the employer to follow up with an interview. Ask yourself: will this factor help the recruiter decide to interview you? If yes, use the subjective factor.

Excite the Reader!

Key Words Count

With such limited space, every word must count. Extraneous words and cliches must be eliminated. Every word must be analyzed for its contribution to your objective. Does this word create the impression you want? Does that word say positive things? Can a word be substituted there that has a broader meaning? Have you used words that seem to expand meanings?

The impression you leave depends upon the words you use. You obviously must mention the basic qualifications you have placed on the resume, but putting them into sentence format gives you the chance to add important "adjectives" that expand the meaning of your basic credentials. The free-form writing style permits you to be more creative in your presentation.

CORPORATE CULTURE

"Establish Tie to the Work Environment"

All employers are proud of their people, facilities, and basic organizational culture. One screening criteria is to ascertain if you fit their unique work environment. Your cover letter might allude to your awareness of their orientation and/or how you might relate.

Some of these cultural differences are listed below, and your goal should be to show your personal traits.

Pressure and Pace: Do you work well under stress, deadlines, and highly charged atmospheres?

Change and Variety: Do you enjoy frequent changes in duties and work colleagues?

Competitive Climate: Whether from internal or external forces, do you thrive in situations with competitive win-lose outcomes?

Public Contact: Do you thrive on situations where meeting new internal and external work colleagues is routine?

Relationships: Do you prefer the close-knit team work groups or settings which allow more individuality?

Affiliation and Nurturing: Do you prefer a parental close affiliation atmosphere where collegially is a standard?

Security: Do you feel comfortable in a stable and secure environment even though the financial rewards may be lower?

Location and Community: Is the community most conductive to the long-term lifestyle that you desire?

Autonomy and Independence: Are you comfortable in unstructured work and hour arrangements with high levels of ambiguity?

Organizational Missions. Most organizations develop a specific reputation over time that relates to the work group and cultural climate. This is influenced by the basic missions of the organization. Friends in the community and employees are your best sources of information.

When you apply to organizations, you may be able to influence your interview invitation by drawing references to how your background and that of the organization converge.

Convergence. You can acknowledge your awareness by referring to some of the criteria below as they relate to your background and interests.

- Size
- Growth
- Philosophy
- Work Ethic
- Community
- Products
- Advancement
- Pace

The type of employer, the industry, the history, past success, leadership, and many other variables create the corporate culture. Approach organizations where you can draw similarities between your goals, needs, and interests when you write them.

Action Verbs.   Flowery phrases rarely add much and they should be avoided. Action-oriented verbs can bring your letter to life. They serve to connote a spirited, driving personality and a productive person.

Self-Descriptive Adjectives.   When used sparingly and in the right places, self-descriptive words add another dimension to your cover letter. Self-descriptive words add personal qualities to the letter. Their humanistic flavor may inspire the employer to treat you more as a person to be contacted than as a piece of paper to be processed.

Saying a lot in a small space is critical. If the employer were to circle four key words in your cover letter after reading it, what would you want them to be? Have you accomplished this mission with the use of key words? Have you focused the employer's eye on those points?

Using Contacts

Many interviews are obtained by effectively using contacts. Contacts are people with whom you have become acquainted and who are willing to go to bat for you. They write letters, make telephone calls, and permit you to use their names. Contacts can be extremely influential in helping you obtain interviews.

Contacts will not do your work for you. They typically set the scene and then you must take the initiative for the follow-up by letter, email, or telephone call. Thousands of cover letters are written each year on the recommendations of contacts.

Name Dropping.   Always mention the name of your contact if the contact was even in a minor way involved in suggesting a particular employer. Contacts usually personally know the person who they suggested you write. Mentioning the contact's name generates a whole new image.

Upon seeing the contact's name, an employer registers a familiar note. Contacts are important to both employers and employees. The employer quickly concludes that if you were endorsed by the contact, you must be good. Your resume will likely get read, and your chances for obtaining an interview are favorable.

Consulting Others

Not everyone has the ability to write well. The lack of outstanding writing skills is clearly a handicap. If you find yourself in this situation you should first make a series of rough drafts of your cover letter. Take your drafts with your resume to some experts and/or friends.

Advice.   You do not have to be a professional writer to write cover letters, but seeking advice never hurts anyone. The best people to approach are people who you already know well.

The right people might be teachers, relatives, business associates, or neighbors. Most people are willing to give you some advice, and you will find most of the advice extremely helpful when you sit down to do the final copy.

College career counselors, employment agency consultants, and friends in human resource departments are the best qualified people from whom to seek advice. These professionals see all types of approaches. However, do not limit your search for advice to them. You also need to talk to people who know you best, including best friends and family.

Using the name of a mutual acquaintance establishes a commitment for the employer to respond to you.

//WEB.TIP//

www.careerlab.com/letters
Letters for Job Hunters
Form letters for every aspect of the job search/ letter writing coach/time saving resources.

ACTION VERBS

What Have You Done?

Accelerated	Constructed	Fashioned	Operated	Scheduled
Accomplished	Controlled	Filled	Organized	Secured
Accounted	Coordinated	Forecasted	Originated	
Achieved		Formulated	Participated	Selected
Acquired	Corresponded	Found		Served
	Counselled	Generated	Performed	Serviced
Acted	Created		Persuaded	Set up
Adapted	Critiqued	Guided	Pinpointed	Simplified
Administered	Cut	Headed	Planned	
Adopted		Hired	Predicted	Sold
Advised	Dealt	Implemented		Solved
	Debated	Improved	Prepared	Spoke
Advocated	Delegated		Presented	Staffed
Aided	Delivered	Improvised	Printed	Started
Allocated	Demonstrated	Increased	Prioritized	
Analyzed		Influenced	Processed	Streamlined
Applied	Described	Initiated		Strengthened
	Designed	Innovated	Produced	Stressed
Appraised	Determined		Programmed	Structured
Approved	Developed	Inspired	Projected	Succeeded
Arbitrated	Devised	Installed	Promoted	
Arranged		Instructed	Proofread	Summarized
Assembled	Diagnosed	Integrated		Supervised
	Directed	Interpreted	Proposed	Supported
Assessed	Discovered		Proved	Synthesized
Assigned	Dispatched	Interviewed	Provided	Systemized
Assisted	Displayed	Introduced	Published	
Attained		Invented	Purchased	Tackled
Audited	Distributed	Invested		Talked
	Documented	Investigated	Pushed	Taught
Based	Drafted		Questioned	Tested
Budgeted	Drew	Involved	Raised	Touched
Built	Earned	Judged	Read	
Checked		Launched	Recommended	Tracked
Classified	Edited	Lectured		Traded
	Educated	Led	Recorded	Trained
Coached	Effected		Recruited	Transferred
Collated	Eliminated	Lobbied	Reduced	Translated
Collected	Encouraged	Located	Referred	
Communicated		Made	Reinforced	Treated
Competed	Established	Maintained		Trimmed
	Evaluated	Managed	Reorganized	Troubleshot
Compiled	Examined		Repaired	Uncovered
Completed	Exhibited	Manipulated	Reported	Updated
Composed	Expanded	Measured	Researched	
Conceived		Mediated	Resolved	Upgraded
Conducted	Expedited	Motivated		Utilized
	Explained	Negotiated	Responded	Visualized
Confronted	Expressed	Observed	Reviewed	Won
Consolidated	Facilitated		Revised	Wrote

Figure 13.2

Cover Letter Design 307

SYNTHESIZE YOUR PERSONAL QUALITIES

How would you describe yourself using only five words? Cover letter readers must draw quick images of you after a 30 to 60 second rapid scan of your cover letter. What impression do you want your cover letter to leave?

After reading your cover letter, can you step away and write down five words that *accurately* describe your most important qualities? Every reader conjures up some picture about the person whose cover letter and resume (if it was read) was just reviewed. Most cover letter readers boil their evaluation down to about five key descriptive words. Some of the most frequently used positive words are listed below.

Analytical	Energetic	Persuasive
Assertive	Enterprising	Productive
Charger	Enthusiastic	Responsible
Confident	Expressive	Skilled
Creative	Extroverted	Tactful
Disciplined	Manager	Team player
Efficient	Personable	Technical

It is not practical to directly state: "I am . . ." You must imply those personable qualities by how you describe your academic experience, activities, events, achievements, recognitions, etc.

A clever way of accomplishing this attitude is to first pick the five most important qualities that you possess and wish to communicate. You use these actual words at least one time in the body of the cover letter.

A most effective approach is to describe an event, course, work experience, or personal activity using one or more of these adjectives. For example, you could state, "The team took a hard line approach that tactfully avoided conflict with . . ." or "The energetic group rallied 30 members in a productive enterprise that . . . ."

The incorporation of action verbs and adaptive functional skills with descriptive adjectives presents an appealing candidate when these are sublimely transferred upon you. Challenge yourself in finding ways to choose insightful and accurate words that bring out your true personal qualities.

• Action Verbs	• Adaptive Skills	• Descriptors

Structure and Content

The cover letter follows the format of a basic business letter. Whenever possible, it should be addressed to a specific individual. In the rare instance where it is impossible to write to a specific person, the salutation should be "Dear Sir/Madam." The impersonal approach is used only as a last resort and its effectiveness is not likely to be strong.

If you do not know the proper person to write, call the firm and request a specific name by giving the receptionist the title of the person you wish to address. Also surf the web for specific names.

TYPICAL BUSINESS LETTER FORMAT

Street Address
City, State, Zip
Telephone Number
Current Date

[4 spaces]

Employer's Name
Title
Department
Organization
Street Address
City, State, Zip

[1 space]

Dear Mr./Ms./Dr./Individual's Name:

[1 space]

Introduction: Reference previous conversation of correspondence . . . give specific dates if possible . . . state appreciation for past consideration . . . succinctly state current business . . .state your credentials . . .mention a specific job title . . . mention name of recommendors.

[1 space]

Body: Give details on purpose of letter . . . make reference to attachments . . . write short but complete sentences . . . avoid large and unnecessary words . . . cover the central theme completely . . . make paragraphs two to five sentences . . . list your accomplishments.

[1 space]

Close: State the action you expect from the recipient . . . keep paragraph short . . . . . . indicate your next plan of action . . . offer specific date of expected action if appropriate . . . thank the recipient.

[1 space]

Very truly yours, (Sincerely, Sincerely yours, Truly yours, etc.)

[3 spaces]

Typed Name

[1 space]

P.S. Information that came after the letter was written.
Sometimes used for emphasis.

[1 space]

Encl. (Indicates that there is an attachment)

[1 space]

cc: Placement Office (Indicates others who are kept informed)

Figure 13.3

EMPHASIZE YOUR FUNCTIONAL SKILLS

How can you best contribute to the organization? What do you offer that is unique to you? Why are you among the best group of individuals who should be interviewed? Organizations are comprised of a variety of jobs which require specific skills.

Your cover letter should specifically address your strongest set of skills. You clearly cannot cover all of the skills that you possess so you must rank order them in relation to what you anticipate the employer's top screening criteria might be. The most common functional skills include the following:

Accounting	Fact-finding	Planning
Advising	Implementing	Problem-solving
Analyzing	Influencing	Promoting
Budgeting	Initiating	Relating
Delegating	Managing	Reporting
Designing	Motivating	Serving
Engineering	Operating	Speaking
Expediting	Organizing	Teaching
Expressing	Performing	Troubleshooting
Evaluating	Persuading	Writing

Your resume probably incorporates many of these words in the explanation of your academic background, part-time and full-time job descriptions, and other extracurricular, social, and civic activities. Nonetheless, you should draw attention to your skills in the body of your cover letter.

• • • Bullet Points • • •

The most effective method to accomplish this is to draw attention by using bullet points in the middle of your cover letter where you acknowledge your achievements. The achievement should use words that describe your strongest skills. Use as many of the functional skill words as you can to aid in capturing the reader's attention.

The cover letter is made up of three to five paragraphs, each of which has a specific purpose. The first paragraph is called the *introduction* and the last paragraph is called the *close*.

The middle paragraph(s) form the *body* of the letter and describe your qualifications and interests. Material in the body paragraph(s) is often intertwined.

Introduction Paragraph

The introduction establishes the purpose of your letter, which is to apply for a specific job opening. The introduction normally comprises a maximum of four sentences.

Goal. One of the sentences describes the position for which you wish to be considered and, if appropriate, how you learned of the opening. Another sentence succinctly states your immediate job objective and longer-term career aspirations.

To interest the reader, many people also insert a brief sentence that gives their degree, major, graduation date, and years (if any) of relevant work experience. One of the sentences mentions the mutual acquaintances you have (if applicable) or the contact that suggested you write to the potential employer.

Attention. The goal of the introductory paragraph is to attract attention. You do this by stating your purpose and lucidly explaining how your credentials can help the employer.

Strong opening sentences excite the employer and motivate him or her to continue reading your letter and the accompanying resume.

The opening paragraph must capture attention by establishing common goals and relationships.

Body Paragraphs

The middle paragraphs sell your credentials to the employer. While urging him or her to read further, you are showing how your background perfectly matches an opening that you believe is available. Your mission in the body is to prove to the employer that you should at least be invited to interview for the assignment.

Sell. One of your sentences states your reasons for wanting to work for this organization. The employer is loyal to her or his organization and takes pride in it. You appeal to this pride in indicating the reasons why you feel it is a top-notch organization.

Another sentence specifies why you believe your background is relevant to the position being sought.

Briefly describe your key assets without repeating too much of what is already on the attached resume. This personalizes your potential relationship with the organization in a manner that describes you in a more humanistic way than the facts on the resume.

Identify. One sentence in the body appeals to the employer's needs. In essence, you are making a proposition of employment, so you must show how you can help the employer achieve organizational goals in your area of specialization.

The goal of the body of your cover letter is to convince the employer that there is merit in thoroughly reading your attached resume.

Examples. In a separate paragraph within the body, stress your accomplishments. This goes beyond stating your education and experience. You want to point to some specific examples in your education, extracurricular activities, and work experience which addressed a problem and solved it. It would be helpful to illustrate how these problems you solved earlier relate to possible assignments within the employer's organization.

Interest. Another paragraph is interest-oriented. It shows some of your more personal qualities which are more difficult to highlight on a resume. Including self-descriptive words helps. The most effective technique for accomplishing this is to discuss some episode in your background that brings out some of the personal qualities that you know the employer needs in the person filling the position you are seeking.

...EVEN ROCKEFELLER WARNED ME NOT TO NAME-DROP.

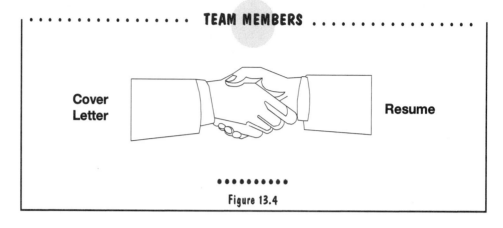

TEAM MEMBERS

Cover Letter

Resume

Figure 13.4

Refer. One of the body paragraphs refers the reader to the resume. Indicate that the resume is only a brief summary of your background and that you would like to personally expand on your credentials.

Imply that there is a lot of additional information about your background that is relevant to the position you are seeking.

Close Paragraph

The last paragraph closes the sale. You have made your pitch, so now you must ask for the order.

Successful sales people will tell you that most of their colleagues who fail do so because they do not effectively ask for the sale. You have to assume that you have done a perfect job of selling; now show the employer how he or she can take advantage of the opportunity you have just presented.

Ask! Ask for an interview. Do it straightforward. Ask for it in a positive, convincing manner as if you will not accept no for an answer.

The close should never exceed four sentences: effective closes are often much shorter. The close is aggressive.

Ask for the interview!

You want to sound like you are in command but that you recognize the employer must make a decision to invite you for an interview. You want to let the employer know that although the ball is in his court, you are still prepared to serve again.

A close that says, "If you feel a match is present, please contact me," is not strong enough. You can avoid a "no interest" form letter by asking the employer for more information, or by stating that you will call for an appointment, or that you will stop by in a few days.

Match. Leave the impression that there is a mutual concern. It is only a matter of the two of you agreeing on a time and place for the interview.

Let the employer know that you do not ex-

AND IF YOU HIRE ME TODAY, YOU'LL RECEIVE THESE LOVELY STAINLESS STEEL STEAK KNIVES ABSOLUTELY FREE.

·········· ACHIEVEMENT HIGHLIGHTING METHODS ··········

First Paragraph: Capture attention

Body Paragraphs:

- Highlight Your Achievements
- Give Specific, Qualifiable Results
- Draw From Examples Like These

School

- Worked with a seven member team of students
- Earned highest grade on senior class project
- Led a group of 150 students who raised $50,000 for . . .
- Maintained a 3.5 GPA the last two years
- Earned a 3.6 GPA in my major
- Made six presentations in my senior project class
- Received a recognition trophy on . . .

Work

- Hired 28 people in three months
- Sold 10,000 gizmos in five months
- Delivered 220 prospects on a minimal budget
- Wrote three articles for two different journals
- Supervised a team of 20 staff with a $500,000 budget
- Increased earnings by 40 percent in six months
- Saved firm $50,000 via cost reduction efforts
- Increased productivity 15 percent

Closing Paragraph: Ask for the interview

·········
Figure 13.5

pect the organization to pay your expenses for an interview trip for a preliminary interview. Very few employers will invite you to travel a long distance for an interview and pay your expenses prior to a preliminary interview unless you have very unusual job skills which are in high demand.

An exception might be made after you are interviewed by telephone or after they have contacted some mutually known references.

Next Step.   Close the letter by informing the employer of your next action. You might go as far as suggesting a date and time for an interview and calling a secretary to confirm it. Your taking the initiative relieves the employer of immediate action. This approach could stall a "no interest" letter.

The second initiative gives you a second chance at the organization. The second initiative can also force the employer to hold your file for a day or two, which might generate a more thorough reading during a later and slower part of the day.

Be assertive by suggesting a date that you will call to set up an interview appointment time.

//WEB.TIP//

www.careerlab.com
Career Lab
Sample cover letters/career articles.

Your Address
City, State, Zip
Telephone Number
Date of Letter
        [4 spaces]
Contact Name
Contact's Title
Contact's Department
Employer Organization
Street Address
City, State, Zip
        [1 space]
Dear Mr./Ms./Dr. Contact's Last Name:
        [1 space]

Opening Paragraph:

- State purpose
- Capture attention
- Name position seeking

- Use recommender's name
- Use name of mutual friends
- Consider opening with a question

- Mention source of lead
- State top credentials
- Be Assertive

[Capture Attention — Build Match]

Body Paragraphs:

- Create interest
- Show enthusiasm
- Stress skills
- Use self-descriptive words
- Use action verbs
- Emphasize excellence
- Show commitments honored
- Present confident tone
- Humanize
- Tell a brief story
- Give rationale for decisions

- Illustrate personality
- Point to achievement
- Don't repeat resume
- Use adverbs for time constraints
- Put adjectives with activities
- State performance levels
- Identify how skills obtained
- Build credibility
- Create warmth
- End at three paragraphs—maximum!
- Give reasons for interest

[Read More of Novel . . . Refer to Attached Resume]
[Explain Why You Are Best Qualified]

**[Create Excitement And Interest In Wanting To Know More
About Your Education, Experience, And Activities]**

Closing Paragraph

- Close strongly
- Stay confident
- Avoid wimpy close
- Make response easy

- Restate solid match
- Refer to resume
- Call for appointment soon
- Initiate follow-up plans

- State your next step
- Give specific dates
- Avoid "If you have . . ."
- Take charge

[Ask For The Interview!]

        [1 space]
Sincerely,
        [3 spaces — Sign Letter]
Type Your Full Name
        [1 space]
Enclosure: Resume **[Always Attach]**
cc: Copy mutual acquaintances

• • • • • • • • • • •
Figure 13.6

Your Address (home or campus)
City, State, Zip
Telephone Number
Date of Letter

[4 spaces]

Contact's Name
Contact's Title
Contact's Department
Employing Organization
Street Address
City, State, Zip

[1 space]

Dear Mr./Ms./Dr. Contact's Last Name:

[1 space]

Opening Paragraph:
- Type individually; never use a form letter
- Address to a specific person
- Use 8-1/2 x 11 paper only
- Use standard white bond paper

- Use perfect grammar and spelling
- Stick to one-page limit
- Provide ample margins and white space
- Center on page for appearance

Body Paragraph(s):
- Use bullet points for emphasis
- Graphically lay out paragraphs
- Center key accomplishments
- Display job related courses as a group

- Limit total letter to a five-paragraph maximum
- Limit paragraphs to a five-sentence maximum
- Emphasize accomplishments and recognition
- Highlight skills that match job

Closing Paragraph:
- Ask for the interview!
- Be bold, convincing and assertive
- Express positive match
- Refer to resume attached

- Make employer's reply easy
- Advise that you will call on a specific date
- Ask a friend to proofread your letter

[1 space]

Sincerely,

[3 spaces — Sign Full Name]

Type Full Name

[1 space]

P.S.
- Sometimes used for emphasis
- Limit to one brief sentence

[1 space]

Encl(s).
- Resume enclosed (always)
- Other supporting documentation enclosed (occasionally) (like unofficial transcripts)
- Portfolio (if appropriate for profession) (evidence of abilities)
- References (To Whom It May Concern letter) (rarely used here)
- Unofficial transcript (rarely used at this point)

cc: Copy mutual acquaintances

· · · · · · · · · · ·

Figure 13.7

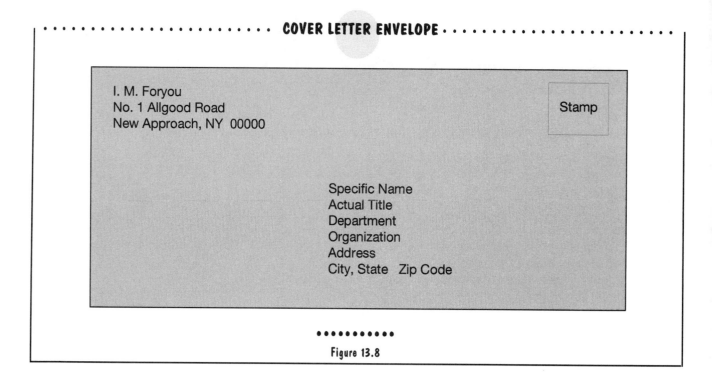

I. M. Foryou
No. 1 Allgood Road
New Approach, NY 00000

Stamp

Specific Name
Actual Title
Department
Organization
Address
City, State   Zip Code

· · · · · · · · · · ·
Figure 13.8

Follow-up Approaches

Follow-up Options

A little empathy can tell you what an employer's potential options are after reading your resume and cover letter:

- No reply
- No interest
- No opening
- Hold in file
- Call for appointment
- Stop by
- Invite call

The potential for negative replies greatly outweighs that for positive options.

Potential Responses.   Your goal is to get a personal call or written letter. You do not want a form reply. You can influence the employer's action with several techniques.

To insure obtaining a reply in as short a time as possible, consider enclosing a reply postcard. Make the employer's task easy. The postcard could lay out boxes for the employer to check for the options listed above. If you do not already have it, you can indicate a space for the employer's personal telephone number, as well.

Be careful about suggesting an email reply. It makes it almost too easy for the employer to give you a "no interest" reply. By telephone, you at least get to ask why.

Dates.   Another approach is to suggest some dates and times for an interview in the letter. Follow up with a telephone call in which you simply ask which of these times would be acceptable.

Request. Many employers require a completed application blank before an initial interview. One technique occasionally used to avoid an immediate turndown is to request an application blank.

After getting a reply and completing the application blank, you can call and ask when it would be convenient for you to return the application blank and discuss your credentials in more detail in person. This technique can also give you the name and title of a specific person to contact.

Call. The most common approach is to advise the employer that you will telephone on a specific date to negotiate a convenient interview time. On the appointed day, you call and make appropriate arrangements.

Call for an appointment on the date indicated.

Some experts recommend that you establish the appointment with a secretary to avoid the possibility of a turndown after a brief telephone interview. The assumption is that telephone interviews are rarely as successful as personal face-to-face interviews.

The specific follow-up approach which you employ should fit your personality and judgment. The main idea is for you to take some initiative and not allow the decision to be based solely on your cover letter and resume.

Telephone Finesse

Once you call an employer, getting through to the right person can be a significant challenge. Most of the key decision members often have a clerical person who screens calls. You need to develop a technique that will get you past the receptionists.

In most cases you must first explain the purpose of your call to the secretary. The secretary will decide on behalf of the boss' time whether your call should be put ahead of current activities being conducted.

Be careful in explaining your *whole* story or the person you are talking to may make a decision you do not want. You must give requested information but do not volunteer a thorough background description unless this is the initial decision-maker.

Lower level employees often have a penchant for making decisions in order to protect a supervisor's schedule.

You should also expect voice mail. Plan your response ahead of time. Be specific about when it is best to reach you. Leave a tone of urgency, but do not give too much more screening data. Be positive and enthusiastic. Practice the message.

The telephone is one of your most potent job finding tools. Your goal is to get an appointment, not to be interviewed. Keep the conversation moving toward your goal of getting the appointment with the right person.

If you are not certain of who the proper person is, call the

SHALL I CALL YOU OR WAIT FOR
YOU TO IGNORE ME?

```
..............TELEPHONE BARRIER BUSTERS..............

    • Be prepared with extensive notes
    • Get a hook in with your opening statement
    • Avoid the secretary screen
    • Entice but do not interview via telephone
    • Press for an appointment
    • Use hard hitting, short verbal commercials
    • Write notes as you listen
    • After appointment, get off the line quickly
    • Be available late afternoons and early morning
    • Use names of mutual acquaintances
    • Smile when you talk — be upbeat

                  ••••••••••
                  Figure 13.9
```

switchboard number and ask who runs the function which interests you. Be sure to get the name spelled correctly, a full title, and the telephone number.

The telephone is so important to you primarily because of speed. You get results, one way or another, almost instantly. Unfortunately, telephone tag is also your greatest enemy. Give a person a reasonable time in which to call you back, but do not hesitate to call again if you have not received a reply within 24 hours. The employer may not be in the same rush as you.

One way to avoid telephone tag or message ignoring is to not leave a call back message. Try to find out when the employer is available and advise that you "will call back since you are so difficult to reach." Call back promptly. Be courteous and sensitive by asking if this is a good time to talk.

Be prepared for brush-off lines like the following:

- "Send me a resume"
- "I am busy right now"
- "Talk to Personnel first"
- "No needs right now"
- "Great credentials but . . ."
- "Call me in a few weeks"
- "Committed to another"

You must be prepared to address the brush-off lines with previously prepared routines. You can always acknowledge that you understand their situation by showing sympathy and understanding while acknowledging agreement.

You must presume that your talents are needed in the organization, so you should offer some solution to the objections by pointing out some alternatives.

One method to deal with the brush-off is to keep on the telephone by asking questions where you learn about the job and thus can respond by pointing out how your strengths merge. You should always close with a request for a personal appointment.

One effective preparation technique for telephoning is to develop a one to two minute commercial about yourself. Nearly everyone will ask you to tell about yourself, and the better prepared you are, the more organized you appear. Try to

DIRECT MARKETING CONCEPTS

- Market research
- Advertising design
- Target customers
- Ad layout
- Mail distribution
- Telemarketing follow-up
- Sales presentation
- Close the sale

        ••••••••••
        Figure 13.10

rehearse your commercial by listening to yourself on an audio tape recorder. Do not read it.

In closing, you should ask for the appointment by volunteering some specific times, even if it is after normal working hours. Repeat the date, time, and place as you write it down for your records.

Direct Mail Campaign

Many experts object to the idea of waiting until you have a firm job lead before you start your job campaign. These experts suggest a dynamic, aggressive, direct mail approach to the job search process. Waiting for job leads to materialize is much too passive.

This traditional method of job search aggressively goes after the hidden job market. The direct mail job campaign is a job finding approach with overtones of a mass media blitz.

The direct mail approach may also be used in smaller, targeted mailings. The odds of success are improved significantly by the more targeted approaches where the likelihood of a job match is much higher.

The WWW will help you identify both a narrow band or broad base list of contacts to distribute the cover letter and resume. The initial decision is how to best segment the "world of contacts" with a realistic search strategy.

Basic Concept

The direct mail approach is the number one method used by most people. It characterizes our society's free enterprise spirit. The idea is to advertise the product and if it has value, the public will buy it. The direct mail approach is a time-tested, effective marketing technique.

Some products sell better than others. Sometimes the difference in marketability is due to the quality of the products. Sometimes it is due to the quality of the advertising. There are as many marketing strategies as there are products.

A look through any basic marketing textbook reveals a massive array of marketing concepts that help to sell products. Some of these concepts might have application for persons interested in selling themselves.

These concepts include:

- market research
- market segmentation
- product presentation
- brand management
- advertising strategy
- advertising design

- media utilization
- channels of distribution
- selling techniques

Are these ideas applicable to you? Can your credentials be marketed? How does market segmentation differ from career objectives? This whole subject is repulsive to many people. Yet there is a significant amount of validity in applying marketing concepts to the job search process.

The experts can prove that these sophisticated approaches greatly aid people in finding nearly perfect career matches.

The direct mail job search strategy is controversial. Many experts label it as archaic, backward, ineffective, and disgusting. You must decide if your values and the techniques are compatible. However, you cannot decide whether the approach is for you unless you understand it.

Definition. A direct mail campaign involves the preparation and dissemination of a qualifications package to potential employers. The qualifications package (the presentation of the product) usually consists of a uniquely designed cover letter and resume.

The dissemination of the package is usually done by direct mail, but occasionally other media are used such as "position wanted" ads in appropriate publications. The decision on which dissemination method to use involves an analysis of the market to be targeted.

The letter is referred to as a personal sales letter, a broadcast letter, or simply a cover letter. Actually, the format of sales letters is no different from that of regular cover letters, but the content is more general.

The "sales" letter hits a broader market. You do not always know the types of persons who will receive the letter, so you must write the letter in a way that will capture the attention of people serving a variety of functions in your career field. The same thinking applies to the resume. It is general and follows a standard format.

Usually, the direct mail campaign strategy is more of a mass market appeal. It cannot be as finely tuned as the individualized cover letter and resume prepared for a specific job lead.

An interesting takeoff of the direct mail campaign is an email campaign. You identify your "contacts" in the usual way but using the www as your primary resource. You use your same carefully crafted cover letter and attached resume. Once you learn the web and email technique, it is very simple and effective to broadcast your sales package.

In practice, you can also use the direct mail approach in a much more targeted, or segmented, market approach to cut costs and increase your odds of a higher return rate.

Objective. The objective of a direct mail campaign is to generate job leads. It does not create jobs but tries to find the ones available. The odds of making a direct hit with each piece is extremely low.

The whole concept plays the percentages just as any advertiser does. Direct mail has traditionally been a better medium to use than television, radio, newspaper, etc. for obvious reasons. Advertising can be targeted on a finite base of employers which is of a reasonable size and which is potentially productive.

Once a job lead is noted, the goal is to obtain the interview. The procedure is then the same as with any other lead. There must be a telephone call follow-up for each lead generated. The telephone call often serves as a preliminary interview, but your goal should focus on an appointment.

Like the cover letter, a sales letter is likely to be far more effective if it is addressed to a specific person.

One problem is that many people expect to hear that the employer is interested and wants to interview them immediately. Although that does occur occasionally, a more realistic expectation is simply to expect that the employer desires more information. Hopefully, you will be able to determine if there is a *possibility* for an opening with the employer.

Usually, you can expect *no* response unless there is a job possibility.

When you receive direct mail at your home, you normally do not respond. Unless you are interested in the product, you do not return the easy reply envelope.

Employers are not likely to respond to your unsolicited cover letter and resume unless there is a possible match. Direct mail advertisers often do a follow-up by mail. Your follow-up will need to be done via telephone.

Response

The ideal response from an employer implies that the organization currently has a job opening that matches your job objective and fits your background perfectly. Ideally, the employer calls you on the telephone for the purpose of discussing your background and interests in more depth to ascertain your current status, personality fit, communication abilities, and skill level.

Assuming that there seems to be a match, the employer establishes a mutually agreeable time for the two of you to get together for an interview. If there are any expenses to be incurred, the details of who pays them are discussed.

The perfect scenario happens infrequently. You learn to "roll" with the response and even take a more aggressive action toward any employer who gives even the slightest hint of a possible match.

Rate of Return.   One major criticism to the direct mail approach is the low rate of return. Most employers do not respond at all. Do you go down to the store and indicate that you do not want to buy an advertised product? Expecting employers to respond to the hundreds of letters they receive annually is unrealistic. Just hope that you can get your material read.

The response rate varies greatly. In soft job markets, it will be lower. For highly sought-after candidates, it will be high. For carefully targeted populations of employers, it may be higher. Well-designed materials (the presentation) get read more frequently and more completely. Personally typed and signed letters get more attention than mass-produced letters.

With all of these variables, it is impossible to predict what your response rate

The rate of return is always low.

will be. Mass surveys suggest that three percent is average. Some people get ten percent, which is phenomenally high. Others are lucky to get a one-percent reply. Your best estimation is the three-percent expectation that a job interview possibility will result.

Cost.   Although these rates of return sound low, you must ask yourself, "compared to what?" Before

I THINK IT'S A REJECTION. LISTEN...
"DEAR SCUM-BAG."

you compare approaches you need a common base to which to relate the results. Your results can be defined as interviews. Your common base can be dollars per interview.

The cost of a direct mail campaign is not minor. A typical mailing might include 1,000 letters. At an average cost of $1 each, you will have invested $1,000 plus a lot of time. It is better to spend your time on this approach, however, than on just sitting and hoping.

If you get a three-percent positive acknowledgment and half turn into interviews, you will have paid $67 per interview for 15 interviews. The amount of time you have spent plus $67 per interview may make this a relatively inexpensive method for you to use to generate job leads and interviews.

What you include in the cost is important. How many letters will you send out? Will you do all of the work yourself or hire it to be done? Will you use professionals to design the cover letter and resume? How many long distance telephone calls will you have to make? These questions impact on your particular cost situation.

Type of Responses. The type of responses that you get depends upon how you close your letter. Return postcards increase your response rate but also increase your costs because you must then follow up with a telephone call. Leaving open-ended replies (like, "If you have an interest, please. . . .") decreases your chances of replies.

Very few, if any, reply letters are going to say, "We like your background and want you here for an interview." A more likely positive reply is a telephone call to get more information about you and discuss your interests. After this brief telephone interview, there may be some discussion of your coming in for an interview.

If you use the direct mail approach, you must have a telephone answering machine. Do not use cute "we are out" messages. Be brief. You do not want to miss a very expensive telephone reply or turn off a potential employer.

For senior management-level openings, employers may pay travel costs to the first interview. Usually the candidate must pay the first interview expenses. If negotiations continue through to the offer stage, most employers will later pick up expenses. Expenses are a negotiable item.

Most of your positive replies will state, "If you are in the area, please call." That is your clue that there is probably a job opening now or one is anticipated for someone with your credentials. You should follow up with a telephone call immediately.

Most replies simply state that there are "no openings consistent with your background at the present time." Some may indicate that your resume will be kept on file. Keeping your resume on file usually guarantees nothing until you write again in eight to ten weeks to reactivate the employer's memory.

Techniques

All who have used the direct mail approach have learned from their successes and failures. Upon analyzing the results, everyone comes up with a few ideas that would have greatly increased the quantity and quality of their results. Most of these ideas are specific to the individual or career field.

Many ideas can be gained from others who have used this approach. The gimmicks that have been tried number into the thousands and everyone seems to think his or her approach will work for everyone else.

The simple fact is that there are no universally successful techniques. If there were, employers would be inviting everyone who writes for an interview.

Although the rate of return is low and the cost per interview may also be low, your personal time commitment may also be high.

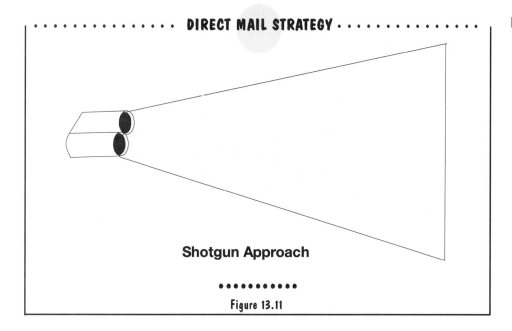

········· **DIRECT MAIL STRATEGY** ·············

Shotgun Approach

●●●●●●●●●●
Figure 13.11

Most positive responses are likely to be a "send application," "call," or "stop by" reply.

The odds are extremely high that an employer is not going to have an opening at the specific point in time when you apply. Direct mail plays the percentages.

The most successful techniques employed by others relate to three things:

1. Improving the qualifications package
2. Improving the target population
3. Improving the quality and appearance of the sales letter

The techniques below describe your options in two of these areas.

Shotgun Approach.   In any approach, you have to zero-in on some population's target. The targeted employers must be in the geographical area of your concern and normally offer some opportunities in your field of expertise as stated on the resume you plan to send.

A shotgun approach takes a wide and large population and broadcasts your credentials to a diverse group of people. Your resume may be sent to hundreds of employment managers or sent to everyone employed in your profession.

This is akin to using a sawed-off shotgun to hunt game if you are not a particularly accurate shooter. A shotgun spreads the pellets into a large circle of fire. Although some pellets may hit the target, they won't necessarily kill it, but you will still have a chance to stalk down the target.

If you employ this strategy, you are simply hoping for a very small percentage return from a large sample. Although the response *rate* may be lower, the *number* of subsequent replies could be larger.

You may have to employ this approach if you have limited time to sort out the most likely employers or if you cannot find narrow mailing lists.

Rifle Approach.   The rifle approach takes aim on a population group that you feel has a high probability of employing people with your credentials. It is in the middle ground between the personal cover letter and the shotgun approach.

To a major degree, your occupational field dictates the approach you use. For example, if you were seeking a history teaching position in higher education, there would be about 3,000 colleges that might hire you. You could write the chairman of every history department. That would be a shotgun approach.

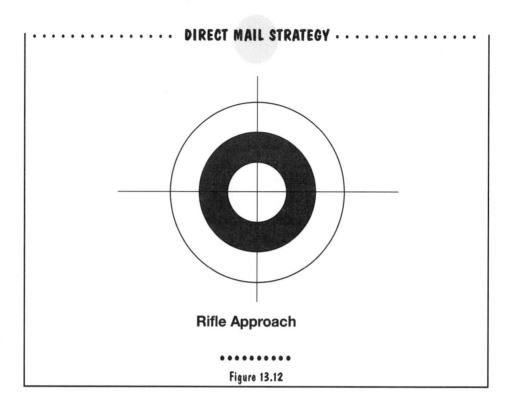

Rifle Approach

· · · · · · · · · ·

Figure 13.12

The rifle approach is just a small step above the individually typed cover letter.

However, given the declining enrollment in colleges, the financial plight of small private liberal arts schools, and the strong economy in the Midwest, you might elect to mail to chairmen only at public institutions located in 12 midwestern states. That would be taking a rifle approach based on a realistic appraisal of job probabilities.

The goal behind the rifle approach is to raise your percent rate of return from one percent to the five percent range. This approach makes more economic sense, but it is not always practical to employ if your target population is not readily identifiable.

Appearance.   Individually typed letters make the receiver more likely to respond. Many employers make it a policy to respond to all personalized correspondence, especially if it is addressed to them specifically. With today's word processing equipment, personal letters are not the laborious chore they once were.

Mailing services provide typed letters for a fee. For as many letters as you might need to send, the cost is significant. Other than pay the bill, all you need to do is provide the date, inside address, and salutation. The service does the rest.

The least expensive and far less desirable approach is to use a printed broadcast letter. The salutation would simply be "Dear Sir/Madam," "Dear Employer," or be omitted altogether. This is *not* recommended!

The ideal approach is to have all of your broadcast letters individually prepared and personally signed. Whether the cost is worth the increased response depends upon your financial resources and personal judgment.

Most experts suggest that if you cannot write "personalized" letters, the direct mail approach is not worth the effort. A word processor can alleviate much of the drudgery but not everything.

Mechanics

The real success in direct mail campaigns often lies in simple mechanics. A job worth doing is worth putting time into. If you decide to employ this approach, prepare yourself to do some plain old hard manual work.

It takes some ingenuity and research to obtain the most effective mailing labels, but the real work is involved with the mundane clerical duties. And the quality of the performance of the mundane duties is a major factor in the rate of success.

Mailing Lists.   The mailing list you use depends upon your background and career interest. You will find membership directories in your career field on the www. You can obtain many names from directories in your public library if you are not web efficient.

Since this is a play-the-numbers game, you must make the size of the list worthwhile. Mailing out 100 letters to get three replies is marginally fruitful. Most experts recommend a start of at least 250 names, which might generate about ten interviews.

Distribution Duties.   The boring part of the direct mail campaign is the clerical operation of putting the materials together. Printing letters, addressing and stuffing envelopes, printing labels for envelopes (or pasting on preprinted ones), affixing postage, and mailing take a huge amount of "nitty gritty" time.

The outcome is worth the effort. You have the option of hiring a part-time clerical person or paying a mailing service to do this if you have the financial resources.

Try to use a good word processing program for your letters. Use a letter quality printer. Always personally sign each letter. It cannot look like a copied letter.

COMPUTERS IN THE JOB SEARCH

There are literally thousands of software programs written for personal computers. If you have computer skills and access to a PC, you will find this an enormous time saver. For more generic tasks, there are three types of programs that can be especially useful in the job search process.

1. **Word processing** — Use for letters and possibly the resume. (WORD)
2. **Database managers** — Use for tracking your contacts. (ACCESS)
3. **Spreadsheets** — Use in making lists and tracking efforts. (EXCEL)

There are a number of other specific software packages that are dedicated to the search process. These software packages contain form letters, tests for personal analysis, checklists for self-assessment, target contact lists, special form letters that are easily modified, resume writing assistance, and interview results evaluations.

Computers help you take a more rifle oriented approach to the direct mail job search strategy. You can customize your promotional materials to a specific targeted market.

The market is proliferated with a variety of software aids. These are available in many bookstores, college placement offices, employment agencies, and in retail software supply stores. The WWW has an impressive array of related tools.

Summary. When your accomplishments and qualifications are written and packaged in a professional manner, direct mail job campaigns can be extremely useful. They take much work, but positive results are possible.

The great appeal of direct mail is its potential ability to generate a number of interviews with a minimum amount of work. Unlike responding to an advertisement, when you do make a hit, you may have little competition for the job because you have tapped part of the hidden job market.

The other major appeal is that you do all of the work. Relying on others can be disastrous. With the direct mail approach, you are on your own more than with any other type of job search technique.

Remember that this is a "play the odds" strategy. By definition, your percentage return is low. Quality cover letters and accurate, specifically targeted lists greatly improve your success rate.

//WEB.TIP//
www.four//.com
Information Directory
Need contact info?/try 411/explore where to send resumes and cover letters.

Career Action Projects

The best way to learn how to prepare a cover letter and a direct mail job search strategy is to do it. Listed below are two similar career action projects which, after completed, will provide you with a sound understanding of the activities involved.

You should approach these as if they were your real campaign. Once you design the approach, modifying it for later update and use is very convenient.

Access to a computer word processor is an essential requirement. If you intend to utilize this approach, you will find a word processor to be extremely rewarding. You undoubtedly will be changing addresses and your cover letter frequently to be most effective.

Contact Data Base

Using directories, classified ads, trade publications, association membership lists, the WWW, and other sources of job leads, make a 100-name list of potential contacts and job lead prospects that are consistent with your career objectives. The address list should include organization name, division (if appropriate), contact's name, title, telephone number, city, state, and zip code.

Enter data into a word processor so it could easily be updated. You might also want to set up a field for the date you mailed your letter for record-keeping and follow-up purposes.

Develop a one-page cover letter that you intend to actually use. Insert this into your word processor, so that you can do a mail merge routine to develop your addressed and typed letter.

WHAT'S THE POSTAL SERVICE GONNA DO FOR REVENUE WHEN YOU DO FIND A JOB?

Contact Career Action Project. Print out a complete listing of your database. Print the date you intend to mail the letter and the follow-up date for your telephoning. Prepare a cover letter and a page explaining the sources used to develop the contact list.

Discuss why you feel this mailing list is best for your situation. Describe which technique for preparing your cover letter you plan to use and discuss why you adopted that approach. Give an estimate of the expected percentage of response you expect and how you arrived at this figure.

Prepare the advertising package that you plan to use to send to potential employers. Write your sales letter and resume in a broad enough style to apply to a variety of types of jobs but narrow enough to give employers an idea of your specific career interests.

Cover Letters

The cover letter is one of your most important tools in your job campaign. It is wise to experiment with several different designs initially. You may wish to customize a given design with a specifically prepared mailing list.

It would be wise to solicit the advice of your friends and career advisors on which design might be most appropriate for your unique data bases. Review the various formats suggested and review all of the samples before you start this project.

Make a list of your best action verbs, accomplishment statements, and personal qualities. Preparing the items to include before writing your rough draft aids you in making the letter flow smoothly and still cover all of the essential qualities.

Write your 3–5 achievement bulletpoints before you draft your first and last paragraphs. Step away and see what must go into 2–3 body paragraphs and/or your highlighted bulletpoints.

Cover Letter Action Project. Prepare three different, perfectly typed, one-page cover letters that you intend to consider using. Graphically format each letter differently by using bullet points with one and paragraphs with others. Highlight courses and functional skills differently.

Force yourself to use different formats and style. Remember that each one is a sales tool. Avoid just repeating the resume by expanding or summarizing only the most relevant and important skills and achievements.

Address each letter to a different person but one that is realistic for your potential situation. On a separate page, present an analysis of the three different letters. Are your qualities all noted? Did you include your key functional skills and highlight your accomplishments? Why would you select one of the designs over another design? Does one simply repeat the resume more than others?

Try to be very critical of each letter. Get a friend to help you with the critique. How do you intend to use these letters? What is your plan for dissemination (timing, targets, etc.)? Use a separate page for your distribution plan.

Writing this analysis should prove to be your most effective method of learning how to write cover letters.

This project should end up with 3 differently styled cover letters with a single page attached to each letter that explains its purpose, attachments, mailing lists, etc. Describe how and when you plan to use each letter.

125 S. Park Avenue
Salem, NC 00125
333-333-3333
June 20, xxxx

Mr. Scott Purdue
Vice President, Finance
ABC, Inc.
125 SW Research Park
Raleigh, NC 00245

Key Points

- Position

- Experience

- Reducing costs

- Increasing margin

- Leadership

- Technical skills

- Larger goals

- Get together

Dear Mr. Purdue:

I am seeking employment as a senior financial analyst, preferably in the electronics industry where I have two years of experience. ABC Inc. has been repeatedly recommended to me by Professor James Wine of Duke University who is a leader in the industry and in my area of expertise. Your respected development program and expanding growth potential prompts my inquiry.

My forté at XYZ has been responding to difficult problems and creating solutions to the problems. I have met several challenges by reducing cost overruns and increasing profit margins on marginal products. I believe that my efforts have helped us turn the corner.

A strong academic performance in my academic program and extensive leadership activities positively address my motivation and work ethics. My corporate internship further supports my interest in the industry. The course content below illustrates my skill base.

- Accounting — 9 hours
- Finance — 12 hours
- Computer Analysis — 6 hours
- Communications — 12 hours

The insightful two years at XYZ provide me a learning base, but I also want the longer term potential offered by a firm in a more growth oriented environment. Your firm would complement my academic and work background very well which would enable me to make a significant contribution in your financial area. The route to a controllership assignment in an operating facility is much more feasible than at XYZ.

I request an opportunity to show you how my credentials and your needs fit together. Would it be possible for us to get together someday next week? I will call you on Friday to see when a suitable time might be scheduled.

Sincerely,

Robert S. Wallstreet

Enclosure: Resume

Key Points

- Graduating

- Commercial sales

- Financial orientation

- Industry knowledge

- Leadership

- Transcript skills

- Relevant hobby

- Local contact

125 S. High Street
Columbus, OH 43210
333-337-3337
May 1, xxxx

Mr. James R. Big
Director of College Relations
Hewlett-Packard
Palo Alto, CA 94444

Dear Mr. Big:

In May I will be graduating from Ohio State with a degree in marketing supported by a strong set of courses in finance and computer applications. I am seeking a position in commercial sales which draws equally from my marketing and finance strengths. Your opportunity in calling on corporate financial managers for the purpose of selling financial software and hardware solutions excites me.

Hewlett Packard and other hardware vendors in the computer industry offer a unique opportunity to use many of my skills. My elected leadership activities and involvement in intramural team sports give you some clues to my personality and spirit. My unofficial transcript illustrates the depth and breadth of my skills and interests in your opportunity.

I read several popular computer magazines regularly and have stayed attuned to recent developments in microcomputers and related equipment throughout college. I work part-time at a local computer retailer dealing with everyone from hackers to local business owners. I follow e-commerce developments regularly.

The enclosed resume provides detail about my credentials and interests, but I need an opportunity to personally talk to you to best express how I can contribute to Hewlett Packard. Even if you could put me in contact with a local representative as a shadow for a day, my talents would be clearer. I will call you on Wednesday to see when we might be able to get together.

Sincerely,

Edward R. Bell

Enclosures: Resume
                Unofficial Transcript

Key Points

- Source

- Credentials

- Skills

- Self-description

- Alternate to
  experience

- Weak close

12345 Mason Parkway
Greenwood, IN 44444
812-444-4444
August 20, xxxx

Mr. U. R. Big
Employment Manager
Professional Software
111 Downtown Highrise
Pittsburgh, PA 15300

Dear Mr. Big:

I am interested in the analyst position which you advertised in the *TIMES* on
October 15. The requirements match my credentials extremely well. My
strengths and talents include:

- Earned a BS degree in finance from Purdue recently
- Worked 20 hours per week in college computer retail store
- Proficient with spreadsheet, data base, and desktop publishing software
- Proficient with many financial software packages
- Created several webpages
- Sold and serviced hardware and software to students
- Consistently ranked in top 10 percent of most of my related courses
- Excel in intramural team sports

Your position and my goals and abilities complement each other well in spite of
my lack of the two years of full-time experience you prefer. I learn fast, build
friendships easily, work well with colleagues, and assume responsibility carefully
which I feel may make up for my lack of the experience you want.

Please review my resume. I would appreciate a chance to tell you how I can
contribute effectively and produce handsomely in this job. My email is
jenkins.email.com which is the best way to reach me. I will call you soon.

Sincerely,

Bernice Jenkins

Enclosure: Resume

Key Points

- Name of recommender

- Technical orientation

- Degree and major

- Technical experience

- Industry relationship

- Skill support

- Meeting location

125 University Quad
Indiana University
Bloomington, IN 47400
812-735-5555
February 1, xxxx

Dr. Mary Brian Vice President of Research
New Horizons Communications
Research Center Park
Columbia, SC 27100

Dear Dr. Brian:

Dr. Charles Smith in the Indiana University Telecommunications Department informed me of your expansion plans into the satellite transmission business. The University has had a prototype project for the past two years that uses some of the technology that you may be employing, and I have been working part-time with the research equipment. I am interested in opening discussions with you about my possible employment in this new field. Your approach will add some needed competition in the industry.

I will earn a BS degree in physics from Indiana where I also did an interdisciplinary program with the Telecommunications Department. I assist two different professors with installation and research applications in both physics and telecommunications. We have been experimenting with both fiber optics and satellite data communications in conjunction with the University Research Computing Center.

My practical experience coupled with technical report writing and analytical skills has provided me a unique insight into the industry. My senior project involved intersatellite communications. My leadership in the Physics Club enabled me to attend the last National Telecommunications Association meeting in New York City.

My resume and detailed transcript are enclosed which should give you a strong assessment of my potential. I will call you next week to see if we can get together soon. Since I plan to attend the upcoming TRC meeting, which is being held near your facility, perhaps that might be an appropriate meeting time. Please email me at Lau@email.edu if you want further details on my skills before our meeting.

Sincerely,

Richard L. Lau

Enclosures: Resume
               Unofficial transcript
               Letter of recommendation from Professor Smith

University of Notre Dame
123 Blue Ridge Road
Notre Dame, IN 45555
January 10, xxxx

Key Points

- Capitalize on university

- Systems opening

- Technical qualifications

- Self-description

- Non-technical talents

- Follow-up plans

Mr. Ned Hill
Director of Information Systems
Aim Financial Services
INB Financial Center
Cleveland, OH 44444

Dear Mr. Hill:

The University Placement Office at Notre Dame recently posted an opening for a systems analyst in your computer center in Cleveland. Being from the vicinity, I know your organization well and feel that my June computer science degree might be of interest.

I have tried to merge my technical skills with some marketing and communication courses. Although I am proficient with several computer languages, my other strength is my ability to work with others, define problems, and present alternate solutions. I am very web proficient.

My activities reveal my talents in working in teams, prioritizing my time commitments, and communicating to large groups. My resume shows the wide variety of experiences that I have enjoyed at Notre Dame.

I would appreciate discussing my interests with you. I will call you within the week to schedule an interview. Please contact me via email at mills@email.com.

Sincerely,

Scott Mills

Enclosure: Resume

Key Points

- Name dropping

- Labor position

- Confidence

- Related experience

- Commitment

- Targeted resume

- Strong wrap-up

- Anxious to talk

- Postscript emphasis

Rock Berry Hall
Evansville, Illinois 47205
812-344-8888
May 5, xxxx

Mr. J. B. Price
Labor Relations Manager
Golden Enterprises, Inc.
Chicago, Illinois 50121

Dear Mr. Price:

Dr. C. Randall Powell, Professor of Business Administration at Indiana University, recently suggested that I write you concerning your opening and my interest in a labor relations assistant position. With a B.S. degree in human resource management and courses in labor economics, collective bargaining, and labor law, I am confident that I could make a positive contribution in the position.

The last two summers, I worked as a general laborer on a production line, once in a unionized shop and once in an unorganized plant. My ability to appreciate several points of view on labor problems should prove to be a major asset in my future career performance. Before I left my last summer job, my supervisor had recommended that I be hired as a first-line foreman after graduation. Although I am enthusiastic about the foreman's position, I think my energies and resourcefulness might be better suited to tactfully handling union-management problems as a third party in the grievance steps. This assignment has been a four-year goal for me in college.

My attached resume better highlights my education and experience. My leadership roles in campus politics should strengthen and support my abilities to serve as a labor relations assistant.

I am anxious to talk with you because I feel I can show you why I am a strong candidate for the position. I have friends in Chicago that I could stay with on weekends so any Friday or Monday would be ideal for an appointment. In three days I will call you to see if your schedule might be open. I look forward to our getting together soon. If you need additional information, please call, write, or email me.

Very truly yours,

James J. Aggressive
aggressive@email.com

Enclosure

P.S. Dr. Powell indicated that it was okay for me to invite you to contact him for a recommendation at 812-336-5317 or powell@email.com.

Marketing Opportunity

1400 N. Maple Lane
Bloomington, IN 47401
812-335-5555
outgoing@email.com
January 13, xxxx

Key Points

- Contact source

- Credentials

- Work ethics

- External
  orientation

- Achievements

- Specific
  appointment

- Copied contacts

- PS for credibility

Ms. U. R. Fashion
Manager, Organizational Development
High Fashion Stores, Inc.
Chicago, IL 60601

Dear Ms. Fashion:

I received your name from the Career Services Office at Indiana University where I am earning a bachelor degree in English. Professor Smith encouraged me to write you about being considered for your executive development program which starts in June.

Although I am not a business graduate, I have many of the other qualifications which you outlined in your website. I have been involved in a leadership capacity in several activities on campus and have worked as a part-time sales clerk in a local specialty shop for the past year. I am familiar with the basic retail sales functions of display, marking, inventories, cash control, advertising, etc. but I need the buyer's perspective.

I really enjoy the public contact and servicing the customer, but I want to get more experience in the buying function, supervision, and general management. As vice president of my sorority, I learned much about management skills. This encouraged me to take two courses in business (accounting and retail marketing) which should help my understanding of your business operations.

I hope to graduate in the top twenty percent of my class. My resume is enclosed.

I hope that we can get together. My personal plans call for a trip to Chicago later next month. Would it be possible for us to meet on February 20? I will call you or your secretary next Tuesday to set up a specific appointment time. Please feel free to contact me at 812-335-5555 or email me if that date is inconvenient. I sincerely appreciate your consideration.

Sincerely yours,

Susan Outgoing

Enclosures

cc: Professor J.B. Smith
University Career Services Office

Pleasant View Hall
Floyd Knobs, Indiana
812-427-7777
career@email.com
February 24, xxxx

Key Points

- Trade journal

- Credentials

- Career interest

- Personal
  orientation

- Related work

- Skills

- Request material

- Call for
  appointment

Mr. J. B. Money, President
First National Bank
First and Walnut
Hoosierland, Indiana 45201

Dear Mr. Money:

In reply to your classified ad in the *Hoosier Banker,* I would like to apply for the Branch Manager Trainee position. I will graduate from DePauw University with an economics major in December.

Because of some part-time work experience in related areas and academic courses in the field, I am very familiar with the various assignments in banking which is my basic career interest. I read the book, *The Money Changers,* last year, which was recommended by a professor here and was very unhappy with the journalistic liberties taken by Mr. Haley, but I learned a lot which stimulated my interest. The recent article in *Fortune* on women officers in banking convinced me that I made the right decision.

During my first three years at DePauw, I worked as a part-time teller at the University Credit Union. During summers, I worked as a clerk/secretary, basically filling in as vacation relief in several jobs. Beginning my senior year I worked part-time in the Bursar's Office doing odd jobs dealing with dash balances, fee collections, auditing statements, calling on bad debts, report writing, etc. I have taken courses in money and banking, financial institutions, and two courses in accounting and finance which I took at night school during summers at home.

Because of my desire to locate in a smaller community like yours, I am especially interested in your job. Although it is three months before graduation, I want to make a decision fairly soon. Would you please send me an application and more information about the job and community? I am available for an interview any Monday or Friday, which are my lightest class days. I will call you for an appointment as soon as I receive the application.

Sincerely yours,

Jane Career

Apartment 22
Stone Hill Estates
Arcola, Ohio 32064
317-222-2222
catt@email.com
February 27, xxxx

Key Points

- Question opening

- Targeted field

- Personal qualities

- Industry interest

- Maturity

- Regional interview

- Will call

Mr. C. B. Executive
Human Resources Manager
Professional Pharmaceuticals
Middletown, Michigan 47720

Dear Mr. Executive:

Do you have an opening for a sales representative? With a B.S. degree in marketing and ten hours of chemistry courses at Ohio State University, I think that my academic qualifications and personality are well suited for a career in pharmaceutical marketing.

Two summers and many part-time jobs in sales-related positions have convinced me that sales is the best entry-level position for me to begin my career as a future marketing executive. I value the freedom and independence that you offer an individual after your training program which I read about on your careers website. Each of my previous employers will tell you that I work hard and thrive under pressure and challenge. Although I have not been active in campus life as a leader because I have had to work to get through school, every work supervisor has expressed pleasure at my enthusiasm to serve customers.

In my last experience at Super Drugs, I worked for a pharmacist and talked with several salesmen who called on us. They all commented on the individual rewards of working in the health-related industry. The attached resume only brushes the surface of my qualifications so I hope I have the opportunity to elaborate on my credentials in person.

I am willing to work hard, study, learn, and take responsibility. May I have the privilege of an interview? Since we are several hundred miles apart, would it be possible for me to schedule an initial interview with any of your salesmen in this region? I plan to call you within the week to see if something might possibly be arranged. I need a chance to start as a sales representative because I know I can advance on my own merits with Professional Pharmaceuticals. Please contact me if you need more information.

Very truly yours,

Morris Catt

Enclosure

Key Points

- Attention
- Humor
- Credentials
- Confidence
- Self-description
- Personal ad
- Comparing
- Contact

301 N. Indiana Avenue
Bloomington, IN 47401
812-333-3333
funn@email.com
October 4, xxxx

Mr. A. G. President
President
President Advertising Agency
1000 N. Michigan
Chicago, IL 60604

Dear Mr. President:

Advertising's my bag and I'm ready for your game. Aim at me if you want a self-starter and go-getter. For a job as a copy writer/account executive, I offer the following credentials.

- Degree in communications
- Top grades
- Marketing orientation
- Leadership potential
- Gregarious personality
- Pleasing appearance
- Aggressiveness
- Determination

They tell me that no jobs exist in advertising unless you know somebody who knows somebody important. Unfortunately, the important people who know me don't know you. But I am important and I want to work for you.

Getting a job in advertising is exciting, challenging, and real hard work. It is really testing my communication skills.

Notice the advertising brochure on Roger (some call it a resume). This tacky approach is unique, original, and funny, yet truthful, and I hope it gets my foot into your door. The ad I write for *Advertising Age* cost too much to print, and my old resume wasn't me and hit too many circular files. I'm bettin' on this approach.

I want to work for you and need an interview. You can contact me by returning the handy tear-away order form on the resume brochure (the enclosed coupon will get you a discount). I would like to hear from you soon. To avoid C.O.D. charges, you can expedite matters by calling 812-337-6660 collect today. You can also visit my flashy website at www.funntimes.com and email comments from the site.

Very truly yours,

R. U. Funn

Enclosure

Key Points

- Ad source

- Achievement

- Mutual interests

- Credentials

- Recognition

- Leader

- Match

- Get together

1000 S. Montana Road
Covington, Virginia 20000
525-525-2525
success@email.com
May 1, xxxx

Mr. James Wise, President
ABM Corporation
1 City Square
Superdeal, Wisconsin 10229

Dear Mr. Wise:

Your ad in the *Wall Street Journal* for a vice president of marketing caught my eye. Last year my management ability helped double the sales output of my division while we cut selling costs by 20 percent. A much-needed system of cost controls and implementation of an incentive pay program helped turn around a stagnant growth record in my new division.

I would like to discuss our mutual interests. Although our industries are very different, there are many striking similarities. I believe that my ten years of sales and marketing experience can produce results for you. Briefly, my credentials include the following:

- Technical product knowledge
- Sales management experience
- Record of sales achievement
- Hundreds of recognitions
- E-commerce experience

- Purdue University
- Industrial management
- Salesperson of the Year
- Competitive spirit
- web expertise

My enclosed resume fills in some details which I know you will want to confirm. I am proud of my record. I am looking for the "right" step upward. Your company is a recognized leader in the industry, and I have admired the professionalism of your people that I have met. Your job description given in the ad matches my qualifications and goals precisely and I like the web based marketing that you have been using.

We need to get together. I will call you next week for an appointment. If you need to get together sooner, call me at home any evening (7:00 – 10:00 p.m.). I look forward to our getting together.

Sincerely yours,

J. R. Successful

Enclosure
P.S. Please browse to www.abm.com/products to see some of my recent innovations.

421 E. Fourteenth Street
Apartment D-4
South Bend, Indiana 47401
317-317-3131
favors@email.com
April 2, xxxx

Key Points

Mr. U. I. Alumnus, Partner
CPA & Associates
Woodward and High Streets
Detroit, MI 38251

Dear Mr. Alumnus:

- Alumni referral

- Guidance

- Solid achiever

- Strong work
  ethic

- Location
  rationale

- SASA easy
  reply

- Collect call

- Request leads

My accounting professor, Dr. Curt Brown, was recently counseling me on my interest in joining a regional public accounting firm in the Detroit area. I expect to receive a bachelor's degree in accounting from Notre Dame in June. Professor Brown said that you might be able to offer some guidance since you had the same problem a few years ago when you were here.

I have not been an academic superstar, but I have never earned anything less than a "B" grade in accounting, either. I have worked 20 hours each week as a night auditor for the University Union for the past two years which has limited my extracurricular activities, but working got me through college. During my first two years here, I was quite involved in organizing an intramural softball league for women but wound up umpiring because I needed the money.

Because my fiancé has found an excellent job opportunity with an automotive firm, we have decided to locate in the Detroit area. I am interested in joining a small to medium size public accounting firm. Since few firms that size actively recruit, I need some help in identifying some of the better prospects in the area. My enclosed resume explains why I think I am best suited for this type of firm.

Enclosed is a stamped, self-addressed envelope. Could you take a minute of your time to jot down some appropriate contacts for me? Based on Dr. Brown's comments, I would especially be interested in learning more about your firm. If you think that there is a chance for employment in your firm, would you please give me a collect call? I can get to Detroit on a day's notice. I thank you in advance for any help you can give me. If you prefer to use email, I can get back to you even faster.

Sincerely,

I.O.U. Favors

Enclosure

Key Points

- Credentials
- Position referenced
- Extensive experience
- Job knowledge
- Specific week
- Calling for time

3950 Forest Avenue
Columbus, Ohio 42222
317-317-3131
hall@email.com
May 15, xxxx

Mr. Robert Nelson
American Machine Tool Company
639 Christopal Drive
Boston, Massachusetts 00231

Dear Mr. Nelson:

I will be graduating from the Ohio State University with a Bachelor of Science degree in Mechanical Engineering this June. Dr. Green, Career Services Director, advised me to contact you directly concerning a position you have open in Research and Development Engineering.

As my enclosed resume indicates, I have had extensive experience in the machine tool business. My work has included the use of physical test equipment, calibration and application of such equipment to solve manufacturing problems, investigation of field service complaints, and complete engineering tests of prototype numerical control lathes and new design machine units.

My experience covers a broad range of engineering functions which I can further develop with your company to our mutual benefit. I am great at using the www to find technical solutions.

I will be in Boston for about five days in early July. If acceptable, I will call you on June 15 to arrange a convenient time for an interview. I am very interested in working for your company, and I am eager to discuss how I might contribute to your further development.

Very truly yours,

Tom T. Hallgreen

Enclosure

P.S. My website URL is www.hallsshop.com. It will illustrate some of my R&D interests.

Key Points

- Establishes experience

- Academic background

- Related experiences

- Management talents

- Sensitivity

- Quality references

- Calling soon

25 N. University Avenue
Columbia, Missouri 50250
314-314-3131
bragg@email.com
February 15, xxxx

Mr. James Shoemaker
Director of Platform Engineering
General Motors Corporation
11 Grease Street
Detroit, Michigan 42051

Dear Mr. Shoemaker:

I graduated five years ago from the University of Missouri with a degree in Mechanical Engineering and a minor in Business Administration. After reading your advertisement for the "Engineering Supervisor" position posted at the University of Missouri, I am pleased to submit to you my qualifications in the attached resume.

The key to the success of any operation, I feel, is in the attitude of the workers. My experience in construction management, as a construction supervisor on the Valley Nuclear Power Project, has allowed me to develop effective supervisory and motivational skills. I have established a functional rapport with organized labor on site, from labor superintendents to trade apprentices. This job has demanded accurate problem solving and crystal clear instructive communication.

My experience at Chrysler Corporation in St. Louis has not only provided me with insight into large-scale production procedures and problems, but has allowed me an overview of production from the corporate management point of view. As a result, I am aware of the capabilities along with the limitations of a large-scale automotive production operation.

Having some background in football coaching and as a classroom instructor, I am sensitive to the special obstacles encountered in transforming an inexperienced worker into a productive one. Human relations is one of my strengths.

The experiences mentioned above could prove to be most beneficial in the effective management and smooth operation of your work force. I urge you to contact my former employers listed in the reference section of the attached resume. I look forward to having a chance to talk with you further on this important matter. I shall call you next week after you have had an opportunity to review my application.

Sincerely yours,

James R. Bragg

Enclosure

2375 N. College Road
Pace, New York 00900
919-919-9191
hope@email.com
May 20, xxxx

Key Points

- Employee referral

- Prestigious institution

- Technical talents

- Design engineer

- Calling date

Mr. Frank Short
Director of Engineering
Aerospace Design, Inc.
Phoenix, Arizona 89345

Dear Mr. Short:

At the recent manufacturing exhibit in New York City, I became intrigued with your new nose cone design. One of your engineers (Mr. Charles Shears) and I had some interesting discussions about some potential applications which I have been investigating. When I told Mr. Shears that I was a recent graduate of New York Technical Institute, he mentioned that you might have an opening on your staff.

I have just received a master's degree in mechanical engineering. I have some experience from my co-op work and a graduate assistantship which relate to the type of work you are doing. My attached resume explains this in more detail. When you visit my website at www.hope.edu you will see my fascination with satellite launchings.

Mr. Shears indicated that he would recommend that you follow up with me. I would very much like to come to Phoenix and discuss the possibilities of my employment as a design engineer with you. After reviewing my resume and talking with Mr. Shears, I hope that you will decide to allow me the privilege of an interview. I will call you on June 1 to see if we can arrange a suitable interview date.

Very truly yours,

I. M. Hopeful

Enclosure

Key Points

- Source

- Family reasons

- Background match

- Achievement record

- Specific date

11 S. High Street
Macon, Kentucky 42000
502-502-0202
hart@email.com
May 5, xxxx

Mr. U. R. Big
Employment Manager
International Chemicals
1000 South Grant Street
Chicago, Illinois 60601

Dear Mr. Big:

Your ad for a Chemical Engineer in the *Chicago Tribune* prompts this inquiry. For family reasons, I find I must leave Kentucky Chemical under the most amicable conditions to return to the Chicago vicinity.

My enclosed resume presents certain aspects of my technical background which appear to coincide with your needs. My technical training at Illinois Tech and work experience in industrial solvents run parallel to the description you provided in the ad.

My chemical engineering degree includes an internship in the laboratory of one of your major competitors. My two years of chemical engineering experience includes brief exposures to field technical service, product analysis, and, most recently, process control and supervision. My two promotions indicate the positive achievement record which I have earned.

I can be in Chicago any Friday or Monday with a minimum amount of notice. I would like an interview to show you my credentials. I will call you or your secretary on May 10 for a specific appointment time. Please feel free to call me at work at 502-666-1333 if you need to reach me before May 10. My employer is aware of my need to relocate to Chicago soon.

Very truly yours,

Jane Smith-Hart

Enclosure

R. R. 13, Box 64
Minniville, Ohio 34260
525-525-5252
around@email.com
December 10, xxxx

Mr. J. Paul Big
Manager of College Relations
Gusher Petroleum
Houston, Texas 76106

Dear Mr. Big:

Your advertisement on the Jobtrak website prompted me to contact you about consideration for a position in chemical engineering. I will receive a bachelor of science degree in biology from Ohio State University in June.

Before you pitch this letter because I am not an engineer, please take a look at my credentials on the enclosed resume. I rank near the top of my class, am senior class president, am captain of the reserve rugby team, am experienced in laboratory techniques, and have organized and supervised a student government project of leasing mini-refrigerators to dorm residents.

I have read the job descriptions for chemical engineers in various employment websites for companies in the drug, chemical, petroleum, and agri-business industries. I have also reviewed some engineering textbooks of my chemical engineering friends. I have the courses, skills, and interest to handle all work assignments even though I don't have the exact degree you are seeking.

My background consists of 18 hours of chemistry, 6 hours in physics, 12 hours in math, and 30 hours in the biological sciences. My advisor, Dr. I. M. Smart, is encouraging me to go to graduate school, but I am more interested in utilizing my background in a practical setting than in a research setting. I also have interests in quality control and production supervision of technical products.

I prefer to locate in your area and am trying to determine if a 1,000-mile trip in late January is worth the cost. I do have relatives with whom I can stay. If you can offer the slightest encouragement to me, I am willing to pay for a trip to the area. Please check the appropriate boxes and return via email. I shall look forward to your reply and hopefully a personal interview. Thank you for your interest and consideration. I will call you after you return this note.

Very truly yours,

C. U. Around

☐ Call for an appointment   ☐ Recontact in _____ weeks
☐ Stop in when you get here   ☐ No present background match
☐ Call when arrive in town   ☐ Return application blank
☐ Click here to launch back to me.

Encl.
P.S. Visit my web to verify my credentials at www.around.com!

Key Points

- Source

- Not perfectly qualified

- Achievements

- High interest

- Courses

- Location

- Survey

- Follow-up

Job Search Systems:

Process — Market — Services

Where are the best job hunting grounds? You need a hunting guide. Your best guide is an understanding of how the job hunting systems work.

The career search system is a complex *marketing* concept. Several components form the framework around which you must design a strategy to find an immediate job opening.

Your goal is to make the job search system work for you. The degree to which you will have success in finding the right job depends upon your awareness of the job search system and how to make it work for your unique situation.

The system involves the following activities:

1. Setting your goals
2. Understanding your needs
3. Developing your tools
4. Knowing the process steps
5. Attacking job leads
6. Influencing the hidden market
7. Designing the role of others
8. Executing a plan

Your approach involves both strategic considerations and tactical plans. The longer viewpoint sets the overall parameters and the shorter plan addresses your more immediate actions.

Planning the Job Search Process

A job search strategy starts with an *objective*. No plan ever reaches fulfillment without a goal.

Far too many job seekers plunge into job hunting without setting meaningful goals. Most of them simply want better jobs and more money. Life is too short to spend it wandering around from job to job trying to just earn a living.

Effective job hunting begins with career planning. Personal satisfaction comes when you find a position that perfectly matches your skills, values, interests, and personal qualities.

Establish a Job Goal

When you approach the job market, broad career goals must mesh with reality. The job market is composed of specifics. The specifics range from entry-level jobs to top-level executive assignments in hundreds of different types of organizations and functions.

Assessing where you are, exploring the options, and setting a goal that is a reasonable compromise between reality and personal concerns is the essence of career planning.

Jobs are filled by job title. Acceptance of a specific job today does not pigeon-hole you for a lifetime. A specific job should be selected because of the options it will open later. Planning ahead is important.

Obtaining multiple offers for a particular type of job is your short-run goal. A job search strategy is a short-term method that fits within an overall long-term career plan. A career often implies many jobs with many different employers.

Function. Many immediate job objectives are very specific. Even the function and department is often specified. Accounting, finance, marketing, manufacturing, engineering, research, and administration are the basic functions of any type of organization.

Being specific narrows the choice to such a degree that an employer's decision is greatly simplified and thus more likely to produce the results you desire.

Industry. Many jobs exist in only certain industry groups. Most teachers are employed by local school boards, and most retail store buyers work in the retail industry. Many people develop expertise in their functional field and then further relate it to a given industry which builds in job security and career potential.

In many cases, it is unwise to leave an industry where such an accumulation of knowledge has been beneficial to career advancement because employers within the area of expertise are much more willing to pay more and recognize your unique combination of abilities.

Location. Not only must you decide what you want to do, but you must also decide *where* you want to do it. In our society, employment is often localized. Even in an organization with international operations and scores of locations, hiring decisions invariably are made at the local level.

Supervisors want to personally hire the people who will work for them. If they do not specifically hire the new person, supervisors want to feel that they had some input into the decision. It is a rare situation where a manager in one location, even the home office, can hire for a manager in another location.

This grassroots hiring concept means that you have to make a decision about *where* you want to practice your particular expertise before starting the search

Most resumes and cover letters state the title of the position which you are currently seeking.

You must interview at the specific hiring location because supervisors prefer to personally hire their own staff.

RIGHT NOW I'M LIVING IN A TEEPEE IN THE AZORES, BUT YOU CAN REACH ME BY MOBILE PHONE.

process. Once you have decided on what you want to do and where you want to do it, the stage is set for implementing a basic job search.

Job Hunting Process

Have you ever wondered how the phrase "job hunting" ever got started? Hunting implies that there is an adversarial role: a hunter and a prey. The job search process does involve two parties, but the goal is one of mutual satisfaction. Two parties are attempting to get together to help each other. An adversary relationship is about as far from the truth as it can be.

Your Problem. Some of the hardest work you will ever do is the work you put into finding employment. The right employer often seems to elude you. The search process is not always an enjoyable activity. Rejection for a job is a major ego-deflating experience.

The search process can take months and cost several thousand dollars if you include lost earnings during the search process. Job hunting is so discouraging and frustrating for some people that they choose to remain in less than ideal job situations rather than attempt to change.

Employer's Problem. The employer often reads through mountains of paperwork and conducts hundreds of interviews just to find one person for a given job. Once an employer generates a job opening for which you are the perfect match, that employer has no systematic way of identifying you from the masses of people (most of whom are unqualified for the position).

The employer can only publicize an opening and hope that a person like you will apply. That is an extremely passive role. In addition, publicizing the opportunity only adds to the problem because so many unqualified applicants respond hoping that the employer will compromise the publicized specifications.

The employer is locked into screening applicants—talking to whomever happens into the office and reading whatever resumes come across the desk or in the email file. In an effort to find you, the employer sorts through hundreds of poorly qualified applicants. Because of a pressing need and a deadline, the two of you may never connect.

Clearinghouse. There is no central clearinghouse. Even when computerized, the right matches seem to elude employers and applicants. The *subjective* factors needed in a job often play havoc with sophisticated computerized matching systems.

Although the internet has greatly facilitated the search process, the volume of information to review is still overwhelming.

The www is very important in your job search but it is not a perfect solution. You still must get your credentials to the right person.

Finding the solution to this dilemma is your responsibility. You must throw your qualifications into the path of the employer's often undirected search.

By following some time-tested strategies and employing some effective techniques, you can bring the right parties together. There are many fewer employers than employees, so you have a far better chance of finding the right employer than vice versa. The www facilitates your locating the right decision maker.

Cost Considerations. A good job search plan takes time to develop and implement. It is also expensive. If you are unemployed, that cost can be an emotional barrier.

To avoid adding stress to an already difficult situation, you must make plans ahead of time to deal with the financial aspects of job searching.

The "Estimated Search Expenses" provides a list of the expenses normally incurred in a job campaign. Look at the items that pertain to your situation.

Your mission is to bring your desires to the attention of people who need the talents that you have to offer.

```
. . . . . . . . . . . . . ESTIMATED SEARCH EXPENSES . . . . . . . . . . . .

        Resume typing/software          $_____
        Resume printing                 _____
        Cover letter typing             _____
        Postage                         _____
        Telephone calls                 _____
        Travel                          _____
        Personal expenses               _____
        Periodicals                     _____
        Publications                    _____
        Career seminars                 _____
        Agency fees                     _____
        Counseling fee                  _____
        Clothing                        _____
        Other                           _____
                            Total       $_____

                    . . . . . . . . . .
                        Figure 14.1
```

Rough-out a plan for eight to twelve weeks—the normal time frame for changing jobs.

The typical job search takes 90 to 120 days, or about three months for budgeting purposes. After looking at the bottom line, make a detailed source of funds statement for estimating your financial resources during your search period. Planning ahead will greatly relieve some major stress later. Always try to hold your current job while looking for a new job.

You should keep very accurate records of what you spend on your job search. All legitimate expenses are often tax deductible if you are currently employed.

Communication Tools

Your *resume* represents your skills, interests, and aptitudes. It helps you be many places at once.

Your resume is disseminated in such a manner as to "get in the way of" the right employer. All that you have to do is to get the employer's attention for the few seconds it takes to realize that you are the perfect person and ideal match.

A *cover letter* should be the extra pizzazz that opens the employer's eyes. It brings your resume to life. A well-prepared cover letter motivates the employer to read your resume in depth.

Your resume and cover letter are the main features in your personal promotion materials.

In essence, these two brief documents team up to serve as your personal advertisement. The package permits the employer to screen out unqualified applicants and screen you into further consideration.

A well-designed resume and carefully worded cover letter are your most important means of communicating with potential employers. Your investment of time and money in this sales and promotion package returns benefits for years if it is properly formulated and disseminated.

Hiring Sequence

The employment process is simple in concept but cumbersome in practice. Two parties must recognize the contribution that each can offer to the other. Both parties *want* to get together.

Both parties mobilize their efforts to attract each other by extending "antennas" that reach into each other's world. This continuous, directed, yet random reaching eventually results in contact. Once there is contact, communication begins.

Many critics of this hiring sequence stand aghast at the inefficiency of it all. Critics for decades have decried the seeming chaos of the system but, in spite of the outcries, the archaic monster rides on. The critics have yet to offer any better solution despite the fact that their words often sound good.

Most critics admonish you to take charge of your life rather than let the system dictate your fate. Nonetheless, whatever advice unfolds, the bottom line is always bringing together the two parties. Advice only differs on how to improve the likelihood of the paths of the parties crossing.

Once the awareness of a possible match occurs, a sequence of hiring steps occur. These steps are direct and simple to comprehend and influence.

Introductory Interview. Based upon the resume and cover letter, the employer contacts you and invites you to interview for the position you are seeking. A time and place for the meeting is arranged.

In some instances, a third party is instrumental in making the physical arrangements. The employer may be represented by a personnel representative, the employee to whom the hired person will report, or another employee of the firm.

The purpose of introductory interviews is to initially screen candidates. They are normally less than an hour in length and sometimes they are conducted by telephone. Rarely do job offers for technical, professional, and managerial positions immediately follow introductory interviews.

An evaluation is completed on the candidate. A recommendation is made to continue discussions or to conclude considerations at this stage.

Follow-up Interview.   If the introductory interview is successful, you will be invited back for more extensive and intensive interviews. You are normally interviewed by several people, including your potential supervisor and someone from the human resources department.

Some organizations pay for any expenses you may incur for travel, lodging, and food when discussions reach the follow-up interview stage. This is not a universal policy but it has wide acceptance.

Job Offer.   The decision to extend a job offer is normally a *consensus decision*. In education, the decision is often recommended by a selection committee. In business and government, there is an evaluation by each person who interviewed you. Your acceptance of the job offer completes the hiring sequence.

The Decision-Makers.   The most important person you have to impress is the key job decision-maker, usually the person to whom you would eventually report. That is the person who has the power to hire or fire you. The smaller the organization, the more likely it is that this is one person.

Organizations employing 50 or more people (or smaller government units) usually base an employment decision for managerial-level personnel on the consensus of two to five people.

Be careful in trying to identify who the chief decision-maker really is. Power in an organization rarely rests with only one person. Higher-ranking people are frequently strongly influenced by the well-reasoned opinions of subordinates. As an interviewee, you must please everyone because any one person could have the influence to blackball you.

Web Job Contacts

Contacts are everything in the sophisticated job search. Networking and targeted job search strategies only work well when the "customer" is pre-selected. The secret is boiling it down to the right contacts and wisely approaching the best assets.

The web is invaluable in finding the needle in the haystack. The needle locator is the search engine. The haystack is the mass of databases. The needle is the perfect job for you.

Your task is to learn to use the web to locate the perfect set of contacts. It is not complicated but it does take time. Some job-hunters and employers will always pay others to do this not so exciting work. Employment agencies and search firms will not disappear but you can bet they will do much of their research on the web also. Whether you are a job-hunter or employer, you now can opt to do your own work.

The web is making the job market much more efficient. It is another tool. It is not a panacea. Contacts are everything!

To aid in your search, a tidbit of information is offered on each site but your best choice is to click the sites that even come close to meeting your needs. One person's joy is another's loathing so beware of the "site ratings." It only takes a few seconds to check out each site.

Most sites stay alive on revenues from ads online. If the site stinks, the marketplace will force it to disappear.

The best sites bring job seekers and employers together. The communication links vary widely.

- e-mail (very common)
- confidential "headless resumes"
- snail mail exchanges

- telephone linkages
- middle people facilitators

The old cover letter and resume are not dead. The exchange media is simply changing for certain parties. That clever cover letter and creative resume usefulness will probably never disappear. The delivery vehicle is just changing. In spite of the chat room hopes, the interview is hardly going to disappear either.

The number of search variables is massive. You name your search criteria and you can bet that some job search engine has it. Some of the most common search criteria are listed below.

There are basic components in most sites:

- job listing
- resume posting
- search advice
- virtual career fairs

It is captivating. You can easily get absorbed in information overload. Job hunters and employers used to pay dearly for this virtually unlimited information and databases. Rarely should you have to pay anything. Beware of sites asking for fees. There is a lot of good stuff for free.

A growing number of job listing and resume available sites provide overlapping links to each other. The online job seeker is often swamped with a vast array of job posting indexed by location, industry, job function, skills desired, experience factors, salary, etc.

Online job hunting involves lots of keyword searching and page hopping. Flashy graphical images attract your interest. Incidently, you may want to set your browser to *not* automatically load graphical images. If loading time is not of major importance though, let these glitzy images flow. They can be fun to watch and they might serve their purpose: to help identify the right job for you.

Making Contact

You have identified those special organizations and people who can help in your job search. Now, how can you get the all-important address, phone, fax, email, and other contacting data?

The WWW can help there also. Let your computer mouse do the walking. The many web sources will help you track down the perfect contact. You only need to visit the website of a major college career services office to help you identify the best links for specific contacts. Start with your college's website.

Influencing the Job Market

At any point in time, positions needing your qualifications exist somewhere. The job market is one vast pool of available job openings. For a number of reasons, some labor market job pools are less visible than others.

Not all job opening notices reach the mass publicity market. Many experts refer to this less visible pool of jobs as the "hidden job market." Other jobs may not ever be publicized because a unique job is created to fit a special person's credentials.

Visible Openings

Most experts acknowledge that less than 15 percent of all job openings are ever listed. Therefore, it is not surprising that about 90 percent of all job seekers ask for consideration for only 15 percent of the jobs. Just because a job is not advertised does not mean you cannot be considered for that opportunity.

The visible openings are the job openings which the average person sees advertised. You may see them advertised in various media, read of them on the www and in newspaper articles, or hear stories circulating about jobs in certain organizations or career fields. The visible openings are the jobs about which you are most likely to hear information.

Most jobs are never advertised.

The reason certain openings are so visible is that employers must use the mass media to attract qualified applicants to apply. In most occupations at the technical, professional, and managerial level, that approach is not usually necessary.

An arrangement of publicizing the job to a *specific* target audience may exist. You have access to information through avenues other than the mass media channels of communications. This is your hidden market access.

Hidden Job Market

Only a very small percentage of jobs are ever widely publicized. Many jobs are publicized in less obvious ways. However, the fact that all jobs are not widely advertised does not imply any sinister, underhanded dealings by employers either.

Most estimates place the number of "hidden jobs" at about 85 percent of all available openings during any time period.

The hidden job market represents about 85 percent of all jobs open in a year.

What are these "hidden jobs"? There are several categories. Jobs for which there are always more applications on file than could reasonably be made available form one group. Why publicize an opening if you already have a file of well-qualified applicants?

Publicizing some types of jobs on an open basis invites hundreds of unqualified applicants to apply. For example, publicizing an opening for a "personnel assistant" would generate several hundred resumes. A more prudent publicity effort might be to identify five schools known for turning out top-notch human resource graduates. It might be wise to approach only two faculty members at each school for referrals. Another approach might be to limit recruiting to a national HR association meeting where many well-qualified people would be present.

The internet certainly has opened access to formerly "hidden" jobs. Yet the number of employers not using the job media is still high. Even within the web community, you need to know how to source the specific job lead.

Specialized channels of information distribution characterize the hidden job market. It is not the "old boy" system of yesteryear that restricted entry to the better jobs to a special clique, but it is true that only certain people know about job openings.

```
· · · · · · · MOST COMMON INTERVIEW GENERATING ACTIVITY · · · · · · ·


        Direct Mail Solicitations          5 – 10%
        Responding to Ads                  5 – 10%
        Responding to Web Ads              5 – 10%
        Job Fairs                          5 – 10%
        Third Party Reference             10 – 20%
        Networking                        70 – 80%

        (percentage varies by size and type of employer/function)

                    · · · · · · · · · · ·
                        Figure 14.2
```

The informal grapevine information network is often more productive than the sophisticated advertising techniques used in the popular media.

Another reason some positions are not publicized is because some employers have internal posting systems. Current employees, regardless of rank, get first shot at higher-level positions

The promote-from-within policy is popular. Over time, this policy will cause most openings for technical, professional and managerial positions to be at the entry level in mature organizations. The new, smaller, rapidly-growing organizations offer opportunities to higher-level job seekers, so they tend to recruit employees from the more established firms.

It is useless to publicize some openings. Some jobs are not desirable, and the talent for others is so sparse than no applications would be generated via the listing anyway.

Some jobs do not receive publicity because the employer elects to assign the selection chore on an exclusive basis to an employment agency or search firm. Job agencies may already have well-oiled machines of contacts by which they spread the word, so there is no need to advertise openings by either the employer or the placement service.

Hidden Market Entré

Regardless of the reason, most jobs are not listed. Consequently, you will have to find a way around that roadblock.

The main way to get into this market is to market yourself. You can gain entry by publicizing yourself to people who are in the channels of information dissemination used by employers. The secret is to get your credentials to the right people. This involves a continuous and systematic approach of reaching out to others.

The most used publicity technique of employers is simple: *It is word of mouth.* Word of mouth publicity is thus the most important technique you can use. It is the most important technique for employers, so you must enter that scene too. Manage to get your story told in the right circles.

The internet facilitates the networking but it cannot replace word of mouth. You must learn to use the www as another one of your job search tools but recognize the word of mouth power.

Most job openings are filled through the informal grapevine.

Your access to the hidden job market is through other people. Word of mouth fills most jobs.

Job Creation - Timing

Not only are most jobs seemingly hidden, but some do not exist at the *time* you apply. Your skills and background may have great value, yet there may not be a traditional job for which employers have recognized sufficient economic return to justify hiring your kind of talent.

Occasionally, an enterprising employer may see a lucrative monetary return from a certain unique talent possessed by you. When this happens, the employer may make a spot for you by creating a position that fits your credentials.

Would you hire yourself and work on commission? Do you have confidence in the contribution you can offer? If you have a unique skill, would you like to work for yourself? You might make more money than if you work for someone else.

An employer must make a profit to remain solvent. The profit motive is what causes an employer to create a new position.

There are many reasons why you might prefer to work for an employer rather than attempt to go into business on your own. The unique service you offer may not be easily marketable to the public.

If the service is marketable, working for others relieves you of the accounting, marketing, and other functions which may not be your strong suits. It is often worth it to work for someone else rather than do all the other things that you are not capable of (or do not enjoy) doing.

Employers rarely create a job just to fit your credentials but it does occasionally happen if you have a significant contribution to make.

Jobs are not created easily. An employer analyzes the situation a long time before adding a new expenditure. After all, the organization is probably running well without your skills. How much more can it accomplish by adding you? If the answer is "a lot," you have a new position.

New positions represent a very small fraction of the hidden job market. For established organizations, creating a new job is not a simple task. Here is how the job creation process works in most organizations.

1. *A Need Develops.* A new product or service brings about the realization that new problems face the organization. A need may result from growth and expansion or when a key employee retires or leaves.
2. *Reallocation.* One solution is to internally shift resources and people from one function to another. Sometimes this "internal reorganization" eliminates the need.
3. *Realization Strikes.* Management recognizes that a new position is needed and puts together a new job description.
4. *Employee Referrals.* Management asks current employees for referrals or internal upgrades. Management usually interviews internal candidates who believe they may be qualified.
5. *External Publicity.* The availability of the opening is publicized. The publicity may initially be via a very narrow channel and then be gradually expanded as the need for more or better qualified applicants increases. The publicity may eventually hit the newspapers or employment agencies if word of mouth fails.

This creation of a position process can take one week to six months. The larger the organization is, the greater the red tape, internal procedure, legal considerations, budgetary concerns, etc. Small organizations face many constraints as well. If you show up with perfect credentials for a new position that the organization desperately needs, it still may take considerable time for you to be hired. Whether it is a "Mom and Pop" consultant or Fortune 500 firm, job creation is no simple matter.

Job creation does occur. It is an option, but not an entirely prudent one for you to rely upon. Your job objective should be geared to what is currently available in the real marketplace. Do not put all of your efforts into "maybe's." Keep your eyes open. Jobs do get created.

PERFUME

GOT ANYTHING THAT ATTRACTS GENEROUS EMPLOYERS?

Market Awareness

The labor market pool is big and open, even in time of severely restricted economic growth. Sometimes the right job is a compromise which is made because the market is soft at the time.

The concept behind a labor market pool is the fluid movement of people. People change jobs. The economy fluctuates. People take certain jobs for expediency. If the job you must accept is not the job that leads to where you think you want to go, perhaps you can make it lead you to the proper sources of contacts.

Job hunting is a complicated game. It is an on-going business because one thing leads to another. An awareness of visible, hidden, and non-existent position possibilities is a first step to getting where you want to go.

Your understanding of how the labor market really functions helps you focus on specific execution activities that work best.

Hunting Advice

Know how to get hunted. Be the prey. Let the hunter find you. That technique does not mean to do nothing but hope. For most people's personalities, adopting the role of the prey, in practice, is actually somewhat difficult.

By posting your credentials on the www, you create a larger bullseye. But you still must be in the right field/sight for the hunter to notice you.

The most successful job search technique you can employ is putting yourself in the right place at the right time. This does not come about by accident, nor by luck! Being in the right place at the right time takes planning and hard work.

Never hunt for a job. Make the job come to you. Get hunted!

The Job Search Team

Understanding job search basics involves knowing who the participants are. Every job campaign plays to a supporting cast. The supporting cast of participants creates the excitement, reality, and final success.

Yourself

Neither you nor the employer could survive without a cast of lesser players. Individually, you and the employer swim in a giant sea. Neither knows the other exists. Neither can see the other initially. Something (or somebody) often serves as a catalyst to bring the two of you together.

Starting a job campaign without recognizing your back-up players is like trying to swim with both legs tied. You can stay afloat, but it zaps a lot of your energy.

Doing everything on your own is possible, but it is foolish. Proving that you are independent to that degree pleases no one but you. That attitude scores few points and may not be the most efficient way to get you a job.

Regardless of your age, you have a lot of future left, and you probably want a career, not just a job. Recognizing that you need others in the search process makes your chances for planning and implementing your career goals better.

People who you know and learn to know form the most solid foundation upon which you can build a total career plan. Managing a life plan involves many other people.

> *You are the most important person in your search team but not the only team player.*

The Employer

The employer is in the same boat. Without people to help find the talent it needs, no organization can succeed. Many organizations have collapsed even though their financial resources and capital goods were more than adequate.

Organization life depends on people. Without good people, few organizations survive. Employers must develop a strong cadre of people within the organization and on the outside. Employers need a way of drawing outstanding people to work for them.

A system of contacts is like an underground information network that continually feeds information about talented potential employees into the best managed organizations. These "people networks" largely explain why some organizations tend to consistently be top performers in their fields.

An organization's success depends upon people. The best organizations develop the people they have and aggressively recruit additional strong talent. The recruiting process is not a "hit or miss" approach. It is a consistent effort that draws on input from people internally and externally.

> *The employer also needs to find you.*

Human Resource Departments (HRD)

The best employment contact for you is the person for whom you would work if you got the job. Unfortunately, you cannot always determine who that person is.

You may need the HRD to direct you to the right path. Many employers have strong corporate policies against the hiring of technical, professional, and managerial employees without first going through HRD.

Because of government compliance regulations, the trend is clearly in the direction of requiring all applicants to see HRD first. Most decision-makers do not want responsibility for the paperwork which the government often requires prior to initial interviews.

In today's parlance, the old "Personnel Department" is often called the "Human Resources Department" or H.R. for short. The key H.R. manager in a medium-size organization is the "salaried employment manager." It is this person who signs-off on or approves 90 percent of all offer commitments made to professional and managerial-level employees.

The term "salaried" employee is gradually being replaced by the term "exempt" employee. That simply means that your employment is not legally covered under the Fair Labor and Standards Act (FLSA) as amended repeatedly. FLSA primarily covers employees paid on an hourly basis (non-exempt employees).

Role. The HR department's role is to protect the manager's time. To accomplish this they can carry out the initial screening and handle all of the necessary paperwork. If necessary, they can do both internal and external searches for the manager and at the same time stay within affirmative action guidelines.

Knocking on the doors of HR offices can be nerve-wracking. HR people can make "no" decisions but have little power to make "yes" decisions. Nonetheless, in most cases it is unwise to try to bypass the HRD.

In most medium and large organizations, the HR departments carry a significant amount of weight in the hiring decisions for all salaried employees. Technical, professional, and managerial openings at the entry level for college graduates are almost always dealt with first in personnel departments. HRD's influence in top-level jobs is not as extensive.

Smaller employers put much less weight on HR functions. The operating managers make most hire-and-fire decisions involving salaried employees in smaller organizations.

Tactics which circumvent the HRD often alienate its staff. In addition to the short-term resentment, there are some long-term negatives.

Even if you obtain the position, you will still need the support of the HRD as you advance. Although HR is not the most powerful function in most organizations, HR staff do carry considerable influence in things that may matter to you later.

Alienating the HR staff is a serious action. Study the ramifications before you undertake actions that will upset this group of people. Just like your next boss, they can be important career makers or breakers.

Writing Executives. Some experts suggest writing the top executive for all positions paying over $100,000. If you cannot locate the appropriate decision-

Human Resource representatives are your roadmap within the organization.

Personnel staff can open internal doors for you.

maker, you can usually insure that your inquiry will get funneled to the proper person by directing it to the top executive officer.

Most letters, though, even when noted as personal and confidential, never get to the chief executive. In most cases, an administrative aide sorts the mail and routes it to the proper person or department.

There is subtle pressure on a subordinate when he or she gets such a letter from "upstairs." The attitude can be resentment just as much as a desire to satisfy the boss, however.

Teachers

Good high school and college teachers and counselors make it a point in their work to get to know potential employers. Teachers train talent that employers need. If there is no market for that talent, some of the teachers' drive and interest dies.

Most studies of students' goals show that a major motivation for schooling is upward mobility. Students attend school to obtain skills that will improve their ability to accomplish their goals in life.

People who go into the teaching profession tend to be helping, caring persons. They try to get to know their students well. Employers needing the type of talent that certain teachers produce want to get to know those teachers too.

Teachers make more job recommendations than any other occupational group, so try to get to know several very well.

Many teachers are in unique positions with much potential for playing broad roles if they elect to exercise their influence. They can be major participants in the flow of the labor market talent because they help both students and employers. You should get to know your teachers and mentors well.

Work Associates

The people you meet in your current full-time (or part-time) work setting are the next most influential participants in your search process. These associates may be colleagues or customers. Colleagues occasionally leave for greener pastures and they may come back for you. Customers can occasionally see your potential better than your present employer.

All of your work associates have lives that extend beyond the current work environment. They can be influential participants in your job search process. Get to know them well. Employers use them very effectively and you should, too.

Friends

Friends are the small group of people with whom you have become close through sharing your life with them. They should be among the first people you go to for advice.

Friends play an important role in your job search process. They can offer advice and suggest job leads. They also may be in positions to share your resume with their other friends at clubs, civic groups, church, etc.

Acquaintances

Acquaintances are people who you know and who know you, but your relationships with them are not of a close personal nature. Acquaintances can nonetheless influence the thinking of others about you.

If you advise acquaintances of your desires, they can help. Their role can be very important in your search process. Taking advantage of the influences of acquaintances is an important strategy in a job search plan. It is extremely important in the construction of the elaborate network of people who are capable, in small and large ways, of influencing others to offer you job interviews.

Summary
• • • • • • • • • • • • • • • • • • •

The job search system is not as complex as it might at first appear. You have many people willing to help you move through the job search process. Unfortunately, too many job hunters approach the process without an overall awareness of how the process can work for them.

The internet introduction into the employment function has been a great asset in managing and improving the efficiency of the marketplace. It will not however replace "networking" and "word of mouth" communication. Recognize it as an important tool for you to use but do not rely on it to solve your contact communication concerns.

You should set your goals, develop your job search tools, and approach the proper acquaintances and contacts to get yourself into the mainstream of the hidden job market. You have hundreds of contacts who are willing to help you with your plans.

//WEB.TIP//
www.careermag.com
Career Magazine

Your personal contacts are your very own unique sales force. Help them help you.

//WEB.TIP//
www.monster.com
The Monster Board
One of the most hit job sites/job listings/employer profiles/resume posting/ search resources/user friendly/many links.

Prospecting for Job Leads:

Sources — Systems — Agencies

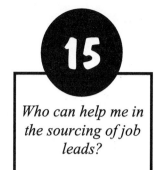

Who can help me in the sourcing of job leads?

One of the hardest parts of job hunting is just identifying people to contact about an interview. You may have an excellent resume, cover letter, and interview pitch, but those are not much use if you can't locate several hot job leads.

Most of us believe that we must know that a job exists before we attempt to contact a potential employer. Unfortunately, only a small percentage of jobs are ever listed.

Most jobs are filled via word of mouth. It is unrealistic to assume that there must be a known job before you take time to talk to the employer.

This is not to suggest that no jobs are ever listed. Obviously, the web and newspapers list hundreds of jobs every day in classified ads. But the odds are long on you finding the ideal job that perfectly fits your background and interests.

Any good job search campaign must take advantage of all employment options even if the odds might appear to be a long shot. You want to work smart in this effort. That means making direct contact with a potential employer, even if the odds are not in your favor.

Traditional job search methods take advantage of all job leads. The traditional approach goes beyond just waiting for these job leads to be brought to your attention. It involves a proactive effort designed to flush out all such opportunities. Sourcing real job leads is a fundamental part of an effective job search strategy.

Job Lead Sources

How do you find out about job openings? The major sources are publications, the internet, services, employers, contacts, and your own initiative. College Career services do some of this work for you. They canvas potential employers and collect job openings. These services bring you and the employer together.

Job Websites.   Are the days gone when your "perfect job" depended upon who you knew, how slick your resume was, clever ads to rifle through, and networking contacts? Probably not, but the job hunting rules have certainly changed with the introduction of the "World Wide Web" into your job search efforts.

A plethora of Internet sites have sprung up which offer job search information, resume advice, and job listings. Perhaps you want your mouse to do the walking.

Surfing for jobs is today's reality and you must learn the ropes in this new job search world. The WWW brings together "job providers" and "job seekers" in a virtual HELP-WANTED and JOB-WANTED forum. Articles sharing career advice and job information abound on the web. Check out your various options.

Placement Services.   Whether it is a college service, a government agency, or a private service, a placement service is the most convenient and easiest way for you to seek employment. Your first step in using that process is to prepare for the interview. Much of the hard work has already been done for you.

Your goal is to find job openings before they are ever advertised and initiate contact whenever you learn of any opening, whether advertised or not.

Why doesn't everyone use only that approach then? A person is indeed foolish to not take advantage of this opportunity. Unfortunately, for a variety of reasons this does not work well for everyone.

College career services and private employment services solicit job openings and provide these listings for you.

Placement services have access to only a limited number of jobs. At the entry level for business and engineering college graduates, less than half of the job openings are listed. The percentages go down drastically from there.

Experts suggest that fewer than 15 percent of all job openings are ever widely publicized. Services only get a portion of those because many employers advertise jobs themselves. They also get access to a few unpublished jobs as well.

The jobs that are listed with services are sought by almost everyone who is looking. Logic suggests that only the very best qualified candidates (however you measure best quality) get selected for interviews and offers. For the best qualified applicants, placement services are ideal. Average candidates often have to look elsewhere.

Publications. Jobs are advertised, people like you apply, and offers are extended. Scouring want ads in newspapers, the web, trade magazines, association newsletters, and professional journals pays off for many candidates.

The purpose of an employment advertisement is to generate the largest possible pool of qualified candidates. By definition, about 90 percent of the people applying are screened out. The best 10 percent are screened in and interviewed.

Respond to all relevant want ads but realize that only a small percentage are called for an interview.

Respondents to employment ads rarely fit the job descriptions perfectly. Most employers and applicants realize that there is some give and take on acceptance of qualifications.

Any time you see an employment advertisement that closely matches your credentials, you should send a cover letter and resume. For best results, write the cover letter and resume in such a manner that it is obvious to the employer that you have almost the exact credentials requested.

This force-fitting yourself technique is the best way of insuring a positive reply. The total you, with all your liabilities, will be discovered in the interview.

It is in your best interest to get the interview; you can best defend their qualification in a face-to-face setting. A simple piece of paper rarely talks back. You need to talk.

Respond to all ads _immediately_ even if you are only marginally qualified.

Some experts suggest waiting about one week after an ad runs to reply. The logic is that employers are flooded with applicants the day after the ad breaks. By waiting a few days, your resume will not be in the stack with hundreds of other replies and thus may get a more thorough review. The disadvantage to this approach is that you run the risk of the opening being filled by the time you apply.

Do not wait to find a perfect match between the qualifications desired in an ad and your background. Play the odds. Your goal is to get as many interviews as possible.

If you are currently employed, you run a major risk of your current employer finding out that you are looking around. Few ads on the web or print media give employers' names and addresses. They often give email or post office box numbers. Because of this, you could unknowingly respond to your current employer's ad.

One reason employers often use email and post office boxes is to avoid tarnishing their names. Many firms do not ever reply to people answering blind ads. One ad in a Sunday edition of a large metropolitan newspaper will generate 300 to 500 responses, depending upon the supply and demand situation for the listed opening. Obviously, an employer must be slow in responding. They often respond to only the most likely matches.

Most ads are placed by human resource departments. In many cities there is an association of employment managers who tend to know each other well. They may be friends outside the job. The grapevine may spread the fact that you are looking around.

Whenever you reply to an ad, you run the risk of your employer learning of your action. Be prepared to explain this to your employer.

Personal Contacts. Your best source of job leads is your personal contacts. When you are ready to begin your job lead development activity, it is time to call your contacts. Personal visits to them or telephone calls asking if they know of specific job openings is in order.

Contacts should be used frequently and regularly to help generate job prospects. Weekly calls to them may turn up many "no's," but they keep your contacts informed of your status. The calls give them a chance to do some digging on your behalf, which most are willing to do when you ask.

Your contact network should produce a number of excellent job leads.

> **Responding to blind ads runs the risk of your employer indirectly discovering that you are looking for another job.**

Employer's Applicant Sources

How do employers find applicants? What sources do they use? If you know a little bit about their business, you have a better chance of adopting a strategy to fit your circumstances.

There are seven basic sources available to employers. Which source they use depends on the type of job, the level of responsibility (salary level), and the supply of candidates in the community. The seven primary sources are:

- College recruiting
- Job fairs
- Referrals
- Advertisements
- Walk-ins
- Write-ins
- Employment agencies

A very high percentage of entry-level hires in business and technical fields come from college campuses through on-campus interviewing or job listings on campus. A high percentage of the jobs requiring one to ten years of experience are filled by private agencies. The middle of the market is in the $30,000-$80,000 salary range for technical, professional, and managerial openings.

Referrals come from employees and friends of the organization. Referrals and write-ins constitute the largest percentage of hires in the mid-range group and a smaller, but important, percentage of hires for top paying jobs.

Because of the discouraging nature of the approach for the applicant and time commitment required by the employer, few hires result from walk-ins in all categories.

Advertisements, web or print, are usually used only as a last resort. When the supply of applicants is very low, a need to advertise becomes evident. Advertising is normally confined to highly skilled technical people and sales personnel in the middle and upper ranges of exempt personnel.

Large well known firms rarely advertise except in situations where applicants are very scarce. Smaller firms advertise more frequently.

Classifying Job Leads

Job leads are the bread and butter of your job search, and they are what you are working to find. When you discover a job lead, your mission is to convert the lead into an interview. The action you take immediately upon learning of an opening is critical.

How swiftly you respond and how much time you devote to your strategy of responding should relate to your perception of how important the job is to you and of how "hot" the lead is. Some leads need to be followed up more quickly than others, so you need to be able to read "temperatures."

Hot Leads.   Extremely hot leads are those you receive through your contacts, advertisements, listings from a placement service, or direct referrals. On hot leads, you call for an appointment within the hour. If a letter and resume are requested, you personally deliver them if possible.

Your goal is to obtain an interview that day or, at the latest, the next day. The very best jobs are often filled within hours.

Lukewarm Leads.   Employers who advertise in annuals, journals, association newsletters, and other publications with a week or more lead time before printing, are usually not in a hurry to fill their jobs. They want to develop a good pool of applicants, review them, and select the best to interview.

You want your resume to get into the pool. Sending it immediately is not necessary in most cases. Since you have some time, find out through web reviews, telephone calls, and personal contacts as much information as you can about the opening.

After you know precisely what the employer is seeking, write your cover letter and resume to fit the opening. Make your qualifications appear to be most outstanding.

Lukewarm leads are common for jobs with government agencies, teaching jobs, and training programs. The employer may not be sure of the exact nature and number of the job openings, but usually there are several openings when such an ad is placed.

Prospect Systems

There are several different types of prospects. Prospects are job leads and potential job leads. Some prospects are more important to you than others.

Prospects come from employment services, the internet, publications, and personal contacts. Through one of these sources you have learned that a job or potential job opening exists.

Your mission is to establish a system of sourcing, building, maintaining, and following-up on all of your job leads. There are many methods of accomplishing this recordkeeping function but the important point is to keep the leads current and well organized.

· · · · · · · · · · · **PUBLISHED SOURCES OF JOB LEADS** · · · · · · · · · · ·

- The Internet (direct or via vendors)
- Metropolitan newspaper classifieds
- National newspaper classifieds
- Small town newspapers
- Financial newspapers
- Business magazines
- Trade association publications
- Professional association publications
- Industry trade magazines
- Technical journals
- Employment agencies
- College placement offices
- Career fairs/conferences

· · · · · · · · · ·
Figure 15.2

COMMON PROSPECTING MISTAKES

Prospecting for job leads and interviews is never a fun job for anyone. Even with the best of friends, relationships, solid leads, and supportive environment, this can be a discouraging task. No one likes to be turned-down for an appointment.

Your plan is important in turning the writing, telephoning, and personal visits into a more pleasant activity. Unfortunately, many job hunters even dislike asking for advice. There is no good way to avoid the very personal nature of prospecting.

It helps if you understand the pitfalls that others have experienced. Anticipating problems and taking action to avoid them improve the success of your job search.

Wrong Assumptions:

- *The acquaintance knows your background.* You must explain your credentials.
- *The person understands what you want.* You must state your job goals succinctly.
- *The contact has read your resume.* You must review it with them.
- *You are capable of winging a conversation.* You must plan your presentation and approach carefully.
- *The employer is rejecting you personally.* It is your credentials, not you, that are not as competitive as others.
- *People will do what they say.* You must initiate most follow-ups and be persistent.
- *Your job goals are clear.* Your integrity depends on specific, delineated goals.

Over-reliance:

- *The search agency will get you a job.* Your personal efforts are far more likely to produce results.
- *The job for you will be advertised.* Over 80 percent of job openings are never advertised.
- *An offer from a specific employer is imminent.* The offer is not an offer until all details are closed conclusively, so do not stop looking.
- *The salary will be competitive.* Premature discussion can be damaging, but never to bring it up is foolish.

Wrong assumptions and over-reliance kill prospecting hopes frequently. There is a strong human tendency to wait and hope. Actions speak louder than hopes.

Be aware of the pitfalls of prospecting. Plan ahead.

Many good leads disappear through lack of management care. Leads get lost and turn stale quickly. You need a support system that organizes the nitty-gritty filing so that your daily activity can automatically return to prospects and keep them active.

Prospect File.   A prospect file is a collection of all of your job leads. It differs from your contact network in that it is used for a different purpose. Your contact network is an information-generating and advice-seeking collection of important people.

Your prospect file is a collection of individual names and specific organizations who may have specific job possibilities for you. It is a product of your network of contacts.

Building a prospect file requires an approach similar to that for building your contact network, but their purposes make the two lists substantially different. The method of developing the prospect file has similarities to the network, but the names included must be bona fide employment prospects.

Many contacts in your network are not employment prospects. Conversely, many names in your prospect list are not on your contact network list and never should be. There could be some overlap in names but that is not the norm.

Organization.   Many people prefer to maintain their prospect files on 5 x 8″ index cards because of the way the files are referenced. There are hot, lukewarm, and downright cold prospects in the file. From time to time prospects' cards can be removed from the file.

The purpose of using a card system (or a computer database) is to have the capability of shuffling through them on a daily basis. Of course, this shuffling can also just as easily be done using a good computer word processor, database, or personal information manager like ACT!, NOTES, OUTLOOK, ORGANIZER, etc.

Many people maintain their prospect cards in four sections:

- Hot
- Lukewarm
- Cold
- Terminated

New leads, from whatever source, immediately go into the hot section. The hot file is worked regularly; usually daily. You are talking to or have recent correspondence out to these people. You may have had interviews with them and/or are waiting for replies.

The lukewarm section contains job leads which you have worked but are now getting old. On a less frequent basis you go through these and recontact the employers. You may be on an active "hold" status with some of these employers. You may use a weekly status update.

The cold section contains those leads which still have some spark of life but which are not very promising. Perhaps, for example, an employer never responded to your inquiry, but you have some reason to believe that you are still being considered. In another case, the employer may have told you your qualifications look great, but that the timing is not right; you have been told that there is a reasonable chance that something will materialize later. The cold prospects are not likely to turn into interviews, but they may.

The termination section contains the burned-out job leads. You received a "no interest" response before or after the interview. You know that the "hold your resume in file" phrase is worthless.

All old leads (those 60 days or older) eventually rest in this section. You do not want to throw these away because some of them might rekindle, and they contain excellent information for a review and evaluation of your job search strategy on a periodic basis.

Content. Prospect file cards should contain: organization, division, branch, personal name, personal title, address, city, state, zip code, and telephone. Each time you have any type of contact with the employers, it must be noted on the card with the date, person, result, current status, and expected next action.

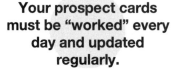

SINCE YOU ADVERTISED FOR THE POSITION I ASSUME YOU'RE AS DESPERATE AS I AM.

This includes both your contacting of the employer and the employer's contact with you. If you have had an interview, you should record your impressions of the interview.

The prospect file should be updated daily during an active job search campaign. It is maintained in alphabetical order by organization name within the four classifications of prospects. The file is a running summary of your discussions which can be readily accessed and evaluated.

Your prospect cards must be "worked" every day and updated regularly.

File Folders. When you have two or more pieces of correspondence from an employer or just before you have an interview, a manila file folder should be prepared for the employer. These folders are kept separate from the prospect file and contain much more detail.

Those (alphabetically maintained) folders are not something you shuffle through on a daily basis, but you do refer to them whenever you write, interview, or receive correspondence from an employer.

The prospect file does *not* include a card for each of the mass direct mail feelers that you have sent. If the cover letter for any of these was a personally typed letter or the lead for it came from an important contact, it would go into the prospect list immediately.

Function. The main function of the prospect file is to organize your approach in dealing with potential employers. It provides a system for classifying your job leads which, if you have done a good job of creating them, are a sizable number of prospects.

Some priorities in terms of quality and timing must be established in order to avoid spending too much time on your less promising leads.

Hi-Tech Contacting. A number of electronic contact managers are available for your use. The contact managers run on Palm Pilot devices to large network servers. The concepts for organizers is the same whether electronic or hand copy. Use whatever you are most comfortable with.

```
..........................................                ...........

                                   ┌─────────────────────────────┐
                                   │      Prospect Card           │
         ┌─────────────────────────┘                             │
         │  Type Lead _____
         │
         │  Name _____  Title _____
         │
         │  Organization _____
         │
         │  Address _____  Phone _____
         │
         │  Job Title and Description
         │
         │
         │
         │
         │  Date       Person Contacted    Result, Status, and Next Action
         │  _____     _____     _____
         │  _____     _____     _____
         │  _____     _____     _____
         │  _____     _____     _____
         │  _____     _____     _____
         │  _____     _____     _____
         └─────────────────────────────────────────────────────────┘

                        ●●●●●●●●●●●●
                        Figure 15.3
```

Prospect Calling

Contacting Prospects

An important aspect of prospecting is sourcing the job leads and then turning the lead into a bona fide job opening. Leads, including job opening advertisements, do not turn into a job offer without a preliminary interview and subsequent secondary interviews.

You must do two things. You must investigate the lead until you discover for certain that there is a real job opening. Secondly, you must be one of the few applicants who gets the opportunity to interview for the bona fide job opening.

Many employers simply pass the word along that a job opening may be forthcoming. They may be in the process of getting an "opening approved" through their superiors but they have confidence that the opening will eventually materialize. Their pre-advertisement reason for "passing the word" is to get a feel for the strength and quality of the potential applicant pool.

Many employers prefer to interview for "anticipated" openings. They may not have an immediate opening but realize that the business is growing and that within a reasonable period of time an opening will be created. Others realize that turnover is inevitable, and they want to maintain a reasonable size applicant pool so that if someone leaves after giving only a two-week notice, the pool can be quickly accessed.

//WEB.TIP//

www.vjf.com
Virtual Job Fair
Search jobs by function/
view job descriptions/links
to company site/specialty
in IT but the VJF concept
is universal.

Some employers interview for training programs. They know that the organization typically hires a number of entry-level management trainees into a given function. The openings typically occur around January and June when many college graduates complete their degrees.

Anticipatory interviewing is not the norm but it is not unusual either. The majority of employers interview applicants only when they know that a job opening exists. Since the opening needs to be filled as soon as possible, the "interviewing window" for a given job may only be two or three weeks long at the most.

Timing is what makes job hunting so difficult. Being at the right place at the right time makes a great deal of difference. Candidates who are available are the only ones interviewed. Better candidates might be available, but the timing may not be appropriate and both the candidate and employer lose.

Timing plays a significant role in the hiring decision.

Ironically, employers do not want to hire unemployed candidates. The assumption is that they do not have a job because of a lack of strong credentials (otherwise, they would be employed). This vicious cycle hurts unemployed job hunters.

The "golden rule" is to never quit one employer until you have another job already lined-up.

It is better to be working part-time in a job beneath your capabilities than to be unemployed. It is better to be in school and working part-time than to be unemployed.

BREAKING THE SECRETARY SCREEN

A major job duty of any secretary is to protect the time of superiors. Whether you are contacting the personnel department or a functional line operating manager, you will inevitably have to deal with the secretary screen.

Your goal is to avoid the block and persuade the secretary to give you a few minutes of time. Expect to be asked about the nature of your call. Some of the most common responses are as follows:

- Indicate personal: "A mutual friend, Dr. Smith, suggested . . ."
- Telephone tag: "We have been missing each other . . ."
- Returning call: "She called me on . . ."
- Correspondence follow-up: "Regarding the letter he wrote . . ."
- Establish rapport: "Strike-up conversation with secretary"
- Embarrass: "Has not returned three other calls and . . ."
- Busy schedule: "I am tough to reach so . . ."
- No message: "When is a good time to call back?"
- Direct: "Seeking an appointment. Can you . . ."
- Message: "I am seeking . . . and . . . please call on . . ."
- Polite: "Keep missing each other"
- Friendship: "Can you help me with . . ."

The secretary can be your best ally if you establish a proper dialogue. You will likely talk to this person several times before you get the appointment and after the interview. Try to establish a positive relationship so that once you break the initial barrier, follow-up contacts will be much smoother.

Prospecting regularly addresses the timing issue. Building a base of job leads is called prospecting. Prospecting is calling or visiting an employer. It can be done via telephone or in person.

Some people view prospecting as cold calling. You have an inkling that the customer needs what you have to offer. Your degree of certainty varies from 10 percent to 90 percent.

A personal, unannounced drop-in or walk-in does not have a high success rate. However, if you are the type of person who tends to make a very pleasing first impression and if you can get to the decision-maker, cold calling often works well. Most employers like to see the hard-charger, go-getter, want-the-job type of job applicant.

The most difficult part of the walk-in is getting past the clerical screen of protection. If you have patience, it may be right for you.

Both personal prospecting and telephone prospecting work. The purpose of prospecting is to obtain an interview appointment.

Personal Prospecting.   Prospecting takes planning if it is to be successful. You could find yourself in the midst of an interview for which you are unprepared. In such a case, even though you would have succeeded in the battle to obtain the interview, you could lose the war because the interview could be a real flop.

Cold calling is prospecting for job leads. If you are to be successful, you need to be prepared to fill out an application, get screened initially, and set up a return appointment.

Personal prospecting works. People do get hired this way every day. This method is not common or popular among technical, professional, and managerial hires. When it is successful, it requires finesse.

Cold calling can be a tough, discouraging proposition. Being told "no" to your face is a major confidence-destroying experience. Only if you can handle this type of unpleasant situation time and time again should you attempt this.

One of the reasons cold calls work is the very reason many people do not try it. It is threatening. It takes guts. Only aggressive people try it. Ironically, that is a quality that employers like to see in applicants.

Another reason it works is because you may happen to show up at the right place at the right time. When some openings materialize, employers cannot afford to go through a long, drawn-out search process.

The supervisor may need a new person immediately and pressures mount fast if it is a key job. Even if you are not the perfect match but you are available immediately and have training potential, an employer may jump at the chance to hire you.

Walk-ins often immediately get to see the chief decision-maker. Busy people often do not like to get locked into an appointment schedule, and they tend to postpone setting up job interview appointments. If a person is right there, many will take a break from the routine and talk to the person.

Getting to see the decision-maker on the spot is important. If he or she happens to like you, other candidates for the assignment may never get to see the employer. Cold calling frequently puts you near an important power figure.

Telephone Prospecting.   If you can use the telephone (instead of walking in) to arrange a meeting over lunch or meet at a social function, there will be less tension.

Prospecting is an aggressive approach which works!

DELIVER YOUR TELEPHONE MESSAGE

Purpose:

Seeking a job
Plan to change jobs
Need your help
Seeking advice

Plan:

Advising key people
Interest in you
No hurry
Time table

Goal:

Type of job
Locations desired
Industry concerns
Organizations like

Why changing:

Graduating
New challenges
Advancement
Completed major task
Good timing
Family or Health
More money
Security

Request:

Explore options with you
Seek advice from you

Sales Pitch:

Deliver one minute
presentation

Close:

Suggest an
appointment time

Follow-up:

Confirming letter
Cover letter
Resume
Request in writing

Figure 15.4

TELEPHONE TIPS

- Rehearse presentation (recorder)
- Plan every call outline
- Limit call to five minutes
- Avoid complete interview
- Introduce yourself
- Establish mutual interest
- State purpose
- Deliver sales message
- Ask for appointment
- Suggest time
- Confirm follow-up meeting
- Leave re-contact open
- Thank for time

Figure 15.5a

Prospecting is preferable for many people who just cannot tolerate the uncertain wait common with direct mail job search strategies. They feel that they must be doing something positive, even if it means facing several face-to-face turndowns each day.

The telephone can be both an ally and a foe. Common courtesy suggests that you should try to get an appointment first, but busy people do not like to bother with appointments. They feel that if you really want the job you should be willing to wait on their doorstep until they can work you into their busy day.

If you employ this assertive search strategy, you should seriously consider establishing a daily call routine. Force yourself to *always* contact at least five different employers each day.

Make good notes after the appointment and always follow up in five to seven days (one week later). You may have received a "no," but persistence often pays. The employer may like your desire, organization, and persistence and give you a chance after a little reflection.

The five visits each day plus the weekly follow-up often pay handsome dividends. Very few employers will be rude to you, but they can be firm, especially the second time.

You must prepare yourself for a tough mental challenge. If you have a thin skin, this approach may not be for you. If you can develop a tough attitude, you will be amazed at how many people you will impress. You may have to settle for a second-choice type of job which may have later potential, but the success rate of this assertive approach works much faster than most other search strategies.

Employers like to make quick employment decisions. Dragging the process out is no more acceptable to them than it is to you. The person present and available immediately most often gets the job even though he or she may not be the very best qualified applicant.

The bottom line in any search strategy is job interviews. Your prospecting actions boil down to three activities with potential employers.

- Writing
- Telephoning
- Visiting

The bottom line in your prospecting is solid job leads. Prospecting is converting your leads into interviews. This is when the telephone becomes your best ally.

Your job lead provides you with a name and telephone number. If you did not obtain the specific name of the key contact, try to obtain it. The simplest way to obtain it is to call the organization's receptionist and ask for the name and number of the person heading up the function where your new job is likely to be.

If that does not work, call the HR office and explain your situation. One of their functions is to help you reach the proper person. Your goal is to get an interview with the key decision-maker in the department or unit to which you are seeking entry. If that fails, the personnel department can help you get your foot in the door.

You want to avoid a lengthy telephone interview with anyone. The best plan is to get a face-to-face meeting so that you can present your qualifications and interact in the most favorable light. Rarely can you obtain a job offer after a telephone interview.

An air of confidence, tact, and a positive mental attitude will suffice on the telephone. Sometimes your telephone technique can hurt you. If you feel you might have that problem, the best solution is advance preparation. Think of the possible questions you will face and have answers for them ready. Try to maintain control by moving toward setting up a specific time for an interview.

Your goal on the telephone is to establish a specific time and date for an interview.

The best laid plans sometimes fall apart in the reality test. Because of their fear of failure, some people fail without ever playing the game. If your plan is established, you must at least give prospecting a fair chance of succeeding.

You have worked hard to generate job leads and convert these into specific interviews. Your next task is to make all of your interviews turn into job offers.

TELEPHONE MANNERS

- Brief greeting
- Friendly tone
- Nice day
- Establish rapport first
- Polite and patient
- "Good time?"
- Short commercial
- Mutual acquaintances
- Appreciation

••••••••••

Figure 15.5b

Use the telephone and email to set up the details such as the time and place of the meeting.

//WEB.TIP//

www.cweb.com
Career Web
A career hub with services for employers and job searches/job listings/ resume postings/e-mail to registrants/highly visited/ lots of articles and links.

Try to avoid getting screened out by a telephone interview.

Prospect Career Action Project

Prospect File Project. Develop a 100-name job prospect file based on your career job objectives and contacts. Use at least three different sources for the development of job leads. On each card, indicate the information suggested in the text and summarize as much information as you know about each job. Use a copy of Figure 15.3 in creating this database.

Select three of your hottest job leads and write a cover letter and resume for each. Indicate that you will be calling within a reasonable period of time if that is appropriate.

Recontact each of the prospects within four weeks by telephone or email. Do your best to obtain appointments. Evaluate the process that you have just gone through. Is it something useful for you that you wish to continue or is it a waste of time in your unique situation?

Prepare a two-page, single-spaced prospect telephone conversation. Open with a greeting, present a personal message, make a request, and close with a confirming follow-up.

Copy the "Prospect Card" format from the text. Complete it for the three prospects. Be thorough on the job description and the status and next action. Record each of your follow-up actions. For the teckies use your PIM software to handle this process.

Employment Services

Employment services are designed to support your efforts in prospecting for job leads.

Job referral agencies also participate in the job search process. The degree to which you use these services is a matter of personal choice based upon your perception of the cost/benefit ratio. The obvious benefit is the variety of job possibilities they offer. The cost is computed in terms of the time and money one invests in utilizing the agencies' services. Rarely will you have to pay a fee.

Employment agencies are used by many employers. Some employers use them exclusively to avoid the initial screening process. They find it less expensive to let another party handle that phase of personnel selection for them. They essentially outsource this function to save costs.

If the employers you want to work for use placement services, you should seriously consider using them. Employment services include college career counseling and placement services, employment agencies, executive search firms, government agencies, private career assessment and counseling services, internet vendors, and paper processing operations.

These agencies will participate in your job search campaign to the extent that you elect to ask them to participate. The only difference between you and them is that they get paid for performing a brokering and advising service.

College Career Services

The college career office is an organization located on campus with the express purpose of getting potential employers together with potential candidates. Depending upon the college or university, the services which are provided vary widely, but most of them offer on-campus interviewing with employers, career counseling, and job referral. Most offer services to both current students and alumni.

College career services provide extensive aids to assist you in your career planning efforts. Most have areas where you can go to read employment brochures, annual reports, access the internet, current job listings, and descriptions of hundreds of jobs as well as the standard sources of names for various employing organizations.

Most provide considerable assistance in accessing the world wide web for employment purposes.

There are usually very low charges for assistance to either the registrant or the employer.

Most of the major employers in the United States work through and cooperate fully with college career offices. Both are members of a non-profit professional organization called the *National Association of Colleges and Employers. NACE* publishes a code of ethics to which both parties subscribe. Forms are jointly developed by the parties and are standardized throughout the nation.

The college career service provides a number of services which are free (or nearly free). As appropriate, the major services—including campus interviewing, referring, counseling, web access, job listings, and career libraries—should definitely be utilized. These services should make your college placement office high on your list of resources to use.

Campus Interviews. For most graduates, on-campus interviewing is one of the easiest and most effective means for landing the first assignment after college. Alumni under 30 years old can also find this system useful if they are seeking entry-level positions.

Employers often prefer to fill their needs through on-campus interviewing for a number of reasons. They can see large numbers of applicants at a time, it is inexpensive for them as compared to other means, and they see the top talent in the nation first.

Some employers have hundreds of job openings located throughout the country. Their college recruiting is usually national in scope, and these large employers refer graduates to several different locations after initial on-campus interviews.

Most other methods of employment are localized, and applicants must be available in the geographical areas of the openings. Employers often pay for candidates' transportation to a second interview that is hundreds of miles away when the candidates were first interviewed on campus.

Teams of college recruiters usually visit campuses during the fall months of October, November, and December. During the spring, they are on campuses during January, February, and March to hire spring and summer graduates.

THE JOB SEARCH IS GOING WELL...FOR THE FIRST TIME IN MY LIFE I REALLY FEEL IN CONTROL OF MY OWN DESTINY.

Although the policies at schools differ, most spring graduates register for placement assistance near the beginning of the last year in school. Many take interviews both in the fall and spring periods.

Students who wait until one or two months before graduation to contact employers have a far tougher time finding employment. An early start is a good idea.

Employers often try to fill all of their openings through college recruiting by April; therefore, there are few professional jobs left for late applicants. Those individuals about to graduate must plan early for the better opportunities.

Referrals. Not all college career offices operate extensive on-campus recruiting programs. The number of graduates at some schools is not large enough to attract large numbers of employers, and the mix of academic majors may not be in high-demand fields.

The roles of career officers at small colleges and liberal arts schools are somewhat different from those of directors at large universities and in business and engineering curriculums. They usually serve as referral agents for graduating students.

Directors at these smaller, primarily liberal arts institutions, maintain close touch with alumni, local employers, and a selected group of national employers. Referrals to job possibilities are handled on a personal basis.

You must get to know the counseling staff on a personal basis if you are a student at these schools. Only if the staff knows you will they place their credibility on the line with employers.

The one-on-one personal referral is often more effective than mass interviewing. The referral approach accomplishes the same goal; it gets you interviews.

Counseling Service. The placement office is not simply an agency that lines up interviews. The key to finding success in a career assignment lies in prior preparation. The career office assists you in many ways by offering job search advice, job leads, group programs, personal counseling, and web access.

Many people engaged in the job search process find themselves making the same mistakes as their predecessors. College career professionals see common mistakes repeated over and over. The college career counselor is in a unique, pivotal position.

Whether you are an alumnus or a current student, you will find that their advice is some of the best available anywhere at any price. Use it.

Job Listings. As has been pointed out earlier, not all employers recruit on campus. Many prefer to send career officers a list of their openings every month or

Placement offices at the larger universities often schedule several thousand interviews each year and refer hundreds of resumes using sophisticated computer referral systems.

Graduates from smaller colleges need to get well acquainted with the counseling staff because referrals are made on a very personal basis.

Job search advice and personal counseling aid thousands of college graduates every year.

so. Others send a special letter, email, or telephone message when an opening requiring an inexperienced graduate or experienced alumnus materializes.

All career service offices publish and/or post job openings with the information needed for contacting these employers directly.

Publications. The placement office distributes many informative materials on employers. Those materials are available through the career service office career libraries.

The materials give the current names and addresses of the people to contact in hundreds of employing organizations. Many employers advertise in them. They identify types of positions, employers, and are cross-classified by college major and geographical location.

Placement offices keep a wide variety of literature available for reference. Most major government and corporate employers keep placement offices well supplied with recruitment brochures.

Even for new graduates undecided about careers, these can be helpful because they often discuss the duties, responsibilities, future potential, and qualifications for many different types of openings. The pictures and descriptive materials help provide focus on given fields.

Most offices also have on reference a copy of the Department of Labor's two-inch-thick *Occupational Outlook Handbook* and the special edition of it which is directed to college graduates.

The *Handbook* contains several hundred job titles with descriptions for each of the work involved, the places of employment, qualifications, earnings, employment outlook, and sources of additional information. It is a useful planning tool.

You should cultivate a working relationship with your college's career personnel. They personally know hundreds of employers and their recommendation can secure an interview for you. Their potential aid and influence should not be underestimated.

As good as it is, however, you cannot rely solely on your college career service. What works well for some people may not work well for you.

If you have less than five years of work experience, use the office on an aggressive basis. The more work experience you have, the more you should incorporate other approaches into your job campaign.

Your career services office publishes a list of jobs on a regular basis.

Employment Agencies

Private employment agencies should not be overlooked. Even if it costs 15 to 25 percent of your first year's salary, the services of one of these agencies may be worth it. In fields where there is a shortage of talent, employers almost always pay the fee.

In simplest terms, an employment counselor is a person who maintains two files: one of job openings and one

WHAT FOR?... WE'RE ALREADY *IN* COLLEGE.

SPECIALIZED EMPLOYMENT AGENCIES

- Accounting
- Financial institutions
- Data processing
- Engineering
- Sales and marketing
- Health organizations
- Government
- Human Resources
- Education

• • • • • • • • • • •

Figure 15.6

Employment agencies serve a brokerage function for middle management jobs that pay $30,000 to $80,000.

of applicants. In an ideal situation these two lists match, but in reality this is seldom the case.

The employment counselor is many times a salesperson working for two parties at the same time. The counselor may try to convince you to take a job which requires fewer skills than you possess (downgrade), and/or convince an employer to accept a compromise applicant.

Career counselors are often caught up in the role of salesperson because they work on commission and make their living only when creating job/applicant matches.

Agencies build up their candidate files by placing newspaper ads offering nice-sounding jobs to stimulate job seekers' interest. They build up their job files by contacting employers on a regular basis asking for openings.

Many firms supplement their placement business by having applicants sign contracts for certain resume, testing, and counseling services. Even if employers pay the placement fees, applicants pay for these other services.

Registration fees are considered unethical. Before signing a contract with one of the agencies, make certain that all of your questions have been completely and adequately answered. The law is "let the buyer beware."

Employment agencies normally confine their search for jobs to a local area. Usually only local employers list with them. If there are branch offices in other cities, arranging for interviews in those other areas is difficult. You might as well go to the other city and work with an agency there.

The service that you receive depends on the interest that an employment counselor is willing to take in you. Choosing an agency to use is just like shopping for any other service you purchase, and shopping around is a good practice. Only you can evaluate the quality of service that you are likely to receive.

Most agencies charge employers for the placement. Always ask about "fee paid jobs only." If you have to pay, plan on handing over 15 to 25 percent of your first year's earnings to the agency. Usually you do not pay.

Executive Search Firms

What is the difference between an employment agency and a search firm? The original distinction was that an agency charged the applicant, and the search firm billed the employer. Many agencies today accept only fee paid jobs, however, so that distinction is slowly fading.

Another difference is that agencies "registered" applicants. Search firms, on the other hand, did not accept registrants because they "recruited" the best talent. Today, many of the large search firms maintain extensive files of potential job candidates, so the distinction here is beginning to fade also. All firms are setting up websites to solicit quality resumes.

A major distinction between employment agencies and search firms has been the responsibility level of the positions they attempt to fill as reflected by the salary levels. The majority of the employment agency business is placing people in positions paying under $80,000. Only in rare instances do reputable search firms accept jobs in the under-$80,000 salary level.

GREAT NEWS, MOM! THE EMPLOYMENT AGENCY FOUND ME A JOB.

Most of the work of search firms is in the over-$100,000 salary range.

Fees. An executive search firm is hired on an exclusive basis by the employer to identify, screen, verify references, and arrange interviews. The firm is paid an initial fee which is retained whether or not a suitable candidate is found. The final total fee charged the employer ranges from 25 to 33 percent of the annual salary.

There is a clear bias on the part of search firms. They work for employers. Unlike agencies who encourage applicants to come in, search firms almost close their doors. There is no monetary return in seeing hundreds of job applicants.

Search firms are often called "head hunters." They go after the best-qualified talent for their clients. That means more than rifling through a file of resumes. The best candidate is probably already working for a competitor in an assignment similar to the one to be filled.

Sourcing. A search firm professional spends hours on the telephone talking to people already successfully employed and who rarely are in the job market.

Search firm professionals are not looking for resumes. They spend their time talking to leaders in professions, career specialties, and/or industries. They intuitively know when people are ready for promotion or movement. Their business is to track star performers and at the proper time play matchmaker.

The search professional's job is extremely personal in nature. Headhunters spend hours on the telephone asking highly-paid people if they know of candidates coming along who might be ready for truly major assignments. Consequently, these search professionals run in circles of people earning very high incomes.

A search firm could become one of the participants in your job campaign. If you are moving toward the appropriate income level or are already there, you might explore how you can get your name circulated in the right places.

Contingency Firms. A spin-off of the search firm business has been the development of "contingency" firms. In this situation, an employer may "list" a $50,000–$100,000 job with several contingency search firms. The search firm receives a fee, usually 30 percent, only if and when a candidate that they have sourced and referred to the employer is hired. They do not operate on an exclusive listing basis.

Use. Sending your resume to a search firm is not normally the best technique. You have to prepare such a general resume that your goals come across as weak and vague. That is not the type of resume that you want circulating. At that salary level,

EMPLOYMENT AGENCY CHARACTERISTICS

- Charge 15–20 percent of annual salary
- Set up appointments for you
- Some counseling available for a fee
- Effort depends on client's marketability
- Assist in resume preparation (fee)
- Focus on middle management jobs
- Often specialize

• • • • • • • • • •

Figure 15.7

TWO TYPES OF SEARCH FIRMS

- **Retainer:** Paid by the employer on an exclusive retainer basis to locate people for a specific position
- **Contingency:** Search is not exclusive to one search firm only and agency is paid only upon successful placement

Figure 15.8

it could easily come together with a more specific resume of yours from another source and thus be counter-productive.

The best way to deal with search firms is not to deal directly with them. Let others speak for you or wait until the search firm calls you. If you properly and skillfully use the contacts you have, and if you are a "star," search professionals will "crawl all over you." Ask your key contacts to mention your background to a respected search firm.

If the position to which you now aspire is in middle management or technical, spend your time working with employment agencies and your college placement service and nurture your own contacts. If you make a positive track record and are ready for top management, the search firm people will find you.

Whether you are planning for the future or just for now, include the use or potential use of search executives in your overall career plan. These professional participants could greatly aid you in meeting your long-term career goals.

State Employment Services

Traditionally, state employment offices have served primarily clerical workers, retail clerks, and blue-collar personnel. There has been an increasing interest in serving people seeking technical, professional, and managerial positions recently, however.

EXECUTIVE SEARCH LISTINGS

Directory of Executive Recruiters
Consultant News
Templeton Road
Fitzwilliam, NH 03447

National Association of Personnel Consultants
Roundhouse Square
1432 Duke Street
Alexandria, VA 22314

Figure 15.9

The effectiveness of employment services varies greatly from location to location, so it may be worthwhile to walk in and see what type of service your local organization is providing.

Many employers are now required by law to list all openings with government employment services. Employers holding government contracts over a certain size must comply with this regulation to insure that adequate consideration has been given to veterans, minorities, the handicapped, and other protected classes.

The services are free to both you and the employer. Offices are located in most cities. These offices are doing their best to shed the old stigma of being "unemployment" offices. The service is a possible, if not likely, participant in your job campaign.

State Web Services

Nearly every state in the USA has a government-funded employment service. The quality of services, especially those dealing with college graduates, varies greatly. Thousands of employers have vendor relations with governments and thus are often "required" to list any job openings with their local government employment agency.

If you have a special geographical location job requirement, you should check out this resource. Although it may take a minute or two of surfing to locate these listings, it can be worth the time. The search surf should start with this URL:

www.state.XX.us/

The XX is the 2-digit postal code for your state. Usually key words like the following after the slash get you to the listings:

- employment
- personnel
- jobs
- job search

Many cities also have major job agencies within specific departments. These cities often have cooperative employment programs with local Chamber of Commerce organizations. The State employment agency almost always has links to these city jobs. Major cities like San Francisco, Los Angeles, New York City, Chicago, Atlanta, Dallas, Phoenix, etc. have their own sites.

Another excellent link that you often find is to the major local newspapers who have their employment ads in a database. The larger newspapers are in a consortium called .careerpath.com which also focuses upon city and regional area employment.

A Directory of all State Employment Offices by State can be found at this URL: www.fedworld.gov

Career Assessment Services

Career assessment services are private career counseling programs. They work with people on an individual and group basis covering all phases of career planning.

Clients go through exercises in self-assessment and take batteries of psychological tests. Professional counselors work with clients in guiding them through various potential career fields. The goal of these firms is to assist clients in the career decision-making process.

//WEB.TIP//

www.doleta.gov
U.S. Department of Labor Employment and Training Administration.
Government training centers use this site to help job applicants write resumes, cover letters, search job banks, and help themselves.

When a career assessment firm works for an organization which is downsizing, the same firm may be called an "outplacement" firm.

WHEN THE HEADHUNTER CALLS

Headhunters make no money until they find the right candidate for the employer who is paying the fee. If they call you, they received your name from a reliable source who advised the headhunter that you might be a viable candidate.

The caller will tell you about the job opening and then ask if you might be interested. Indicate that you are pleased with your progress at your present employer but that you would like to have some additional information about the job. There are a number of questions you should be prepared to ask.

- Ask for more information
- Ask about salary level
- Indicate that you are near that level now
- Inquire about location
- Employer's name will not always be revealed
- Why is there an opening?
- What is the work environment?
- When must the job be filled?

Based upon this information, decide if you want to pursue it further. If you do, ask if you can have a day to discuss it with your family. Agree to call the recruiter the next day. After buying some time, use it wisely to decide if you really want to pursue the option.

If you are only marginally interested, you may wish to discuss the call with your superiors or work colleagues. Make it clear that you did not initiate any contact and that you have no interest in the job. The fact that outsiders are interested in pursuing you cannot hurt your internal salary and advancement potential. That still does not preclude you from following up with the headhunter.

If you are interested, call the headhunter and advise that you would like to talk further. Do not permit a telephone interview. You want the opportunity to meet and impress the headhunter personally.

The headhunter will usually agree to meet you for lunch or after work at a neutral site. It is at this time that you must get the name of the employer if you do not know it. The headhunter interview is very important so you should plan for it like any other formal interview.

The headhunter will usually recommend that the firm interview two or three candidates that have been interviewed and screened. If you are one of those recommended, you will still negotiate the interview date with the headhunter but the interview will be at the employer's facilities by their personnel, including the person to whom you would be reporting.

Usually the headhunter is involved in the salary negotiation. You probably discussed it with the employer but the headhunter's role is not insignificant. The offer will usually come directly from the employer, but the verbal offer could come via the headhunter. A 20 percent increase is not uncommon.

After you receive the offer in writing, it is time to discuss your options with your current employer if you have not already made a firm decision. It is not uncommon to use the offer as a bargaining chip with your current employer. Assuming that you are serious about leaving, you have nothing to lose.

Whether the headhunter is with an employment agency, contingency search firm, or retainer search firm, your career can be enhanced when the headhunter calls.

An extensive part of this business is helping clients define their long-term goals in a manner that is consistent with their background and reality. The counselor then aids the client in transforming these long-term goals into some real job possibilities which might be stepping stones to his or her personal career and life goals.

The second major phase of these services is helping the individual prepare a marketing plan for achieving the short-term goal of getting a specific job. A significant amount of help is given in resume preparation, cover letter design, and developing an effective approach to disseminating information about themselves to prospective employers.

Most of the services do promise to *assist* the client in finding a job. The most reputable firms, however, make no guarantees nor imply any guarantees. In no way do they get involved in the placement process.

Many reputable firms would consider it unethical to get involved in an employer referral process. If a counselor did become involved that way, he or she would be vulnerable to a charge of manipulating the client's interests and career plan into a direction that led straight to a given employer.

There could well be a legitimate charge of collusion if the job did not work out as planned.

As a result, most career assessment firms stay out of the placement business. They are career counselors and advisors only. Beware if they offer claims that sound like functions of an employment agency or executive search firms.

The most they should offer is to provide contacts and listings of potential employers. Some may propose to get into offering specific job leads. Be cautious about the job lead business.

Outplacement firms rarely assist in arranging personal interviews. Their role is one of assistance, not placement.

If you feel you need this personal attention, career assessment firms can be the perfect thing for you. As with many other subjects, however, it is possible to learn much of what career assessment firms present out of a book or a self-programmed learning experience.

Some people learn better within the structure of a classroom, seminar, or individual guidance study program. If you do not have the

IT HURTS TO BE TOLD YOUR BEST SHOT IS AS A PRO WRESTLING REFEREE.

. . . UNSOLICITED LETTER TO SEARCH FIRM OR EMPLOYMENT AGENCY . . .

Dear ***[specific name]***:

As a director-level marketing manager at ABC Inc., I have made considerable career progress as you can see from the attached resume. However, the time is ripe for me to seek a broader range of responsibilities in a new environment at the vice presidential level. My most significant accomplishments of interest to your clients are likely to be the following:

1. Manage bottom line P&L responsibility for our largest group of brands.

2. Prepared and implemented highly successful marketing plans that moved our market share penetration up 5 points, increased profitability 20 percent, and managed all resource allocations for a new product that now grosses over $20 million annually.

3. Evaluated and managed three product line acquisitions including an overseas joint venture in the past five years.

With incentive compensation, I would be seeking an opportunity in the $80,000–$100,000 range. Should you run across a client assignment matching my credentials, please call or email me.

Sincerely,

Figure 15.10

discipline to apply the principles yourself, the career assessment services may be ideal.

The cost of individual counseling varies from $50 to $100 per hour. Complete programs usually cost well over $3,000. A one- to five-day seminar costs from $500 to $2,000.

The charges may be broken down by the individual services rendered. The cost is not minor. Be sure you know what you are paying for and that you are willing to pay the amount for the service provided.

The charges are legitimate and well worth the investment for thousands of people. In all industries there are rip-off artists, but the majority of organizations are extremely reputable. The good firms are earning a handsome profit as they should. Very few are making "obscene" profits, and they won't be for long in our competitive society. Check these firms out just as you would other firms that provide personal services.

//WEB.TIP//

www.jobsamerica.com
Jobs America
Organizers job fairs/usually a job focus/virtual job fairs online.

Summary
• • • • • • • • • • • • • • • •

The job search process is clearly defined in our society and contains built-in checks and balances to guard against nepotism and discrimination. Once the process is understood, it is relatively easy for one to operate effectively within the process.

The job market itself is a pool of available job openings which may or may not be advertised widely for a variety of reasons. You and the employer are the principal actors in your job search scenario, but a strong supporting cast is made up of human resource departments, teachers, work associates, friends, relatives, and acquaintances.

A number of professional services aid in the process of bringing you and an employer together. College career services, employment agencies, executive search firms, state employment offices, websites, and career assistance services all can be used in your employment search strategy.

The key to success is your ability to wisely prospect for job leads and job interviews. The supporting team aids in your prospecting but in the final analysis, your efforts pay the biggest dividends. Applying the techniques and knowledge here will improve your prospecting success.

//WEB.TIP//

www.jobtrack.com
JOBTRAK
One of largest job listing services for college graduates/full and part-time jobs/internships/links to MBA programs/past resumes.

Networking Search Strategies:

Networks – Infosearch

*Who should
I contact?*

The approach you use for achieving your short-term goals must be based upon a solid understanding of the employment world in which you must operate. The employment process is basically a given, but there are many innovative and exciting things you can do to make the system work better for you.

How you choose to utilize the employment system determines the degree of your success. If you understand the basic process, you can enhance your success by creatively manipulating circumstances.

A Creative Search Strategy

An effective job search requires the development of a strategic plan. A strategic plan is a long-term, systematic, and logical approach for achieving a pre-planned objective.

Strategic job search planning establishes a pattern of behavior that will insure your successfully reaching your goal. That goal is to obtain as many job interviews as it is physically possible for you to conduct.

Strategic planning looks at the big picture. Achieving a short-term goal insures the greater possibility of achieving the long-term goal of job satisfaction and career advancement.

As employers screen cover letters and resumes, what factors do they use for deciding who they want to interview? Past performance as highlighted by significant achievements is one important factor. Your education, skills, and abilities can point to the fact that you are capable of doing the assignment for which you are applying.

In spite of your other assets, however, one thing can shine above them all. *Motivation* ranks higher than anything else in an employer's mind as a predictor of performance on the job. You can have the strongest credentials in the world and yet not be *willing* to work hard.

Willingness to work. Attitude. Outlook on life. How is an employer ever going to measure those elusive qualities? There are no psychological tests which measure them accurately and confidently.

What do other people say about you? How do people describe your willingness to work? How do people talk about your attitude? What other people say about you *is* important!

Competence is important, too, but the proper attitude with less competence may still get you more interviews and job offers. Hard work can make up for a lack of competence. Ideally, superior competence and proper attitude come in the same package.

Your immediate goal is to create a plan for getting you the right type of job interviews.

What people say about you impacts getting job interviews.

389

Other people open doors for you by touting your motivational qualities.

An employer is definitely influenced by what others say about you. Other people can open the door for you. Think of the doors that you have personally opened for others. Opening doors is fun and rewarding, and other people enjoy helping you.

Employers hire successful people that they personally know. Even when people who have the "right" qualities are not totally successful, employers prefer to hire them if they know and like them. Hence, *liking you* is an important attitude that you must create in the employer's mind.

When employers do not know job candidates, they must turn to people they know and trust. Employers often ask their friends who they know with credentials appropriate for the open position. Relying on recommendations from friends (or employees) is still the number one way employers fill jobs.

It is who you know that counts!

Many people know you. They are the people who count. They are important because employers will listen to them. They may be "high brows" or "low brows," executive-level or lowest-level, but they may be just the persons on whose opinions an employer relies.

Never underestimate the power of people you know! They will always be your greatest asset.

Contact Networks

A network of hundreds of people is waiting to go to work for you. Who are they? They are people who know and respect you.

The most effective job search technique never had to be invented. It is human nature. It is human nature to want to help others, so you only need to learn how to help others help you.

Recommendations create job interviews.

You have to let others know of your situation and then let human nature take over. People naturally exchange information about other people. It is fun. Use this to help yourself. These people won't ever charge you a fee for helping you, either. They will do it for free because they like you.

Now, there are a few selfish folks in this world, but their numbers are small. All you have to do is deal with your warm, loving, kind, normal, everyday fellow human being.

It is also human nature to talk about jobs. When people hear about an opening, they immediately try to think of who they know that would be "good for that job." Many kind people, when they learn of your situation, will go out of their way to ask others if they have "heard of anything" for a nice person like you.

Get known by people who are willing to work for you.

You are probably saying that it is not that simple, and you are right. Job opportunities given to you on silver platters are not worth any more than the time it took for you to get them.

People whom you have not met cannot like you. People whom you have not met cannot recommend you. It behooves you, therefore, to get out and meet people.

Meeting people is often difficult. A very few of us feel we have "too many" friends and acquaintances. So you probably need a "system" for meeting new people and making new friends. That is where the network idea comes in.

Meet people!

Network Concepts

A network is a series of interlocking connections. Have you ever heard the word "connections" before? Connections facilitate the flow of communication. They make commerce successful and stimulate trade. Connections can shrink the whole world into somewhat of a small community.

You need connections! A network provides those connections. A properly constructed network directly touches thousands of lives. Many of these people can work for you. You need to develop a personal network over time which will make connections for you.

Network Power

The geometric concept is what makes networks so powerful. Each link between two people creates a geometric expansion. If those two people talk to two people and so on through only four sequences, you have potentially shared your situation with 256 people ($2 \times 2 \times 4 \times 16 = 256$). If you share your concerns with 100 people, the potential magnitude of your network is staggering to consider.

This contact network operates on the same principle as the chain letter. It can and does break down at certain points. Nonetheless, whatever action is generated produces good. The "power network" is a win-win situation. You cannot lose by employing it.

You can repair broken links. All you have to do is prepare a routinized follow-up system. Each follow-up contact restores the potential of the geometrically expanding contact network. The odds of its breaking down the second time are smaller, and you will have enhanced the value of your relationship with contact.

Connections

Contacts are your connections and they are participants in your job search strategy. Your initial contacts are your family, relatives, personal friends, general acquaintances, teachers, and work associates.

These contacts are not necessarily in your job lead prospect file. They may eventually become part of that powerful and influential group, but you are not yet at the job contact phase of career planning. You certainly do not want to employ a search technique that immediately starts twisting the arms of those people who are closest to you.

Your acquaintances are your personal sales force to manage.

Network Development

Your first task is to build a strong network of contacts that can be relied upon to work with you. You start this by personally contacting every person close to you.

Contacting people requires a motive. Your motive is not to ask your contacts for a job. A job interview is your ultimate goal, but before you can begin working toward that you must have a network of contacts.

Your first step in developing this network system is to map out your strategy for contacts and write it down.

Create your own network of contacts.

NETWORKING CREATES LIFELONG MENTORS

Networking is an extremely powerful concept. The number of lives that can be touched in the network concept is geometrically expanding. Word of mouth publicity is extremely effective, highly credible, and long living.

Any job search strategy is a long shot. You must be at the right place at the right time with the right credentials. Some would argue that a successful search takes a lot of luck. Yet, the number one method used by employers to source talent is referrals and recommendations.

The informational interview is often used in re-establishing contact with network participants. Although the expressed purpose is to gather information, the main thrust is simply to renew acquaintances and advise of the new status. The interview is not an informational exchange or a job interview.

The purpose is to renew the relationship or create a new one. The goal is to develop lifelong mentors. This is not a one night stand that uses people indiscriminately. A well-developed network represents a smooth functioning set of mentors who may not even know each other. The network is held together by the word "thank you."

The mentors serve as counselors, peers, colleagues, confidants, and resume referral agents. It functions as both a sales force and a personal support group for you. The dynamic mentors serve when needed.

NETWORK CONTACT CARD

Name: _____

Title: _____

Employer: _____

Address: _____

City, State, Zip: _____

Telephone: _____

Last date contacted: _____

Relationship: _____

Purpose:

Next date contacted: _____

Purpose:

Date prepared: _____

Figure 16.1

New Personal Contacts. To create personal contacts you need to be involved. Be a person who gets involved in activities for the enjoyment of meeting others. For an activity to be successful and enjoyable, pick activities in which the people in attendance at the function or activity have interests similar to yours.

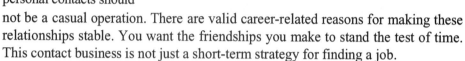

Developing these personal contacts should not be a casual operation. There are valid career-related reasons for making these relationships stable. You want the friendships you make to stand the test of time. This contact business is not just a short-term strategy for finding a job.

Career progression and career management depend upon other people. The most expedient way of burning important bridges is having people discover that you are using them. Developing personal contacts should be a long-term, life-enhancing experience which will benefit you and your circle of friends for many years.

Professional Societies. Professional societies bring people of like career concerns together. Engineers, educators, scientists, salespeople, retailers, and practically every other occupation has such a society.

Most societies have local chapters as well as regional and national groups. Getting to know your work colleagues is one of the best career advancement insurance policies you can purchase. Career and life go together, and members of these groups usually strongly support one another.

If you are not involved in this type of professional organization, you should seriously consider joining one or several. More than just joining, you should try to get involved in a leadership capacity. Your professional association is career insurance.

Social Organizations. Social organizations are clubs. People have joined clubs and created special interest groups for thousands of years. College alumni groups are often some of the most active.

There are some very exclusive social clubs like yacht clubs, country clubs, athletic clubs, and similar groups. Being part of these "in" groups can open an amazing number of doors. It is expensive to join and maintain membership in most of these groups.

Some very popular social clubs are springing up in the form of sporting clubs. There are aerobic, tennis, racquetball, bowling, swimming, handball, etc. groups that are perfect for many people. Many of these have pairing programs for matches and meets that make getting acquainted very natural.

Service Clubs. Nearly every city has numerous service organizations which are always seeking to recruit new members. The fellowship in these is enjoyable, and the projects they carry out are rewarding to the community. As

> **Networking is a long-term strategy for career development.**

> **Your professional colleagues want to work for you.**

DEVELOPING THE NETWORK LIST

- Family relationships
- Work colleagues
- College classmates
- Friends and acquaintances
- Association acquaintances
- Social organizations
- Fraternal organizations
- Civic and political groups

• • • • • • • • • • •

Figure 16.2

Keep your friends and acquaintances in your network in touch with your current job plans.

Your network is your entry into the hidden job market.

these organizations often meet over a lunch or dinner hour, the necessary time commitment for them is minimal.

Religious Institutions.   Churches and synagogues bring people together to worship, but more than any other type of group they inspire friendship. Most churches have many programs outside the normal worship period.

Religious groups have a mission of helping others. Although the members' career advancement is hardly ever one of their stated missions, the fellowship which evolves in religious settings makes for strong friendships and thus contacts.

Network Maintenance

People networks are not developed solely for job search reasons; their friendship extends far beyond career concerns. Nonetheless, networks can greatly aid careers. Some good motives have a natural way of spinning off other good motives.

People networks die if they are not nurtured. They do not demand a lot of care to remain healthy and viable, but some care is necessary. People like to hear from you and to hear that you are doing well.

This talk of nurturing may sound extremely self-serving, but friendships and people networks are mutual associations. Each party enjoys and grows just as the other does.

Keeping friendships and other contacts current is a relatively simple task. It means having lunch with old friends occasionally. It means exchanging holiday greetings. It means small courtesies that show you care about each other in a sincere way.

Using Networks

Your contact network is a precious asset because it is made up of people who know you and respect you. You help them and they help you. Part of this helping is understanding each other's concerns, and a career concern is a very important part of life. Ordinary, friendly people who know you best are the ones most likely to help you the most.

You do not necessarily go to your friends when you need a job. Chances are that they are not in positions to give you a job anyway. But they are usually in touch with people who can help.

There is some therapy involved in talking to your friends about your career concerns. That aspect should not be minimized. From a more pragmatic point of view, you also need some concrete answers.

You must become known by people who count in the job world. You use your network to break into that huge reservoir of often hidden jobs.

NETWORKING BUILDS RELATIONSHIPS

Developing a network support system is a process that should continue throughout your life. It is important to develop these support groups for the purpose of job searching, but it is a far broader goal to establishing lasting bonds. In more cases than not, in the final analysis you may be the person helping others most frequently.

Networking is a mutual helping concept, not a one-way street. Your network participants may not be your best friends but they are good acquaintances who over time can help improve your station in life. As you grow in your career, you, in turn, should be of assistance to others in the group or who might subsequently join your groups.

The network participants are your private sales forces. As your ambassador, they are willing to take action to advance your career. Unfortunately, the network is an indirect entry or re-entry into a new job and thus a slow process. If you employ this approach, plan several months ahead.

Networking is a two-way street. It is a dynamic use of relationships for both personal and professional growth. This partnership arrangement is a creative, "right brain" strategy that occasionally might deviate from accepted norms.

The primary objective in networking is to become better known so that you will be referred for jobs often. Your network representatives have a genuine concern for your interests and identify with your concerns. Since you are not requesting a job, there is no negative turndown, and there is a positive feeling about your interest in them.

Going after job interviews is hard work and it is often mentally depressing. Receiving turndown after turndown without so much as getting a formal job interview is ego-deflating. This is where your contact network can come to your aid.

Your network opens doors for you.

You need information. You need advice. You need to open some doors. Many avenues to job interviews are not as simple as might first appear. Waiting and hoping for the right opportunity to come along is futile unless you start to make things happen. If you employ the network concept, you will never have to job hunt again. Your network, if cultivated regularly, will cause jobs to hunt your talents.

Interviewing for Information

The word "no" is an extremely damaging word. The traditional job search strategies invite potential employers to say "no." How can you get away from the negative syndrome and into a more positive environment?

You must remove yourself whenever possible from the negative world. Your network contacts help you do that by offering to speak positively on your behalf.

Your goal should be to avoid getting yourself into a situation that calls for a firm "yes or no" decision. The type of decision required after a job interview is a "yes or no" response. Some decision situations are unavoidable, but you can avoid many of them.

Many people get turned away before they ever get to the interview stage. You can avoid much of that negative environment.

The secret is to avoid putting others in the position of having to give you a negative decision. You accomplish that by avoiding the job interview until you firmly know that a job exists and that you want to be a candidate.

You rarely ask your network contacts directly for a job. You invite them to help you in the job search process which they rarely will refuse to do. Some contacts may not work hard on your behalf, but they do not have to tell you "no" either.

Your goal is to get your name passed along to others in a positive manner. You expect them to describe you as a highly motivated, hard working person with some excellent job skills. If they cannot do that, they will simply politely not speak negatively on your behalf.

Interviewing for information is another way to gently add to your network. You select people who are in a position to help you in your job goals if they elect to do so.

Interviewing for information relative to your career is referred to as "infosearch." Interviewing for information makes things start to happen. You might not believe that you need information or advice, but ask for it anyway.

Infosearch is a basic employment strategy. It is sincere and honest, and it accomplishes things that job interviewing has no chance of doing.

You interview when you know a job exists. The goal of interviewing is to obtain a job offer.

The goal of infosearch is to collect information. It is a preliminary step to job interviewing. Interviewing begets job offers. Infosearching begets information which may *lead* to job interviews.

Interviewing for information makes important things start to happen for you.

Infosearch indirectly produces the real job interviews which you need. Job interviews result when you are at the *right* place at the *right* time with the *right* qualifications. Infosearching produces right situations.

The results are not accidental, nor are they due to luck. The results are the outcome of a carefully orchestrated career search strategy.

NOW JUST RELAX... THE BOYS AND I ONLY WANT A LITTLE INFORMATION ABOUT YOUR JOB.

Infosearch does not produce job offers, but it can help you get your foot in the door.

Infosearch Objectives

The purpose of infosearch is three-fold. You need information to gain new facts and to confirm your views about your career goals. Infosearch is a real-world feedback system that gives you a

UNDER "BIG" COULD YOU CHECK ALL THE WHEELS, SHOTS, WIGS, AND CHEESES?

chance to re-assess your basic career objectives that emerged from your earlier self-assessment and career exploration. Infosearch data helps you clarify and further specify your career plans based upon some real world input.

Infosearch, when followed out according to a plan, will greatly expand the size of your contact network. As the infosearch process systematically and continuously progresses, more and more people become involved in your network.

This networking process will eventually become the base of your operations for obtaining specific job leads. Once you have firm job leads, you can gear up for an altogether different approach to interviewing.

Hidden Agendas. Your basic agenda is to get better known in the circles that count. If you are operating in the right circles, job leads will come almost automatically.

In most cases you want to go in and talk specifically about the career field in which you have an interest. However, you may want to narrow that and simply seek advice on job hunting approaches.

There may be instances when you do not want the participant in your infosearch to know that you are in the job market. You still need to make use of your contact so that he or she can get to know you better. In those cases, you will need a rationale for setting up an appointment.

There are hundreds of topics you can use as legitimate rationales for getting together. If you are in school or taking a continuing education class, you can approach your contact as part of an educational learning project. You can even offer to show him or her the results of your project at a later date.

If you are currently employed, you could approach contacts on behalf of a product to which you want to introduce them. You could solicit opinions as part of a market or product research effort. You could even try to sell the product or service to them on a low-key basis.

It is common for people to get together to discuss an avocation. You may have some mutual friends or you may be supporters of the same sports team. You may be approaching contacts on behalf of a civic responsibility that you have. You may want to talk politics or religion.

The rationale for the meeting is relatively immaterial from the infosearch standpoint. You need about 30 minutes to help the person to know you better. You need to guide the conversation sufficiently to allow you to talk enough about yourself so that you are better known by the person.

INFOSEARCH GOALS

- Provide information
- Expand network size
- Create job interview later
- Open hidden job market

• • • • • • • • • • •

Figure 16.3

Create realistic situations for personal interaction that permit you to become better known.

Your hidden agenda is to get known better by influential people who you want to add to your network.

Advantages.   Infosearch has some major advantages over job interviewing. If you were job interviewing, you probably would not get the audience. Job interviewing is a pressure generating situation for both parties.

Infosearch takes the heat off of both parties. You each have a greater chance of just being yourselves.

There is no point where you have to deal with rejection. The contact does not have to handle a delicate situation by sending you a rejection letter.

Infosearch permits both of you to create and leave a positive impression of each other. The positive feeling you can leave with the contact means that he or she can relax and say, "I like that person."

Infosearch costs you and the other party nothing but time. Hopefully, it will turn out to be a pleasant experience for both parties. In many cases, your contact will be flattered that you called and took the time to seek counsel. You very likely created important goodwill.

Most important of all, you are building an effective network of people who know and respect you.

One of the side benefits could be a job lead or an interview recommendation. It also creates another possible mutual acquaintance that you and a potential employer may someday share.

Targets.   Infosearch starts with the people. Those people will lead you to other people. The starting points are teachers, work colleagues, relatives, friends, acquaintances, and friends of friends.

In addition to these people, you need to begin to develop additional infosearch people who will become part of an expanded contact network. You want to look toward leaders and highly successful people for this next group.

Career Participants.   You want to begin to focus on people in career fields to which you aspire or people in related career areas. You want to ask these people questions related to your career interest. Some of them could eventually turn out to be decision makers that you will interview with for jobs.

You may not know many of these career participants. Some of them may not be known by people in your contact network either. You will need to employ an additional approach for expanding your infosearch network.

This additional approach is not unlike that of searching for job leads. In fact, you might want to develop names in a job lead prospect file simultaneously since you are contacting the same sources.

Your infosearch network will be much smaller than your contact network. It will also be more specific-career oriented.

People in your career field are likely to be most helpful to you.

Contact Sources

Who you approach largely depends upon your career thrust and your specific job target. Contact information is also available from persons outside your network who make it a profession to develop contacts.

Professional Counselors.   These people work for college career services, educational institutions (teachers and counselors), government employment services, government social work agencies, and private employment agencies or search firms.

Approach these groups directly. Give them a telephone call, set up an appointment, or walk in to visit with them. The services and institutions deal in jobs. They will provide you with specific names of people to contact if you can give them some guidance on specific types of people you wish to contact.

```
· · · · · ·  CONTACT RESOURCES FOR NAMES OF INDIVIDUALS  · · · · · ·

    — Guide to American Directories
    — Encyclopedia of Associations
    — Standard and Poor's Register
    — Directory of Corporate Affiliations
    — Standard Directory of Advertisers
    — Federal Directory
    — Polk's World Bank Directory
    — Directory of Directors
    — Dunn and Bradstreet Million Dollar Directory
    — Standard Directory of Advertising Agencies
    — Thomas Register of American Manufacturers
    — Taylor's Encyclopedia of Government Officials
    — Directory of American Firms Operating in Foreign Countries
    — World Wide Web

                    · · · · · · · · · ·
                    Figure 16.4
```

Do not ask them to give you a list of all their contacts. That could be thousands of names. Help them sort out the specific group of contacts that are relevant to your situation. Try to obtain telephone numbers as well as addresses.

You are likely to still need more names to approach. Your next source is a career library, the internet, or the public library. Thousands of names are available there for you to view.

Newspapers.   Classified ads for employment frequently give specific names of job decision makers. You do not need to confine your search to the most up-to-date newspapers. Back issues are just as good. You are not going to apply for a specific listed job so you do not even need to concern yourself with whether or not a job listing is in your area of specialty.

What you need to look for are organizations that you feel might have the position to which you aspire. You want to contact someone in that position to whom you can go and talk.

Normally, a want ad gives the HR department's employment individual as a contact. You will need to call that person and obtain the name of someone working in your field. Try to obtain complete contact information, including the telephone number.

Telephone Book.   In many instances you can identify the organizations or at least types of organizations that are most likely to employ people in the capacity you are seeking. The telephone book's yellow pages should help you in this identifying process. These are available on the internet.

The only information about the organization you need to get from the phone book is its address and telephone number. You can call the switchboard to obtain the name, title, and telephone number of the person or persons working in your area of specialty.

Many times you can go to the plant or office building and see a directory in the lobby. If there is a receptionist, he or she may share the internal telephone directory with you for a limited period of time. Scanning through the lobby directory or the internal telephone book will greatly aid in identifying the right people to contact.

— Business Periodical Index
— Readers Guide To Periodical Literature
— College Placement Annual – Job Choices
— The Wall Street Journal
— Barron's
— Business Week
— Forbes
— Fortune
— Money
— Nation's Business
— Inc
— The Internet

· · · · · · · · · ·

Figure 16.5

Professional Associations. Your area of competence may have a professional association (or several of them) which many of the people in the position you seek belong to. If you could obtain that membership list, you would have one of the best potential infosearch networks imaginable.

Chances are very good that your P.A. has a website. There is often a membership directory on it. It typically provides links to contact data.

Public libraries can help you identify relevant associations and professional societies. Obtain the name of the executive secretary of one or more of these. Call and see if you can join the association as an aspirant. Before asking about joining, you might simply ask if you can obtain a membership directory. It may be on the www.

Do not indicate that you intend to use this as an employment prospect list. You want to use it in your infosearch process. Your purpose is to become known by people who count in your area of interest.

Geographical location may be a limiting variable. If so, select the names of those people in your region. If geography is not a problem, try to identify the current and past leaders in the profession. These are often older people who are more willing to help others break into and move up in the profession.

Directories. Public libraries maintain extensive collections of various types of directories. Whether you are seeking a job in education, government, business, or the non-profit sector, you may well find a directory pertinent to your inter-

KINDLY SEE THAT NOBODY ELSE GETS A FOOT IN THE DOOR PLEASE.

ests. You are particularly interested in directories which are updated annually. There is even a *Directory of Directories!*

In the business sector, you will find directories like *Thomas' Register, Million Dollar Directory, Standard and Poor's, Moody's,* and those of a variety of investment services. There is an *Encyclopedia of Associations* and a *Foundation Directory.* One very useful directory is the *Directory of National Trade and Professional Associations.*

You need specific names, preferably names of people one or two levels above the position you will be seeking. Nearly all of these directories are on the internet. Surf to these sites for the specific contacts you may need.

Other Publications. A librarian or career center counselor can direct you to a variety of sources of names. Many specific career publications contain leads for you to follow.

Opening Doors

Begin your infosearch by telephoning your contact. If the contact is someone you know, you only need to indicate the subject and how much time you need.

Most infosearch interviews last 30–45 minutes. If your contact has been recommended by another person, be certain to mention that person's name. In asking for a few minutes of someone's time, you are appealing to their desire to help you with your project or concern. Most people are flattered when you seek their advice, so that helps you get your feet in the door.

Very busy people may want to put you off. Do not push. Being a pusher will not help you meet your objective of getting known *and* liked. Volunteer to meet them after work or for lunch, but do not be persistent. If you get a "no" answer, close the conversation by saying you want to keep the door open. Leave your name and number. You should even follow up with a letter and a resume later.

Conducting. An infosearch appointment requires planning. You want the interview to flow in the direction that is most advantageous to you. You set up the meeting and thus you are responsible for controlling it. You will look disorganized and ill-informed if you let the interview take its own course.

Infosearch planning involves setting up a strategy. If you set up a 30-minute appointment, you need to break the time into at least four components with time frames tied to each section.

After a brief introduction and some rapport building, you will need to take charge. Taking charge means knowing what you are going to do in an organized sequence of events. You cannot afford to waste the other person's valuable time.

Format. Most infosearches follow a question and answer routine. An exception is where you take time to make a presentation. Your questions should be written

//WEB.TIP//

www.ajb.dni.us
America's Job Bank
One of the largest job sites in the world/maintained by U.S. Dept of Labor/extensive search capability by location, function, requirements, etc./links to public and private employment sites.

INFOSEARCH PROCESS

- Telephone for thirty-minute appointment
- Send confirming follow-up letter or email
- Prepare presentation
- Make list of questions
- Conduct informational interview
- Leave a feeler
- Ask for other names to contact
- Send thank-you letter or email
- Maintain regular contact

• • • • • • • • • • •

Figure 16.6

down in advance. You need to convey the impression that you have a definite purpose and want to cover a lot of territory in a short period of time.

Take a note pad. Have your questions written down. Make notes if necessary as the contact speaks. By nods, gestures, and writing, you will be showing great interest in what is being said. People like to sense that you are accepting what they say as important.

Watch for areas of obvious pride. Begin to probe into these areas even if it means temporarily deviating from your interview outline. If the contact puts great importance in a given area, take the time to explore it in sufficient depth. It may be an area of importance to you that you have overlooked.

Questions. The questions you ask largely determine the impression you leave. They must be well thought out and relevant to the situation. You are being evaluated more on the basis of your questions than anything else.

If you are infosearching someone who is working in a field or job to which you aspire, you need to focus your questions in this area. The following questions (and those in Figure 16.7) are representative of the line of questioning that you should take.

What do you do? What is a typical day like? What is a terrible day like? May I tag along for a day? What do you like and dislike about your job? How did you get into this field? What has been your line of advancement?

What is your academic training? What will be your next promotion? What would you recommend for me? What do employers in your career field look for in interviews?

Close. Before you end the interview think back on your original objective. Has it been met? The close is the time you begin to pull everything together. Let the person know that you have been carefully recording (mentally or in writing) what was being said. Summarize the results.

Be sure to close on a happy note. Tell your contact that it was an enjoyable and truly enlightening learning experience for you. Thank the person for the time and information. Let him or her know how you intend to use the information and factor it into future decisions.

Keep the door open for a return visit. Ask for permission to visit again if you should find you need more information at a later time. The memory of your pleasant attitude and smiling face is the best thing you can leave with the person.

Leave some information with your contact. At a minimum you will leave a business or calling card. Encourage the person to contact you if anything important was not covered. If appropriate and subtle, you might even ask the person to review your resume with you and then leave a copy.

You are going to need more infosearch contacts. Before you leave, ask if the contact knows other people in similar capacities who would be good to "touch base with." If you keep expanding your network, your objective will soon be met.

Feelers. Many times a "feeler" is appropriate. A feeler is a subtle way of saying that you are interested in employment in such an area. Feelers are not direct requests for job leads, but they come close. A few examples are listed below.

- Not looking now, but . . .
- If you hear of something . . .
- Might consider a move if . . .
- Keep me in mind if you . . .

You are in charge and asking questions, not the interviewer. The tables are turned and yet you are still getting better known.

Prepare your questions in advance.

- What are some important long-term trends affecting your industry?
- How aware are others in your profession of (cite an important trend) and what impact might it have?
- How do you see (a problem or issue) affecting your (industry or profession) in five years?
- To what extent do (trends and issues) impact upon hiring policies?
- What educational qualifications are necessary before starting a career in (occupation or industry)?
- Which of my credentials should I emphasize if I interview in this field?
- What actions should I take to better prepare me for a career in this field?
- How much competition am I going to face if I elect a career in your field?
- What good sources of further information about this trend would be good for me to read?
- Can you recommend some other good people for me to talk to?
- If I got into your field, what would my co-workers be like?
- What level of recognition do most organizations give to this endeavor?
- To what extent do other organizations invest in further training in your field?
- What are some of the typical advancement paths in your field?
- How secure is the field in most organizations in terms of contributing to the bottom line?
- Can you give me some idea of the entry level compensation and what might be possible later?
- What types of opportunities outside of the field have people gone into later?
- Why do people accept less money in this field when they could be earning a lot more elsewhere?
- Based upon my background, where do you think that I would have to start?
- What would you suggest for me to do right now?
- How might I re-position my resume to improve my chances for success?
- How could I use my accomplishments to tie myself more directly to the field in an interview?
- Do you feel that I should go back to school to pick up additional training in the field?
- What is the best way to get through the tough resume screen in the field with so many applicants?
- Could you identify some organizations which employ large numbers of people in your occupation?
- How important is an advanced degree in this field for long-term advancement?
- If you had to start your career again, what education and experiences would you try to obtain?
- What is a typical day (week or month) of specific duties and job activities like?
- What do you really like and dislike about the field?
- Can you recommend some specific websites that will keep me current?

· · · · · · · · · ·

Figure 16.7

Feelers keep the door open for later follow-up.

Feelers do not work immediately, but when properly followed up, they can be very positive statements.

Feelers let your contact know that if the right circumstance was identified, you might consider a move. Feelers do not say, "I need a job." Feelers do not ask for a job but their message is clear.

ACTUALLY SOME DAY I'D LIKE **YOUR** JOB.

Infosearch Follow-up

In preparing and conducting an infosearch, you invested several hours. Hopefully, there was an important payoff at the time of the appointment. You need to have longer-term payoffs as well. A follow-up can significantly increase the contact's effectiveness for you.

Your conversation revolved around a topic of mutual interest, but since you called the meeting, you are the one who should send a note of appreciation. Let the person know how you felt about the meeting in a positive way. If you send a follow-up note, your contact will assume that your goals for the meeting have been satisfied.

After the infosearch you will better know if your contact might prove helpful as a source of future job leads. Regardless of who the contact is, the odds are very

- - - - - - - - - - - - - **CONDUCTING THE INFOSEARCH** - - - - - - - - - - - - -

Plan expected results in advance
Prepare an introduction or purpose
Give a brief background bibliography
Prepare a list of questions
Focus on three to five topics
Ask specific questions, not generalities
Confine the interview to thirty minutes
Request advice frequently
Listen attentively
Write notes in your notebook
Follow up on questions after listening attentively
Ask for names of others to contact
Avoid "Do you know of any jobs?"
Leave a feeler about job options
Close with "Thank you"
Follow up with letter and resume with thank you
Build a bridge for future follow-up

- - - - - - - - - -
Figure 16.8

high that he or she has the power to influence others who can help you later in your job search.

In all probability, you will want to send a resume with a brief note leaving a "feeler." An attachment as an email thank you might be appropriate.

Immediately after the infosearch you have an obvious reason for getting back in touch because you want to say thank you. You need to maintain the relationship through periodic contacts. The best way to do this is to let the person know of your progress on a regular basis, probably monthly.

Send the results of any project that you may have discussed in the interview. Is there something you have or know that would be of value to the contact? Use it as another reason to re-establish contact.

Always leave feelers whenever you contact these persons. Encourage them to "keep in touch" and promise to keep them informed of your plans and progress. Keep current resumes in their hands. Always acknowledge how appreciative you are of their help.

Keep in touch on a periodic basis.

Infosearch is part of your exploring stage of career planning and an integral part of your employment strategy. Infosearch is the best tool you have for learning about the field in which you want to work.

Infosearch is one of the most effective means of tapping the "hidden job market." The job market is hidden partly because people want to keep what they say about others a secret. If you can keep people whispering nice things about you to others, the hidden job market has a good chance of opening its doors to you.

Like most employment strategies, infosearch has some upper limits. It has pluses and minuses. You can improve on methodology, strategy, and technique, but yet you are limited by some constraints which are beyond your control, such as the economic environment.

On the other hand, the beauty of infosearch is that there are no limits placed upon your resourcefulness, creativity, competence, achievement, and contribution. If you keep putting those together in packages for others to see, evaluate, and discuss, you have achieved a major breakthrough in your job search.

Career Action Projects
• •

Contact Network Project

Prepare a list of all of the people you know who might possibly be influential in your job search process. Include name, title or occupation, address, and telephone number for each of them. In developing this list, incorporate the ideas for generating this list discussed here.

To aid in the development, categorize your list by teachers, work associates, friends, relatives, acquaintances, and friends of friends.

Network Action Project. Make a network list go down a three-inch column on the left side of an 8-1/2" x 11" sheet of paper. Label this column "Contact."

Beside each name, indicate what action you expect to carry out to involve that person in your career planning program. You may be giving them your resume, job interviewing, infosearching, requesting advice, etc. Make this list go down the middle three inches of the 8-1/2" x 11" sheet and label it "Action."

You should have about 50 names in your list. Leave about one-half inch between names. You should have their name, title, employer, address, telephone number, and any other relevant data on this list.

Beside each name and action indicate the approximate date that you believe would be most appropriate for you to make your move. Note this date in the 1-1/2" column on the right side of the page.

You should now have an action plan for involving your contacts in your job search strategy. Follow this plan and build a follow-up system into it. You later should tape a second 8-1/2" x 11" page beside the first to record the "Date" and "Action/Results" of future contacts.

Your goal is to encourage the contacts to work on your behalf in sharing your resume, providing infosearch people, and making specific job referrals. This network will only continue to work for you as you continue massaging it.

Infosearch Project

Develop a list of all people who you feel are candidates for your infosearch based upon your contact network. Add to that list names of people currently working in the career field to which you aspire who would be likely infosearch prospects.

They must be located within a reasonable driving distance for you to accomplish your concerns. Include the name, title or occupation, address, and telephone number of each of your infosearch people.

Infosearch Career Action Project. Based upon your specific background, develop a series of twenty questions which you plan to ask each person. Preface each question with one or two sentences that say something about you and indicate a reason for asking the question.

Each question, with its informative preface, should be about 5 to 10 single-spaced, typed sentences with about two inches between questions for later responses.

For example, "I studied English for four years in college and worked as a reporter for two years. I believe that I have pretty fair writing abilities. What was your training and how much did it help you in your career?"

Conduct at least one infosearch using your questions as a guide. Prepare an evaluation of one single-spaced page explaining the circumstances and the results. On a separate page evaluate the potential use of this resource in helping you gain

CULTIVATING CONNECTIONS

Contacting individuals who can help you identify potential employers and/or tell you about potential job openings for which you might be qualified is fundamental in career networking activities.

Most employers who need to hire someone to help them usually start informally identifying potential candidates long before the position is formally announced.

Your best job interviews may well be informal chats with individuals giving you job information for you to use in finding employment elsewhere. You should recognize that you are continually cultivating connections.

The informal "advice sharing" session can be your job interview. Do not leave these important events as an unplanned chance meeting.

Making the right connection does not insure a job offer. No matter how powerful your contact is, you still have to compete and prove that you are the best candidate for any opening.

Regardless of how an employer sources candidates for a job, you can be certain that you face competition. You could embarrass your connection if you fared poorly in subsequent interviews with others in the organization.

One of your strongest connection creators are university alumni. Many universities provide graduates and alumni mutual access to each other by distributing directories and presenting meetings for mixing purposes in selected locations. Investigate the possibility of cultivating that connection opportunity. You may find alumni names on the internet for your college.

Cultivating connections goes far beyond career concerns. Successful people constantly nurture and go out of their way to build lasting relationships with many people.

Relationship building activities occur at regular business activities, conventions, trade shows, alumni gatherings, professional association meetings, athletic clubs, civic groups, political events, religious organizations, social friendships, and even family reunions. The need to cultivate your connections never ceases.

Whatever your career endeavors (most of us have several), success depends on other people. How effectively you get your ideas and thoughts across to clients, subordinates, supervisors, and personal acquaintances impacts upon your ultimate success.

Cultivating connections is fruitless without an ability to subsequently deliver a well-organized, articulate, and meaningful message.

entry into the position you desire. Particularly comment about the feelers that you may have left.

As a follow-up, write a letter of appreciation to your infosearch contact. Mention some important points which were established in your conversation. This letter should not be more than two pages.

Re-evaluate your use of the infosearch technique in your job search strategy. Will it work for you? Why or why not? What would be the long-term advantages and disadvantages of your adopting this strategy? Come to some decision with a written rationale of how you intend to use the infosearch strategy. Write on a separate sheet of paper what you learned from this infosearch project.

Preparing for Your Interviews:

Before – During – After

The development of the proper tools necessary to obtain the interview requires considerable time and effort. Your resume concisely summarizes your background so that the essentials can be readily identified.

The interview is not the place to restate the resume. Employers can read! You should dive into the meat of your resume (your strongest points) and expand upon them. Your resume is a written presentation of your credentials while the interview is an oral presentation of them.

The employer is interested in what makes you think and react and, more importantly, why you behave as you do. The employer will also want to probe into the major activities listed on your resume so they can appraise the type of qualities not revealed on the piece of paper.

What motivates you? What are your values? What kind of personality do you have? Are your verbal expression abilities consistent with your background? Are you a leader or a follower? What excites you? What are your ambitions? How much thinking have you done about your career plans? What do you have to offer? What are you willing to do?

Why should I hire you?

Interview Preparation

The secret to successful interviewing is a sound presentation. All successful salespeople develop personal presentations. You are attempting to sell yourself and should follow the same presentation strategies.

Development of the Presentation

A good presentation requires preparation—much preparation. By following sound career planning strategies, a major step has been taken in the presentation: your self-assessment. A good interviewer has been trained to probe until an appreciation of both your strong and weak qualities have been established.

Relative size of firm in the industry
Potential growth for the industry
Annual sales growth
Array of product line or services
Current customer base
Potential new markets, products, or services
Various price points in product or service line
Competitive products
Competitive organizations
Age of top management
Organizational structure
Geographical locations
Number of plants, stores, or sales outlets
Short-term profit picture
Type of training program
Average time in non-management assignment
Recent items in the news
Structure of assets
Relocation policies
Percentage of annual earnings growth
Present price of stock
Recent trend in stock price
People you know in the firm
Formal versus on-the-job training
Typical career path in your field
Location of home office
Name of recruiter and other contacts
Website URL

• • • • • • • • • •

Figure 17.1

If you conducted a self-assessment, you should know what conclusions the employer will make. Knowing what the employer will find makes it relatively easy to direct the interview toward your strengths rather than let recruiters focus on your weaknesses. You should never offer explanations and apologies for weak points; you should direct the interview to emphasize your strong points.

The secret to successful interviewing is developing a presentation that allows *you* to *control* the interview.

Your planned presentation allows you to control the interview.

Many employers are not expert interviewers. In this situation, a well-prepared presentation is most important because *many* employers emphasize reasons why *not* to hire. You should plan to support reasons why you *should* be hired.

Preparation Strategies

Why should I hire you? If you don't know the answer to this question, you are *not* the person for the job. Regardless of your background, you can make a strong verbal presentation for a given assignment if you have done adequate advance preparation.

DEVELOP YOUR STRATEGIC MARKETING PLAN

Your interview is an integral component in your career plan which is analogous to your personal strategic marketing plan. In arriving at the interview stage, you completed a major part of your marketing plan. The typical strategic marketing plan has seven basic elements:

1. Define the product
2. Choose the market
3. Prepare promotional materials
4. Design the selling techniques
5. Deliver the message
6. Negotiate the details
7. Close the deal

The interview process picks up at Step 4. Your focus is now on designing your presentation, executing it in the interview and then negotiating your offer and starting date as you close the deal.

Preparation includes homework about *yourself*. It also involves homework about the *employer*.

Annual reports, websites, investment services, faculty, friends, employment brochures, news articles and personnel of the employers can all help you understand both yourself and the employers.

If you know what the firm is seeking, your presentation can emphasize all your relevant strong points. Figure 17.1 identifies some of the information you should have on the employer prior to the interview. If it is impossible to obtain some of this information before going to the interview (after a massive search), request some of it during the interview.

Having this information before the actual interview will enable you to spend a few hours developing a presentation that will interweave your background into what the employer has to offer. Thus, by adequately researching the organization, you will stand a much better chance of creating a positive impression.

Being knowledgeable about the employer prior to the interview leaves you free to explore other possibilities during the interview. If the employer is spending time providing information that you could have found out through research, very little is being said about *why you should be considered* for the job.

The employer is there to evaluate you. It will be your turn to evaluate the employer after getting an invitation for an in-depth interview or receiving an offer. Interest is shown by asking relevant and pertinent questions. Develop a presentation that includes questions requiring specific answers about the organization.

Knowing yourself and how you can relate to the employer's needs strengthens your presentation.

Purpose of the Interview

The first interview with an employer is normally only an *initial* screening. Applicants can be told "no further interest" at first interviews, but seldom are they hired then.

- Tell a story
- Relate a life episode
- Create an action photo
- Share a class example
- Present a relevant term paper
- Illustrate with examples
- Develop a team illustration
- Use humor for emphasis
- Poke fun at yourself gently
- Show a project result
- Interject values
- Tell an achievement story
- Point to performance numbers
- Quantify your presentation
- Mention mutual acquaintances

Figure 17.2

Personnel department staffs often conduct these initial screening interviews and then refer applicants to specific department heads who actually make the decisions to hire or not to hire.

The second interview with the department manager is not much different from the one with personnel—the department manager simply sees fewer candidates. Consequently, preparation for subsequent interviews differs very little.

It is possible in the second interview that the interviewer will ask more specific questions about a specific skill level for a technical field like accounting, data processing, or engineering. The same interviewing techniques and strategies apply to both interviews.

The initial job interview is one of the most important events in the employment process. The twenty or thirty minutes spent with the interviewer can determine, or at least influence, the future course of your life.

Interviewers are continually amazed at the number of interviewees who drift into job interviews without any apparent preparation and only the vaguest idea of what they are going to say. This suggests the attitude of, "Well, here I am. What do you have for me?" And that is often the end of it.

Interview Results

Interviewers often speak with ten to fifteen job applicants each day, so they become quite adept at identifying talent and potential managers. They often have undergone extensive training in interviewing techniques as well.

Perhaps some knowledge of interviewers' objectives and problems will help you understand their role and help shape your interviewing behavior.

Although there are no established norms for determining what a company's success ratio in interviewing should be, a random sample of twenty interviews for an entry-level assignment might reveal the results shown in Figure 17.3. This implies that an employer must speak with twenty applicants for each hire. Two-thirds of the applicants who receive offers turn them down.

TYPICAL EMPLOYER INTERVIEW RESULTS

- 20 Interviews
- 16 Turndowns
- 4 Follow-ups
- 3 Offers
- 1 Acceptance

Figure 17.3

SELLING TECHNIQUES PRODUCE OFFERS

The accepted secret to successful interviewing is the ability to sell *yourself*. But often an *indirect* way of getting to the final sale can be more successful than a *frontal* sales assault. The important clue is to be adept at creating a "buying opportunity" during the interview.

Professional sales personnel like to refer to themselves as "problem solvers." In sales terminology the interview is a "solution sale." The employer has a problem and is going to make an offer to the person who seems to be the best solution. Solution selling uses concepts that are also applicable in interviewing.

Concept 1: Determine Customer Desires. You cannot sell a customer something until you know what the customer is looking to buy. Your first task is to find out what the interviewer is "looking to buy." You need more than a job title. You need the individual profile, including specific traits as well as skills.

Proper interview preparation before the sale generates some of this information. The rest of it must come in the early phases of the interview so you can adjust your presentations to fit the customer's desires.

Concept 2: Make the Sales Pitch and Close. Many job candidates fail to ask for the offer in a professionally accepted manner. You do not bluntly say, "Can I have the job?" but you can say, "I believe this job matches my credentials and I want you to know that I am very interested."

The close can be awkward. If you ask, "Where do you think I stand in relation to other applicants?" you are not likely to get a definitive answer. But you may receive some clues as to where your qualifications need some enhancements. Another phrase you can use is "What do you see as my major weaknesses for this job?"

Concept 3: Overcome Objections. No applicant is going to be perfect. Hiring is an art that requires compromises. If you can obtain clues as to your interviewer's reservations about you, you can deal with them directly.

Addressing objections is an empathic process. You try to help the interviewer see your limitations while emphasizing your strengths. Never force an interviewer to defend a statement, especially by asking "why."

Instead, absorb the objection by repeating the objection and indicating that you understand this reservation. Repeating it psychologically waters it down for both of you. Then insert the key word.

The key word is "however."

This simple word places the objection on the shelf while you follow with a statement about your unique abilities that another person might not be able to offer.

Dealing with objections in this non-threatening manner keeps the door open instead of closed. As the dialogue continues, more and more obstacles can be removed from the path of an offer. You can repeat the question, "How do you feel about me?" a second or third time to give you a chance to deal openly with objections.

Rather than dealing with objections so openly, you may feel more comfortable approaching the objection from the positive angle. This approach is to minimize objections by maximizing your other qualities that might solve the same problem caused by your limitations.

This sales technique may not always work, but it should enhance your chances. When it does not produce perfect results, you still learn from the interview experience which should increase your odds for success in future interviews with other organizations.

Successful interviewing requires successful selling. Perhaps learning and applying a few "proven" sales techniques in the interview will work for you.

The information does not imply, however, that you can expect one offer for every seven interviews you have. It is hard for employers to improve their batting average (whether above or below that suggested in Figure 17.3), but it is relatively easy for you to improve *your* success ratio.

Following the ideas suggested here will definitely improve your interviews. There are many applicants, some with poorer qualifications than others, who receive positive feedback from each interview they take.

Preparation and presentation are the most important elements of your job search. Success involves hard work. Planning an interview is easy. If you follow these suggestions, you will not necessarily get an offer from every interview, but you will significantly improve your chances of doing so.

Interview Evaluation Criterion

How important is the interview? Most recruiters contrast it to the last game of the league playoffs. If you don't win, you can't play in the World Series.

The initial interview is not the World Series. If you are successful, you get a chance to continue. If you fail, you are usually through with that employer.

Your cover letter, resume, and contacts helped get you to the *initial* interview. But it is a solo event from that point forward. No one else can "get you a job." Others help "get you an interview," but "pull" and "pizzazz" rarely help convince the person who must rely on your future performance to hire you if you are not the "best" qualified person.

What criteria do employers use in defining the *best* qualified person? The unenlightened often guess that job-related skills are most important. Wrong!

Everyone interviewed for a given assignment usually has the skills needed to do the job. Otherwise, they would not have gotten through the initial resume screen. The interview would not be needed if "skills" were the main criteria.

The more important *subjective* factors come into the decision at the time of the initial interview and subsequent follow-up interviews.

The initial interview is a rigorous screen for these non-qualifiable variables. Your attributes that are relayed in the initial interview reign paramount over your basic skill set. Many employers have a difficult time articulating these subjective factors, but they all say, "I know what I am looking for."

The purpose of the first interview is not to sell you on how great the organization is so that you will say "yes" to their offer. The "sales pitch" comes after you pass the first interview and often after several other screening interviews.

What are the subjective factors? The interviewer's task is to *predict* how well you will perform in the next three to five years. The subjective factors are really longer-term predictors of success.

Figure 17.4 lists some of the most frequently stated factors that employers use in assessing interviewees.

Researchers take pleasure in asking recruiters to rank the most important personal qualities sought. Whether you are reading the most recent evaluation in *The Wall Street Journal, The Journal of College Placement,* or the *HR Journal,* the web, etc., the results are always a little different. The differences in the ranking of importance vary by type of position sought, industry, and job level.

Advance preparation and a planned presentation greatly increase your chances for a successful interview.

Subjective factors are far more important than skill factors in the employer's evaluation of you.

The important point is that these five factors always appear in the rankings:

- Communicative Abilities
- Realistic Career Goals
- Personality Congruence
- Leadership Characteristics
- Motivational Achievements

Research suggests that if you address these five factors you will succeed in the interview. Your success can be measured by how effective you demonstrate your qualities vis-a-vis the position which you are seeking.

Your goal is to *prove congruence* between your attributes and those needed in the initial job and in potential jobs that later follow from the initial assignment. Interviewers are hiring you for your *potential* performance as much as they are for your current abilities for the job. Therefore, you need to impart information about your attributes that impact on *both* the initial job as well as those to which you aspire.

Of course, you cannot come out and say:

> "I consider myself a great communicator, with solid future career plans. My personality closely matches what you seek, and I have the leadership abilities to excite others to follow me. I am a strongly motivated person who works hard to achieve significant performance levels."

You would be laughed out of the interview. Yet, recruiters are trying to boil things down to that simple analysis. It behooves you to leave that impression without an overbearing attitude.

You get your message across by telling *stories*. Your goal is draw upon an episode or event in your life that will illustrate your ability to plan, take charge of an activity and, through others, produce a successful outcome.

As you relay the event, your ability to organize your thoughts and articulate your message in an assertive, confident style will become evident. As you get enthused about the event with its peaks and valleys, your personality attributes are also likely to come forth.

If you plan these stories in advance and make a point to illustrate each of the five basic evaluative factors, the message you leave with the interviewer will show you as the exact type of person sought for the job.

Before the Interview

Get the Facts

Prior to the interview, it is important that you adequately research the organization. You should try to find out about the organization's products or services, what its growth has been, and how its prospects look in the future. Also, it would be helpful to know where its plants and offices (or stores) are located and to determine to what degree the company has established itself as a leader in the field.

This information assures points to discuss in the interview besides your own interest of finding employment. The employer believes in their organization and expects you to share some of this enthusiasm. Try to identify how all of this information relates to your interests and perceived job duties. Figure 17.1 illustrates the type of information you need to have about the employer.

PREDICTORS OF SUCCESS

- Ambition and motivation
- College grades
- Related work experience
- Creativity and intelligence
- Teamwork capabilities
- Initiative and responsibilities
- Good personality (outgoing)
- Job skill match
- Specific courses
- Adaptability
- Leadership ability
- Ability to communicate
- Work habits

• • • • • • • • • • •

Figure 17.4

Use stories to get your key points across.

//WEB.TIP//

www.fortune.com
Fortune Magazine
Articles/stories/rankings/
Fortune 500/links to job
search engine/surf to career sites they endorse.

THROAT SLITTERS

What you say in an interview can burn you. Positive statements about your previous employers and academic progress attract attention more readily than negative gripes.

One sure way of slitting your own throat is to speak derogatively about former employers, schools, facilities, or other people. Here are some examples of throat slitting interview comments.

Throat Slitting Interview Comments

The politics were terrible there.
Morale was very low there.
My boss was a poor manager.
There were personality conflicts.
They suffer from indecision.
The marketing plan was ill-conceived.
There was no strategic game plan.
My co-workers were not strong.
The classes were too large (too small).
The program stinks and needs a major overhaul.
I hated that class (or program).
The requirements were too tough (too weak).
The compensation was peanuts.
That was a sweat shop.
They really didn't care about the staff.
It was a no-growth situation.

No one intentionally cuts their own throat, but alibis and excuses often come across as sour grapes. The implication is that if you say comments like that about others, what would you be saying about us if things did not work out?

All of the above statements can be converted to a positive reflection about you with a bit of clever re-wording. Never apologize for your past, even if things went awry.

Your best approach is to acknowledge that there were problems and that you attempted to find appropriate solutions. Discuss your positive solutions rather than other's failures to avoid the throat-slitters.

Know the organization.

The web should be your primary source of employer information. Annual reports should be your next source of information when researching the company. Detailed information about a company can be found in an annual report or in a prospectus from a stockbroker both of which are also likely to be on the web.

There is no excuse for going into an interview ill-prepared. Nothing will turn the employer off faster than expressing ignorance about the company. Some traditional sources of information are listed in Figure 17.5.

Why This Organization

It is important that you are prepared to answer why you are interested in the organization. You can trace your interest to the employer's overall reputation, the

//WEB.TIP//

www.hoovers.com
Hoovers Online
One of the largest company data bases/in depth profiles cost/search by industry, location, sales, etc./ links to other sites with job related info.

size of the firm, its location, the type of products or services produced, or people you have met. Whatever the reason, you should have formulated an effective answer to this question.

Be prepared to address *why* you think this particular firm is different from others that you are interviewing. The interviewer takes pride in working for that firm and expects you to also show a similar degree of enthusiasm if you also expect to work there.

You cannot give a convincing answer if you do not sincerely want the job. Your lackluster attitude will become apparent. If you have not convinced yourself, you will find it impossible to convince others of your sincere interest.

Know why the organization is right for you.

Arrive Early

It is essential that you arrive at the interview location at least 15 minutes early. It is preferable to arrive 30 minutes early just to review your notes and show your excitement about the interview.

Tardiness is inexcusable. An early arrival will provide you with the time needed to recall items about the interview, particularly those points you want to emphasize.

The first impression you create is extremely important and being punctual is the first step toward creating a positive impression. Use the time to get mentally prepared for your organized presentation of your key points.

//WEB.TIP//

www.cnnfn.com
CNN Financial Network
Latest news on business organizations/Links to specific business articles/ industry stories/headline business news.

Professional Dress

There are too many other important factors to belabor the point of proper dress, hair length, etc. The best guideline in personal appearance is to come prepared to the interview in an attire appropriate with the type of position for which you are applying. Thus, you would wear clothes that you would wear on the job.

Try to emulate the dress that you expect the interviewer will be wearing. It is always preferable to be overdressed for the occasion than underdressed.

In many business professions, this means that you will come dressed to the interview in a dark suit, white blouse or shirt, and sensible shoes. This is the standard uniform that is acceptable in the various professional fields. While some areas are more flamboyant than others, it doesn't hurt to dress conservatively.

SOURCES OF EMPLOYER INFORMATION

- Websites
- Annual Reports
- Employment Brochures
- Investment Service Publications
- Product Brochures
- Business Periodicals
- People

• • • • • • • • • • •

Figure 17.5

Enthusiasm Is Important

You must stress the importance of each interview to yourself before trying to convince the employer that you are right for the firm. Anticipating questions and phrasing answers beforehand in a well-organized fashion is helpful. The mood may not be serious, but it will be a formal business atmosphere.

Emulate the interviewer's appearance.

It is normal to be nervous and a little anxious prior to each interview. You do need to prepare yourself for a competitive interview. Most employers will overlook your initial nervousness and will attempt to put you at ease.

It may help to undergo some "practice" interviews with your friends before the actual interview. If you formulate answers to some questions and actually hear how they sound out loud, you may decide to change some of your responses. The more times you interview, the easier it will be for you.

GREAT LOOKING SUIT SON... OF COURSE THAT ALONE WON'T GET YOU A JOB.

IMAGE TUNE-UP

Your first appearance impacts the interviewer's evaluation of your interview performance. What image do you wish to project?

First impressions count in the final interview evaluation. Some research studies prove that professional interviewers make 90 percent of the selection decisions within the first ten minutes of the interview. Much of that cursory impression must be influenced by how you dress and look.

Standard advice is to dress in a manner that emulates the interviewer. Other sound advice is to dress in a manner that emulates other professionals in your field in their everyday working attire. Still other advice suggests to err on the side of being overdressed for the occasion, but short of formal attire.

Many retail stores cater to the professional business person. Some are oriented to both men and women. You often see the words "professional," "executive," "career," or "corporate" in their advertising. The clerks in these specialty stores can be very helpful, assisting you in putting together an appropriate interview "uniform" and complete business wardrobe for later work situations.

For emulation purposes, you might wish to review the **photographs** of professional business leaders in magazines like *Business Week, Fortune,* and *Forbes.* You are more likely to discover **articles** in magazines like *Gentlemen's Quarterly, Glamour, Cosmopolitan,* and *Working Woman.* Watch the pictures in the ads for clues on how to dress.

Newspaper advertisements on professional dress can also be helpful. The major metropolitan papers like the *New York Times, The Chicago Tribune,* and the *Los Angeles Times* regularly feature ads using professional business attire regularly. The major department store ads often feature models appropriately dressed for the business world.

Fashion trends tend to vary by regions of the country, time of year, and even by occupation group. Your goal should be to focus on new clothes, top quality materials and tailoring, current styles (but not trendy fashions), and advice of your colleagues.

Keep sex out of the interview. Watch hemlines, necklines, make-up, hair styles, perfume, and jewelry. Whether you are interviewing a male or female, these items can influence the evaluation.

Your goal is to leave the impression of a modern, sophisticated, professionally-poised employee. Venturing into casual clothes or trendy looks risks potential damage to your case.

Conduct an image check-up before your interview. First impressions weigh heavily on the final impression.

Practicing your interviewing will improve your effectiveness. Practice builds confidence by eliminating much of the uncertainty of the event.

Getting psyched up for the interview is no different than what a coach of a championship team attempts to do before a big game. Every interview is a major challenge. If not, there is no reason for you to waste both your time and the employer's time.

One excellent method to use in developing your confidence is to role play the interview with a friend. Professional speakers often use audio tape and videotape to rehearse their presentations.

If you find yourself experiencing problems in the interview due to anxiety, you may wish to videotape your various presentations. It might be helpful to go through these vignettes with a friend or professional counselor who could offer some constructive criticism and positive suggestions.

Talking to yourself about the importance of the interview can help. If *you* are convinced you are the best candidate for the job opening, you will be more convincing to the employer. Confidence will help you develop the psychological state needed to have a successful interview.

During the Interview

Follow the Lead

You will probably be surprised at how fast your nervousness disappears once the interview begins. Cues can be taken from the employer. You should shake hands and pronounce the name correctly. If you did not clearly understand the employer's name, ask again.

The interview will begin with small talk destined to set you at ease. It may focus upon your name, the weather, athletics, news, recent activities, etc. The purpose is to establish a warm rapport so that rigid communication barriers can be broken. Be yourself during the two to three minute warm-up.

IMAGE CHECK-UP

- Minimal cologne
- Business hair style (not trendy)
- Minimize wardrobe color
- Natural look make-up
- Fresh haircut or style
- Slim is in
- Manicured nails
- Quality clothes
- Minimal jewelry

• • • • • • • • • • •

Figure 17.6

Get excited about the interview.

• • • • • • • • • • • **POWER WARDROBES** • • • • • • • • • • • • •

Men	Women
Dark suit	Tailored suit
Single breasted suit	Oxford blouse
Current style suit	Floppy bow tie
Solid or pinstripe suit	Tailored dress
Conservative tie	Silk blouse
Red or blue tie	Knee or lower hemline
White or blue shirt	Quality, not fashion
Dark mid-calf socks	Neutral hose
Dark polished shoes	Dark closed-toe pumps

"These vary by trends and regions of the country."

• • • • • • • • • • •

Figure 17.7

Be Prepared for Questions

Questions start soon after the door closes. Questions regarding qualifications, career interest, achievement, grades, activities, and so on will be asked. Expect to hear questions that will help evaluate subjective factors, including your personal qualities. It is extremely important that you are prepared for these questions so you are not caught unaware. Figure 17.8 gives a list of "Twenty Frequently Asked Questions." You should prepare complete and thorough answers to each question before your interview.

Rehearse. Each question should be reviewed in depth along with your prepared response. You will not be expected to memorize a response, but you should have a series of points to cover for each question.

It is a good idea to rehearse each of these answers by sitting in front of a mirror and watching your response, including your expressions, mannerisms, and delivery. Observing yourself on videotape is helpful but is a bit much unless you are experiencing some difficulties.

Most interviews follow a simple question and answer routine. If this is the case, your ability to answer quickly and intelligently is of great importance. If you do not know the answers to any of the questions the employer asks, do not try to fake an answer. Honestly admit that you do not know the answer.

· · · · · · · · · · **TWENTY FREQUENTLY ASKED QUESTIONS** · · · · · · · · · ·

1. Tell me about yourself. Expand on your resume.
2. For what position are you applying and why?
3. What are your long-term goals? Where do you hope to be in ten years?
4. Why do you feel that you will be successful in . . .?
5. What supervisory or leadership roles have you held?
6. How do you spend your spare time?
7. What have been your most satisfying and most disappointing experiences?
8. What are your strongest (weakest) personal qualities?
9. Give me some examples that support your stated interest in . . .
10. Why did you elect to interview with us?
11. What courses did you like best? Least? Why?
12. What did you learn or gain from your part-time and summer job experiences?
13. Which geographic location do you prefer? Why?
14. Would you prefer on-the-job training or a formal program?
15. What can you do for us now? What can I do for you? What motivates you?
16. What are your plans for graduate study?
17. Why did you choose your major and other academic pursuits?
18. Explain your academic grade performance levels.
19. Tell me about your activities and interests outside work and school.
20. Why did you leave your various jobs and what did you learn from each?

· · · · · · · · · ·

Figure 17.8

Empathy. An effective technique in answering questions is to use empathy prior to responding. You should think, "If I were in the employer's place, what would I like to know about myself?"

The answer should relate both to your situation and the employer's situation. Giving an answer showing the interrelation between the two is most effective. You should not memorize your answers. Avoid sounding like a robot who is on the 35th interview.

Outlining. It helps to outline responses to each question before the interview. The tricky part is to give the employer the answer being sought without appearing that the answer was contrived. If the employer perceives that your answer is contrived, you will be interpreted as being an insincere person.

//WEB.TIP//

.vaultreports.com
Vault Reports
In-depth company profiles/ hard to get info/top experts offer advice on job hunt/ online fair links to jobs.

Watch Your Ethics

No one would intentionally lie in any interview. It is too easy for an employer to verify course, grade, work, activities, and other information. However, it is easy to get lulled into "fluffing" your experiences because they might be somewhat harder to verify.

A great deal of emphasis is being placed on ethics in our society. However tempting it may be to exaggerate the truth, you should recognize that you live in a small world and improprieties frequently have a way of being exposed.

Emphasize Your Strong Points

Strong points impress employers. Your strengths should be emphasized at every appropriate opportunity. *All* your strong points should be conveyed to the employer. They may not come out unless you bring them up. Your answers must be factual and sincere without conveying conceit. There is a fine line between appearing cocky and appearing confident. Being informative without boasting is possible.

Express your confidence by using concrete examples.

Walking this tightrope is difficult but the success pays handsome dividends. It might be wise to identify your best qualities with a personal example. Rather than saying, "I am a hard worker and I want to get ahead," you might instead say, "I worked throughout college with part-time jobs plus full-time during the summers to put myself through school. In addition, I took some extra courses to prepare myself better in my major area." The second response is much more effective than the first, and the impression you desire is delivered in a humble manner.

Emphasize Future Goals

One of the favorite questions asked by employers concerns employment desires in five or ten years. When you encounter this question, remember that the purpose is to determine your ambition, ability to get ahead, and the soundness of your thinking. It is important to provide an answer that

I COULD TELL BY THE INTERVIEWERS BODY LANGUAGE THAT I WASN'T DOING WELL... SHE GOT UP AND LEFT THE ROOM.

STRESS INTERVIEW TECHNIQUES

Most interviews are stress interviews. Almost all interviews contain a certain amount of uncertainty that generates pressure. By its very nature, an interview is a tense, pressure situation that makes you uncomfortable and less confident of your abilities. The "stress interview" is different.

The very intent of the stress interview is to create an intense feeling of pressure. The interviewer's goal is to observe your reactions and performance under stressful conditions. The uncertain conditions may be similar to what you might find on the job after being hired.

Why would an interviewer want to subject you to this technique? The reasons cited most frequently are listed below.

- To destroy canned replies
- To throw you off balance
- To reveal the real you
- To discourage you if possible
- To observe your reaction
- To test your inner strength
- To probe your judgment
- To evaluate emotional maturity
- To force disjointed reasoning
- To incite reaction to criticism
- To intimidate to evaluate poise
- To simulate real job pressures

A stress interview is any interview where the volume has been artificially turned up. The typical reporter type of questioning using probing questions beginning with the following are very common.

- What
- Where
- When
- Who
- Why
- How
- Explain
- Tell

There are literally hundreds of techniques that stress interviewers use to turn up the volume. The most common approaches are listed below, but many more are illustrated in Figure 17.9 on "Stress Interview Techniques."

- Focus on negatives
- Challenge replies
- Probing questions
- Use silence

demonstrates you have conducted sound, rational thinking in a realistic work environment.

The number one reason given by recruiters for rejecting otherwise qualified job applicants is "ill-defined career plans." Lack of attention to personal goals is a sign to recruiters of immaturity. How can they expect you to make plans for their organization if you have not done it for your own life?

Express confidence in your career plans.

Never convey the impression of not being sure of your career direction. Employers are not career counselors. They have specific jobs to fill and are looking for specific qualities in people. The primary objective is to hire people who fit the

- Belittle credentials
- Interrupt frequently
- Criticize constantly
- Intimidate
- Use body language
- Set time limits

Most stress interviewers use four main strategies during the process. The questions are *planned* in advance and asked of every applicant. The questions are *targeted* to a specific topic, often an embarrassing topic. The questions follow in a specific *sequence* to add order to the inquiries for validity purposes between applicants. The responses are *layered* on top of each other so greater and greater depth can be built into the replies.

The well-trained interviewer will waste few words as preface to the questions asked to maximize the amount of time that you will spend talking. There will be no editorializing, few extraneous comments, and no hints of your performance. The information flow will be maintained and controlled by constantly exerting steady pressure for better and more complete responses from you.

How do you effectively respond to these tactics and to the tough "stress interview questions" listed in Figure 17.10? The simple answer is preparation. The complete answer is nothing more than planned hard work prior to your interviews.

The interviewer wants the best qualified applicant to respond in an aggressive, determined style. Timid replies signal failure. You must confidently answer in an assertive manner with a factual story. Use examples. Buy time to think about a better response. Always turn a negative question into a positive question by repeating the positive question that you intend to answer.

In order to wrestle control back, you must start talking with authority. Be long-winded but with your points clearly mapped-out. Do not ramble or go off on tangents.

If you are like most people, you cannot compose your responses off-the-cuff, and the recruiter realizes that. You cannot afford to deviate from your interview plan. What were the 10 to 15 key points that you wanted to get settled? Stick to your mission even if it means starting off toward right field and swinging back to left field where you perform best.

Your best defense is a strong offense. Your offense should have been planned before the interview. You need to return to your plan if you at first let the interviewer lead you astray.

Study both the "Stress Interview Techniques" and "Stress Interview Questions" figures. It is impossible to address every tactic and prepare a response to every question. What you can do is to prepare an approach and prepare responses to the most common form of questions.

Stress interviews are not common, but if you plan for this approach, nothing should deter your progress in a normal probing interview.

organization's needs. If the employer starts giving you career advice, it's a sure sign you are no longer being considered for employment.

You must not convey the impression to the recruiter that you are not sure of career direction. Never say, "I'll do anything if I have the interest and if I'm given a chance to learn," or "I was hoping that perhaps you could identify some areas for which I am qualified."

These statements will kill you about as fast as you make them. Why? The employers are not job counselors. They have specific jobs to fill or are looking for people in a specific field of work. Their job is to hire people to fill organizational

Interviewer: How can I test reactions, evaluate credentials, and observe personal traits? These goals can be met by simulating a stressful interview situation similar to that required on the job.

Purpose: Create stress to observe performance under pressure. Destroy pre-rehearsed responses to typical questions and force a truer, spontaneous answer by inciting a more emotional reply.

Ask a question and cut the response short.
Demean the answers to interview questions.
Belittle credentials such as grades (even if great).
Challenge applicant to support their best (not worst) credentials.
Put a time limit on a response.
Discuss the unfavorable odds of getting an offer.
Discourage the applicant; from position, career choices, firm.
Why should I hire someone with your meager credentials?
Sell me this article.
What is the worst thing you have heard about my employer?
It's your 30 minutes; let's hear your story.
How do you react to extremely negative criticism about you?
Write or read while the applicant is talking.
Use silence to create awkwardness and ambiguity.
Give a poker face throughout the interview.
Avoid eye contact by staring at an object.
Display non-verbal gestures that imply impatience and disgust.
Keep applicant on defensive by constantly probing weaknesses.
Criticize appearance such as clothes, weight, odor, etc.
Your experience and courses were a waste of time.
Use comments like "dumb idea," "fruitcake," "wimp," "baby-kisser."
Prove to me you can earn your salary.
What a stupid question—why would you ask that?
Intimidate by showing disrespect.
Fire questions rapidly without time to respond.
Ask a demeaning question.
Keep probing answers in increasing depth.
Give expressions of being disgusted and bored.
Gaze or stare in silence.
Abruptly interrupt a legitimate reply.
Frequently interrupt responses.
Challenge validity of answers.
Forcefully test technical competence.
Impune the honesty and integrity of a reply.
Parrot a reply in a simplistic manner.
Use negative questions consistently.
Whipsaw topics and responses.
Ridicule responses.
Give curt replies to all questions.
Give face to face rejection.
End abruptly.

· · · · · · · · · · ·

Figure 17.9

Use stress questions to provoke a thoughtful, unrehearsed, possibly emotional response to unanticipated questions like these to exert a reasonable degree of pressure in the interview environment to observe job-related personal qualities.

Analyze the position you are seeking.
Why would you leave your good job?
What is your work philosophy?
Why do you think that you are worth this amount?
How long will we pay you before you add to profits?
How long will you last with a firm like ours? Why?
How do you feel about minority groups?
How did more education change your life?
What do you think of your last supervisor? Professor?
Which professors contributed most (or least) to
     your education?
Why aren't you employed yet?
How many other offers do you have?
Evaluate your latest educational experience.
Give me a situation where your performance was
     severely criticized.
Give me three problems that you have not yet solved.
How long before you will want your boss's job?
Give an example of your creative skills.
What do you think thwarts most innovative ideas?
Give me a situation where you reprimanded
     another person.
How do I know that you have good analytical skills?
Describe your managerial leadership style.
What other types of job and specific firms are you
     interviewing?
Prove to me that you have top management potential.
How important is money to you?
How well do you work in ambiguous situations?
Describe your ideal work climate.
How could someone with your demeanor be
     successful in this field?
How important are status, prestige, and power
     to you?
Give me some examples of your concern for
     human suffering.
Justify your salary expectations.
What are the key reasons for your successes? Failures?
Describe your ideal, typical work day.

Use a situation to describe your energy level.
What things do you dislike the most about your job?
Why haven't you earned more external recognitions?
What are your best and worst personal qualities?
Why do you work so well under enormous pressure?
How do you define challenge in a job?
What is the difference between opportunity
     and advancement?
Describe your three most important motivators.
What is the most challenging aspect of your life? Why?
What type of decisions do you find most difficult
     to make?
Describe the difference between goal-driven and
     task-driven.
How did you handle the toughest boss you ever had?
How did you recently resolve a difficult problem in
     your life?
What kept your accomplishments from being
     super superior?
What are you working hardest at to improve?
What can you do to get better qualified for this job?
Why were your college grades not in the top five
     percent?
What job-related tasks do you really dislike?
Just how unhappy were you with college?
Just how unhappy were you with your job?
What type of people really turn you off?
What have you done that shows initiative?
Were you ever involved in any controversy?
Describe the major difficulties that you most
     encounter with others.
Why was your performance below your expectations?
How do you react to intense criticism?
How do you resolve conflict between other people?
Describe how you responded to an unethical situation.
What do you do when the subject of politics
     comes up?
What negative things do your references say
     about you?

The answers to the questions may not be as important as the very reaction, mannerisms, and behaviorisms incited by the stress-induced questioning techniques, designed to elicit an evaluation of personal traits.

. . . .
Figure 17.10

needs. Some professional recruiters do give sound advice, but when they start giving advice they are probably through considering you for a job.

In reality, career goals are always in a state of revision. This dynamic process presents a moving target but at any given moment you must take the snapshot and state your plans at that specific point in time.

Whenever possible, you should apply for a *specific* job or field of work. Most employers have established specific job openings. The important point is to get into the type of firm that meets your established qualifications and that will allow you to work hard and show your abilities. After you have succeeded on your first assignment, different avenues within the organization may open.

Playing Coy Is Unwise

Playing coy is one way to destroy your employment chances. In each and every interview, you should be determined to get the job available. You may have other irons in the fire, but it is important to stress to the employer that your interest is in the particular position available now.

If you are playing hard-to-get, the only person you are fooling is yourself. It will not motivate employers to increase their efforts to hire you. Instead, you will find that it will be an immediate turn-off for most employers. Playing coy could materially dim your chances for a successful interview.

No matter how ideally you think that your credentials fit the job, there is usually someone else equally qualified. An egotistical attitude, even if not intended, is a turnoff for most employers.

Ask Questions

As appropriate openings develop in the interview, you need to ask concrete questions. Ask questions that may have a bearing on whether or not an offer would be accepted if it was extended.

YOUR BODY TALKS

Non-verbal communications influence the outcome of your interviews. *What* you say and *how* you deliver the message are important aspects to develop in your interview presentations. Your body language impacts the final evaluation of all employers.

We all have seen actors, speakers, singers, comedians, and other performers imitate the "stars" and fall flat. It is not only *what* you say but *how* you use your unique features in making your statements.

Body talk includes a variety of things. Some of the items that recruiters mention in their evaluations include the following.

• Smiles	• Sharp dresser
• Laughs	• Gestures appropriately
• Nods in agreement	• Fidgets nervously
• Eyebrow movement	• Wringing hands
• Inquisitively scratches head	• Makes eye contact
• Controls voice	• Excessive blinking
• Has a twitch	• Crosses legs frequently
• Chews gum	• Positive expressions
• Needs manicure	• Non-conforming hairstyle
• Frequent swaying	• Smokes
• Sweaty palms	• Loud clothing
• Excessive cologne	• Poor hygiene
• Positive poise	• Strong posture
• Sleepy appearance	• Alert and bright
• Optimistic	• Pessimistic
• Nervous actions	• Confident
• Puzzled expression	• Phony appearance
• Mumbling	• Cracking, nervous voice

Your body talks. You can tell it what to say with some attention to this form of communication. Non-verbal signs signal both positive and negative messages.

These signals can best be interpreted by role-playing experiences conducted by critical coaches. A less obtrusive approach is to watch your planned presentation on videotape and critique yourself.

Employer attitudes can be changed by proper attention to body talk.

Tell your body what to say!

Questions to be avoided are those for which answers could have been obtained in preparing for the interview. In many cases, the interviewer is the person who wrote the employment brochure and one who knows the annual report very well. Asking a question that could have been looked up does not show much industry on your part.

Questions to ask are those that relate to the type of position for which you are applying, the geographical location, potential product line growth, etc. Questions should be prefaced with statements that indicate your extensive homework and that show you need additional information for decision purposes.

Ask questions that elicit *positive* replies from the employer. An example of such a statement and question follows.

Planned questions reinforce your interest in the job and organization.

"I noticed in the job description printed in your employment brochure that all candidates enter into a rather structured two-year program of on-the-job training and classroom instruction. This implies that most new sales representatives are expected to progress at the same pace. With my prior experience in sales, would it be possible for me to move faster into a marketing management position?"

In this question, the employer is informed that you have investigated the firm and its training. The question assumes that an offer will be forthcoming. It shows confidence and ambition. It is a question where the answer may determine whether or not the applicant is interested in pursuing the position further.

Every question you ask should bring out facets of your interests and knowledge of the organization. Try to ask "telling questions." Figure 17.11 offers some of the typical subjects around which such questions are frequently constructed.

If you preface your question with a brief statement about yourself or something you read about the firm, you let the employer know that you have prepared for the interview and that the answer is important to your future decision.

The number of questions you ask should not be so great that the interviewer fails to learn enough information about you. The interview is a mutual proposition, remember.

Have several questions in mind before reporting to the interview. Make certain that they are pertinent to your employment decision.

Maintain Enthusiasm

If the impression develops that the interview is not going well and that rejection is likely, you must still keep your enthusiasm high. Nothing is lost by continuing the appearance of confidence, and much can be gained. The last few minutes of an interview can change things.

Your remaining confident and determined will make a good impression on the interviewer. Few employers want to hire in-

Preface your questions with telling statements that reveal positive facets of your background and why the answer to your question is important to you.

TELL ME, KIP, WHAT PERCENTAGE OF THE "FORTUNE 500" DO YOU THINK **DOES** GIVE "NATIONAL HOT DOG WEEK" OFF WITH PAY?

How much travel is normally expected?
Do employees normally work many hours of overtime?
Can I progress at my own pace or is it structured?
How frequently do you relocate professional employees?
What is the average age of your first-level supervisors?

Is the sales growth in the new product line sustainable?
How much contact and exposure to management is there?
At what level is an employee placed in the "exempt" status?
Is it possible to move through the training program faster?
When does the training program begin? Only in June?

About how many individuals go through your program each year?
What is the housing market for young married couples in . . .?
How much freedom is given and discipline required of the new people?
Would I have to cut my hair and trim my mustache?
Does the firm recommend any night courses the first year?

How often are performance reviews given?
Is it possible to transfer from one division to another?
How much decision-making authority is given after one year?
Have any new product lines been announced recently?
How soon after graduation would I expect to report for work?

How much input does the new person have on geographic location?
In your firm, is this position more analytical or more people-oriented?
In promotion, are employers ever transferred between functional fields?
Does the firm provide employee discounts?
Are cars provided to traveling personnel?

Is the city difficult to adjust to compared to this campus community?
What is the average age of top management?
What is the normal routine of a . . . like?
Is public transportation adequate?
What is the average time it takes to get to . . . level in the career path?

Preface every question with revealing statements

Figure 17.11

dividuals who get discouraged easily, particularly in a brief interview. Some recruiters even try to discourage applicants to test their tolerance, so beware of that tactic.

If, on the other hand, the recruiter makes it quite evident that your interests and qualifications do not match what is available, use him or her as a sounding board to help you improve future interviews.

Discussing your problems, interests, and ideas with interviewers may assist you in obtaining helpful suggestions. You should consider, however, that the interviewer's context may be quite limited and not nearly as broad as that of a

Professional composure even under stress reveals great poise and maturity.

professional counselor. All information obtained from employers, counselors, and other professional personnel must be integrated to benefit you in the most productive fashion.

THANKS SO MUCH, MR. BLANDLY... I REALLY HOPE TO HEAR FROM INTERNATIONAL FOOLS.

You will usually be able to tell if the interview is going poorly. If you develop the impression that the interview is not going well, try to keep your enthusiasm level high.

Nothing is lost by continuing the appearance of confidence and much could be gained. The last few minutes of the interview may change things drastically. Remaining confident and determined will make a positive impression with the employer.

If the interview has gone well, don't blow it by lack of attention to the follow-up details. You may be on a major high, but if you miss important deadlines as follow-up information, your chances for the firm offer may be lost.

Close Confidently

Most initial interviews last about thirty minutes. If the interview has been successful up until the close, it is possible to reverse this success and talk yourself *out* of the job in the closing minutes.

Sum up your interests briefly and express them to the recruiter. Let the interviewer know *without* a doubt that you are still very interested in the position.

As the conversation closes, make certain that you understand the *next response* required. Most recruiters will say that they will be in touch, one way or the other, within three or four weeks.

Some interviewers, however, say that if further interest in you develops, they will contact you within three or four weeks. Therefore, if you do not receive a letter by then, it means the employer is not interested in you.

In some cases, the recruiter will close the conversation by giving you an application form or requesting a transcript. That means that the next contact must be made by you in letter form to the employer. In such situations you must take the next initiative. Clear up the situation in the close. Get the facts right before leaving.

After the Interview

Make Notes

After leaving the interview, jot down your immediate impression of the interview. Also get the interviewer's name, title, telephone number, email, and address. You should also record the type of position you applied for and some of the major responsibilities and duties of the job.

Make notes of any follow-up that was requested, such as returning an application blank or forwarding a copy of your transcript. Other important information to record

HOW DO YOU SOUND?

What you say in the interview clearly impacts the selection decision, but *how* you say it also influences the message delivered. You can *say* the right words but *come across* in an unintended manner.

How you project your voice influences your evaluation after the interview.

Voice control techniques can redirect your interview efforts. The act of exercising control over your voice implies that you recognize the potential influence and that you know how to manipulate the proper variables. There are at least eight aspects of your voice that you can control.

Pitch: Does your voice sound squeaky? Is there a mumbling sound when you get nervous?

Tone: Does your voice sound bright, upbeat, and friendly? Do you sound rushed in trying to get your thoughts out before you forget them? Do you come across as patient, slow, and thoughtful?

Modulation: Is your voice a monotone or do you vary from high and lows to emphasize key points?

Volume: Do you sound very loud when you are under pressure? Do you talk so softly that others find it difficult to hear you?

Intensity: Do you come across as under a great deal of stress and pressure or as a timid person?

Quality: Is your voice unique enough so that when you are heard from a distance people automatically know you?

Nasality: Do you sound like you are talking through your nose?

Pauses: Are you good at managing the silence (or lack of it) in your speech?

The most common complaints by interviewers are:

"Talks too softly"	"Heavy accent"
"Sounds cocky"	"Mumbles"
"Too serious sounding"	"Uses uh . . ."
"Uses y'know"	"Uses junk words"
"Cannot understand"	"Rambles"
"Sounds hissy"	"Blasting voice"
"Too nasal"	"Poor grammar"
"Monotone"	"Too authoritarian"
"Sounds downbeat"	"Too much silence"
"Won't talk"	"Timid and shy"

If you understand what to look for, it is not difficult to positively influence your ability to project your thoughts in an assertive, bright, friendly, and smiling manner.

Spend some time analyzing "how" you say things in addition to planning "what" you say in the interview. Review your presentations several times with a recorder before delivering them in a live interview.

Critique yourself each time. Make your voice work in concert with your thoughts.

Your attention to closing details makes follow-up plans more definitive.

includes the position for which you applied and some of the major responsibilities and duties of that particular job with that employer.

If you obtain an invitation to follow up with further interviews with other decision makers, you will be in a better position to recall events that transpired in the initial interview. If you have had several initial job interviews and have not made a record of facts immediately following each interview, it is possible you could lose track of what was said in the various interviews.

No Answer

If the employer seemed interested or indicated further contact and you do not hear from them within a reasonable time frame, recontact the interviewer by letter. A reasonable time period is about two to four weeks unless the employer indicated otherwise. Express your continued interest in the organization and indicate that further interest from them would be appreciated.

A subtle approach to this delicate situation is to tell them that you are calling, emailing, or writing for another purpose. Tell them that you would like to add additional information if needed.

Include any new information that may have developed and which might have a bearing on employment. It never hurts to tell people how much you appreciated their interest in you.

At the end of the letter, request a response from them indicating the level of their interest in you. Little is to be lost at this point, and this might secure a favorable response. Although it does not pay to become a nuisance, there are some things which you can do to help keep your resume and interests in the foreground in the event that a job requiring your qualifications opens. Walk that fine line.

Before becoming too angry at a slow response from a particular employer, remember that many people are interviewed in a very short time period. It takes much time to stay on top of this massive flow of communications.

I'M PRACTICING ACCEPTING REJECTION... DINNER?

THE FINAL SALES PITCH

Thank you letters are not necessary for every initial interview you take, but where things went especially well for you and the interviewer, they can have a major impact. Thank you letters are your final sales pitch.

The final sales pitch starts with a recount of the situation (where, when, position) and how well that you felt the interview went. The first paragraph shows a sincere appreciation for being selected for an interview and for the courtesy and time granted by the interviewer. Try to make it sound personal.

Your enthusiasm for the organization and job must radiate as you tell what points covered impressed you most. Acknowledge where the uniqueness of the organization's program most reflected your interest.

Another paragraph provides supporting evidence and documentation of the solidness of the match between the opportunity and your credentials. In addition to your restatement of the items covered in the interview, include some new information. You could, for example, enclose some recommendation letters, a re-grouped unofficial transcript, or a school or work project that supports your claim for the match between both parties.

As you begin your close, your desire to work for the employer and your high interest levels need to illustrate your excitement about joining the work team. Point out some work of excellence on your part that was performed under pressure that relates to the qualities that you feel the work group would be seeking in you.

In your close, express your desire for the job. **Ask for the job.** Close the sale. Indicate your outstanding commitments where you are (job notice, graduation, etc.), when you expect to make a job decision, and how much you appreciated the opportunity for the interview consideration.

Your final sales pitch should be upbeat, confident, positive, and assertive. It adds the icing to the cake. It will not turn bad interviews around, but it can turn lukewarm evaluations into positive ones.

Do not do this via email unless the employer specifically requested email communications.

Also recognize that you may be the number two choice and that the firm may be waiting on an answer from number one before getting back to you. Pushing for a premature answer too aggressively could cause you to lose an important opportunity.

No Interest

If you receive a "turndown" letter, try not to read too much into the letter. They are simply saying, "You are not for us, but thanks for your time."

Some employers may send out a letter indicating that they will keep your name on file if anything opens up. If this is the case, it would be beneficial for you to contact the employer at a later date by letter or email. Refresh their memory and reiterate your interest. Unless you stay on top of this opportunity by being the *assertive responder*, the odds for them contacting you are minimal.

Persistent follow-up can turn marginal interview performances around.

If an outright turndown is not received and the employer indicates that their economic situation may soon improve or that they may be interested later, there is still a possibility that you might land a job with them. Keep in touch with such employers. Cultivate this type of employer even though only a small degree of interest is expressed.

Employers do not give you reasons why they turned down your application. In the majority of cases they found other contacts whom they feel would be more productive in the assignment.

Do not press the employer for a justification or reason for your turndown. He or she may not give you the truth anyway; thus you could make an inappropriate decision. Seek advice from others, not from employers that you interview.

You did your interview preparation, had an excellent interview, and received a positive "further interest" letter. Don't break out the champagne yet. This is merely a base hit; it is not a home run.

The normal procedure is for an employer to then extend you an invitation to visit their facilities for interviewing with people in your stated area of specialization.

If there are any expenses to be incurred for the second interview, the employer normally pays them. If this is not completely defined in the invitation letter or calls, clarify this point by telephone. Local employers and about ten percent of other employers do not pay any of your expenses incurred at the second interview.

Your home run letter comes when the firm has interviewed several applicants and the manager extends a firm offer to you in writing.

Solicit Feedback

Problems can arise during the interviewing process, and the best person to answer these questions is a career advisor.

Many college career offices, employment services, and search firms have an interviewing feedback process whereby the applicant may share in the interview comments. Request this service.

Counselors will not normally identify the comments of specific employers. Even employers expressing continued interest often give considerable criticism, hoping that applicants' faults can be corrected before their secondary interviews.

Employers hesitate to give positive or negative feedback at the time of the interview because they want to see all candidates before making even tentative decisions. If an employer were to express interest and for some reason the position is eliminated or filled by a better candidate, the interviewer would be embarrassed.

In other words, a career counselor can provide some anonymous, constructive criticism. It will only be constructive, however, if you use it.

Consult a career counselor for advice, not the employer.

Managing Your Interviews:

Organize — Control — Evaluate

The interview is supposed to be a 50–50 proposition. You do half of the talking. In the final analysis, most people assume that the interviewer is in charge of the interview.

You probably look to the interviewer to take charge and lead you through the flow of questions. The direction is too often totally in the hands of the employer. It should not be that way!

The most successful interviewees take charge of this 30-minute conversation. They decide what is to be covered and when it will be addressed in the sequence of events. Interview management is a goal to which you should aspire.

Interview management is a bold concept. By applying certain controlling techniques, you can put yourself in charge instead of the recruiter.

Interview management is for every interviewee, including you. The concept behind interview management is simple. You set several short-term goals for each three to four minutes of the interview. You next look at how you can get your goals achieved.

Executing certain techniques that are planned prior to your interview and which are practiced ahead of time permits you to thoroughly cover your planned agenda.

Several ideas on methods and techniques are offered here which should help you manage your interviews much more effectively.

Interviewers tend to move your conversation to your weak points. There is a natural tendency to look for characteristics that knock you *out* of further consideration instead of looking for factors that screen you *in* for further consideration.

Your goal is to continually move all conversations away from your weak points and toward your strengths.

Once you recognize that the flow of information can be manipulated, you are well on your way to managing all of your future interviews. Planning ahead is step one. Execution is step two.

Interview management is accomplished via an advance plan, a carefully rehearsed presentation, and precise execution.

Controlling Techniques

Anticipate Questions

Knowing the questions that will be asked is only half the problem; the answers are needed also. If you get together with friends and do some role-playing, you will discover how easy interviews can be.

Outlining answers to the key questions the interviewer is likely to ask also helps. With this outline in mind, have a friend ask the "Twenty Questions" in Figure 17.8.

Practice the answers until it is not necessary to use your outline as a crutch and you develop the ability to respond to questions quickly, concisely, and in a

TEN INTERVIEW TOPICS

- Career Objectives
- Type of Job Sought
- Knowledge of Organization
- Personal Qualifications
- Reasons for Career Choice
- College Preparation
- Geographical Concerns
- Achievements
- Activities and Interests
- Special Skills

• • • • • • • • • • •

Figure 18.1

well-organized fashion. Most questions revolve around the topics listed in Figure 18.1. Use these as your guide.

Interviewers invariably focus their questions on the "Ten Interview Topics" shown in Figure 18.1. What do you want the recruiter to know about you under each topic? Since you do not know which of the ten topics the recruiter will target, you must decide in advance what you want discussed under each topic.

Many employers are trained in Behavior Based Interview (BBI) techniques. The idea is to ask you questions about how you handled certain types of events in the past. How do you handle problems and decision points?

Recruiters assume that your past behavior is indicative of your future behaviors. BBI assumes that the past is the best predictor of the future. Recruiters are trained to ask questions related to past events. Anticipate the event and have a story ready.

Your responses should be prepared in advance. Under each topic, prepare a two- to four-minute statement (about 15 to 25 complete sentences). An excellent way to accomplish this is to draw on about three different experiences (short stories) in your life that best illustrate the most important points.

For example, under achievements you might want to describe three examples where you were recognized by others as having accomplished a significant task.

In addition to achievements, this description might also illustrate an activity, personal qualities, and communicative ability. You can avoid saying, "I am a great communicator," by developing that skill by example instead.

Illegal Questions

Illegal questions are difficult to define. What may be illegal in one situation may not be illegal in another situation. In a general way, employment laws protect certain classes of people from being discriminated against. The most common protected classes are:

- Sex
- Race
- Age
- Religion/creed
- National origin
- Citizenship

Employers may ask questions related to a protected class if there is a bona fide occupational reason and provided that the same questions are asked of every applicant. The applicable laws are often general and subject to different interpretations.

There are certain questions that may be illegal to ask before you are hired but perfectly legal to ask after you are hired. For example, after you are hired you can legally be asked the age of your children for medical and tax purposes.

Marital, child care, age, religious affiliation, race, etc. are generally unacceptable. When in doubt, check with authorities in a local employment service office for guidance. The laws are sufficiently strong to cause an offender to reconsider if challenged.

Practice Interviewing

Experienced job seekers have usually obtained much interviewing experience whereas college graduates have minimal experience. Few employers like to provide interviews for practice. They interview because they must locate potential employees.

If you need experience, how do you get it? Interviewing for experience is not the proper answer.

Interviewing for practice has some major disadvantages and should not be tried. Interviewers are experienced at spotting the phony and insincere practice interviewer and most give these people the quality of attention the situation deserves. Some will even challenge such "applicants" with stress interviews or with interviews most unrepresentative of what might be expected later.

Employer representatives in a given locale usually know each other well through professional associations and traveling together. It is not uncommon to hear comments over a lunch table about some inconsiderate applicant with whom a recruiter recently spoke. There is no advantage in incurring the wrath of a recruiter with a job to do (to hire qualified talent; not career counsel). They may pass negative thoughts about you on to others.

Even if the recruiter is unable to spot you "just shopping around," you are still likely to get negative feedback if your interest is not genuine. The intense psychological attitude in interviewing is critical.

Without a high degree of confidence, zeal, and enthusiasm toward the employer and the position, the chances of a successful interview are hampered. If you know that the interview is just for practice and that you have no real interest, how can you convey sincere desire for employment?

The only purpose in taking practice interviews is to get some idea of which approaches work best. Unfortunately, in nearly all cases, all that is likely to be gained is negative feedback: "Thanks, but we are not interested."

When you need positive, not negative feedback, why should you guarantee yourself a negative response through practice interviewing? The first two or three interviews are likely to be rough enough without the additional negativism gleaned from practice interviews.

To be sure, your first interviews may not be the most effective. After every interview—even the 50th—additional polish of the presentation occurs. Interviewing with an organization in which you have little or no interest does not help.

Practice interviewing angers recruiters and generates negative, unproductive feedback for you.

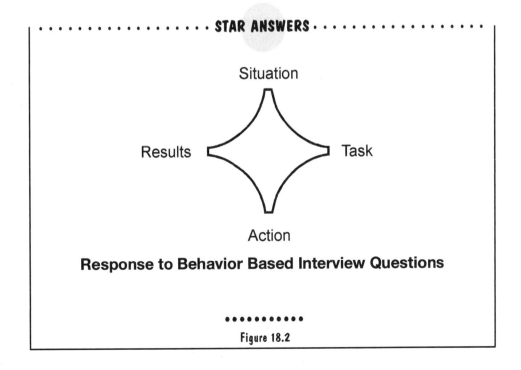

· · · · · · · · · · · · · · **STAR ANSWERS** · · · · · · · · · · · · · ·

Situation

Results   Task

Action

Response to Behavior Based Interview Questions

· · · · · · · · · ·
Figure 18.2

CONTROL YOUR INTERVIEWS

The first step in directing the flow of information in an interview is an awareness of the parts of the interview. You can control the interview only if you allow the interviewer's objectives to also be achieved. The six main elements are:

1. Establishing a rapport
2. Expanding on your resume
3. Proving your case
4. Selling your achievements
5. Concluding with a fit
6. Closing positively

The rapport begins by establishing a warm, mutual, supporting relationship. Warm-up examples include conversations about athletic events, the weather, physical facilities, mutual acquaintances, schools, etc. The purposes of the informal chit-chats are to break the ice, smooth normal tensions, and create a sharing atmosphere.

The conversation naturally flows into a fact-finding probing set of questions designed to investigate the scope of your functional skills. Your responses draw upon facts in your resume but provide some depth of analysis based upon your experiences. Your goal is to emphasize accomplishments that emphasize excellence.

Once the facts are on the table, you must prove your case. By drawing upon examples that show more than just awareness, you use a story that proves that you are highly proficient in the skills that you possess. If your pre-interview research revealed that the job required a specific set of skills, you need to demonstrate how you attained the skills, the depth of your knowledge, and an application example of the regular use of those skills.

Selling yourself is as important as proving your skill capacities. Employers must be convinced that you *will* do the job, not only that you *can* do the task. Once your credentials are established, you should offer some motivational examples. Most of these focus on how well you achieved a project within a given time consideration. These examples illustrate hard work, discipline, commitment to goals, reaction to pressure, and top performance under stress.

As you describe your commitment to excellence, you interject your personal qualities. Describe yourself. Think about how others describe your personality. Add these descriptors onto the examples that you use to illustrate skills and motivations. By implication, these descriptors will be subliminally ascribed to you.

Both you and the interviewer must draw your thoughts together for evaluation purposes near the end of the interview. You can control your own evaluation by doing it for the recruiter as a summary of your discussions. If *you* bring the fit together, the natural tendency of the evaluator will be to draw upon your summary in completing the formal interview record.

At the final closing stage, you need to repeat and verbally confirm the follow-up steps. Volunteer to provide more supporting documentation if necessary. State your goal. Your goal is a job offer or further interviews. Be positive by using the word "when" rather than "if" as you discuss the follow-up.

This scenario puts you in charge. You control the movement forward and influence the judgment of the evaluator. If you are well prepared, there will be no doubt at the end in the interviewer's mind that you are the best qualified person for the specific job opening and that you have the potential to move up several levels beyond that specific assignment.

Practice interviewing shows up weak spots in your presentation and insures rejection due to your obviously low interest level.

Your first two or three interviews must be with employers whose job requirements closely meet your qualifications. Your first interviews may not be rated among your five most important, but the results of their outcome are meaningful

ASK ME!

Confident interviewees challenge interviewers. The "ASK ME!" interview technique works in most interviews.

Advertising experts claim that the one-minute radio or television ad provides great impact on most audiences. Long commercials bore people. Short commercials lack decision-making information. One minute offers balance.

Your answer to each interview question is one of your personal commercials. You need several commercials to run. The test on their potential impact is the "ASK" evaluation.

Accomplishments

Skills

Knowledge

Ask yourself the following question: Does my commercial . . .

> . . . Emphasize my accomplishments?
> . . . Reveal my skills and proficiencies?
> . . . Represent my intellectual capacity fairly?

Interview success is directly related to the "ASK" test.

and helpful. You should go into even your first interview with the determination and desire to get a job offer.

Obtaining interviews is tough. Every interview must count. The cost of interviews is high. Interviews are hard to get, so make every one count.

Recognize Your Multiple Interests

Even after four or more years of college, many graduates still do not know what type of position they would most like to hold. Many people are not sure of this even after working ten years.

You may have investigated the wide range of assignments in a number of different industries and still have come to no firm conclusion. Simply pick two or three fields in which you have an interest and begin talking to employers. It is important to specify the type of position for which you wish consideration.

It is appropriate for you to tell XYZ Employer of an interest in an assignment in sales while telling ABC Employer that you are interested in an assignment in retail management. If you have an interest in a field and wish to investigate it, then make every effort to land a job offer in that field.

When evaluating job offers at a later date, you can decide which of them is best for you. Avoid making the decision until your options are real.

The logic behind this approach relates to the employer's eagerness to see your level of career planning. If you have done little thinking about what you want and

ASSERTIVE INTERVIEWING

- Prepare intensively
- Project confidence
- Rehearse your goals
- Defer greeting and sitting
- Establish initial rapport
- Get recruiter talking
- Appear to be happy— smile
- Make the interviewer smile
- Control the content
- Focus on employer needs
- Speak with authority
- Ask revealing questions
- Be positive and enthusiastic
- Use non-verbal tools well
- Stick to a planned agenda

• • • • • • • • • • •

Figure 18.3

Quality listening is as important as presenting your case.

Stress your problem solving abilities.

why you might be successful, the employer will conclude that you are not worth the risk.

An employer is not likely to appraise your interests, personality, values, and other qualities for you and decide that a certain job in the organization is the best match. You do not want that either. The employer is looking for direction from you as to why you will be successful in that field. A tentative decision is much better than no decision.

This advice to vacillate is not extremely wise, particularly if the two fields you selected are unrelated. In the example used on the previous page (sales and retailing), there are many cross-qualifications and similarities.

But there are not many commonalities between such diverse fields as sales and computer programming. One may be a highly unstructured environment and the other may require a high level of analytical talent and interest in working behind a desk. Few people are capable of being successful to the same degree in such different types of jobs. Take care in how you deal with multiple career interests.

Listening is Learning

The interview is a mutual, two-way conversation, not a monologue. You need to take your part in the interviewing situation, or you will not be in a position to make some important decisions at a later time. This does not mean that you should do all of the talking.

Listening is as important as talking.

The interviewer's objective is to ascertain your credentials and to deliver some information to you. It is important to understand and remember what the interviewer says. It could be quite embarrassing later to find the assignment is not what you anticipated.

Not listening to another person because one is thinking about what to say next is a bad habit at best.

Philosophic Attitude

Some people may consider that they just are not future executive material. They are not willing to fit into a mold that the organization image dictates. All too often, however, stereotyped views are wrong. Individuals who feel that they are mavericks will be making a great mistake when interviewing if they do not let the employer know their true feelings.

Interviewers are seldom looking for the "dark suit" mentality. Their organizations may very well have too many of those already.

Intelligence, personality, drive, and the ability to recognize a problem and develop a means for helping solve it are the characteristics of the candidates most interviewers seek. In fact, many of the top executives of today arrived where they are because they expressed different ideas. The ability to communicate these ideas to others is one of the best qualities you can possess.

Exude Confidence

A thin line exists between confidence and cockiness. Being a little overconfident in an interview is more of an asset than a liability, but guard against appearing conceited. However, if in doubt, toot your own horn —no one else will toot it for you.

Don't run the risk of seeming like a meek, passive, indecisive person in an interview. Your best bet is to project an air of confidence.

◗ USE THE "ZAP INTERVIEW" FOR IMPACT

Every interviewer claims to hire only candidates who display charismatic, energetic, determined, confident, and responsible qualities. In addition, candidates need to possess the analytical, technical, and/or managerial skills to handle the assignments. How can you say that you have all of those skills and qualities with a straight face? You can't.

Zesty **A**necdotal **P**resentations (ZAP) interviewing is one method to address this issue. You indirectly imply you possess the appropriate skills and personal attributes by projecting the qualities sought into an experience. The experience is your anecdote.

Rather than describe a boring event in your life, you must think of ways to add spice to your story. This lively example, taken from your classroom, work, or activities experiences, forms the foundation for your interview presentations. The descriptive adjectives that you use to add zest to your example will permit the recruiter to project these qualities into your background.

The "ZAP Interview" technique focuses on what you have learned from what you *did,* which is one of the best ways to learn anything. Rather than memorizing responses to interview questions, you are remembering the real event as it honestly happened. No matter how many times you tell the story you are likely to give a consistent response.

Memorizing answers to questions runs the risk of giving different answers from recruiter to recruiter. It is easy to forget your "canned pitch." The advantage to ZAP examples is its consistency (you can easily remember your story) and interesting nature. The recruiter will find being "ZAPped" much more exciting. The interviewer's recall of you will also be easier after the evaluation record is written.

The "ZAP Interview" technique allows you to come across with the attributes the interviewer is seeking. Your descriptive adjectives add zest to your life and zip to your presentation.

Start worrying about confidence turning into cockiness only if rejection letters start arriving from employers who previously had expressed an interest. If that should happen, it is advisable to consult a career counselor.

Keep Your Perseverance

Seeking the right career position can be one of the most *discouraging* activities ever undertaken. As success begets success, failure generates failure to the point where some people just give up. Continuing to get rejections indicates a special problem that should be discussed with a counselor—but do not quit!

Counselors offer feedback advice. A counselor may suggest a change in strategy in the interview situation that can begin a new course of success.

It often takes time to find the type of position with which you can be happy. You will reject many employers before they reject you. You can only accept one job, so it must be one with which you can be happy and can see a bright future. Giving up means settling for a less desirable choice on one of the most important matters affecting your future happiness.

It often takes more than twenty interviews before a mutually satisfactory match is made. Interviewing is not simple. Each interview should be a learning experience.

Some employees get one year of work experience ten times instead of ten years of experience at one job. Some interviewees fail to learn from their interview experiences and continue to make the same mistakes over and over.

Perseverance is essential, but it is not always the solution. As soon as success is below your expectations, ask for help. It is usually beneficial to review your strategy with others. It may be necessary to rethink your self-assessment and its relation to the position(s) for which you are interviewing.

Rejection letters are very common so keep your spirits high but seek advice if you sense special problems.

Addressing Issues
. . . .

Salary

The salary question is the most frequently discussed issue among job applicants as well as the most widely misunderstood. In nearly all studies that have been conducted, few people make an employment decision based solely upon salary considerations.

To be sure, it is important for the salary to be within a general "ball park" range. The overwhelming majority of offers for the position you are seeking probably fall within a competitive salary range with which you would be happy.

The salary issue is addressed after there is a general agreement that an offer is imminent. Rarely is it an issue in the initial interview. For entry-level assignments for college graduates, the starting salary varies only slightly between different candidates. The job, not the candidate, influences salary most.

Although some employers do pay premiums for such things as exceptional college grades, previous related work experience, military service, maturity, and

Do	Don't
Smile, smile, smile	Discuss past compensation
Express confidence	Press for a quick decision
Listen intently	Reveal disappointment
Appear excited	Request why rejected
Make eye contact	Take notes in the interview
Ask for the job	Show your nervousness
Show decisiveness	Smoke in the interview
Stay on task	Discuss politics or religion
Maintain professional poise	Bad-mouth others
Project a positive attitude	Apologize for weaknesses
Emphasize accomplishments	Discuss graduate study
Sell your skills	Ask for career advice
Stress personal interests	Appear timid or shy
Give thoughtful responses	Get emotional
Show enthusiasm	Rush through answers
Appear positively assertive	Shun responsibility
Appear highly organized	Reveal disorganization
Project confidence/presence	Alibi about your record
Record notes later	Sound rehearsed

· · · · · · · · · · ·

Figure 18.4

other factors, the differential seems relatively unimportant at the end of one year of work experience with that employer.

The job and what goes into it ultimately determines the salary. Financial success with any employer is usually based entirely on merit, not seniority. Salary increases result from doing an outstanding job.

If the salary question occurs, your best reply is to state that a salary competitive with others you have received or anticipate receiving is expected.

Career counselors normally can provide guidelines regarding the normal range of salaries for people with your particular type of background. In the majority of cases, employers offer a standard salary for a given assignment for individuals with similar backgrounds. There often is not much "negotiating room" as a result.

When you question an employer about salary, the reply is normally very general. It is apparent only that the organization is competitive. Salary should not be discussed in the initial interview unless the subject is forced upon you by the interviewer. What employer would admit to being non-competitive?

If you possess a significant amount of work experience and/or an advanced degree, give the employer some guidelines with regard to the salary range you expect.

Individuals with salary requirements substantially above the standard rates and individuals who possess the credentials to demand a high level of remuneration rarely find themselves in non-competitive salary interviews. If you find yourself in such a situation, ask about salary but realize that the employer may well advise that they are not in the position to offer that remuneration. Thus, you may not receive

Generally, the salary issue comes up only after several interviews, when an offer is imminent.

an offer, but there is little value in pursuing dead-end routes by continuing a "fake courtship."

Be Frank About Limitations

It is discouraging to answer questions that probe into areas where you lack success or have other limitations. By facing the challenge, and without showing disappointment, you can welcome the opportunity to set the record straight. Many times a frank admission can be turned to your advantage.

For example, an interviewer may ask a question concerning poor grades in college. It is proper to reply that although your overall grades may leave much to be desired, more recent grades and grades in your major are significantly higher. This frank reply shows the interviewer that you have matured since you first entered college.

You might also identify extracurricular activities and emphasize the part-time jobs you have held. The score could then be three big pluses with one not-so-embarrassing minus.

It is important that the interviewer identify your limitations. It would be unwise for an employer to place you in a situation where you would be likely to perform poorly. If you are not a Phi Beta Kappa, admit it and point out your other strengths. The employer will be impressed if you candidly discuss your weak points while pointing out your strengths.

Face Personal Questions Directly

Few people appreciate the personal question approach that a number of employers use in identifying potentially successful managers. Questions regarding home life, family, friends, and outside activities appear to infringe on personal privacy. This line of questioning is not very common, but it does occasionally occur, so be prepared for it.

If such questioning is offensive to you, politely inform the recruiter that it has no bearing on the qualifications for the job in question. This will convey your message. If not, it is probably not worth sacrificing your principles to seek employment with that particular employer. Personal questions may not be illegal.

It is important to realize, however, that success in any organization—whether business, education, or government—may well depend upon factors other than basic skills. When a big job change or promotion is imminent, you may well find yourself taking a number of interest and personality tests in addition to visiting psychiatrists.

Grades

Nearly all employers state that they wish to hire only candidates in the top half of their college graduating classes. Each year, however, most graduates, regardless of their academic standing, find careers compatible with their qualifications. In other words, few employers hold to their grade standards because other factors often override grades.

Some employers use grades as a crutch to help them identify talented people. They assume that grades are the best quantitative measure of a person's ability and initiative.

Grades are quite important, but they alone do not qualify an individual. This means that people with high grades should not rely on their scholarship alone.

If you have poor grades, you should capitalize on your other assets. The smart applicant turns the grade question into a discussion of other activities. This technique shows interviewers that you have not been spending day and night reading only textbooks and helps minimize the impression of narrow interests.

If you do have low grades, you should show how other factors, such as work experience, leadership responsibility, social organization activities, sports, hobbies, etc., have contributed to make you a total person.

Fight Nervousness

With friends, relatives, faculty, and counselors emphasizing the importance of getting a job, you may become quite tense before your first interview.

Many college students never take an interview on campus simply because they are afraid they will embarrass themselves or others in their first interview.

Waiting until after graduation is generally disastrous if you want to go to work for one of the better organizations. Many of those employers' openings will be filled by that time.

The first interview in a job search is always the most difficult. Interviewing gets easier with each successive interview until eventually it becomes a routine exercise. Some people become so professional at it that they can go into any interview situation and come out successful.

It is normal to be quite nervous before the first two or three interviews. This nervousness usually disappears once you are into the interview. A good recruiter helps you to relax. In many cases, tenseness helps to keep you alert and prepared for circumstances as they develop, so a certain amount of nervousness can be good.

Interview two or three employers before taking on the employer who is your number one objective for employment. Confidence also plays an important role in helping you overcome nervousness, and adequate preparation brings confidence.

The best antidote for nervousness is a planned presentation and a confidently delivered message. This eliminates much of the uncertainty.

The Selection Decision

Every interviewer must come to a definitive YES or NO decision about every applicant interviewed. Temporarily, "maybe" may be appropriate but within a brief time parameter, even "maybe" gets turned into a definitive statement.

Good interviewers are well trained on how to handle the selection decision. In order to make the decision *reliable*, the same basic information must be obtained from each applicant. Interviewers and their employers work hard to improve the *validity* of every interview. High *validity* means that the information from the interview is relevant and will measure the potential success of the applicant on the job.

RECRUITER'S GUIDE FOR SUCCESSFUL ON-CAMPUS COLLEGE INTERVIEWING

1. **Preparation for the interview** (five minutes)
   a. Know the school and its basic program
   b. Know the opportunities available in your company
   c. Read each interviewee's resume prior to the interview

2. **The interview** (your information—ten minutes)
   a. Warm-up (setting the applicant at ease)
   b. Obtaining additional information that expands on the resume (abilities and skills)
   c. Ask questions that focus on personality
   d. Ascertain goals—present and future

3. **The interview** (interviewee's information—ten minutes)
   a. Relate information on your company
   b. After applicant identifies the area of interest, explain your programs or openings in his/her area of interest and competence
   c. Counsel if no interest

4. **Interviewing skills**
   a. What data to collect—ability, interests, personality
   b. Interviewing techniques—patterned, behavioral, directive questions, stress, hypothetical cases
   c. Knockout factors
   d. Showing interest but not committing

5. **Evaluation** (five minutes)
   a. Complete your evaluation form
   b. Inform the placement office of your evaluation for their counseling program
   c. Make recommendations for further interviews or a rejection

Figure 18.5

Interviewing Styles

Interviewers come in all types of packages, but nearly all of them are trained in interviewing techniques before being given the responsibility.

The interviewer may be a manager or even president of the organization and has the responsibility to select the best qualified talent for the organization. Recruiters vary widely in age, and there are good recruiters at all age levels.

The ability to communicate effectively is probably the most important quality for an interviewer. Professional interviewers know about each school's academic programs.

They know what their organizations have to offer and the positions which are presently available.

Empathy with the interviewer's problems is important. Generally speaking, interviewing at branches and plants is coordinated through a central corporate office which may use professional personnel that enlist assistance from individuals working in specific fields.

For example, if ABC Company had openings only in the sales area, they might use a sales manager to interview. On the other hand, if ABC had a wide range of different types of positions to fill, such as in finance, production, and sales, they may very well use someone from the HR office. Whoever is used will be trained to handle the job interviewing situation.

Although recruiters come in all ages and from a variety of backgrounds, there are certain classifications used by some applicants to describe the more undesirable recruiters.

The "yakker" wants to do most of the talking and judge the applicant's reactions—interest, comprehension, and intelligence—shown in the interview. The "yakker's" evaluation centers around information given on the resume and job application form.

"Yakkers" are often disliked because they do not give you the opportunity to show your assets which are not listed on the pieces of paper. You may find it necessary to break into the conversation whenever you can, because a decision based only on printed information may not be desirable to you.

Contrastingly, the "deadpan" recruiter hardly speaks at all but merely guides conversations in the desired direction. This may be disappointing because it is difficult to determine what information the interviewer is seeking. The "deadpan" gives little positive or negative reinforcement during the interview.

The "deadpan" forces you to sell yourself and call on your knowledge and interest in the position being considered. Preparation prior to the interview will prove to be very worthwhile if you should find yourself being interviewed by a "deadpan."

The "questioner" rapidly runs through a standard set of questions for you to answer. Since the pace is rather hectic, it is difficult for some people to organize their responses. Prior preparation is important.

You may not enjoy the structured set of questions, so your image of the recruiter may be negative. The "human" element often seems to be missing in "questioners." The approach may be dictated by the firm, however.

Complete answers, never just "yes" or "no," are necessary for each question. Interjecting humor into responses, where appropriate, can help you to obtain better results with this type of interviewer.

Interview Methods. The interview is a series of questions designed to get you talking about yourself. As you talk, the interviewer is mentally evaluating you on a scale or ranking form. The form contains many traits that describe you on different performance dimensions. The interviewer can use several methods to elicit information from you that will allow completion of their evaluation forms.

Traits. The questions are designed to get you to describe yourself using personal characteristics. The idea is to understand what motivates you and if the new work environment will allow you to excel.

Behaviors. The questions focus on probing given behavior skills needed on the job which you might have previously exhibited. What you have done can be observed and measured. The idea is to predict future behavior based upon your past behaviors. You describe a situation, and the interviewer evaluates your past actions and also learns about your traits.

WORKPLACE ATTITUDES INFLUENCE HIRING

After the employer hires you, what type of person will you turn out to be? The recruiting team that made the recommendations to hire you tried to assess the attitude that you will bring to the workplace.

Your goal in the interview, especially the second set of consensus interviews, is to give some insight into your attitudes. You surely have a better picture than anyone else on how you might behave after being hired.

Your attitudes and how they conform to your new work group matter as much to you as they do to the employer. The type of attitudes most sought are listed below, but your goal is not to emulate the ideal.

Are you the type of person that . . .

- Approaches confrontation directly?
- Accepts responsibility regardless?
- Self-starts everyday?
- Walks away from rumors?
- Communicates best by talking?
- Listens to all viewpoints?
- Supports the existing team?
- Creates enthusiasm in others?
- Responds positively to criticism?
- Normalizes tense situations smoothly?
- Uses diversionary tactics?
- Toughens-up in a non-threatening manner?

Your goal is to locate the situation where your attitudes can best be tolerated and your ideas readily accepted. Emulating a false ideal places you in future jeopardy.

Before you find yourself in an untenable situation, determine your attitudes and make a determined attempt to put yourself in a mutually supportive work setting through a sound interview approach.

Your attitudes influence your workplace success later. Help insure compatibility. Reveal the real you.

Case Interview Method. The goal is to assess your ability to size-up information given to you and observe your recommendations based on the hypothetical "case." This situational style of interviewing forces you to think and act so traits, past behaviors, and future actions, based on your reasoning process, can be evaluated.

Approach. Each approach has its merits. You can do well by practicing each technique before your interviews. Many employers will use a combination of these 3 methods. You must anticipate and plan to discuss past circumstances and show how they relate to the job requirements for which you are interviewing. To crack a case, you need a framework around which to present your plan. Your logic and approach may be just as important as your hypothetical result or action.

Plan. Interviewing success relates directly to the time you spend in preparing responses. You should always draw upon real past situations in your life. Think about what the interviewer needs (factual info) to complete some type of evaluation form provided by the employer.

In a planned, but abstract way, you are writing this form for the interviewer. The self-assessment tests will confirm what you say in the interview so take several of them before you take your key interviews. You need to confirm consistency and reliability between the two approaches: Interviews (regardless of method used) and assessment instruments.

The web will give you additional information on each interview method and other assessment tests to take and self-evaluate. Plan ahead!

Evaluation Factors

The recruiter will evaluate you following the interview, and it is good to know what factors will be considered in this evaluation. Not surprisingly, most recruiters use a similar format regardless of the type of position for which they are interviewing.

The "Interview Evaluation" shown in Figure 18.7 is an adaptation of forms used by many employers. Several other examples of typical evaluation forms used by employers are also illustrated. Study all of these carefully to understand the criteria employers use to assess potential.

Knockout Factors

Each time an employer says "no" to you, a basic problem has motivated the decision. Surprisingly, the same "knockout factors" continue to be prevalent in the majority of rejections.

When applicants receive rejections, their natural tendency is to ask, "Why?" The knockout factors identify the more common reasons. By thoroughly and carefully reviewing these you can begin to answer the question, "Does that identify me?"

· **FIFTEEN KNOCKOUT FACTORS** ·

(Reasons *why* candidates receive rejection replies)

1. Lack of proper career planning—purposes and goals ill-defined—needs direction
2. Lack of knowledge of field of specialization—not well qualified—lacks depth
3. Inability to express thoughts clearly and concisely—rambles—poor communicator
4. Insufficient evidence of achievement or capacity to excite action in others
5. Not prepared for the interview—no research on organization—no presentation
6. No real interest in the organization or the industry—merely shopping around
7. Narrow location interest—unwilling to relocate later—inflexible
8. Little interest and enthusiasm—indifferent—bland personality
9. Overbearing—overaggressive—conceited—cocky—aloof—assuming
10. Interested only in best dollar offer—too money-conscious—unrealistic
11. Asks no or poor questions about the job—little depth and meaning to questions
12. Unwilling to start at the bottom—expects too much too soon—unrealistic
13. Makes excuses—evasiveness—hedges on unfavorable factors in record
14. No confidence and poise—fails to look interviewer in the eye—immature
15. Poor personal appearance—sloppy dress—lacks sophistication and poise

· · · · · · · · · · ·
Figure 18.6

The best people do not always get the best jobs. You may get turned down while you watch a person with lesser credentials get the job you wanted. Why?

Interviewing success is not solely a skill-based decision-making process. If you eliminate "pull" (and pull usually only gets you an interview, not the job offer), personal qualities influence candidate judgment calls far more frequently than anything else.

Certainly, most jobs do have a required set of functional skills needed to handle the assigned tasks. But, *many* people often meet the *minimum* level of skill requirements. Recruiters must look beyond the *basic* set of skills needed to handle the specific tasks.

You may be the *smartest* person but high mental ability is only one of many screening criteria used by employers. The factors of maturity and motivation enter the equation at a comparable level. It takes a high score on *all* of the "Three Ms" to be a success in interviewing.

The Three Ms:

- Maturity
- Mental Ability
- Motivation

The difficulty with interviewing is the inability of employers to be exact about what is needed. Some interviewers admit that maturity and motivation are amorphous qualities and, yet, a definitive evaluation is required. It is tough to even explain. What do these three words mean?

You will probably be qualified for every interview you take, but you will not get a job offer every time. There will always be more than one possible candidate for any job. You face more competition for some jobs than others.

A recruiter must select from among several qualified individuals. You may be qualified, but are you the *very best* candidate?

The best is defined in many ambiguous ways. What is best to one recruiter is not best to every recruiter. Therefore, there must be some highly elusive qualities that are defined differently by different employers.

The basic concept underlying interviewing is discrimination. How can you discriminate between what on the surface appears to be two equally qualified applicants?

If all talents could be reduced to qualifiable traits, employers would need only to plug the proper variables into a computer and up would pop the most desirable candidates, conveniently ranked. Fortunately, you are not a computer. You have qualities that when packaged together make you a *unique* person. No one else has your special qualities.

Employers do not seek perfectly square pegs. Employers frequently must adjust both the holes and the pegs to make all activities work smoothly. Finding the right person for a given job who can fill other anticipated higher-level jobs later is an art, not a science.

Selection is an art. Being smart is not the only factor. There may be thousands of evaluation factors.

Smart people must become artists, not simply tacticians. Like the employer, you must also become an artist. You need to aid in the process of finding the unique clever match between your total complicated background and an equally complex set of job openings.

Smart people win too!

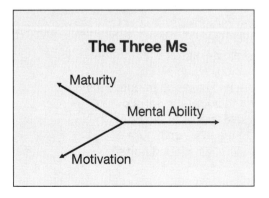

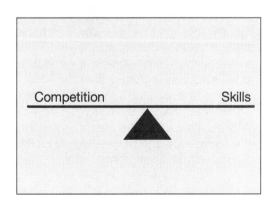

The knockout factors are important because they can influence the interviewer's perception of all of your other qualifications. It is common to find a "halo effect" in reviewing employers' ratings.

Although personal appearance may not be as important as the ability to communicate effectively, when a recruiter marks you low on appearance, the halo is likely to influence other characteristics as well.

Of course, you may get turned down for a given job through no fault of your own. Often an employer finds other candidates with overall stronger qualifications. There are also situations in which the qualifications of two or more candidates are identical and employers' decisions are toss-ups. There is not much you can do when you are turned down for these reasons except to keep persevering until the toss of the coin favors you.

INTERVIEW EVALUATION

Candidate's Name	Date

Characteristics	Please Use Check or Comments				
	Outstanding (A)	Above Average (B)	Satisfactory Acceptable (C)	Limited Potential (D)	Not Acceptable (F)
Appearance Grooming　Bearing Posture　Manners Dress　Neatness	Comments:				
Preparation for Interview Knowledge of Company Knowledge of Positions Open Asked Pertinent Questions	Comments:				
Verbal Communication Delivery and Animation Presentation of Ideas Grammar and Vocabulary	Comments:				
Direction Well-Defined Goals Confidence in Abilities Realistic and Practical	Comments:				
Maturity Responsible　Social Leader Self-Reliant　Judgment Decisive　Work Leader	Comments:				
Personality Enthusiastic　Aggressive Extrovert　Unresponsive Motivation　Noncommittal	Comments:				
Qualifications Academic Preparation Work Experience Position Match	Comments:				
Overall Evaluation Long-Range Potential Drive and Ambition Ability and Qualification	Comments:				

Strong Points Sour Notes Advice Hiring Problems Background Amplify Above Suggestions Plans Personal Hints	*CANDID COMMENTS PLEASE!　EXTREMELY HELPFUL!!*

Probable Action

☐ Invitation　　　　☐ No Job Match　　　　☐ Uncertain at This Time

Figure 18.7

SELECTION SUMMARY

Applicant's Name _____   Date _____

Position Applied for _____

	Out-standing	Good	Marginal	Poor
"CAN DO" FACTORS — **RATING ON EACH FACTOR**				
Appearance, manners				
Availability for this work				
Education as required by this job				
Intelligence, ability to learn				
Problem solver				
Experience in this field				
Knowledge of the product				
Physical condition, health, energy				
"WILL DO" FACTORS — **CHARACTER TRAITS (BASIC HABITS)**				
Stability, maintaining same jobs and interests				
Industry, willingness to work				
Perseverance, finishing what he starts				
Ability to get along with people				
Loyalty, identifying with employer				
Self-reliance; independent; decisive				
Leadership				
MOTIVATION				
Interest in this work				
Economic need				
Need for recognition				
Need to excel				
Need to serve				
Need to acquire				
Drive to succeed				
DEGREE OF EMOTIONAL MATURITY				
Freedom from dependence; independence				
Regard for consequences; responsible				
Capacity for self-discipline				
Freedom from selfishness; ethical attitude				
Personality				
Humor				
Freedom from destructive tendencies; character				
Freedom from wishful thinking; creativity				

<u>Important</u>: Do not add or average these factors in making the over-all rating. Match the qualifications of the applicant against the requirements of the particular position for which the individual is being considered.

Strong points for this position _____

Weak points for this position _____

Overall Rating: [A] [B] [C] [D]

Recommendation to employ: [ ] Yes [ ] No   Rating by _____

Figure 18.8

INTERVIEW REPORT

Name of applicant _____   Date of interview _____
Applying for _____   Interviewer _____

Please report your interview impressions by checking the one most appropriate box in each area.

1. APPEARANCE: very untidy, poor taste in clothes	Somewhat careless about personal appearance	Satisfactory personal appearance	Good taste in clothes; better than average appearance	Unusually well groomed; very neat, excellent taste
2. FRIENDLINESS: appears very distant and aloof; cool	Approachable; fairly friendly	Warm; friendly; sociable	Very sociable and outgoing	Extremely friendly and sociable
3. POISE, STABILITY: ill at ease; "jumpy," appears nervous	Tense; easily irritated	About as poised as the average applicant	Sure of herself/himself	Extremely well composed; probably calm under pressure
4. PERSONALITY: unsatisfactory for the job	Questionable for this job	Satisfactory for this job	Very desirable for this job	Outstanding for this job
5. CONVERSA-TIONAL ABILITY: talks very little; expression poor	Makes attempts at expression; fair job at best	Average fluency and expression	Talks well and to the point	Excellent expression; extremely fluent; forceful
6. ALERTNESS: slow to catch on	Rather slow; requires more than average explanation	Grasps ideas with average ability	Quick to understand; perceives very well	Exceptionally keen and alert
7. INFORMATION: poor knowledge of field of interest	Fair knowledge of field of interest	Is as informed as the average applicant	Fairly well informed; knows more than average applicant	Has excellent knowledge of the field
8. EXPERIENCE: no relationship between applicant's background and job requirements	Fair relationship between applicant's background and job requirements	Average amount of meaningful background and experience	Background very good; considerable experience	Excellent background and experience
9. DRIVE: has poorly de-fined goals and appears to act without purpose	Appears to set goals too low and to put forth little effort to achieve these	Appears to have average goals; puts forth average effort to reach these	Appears to strive hard; has high desire to achieve	Appears to set high goals and to strive incessantly to achieve these
10. ACHIEVEMENTS: **too low to be considered**	Substandard but possibly acceptable	Average	Above average and shows potential	Outstanding

Eligible For Employment:

☐ Yes   ☐ No   _____
                                         Signature of Interviewer

Figure 18.9

POWELL'S TRAIT CHECKLIST

Candidate's Name _____   Interviewer _____

Position Sought _____   Interview Date _____

Please give me an A, B, C, or D grade for each trait listed under each category with your supporting comments and circle the most descriptive words and traits.

Characteristic	Descriptive Words and Traits				Grade	Comments
Personality	Compatible Outgoing Sensitive	Teacher Mentor Resolver	Interesting Adaptable Pleasant	Rapport Flexible Tolerant		
Organization	Planner Organizer Supervisor	Resourceful Analyst Structured	Controller Systems Procedures	Goal Setter Thorough Juggler		
Work Motivation	Ambitious Excels Aptitude	Assertive Energetic Initiator	Achiever Persuasive Hard worker	Charger Influencer Committed		
Expressiveness	Articulate Animated Attractive	Thoughtful Reflective Accents	Eye contact Poise Presenter	Grammar Jargon Worldly		
Learning Ability	Intelligent Aptitude Task oriented	Promotable Competent Potential	Scholar Achiever Worker	Analytic Talker Match		
Leadership	Decisive Responsible Mature	Practical Confident Authoritative	Objective Logical Realistic	Leader Tenacious Solver		
Skill Match	Degree Major Courses	Grades Licenses Certificates	Technical Knowledge Functional Knowledge Industry Knowledge			

Probable Action: ☐ No Interest   ☐ Unsure

☐ Follow-up Interviews   ☐ Offers

OVERALL GRADE

Figure 18.10

TRAIT-BASED CANDIDATE EVALUATION

Candidate's Name	Position Sought	Date	Interviewer's Name

This trait-based candidate appraisal uses key descriptive words for eight selected characteristics of career direction, verbal communication, personal qualities, attitude toward work, job qualifications, interview preparation/presentation, maturity, and appearance. The forced-word evaluation is summarized in an overall evaluation based upon a summary of the key descriptors.

Instructions: Darken the circle beside as many descriptive words as possible. The words selected represent an impression of the candidate's performance in the interview for each characteristic.

CAREER DIRECTION
Please darken the circle beside as many descriptive words as possible that you find reasonably describes the candidate's career direction at this point in time.

O Achievable	O Developed	O Knowledgeable	O Resolved
O Advanced	O Directed	O Lack of specialization	O Self-aware
O Aimless	O Directionless	O Logical	O Self-confident
O Ambiguous	O Disinterested	O Misdirected	O Targeted
O Ambitious	O Driven	O Motivated	O Thoughtful
O Assertive	O Explorer	O Noncommital	O Unclear
O Assured	O Goal-directed	O On-track	O Undefined
O Career-lost	O Good perspective	O Planned	O Unfocused
O Career-oriented	O Idealistic	O Positive	O Unrealistic
O Certain	O Illogical	O Practical	O Unsure
O Clear	O Impractical	O Progress	O Vague
O Concentrated	O In control	O Rational	O Weak awareness
O Confused	O Informed	O Realistic	O Well-defined
O Convincing	O Insincere interests	O Reasonable	O Well-focused
O Defined			

Comments:

CAREER COMMUNICATION
Please darken the circle beside each descriptive word that you feel reasonably describes the candidate's verbal communication abilities.

O Able	O Disorganized	O Nervous	O Slang
O Animated	O Dull	O Organized	O Smiles
O Articulate	O Eloquent	O Personal	O Smooth tone
O Astute	O Expressive	O Pleasant	O Structured
O Attentive	O Familiar	O Polished	O Succinct
O Awkward	O Formal	O Poor grammar	O Systematic
O British accent	O Fresh	O Precise	O Tactful
O Careless	O Homey	O Presence	O Thoughtful
O Clear	O Illiterate	O Rambles	O Timid
O Closer	O Immature	O Rash	O Twangy
O Competent	O Intelligent	O Rehearsed	O Unclear
O Concise	O Laid-back	O Relaxed	O Unfocused
O Confused	O Leader	O Repeater	O Unprepared
O Conversationalist	O Listener	O Robotic	O Used examples well
O Country accent	O Literate	O Rusty	O Vague
O Deliberate	O Mannered	O Scrambled	O Verbose
O Direct answers	O Mixed-up	O Sensible	O Well-spoken
O Disarranged	O Mumbles	O Skillful	O Wordy

Comments:

PERSONAL QUALITIES
Please darken the circle beside as many descriptive words as possible that you feel reasonably describes the candidate's personal qualities and personality.

O Achiever	O Egotistical	O Laid-back	O Poised
O Arrogant	O Energized	O Leader	O Positive
O Artificial	O Enthusiastic	O Likable	O Pretentious
O Assertive	O Excitable	O Mature	O Secure
O Attentive	O Facade	O Motivated	O Self-deprecating
O Avid	O Fake	O Motivator	O Serious
O Belligerent	O Fidgety	O Negative	O Shallow
O Bored	O Forceful	O Nervous	O Shy
O Charger	O Go-getter	O Nonchalant	O Sincere
O Charismatic	O Goal-directed	O Noncommittal	O Unenthused
O Comfortable	O Happy	O Obnoxious	O Unnatural
O Compatible	O Ill-at-ease	O Outgoing	O Uptight
O Confident	O Immature	O Overbearing	O Warm
O Cordial	O Imitator	O Passive	O Weak-willed
O Driver	O Initiator	O Personable	O Wise
O Dull	O Interest	O Persuasive	O Withdrawn
O Dynamic	O Interesting	O Phony	O Witty
O Easy-going	O Introverted	O Plastic	O Zealous
O Edgy			

Comments:

ATTITUDE TOWARD WORK
Please darken the circle beside as many descriptive words as possible that you feel reasonably describes the candidate's attitude toward work.

O Aggressive	O Energetic	O Loose	O Responsible
O Ambitious	O Enthusiastic	O Narrow-minded	O Results oriented
O Artificial	O Fervent	O Negative	O Risk-taker
O Carefree	O Flippant	O Negligent	O Self-starter
O Casual	O Hard worker	O Openminded	O Sensible
O Cautious	O Hard working	O Opinionated	O Sloppy
O Committed	O Unwavering	O Perfectionist	O Solid
O Competent	O Inaccurate	O Perseverant	O Studious
O Competitive	O Inactive	O Persistent	O Successful
O Complainer	O Inattentive	O Political	O Team player
O Cool	O Incompetent	O Precise	O Uncommitted
O Cooperative	O Inconsistent	O Principled	O Unconcerned
O Dedicated	O Indecisive	O Proactive	O Unmotivated
O Determined	O Independent	O Punctual	O Unreasonable
O Diligent	O Industrious	O Reactive	O Value conscious
O Disciplined	O Initiator	O Realistic	O Wholesome
O Distractible	O Intense	O Reliable	O Willing
O Dollar-motivated	O Irresponsible	O Resourceful	O Yakker
O Eager	O Lazy	O Respectful	O Zealous
O Easygoing			

Comments:

JOB QUALIFICATIONS
(Skills, Major, Degree, Experience, Etc.)
Please darken the circle beside as many descriptive words as possible that you feel reasonably describes the candidate's credentials for the opportunity available.

O Academically prepared	O Follower	O Perfect	O Superior grades
O Achiever	O Hustler	O Performer	O Superstar
O Adequate grades	O Impressive	O Poor grades	O Talented
O Analytical	O Inadequate experience	O Problem-solver	O Technically qualified
O Average	O Inconsistent	O Proficient	O Theorist
O Capable	O Innovator	O Qualified	O Thinker
O Committed	O Intelligent	O Related experience	O Unacceptable grades
O Compatible	O Leader	O Requires training	O Uncapable
O Competent	O Mediocre	O Satisfactory	O Unqualified
O Conceptualizer	O Mismatch	O Self-centered	O Unsatisfactory
O Dumb	O Needs improvement	O Self-starter	O Weak experience
O Excellent	O Outstanding	O Sharp	O Weak skills
O Experienced	O Overqualified	O Street-smart	

Comments:

MATURITY
Please darken the circle beside as many descriptive words as possible that you feel reasonably describes the candidate's maturity.

O Accountable	O Flexible	O Loner	O Self-sufficient
O Action-maker	O Follow-through	O Naive	O Serious
O Assertive	O Follower	O Organizer	O Shrewd
O Authoritative	O Giggler	O Participative	O Smooth
O Bold	O Groping	O Poised	O Sophomoric
O Bored	O Haphazard	O Potential	O Sound judgment
O Calm	O Imitator	O Proactive	O Stable
O Capable	O Immature	O Professional	O Street-smart
O Cautious	O Immoral	O Proven	O Talented
O Childish	O Impulsive	O Proven leader	O Team player
O Competent	O Indecisive	O Prudent	O Timid
O Confident	O Independent	O Rational	O Trustworthy
O Confused	O Inexperience	O Reactive	O Truthful
O Decision maker	O Inferior	O Realistic	O Unethical
O Decisive	O Innovator	O Reliable	O Unproven
O Dependable	O Joiner	O Responsible	O Unrealistic
O Dishonest	O Juvenile	O Self-confident	O Unsure
O Emotional	O Leader	O Self-reliant	O Valueless
O Experience	O Logical	O Self-starter	O Witty

Comments:

INTERVIEW PREPARATION/PRESENTATION
(Research, Review, Analysis, Presentation of Facts)
Please darken the circle beside as many descriptive words as possible that you feel reasonably describes the candidate's preparation and presentation for the interview.

O Adequate	O Informed	O Prepared	O Too rehearsed
O Canned preparation	O Inquisitive	O Probing	O Trite preparation
O Careless	O Insightful	O Provoking	O Unaware
O Confused	O Insufficient facts	O Questions	O Understand facts
O Distinctive	O Interested	O Read facts	O Uninformed
O Focused	O Knew facts	O Rehearsed facts	O Unprepared
O Follow-up questions	O Knowledgeable	O Repeats resume	O Up-to-date
O Highly prepared	O Made points	O Sells	O Weak interest
O Homework complete	O Nonchalant	O Superficial	O Well-advised
O Ignorant	O Perceptive	O Surprised	O Well-prepared
O Ill-prepared	O Poor questions	O Thorough	O Well-read
O Indifferent			

Comments:

APPEARANCE
(Poise, Dress, Manners, Mannerisms)
Please darken the circle beside as many descriptive words as possible that you feel reasonably describes the candidate's appearance as broadly defined above.

O Amateurish	O Eye contact	O Poise	O Slouch
O Authoritative	O Firm handshake	O Polished	O Sophisticated
O Average	O Gestures	O Poor body language	O Sparkling
O Businesslike	O Happy	O Posture	O Sweaty palms
O Careless	O Image	O Presence	O Tasteful
O Clean	O Messy	O Professional	O Timid
O Clean-cut	O Military	O Proper	O Tired
O Conservative	O Moderate	O Refreshing	O Unkempt
O Conventional	O Neat	O Relaxed	O Unkept
O Crisp	O Nervous	O Respectful	O Unprofessional
O Dirty	O Obnoxious	O Sharp	O Untidy
O Dynamic	O Personable	O Slob	O Well-dressed
O Excess makeup	O Pleasant	O Sloppy	O Well-groomed

Comments:

SUMMARY
Record evaluative overall analysis below and justify decision

Career direction:
Verbal communication:
Personal qualities:
Attitude toward work:
Job qualifications:
Interview preparation:
Maturity:
Appearance:

RECOMMENDATIONS

☐ Invite for further interviews   ☐ Reject candidate   ☐ Extend job offer   ☐ Delay decision

Decision rationale:

Improving Your Interviews:

Preparation – Presentation – Evaluation

Was my interview a success?

The most effective way to learn any subject area is to physically get involved. Reading alone seldom is the most effective approach to learning. You learn best from what you do.

An interview is a valuable asset that could be destroyed by "practice" interviewing. Before destroying such assets you must do some role playing and simulation.

An interview is similar to an athletic championship event. You get one chance at winning the final event. You prepare for the event by practice. There are many ways to approach the interview practice. *You* need to be *in control* in the interview, not the employer.

One excellent way to approach the interview preparation is to simulate interviews. The "Interview Action Projects" are designed to improve your interview performance.

A well-planned and perfectly executed interview is the backbone of the search phase of career planning. Perfection comes from preparation which includes research, organization, and practicing an approach. One of the best ways to prepare for interviews is by doing practical exercises designed to improve your basic approach to interviewing.

The best way to learn interviewing is to become physically and mentally involved in doing planning activities. This is equivalent to practicing in athletics and music.

Interview Career Action Projects

The purpose of conducting career projects in interviewing is to help assure you the highest level of interviewing success. In many ways, the interview is the most critical element of your career planning because "yes" and "no" decisions by other persons may determine your career direction, not only job possibilities.

A "yes" decision is what your career planning has been building up to. Although a "no" decision is not a catastrophe, it is important feedback. Were your self-assessment, career exploration, and search strategy analysis sound?

Interviews are reality tests. A series of "no" decisions would necessitate a review of your earlier career planning decisions.

A "yes" decision does not complete the process, however. The goal is to get *several* "yes" decisions from your independent evaluators. Your decisions to accept or reject offers may be made on a "rolling basis" or after you've collected several offers. The timing option depends on your specific circumstances. There are many variables which you must consider in your decision of which opportunity to accept.

Simulations and Execution

Up to now, your major activity has been planning. Now it is *execution* time. You are dealing with more than the first ballgame of the year. Although you can afford to lose a few ballgames, the championship will not come to you if you suffer too many losses.

You cannot really afford to lose *any* games. Only with the determination to win (get a job offer) each time will the championship be within your reach.

Once the season starts, there are no practice games. Every interview is for real. Planning, evaluating, role playing, and practicing under *make-believe* circumstances is your only option.

A good contact or a live job lead is a valuable asset that must be nurtured until it can be carefully used. You cannot practice with a real asset because the asset gets used up in the process. Several exercises can help.

There are many things you can do to prepare and practice for interviews. One approach is to use the action projects. Action projects lay the groundwork for successful interviews. They are techniques that will sharpen your interviewing skills to the highest possible level.

Preparation

Your knowledge of an organization is a good indicator to the employer of your real level of interest in it. Most employers believe in their organizations and they are loyal and committed. That is the assumption you must make.

In an interview, the employer is assessing you as a potential member of a close-knit family. Even if the organization is huge, like General Motors, there is a certain *esprit de corps* in overall corporate image and in smaller work groups.

Most employers believe that if you are sincerely interested in working for the organization, you will thoroughly investigate what it has to offer before you take an interview. Assuming that you receive and accept an offer, the organization will become a significant part of your life. It is in your best interest to be thoroughly prepared.

The depth of your preparation for interviews will vary depending upon your time, assessment of your chances, and desire to work for the organization. Preparation is a key variable in interview success.

Cursory attention to preparation usually results in turndown decisions. Few employers hire people for managerial, technical, or professional assignments who do not express a very high interest in working for their firms. Saying that you are interested and proving it by your actions are two very different, and easily evaluated, things.

An in-depth analysis of an organization is the foremost activity that you must do before every interview.

Action projects lead you through a complete analysis of an organization. However, the experience of doing just one action project will help you to prepare for other interviews without the extensive research.

The purpose of an action project is to

OH, DON'T MIND ME... I'M JUST COLLECTING A LITTLE PRE-INTERVIEW DATA.

show you how to approach the task of preparing for each interview. The *method* is the secret. Once you have conducted this method of analysis on a few firms, the data collection in subsequent interview preparations will be routine and reasonably quick.

The two preparation exercises involve three steps:

- Selecting an employer
- Collecting data
- Writing an analysis

Select any employer in business, government, or education. For this exercise, selection of a large, well-known employer makes the data collection process somewhat easier.

By now you have selected a career field and narrowed your selection of a specific job target compatible with your background. Make sure that your specific job target is applicable to the organization you have selected. You will be collecting information on both the employer and the job.

Data Collection. In most cases, there will be a massive amount of information available on the employer you have selected. Your goal is to collect this information from a variety of sources and then to pull it together in a meaningful fashion.

The following sources of information are available in college career offices, the internet, state employment offices, stock brokerage firms, public libraries, and current news publications, as well as from the employer and employees of the organization.

Annual Report. Every public business is required to publish an annual report. It is always available from the employer's public relations department and the internet. Most government agencies and specific departments also publish such documents. Although they are not always called annual reports, many educational and quasi-public organizations make such documents available about their operations as well.

Employment Brochure. Organizations which employ several hundred people usually find it convenient to prepare a publication that describes the organization to potential employees. Usually, these say something about the types of opportunities normally available, and occasionally they discuss job requirements in some detail. They are available from HR offices and can be obtained by writing for them or viewing them on the world wide web.

Investment Reports. Many investment firms make analyses of public business firms whose stock is available for purchase. These firms analyze the stock, and their analyses can be very valuable in assessing the firm's immediate and long-term employment opportunities. If applicable, try to obtain the *Value Line Investment Survey, Standard and Poor's,* and *Moody's* reports. These three firms provide excellent analyses for employment

IT'S OKAY... I'M JUST GATHERING INFO ON HOW TO BREAK INTO THIS BUSINESS.

purposes. The web contains this information.

Job Advertisements. Most organizations regularly place classified advertisements inviting people to apply for jobs. If possible, obtain some that pertain to your field, whether they are current or not. Good sources are Sunday metropolitan newspapers, the *Wall Street Journal,* trade and association magazines, college placement office job bulletins, and the internet.

YOU DON'T HAVE TO **SELL** YOURSELF... THINK OF IT AS A LONG-TERM LEASE WITH THE OPTION TO RENEW.

Advertisements. Other excellent sources of information are product and/or service advertisements. These may be in magazines (popular and trade) and newspapers.

Most firms will send you brochures about their products and services if you write and request them. These give you a much broader image of the company's reputation, quality, and breadth of products and services. The internet typically contains this data also.

News. Most large organizations, whether business or government, are frequently mentioned in newspapers and magazines. Clip out or copy everything you see on your target employer. For business firms, check the library's *Business Periodical Index.* Magazines like *Fortune, Forbes, Barron's, Financial World, Business Week,* and *The Wall Street Journal* frequently contain articles on specific firms. Check issues from the past 18 months. They are on the internet.

Interviews. Many times no information is publicly available especially for small organizations. Many of them will, however, be happy to provide information if you ask for it. Write, call, or visit the head person and ask for some specific information.

Do not mention that your desire for information has anything to do with a desire for an interview later. Keep the interview and preparation separate. You can also obtain information from current employees. Write down all of your findings.

Job Descriptions. You may have collected much information on the organization by this time, but you also need information on the job(s) for which you might be interested. That information is much more difficult to obtain.

Job descriptions are usually only available from specific departments and the Human Resource departments. Write or call the specific department and see if you can obtain a copy of printed material on related jobs.

You need not confine your search for job information to a specific employer. You can do much generalizing from the material in this book and the *Occupational Outlook Handbook.* Try to pull together as much material as possible which is related to your targeted job. Use a search engine to locate job descriptions on the internet.

This material can even be obtained from other organizations. The actual functions do not differ that much from employer to employer. The document that you put together for this interview preparation will also be useful in interviews with other organizations.

Employer Data Collection

The data collection phase of this project is now complete. You should have a very extensive file of information on your targeted employer. The next step is to bring this information together in a way that can be useful for your interview.

Your goal is to develop an informative, interesting, and attractive display of the information. It may turn out to be something you will share with the employer which could certainly have an important positive impact.

Whether you use it in that manner would depend upon considerations such as who the interviewer is, the results of the interview, its appropriateness, the location of the interview, and so forth.

The most important reason for developing this extensive profile is that it will give you concrete data. You do not want to pick a working partner without knowing the facts about it. You may spend years with the employer.

You should evaluate the employer in the same light as if you were picking a business partner and risking all of your financial resources. Much of your future financial resources may derive from your association with this employer.

The selection of an employer is one of the most important decisions you will ever make. Over time, the selection of an employer may be more important than the selection of a career.

Employer Profile Interview Action Project

Prepare an employer profile. The employer profile should be printed to make it more readily accessible, attractive, and useful to distribute. The profile should be three to five pages in length. In essence, you are producing a resume on the employer. You might, therefore, want to follow a simple resume style. The elements of the profile and brief descriptions of them are given in Figure 19.1. Use it as your guide.

Not all of the elements will pertain to all types of employers, and there may be other categories that would be useful to summarize for some employers. The profile analysis is flexible. After you have completed this project you will be very knowledgeable about the organization.

If the employer comes to the conclusion that you are qualified, interested, and strongly motivated to do the job, you will get an offer. Getting the offer is your goal. You need specific job information to best prepare your presentation.

· EMPLOYER PROFILE · · · · · · · · · · · · · · · · ·

Employer: Give name, address, and other contact information on the organization.

General Information: Briefly explain the nature of the business. Mention any international operations and give the approximate number of employees. Note the locations of the greatest concentrations of employees and operations if extensive.

History: Indicate the founding, key early leaders, impact on community and/or public, and the significance of history to today's operation.

Products/Services: Discuss the line of business or operations. Mention all principal products and services and indicate the percentage of their market share and percentage of the firm total sales. Cover the scope of marketing/distribution and the perceived product/service quality reputation.

Structure: Briefly describe the basic organizational structure. What functions report to other functions? Where does the department or function you are interested in fit into the organizational structure?

Industry: Identify specific competitors or employers in comparable operations. Try to indicate the relative ranking of size and quality within that grouping.

Size: Get a handle on the scope of the operation. What is the sales volume or budget? How many employees are there by various groupings? What is the net asset base? Compare figures to other benchmarks to aid in understanding the meanings of the numbers.

Locations: Where is the home office? How large is it? How important is it relative to other locations? Where are the branches and/or plants? How many are there? Is it important to work in several locations? Try to cover all of these points if the information is pertinent and applicable.

Financial Outlook: Investment services provide forecasts of sales and earnings, growth. Look at the various reports. Consolidate their basic recommendations if applicable. If the employer is not a business, try to obtain information on budgets and future and current sources of funding.

Recent News: Summarize any pertinent articles that have been published in newspapers and magazines within the past 18 months. News gives some important ideas on future direction.

Contacts: Give the names and titles of important chief operating officers. Try to learn the names of people who would be superior to you if you obtained a job. If you are applying for general programs or broad training positions, identify the key personnel person who you should contact. If you know the title but not the person, call a secretary for that information.

Positions Available: You probably have a good idea of the job that you want in the organization. Give the title and a brief description of the job.

· · · · · · · · · ·

Figure 19.1

You are unlikely to obtain the exact information you need from the employer. You will probably have to make some educated guesses about job content and other facets of the opportunity.

Title: Make a one- or two-word descriptor, preferably the words used by the employer.

Duties: Describe the day-to-day work activities. Try to hypothesize what a typical work day would be like. Be specific and spell out every single task that is likely to be requested of you.

Responsibilities: How many people might you supervise? What magnitude of dollar responsibility will be on your shoulders? To what position will you report? How closely will you be supervised? Will your decisions impact greatly on the employer's finances and/or image?

Qualifications: Determine the specific skills and background the employer is seeking. What is needed to do a superior job? Discuss the education level and specific formal training required in detailed course work. Get down to the very basic things that create the skills which are necessary to do the job.

Cover the level of work experience required to do a superior, not just an average, job. Keep thinking about how your background fits into this.

If applicable, try to describe some of the personal qualities the employer might be seeking. What personality traits, values, interests, etc. might be very useful in doing a superior job.

Advancement: You have identified the initial job for which you feel you are qualified. The employer will be observing you for growth as well. If all goes well, what will your next three assignments be? Try to think of how you are qualified for these as well, because the employer may be way ahead of you.

What is the time between promotions? What type of training is offered to get you ready? Are you interested in doing the work and study it takes for the next job? Describe some lateral moves as well as upward moves. Keep thinking of what the employer is looking for so you can plan your strategy in your interview presentation.

You now have a good feel for the employer and a better indication of the job. With that much information going into an interview, you are well on your way toward getting the offer. Your next step is to prepare a presentation that integrates what you know about the employer, the position, and your background. The perfect match is then in the making.

Location: Indicate the location of the current job. Where would the next three promotions take you? Would you have to move? Would you be willing to move? Describe all of the potential possibilities. Indicate your willingness to make those moves even if it means several geographic moves.

Compensation: Try to get some handle on the compensation for the job. Is the range reasonable? Could you live on that salary? How fast is salary likely to increase? Is compensation tied to production, bonus, or commission? Identify the type of compensation and how it might change over time. Does the employer seek only highly motivated people? Will money compensation be low? Is that important? What about lifestyle implications?

· · · · · · · · · · ·

Figure 19.2

Job Description Interview Action Project

Prepare a job description. Your career exploration also provides extensive information about this. Write a job description for the job for which you are applying with this specific employer in three to five pages using Figure 19.2 as a guide.

Presentation

If you break an interview down into its basic elements, you will find yourself doing four basic things:

- Preparation
- Presentation
- Execution
- Evaluation

The presentation leaves the most memorable impression in the employer's mind. Why will you be singled out among all the candidates interviewed to receive a job offer? Your presentation has much to do with getting you a job offer.

A previous action project dealt with preparation: getting the facts. This project deals with presenting the facts.

Will your presentation be organized, logical, and convincing? An interview is a lot like a sales presentation. You are packaging the truth.

An interview presentation is similar to a speech. Good speeches are not off-the-cuff comments; they are usually carefully rehearsed. Everyone has heard too many dull speeches. Good speeches require hard work in planning what to say and how to say it. Interviews require the same effort.

An interview has an audience of one. This "speech" before one person would not be more critical to you if it were presented to 100 people. This project asks you to assume a very confident role, one which borders on being cocky.

Presentation Interview Action Project

Tell me about yourself.

Prepare a three to five page, monologue presentation. Use the scenario below as a guide.

Situation. You have been asked to give a speech about yourself.

You have assembled the top five decision makers of the organization for which you want to work. The opening scenario follows.

Introduction. "I know that your organization is seeking top talent to fill positions for which I am very well qualified. I believe that I am among the best qualified people you will see.

"I know you are wondering why I called the five top executives of your organization together today. I appreciate your coming and bringing along with you some of your close associates. This is an important event in my life. I hope it turns into a productive twenty minutes for you. I want a job in your organization.

"I sent you my resume. That will save you valuable time because I will not try to repeat much of the resume information in my presentation so we can focus on my potential contribution.

YOUR RECORD IS EXTRAORDINARY, LORY.
YOUR ABILITIES ARE UNQUESTIONABLY SUPERIOR,
YOUR INTEGRITY IS ABOVE REPROACH, AND
EVERYBODY SEEMS TO LIKE YOU... I CAN'T STAND IT!

THE VIDEOTAPE INTERVIEW COACH

Every interview presentation can be improved. The single most effective method of improving any presentation is to review it via the medium of videotape. Instead of critiquing yourself, a stronger approach is to involve another person in the critique, preferably a career counselor.

Step 1: Practice your responses to common questions before taping.

Step 2: Present your responses in front of a video camera.

Step 3: Review your complete presentation without interruption.

Step 4: Critique your responses one question at a time.

Step 5: Prepare a videotape report card. Evaluate yourself on the following criteria:

- Length of response
- Quality of answer
- Non-verbal communication

Try to be very critical of yourself but recognize that everyone needs another coach. Coaches should not be kind. You need the criticism and recommendations if you expect to improve significantly.

The second videotaping will most likely show a much higher level of self-confidence, stronger motivational qualities, and a true excitement in your voice.

The videotape critique is a superb coach.

"You now know who I am, but I also want you to know why you should hire me. There are many excellent reasons why I can best help you. Let's look at them together. Let me start by telling you the job in your organization which is perfect for me."

Presentation. Plan to continue this monologue with a 20-minute presentation. Prepare a structured outline for the presentation and then write it. It should be roughly 40 to 50 paragraphs of four sentences each. When complete, it should be three to five pages in length, written with several basic, structured outlined points in mind.

Conclusion. At the end, thank the audience for their attention and deliver a forceful close. Ask for the position. Ask them for some commitment of a date when it would be reasonable for you to expect their decision.

This project will be most effective if you can orally rehearse it. Make the presentation to a friend. Ask probing questions about how you can improve it. You should get responses that relate to content, style, organization, mannerisms, etc. Use these ideas to improve your performance. Ask your friend to watch for non-verbal communication.

If you do not have a critic available, tape your presentation as you give it in front of a mirror. Play it back. Critique yourself. Try videotaping it yourself.

Obviously, you are not going to ever give such a presentation to a group of people. What you will do, however, is find yourself drawing on this presentation as you are asked questions in an interview.

Practice makes perfection and perfection is what you must strive for in a job interview. You can never have too much poise and polish. Keep practicing.

Memorize this speech about you. Focus on the outline.

Questions

• • • • • • • • • • • • • • • • • • • •

An interview is a series of questions. The questions are to you and about you. No one knows more about you than *you*. The questions are a given. Although there are thousands of potential questions, they can be grouped into some basic, common themes.

It is not difficult to guess what the questions are likely to be. If you know the questions, how can you *not* be able to give the right answers?

Answers are important, and you can plan them in advance. If you expect to achieve any degree of future success, the answers must be honest. That does not mean they have to come off the top of your head without forethought. Plan ahead.

There are several interview strategies to consider. One is to tell the employer only what you want the interviewer to hear. Another is to tell the employer what you think the interviewer wants to hear. Yet another is to tell only enough so that you get the job.

Some people are experts at second-guessing employers. They are experts at interviewing and get an offer every time. You want to learn to be both an expert interviewee and an expert interviewer.

The essence of this project is to find out what employers want. What are their needs? Can you honestly help? Can you produce on the job? If you can deliver, you are the right person. Further interviewing on your part and further interviewing on the employer's part are a waste of time to both of you if there is not a reasonable match in terms of expectations. Get together.

The essence of career planning is to set a goal and go after it. Your exploring is over, so the interview is not shopping around; it is the real thing.

If you are convinced that you are a match, your motive is to also convince the employer of the match.

The basic assumptions are that you know what the interview questions are likely to be. You know them because

SURE!... I HAVE PLENTY OF OPTIONS IF YOU DON'T HIRE ME.

Prepare your answers in advance.

Your goal is to get an "invite" after every interview.

you have done extensive work on developing the highest possible self-awareness, career awareness, and employer awareness.

YEAH, GRAMPA ALWAYS DID LIKE TO KEEP HIS OPTIONS OPEN.

You know the employer, the employer's job, and yourself. You know that all the pieces fit together. The only remaining objective is to convince the employer that this is the case.

You need to write a plan for telling employers what they want to hear and what you want them to hear in a convincing, logical pattern. Your strategy is to maintain a high level of control over the interview.

Interview questions can be grouped into six basic classifications. If the employer gets the right answers in these six categories, the decision is nearly won. The six areas are:

- Goals
- Education
- Experience
- Interests
- Skills
- Attitude

Nearly every probing question an employer asks is related to one of these six areas. Knowing this, it is not too difficult to anticipate what the questions are likely to be.

This interview presentation technique first anticipates what the questions will be. You next prepare reasoned, logical responses to all of the basic questions. The third step is to write out the responses and study them.

Are your responses honest? Do your responses sound canned? How can you best make them sound candid instead of canned? Effective, planned responses are far preferable to the off-the-cuff comments made by 90 percent of interviewees.

Your objective is to anticipate the interviewers questions and to respond with prepared answers.

I REALLY FEEL THAT I'M READY TO PUT DOWN ROOTS.

It is much easier to eliminate the "canned" and "rote memory" sound than it is to think of effective responses on your feet without a plan.

In essence, you are developing a presentation. After employment, you would never make an unprepared presentation to your boss. You should not think of making an impromptu presentation *now,* either. You are addressing your future boss. You have time to prepare your presentation.

Your job is at stake. You must make every interview count. Interviews are hard to get. When you have a receptive audience, it is critical that you prepare your presentation in advance. Each and every interview is an extremely valuable asset.

Twenty Questions Interview Action Project

Prepare a set of ten questions that you feel an employer is most likely to ask you and give a brief, but convincing, reply to each question. Use the illustration of "Twenty Questions" (Figure 17.8) as a guide, but make each question more personal to your situation.

You might wish to review the stress interview questions (Figure 17.9 and 17.10) for additional question ideas.

Select two questions from each of the six basic categories of goals, education, experience, interests, skills, and attitudes. You should prepare for each question three to five paragraph responses. Limit each paragraph to at least three sentences but not more than five sentences.

You may prefer to print each question and its reply on a separate 5" x 8" cue card which could serve as an excellent review prior to each interview.

Questions on Goals Interview Action Project

An employer uses questions relating to your goals to evaluate your ability to plan ahead and make decisions. Your goals indicate your levels of maturity and initiative.

If you can plan your own life in an objective manner, there is some indication that you can approach high-level assignments with confidence and decisiveness. Ill-defined goals imply "wishy-washiness."

Employers are looking at what you can immediately contribute to the organization. Do you have skills that will help solve particular problems they are facing right now? Do you have immediately usable job skills? Do you have the potential to advance? Are your goals too short-term, or are your long-range goals simply too vague or unrealistic to be meaningful? These are some of the answers an employer is seeking.

Employers may use an indirect line of questioning to get at these answers. Some of the more common questions run like this: What position are you seeking and why do you think you would be the best candidate for it? What

are your most immediate work goals and what makes you think that you will achieve them? What would you really like to do on your first job?

Describe some of the work activities that you would be best at in your first job after college. Give an in-depth analysis of what you really know about the job and how your background fits it.

AND IN COLLEGE, I EVEN RAN MY OWN BUSINESS ...SELLING TERM PAPERS AND FAKE I.D.'S.

In getting at your ability to plan, an employer will start probing into how well you have thought through your own long-term ambitions.

The line of questioning might run something like this: Where do you want to be in ten years? Why do you think that you have the potential to get there? Why do you feel that you would be successful in the long run? Describe an ideal upward mobility career path for you with some realistic timetables on each intermediate work assignment.

A few employers will quiz you on the thoroughness of your planning: How long have your goals been so well-thought-out? What types of lateral moves do you feel would be beneficial learning experiences that would help you in achieving your long-term goals?

The questions on goals are usually your most difficult questions. They may make you uncomfortable. Hundreds of things could later change your plans. You may feel it is unrealistic to plan your life that far into the future. Many people miss the point of this line of questions. No one is going to come back in five or ten years and accuse you of not sticking to your game plan.

This line of questioning probes into the way you approach specific objectives. It gets at factors in your makeup that are quite revealing.

Your approach to planning and organizing can be observed in real-life situations. These are extremely important variables to analyze.

The short-term questions relate specifically to what you can do now. What can you do that will affect the bottom line? How quick can you produce results? Will you stay with the organization? How fast can you advance? Do you really want to do what you say you do?

WELL THAT LAST INTERVIEW WAS EASY.

IF THREATENING INSANITY IS ALL IT TAKES TO GET AN EMPLOYER'S ATTENTION, THEN I'LL HAVE A JOB IN NO TIME.

HI THERE! IF YOU DON'T HIRE ME, I'LL GO TOTALLY BERSERK.

This goal-directed line of questioning is the most important set of questions from the employer's viewpoint. Be prepared to thoroughly respond, realizing that your replies are a test of your reasoning ability, not a long-term commitment.

Summary. Prepare a set of ten goal-related questions and give a brief reply to each question.

Print each question on a separate sheet of paper. Make your typed answer about three to five paragraph responses. Limit your paragraphs to four or five sentences. It would be a good idea to prepare these on 5" x 8" note cards for interview review purposes.

Education Questions Interview Action Project

The obvious reason employers ask questions about your educational background is to evaluate your level of skills and abilities for the required task. Do not forget that they are looking beyond the job you are currently seeking.

Employers do not forget. Employers are evaluating candidates for jobs several levels above the job they are seeking to fill at the moment. Their line of questioning reflects that fact.

Most resumes give the basics on your education. Employers must expand on that limited data, and they do this by probing methods. They try to uncover your interest in learning and growing.

Their probing gets at your basic level of competence and your desire to excel. It gets at your ability to plan, organize, and manage. In other words, probing questions on education go far beyond superficial responses.

The questions you are most likely to hear go like this. Why did you choose your subject area? What subjects did you like best? Why? Least? Why? What did you learn from extracurricular activities related to your studies?

How would you plan your academic studies differently if you could do so? Why? Why did you select your educational institution? Do you have plans for continuing your studies? Why? Where? When?

Are your grades a good indication of your abilities? Why or why not? What major study difficulties have you encountered and how did you cope with them?

There are literally hundreds of questions that you could be asked about your education and extracurricular activities. Your answers are revealing.

Review the questions above. Each question could be answered several different ways. These answers tell different things about your ability and interest in learning. It will pay you to give a studied response. Your answers reveal motivation traits as well as abilities.

Summary. Prepare a set of ten education-related questions and give a brief reply to each question. Expand on your resume; do not indirectly simply repeat it. Discuss rationales for your decisions.

Print each question on a separate sheet of paper. Make your answers about five paragraph responses. Limit your paragraphs to five sentences.

It would be a good idea to prepare these on 5" x 8" note cards for interview review purposes.

Work Experience Questions Interview Action Project

If it is well prepared, a resume documents in a complete fashion the basics about your prior work experience. Dates, job titles, duties, responsibilities, scope, progression, and so forth are all clearly described.

Probing questions focus on your motivations by asking, "Why."

What more could an employer want? Plenty. The brief sketch indicates just *some* of your abilities and skills. An employer is going to probe into your work values, people skills, and personality because these are also important in any work setting.

Work experience questions usually go beyond what you have done or can do. An employer is trying to forecast what you *will* do. By emphasizing achievements and recognitions you offer proof of your motivations.

Some of the skills you have used in past jobs will be consistent with those in the new job, but you may never have done some of the activities required on the job. Are you capable of doing them? A certain technique of questioning can draw out many work-related variables from which an employer can judge whether you *can* and *will* do the job. Employers do not want a recapitulation of your resume.

The questions appear straightforward and up front, but you must consider how your answers will be interpreted. Planned responses can greatly influence the opinions drawn by the employer. Just consider all of the ways you could answer the following questions which are quite common in interviews:

What supervisory roles have you held? Did you enjoy supervising others? Which full-time (part-time or summer) jobs have been most interesting? Why? Why are you changing jobs or careers? Describe the attitude of your last three supervisors toward you.

What has been your greatest or most significant work achievement? Describe what you actually did on your last job. Give me a typical day in your last job. What type of training did you receive on your last job? Identify the specific work skills you acquired from your previous work experiences.

What were your personal objectives in your most recent jobs? May I contact your past superiors for work references? Give me an example of where you took a leadership role. Why did you quit each of your last jobs?

The "Stress Interview Questions" in Chapter 17 offer other excellent questions regarding work experience.

Consider all of the specific responses you could give with very accurate and factual replies. If you sit back and analyze these possible replies, you will find that some give a more positive impression of you than others.

In short, many times a reply that is reasoned and well thought-out in advance greatly influences the impression you leave about your previous work experiences. What you learned is more important than what you did.

Summary. Prepare a set of ten work experience questions and give a brief reply to each question. Discuss how your seemingly unrelated work experience has taught you things that are directly related to the job being sought.

Print each question on a separate sheet of paper. Make your answers about five paragraph responses. Limit your paragraphs to five sentences.

It would be a good idea to prepare these on 5" x 8" note cards for interview review purposes.

WELL, I REALLY HAD MY HEART SET ON THE SUN BELT, BUT I THINK I CAN LIVE IN THE SMOG BELT TOO.

Values Questions Interview Action Project

Some questions take more of a philosophical bend. What do you consider your greatest strengths? What has been the most important turning point in your life? This line of questioning is designed to reveal your commitments to beliefs that you consider most important in your life. What event in your life was the most satisfying to you? The most disappointing? Why? What are your personal five-year goals?

What do you really want out of life? What is your philosophy of life? What makes you work hard? Identify the five things that motivate you most. What do you expect to be earning in five years? Tell me about yourself.

The last question is the most frequently asked question in an interview. The others are occasionally asked but not as frequently. Nonetheless, if they are asked, you should be prepared for them. You can see how an off-the-cuff response to any of them can easily kill your employment chances.

The "Stress Interview Questions" in Chapter 17 will give you some excellent ideas on how professional interviewers might phrase questions related to your personal values.

The responses to these questions quickly reveal your values and ingrained attitudes to some of the deep-rooted, most important aspects of your life. What message about your values do you want to leave?

Summary.   Prepare a set of ten questions on values and give a brief reply to each question. Make sure that your answers reveal that you are a strongly motivated, hard working, committed to excellence type of potential employee. Your motivations and maturity indicators should all be revealed and proven by your past deeds.

Print each question on a separate sheet of paper. Make your answers about five paragraph responses. Limit your paragraphs to five sentences.

It would be a good idea to prepare these on 5″ x 8″ note cards for interview review purposes.

Interest Questions Interview Action Project

Questions relating to values, interests, and personality often run together. It is nearly impossible to identify what a skilled interviewer is after in a given line of inquiry.

Although his or her specific motive may not be clear, the interviewer's goal is to get you talking about yourself.

When you are talking, the employer is learning and evaluating. He or she is learning about your ability to communicate, convince, sell, and work with others.

Your values, interests, and personality are coming out. What makes you tick? A host of factors are being evaluated by some seemingly simple and innocent questions. The questions are unimportant. It is your answers that are revealing.

Questions many times are about your activities outside of education and former work settings. Many of your skills and abilities to do a job come from your outside activities and interests. The questions might include:

How do you spend your spare time? What are your hobbies? Are you interested in any sports? Do you have an avocation? What is the extent of your involvement in civic or professional groups? What leadership have you held outside of education and work? Tell me a little about your background outside of schooling and work experiences. In what type of setting do you feel most comfortable?

Another line of questioning might relate to what you know about the employer. In most cases, the interviewer is trying to assess the sincerity of your interest and your potential commitment to the organization. Questions to reflect these things sound like this: What do you know about our organization? Why do you think you would fit in with our people? Have you heard anything about our training programs? Are you willing to travel? How do you feel about being relocated every three to five years? Are you seeking employment in an organization of a certain size? Why would you like to work for us?

You appear to be overqualified for us; why do you still want this position? What can you do for us now? How can we help you further your goals? What geographical areas most appeal to you? Do you know any of our employees? What kind of information did you find out about us before this interview?

All of these questions get at the heart of your interests.

Summary. Prepare a set of ten questions on interests and give a brief reply to each question. Your answers should show your areas of interests outside the school and work settings. Show how these interests are relevant to the position being sought or how they have contributed to your development.

Print each question on a separate sheet of paper. Make your answers about five paragraph responses. Limit your paragraphs to five sentences.

It would be a good idea to prepare these on 5″ x 8″ note cards for interview review purposes.

Personality Questions Interview Action Project

Personality plays a major role in selection because it greatly influences job performance. Different jobs demand different personality styles.

Regardless of the type of questions asked, personal qualities are being evaluated. Will you fit in with the group? Some questions get at that evaluation more directly than others. Some favorite questions are:

How did you get along with your last boss? Did your teachers respond positively to your questions and answers in the classroom? Do you tend to be the talker in most small groups you are in? How was your classroom participation? Give me a humorous episode in your life. To what positions, if any, have you been elected by your peers? Give me an example of a stress situation and how you reacted to it.

Describe your personality. Are you a team player or a group leader? Do you consider yourself an aggressive, take-charge, type of person?

Personality-type questions usually fit conveniently into the flow of the conversation. There is rarely a planned pattern of questions that follow a specific scheme, but in a roundabout way most of the questions get asked and/or answers are given.

By anticipating all the likely occurrences of personality questions, you can be ready with a proper response. This anticipating strategy puts *you* in control of the interview.

Many of the "Stress Interview Questions" from Chapter 17 are designed to reveal certain aspects of your personal qualities. You might want to prepare responses to these questions.

Summary. Prepare a set of ten questions relative to personal qualities and give a brief reply to each question. Your replies should reveal your commitment to teamwork, ability to work with and for others, assertiveness level, and your approaches to communication with others.

Print each question on a separate sheet of paper. Make your answers about five paragraph responses. Limit your paragraphs to five sentences.

It would be a good idea to prepare these on 5" x 8" note cards for interview review purposes.

Empathic Evaluation Interview Action Project

Immediately following an interview, all employers complete some type of formal written evaluation. They are usually on forms similar to the forms shown in Chapter 17. What would an evaluation form completed on you look like?

The single best way to find out the answer is to do some role playing. You and a friend could develop two hypothetical employers and interview each other. Using a video camera to record the interview would be a special benefit.

The videotaped role play is a super method to use in critiquing and subsequently improving your interview performance. You will find that the second and third time you repeat the simulation, your interview performance will greatly improve.

Many professional out-placement firms and college placement offices regularly use this approach. Being in the role of the employer is just as beneficial as the role of applicant. You get an opportunity to get into the mind of the interviewer to see how and why to formulate specific questions.

Another major asset is just getting a feel on how an employer reviews the interview events and then converts them to a written form. If you can anticipate the factors upon which you will be evaluated, you can direct the flow of the interview in the direction which will more positively shed light on your strongest attributes that the interviewer will be evaluating.

You do not need to role play or videotape an interview to ascertain the most important factors that a recruiter will use in the evaluation. Most evaluation forms emphasize these factors:

- Career direction—goals
- Qualifications—educational skills, experience factors
- Communication abilities
- Personal attributes
- Job-related interests
- Responsibility
- Interview preparation
- Maturity and judgment
- Motivation

Hi-po:	High potential recruit
Empty suit:	Looks good but can't deliver
Charger:	Makes things happen
GQ:	High fashion dresser
Cosmo:	Fashion model
Windmiller:	Appearance of perpetual motion
Guru:	Mentor
Rabbi:	Protector of others
Monk:	Completely work oriented
Air-head:	Not intellectual; dumb
Pretty Face:	Good looking but not street-smart
Hustler:	Achiever
Go-getter:	Assertive

Figure 19.3

Even before your first interview, if you would evaluate yourself on these eight dimensions, you will probably get a sound impression of the interviewer's task. You will better know how to influence a favorable evaluation on each dimension.

Summary. Prepare a three- to five-page *interview evaluation* on yourself. Use as many evaluation forms as you can find to construct the characteristics upon which you feel an interviewer will evaluate you for the specific type of position that you are seeking.

Do not use a specific form *per se.* Any evaluator has words that he or she must put down on paper under each dimension being evaluated, so you need to force yourself to draw upon all of these key words in your analysis.

Review the evaluation forms illustrated at the end of Chapter 18. These will give you an idea of the factors used by employers in their evaluation of you.

Pretend that you just finished an interview. It would be even better if you could use a recent real interview so you could draw upon your performance in that interview in writing the evaluation. After you finish the evaluation, ask yourself what you should have done differently to improve the quality of the evaluation.

You should identify at least eight factors that you feel a recruiter would use in your case. Put two characteristics on each page. Under each characteristic, write an evaluation for each factor. You may do this using key word descriptors or in paragraph form. Explain each evaluation.

Summary

Job interviewing is an extremely important part of the career planning process. You should make great efforts just to obtain your interviews. The dollar value of an interview might vary from $150 to over $500 depending upon your location and area of concern.

You use many contacts to obtain your interviews. Therefore, you must make every interview count. You cannot afford to leave success to chance.

Successful interviewing requires preparation. Many different approaches, strategies, and techniques can improve your performance. By carefully selecting the most valid and reliable strategies for your situation, you can greatly improve your interviewing success.

Preparation is the most important factor in interviewing success. A planned and well executed presentation that draws upon specific content enhances your interview chances for success.

Knowing what factors the interviewer will use in evaluating your responses allows you the opportunity to carefully control your responses toward the most positive directions.

Simulation can never fully replicate a real interview, but practicing projects like this greatly improves your eventual performance. Projects build your level of confidence by eliminating much of the uncertainty about what to expect.

Anticipating what to expect makes your real interview performance much more cohesive. You come across as a person who plans ahead and executes according to an objective set of stops. You are far less likely to be surprised and freeze in pressure situations.

Writing out your plans forces you to cover all aspects thoroughly. A re-reading of your writing not only rehearses the presentation but it allows you to better observe areas needing improvement.

Employment Communications:

Letters – Forms – Decisions

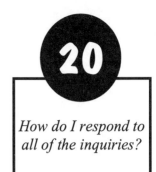

The evaluative process does not end after the initial interview, whether it is on campus or at the employer's facilities. A long sequence of written communications is only beginning for you. The initial interview is normally followed by further interviews at the employer's facilities.

The *secondary interview* initiates a series of further interviews with a number of different people employed in the department that has the actual job opening. Most employment decisions result only after a number of people discuss their opinions about you. Rarely does one person assume total responsibility for hiring. The secondary interview is also referred to as the plant visit, office visit, on-site interview, or call back visit.

If the initial interview is at the employer's facilities, the second set of interviews may be conducted the same day. The current trend is for the initial interviewer to request that you return at a later date. The reason for the later visit is to insure that all of the appropriate decision makers are available.

After the initial interview most employers will contact you by telephone or letter requesting some specific dates which are mutually satisfactory.

Although many employers send turndown letters to applicants in whom they have no further interest, some employers do not do this. As a general rule, if the employer does not contact you within six weeks, little possibility for further consideration exists.

> **The secondary set of interviews are held at the organization's facilities where you are likely to be employed.**

• • • • • • • • • • • EMPLOYMENT COMMUNICATIONS • • • • • • • • • • •

Resume	Thank you for visit
Cover letter	Reaffirming interest
Thank you for interview	Still interested
Keeping in touch	Persistence
Application	Expense statement
Prodding	Terminating discussions
Confirming appointment	Offer
Dear John	Offer acknowledgment
The bullet	Offer stall
Delayed follow-up	Offer acceptance
Invitation to visit	Offer declination
Accepting invitation	Keep in touch (nudge)
Declining invitation	Notes on interview

Figure 20.1

The positive second contact from the employer prompts a detailed sequence of letters, applications, expense forms, and other paperwork. Correspondence takes time.

Even though you are extremely busy interviewing other employers, visiting others, and trying to maintain a normal life, attendance to correspondence etiquette is imperative. One disgusted employer can blackball your chances with many other employers because a close working relationship among employers is very common.

The list of employment communications given in Figure 20.1 gives an appreciation of the scope and magnitude of the problem. As three or more second interviews develop, work builds up rapidly. Since all avenues of employment have to be conducted simultaneously, it is not possible to follow through on one sequence before responding to others.

The time-consuming communication process can be moderated considerably by an advance plan of action. It is far more important to prepare for secondary

VISUAL IMPACT TOOLS

Most letters look dull. You can spice them up a bit by clever graphical considerations. Your goal in doing this is to impress the reader with your attention to detail and to capture special attention to key points in your correspondence. The most commonly used visual impact tools used are listed below:

- Vary two different type styles
- Use bullet points for emphasis
- Boldface (or underline) key words
- Employ an outline format
- Use numbered statements
- Select an off-white paper
- Select a high quality paper
- Use business letterhead paper
- Underline key phrases
- Indent whole paragraphs
- Center top and side margins

Your goal is to deliver a message that will confirm, thank, or call for a follow-up action. Effective use of your visual impact tools increases the likelihood of your mission being accomplished.

interviews than to spend time struggling with letter writing. Yet, the letter writing is very important.

All employers use a standardized set of form letters for the purpose of contacting job applicants. Only minor changes are made in each letter when it is sent to applicants.

Job candidates may also prepare a set of semi-form letters to use in corresponding with potential employers. Of course, letters must be modified each time to fit individual circumstances, but basic construction may vary only slightly.

Required Correspondence

A series of sample letters are included that may be used in contacting employers. The letters, however, represent only a small part of the total communication process. It is important to understand all communication from the perspectives of interviews, itineraries, and employment communications.

Interview Evaluation

The sequence of communication actually begins with the resume and cover letter. The initial interview is followed by an interview evaluation which serves as your personal estimate of future actions. Many effective job campaigns require over thirty interviews. Few candidates can remember the items discussed and the appropriate follow-ups without written records.

Evaluate yourself after each interview for follow-up purposes.

If the response after the interview is positive, the evaluation serves a very useful purpose in planning for future interviews. If the response is negative, the evaluation serves to help you figure out what went wrong. Evaluations should be kept on all interviews—initial and secondary. A sample format is given in Figure 20.2.

Letter Style

Business letter writing style is seldom taught in school, and few people gain any experience in this form of communication. A universal format, style, and etiquette are accepted and used by nearly all organizations.

Each year a large number of job candidates alienate potential employers simply because they do not use appropriate business writing style. Professional communication ability remains a significant factor that employers use in evaluating and comparing applicants.

Figure 20.3 shows the style of a typical business letter. The blocking and spacing may vary slightly. Most people, regardless of the positions they hold, write hundreds of similarly styled letters during their careers.

Each letter must be individually typed and as error-free as the resume. Ideally, a letter should be written after each telephone call or letter received to confirm your understanding of the situation.

Misunderstandings often occur because of the failure to follow up in writing. The employment topic is one that affects a person's entire working career, so attention to details is truly worth the small amount of extra time.

Always keep a copy of every letter sent because it may save later embarrassment. If correspondence is lost in the mail, showing an irritated potential employer the copy may save a job offer. Even better insurance is to send a copy of every letter you write to your college placement office for your file.

Many college career offices maintain a file on each graduating student and alumnus. In due process the files are open for inspection by you. Occasionally an

CONTACT IMPRESSION EVALUATION

Company name ______________________________ Date_______________

Individual contacted ____
Address:

Position applied for ____

How initial contact was made: Campus Interview __________ Letter ____________

Other____

Comments on First Contact

Probable action by recruiter:

No interest ____ Uncertain ____ Is interested _____

Follow Up Procedures

Who will initiate next contact? They ________ Me ________

Date by which contact should be made ____________________________________

Nature of contact:

Actual date of follow-up contact ______________________________________

Nature of follow-up message: ______________________________________

Date consideration terminated ______________________________________

Reason consideration terminated (if self-initiated):

Figure 20.2

◐ BLACKLIST OF SALUTATIONS

All professional business letters start with the salutation "Dear" followed by a colon (:) after the name of the person to whom the letter is directed. To have the impact intended, all business correspondence must be directed to a *specific person.*

Your employment correspondence is no different. You should never use "generic" salutations. The following salutations should be blacklisted in your employment letters. Never use any of them following the word "Dear" unless you add a last name after the title. Titles can never be "dear" to you.

- President
- Dean
- Chairperson
- Gentlemen
- Counselor
- Friends
- Personnel Manager

- Sir/Madam
- Committee
- Staff
- Professor
- Director
- Colleagues
- Any title

If you do not know the appropriate name, call the switchboard number of the organization and ask for the appropriate person's full name.

If you cannot use a formal name, omit the salutation "Dear." In this rare instance you might wish to use the memo format "To:" with the opening in lieu of a salutation. Another acceptable option is to omit the salutation entirely after you type the inside address.

employer calls the career officer to complain about a student's (or alumnus') lack of courtesy. Placement officers invariably pull the file so they can see the true chain of events.

Many major employers also send copies of all their correspondence with students to the placement office. The placement office can often assist students and alumni who have had mail difficulties by showing them copies of letters you should have received from employers.

The importance of proper communication cannot be overemphasized. Written communication is the backbone of every human resource office. A good succession of communication shows the employer that you sincerely want the job. A high level of interest shown by your follow-through can swing the decision your way even though another candidate may have a slightly stronger record.

TYPICAL BUSINESS LETTER STYLE

Street Address
City, State, Zip
Telephone number
email
Current Date

[4 spaces]

Employer's Name
Title
Department
Organization
Street Address
City, State, Zip
[1 space]
Dear Mr./Ms./Dr. Individual's Last Name:
[1 space]
Introduction: Reference previous conversation or correspondence . . . give specific dates if possible . . . state appreciation for past consideration . . . succinctly state current business.
[1 space]
Body: Give details on purpose of letter . . . make reference to attachments . . . write short but complete sentences . . . avoid large and unnecessary words . . . cover the central theme completely . . . make paragraphs two to five sentences.
[1 space]
Close: State the action you expect from the recipient . . . keep paragraph short . . . indicate your next plan of action . . . offer specific date of expected action if appropriate . . . thank the recipient.
[1 space]
Very truly yours, [Sincerely, Sincerely yours, Truly yours, etc.]

[3 spaces]

Signed Name
Typed Name
[1 space]
P.S. [Information that came after the letter was written. Sometimes used for emphasis.]
[1 space]
Encl. [Indicates that there is an attachment or enclosure]
[1 space]
cc: Career Services Office [Indicates others who are kept informed]

Figure 20.3

FOLLOW-UP PHRASES

A number of phrases frequently are repeated in business correspondence. You will find many of these phrases that tie together events, circumstances, qualifications, and actions used in the many illustrated examples.

Most people use a word processor software package to mail all of the required employment correspondence. You will probably put your unique version of your standard replies into your own word processor document files. All you will then need to do is to call up the appropriate letters, make minor changes, retype the inside address, and mail.

In constructing your various letters, you might wish to incorporate some of the preferred follow-up phrases listed below.

> Upon reflection . . .
> Recognize the importance of . . .
> Listening to your advice on . . .
> Impressed with . . .
> Enthused and excited about . . .
> Confident about . . .
> Interested in . . .
> Appreciative of . . .
> Qualifications are . . .
> Important qualities of . . .
> Expect a positive reply soon . . .
> Thank you for . . .
> Contact me if . . .
> However, please consider . . .
> Look forward to hearing . . .
> In reference to . . .
> Enclosures include . . .
> Time and interest . . .
> Please . . .

Employers make ample use of word processing. Given the limited time available during an intense job search campaign, you may also wish to handle much of the processing details in advance. Incorporating some of the follow-up phrases into your letters makes excellent use of your limited time.

Thank You

A thank-you letter after every initial interview is not necessary, but in certain instances where interest is very high, it is appropriate to send a follow-up. A thank-you letter simply restates your interest in a job with the organization.

In some instances, thank-you letters serve another purpose. Some employers fail to respond expeditiously to job candidates and need a nudge. The "nudge" letter is sent under the guise of a thank you about six to eight weeks after the initial interview.

A polite way to nudge the employer to act is to enclose an updated resume or to comment about any new developments since the initial interview. Another approach is to say that another employer is pressing, and a decision is necessary.

Application Forms

Every employer demands that you complete the organization's official application blank. Even if your resume contains the same information, an application is required for legal, data processing, and employer convenience reasons.

The National Association of Colleges and Employers (NACE) has a tacit agreement with most major employers that a completed application is not necessary prior to the on-campus interview if the student has completed the standardized "College Interview Resume" used by the career services office. This resume is of a format adopted and approved by NACE. If there is further interest in the applicant after the campus interview, an application is then required.

The application is an official document. The information must be complete and accurate. If the blanks are inadequate for a certain situation, explain the situation on an attached page.

The application often follows employees for years. Career progress decisions are made on the basis of information contained in applications which may be several years old. Employers tend to update applications by placing promotions, salary progress, and appraisals into the employee's personal file. Thus, a well-completed initial application is in your best interest.

Everyone enjoys reading a document that is free of errors and smudges, neat, typed, centered, and complete. Typing application blanks is not always possible, but if time is available, you should do it. The form is often copied and widely circulated internally; a typed form makes a more pleasing representation.

If you have no significant work experience related to the sought-after assignment, the "salary desired" blank may be left open. For candidates with work experience and/or a minimum acceptable salary, the minimum should be specified. If the employer cannot meet the minimum, an offer is unlikely, so both parties can save much time.

Almost no employers negotiate on entry-level salaries; attempts to negotiate most often are met with offer withdrawals, so be prepared to lose the offer if you decide to haggle.

Accepting Invitation

After expressing your appreciation for the opportunity to visit the employer's facilities and his or her further interest, you should suggest three convenient dates, in most preferable order, for your visit. This is often done via telephone or email.

Invitation

The confirmation letter should be written even if it is only a formality to confirm the dates agreed upon by telephone. It is an embarrassing situation for both the employer and candidate to arrive and find no itinerary arranged.

You should determine with the employer whether overnight accommodations are necessary. If so, it is best to request that the employer make hotel reservations nearby. Advising the employer of your travel plans and time of arrival is standard courtesy.

APPLICATION FORM

Please complete this personal data sheet. Either present it to the interviewer or mail to the office.

Personal: If Employed, This Becomes A Part Of Your Permanent Record.

Name _____
          LAST (Please Print)   FIRST   MIDDLE   NICKNAME

Present Address _____
                  NO. and STREET   CITY   STATE   ZIP   (AREA CODE) TELEPHONE

Permanent Address _____
                    NO. and STREET   CITY   STATE   ZIP   (AREA CODE) TELEPHONE

Social Security No. ____ / ____ / _____   If not a citizen of U.S. indicate type of VISA _____

Have you ever been refused or do you have any reason to believe you might be refused an application for a fidelity bond?

         Yes ☐   No ☐   (If YES, explain in Comments Section)

Education: Scholastic Record To Date (Estimate if not known)

High School	Undergraduate	Graduate
NAME _____	**UNIVERSITY** _____	**UNIVERSITY** _____
CITY AND STATE _____	**CITY AND STATE** _____ FROM_____ TO_____ ATTENDED	**CITY AND STATE** _____ FROM_____ TO_____ ATTENDED
I stood number _____ scholastically in a class of _____, or estimate that I stood in the top 10%☐ 25%☐ 50%☐ 75%☐	**Degree** _____ **Mo. & Yr. of Grad.** _____ Concentration or Major _____	**Degree** _____ **Mo. & Yr. of Grad.** _____ Concentration or Major _____
COLLEGE BOARD S.A.T. SCORES Verbal_____ Math_____ (200-800) (200-800) English___ Math___ Composite___ (1-34) (1-36) (1-35)	**GRADE POINT AVERAGES—** Overall _____ Major _____ Minor _____ Grade point equivalent of "A" _____	**GRADE POINT AVERAGES—** Overall _____ Major _____ Minor _____ Grade point equivalent of "A" _____

	GRADES	NUMBER OF HOURS			NUMBER OF HOURS		
Insert in the appropriate boxes the number of hours of college credits, broken down by grades and subjects as indicated. Use latest degree only.		Major	Minor	All Other	Major	Minor	All Other
	A						
	B						
	C						
	D or Lower						
	Unit of Hours	Semester ☐ or Quarter ☐			Semester ☐ or Quarter ☐		

TOTAL CREDIT HOURS TAKEN UPON COMPLETION OF FINAL DEGREE _____
APPROXIMATE NUMBER OF HOURS PER WEEK OF OUTSIDE EMPLOYMENT DURING LAST ACADEMIC YEAR _____

TEST RESULTS, IF TAKEN —
 Graduate Management Admissions Test—
 	
 VERBAL_____ QUANTITATIVE_____ TOTAL_____
   (0-60)   (0-60)   (200-800)
 	
 Law School Admission Tests—   LSAT_____
                               (10-48)
	LIST UP TO 5 COMPUTER COURSES AND GRADES
	 (If < 5, list last 5)
	 _____
	 _____
	 _____
	 _____
	 _____

SCHOLARSHIPS _____

HONORS: ☐ Beta Alpha Psi ☐ Beta Gamma Sigma ☐ Phi Beta Kappa ☐ Tau Beta Pi ☐ Other _____

PARTICIPATION IN SCHOOL ACTIVITIES (e.g., class organizations, athletics, publications):
COLLEGE _____
HIGH SCHOOL _____

Position Interests:

Have you previously applied to our firm for a position? YES ☐ NO ☐ If YES, _____ and _____
Year   Office

Do you now have any employment commitment with another firm or company? YES ☐ NO ☐ (If YES, explain in Comments Section)

Location Preference—Our firm representatives are seeking qualified personnel for many offices of our firm. Our office locations are listed in our employment brochure. Please indicate your location preferences below:

1st Choice _____ 2nd Choice _____ 3rd Choice _____

Who referred you to us? _____

Starting salary expected _____

Employment Record:

SPECIFICS	LAST OR PRESENT POSITION	NEXT PREVIOUS POSITION	NEXT PREVIOUS POSITION
EMPLOYER			
ADDRESS			
NATURE OF DUTIES			
NAME AND/OR TITLE OF IMMEDIATE SUPERVISOR			
PERIOD–MONTH & YEAR	FROM _____ TO _____	FROM _____ TO _____	FROM _____ TO _____
FINAL MONTHLY SALARY			
DISCHARGED OR ASKED TO RESIGN	NO ☐ YES ☐	NO ☐ YES ☐	NO ☐ YES ☐
MAY WE CONTACT EMPLOYER	YES ☐ NO ☐	YES ☐ NO ☐	YES ☐ NO ☐

References: (Do not include former employers, relatives, or more than one member of college faculty)

NAME	MAILING ADDRESS	TITLE OR OCCUPATION	YEARS KNOWN
1.			
2.			
3.			

Comments: Use this space for any further explanation or information you wish to supply.

If employed, I agree to provide copies of official university transcript(s) or equivalent(s) and a copy of my diploma(s). I understand that you will conduct a routine inquiry into my general character, reputation, and mode of living. Upon written request, I can obtain further information about the nature and scope of this inquiry.

All representations by me on this data sheet are to the best of my knowledge and belief true and correct, and I have not knowingly omitted any related information of an adverse nature.

Date _____ Signature _____

Please attach unofficial transcript (or course/grade listing) with this application.
We Are An Equal Employment Opportunity Firm

COLLEGE GRADUATE EMPLOYMENT APPLICATION

An Equal Opportunity Employer   **TYPE OR USE BLACK INK**

LAST NAME	FIRST NAME	MIDDLE NAME	SOCIAL SECURITY NO.	DATE AVAILABLE TO BEGIN
PRESENT MAIL ADDRESS NO. AND STREET	CITY	STATE	ZIP	PHONE: AREA CODE & NO.
PERMANENT MAIL ADDRESS NO. AND STREET	CITY	STATE	ZIP	PHONE: AREA CODE & NO.

SCHOOL	DATES ATTENDED (Month & Year) FROM TO	GRADUATION DATE	DEGREES	MAJOR	MINOR	Cumulative G.P.A. Out of a Possible	CLASS STANDING (e.g., Top 1%)
PRESENT COLLEGE							
PREVIOUS COLLEGE							

DID YOU RECEIVE ANY SCHOLARSHIPS?   NO____   YES____
IF "YES," DESCRIBE: _____
_____

ARE (WERE) YOU A MEMBER OF ANY HONORARY GROUP(S)?
          NO____   YES____
IF "YES," NAME: _____
_____

SIGNIFICANT MEMBERSHIPS IN AND OFFICES HELD DURING COLLEGE
(EXPLAIN AND INDICATE YEAR):
_____
_____
_____
_____
_____

DID YOU WORK PART TIME DURING COLLEGE YEARS? NO____ YES____; IF "YES," HOW MANY HOURS PER WEEK? _____
PERCENT OF SCHOOL EXPENSES EARNED?   _____%

LIST WORK EXPERIENCE, FULL OR PART TIME (MOST RECENT FIRST), INCLUDING MILITARY:

EMPLOYER	LOCATION	PRODUCT/SERVICE	PRINCIPLE DUTIES	DATES	HRS./WK.

NUMBER YOUR PRIMARY FIELDS OF INTEREST, IN ORDER OF PREFERENCE (NO MORE THAN 2):

__Finance   __Purchasing   __Plant Engineering   __Engineering Planning
__Accounting   __Transportation   __Manufacturing Engineering   __Product Engineering
__Computer Systems   __Production Control   __Production Supervision   __Scientific Research
__Quality Control   __Sales/Marketing   __Operations Research   __Other; Explain:
__Programming   __Industrial Relations   _____

DO YOU HAVE A STRONG GEOGRAPHIC PREFERENCE? NO____ YES____;   If "YES," WHERE? _____

ARE YOU WILLING TO TRAVEL IN CONNECTION WITH WORK ASSIGNMENTS? NO____ YES____
          IF "YES," HOW MANY DAYS PER WEEK? _____

IF YOU FEEL ADDITIONAL COMMENTS WILL HELP IN EVALUATING YOUR APPLICATION, PLEASE ATTACH SEPARATE SHEET.

ARE YOU MAILING THIS APPLICATION AS THE RESULT OF AN INTERVIEW WITH A COMPANY REPRESENTATIVE? NO____ YES____
          IF "YES," WHEN (MONTH AND YEAR) _____ WHERE _____

I UNDERSTAND THAT I SHALL NOT BECOME AN EMPLOYEE OF THE COMPANY OR ANY OF ITS SUBSIDIARIES UNTIL I HAVE SIGNED AN EMPLOYMENT AGREEMENT WITH THE FINAL APPROVAL OF THE EMPLOYER AND THAT SUCH EMPLOYMENT WILL BE SUBJECT TO VERIFICATION OF PREVIOUS EMPLOYMENT, DATA PROVIDED IN MY APPLICATION, AND ANY RELATED DOCUMENTS OR RESUME, AND WILL BE CONTINGENT ON MY SATISFACTORILY PASSING A PHYSICAL EXAMINATION REQUIRED BY THE EMPLOYER. I HAVE BEEN IN-FORMED THAT A REPORT MAY BE MADE WHICH WILL INCLUDE APPLICABLE INFORMATION CONCERNING MY CHARACTER, HEALTH, GENERAL REPUTATION, PERSONAL CHARACTERISITICS, AND MODE OF LIVING, AND THAT I CAN MAKE A WRITTEN REQUEST FOR AD-DITIONAL INFORMATION AS TO THE NATURE AND SCOPE OF THE REPORT IF ONE IS MADE.

SIGNATURE _____   DATE _____

PERSONAL INFORMATION
EMPLOYMENT APPLICATION

An Equal Opportunity Employer   **PLEASE USE BLACK INK OR TYPEWRITER**

Name _____ Social Security No. _____
          Last   First   Middle Initial

PRESENT mailing address, Street _____ Phone: Area _____ No. _____
City _____ State _____ ZIP _____
PERMANENT address where you can always be reached. Street _____ Phone: Area _____ No. _____
City _____ State _____ ZIP _____

Today's Date _____ Dates available for pre-employment visits _____ Date ready for work _____
Height _____ Weight _____ Do you have or expect to have in the near future any family or other responsibilities which
would prohibit or interfere with traveling from one location to another or meeting other demands of employment? No _____ Yes _____ If Yes,
explain _____

Have you had or do you now have any physical or mental health problems such as tuberculosis; epilepsy; fainting spells; hernia; nervous,
mental, or emotional diseases/trouble; diabetes; back ailments; heart condition; amputations; limitations in sight, speech, hearing, or limb;
or any other physical/mental health problems? No _____ Yes _____ If Yes, explain _____
_____

High School _____ City _____ State _____ Graduation Date _____

List all colleges and universities and other educational institutions attended, including military service schools, in chronological order.	Degree	Major	Minor	Cumulative G.P.A. & Base; e.g., 3.2/4.0	Class Standing; e.g., Top 1/10, 1/4, 1/2; or 25/80	Attendance From To (Mo./Yr.) (Mo./Yr.)	Anticipated or Actual Graduation (Mo./Yr.)

List advanced courses in major _____
Languages spoken fluently _____
List college grade point average for each year (not cumulative): 1st _____ 2nd _____ 3rd _____ 4th _____ 5th _____ 6th _____
Future education plans (part-time, full-time, type of degree) _____

Honors, Awards, Scholarships _____
Athletics _____
Organizations and Offices Held _____
Outside Interests and Hobbies _____

List chronologically all work—full-time, military, summer, cooperative, and part-time.

From (Mo./Yr.)	To (Mo./Yr.)	Employing Organization & Location	Describe Duties	Hrs./Wk.

Present reserve or draft status (military only) _____
Branch of U.S. Service _____ Active duty: requested _ ordered _; fulfilled—Mo./Yr. _____ to Mo./Yr. _____ Highest rank _____
Significant achievements/awards while in military service _____

Career areas of greatest interest (such as engineering, manufacturing, finance, marketing, etc.): _____
Specific work interests (such as sales, engineering, quality control, cost accounting, etc.) in order of preference:
1. _____ 2. _____ 3. _____
Product or business areas of interest _____
Geographic interest: None ____ Prefer to work in/near _____ Must work in/near _____

If you have previously discussed employment or corresponded with anyone in our company, please give individual's name, location, and approximate date. _____

Professor with whom we may communicate for additional information _____ Dept. _____ School _____

Not all employers pay expenses for the secondary interview although most of them do. Be prepared to assume the total cost. Call the employer if there are any doubts as to the cost arrangement.

The employer must be notified immediately if changes occur or last-minute emergencies develop. The employer has

YES, I SPENT AN ABSOLUTELY DELIGHTFUL WEEK FILLING OUT YOUR APPLICATION FORMS.

likely developed a schedule for executives to interview you which must be canceled or changed.

Declining Invitation

If you decide that your interests lie elsewhere, thank the employer for the consideration he or she has displayed and state that you have made other career plans. Never ignore an invitation letter. A response, one way or another, is essential within three days. Never burn your bridges.

Reaffirming Interest

After the visit to the employer's offices, a brief note indicating your continued interest should be sent. The expense statement is usually attached and other details of the visit are discussed. The letter should always express thanks and appreciation.

It is common to enclose your expense report in this letter and to indicate that you are enclosing any other information that your interviewers might have requested.

Expense Statements

Many times an employer will request an expense voucher before reimbursing expense money. This could be included in the letter reaffirming your interest. In many cases, the employer refunds expenses at the end of the day of the visit. If the employer does not provide a form for you to complete, the one given in this section is acceptable. Remember that not all employers pay expenses.

I HATE FILLING OUT THESE JOB APPLICATIONS.

BESIDES BEING TIME CONSUMING...

THEY DON'T GIVE YOU MUCH SPACE TO RESPOND.

GUIDE FOR PREPARATION OF EXPENSE REPORT

When you are invited to visit the organization or one of its sales offices more than 50 miles from your present address, you will usually (but not always) be reimbursed for expenses involved in making the trip. Reimbursement is intended to cover actual expenses required to complete the interview. Expenditures for entertainment, tours and other personal activities may not be included. When a visitor elects to visit other firms on the same trip, it is expected that expenses will be prorated among the companies concerned.

1. **Receipts Required:** Receipts for lodging and commercial transportation will be required before reimbursement can be made in accordance with Internal Revenue Service regulations.

2. **Transportation:** In order to reduce time away from campus or job, interviewee may select the most convenient means of transportation (air or rail). Use of private automobile via most direct route will be reimbursed at the current rate per mile. Automobile travel is not recommended if round trip is over 400 miles. Car rentals are not permitted unless authorized in advance.

3. **Hotel-Motel:** Most visits to plants or sales offices will require one overnight stay. Occasionally, where transportation difficulties arise, a second night's lodging will be required. Only charges for room rent will be reimbursed.

4. **Meals:** It is expected that such expenses will not be excessive. Meal charges should include meal, sales tax, and tip.

5. **Local Transportation:** Include airport limousine service, buses, local or suburban trains and taxis with reasonable tips where appropriate.

6. **The Following Items Are Not Reimbursable:**

   - Entertainment, tours, cigarettes, magazines, etc.
   - Excessive tips, personal phone calls unless for emergencies
   - Valet expenses
   - Expenses for persons other than individual interviewee
   - Car rental (unless authorized by in advance)
   - Stopover other than at point of interview unless required by transportation
   - Charges for uncanceled transportation reservations
   - Travel insurance

7. **Read the sample "Interview Trip Expense Report" format**

An effective job campaign can easily cost $1,000 to $3,000 including resumes, letters, travel, and moving expenses. It is an expenditure you should plan for well in advance.

Never pad an expense account. Illegal and unethical conduct is unacceptable. Employers pay expenses day in and day out and know what reasonable costs are. A blackballing letter from an employer to other potential employers could be extremely damaging to you.

Terminating Discussions

If after the visit you determine that you have no further interest in pursuing that employment, advise the employer immediately.

The employer should be thanked for the consideration shown you, and you should state that you have made other plans. This should be done as soon as you decide so that the employer can extend an offer to someone else.

Offer Acknowledgment

After receiving an offer, written or verbal, an immediate acknowledgment of the offer should be made. Thank the employer for the interest shown and discuss your understanding of the terms (salary, job title, duties, etc.) of the offer.

The employer is aware that you may have other irons in the fire; it is proper, therefore, to indicate the date by which you will make a decision. If that date comes and you need more time, an extension can be requested. It must be remembered, however, that an employer has the right to withdraw the offer *any time* prior to its acceptance.

Some employers extend more offers than there are job openings available, and when the first person accepts, they withdraw other offers still outstanding. Most employers, however, will hold an offer open until the date mutually agreed upon.

Acceptance of an Offer

This letter constitutes a contract between you and the employer. An acceptance should again include the terms and conditions. Also, such items as the drug screen, physical examination (if required), reporting date, and perhaps home-hunting plans, should be discussed.

Of course, you can accept only one offer, and the decision is a binding commitment. If a more attractive offer comes at a later time, you must reject it on ethical grounds. The decision to accept should not be taken lightly or done in haste.

If undue pressure to make a decision is exerted by a given employer, do not buckle under if you have other hot irons in the fire. In the final analysis, the decision to accept or reject an offer is your decision, but advice from others always helps.

It is seldom possible for you to collect all potential offers and make a decision after they are all in. Both you and the employer must make decisions in a chronological sequence.

When you turn down an offer, the employer must have enough time left to extend the offer to another applicant. Time can be critical for both parties.

Rejection of an Offer

As soon as you have made a decision to accept a job, immediately notify all other employers of that fact. You should simply advise them that this was a difficult decision but that another employer's opportunities fit better in line with your interests and aspirations.

It is proper to indicate where employment was accepted, but it is not necessary. By courteously thanking them for their interest, you keep the doors open for the future.

JOB DECISION ETHICS

- Honor dates for reply
- Keep your word
- Explain decision difficulties
- Never burn bridges
- Leave doors open
- Write thank you to everyone
- Put everything in writing
- Never renege on commitments

• • • • • • • • • •

Figure 20.4

INTERVIEW TRIP EXPENSE REPORT

Name _____

Address _____

City, State, Zip _____

Telephone _____

Date of Visit _____

Transportation:

From home to airport _____

Airline fare (receipt attached) _____

From airport to home _____

Taxi/Limousine fares _____

Lodging

Hotel (   ) (Receipt attached) _____

Hotel tips _____

_____   _____   _____

Meals

Meals prior to interview _____

Meals en route home _____

_____   _____   _____

TOTAL EXPENSES INCURRED _____

Signature _____

· · · · · · · · · ·

Figure 20.5

STALLING TECHNIQUES

It would be ideal if you could set a date upon which all of your many job offers would arrive simultaneously. On this pleasant date you could review all of your offers, analyze their pros and cons, and then come to an optimal decision.

Unfortunately, reality does not work that way. Your offers arrive over time, and you usually receive two to three weeks' time in which to make a decision. Out of necessity, your decisions must be "rolling" decisions.

Most employers will try to make you an offer about two to three weeks before a date that you name. It requires a considerable amount of coordination of first and second interviews to make your offers arrive simultaneously.

In most cases you will have to make some of your offer decisions before others arrive. This means you must have confidence that a better offer will arrive later if you reject an offer.

Your goal is to evaluate offers against a firm set of criteria that you have established. Rarely can you evaluate offers against each other.

There are some stalling techniques that you can employ that will aid you in planning so that your offers will arrive within your specified "window of opportunity."

These techniques involve calling or writing (preferably writing) each employer explaining your situation and requesting an extension. The most accepted reasons for requesting "only two weeks extension" include:

- Pressing commitments
- Major exams
- Class projects
- Business travel
- Further job details
- Geography concerns
- Consult family
- Consult others
- Work commitments
- Personal plans
- Spouse employment
- Promise to others

Many organizations will need your services immediately unless you are moving into a training program. Others will press you by indicating that they must make an offer to a back-up candidate which they will lose if a delay is granted. Extensions are possible for up to a couple of weeks, but often the employer simply cannot grant extensions and risk losing the back-up candidates.

It is unethical to accept an offer and later renege if a better opportunity emerges. Besides the moral obligation, offended employers have legal methods to address the ethics of an offender, usually through professional associations and personal friendships in the industry. There may be legal actions as well.

The offer process is highly unpredictable. Your best strategy is to pre-identify the "window of dates" during which time you desire all of your offers to converge. Stalling the date of your secondary interviews and requesting decision extensions are the most opportune techniques to insure a convergence of your opportunities.

UNETHICAL EMPLOYMENT PRACTICES

- Inaccurate resume
- Falsifying records
- Incomplete records
- Dishonest recommendations
- Lying in interviews
- Cheating on expenses
- Insincere job interest
- Abusing confidentiality
- Reneging on acceptance
- Leaving job prematurely

• • • • • • • • • •

Figure 20.6

POTENTIAL SANCTIONS FOR UNETHICAL CONDUCT

- Prepare report of situation
- Note in placement file
- Notify current employer
- Advise potential employers
- Inform credit agencies
- Consult references
- Advise Placement Council
- Inform employment agencies
- Contact personnel associations
- Consult legal counsel

• • • • • • • • • •

Figure 20.7

The Secondary Interview

An understanding of what to expect at your secondary interview contributes to your ability to communicate well. Confusion leads nowhere. Each situation may need to be handled differently, but a pattern may be assumed.

Flexibility in the itinerary is a standard procedure. Upon arrival, you usually report to the HR department to learn of the plans for the day. The individual to whom you report may or may not be the interviewer you met previously. Personnel's role normally is that of a liaison and, therefore, the following points may be discussed.

- Outline for the day's activities.
- Organization structure.
- General employment procedures and guidelines.
- Answers to your general questions.

One of the most important reasons for extending an invitation is to introduce you to managers and employers in your field of interest. Expect to be interviewed by four to eight individuals, most of whom work in your area of specialization or interest.

They will evaluate your abilities, competence, and personality. These interviews are quite similar to the initial interview, but there are more of them.

Many of these interviews are copies of each other. The employer wants to expose you to a wide array of people, all of whom will be evaluating you. It is important to not let down in any of them because even one "no interest" can often ruin your chances for employment. Giving the same presentation over and over can become boring but keep a proper attitude.

Most interview visits begin at 9:00 a.m. and continue until 5:00 p.m. Little, if any, free time can be expected, as even lunch is reserved for interviews.

Many employers administer psychological tests during one-day visits. Tests may last from one-half to three hours. There is a trend toward more employer initiating selection testing programs.

Tours of the employer's facilities are not uncommon although it is not always a standard procedure. If it is not, and you have an interest, ask about it.

Near the end of the interviews, you will again meet the liaison person. You may be requested to express your impressions of the day and in return you can expect some feedback on your progress. Many of the interviewers will have returned their evaluation forms to HR by that time.

In many cases, you may get an intuitive idea of how the interviewing is progressing. However, do not plan on receiving an offer at this time. If an offer is extended or the em-

PERHAPS I SHOULD EXPLAIN SOMETHING, KIP. NORMALLY WE DON'T EXCHANGE RINGS HERE WITH OUR EMPLOYMENT COMMITMENTS.

ployer implies that an offer is likely, you can usually expect to receive it in writing within two to four weeks.

If expenses have not been mentioned by the end of the day, ask what procedure should be followed for reimbursement. Many employers refund expenses at the end of the day, whereas others request an expense statement. Nearly all require receipts, so you should save all of them and give them to the employer at the appropriate time.

If you are visiting other employers on the same trip, plan on prorating your expenses. Besides the ethics involved, HR staff seem to have a close local fraternity, and knowledge of excellent candidates rapidly spreads. Do not jeopardize your employment chances by fudging on an expense statement.

If all went well in the secondary interview, you should soon receive a firm job offer in writing. You may have been told such a decision was already made but that it would later be formalized in a letter. These salary offer letters are what you have been working toward, and they deserve your most sincere analysis.

Consensus Hiring Influence

Rarely is an employment decision the domain of a single decision maker. Several managers must be willing to say "yes" to a given applicant's hire in today's arena of consensus decision making. Few managers are willing to take the legal, political, and business risk and responsibility for a hire without the concurrence of other colleagues.

You must pass *several* interview hurdles, not just one. Employment is a "series" of pressing interviews in the majority of cases. Most interviewers have the authority to "reject" you but not the authority to "accept" you without the concurrence of others.

The lesson is simple: you must impress *everyone* you meet. Clearly, in most situations, the decision latitude of the key interviewer is far greater than others, but as an outsider you must impress every person trusting that each will influence other decision makers.

Typically, there are four types of people who will interview you. As a skilled communicator, you must tailor your remarks to your audience. The four interviews are:

- The initial HR screen
- The peer interview
- The boss interview
- The boss's boss interview

These may not be in this order. Each interviewer will grade you on different characteristics. By tailoring your responses to address their unique perspectives, you enhance your ability to navigate each hurdle in the employment process.

Cursory Evaluation

Personnel Screen.   The human resource interviewer is charged with insuring a certain level of quality in all candidates. The referral for the interview may come from outside the organization or even from the boss's boss. Assuming that the recruiter thoroughly knows the job and its qualifications well, this is a *cursory evaluation* to see if you match the stated job requirements. There may be some technical jargon, but an assessment of your technical abilities will be left to others.

Human Resources insures that fair hiring policies are addressed. You will be properly entered into the appropriate data base, evaluated on common forms, appropriately screened for Affirmative Action requirements, medical concerns, legal considerations, etc. There is a cursory personality screen to insure that you will be worthy of the line manager's time.

Technical Competence

Boss Interview.   Upon hiring, you will be placed on someone's budget, and that person is likely to be your future supervisor for some period of time. Ultimate responsibility for the quality of the selection decision rests with this boss.

Bosses usually focus on three issues:

1. Will this person do the job?
2. Does this person have the potential to assume greater responsibility?
3. Will this person fit into the immediate and later work group environment?

The "boss interview" can be more technically oriented than that of the human resource recruiter. Try to speak the unique language of the job. Use buzz words and jargon. Mention names of experts in the field. Reveal your technical abilities and your personal work attitudes, personality, and conversation abilities enough to satisfy the three issues above.

Your questions at this interview should focus on factors that will influence whether or not you will accept the offer you presume will be coming. Common areas of concern include performance evaluation criteria, progress, challenges, reporting relationships, work environment, personal career goals, etc. Come prepared for nitty-gritty job questions.

Work Group Fit

Peer Interviews.   The employees with whom you will be directly working deserves some input on who is brought into the work group. Often very informal

(such as at lunch and dinner), these interviews are frequently non-evaluating. They are, however, important because a weak impression can be an important signal of potential problems to the boss.

The peer-level interview can be a gold mine to you. Your potential work colleagues can offer you an exceptional insight into how life might be if you accept the offer. A great deal of sharing of mutual likes, dislikes, and work expectations occurs. Latch on to this opportunity and show *enthusiasm for joining* this group by asking many presumptive questions about your routine after you are hired.

Keep in mind that some of your potential peers may consider you as competition. Therefore, try to focus your interest on the most immediate assignments, daily routines, management styles, personal frustrations, current challenges, and (most importantly) on getting along with this group. Often you will deal with a recent alumnus from your school, so you may already have a number of things in common upon which to focus.

Future Potential

Boss's Boss Interview.   Assuming other interviews have gone well, you will meet the boss's boss. This manager must give a stamp of approval or you are dead. The focus in this interview will not be so much on whether you can do the job but your *longer-term* potential at the firm. Regardless of the level of your responsibility, higher-level managers assume that your first 10 to 20 months on the job are largely learning experiences.

Your evaluation here is on future capabilities. Your thrust should be on your long-term potential and how your personal qualities fit within the culture of the organization. Are your appearance, intellectual capacities, communication skills, and goals compatible with those expected of executives of this organization?

Play to Your Consensus Audience

Summary.   No single strategy in the interview process can guarantee success. If you can identify the motivations of the different players in the hiring decision process, direct your communications to these concerns, and tailor your presentations accordingly, you stand to increase your odds of interview success.

The Employment Decision
• •

Assuming your interviewing efforts have produced handsome dividends and several job offers are in hand, you are now faced with the task of deciding which offer to accept. How do you choose between offers that provide relatively equal salaries and advancement opportunities?

It is a delightful position, but the choice is not simple. Making the choice can change your lifestyle and move you into a career field that is likely to place an imprint on you for a lifetime. The job decision can influence your career direction and shape your success for years to come. The challenge must not be taken lightly.

How do you make such a decision? From a thirty-minute conversation and a one-day visit, multiple website visits, a wealth of data and facts are not always available from which to draw conclusions.

But with this limited information and other research data, hopefully, a sound decision can be made. Recommendations and ideas from faculty, placement officers, friends, parents, and so forth are additional aids. Collating even this limited information is a big project, especially when you consider the impact of the results on your future.

DECISIVE? SURE, I'M DECISIVE... SOMETIMES
...I THINK... BUT MAYBE NOT.

Factors to Consider

A number of studies have been conducted in which researchers quizzed people about why they accepted the positions they did. The rank order of factors in these studies varies depending on the population used. There are differences in rankings based on sex, race, class standing, and academic major. Consolidating these studies gives a table similar to Figure 20.8.

Whenever an individual is asked to rank the factors influencing his or her job choice, the ranking seldom coincides precisely with views of large surveys. Surprisingly, the top five factors tend to be the same, and the next five factors seldom deviate out of that group of five either. Salary consistently ranks between the sixth and tenth most important factors in most populations surveyed.

You should develop your own ranking scheme depending upon your personal value structure.

Job Comparisons

One purpose of ranking your values is to help you quantify the decision to accept one job over others. Few individuals select the first choice that comes along. An objective scheme to quantitatively rank various choices aids you in your final decision. One useful scheme is the "Job Comparison Form" shown in Figure 20.9.

The "Job Comparison Form" in no way dictates which employer to select. It is impossible to quantitatively rank all factors because one or two factors may be overriding. Some materialistically-oriented people may place salary so high on their lists that other factors become inoperable.

The qualitative approach offers little help to the person who has offers in several different cities but who, for one reason or another, must locate in a given city. Subjective factors greatly influence job choice.

Cost-of-Living Comparisons

Such factors as opportunity for advancement, type of position, work colleagues, type of training program, etc., must be given high priority in a job decision. You are

REASONS MOST FREQUENTLY CITED FOR ACCEPTING A JOB OFFER

- Opportunity for Advancement
- Challenge and Responsibility
- Opportunity for Self-Development
- Variety of Assignments
- Type of Work
- Freedom on the Job
- Salary
- Working with People
- Job Security
- Training Program
- Fringe Benefits
- Working Conditions
- Location of Work
- Job Title
- Reputation of Employer

Rank order varies by candidates surveyed, but most surveys approximate this ranking.

• • • • • • • • • •

Figure 20.8

Factor	Relative Importance to Me	Organizations Compared		
		Employer: Value (0–5) = Product	Employer: Value (0–5) = Product	Employer: Value (0–5) = Product
Prestige and reputation				
Size of organization				
Growth potential (sales)				
Product diversification				
Management caliber				
Industry choice				
Interesting assignments				
Early responsibility				
Location				
Job security				
Salary				
Training program				
Fringe benefits				
Travel responsibilities				
Immediate superior				
People work with				
Recommendations of friends				
Working conditions				
Interest level of firm				
Advancement opportunity				
Point Total				
Relative Ranking				

Rate each of the factors on a scale of 5 to 0 with 5 being most important and 0 indicating no value to you. Place your rating (5 to 0) in the "importance" column. As you gather information about a particular employer, review each factor in relation to the specific employer and assign a value of 5 to 0 to the employer for each factor beside the dotted line. Next, multiply "your importance" ratings and place the product in the column under the employer name. When complete for all factors of each employer, add the points and rank from high to low.

• • • • • • • • • •

Figure 20.9

also probably concerned about salaries and how they compare in different geographic locations.

At first glance, salaries seem much easier to compare than the subjective factors. A true comparison of starting salaries requires investigation of cost-of-living indexes, bonus or commission plans, and any special benefits (such as a car for full-time use, purchase of products at discount, profit sharing, or low home mortgage financing).

...BUT THEN THERE'S ALWAYS THE COST OF LIVING TO CONSIDER IN THIS CITY.

You should investigate the *Cost-of-Living Indexes* for the cities for which you have received job offers. There is a big difference between costs in Dallas and New York City, but how can you interpret this difference? Cost-of-living comparisons are available and helpful, but they can be misleading, so use them *with care*.

The family market basket used in calculating the index may be inappropriate for a recent college graduate who is single and has no dependents. Discrepancies result from the time at which the survey was made, type of survey, family status considered, and whether apartment renting or home ownership was assumed.

Probably the most thorough study available is that provided by the U.S. Bureau of Labor in their monthly publication titled *Consumer Price Index*. Many libraries carry it.

The U.S. Department of Labor's Bureau of Labor Statistics annually publishes a comparison of family budgets in urban areas. These budgets and accompanying indexes can be used to compare differences in price levels for regional variations. The indexes are classified for three different family income levels: lower, intermediate, and higher.

Another index is published by the U.S. Chamber of Commerce based upon the earnings of managerial and professional persons earning realistic salaries. Most Chamber offices have this survey available for viewing.

Figure 20.10 on the next page, is a facsimile of a cost-of-living chart. Given wide monthly fluctuations, this chart is not purported to be current, but it is useful for illustrative purposes. The given index number is of no value except in relation to how it compares with other numbers.

Salary offers in different cities can be compared by dividing each salary by the respective city's cost of living index number. Caution should be used in interpreting the results because personal lifestyles vary greatly and most indexes are based on an "average" family.

Figure 20.11 gives some examples in comparing different salaries in different cities. After equivalent bases have been calculated, the difference in salaries between the high and low may be viewed as significant salary differentials.

FAMILY BUDGET INDEXES

Urban average	100
Metropolitan	102
Non-Metropolitan	91
—	
Atlanta	92
Baltimore	99
Boston	119
Chicago	100
Cincinnati	99
Cleveland	102
Dallas	89
Detroit	101
Honolulu	120
Houston	93
Kansas City	96
Los Angeles	97
Milwaukee	104
Minneapolis	104
New York	116
Philadelphia	104
Pittsburgh	97
St. Louis	97
San Francisco	105
Washington (DC)	108

Source: *Monthly Labor Review,* "Intermediate Budget for a Family of Four."
Indexes are for illustration purposes only. Consult latest publication.

• • • • • • • • • • •

Figure 20.11

Salary Information

Most people want some idea of what they can command now and where they may expect to be, salarywise, in a few years. Experienced people have a more difficult time obtaining this data than recent college graduates. Internet surfing can provide an idea of your likely starting salary because compensation studies are published regularly on the web.

Amounts can vary considerably by curriculum. The exact offer made will depend upon the candidate's prior professional experiences, major subject, degree level, grades, leadership activities, and, of course, the employer's internal salary schedule for the position for which the graduate is being considered.

Many placement offices cooperate with the National Association of Colleges and Employers and send weekly reports to them on offers. This enables a quarterly report to be prepared for all colleges to use based upon a national sample of job offers. Many placement officers share this salary data with students and alumni. It is available on www.jobweb.org.

In addition to getting information from the graduates, several hundred employers keep career professionals informed of salary offers made to their students. The employers

AND THIS IS MY AGENT... HE WILL
NEED A CALCULATOR.

do this by sending a periodic report or sending copies of all letters (invitations, offers, and acceptances) to the school from which the student graduates.

A check with your career counselor will produce an estimate of what salary might be expected after graduation. Given your background, a realistic estimate is fairly easy for an expert to predict. A range rather than an average will probably be given because the mean salary can be very misleading.

Assuming that the mean and the median are fairly close, it should be remembered that one-half of the graduates will be below the median. Students who have grade point averages below "B," few campus leadership activities, and no related work experience generally fall below the mean and toward the lower end of the range.

You should not be misled by averages. This could result in your pricing yourself out of your job market value.

For experienced personnel, very few sources of salary information exist. The best sources are associations of similar career personnel, newspaper ads, and current magazine articles. Surf the web for comparisons.

Inform Career Services

If you are a recent college graduate, always give the college career office information on both your offers and your placement. The Career Services office needs to know the employer, position title, location, and salary amount. This data is kept extremely confidential; most offices do not make it part of a student's file.

The primary use of such data is to assist others in the career exploration part of career planning. The basic source of career information on salaries is past students.

Without complete cooperation from each graduating student, professionals would find it more difficult to help others in this very important aspect of career planning. Everyone wants to have salary information available to assist in career decision making.

Share your placement decisions with your college career service to help others in their career decisions.

The sharing of this information with a source that can pass it along with a high level of objectivity and credibility provides an important service to others.

There are important secondary reasons for sharing offer and placement information as well. Colleges continually face financial problems, and the first items to go out of budgets seem to be student-related services. The simplest method for justification of the career function is to show its results. If an office can show a major contribution to a high percentage of graduates, it may survive the same cost reductions.

Aside from career planning, salary information aids everyone because honest and open salary information tends to raise the overall level of salaries. The average becomes the base which many employers use in determining an appropriate salary offer.

Open salary data tends to narrow the range of offers by eliminating the "lowball" offers; employers do not want to risk getting negative reputations. Employers are less likely to make noncompetitive offers if they know students have knowledge of their job worth.

Desired Salary

Most employers will ask on their job applications what salary level that you expect. Employers have relatively narrow salary ranges for each type of job. An individual's niche in the range will depend on the current supply and demand for people in that field.

There are a number of ways to approach the problem of what salary to request. Asking for too much will eliminate some offers.

If you ask for too little, that may be all the employer will offer. There is less danger with the latter because employers assume other employers might also be interested in you, and they do not want to risk losing a good candidate because of a low salary figure.

One idea is to suggest to the employer a salary *range*. This lets the employer know that you are not overly concerned about an exact amount.

Your perceived range and the employer's given range for the job will probably overlap. Of course, you should be prepared to verbally defend why your offer should be near the top of the range by documenting your above-average qualifications.

Another idea is to give the mean offer being extended to others with the same major, same degree level, and equivalent experience. This gives the employer an idea of your expectations and shows reasonable judgment. The figure can be verbally defended at the appropriate final interview, if you are asked, and additional support can be produced based upon your credentials.

It is not out of line to simply leave the salary line on the application blank. There is no stigma attached to this idea. Most employers have a firm notion of what they will offer regardless of what is written on that line.

One last suggestion is that if you have a minimum salary figure firmly in mind below which you will not accept the job, you should let the employer know this. If, because of certain reasons (such as having other job offers, being on a leave of absence from another position, possessing extensive related experience, etc.), offers below a certain amount are unacceptable, it is best to be honest with the employer and state this.

There is no advantage to wasting time if an agreement cannot be reached.

Salary is seldom the overriding reason for accepting or declining an offer. It is best to let the employer know that salary is an important variable, if it is, but also that it is only *one* of the criteria you will use in a final analysis of which position to accept. There are other variables which may be more important than salary to you.

Negotiating Salary

Salary is not a topic for negotiation with many employers. If it is discussed at all, it will be discussed at the time of the secondary interview. If you are asked, it is best to give an idea of your expectations.

The prospective employer needs a straight answer. Based upon this statement and your credentials, the employer will decide on a firm salary offer that is consistent with the organization's internal salary schedule. Once the figure is offered, it is not likely to change.

COMPENSATION FACTORS

- Base salary
- Commission
- Short-term bonus
- Incentive pay
- Signing bonus
- Stock options
- Cost of living
- Benefits
- Perks
- Overseas adjustments
- Work schedules
- Telecommuting

• • • • • • • • • •

Figure 20.12

Most application blanks request your desired salary.

Initial starting salary should be the least and last criterion used in evaluating which job opportunity to accept after college.

WHAT ARE YOU WORTH?

How much should your new job pay? Salary information can be found with the right resources but not without some significant digging to locate accurate figures. The Internet is full of data.

Compensation is no longer synonymous with salary. Many factors go into the compensation calculations. Most employers turn to compensation experts to help determine an appropriate salary compensation. The compensation analyst keeps track of salary norms within the industry and geographical area.

The experts regularly conduct salary surveys with their competitors in order to establish a fair salary structure within their own organization. These individuals also draw upon a variety of compensation materials published by professional associations such as the American Management Association's "Compensation Review" and "CompFlash."

Evaluating jobs is the first step in a salary structure. Compensation specialists use several methods to compare the value of the job to the organization. The Hay Point System, developed many years ago and regularly used, is the best known job evaluation system. It assigns "points" to various parts of a job, which are then summed. Points are assigned on the basis of responsibility, supervision, budget, complexity, training, and other aspects of each job.

Once points have been assigned, you have in effect ranked all jobs within the organization. A pay structure can then be presented which provides higher financial rewards to those with the highest point totals. A fair and consistent salary structure like this can help avoid the "pay compression" syndrome where supervisors earn only a minimal amount more than subordinates.

An organization can have a fair internal salary structure but not meet the demands of the external market-place. Supply and demand also impacts upon compensation. Consequently, employers must also conduct competitive pay surveys and adjust internal schedules accordingly. They can also tap into giant computer data banks for comparative salary information based on regional factors, organizational size, industry, and other parameters.

In the poker game of salary negotiations, it may seem that employers have the greatest access to information, but you also can strengthen your hand. Knowing the appropriate salary information about your anticipated position is essential for career planning purposes even if you cannot influence the amount offered.

Business, employment, government, and private publications including association journals often release results of salary surveys. Start your research by looking under "Salaries" and "Earnings" in the internet search engines.

//WEB.TIP//

www.jobsmart.org/tools/ salary
Job Search Guide
Career and salary info/ California focus/links to many salary surveys/ Extensive articles/job fairs/ part of Bay Area Library system.

When attempts to renegotiate salary amounts are made by candidates, offers can be withdrawn. An offer can be withdrawn at any time prior to acceptance. If you are certain that an offer you hold is unacceptable, you risk nothing by asking the employer to reconsider. Although the offer may be withdrawn, there is the possibility that if the employer really needs your talents, it may be increased too. Why not try to negotiate in that situation?

Haggling is not always worth the risk. If money must be coaxed from the employer, a bad start is made. The employer may not be happy later because of the issue, or the employer may take the amount from the first raise anyway.

All good employers reward productivity. Showing what you can achieve by work will produce later rewards.

The *National Business Employment Weekly* periodically publishes articles regarding salary statistics that come from various trade organizations, compensation, consulting services, and employment agencies. This *Wall Street Journal* publication is available at most newsstands. The classified job ads also often give salary ranges for current openings which might also be useful.

The U.S. Department of Labor annually publishes the *National Survey of Professional, Administrative, Technical, and Clerical Pay.* Monthly salaries of various managerial jobs are surveyed and reported. Check with your library or the Superintendent of Documents for this publication.

For recent college graduates, the site www.jobweb.org publishes an excellent starting salary survey. It is also available from any college career office. It classifies starting salaries by major, degree level, industry, job function, and several other appropriate categories.

Many times, haggling over a salary offer is a non-negotiable item. You tell the firm what you want and only if they can afford you will an offer be extended in your desired salary range. Even in these circumstances, you need to know some reasonable guidelines in order to avoid pricing yourself out of the market.

One of the worst sources of salary information is your friends. Most know even less than you if you have done your research, and nearly everyone tends to inflate the salaries they quote for personal ego satisfying reasons. Go to the professionals with access to large data bases, not amateurs with very small samples.

The most common negotiating ploy is to have an ace in the hole with a fixed salary. Even if it is not exactly what you want, you can "request" a higher amount from subsequent employers. Your chances of obtaining an offer decline substantially when you advise them that you need 20 percent more than the "ace in the hole" offer amount, but you may be just as happy with your ace if the other offer is not that much higher.

The wisest negotiating advice is to be reasonable if you wish your goals to be obtained. Remember that compensation is only one small part of the "offer" evaluation. Far more important is your personal happiness, and money often does not bring it. In most cases things like job title, location, development, and challenge far outweigh the salary issue. Negotiating pay is a private undertaking with long-term consequences, so a healthy respect for the total process is very important.

Don't forget to factor into your decision items such as discounts (retail), commissions (sales), bonuses, incentive awards, expense accounts, and other perks.

Future Salary Potential

Very little information is available about what to expect after several years on a career path. When questioned about future salary potentials, few employers can give an answer because very few are able or willing to predict the future.

Potential earnings depend upon the person's ability and motivation—also upon being at the right place at the right time. Rather than rely on blind luck, the "movers" in any organization tend to make their own "breaks" happen.

An excellent source of salary information is in the form of the U.S. Government Salary Schedule. The grades and various levels within the grades are closely attached to given job titles for government jobs. Exact salaries are given for each salary grade and years of experience at that level.

These salaries are determined after extensive salary surveys of equivalent jobs in business and industry. There is a conscious effort by government representatives to keep the schedule competitive, yet not below comparable jobs in industry, so the government has a fair chance of attracting equally talented individuals.

Libraries, the internet, career services, and government offices have the salary schedules available.

Another excellent source of salary information in selected career fields is classified advertisements. Many ads give salary ranges for a given number of years of experience for the positions advertised.

You must temper the ads, however, with judgment because many of these ads are "come-ons" designed to elicit a great number of resumes from potential candidates. Nonetheless, many of the jobs are filled at the salary ranges quoted, so they do offer clues about future earnings.

The most extensive listings of want-ads are in daily newspapers of the major metropolitan areas. Large libraries carry newspapers from many cities, so it is possible to review several papers and not have to rely on just a local paper. Sunday editions usually contain the most help-wanted positions. The world wide web covers these at www.careerpath.com.

Also, information can be obtained from want-ads placed by employers in their major trade publications. Most of the industries (automotive, chemical, petroleum, retailing, insurance, etc.) and selected career fields (data processing, accounting, sales, production, etc.) have monthly or quarterly periodicals that offer a classified ad service to members.

For example, *Automotive News* and the *Wall Street Journal* have sections where employers may place advertisements for talent. Most of the positions advertised require experience, so you can guess where you might be on the salary scale with a given level of years of experience.

From time to time, surveys of executive compensation are made by management consultants, university professors, and business research institutes. Major libraries carry reports of these. Some of the major business periodicals (*Business Week, Commerce, Nation's Business,* etc.) summarize these studies in their regular issues. Excerpts can usually be located on the web.

During the past few years salaries offered to new college hires have increased at a faster clip than those given to present employees. Many experts believe that to be due to the changing supply-demand situation between college graduates and entry-level jobs. The next decade will continue to bring greater salary increases to junior and middle management personnel.

The "compression effect" is a great problem for employers. Rapidly rising entry-level salaries push middle-range salary positions into an even slower rising upper salary range position. In other words, the spread between entry-level salaries and top compensation in the salary grades is narrowing.

This contributes to dissatisfaction and high turnover among bright young people. In selected companies and industries, this could be a serious problem in the next several years.

Sample Letters

One of the best ways to learn is to simply emulate. The following sample letters are designed to provide an illustration of typical correspondence required in a professional-level job search process.

The illustrations apply most directly to recent college graduates seeking an entry-level position upon graduation from college. These letters can easily be modified to fit most situations, including those for individuals with significant amounts of prior work experience.

You should not use any of these letters on a verbatim basis. You will want to observe the style and key points and then work your personal situation into the new revision.

The first letter gives you the standard business letter format. Subsequent samples do not show the return address, inside address, or close.

Many experts predict that the current mode of delivery by snail mail will eventually be replaced by email and/or fax. The format, content, and purposes of this communication are not likely to change. Use your best judgment in how best to deliver this information in your employment setting.

Do not handle this correspondence via voice mail or telephone alone. To avoid disasters, written correspondence is absolutely essential. Always confirm in writing!

Appointment Confirmation

Key Points

- Day

- Date

- Time

- Purpose

Your Address
City, State, Zip
Telephone Number
name@email.com
Date

Employer Name
Title
Department
Organization
Address
City, State, Zip

Dear Mr./Ms. *Last Name*:

Thank you for agreeing to a thirty-minute appointment with me in your office. I am confirming the following:

- Wednesday
- October xx
- 10:30 a.m.

I think that the meeting will be productive for both of us. The purpose of our meeting is to discuss my career interests. Your courtesy is very much appreciated.

Key Points

- Last contact

- Still interested

- Support match

- Additional information

- Transcript

- Personal interest

- Follow-up

Dear Mr./Ms. *Last Name*:

Thank you for the interview on Monday, October xx, at *(location or university)*. I hope that you found several mutual interests as I did.

I am enthusiastic about the prospect of joining your organization. Your impressive growth and diversity sparked my interest in you. My familiarity in the field of *(your specialty)* and your client base would enable me to make the transition to your development program with relative ease.

- Enclosed is a more expanded resume which high-lights my education and experiences in much greater depth.

- The unofficial transcript shows how my academic credentials appear to fit within your needed skill base.

- My personal endeavors are similar to others that you have hired in the past. I would really like to work with you.

Should you have any questions, please call me. I shall look forward to your call next week to set up the follow-up interviews that you indicated would be forthcoming.

Sincerely,

Key Points

- Last contact

- Title/Profession

- Action Taken

- Interested

- Qualified

Dear Mr./Ms. *Last Name*:

Thank you for taking time on Tuesday, November xx, to get better acquainted. Your description of the (title) position at *(organization name)* and the long-term opportunities in *(profession)* were very interesting to me.

Since we met, I have done the following:

- Managed a midterm grade of *(gpa)* in *(course)*
- Wrote a term paper on *(topic)*
- Interviewed *(number)* of others in the *(profession)*
- Prepared the enclosed unofficial transcript

I am very interested in the opportunities that you described. I hope that I am still a strong candidate. Please let me know if you need more information on my talents.

Sincerely,

Key Points

- Last contact

- Reinforce good vibes

- No pressure but . . .

- Interest

- Supporting data

- Excited

- Thank you

Dear Mr./Ms. *Last Name*:

My initial interview at *(university location)* was very enlightening and encouraging. Although interviews rarely end with immediate firm decisions, I felt very good about the outcome of our discussions.

I respect your candid response that several items are pending before you can get back in touch with me. I certainly do not want to press for an answer when your response would have to be "no," but I do want to keep you aware of my continuing interest.

Enclosed is some information that supports the ideas which we discussed in the interview. School is going very well and my grades this semester should be quite strong. My leadership activities in the *(organization)* are requiring more time than expected, but the results on the new *(project)* are really worth the extra effort.

I am excited about your job opportunity and really am anxious to hear from you about my employment prospects. I am confident that I can excel in the *(position)* assignment if given a chance. Please call me if you need more supporting evidence of my abilities to succeed in this assignment. Thank you for your consideration.

Sincerely,

Key Points

- Build-up

- Careful review

- Interested
  but . . .

- Difficult
  decision

- Stay in field

- Best wishes

- Appreciation

Dear John:

From your conversations, it sounds as if another Dean's List is in the making. However, I imagine you are now becoming quite anxious for the satisfaction of completion.

During the past week, our management has carefully reviewed your credentials along with those of other candidates. While your educational background, interest in the banking business, and personal attributes were of real interest to us, it is our feeling that we cannot make best use of your strongest abilities.

This was indeed a difficult decision because of your attractive background and ambition. It can merely represent our best current thinking.

I hope this news does not seriously dissuade your interest in the banking business. There is a wealth of opportunity in this field. Unfortunately, we could not get together at this time, but I do want to wish you the best of success in your future endeavors.

Thank you for all your time and interest.

Sincerely,

Key Points

- Appreciate interest

- Impressive background but . . .

- Keen competition

- Best wishes

- On file

Dear Mr./Ms. *Last Name*:

Thank you for your interest in career opportunities with us.

Although your credentials are impressive, we unfortunately cannot offer you a position at this time. We are currently pursuing applicants whose backgrounds more closely fit our needs.

We enjoyed talking to you and wish you the best of success in your job search efforts. If the situation changes, we will keep your application on file and possibly contact you later.

Sincerely,

Key Points

- Last contact recall

- Lacked technical skills

- Initiatives to improve

- State changes

- Ask for re-consideration

- More information enclosed

- Telephone follow-up

- Appreciation

Dear Mr./Ms. *Last Name*:

About four months ago, you were most gracious in meeting with me regarding the position of *(title)* in your *(department)*. At the time, you indicated that my personal skills were excellent, but I lacked some of the technicals needed to do a superior job so you could not pursue employment any further at that time.

I heard the advice you offered and took some initiatives to shore up some of my limitations:

- I took courses in *(subject, subject, and subject)* and am earning excellent grades of *(grades)* in them.
- I have an unpaid internship with a local organization where I really picked up some practical knowledge in *(technical areas)*.

I feel much better about my abilities to handle any assignment that your managers in *(department)* might throw at me. I would welcome a chance to prove myself, even if it was a temporary assignment. I would like to meet with you again to discuss my progress in the event that any related positions might open in the future.

Enclosed are my new resume and most recent transcript. I will call you on *(date)* to see if we might be able to get together in *(location)*. Your help has been most appreciated.

Sincerely,

Key Points

- Recall contact
- Further interest
- Invite
- Suggest dates
- Complete day
- Transportation/ hotel
- Expenses
- Transcripts
- Call us

Dear *Name*:

Thank you for completing and returning our "Application for Employment" form after our interview on October xx. We have now had an opportunity to review your application with several members of our staff. They have expressed interest in your background and would like to further our acquaintance by having you visit us at our general offices.

To insure that we handle your visit in the best manner, we would like you to indicate three dates on weekdays when a visit of this nature would be convenient for you. After we have received these dates, we will review them with our staff to see which is most satisfactory for their schedules.

The program for the day you are here will start at approximately 8:45 a.m. and will continue until 4:00 or 4:30 p.m. We will leave all transportation arrangements to your discretion. However, we would be more than happy to make hotel reservations for you. If you have any questions or problems concerning your transportation, feel free to advise us. You will be reimbursed for your trip expense.

We would appreciate transcripts of your college courses.

We look forward to hearing from you regarding plans for your visit. You can rest assured that we will do everything possible to make your interviewing visitation to our general offices interesting and informative.

Sincerely,

Note: *Some employers do not pay travel expenses. Do not assume that all invitations include the payment of expenses unless you have a statement, such as the one above, of the employer's intent to pay.*

Key Points

- Recall situation

- Decision date

- Suggest dates

- Or confirm date

- Travel plans

- Hotel

- Expense

- Thanks

Dear Mr./Ms. *Last Name*:

Thank you for your telephone call *(letter, verbal offer, etc.)* on March 1, inviting me to Anywhere, USA for further interviews. I was pleased to hear from you because after our initial conversation I was impressed with XYZ's training approach and wanted to be considered further.

I am eager to get together as soon as possible because I hope to make an employment decision around April 1. Since the campus spring break falls between March 11 and 15, would it be possible to get together then? Would March 15 be okay with you? *(Or if just confirming, indicate that you plan to arrive by 8:45 a.m. on March 15.)*

I prefer to make my own travel plans. Since I am unfamiliar with your location in Anywhere, would you please make a hotel reservation for two people for me. My spouse will be coming along to look around Anywhere. Of course, I will pay any additional costs incurred. Please advise me of the hotel accommodations.

Your program appears to be exactly what I am seeking. I will arrive in your office by 8:45 a.m. unless advised otherwise. Thank you for your consideration.

Very truly yours,

P.S. Enclosed is your completed application blank and the transcripts which you requested.

cc: Career Services Office, Indiana University

Key Points

- Situation

- Strong interest

- Great visit

- Information requested

- Confirmation of motivation

- Decision date

- Appreciation

Dear Mr./Ms. *Last Name*:

I really enjoyed the day I spent on Wednesday, November xx, at your facilities talking to your managers. The reception I received was very welcomed. The interest shown in me heightened my excitement about the possibility of joining your management team.

Enclosed is some information which Ms. Jones requested that will give you some indication of my writing ability. A couple of reference letters show some of my commitment to excellence and hard work.

Thank you for your time and for an informative day exploring potential employment opportunities. I shall look forward to hearing positively from you soon. As you know, I would like to make a decision by *(date)*.

Sincerely,

Key Points

- Situation

- Impressed

- Expenses

- Excited

- Supporting information

- Anxious to hear

Dear Mr./Ms. *Last Name*:

Thank you for arranging a most complete day of interviews for me last week. Because of the well-planned and organized day of interviews with so many people, the time seemed to fly by. I hope that your people were as impressed with me as I was with them. I can see why you are so profitable with your high caliber of management personnel.

Enclosed is the expense statement which you requested. The hotel apparently billed you directly because the desk clerk said there was no charge when I checked out.

The visit was truly enjoyable and productive for me. I am even more enthused about pursuing employment with you now. I have enclosed a copy of a recommendation letter from a former employer which you may include in my file.

In my interview with Mr. Smith, he expressed some reservation about my writing and research ability, so I am also enclosing a copy of a term paper which shows my capabilities. *(Any additional information you may wish to use to support your cause should be included, but don't overdo it.)*

I am anxiously awaiting your reply. Of the employers I have interviewed, your opportunity is one of the most exciting to me. If you require any additional information, please call me.

Very truly yours,

Key Points

- Disappointed

- State job seeking

- Still interested

- Preferred employer

- Appreciation

Dear Mr./Ms. *Last Name*:

I was indeed disappointed to receive your letter of March xx informing me that you had selected another candidate for the *(title)* position. However, I must say that it was a pleasure to meet with you and your colleagues who generously gave time to me.

The impression that you made on me was remarkable. Based upon our interviews I have decided to concentrate on exploring opportunities in your field. If there is any chance that you might later be interested in me, please give me a call. You would be my most preferred employer.

I would really be interested in hearing from you if any openings later materialize for which I might be qualified. Thank you for the consideration given me.

Sincerely,

Key Points

- Situation

- Understand

- Still interested

- State why

- Request
  re-review

- Additional
  data

- Achievements

- Relocation

- Follow-up

Dear Mr./Ms. *Last Name*:

I just received your disappointing letter of *(give date)*. I can fully understand your difficulty in selecting the best applicant from among the hundreds that you interview.

(Organization name) was special to me because . . . .

I would like to request another review of my credentials in light of my strong interest in both your firm and the assignment. Enclosed is some additional information about my background that was not fully explained in the interview. These include an elaboration of my three significant achievements listed below that directly support my talents and qualifications for your opportunity.

1. _____
2. _____
3. _____

If the position is filled at this time, please keep my application on file. I would be happy to talk to any other managers at *(location or firm)* who may have similar openings even if it means relocation. I will call you next week to see if we might be able to renew our discussions.

Sincerely,

Key Points

- Review situation

- Express disappointment

- State strong interest

- Request suggestions

- Request appointment

- Career adviser

- Follow-up call

Dear Mr./Ms. *Last Name*:

You cannot imagine the difficulty that I am experiencing with your decision to accept another candidate for the position as a *(job title)* with *(organization)*. My desire to work for you runs deep.

Perhaps you can offer suggestions on how I might better prepare myself for an assignment like this. Of course, I am exploring opportunities with other firms, but you clearly are the leader in the field. I have a strong ingrained commitment to be associated with the best which is why I continue to seek your guidance.

I would like to call you soon to see if we can get together again. I have a number of questions to which your answers would greatly assist in my future career planning. Your thoughts might be extremely helpful in assisting me in achieving my goals and eventually we may find ourselves working together. I hope that you can spare an extra 30 minutes to meet with me after I call.

Sincerely,

Key Points

- Impressed

- Offer details

- Duties

- Training

- Assignment

- Salary amount

- Review

- Relocation

- Contingencies

- Details

- Offer closes

- Decision soon

- Follow-up call

- Positive close

Dear Mr./Ms. *Last Name*:

We were very impressed with your credentials when you visited us on *(specific date)*. As a result, we are pleased to offer you the position of *(job title)*. This will start in our *(specific group)* division which is located in *(specific location)*.

Your initial duties and responsibilities will be identical to those in the attached job description. Your *(specific time)* month-long training program begins here. Upon satisfactory completion of the rigorous development program, you will be assigned to one of our twenty locations based upon an evaluation of your interests and our needs at the time.

Your starting salary will be *($xx,xxx)* per year, payable monthly. Your first review will come after completion of the training program and annually thereafter. If you accept our offer, we will pay a relocation allowance of up to *($x,xxx)* which includes only physical transportation of you (and your family) and temporary housing for up to four weeks. Our benefit handbook is enclosed.

This offer is contingent upon your completion of your academic studies in *(specific area)*, verification by transcripts and diploma, and passing a medical examination which includes a test for abnormal substances at our facilities on or before your reporting date of *(date)*.

This offer is open for fourteen calendar days from the date of this letter, but we hope to receive your letter of acceptance much sooner than that given your expressed level of interest in this assignment.

I will call you in a few days to answer any questions you may have regarding the terms. Please feel free to call me collect if you have any questions. We are looking forward to your joining our management team.

Sincerely,

cc: State University Career Services Office

Key Points

- Restate offer understanding

- Pleased and impressed

- Decision deadline

- Follow-up call/letter

- Appreciation

Dear Mr./Ms. *Last Name*:

Thank you for your telephone call on March 1 offering me a position as a *(title)* in your *(name)* department at an annual salary of *($xx,xxx)*. You cannot imagine the joy with which I received your call. After my visit, I said to myself that yours is the type of organization of which I would be proud to be a part. I was truly impressed with all of the people to whom I spoke.

I understand that you must have a decision within three weeks, and I will call and write you before then.

This is exactly the type of challenge and opportunity that I am seeking. I am pleased that you have such confidence in me. If you need additional information, please call me. Thank you for your consideration.

Very truly yours,

Key Points

- Situation

- Express
  delight

- Other
  commitment

- Request
  extension

- Ethics

- Firm decision
  date

- Strong
  interest

- Appreciation

Dear Mr./Ms. *Last Name*:

Thank you very much for the offer letter that I received on March 15. The pleasure received from that letter was the highlight of my year.

I think you know how serious I am about this job and how much I would love to work for you. I do have some other personal commitments here that I am rapidly trying to bring to closure. These obligations will influence where I go to work, and so I must ask you for a two-week extension beyond March 30, before making a decision.

I realize that it is unethical for me to accept your offer now and later renege on my word. I would not do that. Your opportunity is outstanding, but I must be certain that it is the best decision for me at this time. May I have some extra time to avoid getting myself into a difficult personal situation?

I will give you a firm answer on April 15. Please call and leave a reply on my answering machine if I am not in. I am delighted at this offer and excited about the prospect of working with you. Your understanding is much appreciated.

Sincerely yours,

Key Points

- Repeat situation

- Name influencers

- Tough decision

- Other alternatives

- Firm acceptance

- Repeat other details

- State contingencies

- Personalize

- Reporting date

- Eagerly preparing

Dear Mr./Ms. *Last Name*:

Thank you for all of the time that you have spent considering me for a position as a *(title)* in your *(function)* department. I am very appreciative of your efforts and those of Mr. *(last name)* and Mr. *(last name)* who have given so much of their time and effort in helping me with my decisions.

I have just made one of the most difficult decisions of my life. I have been fortunate in being able to select from several outstanding opportunities. Last week I narrowed my choice to two employers, of which you were one.

I wish to accept your offer as a *(title)* in your *(function)* department at the salary of *($xx,xxx)*. I recognize that this is contingent upon my passing a routine physical examination, and I anticipate no difficulty.

The influence of Ms. *(name)* triggered my decision; I think it will be a pleasure to work with her. I thrive under people who present challenges and have her knack for making one want to do the job.

I wish to report for work as soon after graduation, May 15, as possible. Please let me know an acceptable starting date. My spouse and I plan to take Ms. *(name)* up on her offer to help us search for an apartment. We hope to do that about two weeks before my starting date.

Please advise me if there is any other information you need or if any other details need to be worked out. You may call any day after 4:00 p.m. I am eagerly preparing for my new assignment and look forward to talking with you soon.

Very truly yours,

cc: State University, Career Services Office

Declining Offer

Key Points

- Repeat situation

- Personalize

- Difficult decision

- Respectfully decline

- Better match elsewhere

- Leave door open

- Very impressed

- Ready to work

- Make referrals to others

- Appreciation

Dear Mr./Ms. *Last Name*:

Thank you for all of the time that you have spent considering me for a position as a *(title)* in your *(function)* department. I am very much appreciative of all of your efforts and those of Mr. *(last name)* and Mr. *(last name)* who have given so much of their time to me.

I have just made one of the most difficult decisions of my life. I have been quite fortunate in being able to select from several outstanding opportunities. I narrowed my decision to two employers last week, and you were one of them. I wish I could accept both.

After much deliberation with my wife, friends, faculty, and placement office personnel, I must respectfully decline your invitation to join your *(function)* department. I feel that another opportunity matches my qualifications and interests better at this stage in my career.

In the unlikely event that the other opportunity does not work out as planned, I hope your door might be open to me for possible discussions of something else in two or three years. I am very impressed with your operation and professional way of doing things.

After several years in college, I am ready to energetically meet the world of work. I have advised a number of my friends of your cordial and candid approach to hiring college graduates. A number of them have expressed interest in speaking with you when they graduate. I know that you have other offers extended to graduates of *(name)* University, and I wish you much success in your recruitment efforts. I sincerely appreciate all of your kindness and consideration toward me.

Very truly yours,

Continuing Education:

Decision – Costs – Admissions

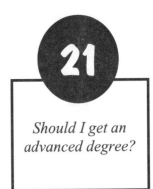

Should I get an advanced degree?

Learning never stops. Regardless of your career status you need to foster the desire to learn new things for career advancement, personal enjoyment, and/or to initiate a change in your career thrust.

The rapidly changing world demands that you make a commitment to the concept of continuing education. You may carry out this learning process through institutions of formal education, informal courses, seminars, or relatively unstructured learning experiences.

Learning is growing.

Where you learn and how you learn are not as important as your commitment and drive to continue your education. Your employer may build learning modules into your work. You may be expected to attend conferences, lead and attend seminars, consult with recognized experts, and learn through your experiences on the job.

Many employers encourage learning by sending their employees to professional, technical, and managerial development programs away from the work environment. Employers pay the costs of these programs and the employee's salaries while they learn.

Other employers provide strong motivation for their employees to enroll in courses at recognized educational institutions by offering to pay for all instruction that is in any way job-related. Even the government permits a tax deduction if job-related training is required and you pay for it.

Employers pay for your learning.

The question is not whether to continue your education; the question is how to do it and what to study. How you do it will depend upon your job, your long-term aspirations, your personal situation, your finances, etc.

You have many options. You can work toward a degree or simply enroll in selected courses. You can go full time or part time. You can keep your job or leave it. There is no one perfect strategy for everyone.

Regardless of your choice, if the study is in any way job-related, you should build it into your career planning model. Education is an important variable that you can manipulate in your career decision-making.

All education can be planned and built into your career plan. Formal education that demands that you quit your current employment requires much career-related analysis because it is a drastic choice.

Plan your learning strategy carefully.

Being a part-time student while you are employed full-time permits you to at least maintain the status quo while preparing for the future; however, there are disadvantages to that approach. If you complete a formal course of study on a part-time basis, your employer may not acknowledge it with earnings increases or job promotions. A return to full-time study forces an employer to recognize your new skills, but then you risk unemployment when you finish your study, and you almost always have to pay for the education yourself.

Decision Analysis

Consider returning to school full-time as a transition to a new job or career field.

You must be truly committed to a full-time course of study in a formal degree program especially since you often must give up your full-time job. Enrolling in an occasional course or going to school part-time for a formal degree is not a critical career decision. If you can afford it and enjoy your chosen area of study, you should probably continue this type of learning throughout your life.

A decision to attend a recognized graduate program on a full-time basis is a major career decision, and such a decision requires a significant amount of analysis. This decision should be an integral part of your career planning, self-assessment, career field exploration, and job search. You need to carry out an extremely thorough investigation to determine if and how graduate study might fit into your overall plans.

Variables

Watch out for becoming over-educated and under-employed.

Unfortunately, there is no clear-cut answer to the question, "Should I attend graduate school?" You need to consider all alternatives. Graduate study is a major career decision.

There is a strong feeling in the United States that the more education one has, the greater are his or her chances for success. This is not necessarily true, however. A person can be overtrained and underemployed. It may be true that additional education will not hurt, but it may not help either.

Position Desired. The answer to the graduate school question largely depends on the type of position you ultimately desire. Many high school graduates earn substantially more money than Ph.D. recipients. If you are measuring success in strictly monetary terms, it may be hard to make a strong case in favor of graduate school.

What do you want to do after your next level of education?

The starting point for making the graduate school decision is to look at the position you desire. Can you obtain the position without the advanced degree? In many positions, you can advance just as far without the graduate degree.

Your full-time graduate study investment demands an annual commitment of at least $35,000 in out-of-pocket cost and lost income each year. The position you aspire to may be well worth the sacrifice if the degree is required. On the other hand, if the position can be obtained now and the degree can be completed part-time or with a leave of absence later, that may be the wiser path to follow from a financial perspective.

Which Degree? There are so many variables to the graduate school question that no one can provide the answer without hedging. The academic community stresses advanced degrees for qualified students. The employment market hedges. It is a difficult choice.

You must investigate your pros and cons, financial commitments, etc., in conjunction with your immediate and long-range career goals. This will put you into a better position for making the decision.

People in liberal arts who wish to continue in their undergraduate fields must question the value of additional education unless they wish to teach in their particular areas. The openings for people with master's degrees are limited in both teaching and other career areas.

Few business firms pay more for master's degrees in liberal arts fields. If you wish to teach in higher education or become a professional in your field (sociologist, psychologist, historian, writer, etc.), you may need a doctorate. Most schools encourage working toward the doctorate immediately after obtaining the undergraduate degree because time can be conserved.

If you are a business undergraduate, the value of additional training for you must be questioned. Would graduate school just be more of the same? To avoid this, you would surely want to earn an advanced degree from a *different* institution. Most business undergraduates take more than two years of business courses which may be equivalent to the two years in many MBA programs.

You may wish to change career direction by choosing a professional or technical advanced degree. The two most popular currently are the Master of Business Administration (MBA) and the Doctor of Law (JD) degrees.

There are other options. Some of them are in the fields of public service, social service, mass communications, journalism, medicine, health, etc. You must keep some perspective on how your abilities and interests relate to the career fields for which these programs prepare people.

The MBA or JD degree is not a panacea for all your career goals.

Employment Concerns

Sometimes more education can *restrict* employment possibilities. Nearly everyone knows someone who has been rejected for a job opening because of being "overqualified"; the individual could have handled the assignment but was not given the chance. Why does this happen?

Is more education really needed to achieve your objectives?

One reason is that the individual's expectations are inconsistent with the assignment. The person would be likely to get bored with the job and be unproductive. Another reason is that the employer figures the job would simply be temporary for the person until a position more in line with his or her education is found.

Considering the high cost of training an employee before he or she becomes productive and the high cost of turnover, why should the employer take the risk on the overqualified person, especially when other qualified applicants are available?

Specialization. Some people approach graduate study as a last alternative. "If I cannot find suitable employment or if I do not like my job, I can always go on

GRADUATE SCHOOL ADMISSIONS

BECAUSE, AS ARISTOTLE SAID... "EDUCATED MEN ARE AS MUCH SUPERIOR TO UNEDUCATED MEN AS THE LIVING ARE TO THE DEAD"... ALSO, BECAUSE I CAN'T FIND A JOB.

to graduate study." That attitude is likely to bring great disillusionment and unrewarding career performance.

Jobs are more plentiful for broadly educated people with wide ranges of career alternatives than they are for narrowly educated specialists.

As the education level increases, specialty increases and the range of alternatives narrows. The number of jobs within the specialty must, by definition, decrease. What employer would hire a master's or doctorate degreed graduate to do a job that an undergraduate can be hired to do? Why risk the dissatisfaction? Why overpay for the job?

Poor Performance. The fact is that some people decide on graduate study when they cannot get jobs. The reason for a person's lack of success in the job market may relate to a poor undergraduate record, personality, or a lack of clear career goals. Graduate study can make that person even more unemployable.

One of the most difficult graduates to place is the person who did not rank high in the graduate class and also did not make an outstanding undergraduate record—a mediocre record all the way around. You are often competing with the very best talents, as well.

There is some validity to the argument that if a person cannot get at least three job offers as an undergraduate, then he or she is not likely to receive even one with an advanced degree. Employers have higher standards for candidates with advanced degrees.

Few people are expert judges of their own abilities. If you have questions in this area, a possible solution is to let employers judge your capabilities as an undergraduate when the standards are much lower.

If you do have employment difficulty, graduate study is not the likely solution for improving your marketability. Rather than acquire more education, you should probably reassess your career goals in relation to your credentials.

Rationales. A very valid reason for returning to graduate study is to change a career thrust. Engineers, teachers, accountants, salespeople, etc., all may return to beef up skills in their area or to switch into new careers such as finance, law, public service, etc.

The old belief that once a student leaves campus, he or she will never return is false. Training in a highly technical society cannot stop with either a bachelor's or master's degree. As continuing education programs in universities continue to grow professionally, so will individuals.

Whether you decide to continue your education now, later, or part-time is not nearly as important as what direction your career should take. Once you decide upon a particular area of graduate study, you get locked into a career path to some extent.

You can always quit working and return to school. All types of potential employers who seek candidates with advanced degrees feel that returning to school for graduate study is an acceptable reason for leaving an employer.

Normally you have that option only once in your life, so you want to be certain you make the proper choice and that the timing of the decision is appropriate for you.

Costs Analysis

Since costs vary considerably among universities, a universal analytical cost for graduate study cannot be calculated. Given a specific university, however, it should be possible to approximate the costs by using the model in Figure 21.1.

Specialization often narrows the number of job choices but makes you better qualified for the fewer jobs available.

Poor graduate grades really hurt your later job search.

Be honest with yourself.

Changing career direction is a major reason for going to graduate school.

It is almost impossible to calculate at what point an investment in graduate school is recovered. Typically, a person with a higher degree will start at a higher rate, but an individual who started two years before would be earning more than this higher starting rate by that time.

It is difficult for an employer to justify paying a beginner, regardless of his or her degree, more money than the individual with two years of experience.

Assuming that the master degreed person shortly catches up with the experienced person, the salary progress of both of them will largely depend on their individual abilities.

Those persons with advanced degrees and superior knowledge are correct in assuming that they should advance faster. If they do not, they cannot recover their investment. If and when they do, the differential between annual salaries begins paying off the principle of the investment.

In other words, it is best to base the decision about graduate study on factors other than financial return. Other than making an intuitive guess about your income potential after further study, no one can help you very much. It is a personal decision.

Most employers will pick up all, or at least part, of the education bill if an employee attends a part-time university program while employed full-time. Almost no employers have scholarship programs whereby they send outstanding employees back to graduate school on a full-time basis, grant them a leave of absence, and pay some portion of their expenses.

Employers *will not pay* the complete bill for an employee's graduate education. Before most firms pay any portion, a person must be employed by them for at least an initial period (often two years) in order to become eligible for this special benefit. In most cases, the field of study must have some relationship to the employee's position.

Many employers will grant an employee a leave of absence to attend graduate school. This is an implied guarantee that the same or a better position will be waiting for the person after he or she completes the degree. In many cases, benefits, insurance, vacation, and seniority continue to accrue during the leave.

This leave of absence is a substantial commitment for the employers who offer this very liberal benefit plan. Do not expect to find this to be a widespread practice.

Long-term salary advancement depends upon job performance, not the degree you hold.

. . . . **MODEL OF GRADUATE DEGREE COSTS** . . . .

Add:	Tuition, supplies, books	$xxx	
	Living accommodations	xxx	
	Sub-total		$xxx
Subtract:	Financial aid, part-time employment	$xxx	
	Sub-total		$xxx
Add:	Loss of salary during years in school		$xxx
	(Use average salary offered or your current salary)		____
	Total cost		$xxx

. . . .

Figure 21.1

Admission Requirements

Admission

Assuming you can afford graduate study, the next step is to determine whether or not you can gain admission. Each university and degree program establishes its own requirements for admission.

There are common elements that all schools and departments share in making the evaluative decision on whether or not to admit students. These elements are used as predictors of a person's ability to succeed in the degree programs.

THEY WERE MORE FAMILIAR WITH MY RECORD THAN THEY CARED TO ADMIT.

//WEB.TIP//

www.gre.org
Graduate Record Exam
Information on test/sample questions/links/financing arrangements/guidance.

Testing

Nearly all degree programs require that a battery of tests be taken to determine your ability to succeed in the program. These tests contain both verbal and quantitative sections. Schools place varying degrees of emphasis on the sections, depending upon their academic orientations.

The most common of the national standardized tests are the Graduate Record Examinations (GRE), the Law School Admissions Test (LSAT), and the Graduate Management Admission Test (GMAT). Any university can provide details on these tests. They require no preparation, although some prior study may slightly enhance your score.

Grades

Grade point average is almost always used as a guide for determining academic abilities. It is really the only measure of past academic performance available. Most schools require at least a B+ average regardless of the area of study to be pursued unless there are special circumstances.

Many schools use your rank in class as a better indicator of ability than overall grades. This compensates for the difference in grading standards.

Transcripts

Applicants are required to send a transcript from each school they have attended. The transcripts are analyzed for specific courses taken, grades in these courses, and any positive or negative grade trends by year while in college.

Faculty References

Most schools require at least two letters from previous instructors recommending you for admission. It is always important for you to get to know as many professors as possible, particularly during the junior and senior years in college.

You need professors who remember you and who are willing to make favorable recommendations for you. Most graduate schools also accept references from previous employers, but the academic references often carry much more influence.

Other Factors

If you do not "make the grade" on one of the points above, some schools may make an exception or admit you on probation. Some favorable points in the factors listed below might give them a reason for considering you as an exception:

- Work experience
- Military experience
- Grade point average the last two years
- Grades in the major subject, particularly if it relates to your proposed field of graduate study
- Maturity
- Personal interviews
- Goals and objective for obtaining the degree

Law School Programs

The U.S. Department of Labor projects that the supply of law graduates in the foreseeable future is likely to far exceed the demand for their services. Yet, law school offers one of the more popular graduate programs.

Apparently many students, correctly or incorrectly, believe that law training is a good background for many types of careers. On the average, less than half of law school graduates find employment in the legal field.

Law has always been a venerable and respected profession. The foundation of the American legal system is the common law of England: legislative acts, court precedents, and procedures. Of the nation's attorneys, about half are engaged

WELL MAYBE THERE ARE JOBS IN LEGAL ADVERTISING.

in private practice. The remainder are in government service (including judges), and most of the rest are in business fields and fields such as stock brokerage, banking, teaching, and politics.

A lawyer studies existing laws, interprets them, and advises clients regarding their financial and legal problems. Many attorneys spend a considerable amount of time in courts and preparing research to use in the courts. Others concentrate on preparing legal documents such as property titles, mortgages, contracts, wills, and trust agreements.

A lawyer may spend much time reading government regulations and ordinances and researching thousands of prior court cases. Lawyers sometimes specialize in criminal cases, real estate, taxes, trusts, corporate law, and other areas.

Currently, nearly one-third of the profession are salaried as associates in law firms, government agencies, or employees in corporations. The others must depend upon fees that vary from year to year depending upon the amount and type of work in which they are involved.

Admission Standards

The standards for admission to any of the law schools are high. The Law School Admissions Test is required. Acceptable scores vary widely. Check the individual schools for their standards.

The American Bar Association does not rank law schools, but member firms sometimes do. By checking with several law professors it is possible to learn which schools enjoy the top reputations.

The best jobs go to graduates of the most prestigious schools who rank in the top ten percent of their graduating classes. Periodically, the ABA publishes a booklet entitled *Law Schools and Bar Admission Requirements,* which you should review before selecting a school. Many practitioners recommend choosing a law school in the state in which the person plans to practice.

MBA Degree Programs

Modern corporate management practices have created a demand for well-trained professional business managers. While many of today's business leaders gained their professional status and competence without the aid of formal graduate business education, opportunities for advancement without professional management training are rapidly diminishing.

The Master of Business Administration (MBA) degree has become increasingly popular as a means of preparing management aspirants. Major graduate schools of

The Official Guide to MBA Programs
Graduate Management Admissions Council
Princeton, NJ 08541-6108

Figure 21.2

business have experienced a dramatic increase in the number of students entering both full-time and part-time MBA programs.

Management is the process of planning, organizing, motivating, and directing human resources for using finances and materials to achieve organizational objectives most effectively. Business management supposes that the process can be

WHOEVER HE WAS, I'LL BET HE NEVER
EARNED AN MBA.

learned in academic settings in addition to real work situations.

Effective managers have developed their skills in decision-making, financial analysis, economics, marketing, operations, and interpersonal relationships. Potential managers are taught how to apply these skills within a system of constraints and alternatives. The modern manager is a forecaster, problem-solver, supervisor, and a personal example to others.

Although the technical expertise taught in MBA programs plays a major role in the initial job search and early career progress, the abilities acquired through organizing the work of others and deciding on major courses of action of the organization become extremely valuable later in the manager's career.

As the environment of the organization becomes more complex in terms of competitive, regulatory, and societal concerns, the need for well-qualified managers becomes more necessary. Many employers look to MBA programs to provide this leadership potential.

Most MBA programs look for people with all undergraduate majors and with prior work experience. The programs draw applicants from a very broad range of backgrounds.

MBA or JD?

Many people ponder whether to attend law school or business school. The choice largely depends upon the type of work the person ultimately desires. Both are excellent and prestigious degrees to possess, but different avenues are opened by completing each degree. The following lists of initial starting assignments indicate some career paths which are available to graduates with the respective degrees.

MBA Degree

- Marketing
- Finance
- Manufacturing
- Public Accounting
- Consulting
- Investment Banking
- Investment Analysis
- Mgmt. Information Systems

MBA FORUMS

Each year the Graduate Management Admissions Council (GMAC) sponsors a series of several *MBA Forums* in several different major cities every fall. This is a "fair" arrangement where member schools send representatives to speak with several thousand potential MBA matriculants.

If you are only vaguely considering the MBA degree, you should attend one of these programs. Your college placement office or any MBA admissions office can provide you with details. The GMAC is the group which develops and administers the Graduate Management Aptitude Test (GMAT). About 100 universities are members of this prestigious Council.

Each participating school staffs a table or booth at the fair with people who can answer questions such as:

- Admission requirements
- Application procedures
- Admission standards
- Application deadlines
- Program starting dates
- Strongest departments
- Length of programs
- Work experience emphasis

- Full and part-time options
- Mathematics requirements
- Importance of GMAT scores
- Size of program
- Curriculum
- Financial aid
- Instructional methods

The purpose of the *Forums* is to help you identify which schools best fit your needs. The contacts you make are informal discussions and are not meant to serve as admission interviews. This is an exploring atmosphere where you can see many representatives, ask all of your questions, and spend as much time as you wish during these two-day, Friday/Saturday events.

The hours are usually 2:00 p.m. to 8:00 p.m. on Fridays and 10:00 a.m. to 4:00 p.m. on Saturdays. Registration in advance is not required, and there is only a very nominal fee.

The career placement of MBA graduates varies considerably from school to school. Most schools will have a placement statement available but realize that these are "sales presentations," not audited annual reports. Many placement reports exclude statistics for graduates who did not report placement and include statistics on those who were employed at high salaries before coming into the program.

For career planning purposes, you should try to collect the following types of data.

- List of recruiting organizations the last year
- List of graduates from the last year
- Starting salary broken down by:
  - Experience level
  - Part-time/full-time
  - MBA major
  - Industry groups
  - Functional field
  - Location

To get some idea of your competition in the classroom, you might want to obtain statistics such as:

- Average GMAT score
- Average undergraduate GPA
- Percent of foreign nationals
- Percent of women

- Percent of minorities
- Average age at admission
- Percent of class attending full-time
- Average months of work experience

Try to attend as many of the special workshops as you can. These general workshops last about 60 minutes and cover many of the several questions you need to ask about various programs of study, job search strategies after the MBA, and potential career paths after the MBA.

The *Forums* are an outstanding source of information for anyone contemplating an MBA degree.

JD Degree

- Attorney at Law
- Labor Relations
- Tax Attorney
- Patent Lawyer
- Trust (wills, estates, etc.)
- Government Administrator
- Politics

For those who desire to go into business immediately after receiving their degrees, the *MBA* is probably the better alternative. For those who wish to practice law for a few years prior to going into business, the law degree is, of course, the better choice.

Few corporations hire people directly from law schools into their legal departments. They prefer to hire people with previous legal experience. Most businesses use law firms on a retaining basis to handle their legal activities.

JDs who have the appropriate background can go into the same functional fields for which employers consider MBAs. In most cases, however, people with law degrees give up working in fields that directly utilize their legal training when they enter business.

The overwhelming majority of top business management people move into key positions from the functional fields of accounting, finance, marketing, and manufacturing. The MBA may be a better choice if top management is your goal. On the other hand, if you like the idea of being an *expert* in a key field, the JD will be the more productive route. The choice depends upon your ultimate career interests.

The purpose behind joint MBA-JD degree programs is to turn out attorneys with business savvy who can thus be better partners or independent practitioners. Very few business employers recruit for this degree combination. The few that do are public accounting firms (tax lawyers), industrial firms (contract administration, interpretation, and labor court cases), banks (trusts and wills), and insurance companies (claims). Business organizations usually take their legal matters to their retained law firms.

The Master of Business Administration degree is very popular among liberal arts, science, engineering, and business undergraduates. Before you consider the MBA degree, you should decide what you really need. The MBA degree is oriented toward business, although government officials, educational administrators, small businessmen, and others may find the degree helpful.

You should decide where your interests lie (accounting, finance, marketing, production, industrial relations, etc.) before selecting a school. Different schools have different reputations. Certain employers may not send recruiters to the school you chose if the program in a given subject area is not highly respected.

Consider the MBA degree if you wish to manage and the JD degree if you wish to practice law. The daily duties are *very* different even though the rewards are nearly identical.

Potential graduate students should do some investigating of schools because all programs are not of equal quality and recognized stature. Not all programs are accredited either. You might wish to write to the accrediting group, AACSB, St. Louis, Missouri, for a list of accredited programs or visit their website.

Advantages of the MBA

Although there are few well-defined employer policies regarding the MBA degree, holders of the degree have several distinct advantages over applicants who do not possess it. In fact, some companies recruit only MBAs for a limited number of openings in special programs.

In most companies MBAs start in the same positions as those with bachelor's degrees but, because of their advanced training, MBAs usually advance at a more rapid pace. The MBA degree usually insures a significantly higher starting salary, as well.

The MBA gives you a competitive edge. With the additional training, you should perform better on the job and, because of the greater initial salary you receive, employers will want to advance you more rapidly. The degree should thus enhance your chances for promotions.

The greater level of maturity due to the two additional years of study should be beneficial to an employer also. Many maturing changes take place within any two-year period of time. In fact, one of the reasons suggested for the higher starting salaries earned by graduates of some of the better known MBA programs is that the average age of the graduating classes has been increasing. Many graduates have prior work experience for which employers are willing to pay a premium.

In any MBA program you will be taught more sophisticated business tools and techniques than are normally covered in undergraduate business schools. Also, the quality of instruction and depth of study are greater than in undergraduate programs. You will find the intensity, competitiveness, and rigor extremely challenging in the top twenty universities.

Limitations

As with any evaluation of alternatives, two points of view exist in the decision of whether or not to obtain an MBA degree. For most graduates, the largest obstacle is obtaining the funds for graduate school.

When considering "lost income" in addition to the high cost of the education, it can be difficult to justify the expense, particularly if it is coming on the heels of an expensive undergraduate education. Aside from cost considerations, several other disadvantages should be clearly understood.

Many employers hire only bachelor's degree candidates, so by getting the MBA degree you might be limiting your chances for employment. This limitation primarily pertains to smaller employers. The MBA degree is occasionally criticized for preparing graduates just for "big" business.

For many employers the MBA degree is simply not required to do the job. These employers are reluctant to pay the higher salary for the degree.

Other employers start the MBAs in relatively the same positions as they do bachelor's degree candidates. Imagine the embarrassment to both the employer and the MBA that occurs when the bright bachelor's degree-holder outproduces the MBA degree-holder. It happens.

The MBA graduate often has high expectations which may be thwarted shortly after being thrust into an actual job situation. Expectations and career progress do

The touted MBA salaries often come as a result of prior work experience *before* the MBA degree.

//WEB.TIP//

www.mbacentral.com
CAREER CENTRAL
Free career management service/started for MBAs but changed/Links to schools/regular email push to registrants/matching.

You can educate yourself out of many fine jobs.

not always keep in step, and it is occasionally a traumatic shock to learn the truth. Actual business experience prior to graduate school can help one to understand this fact.

Some undergraduates are "tired" of school but feel they must continue because of the many tales of people never returning to the academic world once they have left it. This attitude of fear can hurt. Those who fall into this "tired" category should take the prudent course and try something different for two or three years.

Students who force themselves into a graduate program often do only average work. Average and marginal MBAs have a very difficult time finding employment because employers are willing to pay for only the outstanding MBA talent.

Employment Problems

Most people should work a few years before obtaining the MBA degree. If you are out in the work world and find out that the degree is necessary, you can always return to school. You will then know if and how the degree is important in your area of interest.

The MBA degree has grown extremely popular with employers seeking bright, young, potential executive talent. It even appears that the MBA degree had a certain charisma associated with it. The demand has softened somewhat, but jobs are still plentiful in most functional fields.

The MBA degree program normally involves a two-year commitment, which means that the cost including lost income is very high. However, starting rates of MBAs are 20 to 30 percent per year more than those of the bachelor candidates.

Assuming that the MBA is declining in popularity with employers (this may or may not be a true statement), what are some of the reasons for it? The explanations below have been offered by some employers.

The salary demands have forced many employers out of the market. The salary difference between a BS and an MBA is not worth it to many employers.

Business is attracting more top-caliber bachelor degree candidates who used to go on to graduate school. Many faculty members no longer automatically encourage their better students to continue study.

Some employers visit only select MBA schools. The "top-ranked" MBA schools experience aggressive recruiting while many other schools are bypassed. About 25 major graduate business schools are highly courted, thus leaving talented MBAs in less prestigious schools searching for jobs on their own. Often, even at the top schools, students in the lower quartile of their class cannot find employment.

The recruitment of MBA graduates varies considerably by the reputation of the school.

The quality of some MBA programs is declining. There has been a rash of new MBA programs and this has brought widened choices and alternatives. Admissions standards have been bent at some schools to encourage enrollments.

You should consider all of these factors as you decide on whether or not to pursue the MBA degree.

Types of Programs

A large number of universities now offer the Master of Business Administration degree, but not all programs are alike. The differences may be narrowed to the following approaches in instruction techniques.

Case Methods. The majority of the courses follow the class structure of solving general or specific problems through the use of actual business situations. Those students who are strong in class participation should do well. There is much writing involved as alternatives are analyzed and decisions justified.

Quantitative Methods. Curriculums normally follow a pattern of adapting analytical approaches to most business problems regardless of the functional area. Students with good mathematics and statistics backgrounds usually do well in this type of instruction.

Behavioral Approach. These programs relate the wide variety of business problems to the interrelationships between people and/or groups in the organization or society. Students with good psychology or sociology backgrounds usually do well with this mode of instruction.

Combinations. The majority of programs offer combinations of the above basic approaches. Most programs require backgrounds which are strong in many different subjects.

Summary

Graduate programs vary in terms of the length of the program, quality of the program, size of the graduate class, admission requirements, amount of specialization possible, the approach to instructional methods, tuition and other costs, and the placement assistance provided upon graduation. It takes some investigation of various programs to locate the appropriate one for your particular needs.

Each year the organization that administers the Graduate Management Admission Test, the Graduate Management Admissions Council, publishes a book called *Graduate Study in Management*. This book gives general information about applying to most MBA programs and provides one-page descriptions of most MBA programs.

It also identifies which schools are accredited by the American Assembly of Collegiate Schools of Business (AACSB) which is the accrediting body for management education. Even if a college is accredited by a regional association, its MBA program may not be accredited.

If you are considering attending any graduate-level academic program, you need to analyze the decision in the context of your overall career goals. Graduate school attendance is an important decision which has long-term career ramifications. It is a decision that directly influences your self-assessment, career exploration, and job placement.

//WEB.TIP//

www.gmat.org
Graduate Management Aptitude Test
Searchable MBA Program database/links to programs/ practice test/preparation tips.

Graduate School Career Action Project

Identify three specific graduate schools to which you might consider applying. Develop a brief, one-page, typed profile of each school. Stress the strength of each institution as it relates to your goals. Visit each school website.

Make a one-page analysis of why you are considering attending graduate school. Cover such topics as career goals, necessity, part-time versus full-time, location, reputation, placement plans, etc.

On a separate page, describe the admissions procedures of each of these schools. What are the standards for admission? Relate these to your specific credentials. Be convincing to yourself and the admissions staff on this page.

Next, lay out a specific course of study at one of the institutions. Do this term-by-term in as much detail as you are able based upon the school's catalog and your academic and work background.

Starting on a new page, relate your anticipated career path with that of past grades at each school. Investigate the placement success of the program by assessing the number of recruiters, starting salaries by discipline and industry, industry mix, and demographics of the graduating students.

Lastly, summarize why this school would be an excellent choice for you. Upon completion, you should have a very thorough five- to eight-page analysis of why a given program is just right for you. Attach a copy of your resume, complete the school's application materials, and have the package ready to send.

Most competitive programs require admission interviews. This project packet is exactly what you need to study as you visit each school. You will discover that websites and email communication are very wide spread.

Don't decide on any graduate study until you have formally completed this type of project analysis for each institutional program!

Career Management:

Planning – Organizing – Controlling

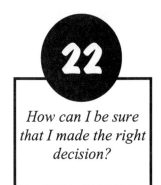

How can I be sure that I made the right decision?

Management is a continuous process of planning, organizing, and directing. A career is a work experience commitment that involves achievement and advancement based upon a high level of significant training and experience in a select field of work endeavor

Career management integrates the principles of career planning, goal setting, and decision making into a framework designed for the specific purpose of helping you understand your working life.

The Career Model Summarized

Career planning is built on three key concepts.

- *Self-assessment* defines the parameters that impact sharply upon your career choice.
- *Career exploration* evaluates your range of potential career options.
- *Search* starts with a career objective and develops a strategy for turning your broad goals into reality through concrete employment.

Decision-making principles form the web that brings together all of your concerns and creates a feedback loop that permits you to make appropriate compromises based upon real world testing. This total career management process continues throughout your working life.

A successful career search, given your career goals, begins with your preparation of the proper tools.

- The foremost tool is your *resume*.
- *Cover letters* which are sent with resumes open doors for interviews.
- Developing *contacts* and using them properly to produce *interviews*.
- Interviews lead to *job offers*.

Productive interviewing requires advance planning. The key factor in interviewing is preparation. An advance strategy, prior preparation of a presentation, and attention to interview techniques are the basics of preparation.

An open, two-way channel of communication is the type of environment that can foster the attainment of both parties' goals.

Achieving that level of communication requires a mutual understanding of each other's position. A common base permits both parties to ask the proper questions and provide reasoned responses in the context of what is expected.

Careers are managed.

Career decision-making is based upon compromises made throughout your life.

The interview is a goal-directed activity.

Career planning is a lifelong revolving cycle.

Career planning does not end with your acceptance of career-related employment. Career planning is cyclical; it continues as you more clearly define your self-concept and as you process new career information. The cycle frequently includes a career search which may lead you to a career or employer change if new circumstances warrant.

Career planning involves you in a continual evaluation of your career progress based upon realistic assessments of your job performance. Continued education throughout your lifetime is a likely possibility for you.

If success in life, (however defined), is valuable to you, you will practice career planning throughout your life. Regardless of your current life status, career planning can be a real and meaningful process. If you permit your working life to roll along without conscious direction, you will neglect an important responsibility and opportunity.

Career Planning Analysis

All of these facets of career management fall together quite naturally once you put the process into action. Once you fully understand the concept, you can implement any of the various aspects by a quick review of the process.

The career planning concept with all of its inherent techniques does not have to be a major project each time you want to review your current career status.

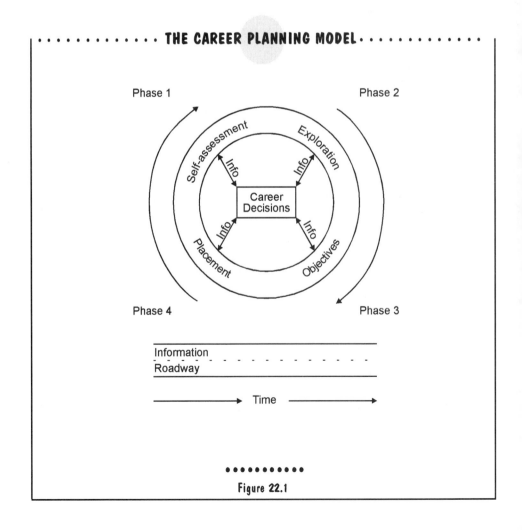

THE CAREER PLANNING MODEL

Phase 1 — Self-assessment
Phase 2 — Exploration
Phase 3 — Objectives
Phase 4 — Placement

Career Decisions

Info

Information Roadway

Time

Figure 22.1

The beauty of the concept is that the overview and the specific techniques are separable. Over time, human resource experts will undoubtedly improve on the techniques used in the self-assessment, career exploration, job search, and career decision-making phases. For example, computer technology use in the career exploration phase will undoubtedly be advanced greatly within the next decade.

The techniques recommended work very well in today's work environment. They will hold up well in the future. New ideas and techniques get incorporated and out-dated ones discarded. Techniques are the tools used to apply the concept. The basic career planning concept (and the system within which it must operate) are likely to be around for many years.

Awareness of the employment system and how to effectively access it complete the career planning process.

When you learn how to put the approach into action, you will be managing your career and your life. Putting the approach into action can become an automatic response. You do not need to go back to the basic elements each time and systematically rebuild the various stages of the career planning process.

As you go through everyday living you will collect new knowledge about yourself and the world of work. There is no finite number of pieces of life like there is in a jigsaw puzzle. You do not easily forget what you learn about yourself and the work world.

Factors Influencing Change

As your information base builds, you will reach a point where you feel there is a need to reorganize your thoughts regarding your career. Any number of factors can trigger the reaction. It may be a sudden personal crisis or a gradual accumulation of information that creates a desire to simply take stock of where your life is headed.

Following a career reassessment, you may conclude that the search phase may or may not be needed. You may only want to test the waters to rebuild your confidence and ego.

A decision to move into the search phase necessitates a more thorough analysis of self-assessment and career exploration. The degree of analysis is a personal decision based upon your judgment of your personal environment.

You alone must decide what factors will force your career planning process to move from low gear to high gear. Many people never get out of neutral. The factors that cause you to shift from a slower moving gear to a higher gear are the things that you deem as important based upon your values, interests, and personal qualities.

Some of the factors which tend to cause people to stop and think about their careers are identified here. Different things spark different people. It may be a single significant event. It may be an accumulation of activities and events. It may merely be a routine inspection of where your life is headed.

Your career analysis may generate a decision to do nothing. You may be in a state of career satisfaction but just want to take a look at how things are going.

Career analysis can also generate many other interrelated decisions. Much confusion can be avoided by using the career planning model. Any career change can bring exciting, challenging, and even stressful situations.

The most fundamental idea to remember is that career planning is understanding yourself and your work options for the purpose of integrating this awareness into a realistic goal statement through a logical decision-making process.

Job search tools and techniques make lifelong career planning concepts into reality.

Sometimes only testing the water may be all the career planning you need.

Changing jobs is a major decision in your life and deserves a very thorough career analysis.

Stabilization

The career planning process is an intense activity if it is followed precisely. The events in the process can move you from very strong psychological highs to lows and back to highs. It is time-consuming, too, especially the first time through it.

This "roller coaster ride" can be smoothed out somewhat by your organized approach to career planning. You recognize what is happening and, as a result, are able to develop a coping plan.

Changing employment or a career is a major decision in life, and by its very nature it can become a psychological problem. The career planning model helps you cope with the situation in an organized, methodical manner. You prepare yourself for a critical life decision.

Once you make an employment decision, you must mobilize your energies to insure that you made a wise decision.

You cannot stay in high gear indefinitely. Your energy is rapidly drained, and you risk burning up your personal engine by dealing with anxieties and stressful situations involving career decisions

You speed up and you slow down. There are continual assessments and reassessments of your personal situation. Sometimes you set goals far too unrealistically and then your reassessment brings about a compromise.

Once you achieve your immediate goal, a stabilization period should set in. The job search process stops. The halt may come about as the result of a decision to remain in your current situation or to accept new employment due to a promotion, a change in employers, or leaving school to take a job.

Ethically, you can take no more interviews once you have made an employment decision. You can ethically not even consider new offers which come in as a result of your previous search process. Your employment decision is extremely important because it is morally binding on your subsequent behavior.

The point of no return is behind you now, and even if a super opportunity comes up after your decision, you must ethically turn it down. Reneging on a commitment is a very serious breach of ethics. An ethics charge is serious business. It can have long-lasting negative effects on a person's future career progress.

You are not alone in making this unequivocal decision. Your new employer is bound to the same ethical considerations. The employer may subsequently interview a better qualified applicant for the position you accepted, but he or she has made a binding commitment to you.

Both parties have exchanged verbal or written words of their intentions. Only extreme hardship or grave consequences should be permitted to influence either party's position.

Plateau. Immediately after your acceptance, the search phase of your career planning downshifts quickly. A plateau is reached. Over time, that plateau will begin to rise, but at no time is your career in a more relaxed state than immediately after you have accepted an

I SUPPOSE ALL NEW EMPLOYEES HAVE ADJUSTMENT PROBLEMS.

CAREER THREATS

Very few jobs are totally secure today. Your only security is your own ability. Your qualifications must be kept current for them to remain secure.

You face many job and career threats. Surprises hit people hard because they rely on the organization and other people to protect them from both internal and external threats.

Reorganization is a common threat. Both service and manufacturing employers face a barrage of forces that cause budget cuts and personnel reductions to meet competition or revenue shortfalls. Middle managers and technical staffs often get hit the hardest.

Merger and acquisition activity is a common threat. There is no need for two separate staffs doing the same job in the new organization. Staff personnel cutbacks of key departments often ensue.

Slow or no growth threaten many jobs. When the product or service life cycle begins to slow, fewer new people are hired. The price of products and services do not rise as before. In order to make a profit, compensation increases are curtailed and staff reductions quickly follow.

Technical obsolescence threatens careers. When the products no longer meet the demands of a changed marketplace, a no-growth situation rapidly follows. These circumstances breed layoffs.

Weak management practices threaten careers. If management is unresponsive to the marketplace or your boss is not satisfactorily performing, an unstable work setting quickly follows.

Discrimination continues to be a career threat. Age, sex, race, religion, and other protected classes seem to be vulnerable in some organizations when times get tough.

Job and career security in our society is not a fundamental right. Even if you own your own business or work for yourself in a legal or medical profession, you are vulnerable to the market forces.

The solution to these career threats is simple. The answer is sound career planning. You must learn how to manage your own career and maintain your ability to move upward as the external (and internal) situations demand.

offer for a position which you feel is an important step toward achieving your career goals.

You must now mobilize your powers and abilities to insure that your decision turns out to be a wise one. By preparing yourself psychologically and intellectually for this new adventure, you move yourself along on the path toward career satisfaction.

Believing that you can handle the assignment and convincing yourself of its "stepping stone" value (if it is not your ultimate employment goal) creates an attitude that almost guarantees success.

JOB SHOCK

- Routine duties
- Definite work hours
- Critical bosses
- Competitive co-workers
- Tight personal budget
- Unfairness everywhere
- Minimal influence
- Colleagues; not friends
- Accomplishment without reward
- Individual (not team) review
- Constant appraisal (daily)
- Amorphous decision making
- Organizational politics
- Daily performance pressure

• • • • • • • • • • •

Figure 22.2

If you are changing jobs or moving from an academic setting to the world of work, big changes are going to occur in your life. Even if you have decided to remain in your present position after your career analysis, a new attitude may be in order.

Vocational theorists view this next period as a transitional adjusting period which may vary from a few weeks to several months in length.

Reality Tests. At this time you begin a reality test of your decisions.

- You will test the *validity* of the self-concept you arrived at through your self-assessment.
- You will test the *adequacy* of your real-world career exploration.

When you made your career decision, you hypothetically merged your self-concept and a career.

Reality is often different from the hypothetical. People and unexpected problems enter the picture. Coping with the unexpected can cause a few problems, but if you have built a sound career foundation, these obstacles should not prove to be detrimental to the satisfaction of your goals.

Starting over, whether real or merely through altering your attitude, presents interesting challenges, and occasionally people "get in over their heads." Recognizing this when it occurs and retrenching because of it can allow one to save face.

It often takes a person about a year on the new job to discover this, and if it happens to you, you only need to recycle through the career planning process once again.

In all probability, you can handle the assignments and responsibilities with ease. After all, your decision was based on much analysis of yourself and the job.

In fact, most people want to assume more and more responsibility before they are really ready for it. The people you work with, not the duties and responsibilities

SUING AN EMPLOYER MAY GROUND YOUR CAREER

The litigious society freely tackles offenders who have brought any type of harm. The newspapers are filled with announcements of layoffs, and age discrimination is often the basis for legal action by an employee against an employer. Indeed the lawsuits run the gamut from sex, race, and religion, to the handicapped.

Most lawsuits are legitimate, and the offender deserved punishment. A settlement is often made out of court. Employers occasionally lose lawsuits but the employee, though legally victorious, may be the real loser. What other employer is willing to hire a litigious person?

Some experts acknowledge that returning to the work force after litigation, whether successful or not, is tough to do. Common sense by an employer dictates that an interviewer avoid undue risks. The interviewer is far more likely to hire another "equally" qualified individual who does not bring negative baggage—a potential lawsuit—to the position.

Before you sue, consider your work future. Analyze the cost versus the gains. Even if you can prove conclusively that you were a victim, evaluate all consequences of the short-term versus long-term gains.

1. Relating theory to practice: the transition
2. Adjusting to work routines: hours, scheduling, deadlines
3. Adjusting to corporate structure: operations, procedures
4. Unrealistic expectations: anticipating too much too soon
5. Developing cooperative attitudes: people differences
6. Accepting responsibility, decision making: completing jobs
7. Understanding management philosophy: profit motive, survival
8. Recognizing inadequacies: finding self unable to cope
9. Adjusting to new location: different lifestyle demanded
10. Learning to communicate effectively: writing, speaking

• • • • • • • • • • •

Figure 22.3

of the job, are likely to be your greatest challenge. They include your bosses, higher level superiors, colleagues, peers, subordinates, and customers.

People Problems. Your attitudes toward others and their attitudes toward you can make or break your well-laid career plans. You can shape others' attitudes toward you as well as your own attitude toward them. A significant part of career management is attitude development and adjustment.

Moving smoothly from one social situation to another requires more understanding of the feelings of others than you probably suspect. You can avoid trouble by anticipating the reactions of others toward you.

Adjustment in a new work environment requires more than obtaining respect for your ability to perform well in all of your assignments. It demands getting along with others as well.

The greatest potential for people problems is other people's fear and apprehension regarding you. The social fabric as well as the work fabric of the workplace is altered by your arrival, and uncertainty is the rule. Be prepared to eliminate the uncertainty when you arrive.

Expectations. Part of your personal adjustment may relate to the expectations you take on the job. What is your internal career path? How long before you will make a move? What will you do? How will you develop friendships? How much will you earn?

You surely have some ideas about the answers to these questions, but your expectations may not coincide with reality.

For example, many people take unrealistic salary expectations to their new positions. The United States is basically a middle-class society where earnings of technical, professional, and managerial employees fall into a relatively narrow salary band. On a percentage basis, most people find themselves in the middle class.

Higher earnings are possible, but expectations of them are not very realistic attitudes. That is a major attitude adjustment problem for many managers.

In all probability, you will face some reality tests that demand changes in your attitude. Over time, facts will be filtered into your career planning model, and when they first hit, a kind of shock effect will touch you. Your adjustments to these "shocks" constitute your career *compromises*.

These adjustment factors can bring about the significant events that ignite your career planning "motor" in the future. When you reach the point where you are no

Learn your job and commit to excellence in it before moving forward.

Career management is a flexible attitude adjustment.

Are your attitudes realistic and do you know how to compromise gracefully?

longer comfortable with the necessary compromises and tradeoffs, you will probably fall back on your career planning model.

Performance Appraisals

Another event that tends to re-ignite career planning interest is the performance appraisal. Few people enjoy sitting down with superiors and discussing their performance limitations over the preceding twelve months. Even strong performers must admit to some failures.

Verbal performance reviews, especially if they turn into harsh critiques, make most people uncomfortable. There is a tendency to put up defenses rather than concentrate on ways to improve performance.

The purpose of performance reviews is to assess the past and lay down some realistic, achievable objectives for the future, but many people only hear the negatives and react accordingly.

The performance appraisal is both an oral and written report card. Are you ready?

Some employers refer to "performance appraisal" as "performance management." Others like the phrase "management by objectives." Regardless of the terminology, it boils down to a job assessment.

Unfortunately, appraisals often have the effect of encouraging some people to begin looking around for other opportunities. People who react in this manner frequently find themselves job hopping from one entry-level

BUT THEN, YOU HAVEN'T MET WOLFGANG ... YOUR DIRECT SUPERVISOR.

assignment to another, never gaining enough credibility to really move up in their chosen careers.

Properly conducted performance appraisals can and do have the opposite effect. Constructive evaluations identify problem areas and help you improve in your weak areas. In effect, they strengthen the whole person. They provide the evaluation that allows you to improve and build a meaningful career path within the organization.

THE PERFORMANCE APPRAISALS ARE COMPLETE, SIR. APPARENTLY EVERYONE CHECKED OUT OKAY BUT YOU.

Upward mobility is not the only route to success. Personal job satisfaction outranks finding yourself appearing successful but inwardly hating your job.

Upward Mobility

Surveys of top executives in all types of organizations invariably indicate a consistent upward mobility. It is slow but steady progress to the top of a profession or organization that distinguishes the movers.

In a very high percentage of instances, the top layer of management has been with their employers for more than 15 years. Superior performance over several years usually is reflected by increased earnings and greater management responsibilities.

Job Hopping. Job hoppers seldom move into positions of major responsibility. Most studies show that the vast majority of top leaders are in their fifties when they assume high levels of responsibility.

Employment with only three or four employers during their career is very common among this group. Most of them have stayed with each employer for seven to ten years and during those tenures experienced several promotions.

In general, job hoppers tend to move from larger, more prestigious organizations to smaller organizations. At the time of a job hopper's move, the new title may be perceived as higher than the old one, but the responsibility in terms of people and resources managed is often much less.

Your career progress (in terms of rank in the organization, salary, and job satisfaction) is enhanced by identifying the most satisfying use of your skills and then building a solid base of performance. Occasional employer changes may be necessary, but frequent job hopping can work against your career progress.

Employer changes that do occur in careers usually come in the early years. When you reach a dead end in terms of your career goal satisfaction, the time is ripe for you to make a move.

You should not attempt a major move without first conducting a thorough career analysis. An analysis should even be con-

THAT'S WHAT I'M LOOKING FORWARD TO ... UPWARD MOBILITY.

Maintain high visibility — be a national authority
Develop reputation for delivering results
Create long-term professional relationships
Look for employment while still employed
Cultivate networks — stay visible to externals
Maintain marketability — stay in demand
Avoid specialization — be a generalist with a theme
Avoid group assignments where credit is diffused
Maintain personal credibility by keeping current
Maintain mobility and flexibility

· · · · · · · · · ·

Figure 22.5

ducted whenever you contemplate a promotion within an organization. Some promotions, especially if they involve a geographical move, may not be in your best career interests.

Turnover.   Turnover has some unpleasant costs for both you and your employer, and if it can be avoided, both stand to gain. In addition to the financial considerations, there are some negative psychological costs which can have lasting negative influences on your career progress.

Is the problem really your desires and not a real problem with your employer?

Turnover usually implies some level of dissatisfaction with the employer. Dissatisfaction emerges when both (not just one) of the parties are unhappy. You may be unhappy because of job content, lack of promotion, people conflicts, etc. This is usually reflected in a lower level of performance which the employer observes.

Whether you are fired, laid off, or see the handwriting on the wall, it is difficult for you to face failure. Your natural instinct is to blame the employer, but you may have some underlying personal problems. As you begin your career planning cycle, you must admit and factor these concerns into your new career objective.

Motivation issues, not competence concerns, cause most turnovers.

Turnover can be very expensive for an employer. It frequently comes about due to underlying people problems in the organization rather than to a lack of competence in the individual who leaves.

People problems are a major disruption to an organization's productivity. In addition, there is the time and expense involved in advertising, interviewing, relocating, and hiring a replacement. Very often, the employer loses a large

investment in the training given the previous employee and must then reinvest in a new person.

A major (and valid) reason employees often give for leaving a firm is the desire to return to school. This implies an unhappiness with job content (or performance competence), and additional schooling can change a career thrust or build a stronger knowledge base.

Returning to school is a common reason cited for leaving. The need for developing new skills in an increasingly information based technological society is a significant reason cited for turnover.

Returning to school is often part of people's broad career plans. Technical, professional, and managerial employees not only want to renew old skills, but they also use education to change the direction of their careers or hasten their upward advancement.

Turnover among recent college graduates varies greatly by industry and occupation. Turnover may be quite low among engineers and very high among data processing personnel.

On the average, many employers of college graduates expect to lose one-third of their new campus hires within the first three years of employment. Some of that one-third leave for educational reasons and later return.

The attrition of technical, professional, and managerial employees who have tenure of more than three years is very small. Major employers expect less than five percent of their employees in this classification to leave within a one-year period.

In the long run, your only security is your own ability. If your abilities are not being fully utilized or recognized, you have a choice to make: either leave the employer, or try to work out a more productive relationship with your current employer.

Some of the more positive reasons most frequently cited include:

- More challenge
- Relocation needs
- Health concerns

Some employers build turnover statistics into their entry-level hiring plans.

Your only security is your own ability.

- Financial security
- More money
- Additional training
- Better opportunity
- Advancement

There are many very legitimate and positive reasons for making an employment change. The most important reason is to further the satisfaction of your long-term career plans. Advancement is the single best reason for making a change.

Internal Politics. Politics play a role in advancement. Regardless of the organization, internal relationships determine who is chosen for promotion.

As the hierarchy narrows, there are many well-qualified applicants for promotion if the organization has done a good job of developing its people. Ideally, every opening should have two or more interested people competing for it.

In any well-managed organization, the first selection of viable, promotable candidates for a given position is made on the basis of competence and previous job performance. This may yield several candidates. Seniority may be a selection factor, but for management-level jobs it is not often considered. The choice is often based on "people skills" rather than technical competence.

How can you win in internal politics? It boils down to getting others (superiors, peers, and subordinates) to know and like you. You must develop feelings of respect, rapport, and confidence among the people who count in the organization. You need to consider your personality, competence, credibility, values, social life, habits, manners, attitude, personal philosophy, and other factors that make you a unique person.

Anyone who gives you advice on how to beat the political game should be held suspect. In some organizations the "Girl Scout" image wins; in others the "hatchet man" wins. In some organizations the motto is, "Do it to others before they do it to you," while in others it is the golden rule.

In no case should you assume that internal politics are unim-

SMITH HERE WILL SHOW YOU THE ROPES.

MENTORS AID YOUR CAREER PROGRESS

A mentor is a career coach who takes a personal interest in you by offering career insights, advising an entry into the social and political environment, evaluating inside information, and promoting your career internally. In selecting potential mentors you should ask yourself these questions:

1. How powerful is the mentor?
2. Is the mentor gaining support?
3. How secure is the mentor?
4. Is the mentor a good teacher?
5. Are your views consistent?
6. How long will the mentor be around?

A good mentor can make your job life more pleasant and satisfying. Evidence suggests that a mentor can influence how far and how fast you rise in an organization.

Mentors open doors to information access from both peers and superiors. Involvement in organizational politics is unavoidable, so the use of a mentor can affect your rewards in terms of raises, promotion, power, and responsibility. A thoughtful selection of one or more mentors can be an essential decision in your career development.

portant for you and your career. Some people literally make a game of internal politics, and some of them win at it too. The level of its importance to you will be based upon your values, interests, personal values, and career objectives.

Teaching you how to succeed in internal politics is a fruitless activity, but advising you that it exists is important. From a career management perspective, succeeding in that area may not be important to you. If it is important, you need to factor that element into your career decision-making framework.

The figure titled "Forty Action Ideas for Advancement" offers advice for those who desire to move up in the organizational hierarchy. Admittedly, some of these sound facetious when they are applied to career planning, and indeed some of them are. Nonetheless, following many of the ideas could contribute to your survival in an organization's political arena. It would be beneficial for you to memorize many of these ideas if the upward "progression syndrome" is a part of your career plan.

Teaching you how to succeed in power politics is a foolish activity.

POWER POLITICS DESTROYS CAREERS

Do unto others before they do unto you. Watch out for Number 1. Success above all. During your career movement you will undoubtedly face many opportunists who unwittingly follow strange advice. Power politics occasionally work in the short run, but the actions described below rarely survive in most organizations.

- Controlling people
- Massaging egos
- Manipulating situations
- Calculating relationships
- Spreading false rumors
- Withholding facts
- Managing information
- Playing favorites
- Name dropping
- Bootlicking
- Yes man
- Playing safe
- Demeaning others
- Back stabbing

This is not to suggest that tough political decisions need never be made. You occasionally must take unpopular stands, establish firm commitments, practice total loyalty, and be aggressive on important issues. But political decisions often boil down to these dichotomies.

- Maintenance versus Greatness
- Acceptable versus Excellence
- Caution versus Courage
- Dependence versus Autonomy

You may discover that politics impact your future success. Organizational politics does not mean a dirty or sinister action. The street-smart, hustling, striver may turn out to be you.

Political savvy builds careers as well. Your role may eventually be to give stress rather than merely suffer stress.

Make your work benefit someone else
Define the value of your work to superiors
Avoid "loose cannon" label
Make your boss a star
Make your subordinates stars
Give yourself minimal credit
Force consensus in work groups
Tolerate inconsistencies
Welcome change
Look forward, not backward

"THE TEN TO DO'S"

. . . .
Figure 22.6

Internal Career Pathing. Career management is not solely your responsibility. More and more employers are sitting down with high-potential employees and helping them map out internal career paths. Career pathing is destined to become a major human resource planning activity within the larger employing organizations in the future.

Your goals and your organization's goals may not be compatible. Within any organization, your upward mobility is dependent upon appropriate openings which cannot always be guaranteed, regardless of the superiority of your performance. For that reason, sound career management must always remain your own responsibility.

Nonetheless, organizational career pathing promises to play an important role in meeting the needs of many employees. The career analysis suggested here may be forced upon you by your employer.

Career pathing will help employers retain the people they desperately need for future leadership. Career pathing will encourage those who find themselves dead-ended, through no fault of their own, to seek greener pastures elsewhere.

Career pathing forces employers to become more aware of the needs and aspirations of their employees. If frank and realistic counseling is given, both parties will come to have more reasonable expectations.

A major cause of turnover is employees' unrealistic expectations. They change jobs only to find that their own attitudes were the problem, not the employer.

Are your goals compatible with those of your employer?

Your employer may hire a professional "out placement" firm to assist you in making the transition to another, more compatible employer or occupation.

Career pathing encourages employers to seek new and innovative ways to reward achievers. Upward mobility is limited by the sheer definition of organizations.

As you move up the pyramid, are you really closer to the top? Mentoring, lateral moves, job enrichment, professionalism, and so forth, are only a few ways to address the inevitable crunch toward the top of the pyramid.

OVER THE LONG HAUL WE EXPECT OUR NEW EMPLOYEES TO TAKE US FOR GRANTED, BECOME COMPLACENT, AND SUPPLEMENT WHAT WE CALL OUR "DEADWOOD".

Career satisfaction is not necessarily compatible with the onward-and-upward mentality. Realistic career planning can be an alternative to it.

Changing Jobs

Factors that cause the career planning process to rekindle are the same factors that can lead people to seek a new career field or a new employer in the same field. The reason job changers most frequently give as to why they change jobs and yet stay in the same field is that they believe it will open up greater advancement possibilities.

Pay, location, boss, job content, and other factors do weigh in decisions to change employers, but the most prevalent reason is advancement.

If the changers are asked why they are changing their career *directions,* there is an even split between job content dissatisfaction and advancement limitations. The plateauing and ceiling restrictions seem to be major change agents.

Sometimes the reasons for changing jobs are underlying personal problems which make coping within the career arena difficult. These problems can make success with any employer unattainable. Until the personal problems are solved, no amount of career planning can be very fruitful.

These problems must be faced squarely and honestly, because running away from an employer or a career field does not solve them. In most cases, the problems resurface later in other settings.

You must recognize the difference between a personal problem and a career problem and then deal with the problem before activating the career planning model.

Employers directly and indirectly terminate professional personnel. The direct approach of firing or laying off people is embarrassing, but it is the most honest approach. It makes people

YES, I HAVE CHANGED JOBS A LOT. I'VE ALWAYS PREFERRED NEW CHALLENGES, BROADER HORIZONS, AND EXPANDED OPPORTUNITIES ... TO BEING FIRED.

wake up and acknowledge the need for career planning. Some employers recognize this and provide professional counseling by outside "out-placement experts" for employees they must terminate.

The indirect approach simply lets people hang on in maintenance capacities. They are productive but they are not utilized to the fullest possible extent. The indirect approach says, "We think you should leave because we see no future for you here."

That signal should be recognized and heeded immediately unless the individual has made a conscious decision to bide his/her time to retirement. Another indirect approach is simply to force the individual to quit by making his/her working life miserable.

Regardless of whether a change is initiated by you or the employer, you risk the same fate again if a solution for the underlying problem is not found. Merely changing jobs or career fields is a temporary, "band-aid" solution that only relieves the pain for a short time. Rather than deal with a symptom, you should tackle the problem head-on in the self-assessment and in subsequent career choices.

Finding cures for career ailments is no simple task, but it is essential if you are going to achieve real career success and satisfaction. If there is no cure, the limitation must be integrated into the self-assessment, the career exploration, and the career objective as a "compromising" variable.

Every employer must occasionally terminate professional employees.

The request for you to leave may come via subtle signals designed to avoid confrontation later.

· · · · · · · · · · OUTPLACEMENT PROTECTION TACTICS · · · · · · · · · · ·

Be loyal to yourself first
Recognize that employment relationships are getting shorter
Rewards are tied to contribution, not years and loyalty
Accept that every organization needs to outplace sometimes
Guard against surprises but lead with strength
Accept the odds—it could happen
Maintain independence—avoid dependence
Prepare psychologically for outplacement
Don't get burned twice—anticipate being outplaced

· · · · · · · · · ·
Figure 22.7

Seek additional responsibilities.
Complete assignments immediately.
Make suggestions instead of critical reviews.
Solve problems instead of just identifying them.
Praise others for good work.

Develop new skills through training.
Seek assignments that offer exposure to managers.
Search for the reason behind each assignment.
Look at problems from a management viewpoint.
Do not underestimate your social responsibilities.

Nurture personal friendships in your peer group.
Ask for certain work assignments.
Study the normal promotional channels.
Develop your personal life outside the organization.
Make professional contacts outside the organization.

Seek line, not staff, responsibilities.
Be patient for rewards, but go after challenges.
Beware of "assistant to" titles. Watch go-fers.
Avoid internal politics and cliques.
Show your enthusiasm for the organization.

Discuss ideas, never people.
Advertise your abilities by superior performances.
Keep records of your work to show later.
Work on your public speaking skills.
Talk to subordinates as friends. They make you.

Never allow pressures to compromise quality.
Maintain personal and organizational ethics.
Make a written appraisal each year for your review.
Ask your superiors for advice about your career.
No negative criticism does not equal positive praise.

Rate your supervisors' potential for promotions.
Get help if an assignment is over your head.
Accept criticism and ask for it. Use it to improve.
Rethink your plans if the pressure bothers you.
Be prepared to relocate if promotion merits it.

Maintain organizational loyalty and advertise it.
Learn to delegate authority.
Accept blame for poor work of subordinates.
Expect two- to three-year plateaus in promotion.
Watch for earnings ceilings.

· · · · · · · · · ·

Figure 22.8

The Career Planning Model

Career changes (and employer changes) are healthy and necessary for most people. Two to six employer changes over a working lifetime are very common. If you change employment more than six times, you need to review your rationale for each change.

Many people do stay with their first employers throughout their entire working careers, however, and many of the firms that actively recruit on college campuses can point to hundreds of instances of this. This is one reason why it is so important to make the employer analysis before making your first employment decision.

Circular Model. The career planning model is a dynamic, cyclical, process. The approach may be used time after time during a career. The techniques you use at given times will differ, but the basic concept remains intact.

For example, early in your career you may carry out the process and decide that your analysis indicates you should return to school to change the thrust of your career direction.

Later in your new career, you may exercise the model to evaluate a promotion you have been offered that would require a major geographical move for your family. At another time you may use the model and decide to make an important job change.

The cyclical nature of the model increases its flexibility because it gives it multiple uses. Many times you may spin off of the cycle before you reach the job search phase. You may access the model, make a thorough analysis, and then come to the conclusion that you should make no career change at that point in time.

The cyclical nature of the model also permits new information to be fed in regularly. The decisions resulting each time are based on the most current information available.

Forward Motion. The career planning model is like a giant snowball rolling down a slope as you progress in your career. As it rolls along with you, you can easily access it at any time, and it collects information about you and your career interests daily.

> **Make every job decision as if you intend to work there for life but realize that changes are not an indictment.**

> **Your career planning model used in analysis should be used on a regular cycle even if you are very satisfied with your job.**

> **Keep your career moving forward based on your definition, not someone else's opinion.**

CREATING CAREER OPPORTUNITIES

Many road blocks face you as you move forward on your road to career success. Solid career *management* coupled with regular and systematic career *planning* destroys many of the obstacles on your way to success.

Your plan demands a take-charge approach. The ten "Career Commandments" listed below can open up many career opportunities for you.

Career Commandments

1. ***Manage Your Career.*** Effort alone is not always rewarded so try to influence decisions made by others on your behalf.
2. ***Strive for High Visibility.*** Create a setting where your abilities can be observed by career enhancers.
3. ***Nominate Yourself.*** Modesty is not necessarily a virtue.
4. ***Evaluate Promotions.*** Avoid positions which expose your weaker qualities or entail activities you dislike.
5. ***Initiate Leaves.*** Make a job move if your supervisor has not moved up in the past three to five years.
6. ***Avoid Specialization.*** Watch getting trapped into narrow job descriptions that limit your sphere of influence.
7. ***Play Smart Politics.*** Establish alliances and fight necessary skirmishes but avoid battles with important superiors.
8. ***Avoid Being Indispensable.*** Watch for reasons why people would be unwilling to promote you.
9. ***Strong Marketable.*** Your professional mobility enhances your external opportunities and increases the organization's impression of your value.
10. ***Evaluate Yourself Regularly.*** Examine your personal values to help identify where you are sacrificing too much for the organization.

These ten "Career Commandments" provide ideas that can mean the difference between success and failure on the job. The ideas cannot replace the "Three Ms" sought by every employer.

1. Mental ability
2. Maturity
3. Motivation

When positioned with your periodic career planning routine, the ten commandments point the way toward upward mobility in your chosen occupation.

This undated model follows behind you, collecting data and picking up momentum as your career progresses.

Building Blocks. Its cyclical nature and its forward movement permit the model to absorb information as your career develops. It can also discard useless or outdated pieces of data about your self-assessment and career exploration. You essentially are building a house of knowledge on a firm foundation which was laid when you first made use of the model.

Your initial access of the career planning model takes an enormous amount of time if it is properly carried out. But once the initial work is done, periodic updating requires only a few hours of time. Your self-assessment and resume should be regularly updated because they are useful for a variety of purposes, many of which are not career-related.

The strategy in this career planning model will help you to manage your career. Management consists of the decisions you make daily and periodically, and those decisions can be planned, organized, and orchestrated.

Career planning takes control of your career away from the hand of fate. *You* can move your career in a direction that will achieve your personal *life* goals as well.

Career management works. It is your ticket to success.

STEP #1: INFORMATIONAL SEARCH

STEP #2: COVER LETTER AND RESUME

STEP #3: RECEIPT OF APPLICATION FORM

STEP #4: FILLING OUT AND MAILING BACK APPLICATION

STEP #5: SWEAT!

STEP #6: INVITATION TO INTERVIEW WITH CAMPUS RECRUITER

STEP #7: ACCEPTANCE OF INVITATION LETTER

STEP #8: BUY NEW SUIT.

STEP #9: INITIAL CAMPUS INTERVIEW

STEP #10: INTERVIEW NOTES

STEP #11: REAFFIRMING INTEREST LETTER.

STEP #12: MORE SWEAT!

STEP #13: INVITATION FOR SECOND INTERVIEW

STEP #14: ACCEPTANCE FOR SECOND INTERVIEW LETTER.

STEP #15: PLANE RIDE

STEP #16: SECOND INTERVIEW BEGINS

Index

C

Campbell Interest and Skill Survey, 22, 43
campus interviews, 377–378
can-do factors of a resume, 206
career, defined, 6
career action projects, 173–186
    accounting, 179
    banking, 178–179
    book review, 183–184
    contacts, 327
    cover letter, 327–328
    engineering, 181
    graduate school, 548–549
    graduate study, 184
    human resource management, 182
    industry, 185–186
    infosearch, 406–408
    interview, 465–484
    management, 175
    marketing, 177
    network, 406
    prospect file, 376
    public accounting, 180
    public relations, 183
    resume, 243–244
    retailing, 178
    sales, 175–176
    self-assessment, 37–45
career assessment services, 383, 385–386
CAREER CENTRAL (website), 546
career commandments, 570
Career Conferences of America (website), 366
career counselor, 11, 13, 21, 23, 380, 383, 385
    source of salary information, 510
career development specialists, 90
career exploration, 6, 8, 17, 47–72, 170, 471, 551
    information sources, 51–53
    job market, 53–56
    process, 48–53, 172–186
    projects, 172–186
    relevant data, 50–51
    salary concerns, 61–66
Career Lab (website), 313
Career Leader (website), 45
Career Magazine (website), 361
career management, 82–84, 169, 551–573
    defined, 551
    See also career planning
Career Mosaic (website), 357
career objective statement, 172, 195, 198, 211, 212–221
    industry awareness, 221
    job titles used on, 215, 217–218
    length of, 216
    placement on resume, 213
    promotion awareness, 221

    samples, 219–220
    targeted, 214
    technical jargon, 216
Career Path (website), 399, 514
career paths, 50, 91
    accountant, general, 123
    accountant, public, 127–128
    credit manager, 136–137
    engineer, 150
    financial institution, 135
    financial planner, 138
    human resources management, 162
    internal, 565–566
    management information system, 133
    operations, 148
    retail, 108
    sales, 105–106
career planning, 169–170
    analysis, 552–566
    assessment (*see* self-assessment)
    defined, 12
    description of, 3–18
    exploration (*see* career exploration)
    model, 551–552, 569–571
    process, 7–13, 49, 551–554
    re-evaluation, 10, 553–571
    search phase of, 6, 8–9, 17, 551
    significance of, 5
    theories, 13–17
    threats to, 555
career plateau, 88, 554–555
career profiles, 96–97
    accountant, general, 122–126
    accountant, public, 127–131
    advertising agency, 113–115
    auditor, internal, 131–132
    credit manager, 136–137
    engineering, 149–154
    financial institution, 134–136
    financial planner, 138
    franchising, 167
    human resource management, 157–163
    insurance, 139–141
    international careers, 165–166
    legal staff, 164
    management information system, 132–133
    management training, 165
    marketing research, 115–117
    operations, 143–149
    preparing, 170–186
    product management, 117–119
    programmer, 133–134
    public relations, 163–164
    research and development, 155–156
    retail management, 108–113
    sales management, 103–108

T

U

websites, 50

U.S. Department of Labor Employment and Training Administration (website), 383

U.S. Government Salary Schedule, 513–514

U.S. Immigration and Naturalization Service (website), 165

U.S. News and World Report (website), 5, 22

USA Today, 167

V

validity
    interview, 27–28
    test, 25

Value Line Investment Survey, 75, 137, 467

values, 25–28, 30–33
    autobiography, 39
    clarification, 30–31
    clarification project, 42–43
    classifying, 32–33
    coworker's tolerance of, 33, 42
    identifying, 42
    in resume, 209

values questions, interview action project, 480

Vault Reports (website), 423

video resumes, 203

videotape, used for interview practice, 473, 482

V.I.P.S., 25–28

Virtual Job Fair (website), 371

vocational theories, 13–17

voice control, during interview, 433

voice mail, responding to, in job finding, 317

W

wage laws, federal, 77

wage and salary administration department, 159–161

Wall Street Journal, 167, 179, 183, 468, 513, 514
    website, 430

warehouse management, 146

web services, state, 383

website resumes, 200–202

websites (utilizing)
    employer, 74
    graduate school, 548
    job, 363
    search firms, 380
    self-assessment, 21–22

Wetfeet Press Insider (website), 422

white-collar workers, 62, 76, 87, 149

wholesale market, 100–101

will-do factors of a resume, 206

word processing
    in business correspondence, 491
    cover letters, 303
    direct mailings, 324, 325, 326
    prospect file, 369
    resume preparation, 200

words in cover letter, 304–308

words in resume
    action, 204–205
    adjectives, 208
    adverbs, 208
    descriptors, 208
    impact, 208
    numbers, 208
    "proven power," 207–209
    self-descriptive, 205–206
    to avoid, 202–204
    verbs, 208

work associates, on job search team, 360

work environments, 16, 73–94
    management, 77–85
    private enterprise, 73–77
    responsibility, 85–94

work experience, 26–27
    autobiography, 39–40
    and salary, 64, 66

work experience listed on resume, 195, 230, 232–237, 478
    descriptive title, 233
    duties, 233–234
    responsibility level, 234
    salary, 234
    training, 234

work experience questions, interview action project, 478–479

work functions, 95

work permits, international careers, 165

work setting, 4, 11
    and job markets, 66–72

world wide web
    contacts, 352–353
    job search, 363
    resume transmission, 201–202

writing services, resume, 197

Z

"ZAP interview" technique, 445

ZDNET (website), 132